D1291484

COGNITION AND THE SYMBOLIC PROCESSES

COGNITION AND THE SYMBOLIC PROCESSES

Edited by WALTER B. WEIMER and DAVID S. PALERMO
PENNSYLVANIA STATE UNIVERSITY, UNIVERSITY PARK, PENNSYLVANIA

 LAWRENCE ERLBAUM ASSOCIATES, PUBLISHERS
1974   Hillsdale, New Jersey

DISTRIBUTED BY THE HALSTED PRESS DIVISION OF

JOHN WILEY & SONS
New York   Toronto   London   Sydney

Lawrence Erlbaum Associates, Publishers
62 Maria Drive
Hillsdale, New Jersey 07642

Distributed solely by Halsted Press Division
John Wiley & Sons, Inc., New York

Library of Congress Cataloging in Publication Data

Weimer, Walter B.
    Cognition and the symbolic processes.

    Includes bibliographies. 1. Cognition. I. Palermo, David Stuart,
    1929- joint author. II. Title.
BF311.W374   153.4   74-13834
ISBN 0-470-92550-7

Printed in the United States of America

CONTENTS

PREFACE

The current revolution in psycholinguistics and cognitive psychology was the point of departure for the conference from which this book derived. The major concern of those who have contributed is with the construction of a psychology of the higher mental processes through the evaluation of past efforts in this direction, summarization of current knowledge in the area, formulation of theoretical ideas, and the projection of fruitful directions for future research. The result is an in-depth discussion of a number of selected topics—ranging from linguistics through learning, memory and perception, to theories of the mind.

This volume is directed toward all those who are engrossed in the problems of cognition and the symbolic processes, with the idea in mind that the papers presented here and the discussion of those papers (both formal and informal) will reveal where we may have established some anchor points, where we are confronted with sharp differences in points of view, and where both theoretical and empirical vacuums may exist which need to be filled. Thus, the conference and this volume have taken the form of a series of major position papers dealing with particular topics followed by formal discussions of those papers and subsequent informal comments raised at the conference. The editors hope that discussion will not end there but that the contents presented here will lead to further discussion, evaluation, disagreement, and eventuate in productive theoretical and research endeavors on the part of its readers. In part, that has already happened in time to be included in this volume. The papers by Brewer, Ross, Mace, Bransford and McCarrell, Franks, Shaw and McIntyre, and Halwes, as well as the discussions of those papers by Dulany, Turvey, and Brewer all were parpared for and presented at the conference. The papers by Halwes and Wire, Anderson, and Miller were prepared subsequent to and, in part, stimulated by the conference. Weimer's overview chapter was, of course, written after the conference as well.

It should be noted that no contributor was asked specifically to review the data in the area. Rather each was asked to provide an opinion of what is going on in the area of his topic, with an eye to issues that should be considered. In particular, the chapters are directed toward theoretical issues with data used as illustrative of theoretical points. These instructions to contributors were not meant to indicate that data were taboo but only that the focus was to be more abstract and, like a tent, tied to the ground only at crucial points. It seems to us that the reader will find that the authors have done rather well on that count.

The Conference on Cognitiion and the Symbolic Processes was held in the Conference Center at The Pennsylvania State University, October 23-25, 1972. It was made possible through the support of the University, the College of the Liberal Arts, the Institute for Arts and Humanistic Studies, the Department of Psychology, and Training Grant HD00151 from the National Institute of Child Health and

Human Development. The editors are grateful for that support and plan to invest the royalties of the present volume in future conferences devoted to the furtherance of cognitive psychology.

We would like to thank Ron Weiss for taping and partially transcribing the conference, and Donna Schimeneck for help in proof reading.

Walter B. Weimer
David S. Palermo

COGNITION
AND THE
SYMBOLIC PROCESSES

1

THERE IS NO CONVINCING EVIDENCE FOR OPERANT OR CLASSICAL CONDITIONING IN ADULT HUMANS

William F. Brewer
University of Illinois at Urbana—Champaign

This chapter argues that conditioning in human subjects is produced through the operation of higher mental processes, rather than vice versa. The individuals most responsible for this chapter are Kenneth Spence and Noam Chomsky. Spence forced me to read, as a graduate student, some fair fraction of the primary literature on conditioning. (The University of Iowa's copies of the *Journal of Experimental Psychology* are literally yellow with graduate student sweat.) Chomsky's insights about language and the nature of psychology have helped me to question the traditional paradigm in psychology and thus question such fundamentals as the existence of conditioning in human beings. Chomsky was also the specific cause of this chapter since it began with a lecture he gave at the University of Illinois on April 1, 1971. Chomsky made a statement to the effect that behavioristic psychology could account for simple behavior, but could not handle more complex behavior. As I sat listening in the audience, I wondered if he was being sufficiently radical. It was fashionable in 1971 to say that Chomsky was outdated; so, to avoid appearing merely fashionable, I set out to do the massive reanalysis of the conditioning literature required to support my speculation that behavioristic psychology could not explain even simple behavior.

CONDITIONING THEORY

The standard view of conditioning is based on an analogy between conditioning and the Sherringtonian reflex. The traditional hypothesis for classical conditioning is that the repeated pairing of a Conditioned Stimulus (CS) with an Unconditioned Stimulus (UCS) will cause the CS to elicit a Conditioned Response (CR) in an unconscious, automatic fashion. For operant behavior the traditional hypothesis is that the probability of occurrence of a response which is followed by a reinforcer will increase in an unconscious, automatic fashion. Statements of the standard view can be found in Dollard and Miller (1950), Logan (1970), Skinner (1963), Staats and Staats (1963), and Verplanck (1962).

Since Watson's 1916 APA presidential address, the general procedure in conditioning studies has been to bring in naive subjects (Ss), place them in one of the standard conditioning paradigms, and subject them to a series of CS-UCS pairings (without telling them what the experimenter (E) expects them to do). After the experiment Ss are not asked what they thought was going on, but are simply excused. It seems clear that experimenters operating in this fashion believe either that the higher mental processes are a myth, or that they are a minor factor that need not be considered in standard conditioning experiments. The "radical" position of this chapter is that the college sophomore does not leave his higher mental processes outside the door when he walks into the experimental room. He not only brings them into the experimental room, but he uses them to try to understand what is going on and what he should do about it. The general mode of attack will be to show that in the standard human conditioning paradigms Ss are not making unconscious, automatic responses, but are developing conscious hypotheses and expectations about the experiment, and that these produce the resulting "conditioning."

To avoid confusion the following terminology will be used. "Conditioning" will refer to the simple empirical fact that repeated pairings of a CS with a UCS often result in the occurrence of a CR, and that responses followed by a reinforcer increase in probability. "Conditioning theory" will refer to the hypothesis that events in conditioning come about in an automatic, unconscious fashion. "Cognitive theory" will refer to the hypothesis that events in conditioning result from S becoming aware of the CS-UCS relationship in classical conditioning or aware of the reinforcement contingency in operant conditioning.

COGNITIVE THEORY

The cognitive hypothesis makes the following assumptions about the processes underlying the conditioning experiment. The naive S comes to the experiment curious about what is going to happen and how he is to respond. During the CS-UCS pairing in classical conditioning, he develops conscious hypotheses about the relationship between CS and UCS (e.g., "Every time the red light comes on I get shocked"). Once S has a hypothesis about the CS-UCS relation, the next stage of the conditioning procedure differs, depending on whether the response system being measured is autonomic or motor.

In classical autonomic conditioning, once S has developed a hypothesis about the CS-UCS relationship, a built-in system is brought into operation, so that S's expectation of shock or food automatically produces the autonomic response.

In classical motor conditioning, an additional process occurs after S has developed a hypothesis about the CS-UCS relation. Having decided what the CS-UCS relation is, S attempts to determine what E wants him to do about it. Finally, having developed a hypothesis about E's expectations, S responds appropriately, to the degree he feels the need to comply with E's wishes.

The cognitive account of operant motor conditioning is the same as that for classical motor conditioning, except that S's hypotheses are about the reinforcement contingency.

In operant autonomic conditioning, S should condition only to the extent that he can develop a conscious cognitive strategy which allows him to bring his autonomic responses under voluntary control.

This form of cognitive theory makes strong claims about the conditioning experiment, and so has the virtue of being easily disproved if false. For example, the cognitive hypothesis for classical conditioning states that S must become aware of the CS-UCS relationship; thus, it implies that he can only be conditioned if he is aware of the CS, the UCS, and the relation between the two. Actually, S's hypothesized CS-UCS relation or reinforcement contingency need not be identical with E's; it only has to have enough correspondence so that responses made on the basis of it will be consistent enough for E to classify S as having been conditioned.

In autonomic conditioning, there is no need for S to be aware of his response, and in fact, in some cases (e.g., GSR) he may not even be aware that he is capable of producing the response. The situation is not as clear in motor conditioning. In most standard motor paradigms, such as finger withdrawal conditioning, cognitive theory assumes that S makes a conscious decision about what response to make, so S must, at least initially, be aware of the response. However, it is possible to conceive of a situation where S isn't aware of his motor response; for example, a slight tensing of the hand when he expects the shock to occur in finger withdrawal conditioning. A motor task with an unconscious response is analogous to autonomic conditioning.

In motor conditioning, S must determine what E expects of him, and then choose to make the response or else the response will not occur, whereas in autonomic conditioning there need be no such decision by S.

In addition to these predictions about the level of awareness of the various components of the conditioning paradigm, a number of other predictions can be easily derived from cognitive theory. For example, telling S the CS-UCS relation should have a very dramatic effect in both classical motor and classical autonomic conditioning—conditioning in zero trials. Telling S that the CS-UCS contingency is no longer in effect should also have a dramatic effect in both types of conditioning—extinction in zero trials for Ss who believe E. Telling S not to make the CR should eliminate the response in motor conditioning, but should have only moderate effect on classical autonomic conditioning, since voluntary control of the autonomic system is probably limited in untrained Ss.

The cognitive approach sketched above is a synthesis and extension of the work of Adams (1957), Cason (1934), Cole (1939), Dulany (1968), Grings (1965), Orne (1962), Page (1969), Razran (1955), Spielberger and DeNike (1966), and Zeaman and Smith (1965). Clearly the cognitive approach is not a theory in the sense used in the more mature sciences. However, since the cognitive view is as rigorous and well articulated as the competing S-R approaches, and the latter approaches have traditionally been referred to as "theories," it seems only fair to use this general sense of "theory" with reference to the cognitive approach.

Conditioning theory provides a nice contrast to cognitive theory on these predictions. On some of the issues conditioning theory makes the opposite prediction (e.g., awareness of the CS-UCS relation not required for conditioning), and on the others it simply is not capable of making a well motivated prediction (e.g., outcome of telling the S the CS-UCS relation).

DISSOCIATION DESIGNS

Experiments designed to distinguish between conditioning theory and cognitive theory ought to be the major focus of investigation in this area, since these alternatives suggest radically different theoretical mechanisms and have very different implications for a general theory of behavior. Yet, in practice, the bulk of the vast conditioning literature is useless for distinguishing between these alternatives, since most experiments have been designed so that either theory can give a consistent account of the data.

However, a number of designs are capable of distinguishing between conditioning theory and cognitive theory. Experiments which are crucial for this purpose will be called dissociation experiments, since they typically operate by dissociating the higher mental processes from the unconscious, automatic effects of CS-UCS pairing or reinforcement contingency. Among the better dissociation designs are the following:

Informed pairing. For classical conditioning the Informed Pairing design simply consists of telling Ss the CS-UCS contingency without giving them any CS-UCS pairings. Cognitive theory predicts that this should be sufficient to produce conditioning in autonomic response systems, since the making of the response is presumed to be automatic after S has become aware of the CS-UCS relationship. An example of this design would be to attach GSR recording equipment and a shock electrode to S and tell him that every time the red light comes on he will be shocked. In practice, leaving the UCS up to S's imagination may not produce a strong enough expectancy, and so it may be necessary to give S a few sample unpaired UCSs in order to produce a robust autonomic response. Telling S the CS-UCS relationship in the case of motor responses should produce immediate conditioning to the degree that he is able to guess what response E expects, and to the degree that he chooses to comply with E. Similarly in operant motor conditioning, telling S the reinforcement contingencies should produce immediate conditioning depending on S's interpretation of the reinforcement and his desire to comply. For operant autonomic responses, telling S the reinforcement contingencies will facilitate conditioning to the degree that it helps him bring his autonomic responses under control.

Informed unpairing. In the Informed Unpairing technique S is put through one of the standard conditioning paradigms, and then, after he has conditioned, is told that the UCS will no longer follow the CS; or in operant conditioning he is told that reinforcement will no longer follow the operant response. Cognitive theory predicts this procedure will produce extinction in both autonomic and motor response systems. The degree of extinction should be directly related to the degree of confidence S has in E's statement.

Instructed conditioning. The Instructed Conditioning design in classical conditioning consists of telling S to produce the CR upon the occurrence of the CS without any UCS pairings. In operant conditioning it consists of telling S to make a specified response. For motor responses, cognitive theory makes the obvious prediction that Ss will respond appropriately. Autonomic conditioning is more complex. Since the response system may be unconscious and automatic in this type of conditioning, cognitive theory predicts that conditioning will occur only to the degree that S develops a strategy to bring his autonomic responses under voluntary control. Thus, if simply told to produce a GSR when a red light comes on, he may fail; but if he uses the strategy of thinking of his last trip to the dentist when the red light comes on, he should condition.

Instructed nonconditioning. In Instructed Nonconditioning Ss are first instructed not to produce the CR upon the occurrence of the CS, or for operant conditioning, not to emit a particular response; then they are put through a standard conditioning paradigm. Cognitive theory predicts that for motor responses and for operant autonomic responses the Instructed Nonconditioning technique will result in no conditioning in compliant subjects. In the classical conditioning of autonomic responses the Instructed Nonconditioning technique should not be very successful, since few untrained individuals will be able to eliminate the emotional state that results from knowing the CS-UCS relationship. For example, to keep from producing the CR in aversive GSR conditioning, S would have to find a way to avoid becoming anxious when the red light occurs, even though he knows that the red light is frequently followed by shock.

Instructed extinction. The Ss in Instructed Extinction are put through one of the standard experimental designs until they reach criterion and then are told to stop giving the CR. The predictions of cognitive theory are similar to those in the Instructed Nonconditioning paradigm. Compliant subjects should extinguish immediately for motor responses and operant autonomic responses, but should show only limited ability to extinguish for classical autonomic responses, especially if the CS-UCS pairings are continued.

Masking. For classical conditioning, the Masking design consists of putting Ss through one of the standard conditioning paradigms, except that the actual relationship between the CS and UCS is masked by some form of misleading instructions. Typically a control group is put through the identical design, but without the masking instructions. Cognitive theory predicts that Ss who are deceived by the masking instructions will develop false hypotheses about the relations of the CS and the UCS and so will not condition, even though they are being subjected to a series of CS-UCS pairings that is known to produce conditioning in unmasked subjects. In the case of operant conditioning, it is the reinforcement contingency that is masked. If S does not become aware of the contingency he should not condition. The predictions for the Masking design are the same for autonomic and motor responses. The effectiveness of the mask in producing false hypotheses should be assessed in this design, especially when the mask has no effect on conditioning.

Awareness of contingency. The Awareness of Contingency design consists of putting Ss through a conditioning procedure in which the CS-UCS relationship or reinforcement contingency is moderately difficult to grasp. After conditioning, Ss

are separated into those who became aware of the contingencies and those who did not. Cognitive theory predicts that only the aware subjects will show conditioning. This should hold for both autonomic and motor response systems, though contingency awareness is difficult to assess in operant autonomic conditioning.

Compliance. One version of the Compliance design is simply an elaboration of the Awareness of Contingency design. Since awareness of the CS-UCS relationship or reinforcement contingency is hypothesized to be a necessary, but not sufficient, condition for the occurrence of conditioning, the aware *Ss* can be separated into those who realized what response was expected by *E* and those who did not. The group who guessed what response was expected can be further subdivided into those who chose to comply and those who did not. The cognitive hypothesis predicts that only the group who were aware of the reinforcement contingency, aware of what response was expected of them, and compliant, will show conditioning.

Compliance can be manipulated also. For example, *S's* willingness to produce the response, once he has realized what *E* expects, can be manipulated by varying the pleasantness or unpleasantness of the UCS or by placing social pressure on *S*. The Compliance designs are applicable to motor responses and operant autonomic conditioning.

Contingency expectancy. There are two different forms of Contingency Expectancy design. One technique is to make the CS-UCS relation or reinforcement contingency ambiguous and then compare the responses made by *S* with *S's* hypothesis about the CS-UCS relation or reinforcement contingency. Cognitive theory predicts that in classical conditioning, responses made by *S* will be in conformity with his hypothesis about the CS-UCS relation, while in operant conditioning they will be in conformity with his hypothesis about the reinforcement contingency. The other technique is to explicitly manipulate *S's* contingency expectancy, and then observe the effect on his responses. For example, removing the shock electrodes from *S* in an aversive conditioning paradigm should immediately reduce or eliminate his expectation of shock, and so cognitive theory predicts that this manipulation will immediately reduce or eliminate *S's* responses for both autonomic and motor output systems.

Response expectancy. There are also two different forms of the Response Expectancy design. One technique is to set up a classical conditioning paradigm in which more than one type of response is possible and then leave ambiguous the type of response expected by *E*. The type of response made by *S* can then be compared to his hypothesis about what was expected. For example, if finger withdrawal conditioning is carried out with neutral instructions, some *Ss* may hypothesize that *E* wants to see if they are capable of keeping their finger on the electrode during the shock, while other *Ss* may hypothesize that *E* wants to see if they can remove their finger fast enough to avoid the shock. Cognitive theory predicts that the response made by *S* will be a function of his hypothesis about the nature of the response expected in the situation and his desire to comply.

The other Response Expectancy technique is to use a conditioning paradigm where several responses are possible and then give *S* information about the responses expected by *E*. Cognitive theory predicts that compliant *Ss* will shift their responses in keeping with *E's* instructions. The effects of response expectancy are probably restricted to motor response systems.

Reinforcement expectancy. There are two types of Reinforcement Expectancy designs depending on the type of reinforcement. With strong aversive stimuli such as shock, *S* can be given information about the intensity of the UCS and then his response can be examined to see to what degree it was determined by his expectation. With reinforcers that do not have a strong natural motivating property (e.g., a click or the spoken sound "mmm-hmm"), it should be easier to show the effects of expectancy. Reinforcers of this type are often ambiguous, and when they are, cognitive theory predicts that *Ss* will respond in accordance with their hypotheses about the purpose of the reinforcer. Thus, for operant conditioning, compliant *Ss* who think the reinforcer "mmm-hmm" is to inform them that they have made the right response will increase the responses followed by the reinforcer, while compliant *Ss* who think that the reinforcer is to inform them that they have made the wrong response will decrease the responses followed by the reinforcer.

These dissociation designs fall into two basic types, depending on how the higher mental processes are dissociated from the presumed automatic, unconscious action of CS-UCS pairings or contingent reinforcement. The Informed Pairing design and the Instructed Conditioning design attempt to produce conditioning through the operation of the higher mental processes, without the occasion for any unconscious, automatic conditioning to have occurred.

The Informed Unpairing, Instructed Nonconditioning, Instructed Extinction, and Masking designs place the operation of the higher mental processes in opposition to the operation of the unconscious, automatic mechanism. The Awareness of Contingency, Compliance, Contingency Expectancy, Response Expectancy, and Reinforcement Expectancy designs also juxtapose the two alternatives, but through the examination of the reported expectancies of certain subclasses of *Ss*.

The findings of those studies that have used one of the dissociation designs can be used to distinguish between three basically different conceptions of the conditioning process.

If none of the results predicted by cognitive theory are obtained in dissociation experiments, and instead only the opposing predictions of conditioning theory are obtained, then clearly the enormous conditioning literature using nondissociative experiments can be safely interpreted as it typically has been, in terms of automatic, unconscious processes.

If intermediate results are obtained with the dissociation paradigms, then a two-factor theory will be required to interpret the standard body of conditioning experiments. For example, if masking the CS-UCS relation reduces the level of responding but doesn't eliminate it, and Instructed Nonconditioning gives a similar reduction, then the results from the conditioning literature will best be conceptualized as resulting from the combined action of the higher mental processes assumed in cognitive theory, and the unconscious, automatic mechanisms assumed in conditioning theory.

If the empirical findings of the dissociation experiments follow the predictions of cognitive theory, then the classic findings of the nondissociation experiments will best be interpreted as resulting from the operation of the mechanisms postulated in cognitive theory.

The following review is extensive, but the literature is so large that many relevant studies must have been missed. However, the studies reviewed have not been selected. All dissociation experiments using the standard laboratory conditioning designs that were uncovered have been included regardless of outcome.

DISSOCIATION EXPERIMENTS: AUTONOMIC RESPONSES

Many writers have felt that conditioning of autonomic response systems is the area where the unconscious, automatic assumptions of conditioning theory are least vulnerable to attack. Yet in fact, the results of studies using autonomic responses are probably even more favorable to cognitive theory than are those using motor responses.

Galvanic skin response (GSR). The GSR is one of the best studied response systems in terms of the number and sophistication of experiments using dissociation designs. There have been seven Informed Pairing experiments using the GSR (Bridger & Mandel, 1964; Cook & Harris, 1937; Dawson & Grings, 1968; Fenz & Dronsejko, 1969; Katz, Webb, & Stotland, 1971; McComb, 1969; Wilson, 1968). In all seven studies simply telling Ss the CS-UCS relation, with no actual pairings, produced conditioning. It is interesting to note that in three of the four studies with appropriate data, the amplitude of the GSR was greater in the verbally informed Ss than in controls receiving actual CS-UCS pairings. This should go a long way toward dispelling the belief that college sophomores show little imagination.

There have been 13 Informed Unpairing studies using the GSR. Twelve of these studies (Bridger & Mandel, 1965a, 1965b; Colgan, 1970; Cook & Harris, 1937; Grings & Lockhart, 1963; Katz, Webb, & Stotland, 1971; Koenig & Castillo, 1969; Mandel & Bridger, 1967; Silverman, 1960, .5-second group; Wickens, Allen, & Hill, 1963; Wickens & Harding, 1967; Wilson, 1968) found extinction, while one did not (Bridger & Mandel, 1964). The technique used to inform S that the CS would no longer be followed by the UCS varied in these studies. Some Es simply told Ss that there would be no more shock, while others used a combination of verbal instructions and actual removal of the shock electrode.

In most of the Informed Unpairing studies the drop in responding is rapid and dramatic; however, it is rarely complete in one trial. This partial deviation from the cognitive hypothesis is not unexpected, since it seems likely that some Ss will not believe that E is really going to stop presenting the UCS – thus these Ss should not extinguish rapidly. Four studies (Bridger & Mandel, 1965a, 1965b; Mandel & Bridger, 1967; Wilson, 1968) have data to bear on this issue. The results reveal much about the typical S in psychological experiments. These studies show that roughly one-third of Ss did not believe that the shock would stop even though the shock electrode had been removed. Those studies that made an objective assessment of Ss' beliefs in the unpairing instructions and then used the data from Ss who stated that they believed the experimenter (e.g., Bridger & Mandel, 1965a; Wilson, 1968) lend strong support to cognitive theory in that they show almost complete extinction in one trial. Wilson's experiment is particularly instructive. He established differential conditioning to a positive and negative stimulus and then told Ss that the positive stimulus was going to become the negative stimulus and vice versa. By the second trial the responses to the two stimuli were completely reversed with the GSR response to the old negative stimulus as high as it had been to the old positive stimulus and vice versa.

Five GSR studies have used the Instructed Nonconditioning technique (Dawson & Reardon, 1969; Harvey & Wickens, 1971; Hill, 1967; Hughes & Shean, 1971; Swenson & Hill, 1970). All have shown a small reduction in GSR amplitude with instructions not to condition, and are thus in conformity with the prediction made by cognitive theory for autonomic responses. The study by Swenson and Hill (1970) showed that Ss can inhibit signaled trials within a conditioning series, and so the effect is probably due to something more specific than overall reduced autonomic activation.

The Masking design is perhaps the most powerful of the dissociation designs, since conditioning theory and cognitive theory make clearly opposed predictions about the outcome. Five GSR studies have used the Masking technique (Block, 1962; Dawson, 1970; Dawson & Grings, 1968; Dawson & Satterfield, 1969; Shean, 1968a). All have found no conditioning when the CS-UCS relationship is masked, and thus all five studies support cognitive theory. Dawson's (1970) study is a good example of the application of the masking technique. The Ss in this study heard sets of five tones. The last tone in each sequence was then used to set up a differential conditioning paradigm, with a high tone serving as the positive CS. All Ss were given a series of CS-UCS pairings in the standard differential conditioning paradigm. The Ss were told that their task was to select the tone from the last four in each series that was most similar to the first tone. One group was also told that there would be a relationship between the highest tone and the shock. The Ss in the masked conditions who thought they were in a discrimination study showed no conditioning, whereas Ss who had been exposed to identical pairings but given instructions about the CS-UCS relationship showed significant conditioning. Thus, the Masking experiments provide strong competitive support for the cognitive explanation of conditioning.

Ten experiments have used the Awareness of Contingency design (Baer & Fuhrer, 1968, 1969, 1970; Chatterjee & Eriksen, 1960; Freeman, 1930; Fuhrer & Baer, 1965, 1966, 1969; McComb, 1969; Morgenson & Martin, 1969). All 10 studies have found that only aware Ss show conditioning. Chatterjee and Eriksen (1960) make the important point that S does not have to be aware of E's CS-UCS relation; he may develop a hypothesis close enough to E's so that he produces enough CRs to reach E's criterion of successful conditioning. The experiments using the Awareness of Contingency technique clearly give strong support to cognitive theory.

A variety of Contingency Expectancy designs have been used with GSR. Mowrer (1938) manipulated CS-UCS expectancy by removing and reattaching the shock electrode. He found that the conditioned GSR was extinguished by removing the shock electrode, but returned immediately if the electrode was reattached. Corn-Becker, Welch, and Fisichelli (1949) and Grings, Carlin, and Appley (1962) have also directly manipulated S's CS-UCS expectancy. The Ss in these experiments saw a series of words on a screen, and after each word the appropriate referent was presented (e.g., after the words "cool breeze" *Ss* would feel a cool breeze). After the series of word-referent pairings, the word "shock" occurred without actual shock. The *Ss* in both studies gave significant GSR responses when the CS (the word "shock") was presented. Epstein and Bahm (1971) and Streiner and Dean (1968) have examined *Ss'* CS-UCS expectancies on a trial-by-trial basis. Both studies found a very high correlation between *Ss'* reported expectation that a shock would occur on a given trial and the amplitude of the GSR for that trial. Epstein and Roupenian (1970) and Hill (1969) have shown that the size of the conditioned GSR depends on the probability with which *Ss* expect the CS-UCS pairings to occur.

Both Mandel and Bridger (1967) and Zeiner and Grings (1968) have found backward conditioning with the GSR. S-R theory has always had difficulty in dealing with the occurrence of backward conditioning (Kimble, 1961, p. 158). However, Zeiner and Grings note that the backward conditioning effect was produced by a subset of *Ss* who had developed hypotheses relating the CS to the UCS, and so cognitive theory gives a natural account of this phenomenon. Thus, the Contingency Expectancy studies using GSR show *Ss'* responses to be in close compliance with their beliefs about the CS-UCS relationship, as predicted by cognitive theory.

Öhman (1971) used a Reinforcement Expectancy design and found that a shift in UCS intensity had little effect on GSR amplitude when it was shifted in keeping with *Ss'* expectancies, but had a large effect when the UCS was shifted contrary to their expectations.

Taken as a whole, the dissociation experiments using classical conditioning of the GSR provide extraordinarily consistent support for cognitive theory. It is quite rare for a large body of experiments on *any* topic in psychology to show as much agreement as do these studies.

Operant GSR conditioning. There has developed recently a wave of interest in the application of operant techniques to autonomic responses. A number of dissociation experiments involving operant conditioning of the GSR have been carried out. Dean, Martin, and Streiner (1968), Martin and Dean (1971), and Shean (1970) have used a variant of the Instructed Conditioning technique and found no operant conditioning of GSR in uninstructed groups, but successful conditioning in groups given either instructions or instructions plus GSR practice. These studies involving the manipulation of *S's* awareness of the reinforcement contingencies thus seem to indicate that awareness of the contingency is a necessary prerequisite for operant conditioning of the GSR.

Six studies have used the Awareness of Contingency design with operant GSR conditioning (Gavalas, 1967; Johnson & Schwartz, 1967; Schwartz & Johnson, 1969; Schell & Grings, 1971; Shapiro & Crider, 1967; Shapiro, Crider, & Tursky, 1964). All six studies report successful conditioning in *Ss* unaware of the reinforcement contingencies. However, this outcome is to be expected, due to the extreme methodological difficulty involved in carrying out an appropriate Awareness of Contingency design with operant conditioning of an autonomic response. Cognitive theory hypothesizes that successful conditioning is not due to the automatic, unconscious action of the reinforcement on the autonomic system being measured, but rather to *E's* inadvertently reinforcing some cognitive activity on the part of *S*. Thus, there are two basic methodological difficulties. First, unlike the case of classical conditioning, *E* has little control over what contingency is being reinforced and so is completely at the mercy of *S*. The second problem is that quite different types of cognitive activity by a single *S* might result in the same autonomic response, while the same cognitive activity in different *Ss* might result in different autonomic responses. Thus if one is going to attempt to use the Awareness of Contingency design in the operant conditioning of autonomic responses, the awareness assessment will have to be very elaborate and will have to be carried out *S* by *S*, trial by trial. None of the six operant GSR studies using the Awareness of Contingency design used anything remotely resembling the assessment procedures outlined above, and so they can be dismissed as counterevidence to the cognitive theory. Thus what minimal evidence there is on the operant conditioning of GSR tends to support the cognitive theory.

Heart rate conditioning. A fair number of dissociation experiments have been carried out using heart rate acceleration or deceleration as the response measure. Nine experiments have used the Informed Pairing technique in this area (Deane, 1961, 1964, 1969; Epstein & Roupenian, 1970; Fenz & Dronsejko, 1969; Folkins, 1970; Jenks & Deane, 1963; Nolan, 1961; Steward, 1962). All nine studies produced significant heart rate conditioning simply by telling *Ss* the CS-UCS contingencies, as predicted by cognitive theory. As was the case in GSR conditioning, a threatened CS-UCS pairing produced as large or larger amplitude responses than did actual CS-UCS pairings.

Two experiments have used the Informed Unpairing technique (Chatterjee & Eriksen, 1962; Notterman, Schoenfeld, & Bersh, 1952), and both studies found rapid extinction. The Chatterjee and Eriksen (1962) study is the only investigation in this area to use the Masking technique. These investigators found no conditioning in a group instructed to give chain associations to the stimulus words, whereas a similar group informed that there would be a relation between one of the words and the UCS did condition.

Deane (1969) and Epstein and Clarke (1970) have carried out Reinforcement Expectancy studies using heart rate. Both found that on the first trial after instructions *S's* heart rate was a function of the intensity of UCS that *S* expected to receive.

Thus, dissociation experiments using heart rate as the response system show excellent agreement with cognitive theory.

Operant heart rate conditioning. The only two dissociation experiments investigating operant heart rate conditioning (Engel & Chism, 1967; Engel & Hansen, 1966) have used the Awareness of Contingency technique, which is difficult to apply to autonomic responses. Both studies reported conditioning in *Ss* unaware of the reinforcement contingency. However, Murray and Katkin (1968) have shown that a reanalysis of the interview data reported in these studies reveals that conditioning was systematically related to the cognitive strategies adopted by *Ss*. Thus the limited data on operant heart rate conditioning support cognitive theory.

Salivary conditioning. Reviewing the dissociation experiments using the salivary response produces some unique problems, since it amounts to analyzing the complex work of one man, Gregory Razran. Razran is one of the few major investigators in this area who saw the full implications of ignoring the higher mental processes in conditioning (particularly in Razran, 1955). Razran held a two-factor theory of conditioning. He felt that what is called cognitive theory in this chapter is necessary to account for some experimental results, while conditioning theory is necessary to account for other experimental results. Because he held the two-factor theory, Razran carried out a systematic set of dissociation experiments using the salivary response. Unfortunately most of these experiments lack crucial control groups and simply do not meet the methodological requirements of current experimental psychology (see Feather, 1965, 1967). A major difficulty with early conditioning studies such as Razran's is the lack of a control for pseudoconditioning or sensitization (Kimble, 1961, pp. 60-65). Most recent investigations in this area have used differential conditioning or an unpaired CS-UCS control group to avoid these difficulties.

Razran carried out one experiment using the Informed Pairing technique (Razran, 1949a). This experiment cannot be interpreted, since it used no pseudoconditioning control to show that specific conditioning occurred and no noninstructed control group to act as a baseline for the group informed as to the CS-UCS relations.

Two experiments used the Instructed Conditioning technique (Razran, 1935, 1949a). In the 1935 study a differential conditioning procedure was used, and Ss were told to try to connect the CS with saliva. One of five Ss seemed to show differentiation, and so this experiment can be taken as weak support for either conditioning or cognitive theory. In Razran (1949a) Ss were told to think of eating when the CS occurred. This procedure gave very large amounts of saliva, but there was no pseudoconditioning control nor a noninstructed control group. If the methodological difficulties were ignored, this study would support the cognitive hypothesis.

The same two experiments also used Instructed Nonconditioning groups. Two of five Ss in the first study seemed to show differentiation, and thus this study gives ambiguous results. The Ss in the Instructed Nonconditioning group in the second study gave very little saliva, but the results cannot be interpreted for the reasons outlined above.

The Masking technique was used in three experiments (Razran, 1936, 1949a, 1949b). In the 1936 study the CS-UCS relation was masked by having Ss learn a finger maze while undergoing classical salivary conditioning. In the latter two studies Ss were told that they were in a memory experiment and given sham memory tests. Razran states that he found conditioning in all three experiments and that none of the Ss became aware of the CS-UCS relations. This is, of course, evidence opposed to cognitive theory. However, the 1936 and 1949a experiments did not use pseudoconditioning controls and so are of limited value. The 1949b study used differential conditioning and so cannot be discounted on this basis. There is, however, a problem with all three studies at a different level. They provide no empirical support for the assertion that none of the Ss became aware of the

CS-UCS relations during the experiment. Thus, none can be taken as serious evidence against cognitive theory.

Feather (1967) carried out a series of salivary conditioning studies with appropriate controls, which he claimed might be the first clear experimental demonstration of human salivary conditioning. He did not use any of the dissociation designs, but stated that the very rapid acquisition and rapid discrimination reversal suggested support for a cognitive theory of conditioning.

If it were not for the methodological difficulties with these studies, the dissociation experiments using a salivary response would give support to both theoretical positions. The masking experiments would support the automatic, unconscious assumptions of conditioning theory, while the remaining experiments tend to favor the cognitive account. However, given the methodological problems, the results cannot be taken to support either position.

Vasomotor conditioning. The final autonomic response system in which dissociation experiments have been carried out is the vasomotor response, or change in rate of blood flow. There have been no clear examples of the Informed Pairing design, but two somewhat analogous experiments have been carried out. Menzies (1941) has shown that asking S to imagine a specific past experience of extremes of temperature causes appropriate vasomotor responses (an increase in skin temperature with imagery of heat, and a decrease with imagery of cold). Shean (1968b) told Ss that only one word out of a 12 item list would be shocked. The Ss showed immediate conditioning after the first trial, as would be expected by cognitive theory, since the first shock presumably informed S of the CS-UCS relationship.

Shean (1968b) used the Informed Unpairing design. He found that the verbally informed group showed immediate extinction of the differential vasomotor response. Shean's study also included a condition using the Masking design. The Ss given a word association masking task showed no differential vasomotor conditioning.

Baer and Fuhrer (1970) and Maltzman (1968) have used the Awareness of Contingency design with vasomotor responses. They both found that only the aware Ss conditioned. Thus, while the vasomotor response system has not been extensively studied, those experiments that have been carried out lend strong support to the cognitive theory.

Overall, the findings of dissociation experiments with autonomic responses are extraordinarily consistent. Almost without exception the experiments in this area support cognitive theory.

DISSOCIATION EXPERIMENTS: MOTOR RESPONSES

As discussed previously, dissociation experiments using motor responses differ from those using autonomic responses. Much of the difference stems from the assumption of cognitive theory that after S becomes aware of the CS-UCS relation or reinforcement contingency, he must determine what E expects him to do and then decide whether or not to comply. Thus, additional experimental designs appropriate to test these two assumptions are required for motor response systems.

Finger withdrawal conditioning. The finger withdrawal response was introduced to American psychology by John B. Watson and has been used as the response system for a number of dissociation experiments. Lindley and Moyer (1961) used the Informed Unpairing technique and found that telling Ss that there would be no more shocks produced rapid extinction.

It seems unlikely that any investigator would carry out an Instructed Conditioning study with a motor response since, in plain English, this would consist of telling S to move his finger. However, common sense is not a good guide when predicting the behavior of investigators operating in an S-R framework. Experiment 6 in Hunter (1938) consists of producing finger withdrawal conditioning by saying, "Lift your finger," or "Don't lift your finger." If Ss didn't make a finger withdrawal response to "Lift your finger," they were shocked. To insure objectivity the commands were presented by telephone. The Ss conditioned.

Three investigations have used the Instructed Extinction technique (Lindley & Moyer, 1961; Moyer & Lindley, 1962; Wickens, 1939). Wickens reported that only one-third of the Ss told to stop making the CR were able to stop making the response, whereas Ss in the other two studies showed the sudden extinction predicted by cognitive theory.

The only study to use the Awareness of Contingency technique in this area was an early, thoughtful experiment by Hamel (1919). He reported that only Ss aware of the CS-UCS relation showed conditioning, but presented no data to support this statement.

One very interesting experiment has used the Response Expectancy technique with a finger withdrawal response (Lindley, 1959). However, in order to understand the significance of this study, it is necessary to review an earlier series of studies by Wickens (1938, 1943a, 1943b). In these studies standard finger withdrawal conditioning was carried out, with palms down. (It is interesting to note that standard finger withdrawal conditioning uses the following "neutral" instructions: "If you get conditioned you will develop a tendency to respond to the tone before the shock goes on. . . If your finger wants to fly up just don't inhibit it [Wickens, 1943a, p. 223] .") After S reached criterion, Wickens used a most ingenious procedure; he turned S's hand over and then presented the CS. The Ss thus had three choices: making the same response they had been making and pressing their finger onto the electrode; achieving the same goal (shock avoidance) by making a new response; or making no response. The results varied from study to study but, overall, roughly 75% of the Ss made the new flexion response that avoided the shock, 20% made no response, and 5% extended their finger into the electrode. These experiments are of considerable theoretical importance, since they are often cited as the classic demonstration of response generalization. However, they are not dissociation experiments, since the Ss' response expectancy was not assessed or explicitly manipulated.

While the Wickens experiments are not dissociation experiments, they can easily be so interpreted, due to a series of experiments by Lindley (1959) using the Response Expectancy technique. Lindley's procedures were modeled after Wickens, but S's expectations were manipulated through differential instructions. One group received the standard Wickens instructions; a second group received instructions which emphasized that a specific muscular response was being conditioned; and a third group was deceived about the location of the electrodes, so that in attempting to avoid the shock they would press into the electrode. The results are most interesting. On the transfer task *Ss* receiving the standard Wickens instructions gave roughly two-thirds responses away from the electrode, thus replicating Wickens. Of the *Ss* given instructions emphasizing that particular responses were being conditioned, only one-third gave responses away from the electrode. During the initial conditioning 100% of the responses made by *Ss* in the first two groups were away from the electrode. During the initial conditioning of the group misled about the location of the electrode, precisely the opposite occurred—100% of the responses made by this group were into the electrode.

In general, dissociation experiments using finger withdrawal as the motor response add additional support to cognitive theory. The powerful effect of manipulating *S's* expectation seems particularly decisive.

Several investigators in the area of finger withdrawal conditioning (Cason, 1935; Wickens, 1939) have attempted to distinguish a cognitive account of conditioning from an automatic, unconscious account, through a design not described earlier. These investigators have compared *Ss* instructed to condition ("voluntary responders") with *Ss* subjected to the standard conditioning procedure ("involuntary responders"). The reasoning is that if the two groups show differences in such parameters as rate of acquisition, amplitude of response, latency of response, etc., then there must be two kinds of conditioning. This is simply not an appropriate dissociation design. The conditioning group must always have a UCS paired with the CS, and this clearly will produce a variety of changes in their expectancies and motivation. Thus, differences or lack of differences between the groups on the basic parameters of conditioning are not interpretable as favoring one position or the other.

Eyelid conditioning. The conditioned eyelid response is usually considered one of the best studied and well-understood areas in psychology. Actually, in terms of dissociation experiments, it is not as well understood as some of the other response systems. There have not been any clear examples of the Informed Pairing design in this area, but Hilgard, Campbell, and Sears (1938) carried out a study in which *Ss* were told the CS-UCS relations and then put through standard conditioning procedure. They showed much more rapid acquisition than did a control group without the verbal information. Cole (1939) carried out an Informed Unpairing study using eyelid conditioning. He found that *Ss* informed that the UCS would no longer follow the CS extinguished almost immediately.

Five experiments have used the Instructed Conditioning technique with the eyeblink response (Fishbein, 1967a, 1967b; Gormezano & Moore, 1962; Hilgard & Humphreys, 1938; Prokasy & Allen, 1969), and all five found conditioning. It is clear that eyelid conditioning lives up to its reputation as one of the most rigorous and tough-minded areas in psychology. Most soft-minded cognitive psychologists might feel that it was not necessary to have five experiments demonstrating that *Ss* can blink their eyes when instructed to do so; nonetheless, cognitive theory does correctly predict the outcome.

The Instructed Nonconditioning technique has been used in 10 experiments with eyelid conditioning (Fishbein 1967a, 1967b; Fishbein & Gormezano, 1966; Hilgard

& Humphreys, 1938; Miller, 1939; Nicholls & Kimble, 1964; Norris & Grant, 1948; Ominsky, 1968a, 1968b; Prokasy & Allen, 1969). All studies found a drastic reduction in conditioning, thus supporting cognitive theory. However, only three of these studies produced nearly complete elimination of conditioning (Fishbein, 1967a; Norris & Grant, 1948; Prokasy & Allen, 1969, .4-second group). In some of the other experiments the groups told not to make responses were making as many as 40% conditioned responses.

However, methodological problems cast doubt on these findings. The Instructed Nonconditioning design is particularly sensitive to pseudoconditioning and sensitization artifacts, since *any* response, produced for whatever reason, is counted against the cognitive hypothesis. Therefore, studies using the Instructed Nonconditioning technique must use either differential conditioning or an unpaired CS-UCS control group. Only Hilgard and Humphreys (1938) and Prokasy and Allen (1969) used such controls. (Presumably the limited use of controls in eyelid conditioning studies compared to other areas such as GSR conditioning is due to the fact that *Es* in eyelid conditioning are convinced that they have experimental control over the phenomenon, and thus need none.) The lack of controls in most of these studies reduces the strength of the findings considerably, especially when taken in conjunction with another common flaw. When the Instructed Nonconditioning technique is used with an aversive UCS, *S* is put in the situation of balancing the *E's* instructions against the aversive effects of the UCS. Therefore, *S's* degree of compliance with *E* must be assessed in order to indicate if the responses are truly automatic or if they are simply the outcome of a decision to disregard *E's* instructions.

None of the Instructed Nonconditioning studies have assessed *S's* degree of compliance, but a study by Ominsky (1968b) certainly tends to support the cognitive explanation. Ominsky carried out standard classical eyelid conditioning with instructions to inhibit the CR and found between 20% and 40% CRs. Conditioning theory would presumably explain these findings as resulting from the gradual increase of habit strength in an unconscious, automatic fashion which eventually overcame a cognitive inhibitory set. Thus, conditioning theory would presumably predict a long, slow extinction of the hard-won habit strength. Cognitive theory would explain these findings as the outcome of *Ss'* weighing the discomfort of the UCS against the instructions not to blink and tending to abandon the inhibitory set over the course of the experiment. Hence, cognitive theory would predict that with the removal of the UCS *Ss* would quickly readopt the inhibitory set and show immediate extinction. Ominsky found immediate, complete extinction in his *Ss,* thus providing empirical support for the cognitive critique of the findings of the eyelid conditioning studies using the Instructed Nonconditioning technique.

Thus, while the Instructed Nonconditioning studies in eyelid conditioning show some possibility of supporting an automatic component in conditioning, the methodological difficulties outlined above cast doubt even here.

The Masking design has been used in three eyelid conditioning studies (Ross, Wilcox, & Mayer, 1967; Spence, 1963; Spence, Homzie, & Rutledge, 1964). The probability matching mask used in the studies by Spence produced reduced conditioning, and the time estimation mask used by Ross eliminated conditioning completely. These results are as predicted by cognitive theory, if it is assumed that the mask used in the Spence studies was only partially effective. The two Spence studies also used the masking task during extinction and found less rapid extinction in the masked group than in a control group with no masking task. Spence (1966) proposed an ingenious cognitive account of this data. He hypothesized that unmasked Ss will become aware of the omission of the UCS almost immediately and thus will extinguish very rapidly. However, masked Ss who are making CRs will be much less likely to notice the shift in the CS-UCS contingency and so will be slower to extinguish.

The Awareness of Contingency design has not been applied in this area, but a study by Hilgard, Campbell, and Sears (1937) did find a direct relation between speed of CS-UCS awareness and degree of conditioning.

The Contingency Expectancy design has been used in a variety of experiments in this area, particularly with respect to extinction data. Eyelid conditioning studies typically show very rapid extinction; for example, Hilgard, Campbell, and Sears (1937) reported that 11 of 14 Ss gave no responses after the first unpaired CS trial. While this is not a completely appropriate dissociation design, Spence (1966) has used this data to argue that extinction must be due to S's becoming aware of the change in the CS-UCS contingency. Porter (1938) interviewed four Ss who did not stop responding during a long extinction series. All four stated that they expected E to introduce the UCS again. Cole (1939) also found that Ss performing in an unusual manner were acting in accord with some unusual expectation about the experiment.

Humphreys' (1939) classic paper demonstrating that Ss given intermittent CS-UCS pairings are more resistent to extinction than are Ss given 100% CS-UCS pairings is probably best interpreted as a study of manipulated CS-UCS expectancy. Humphreys argued that Ss in the intermittent group grew to expect sequences of unpaired CSs followed by paired CSs, whereas the 100% group expected the UCS on every trial. Thus, when the two groups entered the extinction phase of the experiment, it took much longer for the intermittent group to become aware that the CS-UCS relationship had been changed, and so it took them much longer to stop responding. The Ss were asked when they became aware of the change in the CS-UCS relationship, and this awareness data supported Humphreys' expectancy interpretation, showing a much higher percentage of aware Ss in the 100% group than in the intermittent group.

Fishbein (1967b) showed that Ss' expectancies can have a large effect that lasts over time. He had one group perform in an Instructed Conditioning design and another group perform in an Instructed Nonconditioning design. After the initial acquisition these Ss were given standard neutral conditioning instructions and then conditioned a second time. There were large differences in acquisition between the two groups, showing a large effect of initial instructions on Ss' performance, even though the initial instructions had been superseded by standard conditioning instructions. Presumably, these differences were due to different expectations in the two groups, produced by the initial instructions, although no interview data were gathered to support this assumption. Kimble (1967) did obtain extensive questionnaire data on *Ss'* hypotheses and expectations during conditioning and found correlations with conditioning ranging from .75 to .90.

Spence and Goldstein (1961), in a Reinforcement Expectancy design, manipulated *Ss'* expectancies by telling a group that had been conditioned with a weak air puff that they were going to be shifted to an unpleasantly strong puff of air. The *Ss* expecting a strong puff gave as many CRs as did a group actually given a strong puff.

Overall, the data from eyelid conditioning, a stronghold of S-R psychology, provide powerful support for cognitive theory. However, this area, unlike most other standard conditioning tasks, also provides some tentative support for automatic, unconscious mechanisms in conditioning.

Other motor conditioning. Some additional relevant studies have used other motor response systems. Hefferline, Keenan, and Harford (1959) carried out an operant conditioning study of "invisibly small thumb-twitches." This experiment has been considered by some to be opposed to a cognitive approach to conditioning. However, this is due to confusion about the levels of awareness necessary for the various components of the conditioning experiment. The cognitive theory outlined previously clearly requires that *Ss* be aware of the reinforcement contingencies, but not necessarily of the *particular* responses being measured by *E*. The Hefferline study would, in fact, seem a good demonstration of this distinction in a motor task. The *Ss* were rewarded by cessation of noise for very small thumb EMG responses. There were several experimental groups, and in general the more information *S* had about the contingencies that were used to reward him, the better was he able to make the required response. From the limited data presented about the *Ss'* reports, it seems likely that a variety of idiosyncratic responses were conditioned, each of which happened to have the small motor response as a component. Another study which has been interpreted (e.g., by Parton & DeNike, 1966) as showing conditioning without awareness in a relatively unobservable response system is that of Keehn, Lloyd, Hibbs, and Johnson (1965). The title, "Operant eyeblink conditioning without awareness: A preliminary report," and abstract of this paper report successful operant conditioning of eyeblinks in unaware subjects. However, examination of the text reveals no data on awareness assessment. In fact the text contains no evidence or discussion whatsoever in support of the article's title.

One of the popular research designs in Russian experimental psychology has been the Ivanov-Smolensky technique. There are many variations, but one version consists of the following procedure. The *Ss* are presented with a CS and a rubber bulb, and then told, "Press" (UCS). The UCS typically elicits a squeeze (UCR) and after sufficient pairing the CS comes to elicit a squeeze (CR). It is a little hard to deal with this procedure, but it appears to be an example of a Response Expectancy design. Presumably *Ss* eventually decide that *E*, in a very indirect way, is trying to get them to press the bulb when the CS occurs. The Russians have found this technique successful with young children, but it begins to become unstable around adolescence. While this finding is not predicted by cognitive theory, it would take only minimal effort to supplement cognitive theory with a few concepts from social psychology and common sense to account for this strange deterioration of the

Ivanov-Smolensky technique with age. It is interesting to note that even American S-R psychologists have been cautious about including the Ivanov-Smolensky technique with the standard conditioning designs, yet it has sometimes been included (Grant, 1964; Hartman, 1965).

The only well-designed dissociation experiments that have used motor responses other than finger withdrawal or eyeblink are those of Parton and DeNike (1966) and Paul, Eriksen, and Humphreys (1962). Parton and DeNike used the Awareness of Contingency and the Contingency Expectancy designs to investigate operant conditioning of a marble-dropping task in 9-year-old children. They found conditioning only in the children aware of the reinforcement contingency, and the children who developed a false alternation hypothesis responded in accord with their hypothesis, not in accord with the actual reinforcement. Paul, Eriksen, and Humphreys (1962) used a primary reinforcer (cool air for Ss in a heat chamber) to operantly condition gross motor responses, such as hand or foot movements. They found significant conditioning, but only in Ss aware of the reinforcement contingencies. Thus, while there are few experiments with motor responses outside of the standard paradigms, those that have been carried out support the cognitive position.

Operant schedules of reinforcement. Many of the details of human Ss' performance under the various operant reinforcement schedules can be derived from a slightly elaborated cognitive hypothesis. Cognitive theory predicts that Ss in an operant conditioning experiment will develop hypotheses about the reinforcement contingencies and will attempt to maximize reinforcement per unit time at least cost in effort. Thus, Ss with a ratio reinforcement hypothesis should give higher rates than Ss with an interval reinforcement hypothesis. The Ss with a fixed interval hypothesis should give bursts of responses (scalloping) around the moment of expected reinforcement.

Inconsistencies between S's hypothesized reinforcement contingency and the actual contingency may or may not result in changes in performance. If S's responses are such that he never realizes he has a false hypothesis, he should continue to perform in accordance with his false hypothesis. For example, if S is told that he is on a fixed ratio (FR) schedule, but is actually on a fixed interval (FI) schedule and immediately begins giving a constant rapid rate, he will not become aware of his false hypothesis unless he slows up or stops briefly. If he does notice the discrepancy, he should shift from the high FR rate to a slower scalloped rate. If S is told he is on a FI schedule but actually put on a FR schedule and begins giving a consistent scalloped pattern of responses, he will not become aware of his false hypothesis; but if he deviates from the steady scalloped responding enough to receive some inconsistent reinforcements, he should shift from the scalloped FI to the faster FR rate.

A number of experiments lend strong empirical support to the cognitive account of the operant schedules of reinforcement. Four have used Informed Pairing designs to investigate the operant schedules (Baron & Kaufman, 1966; Baron, Kaufman, & Stauber, 1969; Kaufman, Baron, & Kopp, 1966; Lippman & Meyer, 1967). All four studies found that telling Ss the contingency produced the standard curves of performance that have been obtained from pigeons. It is most interesting to note that all four studies are also consistent in that they did not find the usual lawful functional relations between reinforcement schedules and performance in uninstructed *Ss*.

B. F. Skinner has argued that the fundamental goal of science is to establish lawful functional relations. These studies suggest that researchers who accept Skinner's philosophy of science should begin a serious exploration of the cognitive processes of their *Ss*, since that appears to be where the lawful variables are.

Baron et al. (1969) and Weiner (1970) have used the Informed Unpairing design with operant schedules and found that instructions informing *S* that the reinforcement contingencies would no longer be in effect gave immediate extinction as predicted by cognitive theory.

Lippman and Meyer (1967) used a Contingency Expectancy design to study operant schedules. They placed uninformed *Ss* on a FI schedule and found variable performance curves across *Ss*. However, when they interviewed *Ss*, they discovered that the *Ss'* performance curves were consistent with their hypotheses about the reinforcement contingencies.

Two Reinforcement Expectancy designs have used operant schedules (Baron et al., 1969; Kaufman et al., 1966). Both found that *Ss* told they were being reinforced but who actually received no reinforcement showed strong conditioning.

Thus, the dissociation experiments dealing with operant schedules, the stronghold of radical behaviorism, actually give striking evidence for cognitive theory.

Taken as a whole, the dissociation experiments using motor responses provide powerful support for cognitive theory, as did the experiments using autonomic responses.

DISSOCIATION EXPERIMENTS: COMPLEX RESPONSES

Semantic generalization. Cognitive theory gives a very straightforward account of semantic generalization in conditioning. The development of a CR to the initial conditioned word is assumed to be no different from the development of a CR to any other CS. When *S* is presented with the generalization list, he will become aware of a variety of possible relations between the words on the generalization list and the original conditioned word. The generalization responses will be determined by *S's* hypothesis as to the likelihood that *E* will choose to follow a particular word relation with the UCS.

There have been six Awareness of Contingency experiments on semantic generalization. Five (Branca, 1957; Brotsky, 1968; Chatterjee & Eriksen, 1960; Maltzman, 1968; Raskin, 1969) show a strong positive relationship between awareness of the CS-generalization word relationship and semantic generalization, and one (Brotsky & Keller, 1971) does not. Branca carried out a *S*-by-*S* analysis and showed that no *S* who was not aware of the CS-generalization word relation showed significant semantic generalization.

Many writers have felt that the type of generalization exhibited by *S* is a basic characteristic of the *S*. Thus, much theoretical significance has been given to the findings of Riess (1940, 1946) that younger *Ss* tend to generalize more to homophones than to synonyms, while for adults the results are reversed. Cognitive theory suggests that the type of generalization shown by a group of Ss will simply be the result of the pooled *a priori* expectancies of the Ss about the likelihood that E will pair the UCS to words with a given relation. The cognitive approach makes a very strong prediction about the outcome of a manipulated Contingency Expectancy design. The type of generalization response given by S should be easily manipulated by changing his expectations. Thus, it should be possible to shift a group giving semantic generalization to phonetic generalization, simply by telling them immediately before the generalization test, "Look out for the words that sound like the ones you have just been shocked for." Razran (1949c), Raskin (1969), and Peastrel, Wishner, and Kaplan (1968) have manipulated CS-UCS expectancy in semantic generalization, and all three experiments give the results predicted by cognitive theory. Thus, experiments dealing with semantic generalization agree with other areas of conditioning research, lending strong support to cognitive theory.

Conditioned meaning. In 1957 Staats and Staats published a very influential paper on the conditioning of meaning. The experiment reported consisted of pairing certain nonsense syllables with words of common affective values (e.g., "good" words or "bad" words). After a series of trials the affective value of the nonsense syllables was measured through the Semantic Differential technique. The nonsense syllables showed significant changes in affective value, even though only the data from unaware Ss was used in the experiment. The study was replicated by Staats, Staats, Heard, and Nims (1959). This work has been considered to be of considerable importance for two reasons: It has been interpreted as supporting mediational accounts of meaning as an implicit response and as showing the unconscious, automatic conditioning of something as complex as word meaning.

Eleven replications of the Staats and Staats experiment have used the Awareness of Contingency design with more sophisticated measures of awareness (Cohen, 1964; Coles & Leonard, 1969; Freeman & Suedfeld, 1969; Gerstein, 1961; Hare, 1964, 1965; Insko & Oakes, 1966; Miller, Gimpl, & McCrimmon, 1969; Paivio, 1964; Page, 1969, 1971). All but Miller et al. found conditioning only in Ss aware of the relationship between the nonsense syllable and the emotionally valued words. Miller (1967) reported that he found no correlation between Ss' responses on an awareness questionnaire and degree of conditioning. However, in a later study (Miller, 1968), he reanalyzed his earlier data and showed a significant correlation between awareness scores and the conditioning data. Miller and Babcock (1970) found similar results.

Hare (1965) and Page (1971) report data that have important implications for methodology when using the Awareness of Contingency design. Both studies assessed awareness with the general unstructured questions used in the earlier Staats work ("What was the purpose of the experiment?"). With this type of awareness assessment both studies replicated the earlier Staats finding of conditioning in unaware Ss. However, when a more objective, structured assessment procedure was used, both studies gave the usual finding of conditioning only in aware Ss. The lesson is clear. Serious investigators dealing with the awareness issue must spend as much energy and experimental effort on the procedures for assessing awareness as they do on any other crucial aspect of an experiment.

Two studies have used the Masking design to investigate conditioned meaning. Insko and Oakes (1966) used a color naming task as a partially successful mask and found reduced conditioning of meaning. Rozelle (1968) used a sham memory task as a mask and found no conditioning of meaning.

Hare (1964, 1965) used memory errors in an interesting form of Contingency Expectancy design. After each experiment Hare asked Ss to indicate which nonsense syllables had been paired with which types of words. The ratings of the nonsense syllables which had been mispaired in memory provide a crucial comparison, since S thinks they were paired with one type of emotionally valued words, while they were actually paired with some other type. Thus, the ratings of the nonsense syllables can be examined to see if they follow S's beliefs or the actual CS-UCS pairing. The analysis on this subset of items shows that the conditioning followed Ss' beliefs, and not the actual CS-UCS pairings.

Page (1969) carried out a Response Expectancy design with the conditioning of meaning technique. He looked at the small subgroup of Ss who indicated that they were aware of the CS-UCS relations but were not aware that E wanted them to change their ratings of the nonsense syllables on the basis of the CS-UCS pairings. These Ss showed no conditioning. Page also used the Compliance technique and looked at the responses of the small subgroup who indicated that they were aware of the CS-UCS relations and aware of the expected response but chose not to comply. These Ss showed no conditioning.

Thus, with minor exceptions, experiments on the conditioning of meaning show precisely the results predicted by cognitive theory.

Verbal operant conditioning. Greenspoon's (1955) demonstration that word production can be manipulated in an operant paradigm has been followed by an enormous number of experiments. The original popularity of this paradigm was due to its apparent simplicity and direct practical implications. However, for the purposes of this chapter verbal operant conditioning is interesting because it is the only area in the conditioning literature in which the theoretically crucial dissociation experiments have become a major focus of research.

The initial Greenspoon article used an Awareness of Contingency design and found that 10 of 75 Ss could verbalize the reinforcement contingencies. These Ss were excluded from the data analysis, presumably because Greenspoon felt that their change in verbal behavior would not reflect the "true" unconscious, automatic action of the reinforcer. Many of the experiments following Greenspoon also used the Awareness of Contingency design. Krasner (1958) reported that, overall, 95% of Ss in 31 Awareness of Contingency experiments showed unconscious, automatic verbal conditioning. Thus, in 1958 a massive experimental literature appeared to give evidence opposed to cognitive theory.

However, in 1961 two experiments (Dulany, 1961; Levin, 1961) reopened the issue. Dulany (1961) replicated the standard Greenspoon experiment in which Ss are asked to emit single words and then are reinforced with "Umhmm" for plural nouns. He found the usual significant effect of conditioning, and no Ss were aware of the reinforcement contingency. However, he pointed out that this experiment could be looked at as a Contingency Expectancy design with ambiguous reinforcement contingency, and so he assessed Ss' hypotheses about the reinforcement contingency. He found a subgroup of *Ss* who had developed the hypothesis that they were being reinforced for giving items in a semantic category and thus inadvertently gave more plural nouns (e.g., "rubies," "pearls"). A reanalysis of the data showed that only *Ss* who had developed this "correlated hypothesis" showed significant conditioning.

Levin (1961) used the standard Awareness of Contingency design to study verbal operant conditioning with the Taffel (1955) sentence construction task. When he used a four-question interview to assess contingency awareness, he found conditioning without awareness, as had the previous studies. However, when he used a more detailed 16-item interview, he found a much higher percentage of aware *Ss*, and only *Ss* who were classified as aware by the extended interview showed conditioning. The studies of Dulany and Levin were, of course, telling evidence against the earlier studies showing an unconscious, automatic effect of verbal operant conditioning. These two studies replicated the earlier data, but showed that under more sophisticated analysis the same data actually support cognitive theory.

The Awareness of Contingency design has generated an enormous amount of research. Restricting this literature to experiments that used a control group and an extended awareness questionnaire, 15 experiments have found verbal operant conditioning only in aware *Ss* (DeNike, 1964; DeNike & Leibovitz, 1969; DeNike & Spielberger, 1963; Doctor, 1971; Dulany, 1961, 1962, 1968; Kennedy, 1971, Exp. II; Lanyon, 1964; Levin, 1961; Page & Lumia, 1968; Spielberger, 1962; Spielberger, DeNike, & Stein, 1965; Spielberger & Levin, 1962; Spielberger, Levin, & Shepard, 1962). Four studies meeting these methodological criteria have found conditioning in unaware *Ss* (Kennedy, 1970, 1971, Exp. I; Lanyon & Drotar, 1967; Silver, Saltz, & Modigliani, 1970).

A number of researchers have looked at the problems associated with procedures for assessing awareness. The original studies of verbal operant conditioning reviewed by Krasner (1958) often did not report the procedures used in assessing awareness, and those that did tended to ask *Ss* several global questions, e.g., "What do you think it was all about?" Levin (1961) and Spielberger (1962) were able to replicate the earlier findings of conditioning without awareness when they classified *Ss* on the basis of these types of global questions. However, when they used a longer, more structured interview to classify *Ss,* they found no conditioning in unaware *Ss.* Levy (1967) informed one group about the reinforcement contingencies at the beginning of the experiment and found that the responses to general questions at the end of the experiment would have correctly identified less than half of the informed *Ss.* Thus, it is clear that the earlier findings of verbal operant conditioning without awareness were due to invalid assessment procedures.

Levy (1967) and Richman, Riddle, Schneider, and Simmons (1970) have carried out validity studies of several awareness assessment techniques. These studies had a "stooge" inform *Ss* of the reinforcement contingencies before the experiment began and then used the standard Spielberger and Levin (1962) interview to classify *Ss.* Levy (1967) found that 19% of the informed *Ss* were classified as unaware by the interview. Richman et al. replicated Levy, but added an extinction period after conditioning and before awareness assessment. This procedure resulted in 27.5% of the informed *Ss* being classified as unaware. While it is possible that the informed *Ss* may have forgotten the original information about the reinforcement contingencies or developed new hypotheses, it seems more likely that these findings indicate that even the extended interview procedures are not completely valid measures of contingency awareness.

Sallows, Dawes, and Lichtenstein (1971) looked at the validity of awareness assessment by assuming that awareness does underlie conditioning and then examining various measures of awareness to see if they gave the relationships between conditioning and awareness predicted by cognitive theory. These investigators compared a recognition procedure, Dulany's (1968) objective questionnaire, and DeNike's (1964) trial-by-trial "thoughts about the experiment." They found that the recognition procedure classified the largest number of *Ss* as aware and appeared to pick up too many false positives, since the amount of conditioning in aware *Ss* was low compared to the other techniques. The Dulany questionnaire classified an intermediate number of subjects as aware and seemed the most valid measure of awareness, since it gave good conditioning in the aware *Ss* and no conditioning in the unaware *Ss*. The DeNike procedure classified the least number of *Ss* as aware and seemed to give too many false negatives since the unaware *Ss* showed conditioning.

The findings and implications of these studies on the validity of the assessment of awareness in verbal operant conditioning are similar to those dealing with assessment in the conditioned meaning paradigm. The researcher wishing to use the Awareness of Contingency design must devote considerable care to the development of valid measures of awareness. The logic of the Awareness of Contingency design is such that even if the cognitive account is true, improper assessment of awareness or other experimental errors will tend to produce apparent learning without awareness. In fact, examination of the methodological difficulties in using the Awareness of Contingency design makes it quite surprising that the results of experiments using this design in the area of verbal operant conditioning come out so strongly favorable to cognitive theory.

The work of Page (1970) and Page and Lumia (1968) suggests that examination of the distribution of conditioning scores might be a useful procedure in investigating the validity of awareness assessment. Page (1970, p. 295) points out that six or seven misclassified *Ss* can make the group learning curve of "unaware" *Ss* show significant conditioning. Page and Lumia (1968) found that the distribution of conditioning scores in an operant conditioning task was bimodal, with the aware *Ss* giving high conditioning scores and the unaware *Ss* giving scores like the controls. If the finding of conditioning in unaware *Ss* is due to invalid awareness assessment, as suggested by cognitive theory, then examination of conditioning scores of the unaware *Ss* should show that conditioning is due to the high conditioning scores of several (misclassified) *Ss*. Conditioning theory would presumably predict that the conditioning scores of the unaware *Ss* should be unimodal with all *Ss* showing a little conditioning.

A recent counterattack on the generally cognitive outcome of the Awareness of Contingency literature is found in the work of Kennedy (1970, 1971). Cognitive theory makes the strong claim that awareness of contingency must precede conditioning. An earlier series of studies (DeNike, 1964; Spielberger, Bernstein, & Ratliff, 1966; Spielberger & Levin, 1962) supported this assumption. These experiments found that significant conditioning did not occur until the trial block on which awareness was first reported. Kennedy (1970, 1971, Exp. I) has repeated the DeNike (1964) study with assessment on *each* trial and found significant conditioning on the trials just preceding the first report of awareness. While most of the conditioning in these studies comes from the aware *Ss* in the postaware trials, it would still be embarrassing for cognitive theory if there were any significant conditioning before awareness. Fortunately for the cognitive theory, these studies suffer from an obvious experimental flaw. When *Ss* are assessed on a trial-by-trial basis in order to find the exact "moment" of awareness, it is crucial to look at the *S's* very tentative, first speculations, since there probably is no true "moment" of awareness for most *Ss,* just a gradually increasing certainty that a given hypothesis is correct. In both of these studies Kennedy has chosen to classify the trials where *S* had a correct or correlated hypothesis, but was "uncertain" of it, as *preaware* trials. In fact, in Exp. II of the 1971 study Kennedy does an analysis that appears to show that all the "preaware" conditioning effect was due to *Ss* with tentative correct hypotheses. Thus, the Kennedy experiments actually provide tentative support for cognitive theory.

While the Awareness of Contingency design has been the design used most widely with the verbal operant conditioning technique, there have been other types of studies. Four investigations have used the Informed Pairing design (Dulany, 1962; Levy, 1967; Richman, Riddle, Schneider, & Simmons, 1970; Weinstein & Lawson, 1963). As cognitive theory (and common sense) predict, all four studies found that *Ss* told the reinforcement contingencies show strong conditioning.

A series of experiments have attempted to use a Masking design in verbal operant conditioning (Dixon & Oakes, 1965; Oakes, 1967; Thaver & Oakes, 1967). These studies used a color naming mask, reported conditioning without awareness, and interpreted the findings as resulting from the masking task. A number of S-R psychologists (Greenspoon & Brownstein, 1967; Kanfer, 1968; Krasner, 1967; Maltzman, 1966) have considered these studies to be crucial refutations of the cognitive position. While these studies, as they stand, are evidence against cognitive theory, they are certainly not examples of successful use of the Masking design, since in all studies the color naming mask had no effect on either awareness or conditioning. A more practical problem about giving these studies heavy theoretical emphasis is that there have been three replications (David, 1967; David & Dielman, 1968; Dulany, Schwartz, & Schneider, 1966) which are quite consistent in finding conditioning only in aware *Ss*. Thus, the results of experiments using a color naming mask would seem to be at a standoff currently.

Another recent counterattack on the cognitive hypothesis has been the work of Rosenfeld and Baer (1969, 1970). These investigators concede the traditional experimental tasks to the cognitive hypothesis. In fact, in an amusing attempt to rewrite history, they criticize cognitive investigators for being so naive as to expect learning without awareness in simple verbal operant conditioning tasks such as the Greenspoon word-naming task (Rosenfeld & Baer, 1969, pp. 425-426). In order to show conditioning without awareness they attempted to develop a more subtle and convincing masking task. In the 1969 study they informed their S that he was to be E in an operant motor conditioning task. In fact, the "S" in the motor conditioning task was actually a double agent who gave the motor responses as reinforcers for the ostensible E's verbal prompts. Rosenfeld and Baer report successful conditioning of one S's verbal behavior with this procedure. While it was difficult to carry out proper assessment of S's awareness, they give some convincing quotes from the S's interview protocols that he was unaware. The 1970 study was a variant of the double agent technique: Ss were told that they were to act as Es in a verbal conditioning task. The ostensible Es thought they were reinforcing a S for saying words fluently. Actually the "E's" form of request for the next word was being conditioned by the occurrence or nonoccurrence of fluent words. Rosenfeld and Baer (1970) report successful verbal operant conditioning without awareness in two Ss. While there are some difficulties with these studies (clear evidence of conditioning in only 3 of 14 Ss; only limited awareness assessment possible), they should be considered as evidence against the cognitive hypothesis. It is not as clear that they should be counted against the position of this chapter, since the purpose of this review is to demonstrate that none of the standard laboratory experiments that have been used to support the conditioning theory do in fact support it. Whatever the merits of these two studies, the attempt to find new, more subtle, experimental procedures is certainly the way to give a clear laboratory demonstration of learning without awareness, if it occurs.

Several different types of Compliance design have been used in verbal operant conditioning experiments. Researchers have looked at the conditioning of aware Ss who reported that they chose not to cooperate with E (DeNike, 1965; Holmes, 1967; Page & Lumia, 1968; Tatz, 1960). All these studies found that the aware uncooperating Ss did not condition, as predicted by cognitive theory.

Another group of studies looked at compliance by examining characteristics of Ss that should increase cooperation, e.g., desire to please E, desirability of the reinforcer. Six studies have assessed one of these variables and related it to conditioning (Dulany, 1968; Lichtenstein & Craine, 1969; Sallows, Dawes, & Lichtenstein, 1971; Spielberger, 1962; Spielberger, Berger, & Howard, 1963; Spielberger et al., 1962). All six studies found that Ss with high scores on one of the compliance variables showed more conditioning.

Several studies have manipulated compliance in verbal operant conditioning (Kaufer & Marston, 1961; Ekman, Krasner, & Ullmann, 1963; Spielberger et al., 1966); for example, Ekman, Krasner, and Ullmann manipulated compliance by the simple expedient of telling Ss to make E say "good" as often as possible. These studies found that the manipulation to increase compliance produced increased conditioning. Thus, the studies using the Compliance design have produced results favoring cognitive theory.

Levin (1961), Spielberger and Levin (1962), and Spielberger et al. (1962) all report Contingency Expectancy studies in which S was reinforced for the use of two pronouns. Conditioning of the S was directly related to his hypotheses about the reinforcement contingency in that conditioning was specific to one pronoun if S thought that only one pronoun was being reinforced. Dulany (1961, 1962) and Holz and Azrin (1966) report data showing that Ss' responses are in conformity with correlated hypotheses about the nature of the contingencies. Simkins (1963) gave a number of nice examples of the effect of S's expectancy upon conditioning. In an extinction situation Simkins found two Ss who gave a U-shaped conditioning curve. When interviewed, both stated that they noticed the lack of reinforcement and so tried other hypotheses; when none of these worked, they went back to the original hypothesis. DeNike and Leibovitz (1969) have shown that Ss can anticipate when they are to receive a reinforcement. Thus, it is clear that examination of S's hypotheses about the reinforcement contingency leads to results that provide solid support for cognitive theory.

A number of studies have manipulated S's expectancy about the reinforcement contingency. DeNike and Spielberger (1963), Kanfer and Marston (1961), Spielberger and Levin (1962), Tatz (1960), and Weinstein and Lawson (1963) all gave Ss additional information about the reinforcement contingency (e.g., "The experimenter will say 'Umhmm' when you say the right word"). All studies found that the manipulation produced increased awareness and increased conditioning.

While the verbal operant conditioning literature looked like a stronghold for conditioning theory during the 1950s, the more recent developments have reversed this state of affairs, and now this literature lends powerful support for cognitive theory, although there are a few inconsistent studies.

CONCLUSIONS

This review of experiments using the dissociation designs in the standard conditioning paradigms seems open to two possible interpretations. The conservative interpretation is that the bulk of conditioning in the human learning literature is due to the operation of the higher mental processes, as assumed in cognitive theory, but that there is some minimal evidence for automatic, unconscious processes.

However, the most impressive finding is the consistent trend in each of the research paradigms. The early crude experiments seemed to show that all the variance in conditioning could be accounted for by conditioning theory. Then, with increasing experimental sophistication, the results have tended to move in the direction of showing that all the variance in conditioning can be accounted for by cognitive theory. Therefore, a more natural and internally consistent interpretation of these experiments is that all the results of the traditional conditioning literature are due to the operation of higher mental processes, as assumed in cognitive theory, and that there is not and never has been any convincing evidence for unconscious, automatic mechanisms in the conditioning of adult human beings.

Counter-Arguments

Given these rather drastic conclusions derived from the analysis of the conditioning literature, it seems wise to anticipate some possible replies.

Straw man argument. One possible response is to say that no one ever believed that conditioning was automatic and unconscious. This is simply false. For example, see Dollard and Miller (1950, p. 44); Greenspoon and Brownstein (1967, p. 305); Holz and Azrin (1966, p. 807); Kanfer (1968, p. 280); Krasner (1967, p.66); Leuba (1961, p. 281); Logan (1970, p. 75); McGeoch and Irion (1952, p. 269); Saltz (1971, pp. 417-418); Salzinger (1959, p. 84); Skinner (1963, p. 84); Thorndike (1935, p. 62); Verplanck (1962, p. 131); and Wickens and Meyer (1961, p. 68).

The intensity of belief in the conditioning theory can be seen in the title of Verplanck's (1962) chapter, "Unaware of Where's Awareness," or in Crider, Schwartz, and Shnidman's (1969) statement that "it is a currently debatable question that cognitive activity per se produces any marked autonomic effects at all [p. 458]," or in Greenspoon and Brownstein's (1967) comment that "the postulation of awareness as an explanatory construct has not led to the formulation of any meaningful principles of behavior [p. 304]."

Conclusive experiment. Another type of response would be to uncover an ironclad example of unconscious, automatic conditioning. This would force acceptance of the conservative conclusion discussed at the end of the literature review. It would not, however, change the larger theoretical picture. The fact that the core experiments upon which S-R psychology was founded are actually the result of the operation of the higher mental processes would remain untouched. A careful demonstration of unconscious, automatic conditioning would simply become an interesting but relatively insignificant fact about learning in human beings. In fact, given that *Homo sapiens* evolved from much simpler organisms and that the lower brain centers still function, it would seem strange if human beings showed no unconscious, automatic learning at all.

Interoceptive conditioning. The technique of introducing the CS, UCS, or both into some internal organ of an animal or human has been used frequently by Russian psychologists. A number of writers have taken the findings of these studies as support for unconscious, automatic mechanisms in conditioning (Razran, 1961). There are several problems with this literature. First, the Russian studies typically do not meet the usual standards of reporting and so are hard to intepret. This is presumably why these studies are largely ignored in American S-R conditioning literature. Also, Russian psychologists have the same behavioristic biases as do American S-R psychologists and so have not realized the theoretical importance of the dissociation designs. Thus, the case for unconscious, automatic interoceptive conditioning simply remains uncorroborated. However, there is a remark by Bykov (1957) which suggests what sophisticated dissociation experiments in this area may eventually uncover. Bykov stated that when the CS is introduced during interoceptive conditioning, "an orientating reaction on the part of the animal is invariably observed [1957, p. 276]." This suggests that the CS is not as unconscious as it has been made to seem.

Children. The evidence on conditioning in preverbal children has been interpreted by S-R theorists as showing that cognitive theory must be in error (Kimble, 1962; Maltzman, 1966). There are two responses to this argument. The first is simply that it is perfectly plausible that the mechanisms underlying conditioning in children are different from those in adults. However, the more likely alternative is that a cognitive theory of conditioning will also be required for children. The S-R theorists' reasoning rests on the assumption that expectations and hypotheses are restricted to verbal organisms, yet anyone who has observed a young preverbal human in operation will have grave doubts about this S-R assumption. Thus, the arguments based on conditioning in children simply have no impact on the cognitive interpretation of the adult conditioning literature.

Animals. Several S-R theorists (Kimble, 1962; Maltzman, 1966) have suggested that it is unparsimonious to hold a cognitive theory of conditioning for humans and conditioning theory for animals, and since they assume that cognitive theory cannot be applied to animals, it is necessary to adopt conditioning theory for both animals and humans. This chapter suggests an interesting reversal of this logic. Since cognitive theory holds for humans, it is unparsimonious not to apply it to animals. Recent work on thinking and language in chimpanzees (Schrier & Stollnitz, 1971) shows cognitive theory to be a quite reasonable proposal for higher primates. The early work of Zener (1937) on Pavlovian conditioning of dogs suggests the necessity for a cognitive theory of conditioning for animals of this type. Zener pointed out that dogs that are conditioned in one location and then placed in another location will leave the second location and go back to the first when the CS is presented. This certainly looks like a Contingency Expectancy experiment with an outcome supporting cognitive theory. For lower organisms the situation is less clear, but the early work of Lashley and McCarthy (1926) and MacFarlane (1930) with rats suggests that a cognitive theory may even be required to handle the behavior of these organisms. Thus, at least for mammals, the cognitive approach seems not unreasonable, and the use of conditioning in animals as a counter-argument not only fails, but suggests an even deeper penetration of S-R theory by cognitive theory.

Unconscious mental processes. A number of S-R psychologists have responded to this chapter by conceding the laboratory experiments of conditioning, but giving anecdotal examples in which human behavior does not seem to follow from conscious knowledge. They conclude that, even though S-R theory is not supported by the traditional experimental literature, these examples of "real" human behavior show that it will be vindicated in the long run.

It is clear that in adults many kinds of behavior are reflections of tacit, unconscious processes, e.g., speaking a sentence, remembering an event, driving a car. For some unconscious processes, such as the motor skills involved in driving a car, it may be that the actual *learning* required awareness of the task to be learned. However, for other cognitive processes such as learning syntax or learning object constancy, it seems likely that the process goes on in a relatively unconscious, automatic fashion. Unfortunately for S-R theory it does not follow that these real world examples of unconscious, automatic learning will vindicate S-R theory. It seems certain that the theoretical mechanisms required to handle problems such as the child's learning of the abstract structure of language will be totally unlike anything ever proposed in S-R theory.

Experimenter bias. Several S-R theorists (Greenspoon & Brownstein, 1967; Krasner, 1967) have suggested that the results supporting cognitive theory may be due to experimenter bias. In general, researchers ought to be careful about using experimenter bias in experimental clashes—it is a two-edged sword. For cognitive theory the evidence is strongly against this explanation: A number of the influential cognitive theorists appear to have carried out their initial experiments expecting to find unconscious, automatic conditioning (Dawson & Grings, 1968, p. 227; Dulany, 1962, p. 103; Spielberger, 1965, p. 162), and a number of S-R investigators, to their chagrin, have carried out experiments that found strong evidence against the conditioning theory (Insko & Oakes, 1966; Kennedy, 1971, Exp. II). Thus, it actually appears that the cognitive variables are so powerful that investigators find them regardless of their theoretical orientation.

Radical behaviorism. The responses of S-R psychologists with a Skinnerian orientation to the findings reviewed in this chapter has been most interesting. Since awareness is not a construct in radical behaviorism, any attempt to deal with this issue is obviously going to be *post hoc* (an awkwardness that has been pointed out by researchers within the radical behaviorist camp: Krasner, 1967; Krasner & Ullmann, 1963). However, the various types of *post hoc* accounts of the awareness data are instructive and so will be dealt with briefly.

One approach by radical behaviorists has been to argue that the studies that assess awareness suffer from a methodological flaw, in that the assessment procedures elicit awareness reports in subjects (Greenspoon, 1963; Holz & Azrin, 1966; Staats, 1969). This can be easily dispensed with, since it does not account for the fact that only *Ss* who condition give awareness reports. In order to deal with this difficulty a more elaborate *post hoc* account has been developed. Krasner (1967) and Staats (1967) have hypothesized that after *S's* behavior changes, he notices it and then gives the awareness rationale. In addition to suffering from the difficulty of introducing "rationalization," a concept outside of the radical behaviorist framework, this hypothesis is unable to account for the aware, uncooperating *Ss* who do not condition.

Another position taken by radical behaviorists is that responses and awareness reports are both operants and are functions of the same experimental variables (Greenspoon & Brownstein, 1967; Krasner, 1967; Verplanck, 1962). This position is so flexible that it is hard to criticize, but in general it cannot handle the multiple relations between awareness and responses that derive from cognitive theory, e.g., aware *Ss* condition, aware uncooperative *Ss* do not. See Dulany (1968) for an elegant discussion of this issue.

Functional approach. Another possible position is to say that the data from the conditioning literature are what is important, regardless of the theoretical interpretation they are given. The problem here is that the significance of data must be evaluated within a theoretical framework. Without the framework of conditioning theory, it is hard to see the significance of published experiments showing that subjects can lift their fingers, blink their eyes, or give plural nouns when asked.

Cognitive S-R theory. A final possible response to the cognitive theory is to radically modify S-R theory so that it includes concepts such as awareness, hypotheses, expectations, attention, etc. The only reply possible from cognitive theorists is, "Welcome to the fold; it has been a long time since 1913."

The S-R Paradigm

In trying to understand how conditioning theory could have been the dominant approach for 60 years, it is necessary to look at the paradigm which psychology has been using since 1913. Watson's presidential address to the APA in 1916 suggests a number of influences. It is clear that in borrowing the reflex from physiology, psychologists allowed the unconscious, automatic nature of the Sherringtonian reflex to influence their thinking about the Pavlovian conditioned reflex. Watson needed a replacement for the method of introspection for the new psychology to be behavioristic, and he offered the conditioned reflex as the substitute. Concepts such as expectancy or awareness were ruled out on epistemological grounds, and thus there was no longer any need to talk to Ss. In replacing the association of ideas of the British Empiricists with the association of stimuli and responses, S-R psychology retained the belief that the laws of simple association could be extended to handle the higher mental processes. This assumption is just the opposite of the assumption of cognitive theory and so made the cognitive alternative seem quite implausible.

It is instructive to look at the conditioning literature from the framework suggested by Thomas Kuhn in *The Structure of Scientific Revolutions* (1970). Kuhn suggests that the textbooks of a science will select and distort the evidence to fit the prevailing paradigm. The standard reviews of the conditioning literature (Beecroft, 1966; Gormezano, 1966; Gormezano & Moore, 1969; Grant, 1964; Kimble, 1961) deal with the dissociation experiments in a variety of ways. They are either omitted, listed under a heading called "instructions," or given an innocuous interpretation. These studies are never presented as the theoretically crucial experiments that they actually are.

The conditioning literature contains a number of good examples of the way in which anomalous results are made to agree with the prevailing paradigm. Norris and Grant (1948) used an Instructed Nonconditioning design and found that the percent of eyeblink CRs dropped from 70% to 7%. They interpreted this study as showing the automatic and "fundamental character of the conditioning process [p. 48]." McComb (1969) carried out a GSR conditioning study using the Informed Pairing and the Contingency Awareness procedures. He found that telling Ss the contingencies gave conditioning, and for Ss who received CS-UCS pairings, only those who were aware conditioned. With these cognitive findings he concludes, "The notion that GSR conditioning data are purely a function of $S's$ awareness of relevant stimulus contingencies is challenged [p. 96]" because he believes that "To the extent that it is not known how awareness, however defined, controls behavior, it cannot account for any present finding [p. 97]." Lindley (1959) carried out the devastating Response Expectancy study in which Ss in finger withdrawal conditioning made the type of responses they thought were expected of them. In his discussion of the findings Lindley stated, "These results do not contradict the response generalization explanation of antagonistic transfer proposed by Wickens (1943a). Rather, they may indicate the manner in which response generalization is accomplished, i.e., through self-instructions [p. 8]." The *Science Citation Index* shows no references to the Lindley paper in the psychology journal literature for the period 1965-1971.

Another good example of the strength of the S-R paradigm is the semantic generalization literature. The majority of papers in this tradition are attempts to demonstrate the existence of "semantic generalization," i.e., that human Ss can tell if two words have similar meanings. This is particularly bizarre when one realizes that all of the graduate students who ran those Ss had to take the Miller Analogies Test to get into graduate school.

The early paper by Greenspoon (1955) demonstrating the existence of verbal operant conditioning is another good example of the orientation of the prevailing paradigm. In this study the physical characteristics of the test situation are described in minute detail, down to the fact that the room had a 75 watt lightbulb. Yet the specific criteria used to classify the Ss as aware and unaware are not reported.

Kuhn suggests that the members of a new paradigm have to rewrite the history of their discipline to make it agree with the new conceptions of the science. While this is not the place to write a new history of conditioning, it is interesting to look back from the cognitive perspective and see how the early researchers in this area will be viewed. There are a number of individual investigators who suggested a version of the cognitive theory for a particular conditioning paradigm: Cook and Harris (1937), in GSR conditioning; Hamel (1919) and Cason (1934), in finger withdrawal conditioning; and Cole (1939) and Humphreys (1939), in eyelid conditioning.

Of the broader theorists only Razran (1955) and Woodworth (1938) saw some of the implications made explicit in this chapter. However, neither of these men could completely leave the prevailing paradigm, and both held the view that cognitive theory was appropriate for some kinds of conditioning and conditioning theory for other types. For taking what now appears to be a conservative position on the issue both men were attacked by psychologists from within the standard paradigm. For example, Woodworth's (1938) partially cognitive account of finger withdrawal conditioning was called an "extreme position" (Hovland, 1951, p. 618). Razran's (1935) somewhat cognitive theory of conditioning was discarded as not having much explanatory value (Wickens, 1938, p. 119). Thus, it appears that Kuhn is correct, and that totally different weights will be put upon the work of researchers in this field.

A final note about the residual effects of the S-R paradigm on cognitive psychologists is that no one has yet had the courage to suggest an obvious research paradigm in this area. In the fashion of the Würzburg school, have some cognitive psychologists be Ss in a variety of conditioning paradigms, and let them introspect on the degree to which their behavior is due to automatic, unconscious processes.

Implications

The broader implications of this analysis of conditioning seem clear. S-R psychology has been subjected to powerful attacks from outside of psychology (Chomsky, 1959). It now appears that one need not use the abstract phenomena of language to pull the house down. The conditioning curves of Hilgard and Marquis (1940) and Kimble (1961) were the foundation upon which S-R psychology was built. Now it seems obvious that that foundation was one of sand.

REFERENCES

Adams, J. K. Laboratory studies of behavior without awareness. *Psychological Bulletin,* 1957, **54**, 383-405.

Baer, P. E., & Fuhrer, M. J. Cognitive processes during differential trace and delayed conditioning of the GSR. *Journal of Experimental Psychology,* 1968, **78**, 81-88.

Baer, P. E., & Fuhrer, M. J. Cognitive factors in differential conditioning of the GSR: Use of a reaction time task as the UCS with normals and schizophrenics. *Journal of Abnormal Psychology,* 1969, **74**, 544-552.

Baer, P. E., & Fuhrer, M. J. Cognitive processes in the differential trace conditioning of electrodermal and vasomotor activity. *Journal of Experimental Psychology,* 1970, **84**, 176-178.

Baron, A., & Kaufman, A. Human, free-operant avoidance of "time out" from monetary reinforcement. *Journal of the Experimental Analysis of Behavior,* 1966, **9**, 557-565.

Baron, A., Kaufman, A., & Stauber, K. A. Effects of instructions and reinforcement-feedback on human operant behavior maintained by fixed-interval reinforcement. *Journal of the Experimental Analysis of Behavior,* 1969, **12**, 701-712.

Beecroft, R. S. *Classical conditioning.* Goleta, Calif.: Psychonomic Press, 1966.

Block, J. D. Awareness of stimulus relationships and physiological generality of response in autonomic discrimination. *Recent Advances in Biological Psychiatry,* 1962, **4**, 43-53.

Branca, A. A. Semantic generalization at the level of the conditioning experiment. *American Journal of Psychology,* 1957, **70**, 541-549.

Bridger, W. H., & Mandel, I. J. A comparison of GSR fear responses produced by threat and electric shock. *Journal of Psychiatric Research,* 1964, **2**, 31-40.

Bridger, W. H., & Mandel, I. J. Abolition of the PRE by instructions in GSR conditioning. *Journal of Experimental Psychology,* 1965, **69**, 476-482. (a)

Bridger, W. H., & Mandel, I. J. Cognitive expectancy and autonomic conditioning: Extension of schizokinesis. *Recent Advances in Biological Psychiatry,* 1965, **7**, 79-83. (b)

Brotsky, S. J. Classical conditioning of the galvanic skin response to verbal concepts. *Journal of Experimental Psychology,* 1968, **76**, 244-253.

Brotsky, S. J., & Keller, W. H. Semantic conditioning and generalization of the galvanic skin response: Locus of mediation in classical conditioning. *Journal of Experimental Psychology,* 1971, **89**, 383-389.

Bykov, K. M. *The cerebral cortex and the internal organs.* New York: Chemical Publishing, 1957.

Cason, H. The role of verbal activities in the conditioning of human subjects. *Psychological Review,* 1934, **41**, 563-571.

Cason, H. An attempt to condition hand withdrawal responses in human subjects. *Journal of Experimental Psychology,* 1935, **18**, 307-317.

Chatterjee, B. B., & Eriksen, C. W. Conditioning and generalization of GSR as a function of awareness. *Journal of Abnormal and Social Psychology,* 1960, **60**, 396-403.

Chatterjee, B. B., & Eriksen, C. W. Cognitive factors in heart rate conditioning. *Journal of Experimental Psychology,* 1962, **64**, 272-279.

Chomsky, N. Review of B. F. Skinner, *Verbal behavior. Language,* 1959, **35**, 26-58.

Cohen, B. H. Role of awareness in meaning established by classical conditioning. *Journal of Experimental Psychology,* 1964, **67**, 373-378.

Cole, L. E. A comparison of the factors of practice and knowledge of experimental procedure in conditioning the eyelid response of human subjects. *Journal of General Psychology,* 1939, **20**, 349-372.

Coles, G. J., & Leonard, T. B. Conditioned word meaning and the interstimulus interval. *Psychonomic Science,* 1969, **14**, 60-61.

Colgan, D. M. Effect of instructions on the skin resistance response. *Journal of Experimental Psychology,* 1970, **86**, 108-112.

Cook, S. W., & Harris, R. E. The verbal conditioning of the galvanic skin reflex. *Journal of Experimental Psychology,* 1937, **21**, 202-210.

Corn-Becker, F., Welch, L., & Fisichelli, V. Conditioning factors underlying hypnosis. *Journal of Abnormal and Social Psychology,* 1949, **44,** 212-222.

Crider, A., Schwartz, G. E., & Shnidman, S. On the criteria for instrumental autonomic conditioning: A reply to Katkin and Murray. *Psychological Bulletin,* 1969, **71,** 455-461.

David, K. H. Effect of a speed set on awareness and verbal operant conditioning. *Psychological Reports,* 1967, **21,** 549-552.

David, K. H., & Dielman, T. E. Reinforcement schedule, intertrial activity, and verbal operant conditioning. *Psychological Reports,* 1968, **22,** 1037-1040.

Dawson, M. E. Cognition and conditioning: Effects of masking the CS-UCS contingency on human GSR classical conditioning. *Journal of Experimental Psychology,* 1970, **85,** 389-396.

Dawson, M. E., & Grings, W. W. Comparison of classical conditioning and relational learning. *Journal of Experimental Psychology,* 1968, **76,** 227-231.

Dawson, M. E., & Reardon, P. Effects of facilitory and inhibitory sets on GSR conditioning and extinction. *Journal of Experimental Psychology,* 1969, **82,** 462-466.

Dawson, M. E., & Satterfield, J. H. Can human GSR conditioning occur without relational learning? *Proceedings of the 77th Annual Convention of the American Psychological Association,* 1969, **4,** 69-70.

Dean, S. J., Martin, R. B., & Streiner, D. Mediational control of the GSR. *Journal of Experimental Research in Personality,* 1968, **3,** 71-76.

Deane, G. E. Human heart rate responses during experimentally induced anxiety. *Journal of Experimental Psychology,* 1961, **61,** 489-493.

Deane, G. E. Human heart rate responses during experimentally induced anxiety: A follow up with controlled respiration. *Journal of Experimental Psychology,* 1964, **67,** 193-195.

Deane, G. E. Cardiac activity during experimentally induced anxiety. *Psychophysiology,* 1969, **6,** 17-30.

DeNike, L. D. The temporal relationship between awareness and performance in verbal conditioning. *Journal of Experimental Psychology,* 1964, **68,** 521-529.

DeNike, L. D. Recall of reinforcement and conative activity in verbal conditioning. *Psychological Reports,* 1965, **16,** 345-346.

DeNike, L. D., & Leibovitz, M. P. Accurate anticipation of reinforcement in verbal conditioning. *Journal of Personality,* 1969, **37,** 158-170.

DeNike, L. D., & Spielberger, C. D. Induced mediating states in verbal conditioning. *Journal of Verbal Learning and Verbal Behavior,* 1963, **1,** 339-345.

Dixon, P. W., & Oakes, W. F. Effect of intertrial activity on the relationship between awareness and verbal operant conditioning. *Journal of Experimental Psychology,* 1965, **69,** 152-157.

Doctor, R. M. Bias effects and awareness in studies of verbal conditioning. *Journal of Experimental Research in Personality,* 1971, **5,** 243-256.

Dollard, J., & Miller, N. E. *Personality and psychotherapy.* New York: McGraw-Hill, 1950.

Dulany, D. E., Jr. Hypotheses and habits in verbal "operant conditioning." *Journal of Abnormal and Social Psychology,* 1961, **63,** 251-263.

Dulany, D. E., Jr. The place of hypotheses and intentions: An analysis of verbal control in verbal conditioning. In C. W. Eriksen (Ed.), *Behavior and awareness.* Durham: Duke University Press, 1962.

Dulany, D. E. Awareness, rules, and propositional control: A confrontation with S-R behavior theory. In T. R. Dixon & D. L. Horton (Eds.), *Verbal behavior and general behavior theory.* Englewood Cliffs, N.J.: Prentice-Hall, 1968.

Dulany, D. E., Schwartz, S., & Schneider, R. Propositional control and intertrial activity. Unpublished manuscript, 1966. (Cited in D. E. Dulany, Awareness, rules, and propositional control. In T. R. Dixon & D. L. Horton (Eds.), *Verbal behavior and general behavior theory.* Englewood Cliffs, N. J.: Prentice-Hall, 1968.

Ekman, P., Krasner, L., & Ullmann, L. P. The interaction of set and awareness as determinants of response to verbal conditioning. *Journal of Abnormal and Social Psychology,* 1963, **66,** 387-389.

Engel, B. T., & Chism, R. A. Operant conditioning of heart rate speeding. *Psychophysiology,* 1967, **3,** 418-426.

Engel, B. T., & Hansen, S. P. Operant conditioning of heart rate slowing. *Psychophysiology,* 1966, **3,** 176-187.

Epstein, S. & Bahm, R. Verbal hypothesis formulation during classical conditioning of the GSR. *Journal of Experimental Psychology,* 1971, **87,** 187-197.

Epstein, S., & Clarke, S. Heart rate and skin conductance during experimentally induced anxiety: Effects of anticipated intensity of noxious stimulation and experience. *Journal of Experimental Psychology,* 1970, **84,** 105-112.

Epstein, S., & Roupenian, A. Heart rate and skin conductance during experimentally induced anxiety: The effect of uncertainty about receiving a noxious stimulus. *Journal of Personality and Social Psychology,* 1970, **16,** 20-28.

Feather, B. W. Semantic generalization of classically conditioned responses: A review. *Psychological Bulletin,* 1965, **63,** 425-441.

Feather, B. W. Human salivary conditioning: A methodological study. In G. A. Kimble (Ed.), *Foundations of conditioning and learning.* New York: Appleton-Century-Crofts, 1967.

Fenz, W. D., & Dronsejko, K. Effects of real and imagined threat of shock on GSR and heart rate as a function of trait anxiety. *Journal of Experimental Research in Personality,* 1969, **3,** 187-196.

Fishbein, H. D. Effects of differential instructions, differential feedback, and UCS intensity on the conditioned eyelid response. *Journal of Experimental Psychology,* 1967. **75,** 56-65. (a)

Fishbein, H. D. Effects of differential instructions and number of acquisition trials on extinction and reacquisition of the conditioned-eyelid response. *Journal of Experimental Psychology,* 1967, **75,** 126-127. (b)

Fishbein, H. D., & Gormezano, I. Effects of differential instructions, differential payoffs, and the presence or absence of feedback on the percentage, latency, and amplitude of the conditioned eyelid response. *Journal of Experimental Psychology,* 1966, **71,** 535-538.

Folkins, C. H. Temporal factors and the cognitive mediators of stress reaction. *Journal of Personality and Social Psychology,* 1970, **14,** 173-184.

Freeman, G. L. The galvanic phenomenon and conditioned responses. *Journal of General Psychology,* 1930, **3,** 529-539.

Freeman, N. C. G., & Suedfeld, P. Classical conditioning of verbal meaning: The role of awareness, meaningfulness, and evaluative loading. *Psychological Record.* 1969, **19,** 335-338.

Fuhrer, M. J., & Baer, P. E. Differential classical conditioning: Verbalization of stimulus contingencies. *Science,* 1965, **150,** 1479-1491.

Fuhrer, M. J., & Baer, P. E. Effects of intertrial reports on cognitive and GSR differentiation of conditioned stimuli. *Proceedings of the 74th Annual Convention of the American Psychological Association,* 1966, **2,** 53-54.

Fuhrer, M. J., & Baer, P. E. Cognitive processes in differential GSR conditioning: Effects of a masking task. *American Journal of Psychology,* 1969, **82,** 168-180.

Gavalas, R. J. Operant reinforcement of an autonomic response: Two studies. *Journal of the Experimental Analysis of Behavior,* 1967, **10,** 119-130.

Gerstein, A. I. The effect of reinforcement schedules on meaning generalization and on awareness of the purpose of the experiment. *Journal of Personality,* 1961, **29,** 350-362.

Gormezano, I. Classical conditioning. In J. B. Sidowski (Ed.), *Experimental methods and instrumentation in psychology.* New York: McGraw-Hill, 1966.

Gormezano, I., & Moore, J. W. Effects of instrumental set and UCS intensity on the latency, percentage, and form of the eyelid response. *Journal of Experimental Psychology,* 1962, **63,** 487-494.

Gormezano, I., & Moore, J. W. Classical conditioning. In. M. H. Marx (Ed.), *Learning: Processes.* New York: Macmillan, 1969.

Grant, D. A. Classical and operant conditioning. In A. W. Melton (Ed.), *Categories of human learning.* New York: Academic Press, 1964.

Greenspoon, J. The reinforcing effect of two spoken sounds on the frequency of two responses. *American Journal of Psychology,* 1955, **68,** 409-416.

Greenspoon, J. Reply to Spielberger and DeNike: "Operant conditioning of plural nouns: A failure to replicate the Greenspoon effect." *Psychological Reports,* 1963, **12,** 29-30.

Greenspoon, J., & Brownstein, A. J. Awareness in verbal conditioning. *Journal of Experimental Research in Personality,* 1967, **2,** 295-308.

Grings, W. W. Verbal-perceptual factors in the conditioning of autonomic responses. In W. F. Prokasy (Ed.), *Classical conditioning: A symposium.* New York: Appleton-Century-Crofts, 1965.

Grings, W. W., Carlin, S., & Appley, M. H. Set, suggestion, and conditioning. *Journal of Experimental Psychology,* 1962, **63,** 417-422.

Grings, W. W., & Lockhart, R. A. Effects of "anxiety-lessening" instructions and differential set development on the extinction of GSR. *Journal of Experimental Psychology,* 1963, **66,** 292-299.

Hamel, I. A. A study and analysis of the conditioned reflex. *Psychological Monographs,* 1919, 27(1, Whole No. 118).

Hare, R. D. Cognitive factors in transfer of meaning. *Psychological Reports,* 1964, **15,** 199-206.

Hare, R. D. Replication report: Cognitive factors in transfer of meaning. *Psychological Reports,* 1965, **17,** 590.

Hartman, T. F. Dynamic transmission, elective generalization, and semantic conditioning. In W. F. Prokasy (Ed.), *Classical conditioning: A symposium.* New York: Appleton-Century-Crofts, 1965.

Harvey, B., & Wickens, D. D. Effect of instructions on responsiveness to the CS and to the UCS in GSR conditioning. *Journal of Experimental Psychology.* 1971, **87,** 137-140.

Hefferline, R. F., Keenan, B., & Harford, R. A. Escape and avoidance conditoning in human subjects without their observation of the response. *Science,* 1959, **130,** 1338-1339.

Hilgard, E. R., Campbell, A. A., & Sears, W. N. Conditioned discrimination: The development of discrimination with and without verbal report. *American Journal of Psychology,* 1937, **49,** 564-580.

Hilgard, E. R., Campbell, R. C., & Sears, W. N. Conditioned discrimination: The effect of knowledge of stimulus-relationships. *American Journal of Psychology.* 1938, **51,** 498-506.

Hilgard, E. R., & Humphreys, L. G. The effect of supporting and antagonistic voluntary instructions on conditioned discrimination. *Journal of Experimental Psychology,* 1938, **22,** 291-304.

Hilgard E. R., & Marquis, D. G. *Conditioning and learning:* New York: Appleton-Century-Crofts, 1940.

Hill, F. A. Effects of instruction and subjects' need for approval on the conditioned galvanic skin response. *Journal of Experimental Psychology,* 1967, **73,** 461-467.

Hill, F. A. Effects of UCS predictability in GSR conditioning. *Psychonomic Science,* 1969, **17,** 195-196.

Holmes, D. S. Verbal conditioning, or problem solving and cooperation? *Journal of Experimental Research in Personality,* 1967, **2,** 289-294.

Holz, W. C., & Azrin, N. H. Conditioning human verbal behavior. In W. K. Honig (Ed.), *Operant behavior: Areas of research and application.* New York: Appleton-Century-Crofts, 1966.

Hovland, C. I. Human learning and retention. In S. S. Stevens (Ed.), *Handbook of experimental psychology.* New York: Wiley, 1951.

Hughes, W. G., & Shean, G. D. Ability to control GSR amplitude. *Psychonomic Science,* 1971, **23,** 309-311.

Humphreys, L. G. The effect of random alternation of reinforcement on the acquisition and extinction of conditioned eyelid reactions. *Journal of Experimental Psychology,* 1939, **25,** 141-158.

Hunter, W. S. An experiment on the disinhibition of voluntary responses. *Journal of Experimental Psychology,* 1938, **22,** 419-428.

Insko, C. A., & Oakes, W. F. Awareness and the "conditioning" of attitudes. *Journal of Personality and Social Psychology,* 1966, **4,** 487-496.

Jenks, R. S., & Deane, G. E. Human heart rate responses during experimentally induced anxiety: A follow-up. *Journal of Experimental Psychology,* 1963, **65,** 109-112.

Johnson, H. J., & Schwartz, G. E. Suppression of GSR activity through operant reinforcement. *Journal of Experimental Psychology,* 1967, **75**, 307-312.

Kanfer, F. H. Verbal conditioning: A review of its current status. In T. R. Dixon & D. L. Horton (Eds.), *Verbal behavior and general behavior theory.* Englewood Cliffs, N. J.: Prentice-Hall, 1968.

Kanfer, F. H., & Marston, A. R. Verbal conditioning, ambiguity, and psychotherapy. *Psychological Reports,* 1961, **9**, 461-475.

Katz, A., Webb, L., & Stotland, E. Cognitive influences on the rate of GSR extinction. *Journal of Experimental Research in Personality.* 1971, **5**, 208-215.

Kaufman, A., Baron, A., & Kopp, R. E. Some effects of instructions on human operant behavior. *Psychonomic Monograph Supplements.* 1966, **1**, No. 11.

Keehn, J. D., Lloyd, K. E., Hibbs, M., & Johnson, D. Operant eyeblink conditioning without awareness: A preliminary report. *Psychonomic Science,* 1965, **2**, 357-358.

Kennedy, T. D. Verbal conditioning without awareness: The use of programmed reinforcement and recurring assessment of awareness. *Journal of Experimental Psychology,* 1970, **84**, 487-494.

Kennedy, T. D. Reinforcement frequency, task characteristics, and interval of awareness assessment as factors in verbal conditioning without awareness. *Journal of Experimental Psychology,* 1971, **88**, 103-112.

Kimble, G. A. *Hilgard and Marquis' conditioning and learning.* (2nd ed.) New York: Appleton-Century-Crofts, 1961.

Kimble, G. A. Classical conditioning and the problem of awareness. In C. W. Eriksen (Ed.), *Behavior and awareness.* Durham, N. C.: Duke University Press, 1962.

Kimble, G. A. Attitudinal factors in eyelid conditioning. In G. A. Kimble (Ed.), *Foundations of conditioning and learning.* New York: Appleton-Century-Crofts, 1967.

Koenig, K. P., & Castillo, D. D. False feedback and longevity of the conditioned GSR during extinction: Some implications for aversion therapy. *Journal of Experimental Psychology,* 1969, **74**, 505-510.

Krasner, L. Studies of the conditioning of verbal behavior. *Psychological Bulletin,* 1958, **55**, 148-170.

Krasner, L. Verbal operant conditioning and awareness. In K. Salzinger & S. Salzinger (Eds.), *Research in verbal behavior and some neurophysiological implications.* New York: Academic Press, 1967.

Krasner, L., & Ullmann, L. P. Variables affecting report of awareness in verbal conditioning. *Journal of Psychology,* 1963, **56**, 193-202.

Kuhn, T. S. *The structure of scientific revolutions.* (2nd ed.) Chicago: University of Chicago Press, 1970.

Lanyon, R. I. Verbal conditioning and awareness in a sentence construction task. *American Journal of Psychology,* 1964, **77**, 472-475.

Lanyon, R.I., & Drotar, D. Verbal conditioning: Intelligence and reported awareness. *Journal of Experimental Research in Personality,* 1967, **2**, 234-238.

Lashley, K. S., & McCarthy, D. A. The survival of the maze habit after cerebellar injuries. *Journal of Comparative Psychology,* 1926, **6**, 423-433.

Leuba, C. J. Man: A general psychology. New York: Holt, Rinehart and Winston, 1961.

Levin, S. M. The effects of awareness on verbal conditioning. *Journal of Experimental Psychology,* 1961, **61**, 67-75.

Levy, L. H. Awareness, learning, and the beneficent subject as expert witness. *Journal of Personality and Social Psychology,* 1967, **6**, 365-370.

Lichtenstein, E., & Craine, W. H. The importance of subjective evaluation of reinforcement in verbal conditioning. *Journal of Experimental Research in Personality,* 1969, **3**, 214-220.

Lindley, R. H. Effects of instructions on the transfer of a conditioned response. *Journal of Experimental Psychology,* 1959, **57**, 6-8.

Lindley, R. H., & Moyer, K. E. Effects of instructions on the extinction of a conditioned finger-withdrawal response. *Journal of Experimental Psychology,* 1961, **61**, 82-88.

Lippman, L. G., & Meyer, M. E. Fixed interval performance as related to instructions and to subjects' verbalizations of the contingency. *Psychonomic Science,* 1967, 8, 135-136.

Logan, F. A. *Fundamentals of learning and motivation.* Dubuque, Iowa: W. C. Brown, 1970.

MacFarlane, D. A. The role of kinesthesis in maze learning. *University of California Publications in Psychology,* 1930, 4, 277-305.

Maltzman, I. Awareness: Cognitive psychology vs. behaviorism. *Journal of Experimental Research in Personality,* 1966, 1, 161-165.

Maltzman, I. Theoretical conceptions of semantic conditioning and generalization. In T. R. Dixon & D. L. Horton (Eds.), *Verbal behavior and general behavior theory.* Englewood Cliffs, N. J.: Prentice-Hall, 1968.

Mandel, I. J., & Bridger, W. H. Interaction between instructions and ISI in conditioning and extinction of the GSR. *Journal of Experimental Psychology,* 1967, 74, 36-43.

Martin, R. B., & Dean, S. J. Instrumental modification of the GSR. *Psychophysiology,* 1971, 7, 178-185.

McComb, D. Cognitive and learning effects in the production of GSR conditioning data. *Psychonomic Science,* 1969, 16, 96-97.

McGeoch, J. A., & Irion, A. L. *The psychology of human learning.* (2nd ed.) New York: McKay, 1952.

Menzies, R. Further studies of conditioned vasomotor responses in human subjects. *Journal of Experimental Psychology,* 1941, 29, 457-482.

Miller, A. W., Jr. Awareness, verbal conditioning and meaning conditioning. *Psychological Reports,* 1967, 21, 681-691.

Miller, A. W., Jr. The dimensionality of awareness in verbal conditioning. *Journal of Psychology,* 1968, 70, 99-111.

Miller, A. W., Jr., & Babcock, B. B. The operant conditioning of awareness. *Journal of General Psychology,* 1970, 83, 169-177.

Miller, A., Gimpl, M., & McCrimmon, R. Extinction versus counterconditioning for the meaning of words and nonsense syllables. *Psychonomic Science,* 1969, 15, 92-93.

Miller, J. M. The effect of inhibitory and facilitatory attitudes on eyelid conditioning. *Psychological Bulletin,* 1939, 36, 577-578.

Morgenson, D. F., & Martin, I. Personality, awareness and autonomic conditioning. *Psychophysiology,* 1969, 5, 536-547.

Mowrer, O. H. Preparatory set (expectancy): A determinant in motivation and learning. *Psychological Review,* 1938, 45, 62-91.

Moyer, K. E., & Lindley, R. H. Effects of instructions on extinction and recovery of a conditioned avoidance response. *Journal of Experimental Psychology,* 1962, 64, 95-96.

Murray, E. N., & Katkin, E. S. Comment on two recent reports of operant heart rate conditioning. *Psychophysiology,* 1968, 5, 192-195.

Nicholls, M. F., & Kimble, G. A. Effect of instructions upon eyelid conditioning. *Journal of Experimental Psychology,* 1964, 67, 400-402.

Nolan, R. E. Human cardiac conditioning during intense experimental anxiety. Unpublished doctoral dissertation, University of Connecticut, 1961. (Cited in D. Zeaman & R. W. Smith, Review of some recent findings in human cardiac conditioning. In W. F. Prokasy (Ed.), *Classical conditioning: A symposium.* New York: Appleton-Century-Crofts, 1965.)

Norris, E. B., & Grant, D. A. Eyelid conditioning as affected by verbally induced inhibitory set and counter reënforcement. *American Journal of Psychology,* 1948, 61, 37-49.

Notterman, J. M., Schoenfeld, W. N., & Bersh, P. J. A comparison of three extinction procedures following heart rate conditioning. *Journal of Abnormal and Social Psychology,* 1952, 47, 674-677.

Oakes, W. F. Verbal operant conditioning, intertrial activity, awareness, and the extended interview. *Journal of Personality and Social Psychology,* 1967, 6, 198-202.

Öhman, A. Interaction between instruction-induced expectancy and strength of unconditioned stimulus in GSR conditioning. *Journal of Experimental Psychology,* 1971, 88, 384-390.

Ominsky, M. Differential instructions and interstimulus interval in eyelid conditioning. *Psychonomic Science,* 1968, 12, 51-52. (a)

Ominsky, M. Instructions and interstimulus interval in eyelid conditioning. *Psychonomic Science*, 1968, **12**, 49-50. (b)

Orne, M. T. On the social psychology of the psychological experiment: With particular reference to demand characteristics and their implications. *American Psychologist*, 1962, **17**, 776-783.

Page, M. M. Social psychology of a classical conditioning of attitudes experiment. *Journal of Personality and Social Psychology*, 1969, **11**, 177-186.

Page, M. M. Demand awareness, subject sophistication, and the effectiveness of a verbal "reinforcement." *Journal of Personality*, 1970, **38**, 287-301.

Page, M. M. Postexperimental assessment of awareness in attitude conditioning. *Educational and Psychological Measurement*, 1971, **31**, 891-906.

Page, M. M., & Lumia, A. R. Cooperation with demand characteristics and the bimodal distribution of verbal conditioning data. *Psychonomic Science*, 1968, **12**, 243-244.

Paivio, A. Generalization of verbally conditioned meaning from symbol to referent. *Canadian Journal of Psychology*, 1964, **18**, 146-155.

Parton, D. A., & DeNike, L. D. Performance hypotheses of children and response to social reinforcement. *Journal of Personality and Social Psychology*, 1966, **4**, 444-447.

Paul, G. L., Eriksen, C. W., & Humphreys, L. G. Use of temperature stress with cool air reinforcement for human operant conditioning. *Journal of Experimental Psychology*, 1962, **64**, 329-335.

Peastrel, A. L., Wishner, J., & Kaplan, B. E. Set, stress, and efficiency of semantic generalization. *Journal of Experimental Psychology*, 1968, **77**, 116-124.

Porter, J. M., Jr. The modification of conditioned eyelid responses by successive series of non-reinforced elicitations. *Journal of General Psychology*, 1938, **19**, 307-323.

Prokasy, W. F., & Allen, C. K. Instructional sets in human differential eyelid conditioning. *Journal of Experimental Psychology*, 1969, **80**, 271-278.

Raskin, D. C. Semantic conditioning and generalization of autonomic responses. *Journal of Experimental Psychology*, 1969, **79**, 69-76.

Razran, G. H. S. Conditioned responses: An experimental study and a theoretical analysis. *Archives of Psychology*, 1935, **28**, No. 191.

Razran, G. H. S. Attitudinal control of human conditioning. *Journal of Psychology*, 1936, **2**, 327-337.

Razran, G. Attitudinal determinants of conditioning and of generalization of conditioning. *Journal of Experimental Psychology*, 1949, **39**, 820-829. (a)

Razran, G. Semantic and phonetographic generalization of salivary conditioning to verbal stimuli. *Journal of Experimental Psychology*, 1949, **39**, 642-652. (b)

Razran, G. Some psychological factors in the generalization of salivary conditioning to verbal stimuli. *American Journal of Psychology*, 1949. **62**, 247-256. (c)

Razran, G. Conditioning and perception. *Psychological Review*, 1955, **62**, 83-95.

Razran, G. The observable unconscious and the inferable conscious in current Soviet psychophysiology: Interoceptive conditioning, semantic conditioning and the orienting reflex. *Psychological Review*, 1961, **68**, 81-147.

Richman, C. L., Riddle, E., Schneider, G., & Simmons, P. The relationship between awareness and verbal conditioning. *Psychonomic Science*, 1970, **18**, 99-100.

Riess, B. F. Semantic conditioning involving the galvanic skin reflex. *Journal of Experimental Psychology*, 1940, **26**, 238-240.

Riess, B. F. Genetic changes in semantic conditioning. *Journal of Experimental Psychology*, 1946, **36**, 143-152.

Rosenfeld, H. M., & Baer, D. M. Unnoticed verbal conditioning of an aware experimenter by a more aware subject: The double-agent effect. *Psychological Review*, 1969, **76**, 425-432.

Rosenfeld, H. M., & Baer, D. M. Unbiased and unnoticed verbal conditioning: The double agent robot procedure. *Journal of the Experimental Analysis of Behavior*, 1970, **14**, 99-107.

Ross, L. E., Wilcox, S. M., & Mayer, M. J. A simple eyelid conditioning masking task and its effect on differential conditioning. *Psychonomic Science*, 1967, **9**, 333-334.

Rozelle, R. M. Meaning established by classical conditioning: Failure to replicate. *Psychological Reports*, 1968, **22**, 889-895.

Sallows, G. O., Dawes, R. M., & Lichtenstein, E. Subjective value of the reinforcer (RSv) and performance: Crux of the S-R versus cognitive mediation controversy. *Journal of Experimental Psychology*, 1971, **89**, 274-281.

Saltz, E. *The cognitive bases of human learning*. Homewood, Ill.: Dorsey, 1971.

Salzinger, K. Experimental manipulation of verbal behavior: A review. *Journal of General Psychology*, 1959, **61**, 65-94.

Schell, A. M., & Grings, W. W. Avoidance conditioning of the GSR: Nature of the response. *Psychophysiology*, 1971, **7**, 402-407.

Schrier, A. M., & Stollnitz, F. (Eds.) *Behavior of nonhuman primates: Modern research trends*. Vol. 4. New York: Academic Press, 1971.

Schwartz, G. E., & Johnson, H. J. Affective visual stimuli as operant reinforcers of the GSR. *Journal of Experimental Psychology*, 1969, **80**, 28-32.

Shapiro, D., & Crider, A. Operant electrodermal conditioning under multiple schedules of reinforcement. *Psychophysiology*, 1967, **4**, 168-175.

Shapiro, D., Crider, A. B., & Tursky, B. Differentiation of an autonomic response through operant reinforcement. *Psychonomic Science*, 1964, **1**, 147-148.

Shean, G. D. The relationship between ability to verbalize stimulus contingencies and GSR conditioning. *Journal of Psychosomatic Research*, 1968, **12**, 245-249. (a)

Shean, G. D. Vasomotor conditioning and awareness. *Psychophysiology*, 1968, **5**, 22-30. (b)

Shean, G. D. Instrumental modification of the galvanic skin response: Conditioning or control? *Journal of Psychosomatic Research*, 1970, **14**, 155-160.

Silver, D. S., Saltz, E., & Modigliani, V. Awareness and hypothesis testing in concept and operant learning. *Journal of Experimental Psychology*, 1970, **84**, 198-203.

Silverman, R. E. Eliminating a conditioned GSR by the reduction of experimental anxiety. *Journal of Experimental Psychology*, 1960, **59**, 122-125.

Simkins, L. Instructions as discriminative stimuli in verbal conditioning and awareness. *Journal of Abnormal and Social Psychology*, 1963, **66**, 213-219.

Skinner, B. F. Operant behavior. *American Psychologist*, 1963, **18**, 503-515.

Spence, K. W. Cognitive factors in the extinction of the conditioned eyelid response in humans. *Science*, 1963, **140**, 1224-1225.

Spence, K. W. Cognitive and drive factors in the extinction of the conditioned eye blink in human subjects. *Psychological Review*, 1966, **73**, 445-458.

Spence, K. W., & Goldstein, H. Eyelid conditioning performance as a function of emotion-producing instructions. *Journal of Experimental Psychology*, 1961, **62**, 291-294.

Spence, K. W., Homzie, M. J., & Rutledge, E. F. Extinction of the human eyelid CR as a function of the discriminability of the change from acquisition to extinction. *Journal of Experimental Psychology*, 1964, **67**, 545-552.

Spielberger, C. D. The role of awareness in verbal conditioning. In C. W. Eriksen (Ed.), *Behavior and awareness*. Durham: Duke University Press, 1962.

Spielberger, C. D. Theoretical and epistemological issues in verbal conditioning. In S. Rosenberg (Ed.), *Directions in psycholinguistics*. New York: Macmillan, 1965.

Spielberger, C. D., Berger, A., & Howard, K. Conditioning of verbal behavior as a function of awareness, need for social approval and motivation to receive reinforcement. *Journal of Abnormal and Social Psychology*, 1963, **67**, 241-246.

Spielberger, C. D., Bernstein, I. H., & Ratliff, R. G. Information and incentive value of the reinforcing stimulus in verbal conditioning. *Journal of Experimental Psychology*, 1966, **71**, 26-31.

Spielberger, C. D., & DeNike, L. D. Descriptive behaviorism versus cognitive theory in verbal operant conditioning. *Psychological Review*, 1966, **73**, 306-326.

Spielberger, C. D., DeNike, L. D., & Stein, L. S. Anxiety and verbal conditioning. *Journal of Personality and Social Psychology*, 1965, **1**, 229-239.

Spielberger, C. D., & Levin, S. M. What is learned in verbal conditioning? *Journal of Verbal Learning and Verbal Behavior*, 1962, **1**, 125-132.

Spielberger, C. D., Levin, S. M., & Shepard, M. The effects of awareness and attitude toward the reinforcement on the operant conditioning of verbal behavior. *Journal of Personality*, 1962, 30, 106-121.

Staats, A. W. Group discussion. In K. Salzinger & S. Salzinger (Eds.), *Research in verbal behavior and some neurophysiological implications.* New York: Academic Press, 1967.

Staats, A. W. Experimental demand characteristics and the classical conditioning of attitudes. *Journal of Personality and Social Psychology*, 1969, 11, 187-192.

Staats, A. W., & Staats, C. K. *Complex human behavior.* New York: Holt, Rinehart and Winston, 1963.

Staats, A. W., Staats, C. K., Heard, W. G., & Nims, L. P. Replication report: Meaning established by classical conditioning. *Journal of Experimental Psychology*, 1959, 57, 64.

Staats, C. K., & Staats, A. W. Meaning established by classical conditioning. *Journal of Experimental Psychology*, 1957, 54, 74-80.

Steward, J. R. The effect on heart rate of warnings and receipt of pleasant and aversive auditory stimuli. Unpublished doctoral dissertation, University of Connecticut, 1962. (Cited in D. Zeaman & R. W. Smith, Review of some recent findings in human cardiac conditioning. In W. F. Prokasy (Ed.), *Classical conditioning: A symposium.* New York: Appleton-Century-Crofts, 1965.

Streiner, D. L., & Dean, S. J. Expectancy, anxiety, and the GSR. *Psychonomic Science*, 1968, 10, 293-294.

Swenson, R. P., & Hill, F. A. Effects of instruction and interstimulus interval in human GSR conditioning. *Psychonomic Science*, 1970, 21, 369-370.

Taffel, C. Anxiety and the conditioning of verbal behavior. *Journal of Abnormal and Social Psychology*, 1955, 51, 496-501.

Tatz, S. J. Symbolic activity in "learning without awareness." *American Journal of Psychology*, 1960, 73, 239-247.

Thaver, F., & Oakes, W. F. Generalization and awareness in verbal operant conditioning. *Journal of Personality and Social Psychology*, 1967, 6, 391-399.

Thorndike, E. L. *The psychology of wants, interests and attitudes.* New York: Appleton-Century, 1935.

Verplanck, W. S. Unaware of where's awareness: Some verbal operants—notates, monents, and notants. In C. W. Eriksen (Ed.), *Behavior and awareness.* Durham: Duke University Press, 1962.

Watson, J. B. The place of the conditioned-reflex in psychology. *Psychological Review*, 1916, 23, 89-116.

Weiner, H. Instructional control of human operant responding during extinction following fixed-ratio conditioning. *Journal of the Experimental Analysis of Behavior*, 1970, 13, 391-394.

Weinstein, W. K., & Lawson, R. The effect of experimentally induced "awareness" upon performance in free-operant verbal conditioning and on subsequent tests of "awareness." *Journal of Psychology*, 1963, 56, 203-211.

Wickens, D. D. The transference of conditioned excitation and conditioned inhibition from one muscle group to the antagonistic muscle group. *Journal of Experimental Psychology*, 1938, 22, 101-123.

Wickens, D. D. A study of voluntary and involuntary finger conditioning. *Journal of Experimental Psychology*, 1939, 25, 127-140.

Wickens, D. D. Studies of response generalization in conditioning. I. Stimulus generalization during response generalization. *Journal of Experimental Psychology*, 1943, 33, 221-227. (a)

Wickens, D. D. Studies of response generalization in conditioning: II. The comparative strength of the transferred and non-transferred responses. *Journal of Experimental Psychology*, 1943, 33, 330-332. (b)

Wickens, D. D. Allen, C. K., & Hill, F. A. Effect of instructions and UCS strength on extinction of the conditioned GSR. *Journal of Experimental Psychology*, 1963, 66, 235-240.

Wickens, D. D., & Harding, G. B. Effects of interstimulus interval, forewarning, and instructions on extinction of the GSR. *Journal of Experimental Psychology*, 1967, 74, 363-369.

Wickens, D. D., & Meyer, D. R. *Psychology.* (Rev. ed.) New York: Holt, Rinehart and Winston, 1961.

Wilson, G. D. Reversal of differential GSR conditioning by instructions. *Journal of Experimental Psychology,* 1968, **76,** 491-493.

Woodworth, R. S. *Experimental psychology.* New York: Holt, 1938.

Zeaman, D., & Smith, R. W. Review of some recent findings in human cardiac conditioning. In W. F. Prokasy (Ed.), *Classical conditioning: A symposium.* New York: Appleton-Century-Crofts, 1965.

Zeiner, A., & Grings, W. W. Backward conditioning: A replication with emphasis on conceptualizations by the subject. *Journal of Experimental Psychology,* 1968, **76,** 232-235.

Zener, K. The significance of behavior accompanying conditioned salivary secretion for theories of the conditioned reflex. *American Journal of Psychology,* 1937, **50,** 384-403.

2

ON THE SUPPORT OF COGNITIVE THEORY IN OPPOSITION TO BEHAVIOR THEORY: A METHODOLOGICAL PROBLEM

Don E. Dulany
University of Illinois at Urbana – Champaign

I am particularly pleased to comment on Brewer's paper. It is impressive in its depth and scope of scholarship, and I am happy to congratulate him. Yet without diminishing the significance of his review, I disagree with its overall implication, and that disagreement and this conference provide the opportunity to discuss a serious methodological problem. Can we really marshall an evidential basis for the cognitive states and operations we want to investigate? Can we do that, using the standard manipulation—response designs carried over from behaviorism, perhaps venturing a measure or two, and with good old-fashioned parsimony, sticking to one or two hypothetical cognitive states at a time?

All of us have read Thomas Kuhn (1962), and we convene our conferences to celebrate the "new Paradigm"—whatever that may be. We talk mainly among ourselves, with self-congratulatory radical chic; and behaviorism, we snicker, is an idea whose time has gone. How easy it is to believe that scientific history is on our side, that redneck behaviorism must yield to irresistible historical force. But if we rely entirely upon the Kuhnian analysis, putting aside weighty evidential concerns such as the problem of hypothetical states, what is our claim to a *cognitive* psychology? If we *cannot* competitively support cognitive theory in opposition to behavior theory, we cannot support alternative cognitive theories. The methodological problem is the same. Historically, ideological revolution, counterrevolution, and counter-counterrevolution form a common pattern. And in fact, an inability to competitively support alternative cognitive theories was one highly significant cause of Behavioral Revolution I. Could we be setting ourselves up for the next behavioral revolution?

In literally hundreds of experiments, as in life, there are alternatives, stimuli or responses, and outcomes of varying number, likelihood, and value. If the outcome follows a simple response, we call that operant learning. If the stimulus has an outcome that reliably elicits a response, we call that simple respondent learning or classical conditioning. If the outcome follows response to one stimulus but not to another, we speak of discrimination learning. Let the outcome have a probability less than one and we have partial reinforcement. Let the outcome be associated with one stimulus or response with probability P, associated with another stimulus or response with 1 − P, and we have probability learning. And if the critical stimulus or response is really a rule-defined category, we speak of concept attainment − or imitation, observation learning, etc.

This is the Grand Paradigm—grand because it has been the focus of more experimental, theoretical, and methodological analysis over the last half century or so than any other. Work within this paradigm has dominated experimental psychology and great chunks of child, social, personality, and, to a greater and greater degree, even clinical psychology. I use the word "paradigm" here, not in the early Kuhnian sense, but in the sense of a range of experimental procedures with something significant in common. The first sentence of this section characterizes all of these variants, these subparadigms. But perhaps more significantly, in all of these subparadigms there is at least one rule linking some kind of stimulus or response with an outcome—a rule E knows, and must know if he is to conduct his experiment. Furthermore, there is a fundamental question with answers that divide behavior theoretic and cognitive theoretic formulations of the learning process: For S to learn, must he know, or become aware of, that rule too? Must a cognitive process, more specifically, a consciously represented rule, enter into the causal control of the response selected?

Impressive in scope as Brewer's review is, he wisely restricts himself to the first two subparadigms. I sketch the Grand Paradigm in this introduction in order to stress the scope of the theoretical question he considers, and to suggest the scope of the methodological question I raise—a question which may even go beyond this Grand Paradigm.

In this chapter I argue that experiments within the designs that Brewer reviews do not crucially support cognitive theory in opposition to behavior theory, nor even competitively support cognitive theory in the sense of conferring greater credibility upon it. Crucial experiments, I believe, are impossible, and competitive support requires much more than these designs can provide. The principal value of his careful review, in my judgment, is that these experiments show the cognitive account to be equally plausible, rather than less, as many have traditionally held.

GENERAL BEHAVIOR THEORY AND GENERAL COGNITIVE THEORY OF THE GRAND PARADIGM

Anyone with a hearsay acquaintance with learning theory knows that there are several behavior theoretic formulations. They vary in the unseen learning mechanism proposed, and sometimes in the form of quantitative function relating stimulus and response events. They agree, however, in holding that response-reinforcement contingencies and CS-UCS contingencies produce learning by "automatic action" where that term is defined by exclusion–exclusion of a causal role for consciously represented contingency rules and volitional processes. Furthermore, there is an abstraction upon those variants which is in wide use and subject to a fairly precise formulation. The abstraction is possible because the postulates of general behavior theory are formulated on a common description of what happens in two simple kinds of animal learning experiments.

For simplification, let "strength" represent probability, amplitude, or latency. Then two postulates will cover the classical case: (*a*) An unconditioned stimulus will elicit an unconditioned response; and (*b*) as a conditioned stimulus is temporally and spatially associated with an unconditioned stimulus, the strength of a conditioned response increases.

Two simple statements will handle the operant case: (*c*) As a positive reinforcement follows an operant response, in the presence of some set of stimuli S, the strength of that operant response in the presence of that set of stimuli increases; and (*d*) as a negative reinforcement follows an operant response, in the presence of some set of stimuli S, the strength of that response in the presence of that set of stimuli decreases.

Let "outcome" stand for either reinforcement or unconditioned stimulus and two statements will cover generalization and extinction for both cases: (*e*) As stimuli are dissimilar to the set of stimuli S (or the CS), the strength of the conditioned operant response (or the CR) move toward the preconditioning level; and (*f*) as the conditioned operant (or CR) occurs in the presence of the set of stimuli S (or the CS) in the absence of the outcome, the strength of the operant (or CR) in the presence of the set of stimuli S (or the CS) moves toward the preconditioning level.

The general cognitive theory that laces this literature and Brewer's review has a comparable formulation, though I find it a little less definite in a number of particulars. Again two statements will handle the classical case: (*a*) As a conditioned stimulus and unconditioned stimulus are temporally and spatially associated, *S* gradually, or perhaps suddenly, forms an awareness of, or belief in, that contingency. (*b*) Strength of a "conditioned response" (or more precisely, the response that a behaviorist would think had been conditioned) varies directly with, and as a consequence of, the strength of belief in the CS-UCS contingency.

Two more statements cover the operant case: (*c*) As a positive (or negative) reinforcer follows an operant response, *S* forms, gradually or suddenly, an awareness of the reinforcement contingency, and/or an awareness of what he is supposed to do, and/or some kind of disposition to comply. In the general cognitive theory, the relations among these states are not clearly specified. (*d*) Strength of an operant response varies directly with, and as a consequence of, strength of belief in any one, or the conjunction of two or three, of these awarenesses.

(*e*) A generalization principle at about the same level of precision would say that to the degree stimuli are similar they tend to be cognitively categorized together. No more specific principle has been called upon in the designs reviewed. The principle of extinction is fairly straightforward: (*f*) As an operant or "conditioned response" occurs in the absence of the outcome (reinforcer or UCS), strength of belief in the outcome contingency moves toward the preconditioning level.

I think it fair to say that within studies following the designs Brewer reviews, no more elaborate or precise cognitive theory has been presented or used.[1]

BEHAVIOR THEORETIC REINTERPRETATION
AS A METHODOLOGICAL EXERCISE

If confronted with the evidence from the 11 designs Brewer carefully reviews, how might the behavior theorist maintain the credibility of his theory? I offer this analysis as a methodological exercise; I am not playing the devil's advocate. Advocacy of behaviorism is not in short supply and devil's advocacy is a particularly tiresome role. To see what competitive support of a theory requires, we must first understand how it fails. And if we challenge the devil on his own court, we had better understand the devil's game. Suppose we begin by making a few fairly plausible auxiliary assumptions—more precisely, domain assumptions and augmenting assumptions. We should not think it in any way unfair to invoke auxiliary assumptions, since data predicted from theory must always be predicted from theory together with assumptions—most obviously, manipulation and assessment assumptions, control assumptions, etc.—never by theory alone. When critically examining experiments, we judge the credibility of those assumptions, and I submit that the ones I shall offer are antecedently plausible, and in fact technically supported together with the behavior theory postulates by the experiments following the 11 designs Brewer reviews. Some of these assumptions are domain assumptions that would assimilate a number of the cognitive theorist's favorite variables to behavior theory:

1. Let us assume that verbal utterances, instructions from E or covert self-instructions from S, may serve as conditioned stimuli for autonomically mediated responses. Who has not responded *emotionally* – perhaps "without thinking"—to something said? We know that many Es have conditioned autonomic responses to verbal stimuli—Brewer reviews many studies—and we simply use the fact of that conditioning at this point, not its interpretation. Those studies experimentally recreate a plausible history, and if we assume that S brings a cognitive apparatus to the experimental arena, why can't we assume that he brings the consequences of his conditioning history? In essence, instructions are assimilated to behavior theory by invoking postulates a, b, and f as historical assumptions.

2. Assume that verbal utterances may serve as discriminative stimuli or cues—S^D's as the Skinnerians would say—for verbal responses and other motor behavior. Almost everyone has used reinforcement to train a dog or a child or even an adult to respond on command or request or promise, and many experiments

---

[1] Although Brewer reviews my own experiments within his rubric, I would think that they fit a "network design" (Dulany, 1968) rather than any of the 11 designs reviewed.

have shown the same. Again we simply assume that S brings the consequences of his conditioning history with him—a history in which verbal utterances gain control of other responses through selective reinforcement. This time we invoke Postulates c, and d or f, as historical assumptions.

3. Assume that verbal reports of awareness may behave as operants are said to behave within behavior theory, that is, to come under the functional control of reinforcers. Several hundred verbal conditioning experiments have shown that other verbal responses do—why not assume that S's verbal reports should behave the same? In fact, is there anything in the general cognitive theory that would lead us to think otherwise?

4. Assume that fear is a response with stimulus properties—some would say "drive stimulus" properties. Wasn't that Neal Miller's hypothesis in 1948, supported by a classical series of experiments?

Other assumptions augment the theory, but fairly comfortably, since they are assumptions in the public domain, familiar to and probably plausible to nearly all practicing psychologists.

5. Assume that activity of the sympathetic system mediating fear and flight reactions and activity of the parasympathetic system mediating relaxation and vegetative reactions are reciprocally innervated and respond antagonistically. Ask any psychologist.

6. Assume that for conditioning to occur, potential reinforcers, conditioned stimuli, or unconditioned stimuli must be attended to. Nearly everyone assumes that the effective stimulus is the proximal stimulus, not the distal stimulus. But do not think that "attention" sneaks in some sort of spooky cognition. The term in this usage refers only to an orienting response, and James Holland and other Skinnerians have been operantly conditioning it for years.

7. Assume that conditioning has parameters whose values vary over properties of reinforcers, UCSs, responses, and persons. Whether or not conditioning occurs, and in what direction and degree, depends upon the values those parameters take. Some responses are more conditionable than others. Different people respond differently to the same reinforcer, etc., etc. Everybody knows that.

8. Finally, assume that what we call "awareness" is merely an epiphenomenon of some kind of neural process and not causally active upon response selection in any way independent of that neural process. Few if any psychologists think of awareness as disembodied mind-dust. But to be workable for us, that assumption must be slightly more specific: Assume that awareness is an epiphenomenon of the automatic conditioning processes. When conditioning occurs, awareness of the critical contigency, and in the operant case, also of a disposition to comply, just emerges, perhaps in direct temporal parallel, or perhaps sometimes in only a latent and inarticulate form that later appears as a "rationalization" of performace or response to a suggestive interview. Of course, this awareness gets reported in wonderfully novel and varied ways. No behavior theorist, it must be conceded, has yet produced a satisfactory theory of such novel utterances. But then neither, to my knowledge, has any cognitive theorist.

How well then might our behavior theory postulates, together with these assumptions, account for the experiments within the 11 designs Brewer has identified? In order to emphasize that this is intended as a general methodological analysis of *designs,* of their evidential value, I shall treat each as an abstract class of possible experiments, calling anonymously upon procedures from particular experiments for illustration only. At the moment, my concern is not at all with the adequacy of procedures from particular experiments he reviews. Some may be excellent; some wretched. My question is this: could an idealized experiment following each of these designs competitively support the general cognitive theory in opposition to behavior theory?

All are characterized as "dissociative" design by Brewer, since E attempts, with manipulations and assessments, to dissociate awareness from the conditioning process, and then to determine which is related to the terminal responses. This is the method of converging operations (Garner, Hake, & Ericksen, 1956), for many years widely regarded as our strongest method of inference to a hypothetical state.

1. In the *informed pairing* design, E simply tells S the contingency, without presenting that contingency, and observes a consequent effect upon the response. If the response is autonomic, he might attach electrodes and warn S that he will be shocked when a signal occurs. If the response is motor, he might promise a coin for every fourth response. As the cognitivist sees it, these instructions produce an awareness of the contingency which then causes the response, directly in the autonomic case, but indirectly in the motor case, and only for those in whom he common-sensically assumes—in this design it is not measured—that there is some consequent disposition to comply. But the behaviorist might certainly reply, "Haven't these contingencies been repeatedly presented in the past history of the S—warnings and punishments, promises and rewards for responses that meet the conditions of the promises?" Invoke Assumption 1 and we explain the autonomic case: Warnings should be conditioned stimuli. Invoke Assumption 2 and we explain the motor case: Promises should be S^D's. Of course, neither of these instructions may exactly match a prior warning or promise, or it may—if only in highly selective tonal inflection—but behavior theory only requires that the presented stimulus and the training stimulus share a common element, or a pair of similar elements (on Postulate e for generalization). With hundreds of warnings and promises in everyone's past, many may find the behavioral account as credible as the general cognitive theory, which does not even explain how that instruction gets translated into a belief—or for that matter, how the belief gets translated into a response.

2. The *informed unpairing* design is to extinction what the informed pairing design is to acquisition. After classical conditioning of an autonomic response, E informs S that there will be no more UCS (a shock in the experiments reviewed). Typically, extinction is immediate, though rarely complete—just as we should expect, on the cognitive theory, if S believes the instruction with less than complete certainty. But does this finding compel the interpretation of cognitive mediation? Certainly we have all learned to relax in response to all-clear signals and reassurances of many kinds—and been reinforced for that response by fear reduction, an aversive emotional response whose decrement should certainly be reinforcing. Just invoke Assumption 2 for prior discriminative operant conditioning to verbal utterances. Add Assumption 5 for the reciprocal innervation of antagonistic response systems—relaxation should thereby directly reduce fear in the

current experiment—and behavior theory is home free. Isn't it relaxation, the behaviorist might add, that is often used to reciprocally inhibit fear in the remarkably effective systematic desensitization procedures? When the response that extinguishes is a motor avoidance response, as in finger withdrawal studies, we need only add Assumption 4. As the fear response with stimulus properties diminishes, so too should the motor avoidance response it cues.

3. The *instructed conditioning* design, too, comes in operant and classical variants. When E instructs S to perform some motor operant and observes that he does, the behaviorist may once again call upon Assumption 2 for discriminative operant conditioning to verbal utterances. Among the hundreds of requests, commands, and entreaties we have all been reinforced for responding to, there are plausibly some that share a common element or pair of similar elements with the instruction for the experimental response used. At least nothing in the general specification of the design calls for novel instructional stimuli and responses that could never in the past have been conditioned to those stimuli. And even if they did, I am afraid, the general cognitive theory would be about as hard put to explain the response.

In the classical case, E instructs S to produce some autonomically mediated response, typically the GSR, without pairing the instruction with shock and without saying or implying that a punishment will follow. This case presents a little more challenge. But suppose we first invoke Assumption 2 and assume that S has operantly learned to respond verbally to verbal stimuli of E and his own such that he may associatively hit upon "dentist" or "shock" or "failure"—which should, by Assumtion 2, kick in his GSR. Granted that it is difficult to specify the prior operant learning history that sets up just the right chain, but then most Ss take a long time and many fail, as Neal Miller and his associates recently discovered. Unfortunately, the general cognitive theory does not suggest the cognitive strategy for finding a word like "shock" or "dentist" either. The auxiliary assumption of one theory is about as vague as that of the other.

4. In the *instructed nonconditioning* design, E tells S not to produce the CR despite the pairing of CS and UCS (usually aversive), or not to execute the operant response despite reinforcement for the response. This design recalls the informed unpairing design—and a similar behavior theoretic reformulation leaps to mind. In the classical case, it is certainly plausible that S would have learned to relax, through reinforcement by fear reduction, when told "don't be afraid" or "don't show fear" (Assumption 1). Then when responding with relaxation he should, on Assumption 5, reciprocally inhibit the fear that would otherwise be more strongly conditioned. Of course, old conditioning must still compete with new conditioning on this reinterpretation, but as Brewer indicates, instructed nonconditioning is usually not completely effective in the classical case, providing a degree of support for Postulates a and b.

In the operant case, we need only invoke Assumption 2. The S will have had enough reinforcement in the past for not responding when told not to—it is the story of childhood—for this instruction to outweigh an experimental reinforcement like "Right" or "good" or "Umhmm." What does S care about that?

5. In the *instructed extinction* design, successful conditioning is followed by

an instruction not to respond. In the motor operant case, responding stops abruptly; in the classical autonomic case, only to a limited degree. This design is like the instructed nonconditioning design, but instruction is pitted against a presumed perserveration of the conditioning process instead of a presumed accumulation of the conditioning process. The results should therefore yield equally well to the behavior theoretic reinterpretation by invocation of the same Assumptions 2 and 5.

6. In the *masking design*, misleading instructions or procedures are used to divert *S's* attention from the CS-UCS contingency or the operant-reinforcement contingency. Where masking blocks conditioning, this would seem strongly to support the cognitive view. The trouble is, procedures effective enough to mask either of those contingencies may be effective in diverting attention from the elements of the contingency—the CS or UCS or operant or reinforcement—which on Assumption 6 is essential for conditioning to occur. At least I can see nothing inherent in the masking design that makes this possibility less plausible.

7. Unlike the previously discussed designs, the *awareness of contingency* design incorporates an assessment rather than a manipulation of awareness. After a conditioning procedure, or sometimes during the conditioning procedure, perhaps on every trial or after each block of trials, *E* assesses *S's* awareness of the critical contingency, the CS-UCS contingency in the classical case, the response-reinforcement contingency in the operant case. In a large number of studies, only those *Ss* condition who report the contingency—as the general cognitive theory would predict on the view that awareness is necessary for and instrumental in the conditioning. But this design yields readily to a behavior theoretic reinterpretation, either by assimilating the reports of awareness to behavior theory or by calling upon a plausible augmenting assumption. On Assumption 3, that verbal reports behave as do operants, we should expect reports and terminal operants to be conditioned in parallel as *S* covertly articulates the contingency, responds correctly, and is reinforced over conditioning. Furthermore, on Assumption 8, for the classical case, and alternatively for the operant case, awareness of the contingency simply emerges as an epiphenomenon of the automatic conditioning process. Why does it happen that only some *Ss* condition and report awareness? Well, different people respond differently to reinforcers and UCSs, don't they?—just as Assumption 7 says. Within the operant case, this is by far the most common design—there are scores of studies—and the behavior theorist is at least twice blessed with reinterpretational possibilities. Since these assumptions together with Postulates *a–d* predict the results, all might be viewed as supported by these results.

8. The *compliance* design elaborates the previously discussed design by incorporating assessments of both the response-reinforcement contingency and some kind of disposition to comply. In the typical finding, *Ss* who report awareness of the contingency but not compliance do not condition. Only those *Ss* condition who report *both* an awareness of the contingency *and* disposition to comply—as good cognitive common sense would expect. Is this finding crucial? Remember that on Assumption 8, awareness of *both* the contingency and disposition to comply emerges from effective operant conditioning. If *Ss* who condition in the awareness of contingency design only report an awareness of contingency, it is because that

is all that is assessed. Why do a few *Ss* who neither condition nor report compliance still report awareness of the contingency? A suggestive postconditioning interview could raise an only dimly articulated awareness to the light of day. It even happens occasionally with random reinforcement controls. Still, I concede that in obtaining measures of *two* cognitive states, this design makes a small step in the direction of what I believe is required for strong competitive support—a rich *network* of interrelations among experimental variables.

9. I am unable to see a clear difference between some of Brewer's variants of the *contingency expectancy* design and the awareness of contingency design—and believe they submit to the reinterpretation already offered. In one fairly distinct variant, however, a single reinforcer may follow either of two response alternatives, for example, *I* or *We,* depending upon which *S* uses on a particular trial.As it happens, *I* is successfully conditioned for some *Ss*, *We* for others—and *Ss* report a reinforcement contingency upon the response alternative conditioned, just as the cognitivist would expect if *S* acts upon the cognitive hypothesis he happens to form. But on Assumption 8, which served the behaviorist well in the Awareness of Contingency design, an awareness of contingency of reinforcement upon the response conditioned is said to emerge as an epiphenomenon. Why not here, too? We need only invoke Assumption 7 in addition: Different responses are differentially conditionable for different *Ss.* Behavior theory is silent on the next question: why? But the general cognitive theory is equally silent on the puzzle as to why some *Ss* learned a hypothesis formed on *I* and others a hypothesis formed on *We.* Is it any better off?

In a second distinguishable variant, *E* attempts to manipulate *S's* expectancy of a CS-UCS contingency, other than by masking or instruction, and observes that the strength of the CR varies accordingly. For example, removal and replacement of shock electrodes reduces and then restores the strength of a previously conditioned GSR. But this is just what the behaviorist would expect if the electrodes together with *E's* signal have been part of the effective complex CS throughout conditioning. Shock is heralded by signal *plus* electrodes. And would not *S's* attention be drawn to electrodes by a signal associated with shock—a condition, on Assumption 6, for the establishment of an effective CS?

10. The *response expectancy* design evidently differs from preceding ones in that there may be two possible responses with a possible reinforcer for each, and hence two possible contingencies. As the general cognitive theorist would expect, *S* reports the contingency for the response that is made. For example, in finger withdrawl, some *Ss* report the contingency of shock avoidance upon finger withdrawl; others report the contingency of *E's* approval upon holding fast to the shock—and both groups behave accordingly. The problem for behavioral explanation is essentially the same as for the first variant of the contingency expectancy design; and I see no reason why Assumption 8 for emergence of awareness and Assumption 7 for parameters of conditioning, varying over consequences and persons, will not serve equally well in this design.

11. Finally, Brewer reviews a *reinforcement expectancy* design in which the degree and direction of operant conditioning with an ambiguous reinforcer like "Unhmm" is shown to vary with *S's* descriptions of the value of the reinforcer.

Although the general cognitive theory does not make a formal place for subjective evaluation of reinforcement, this finding does accord with good cognitive common sense. Nevertheless, Assumption 7 handles this matter for the behaviorist by telling us that parameters of the effect of reinforcement may vary over persons. Of course, behavior theory does not tell us how S can describe the parameter value the reinforcer has for him, but then neither—I must say once more—does the general cognitive theory. Both make do with the agreeable enough assumption that S knows how to speak his own language.

POSSIBLE REACTIONS TO THE EXERCISE

1. The first thing a cognitive psychologist might do is question the quality of my behavior theoretic reanalysis. Do all of the studies within each design submit as well as the reanalysis as do the few illustrations? Perhaps not. Are some of the auxiliary assumptions a little strained or not entirely adequate to permit behavior theoretic prediction of the experimental results? Perhaps. My heart really wasn't in it. But if turning my own mind to such alien and uncomfortable forms of thought will yield just this much, I feel confident that a dedicated behaviorist could extend the analysis and remedy its deficiencies.

2. Still, one might argue, all those assumptions I call upon are *post hoc*—an especially damning quality to some minds. But *post hoc* for whom? And why does it really matter? All these assumptions have been around for a while, most of them longer than most of the experiments reviewed. I had thought of them all, at one time or another, long before I read Brewer's review. *Ante-* and *post hoc* assumptions may or may not have served science equally well—what is the evidence? Anyway, they could differ on nontemporal dimensions in ways that make the difference. Furthermore, general cognitive theory also requires auxiliary assumptions for prediction of the findings within these designs, as this reanalysis shows—prior assumptions for some, perhaps, but *post hoc,* I suspect, for others. But most fundamentally, the evidential value of a finding for a successfully predictive formulation must surely be independent of the time at which that formulation enters the head of the investigator. Let the assumptions be examined on their own merits.

3. Another possible reply would reject theoretical credibility in favor of theoretical productivity as the goal of this research. Cognitive theory has been experimentally productive, one might say; without it these experiments might never have been performed. Descriptively I do not think this line of argument will wash, and normatively I think this would be a hazardous line of retreat for the cognitive psychologist. Most of the experiments Brewer reviews were in fact performed by behaviorists with behavior theoretic expectations—as he indicates. Moreover, it is perfectly obvious to the reader that nearly all were designed to confer greater credibility upon an answer to the fundamental question on which this literature pivots: Is, or is not, awareness necessary and causal in the production of what we have called conditioning? But more significantly, I think, this reply is illustrative of a well-known line of retreat within the philosophy of science, and one well traveled within psychology. It is the rejection of a realistic interpretation of theoretical

entities in favor of an instrumentalist view of theories. We use theories, on this view, not because we could ever believe their assertions, but because they are experimentally productive. "Model" is a common term we use for a theory we would rather not take full responsibility for—in the sense of supporting credibility claims. But the problem is this: If we abandon realism, if our aim is not a more credible description of cognitive events—not the full story, of course, but a selective abstraction of cognitive reality—what is our claim to a *cognitive* psychology?

4. Psychology as the cognitivist views it is just passing into, or through, or out of a revolutionary paradigm clash between behaviorism and the new cognitive psychology. How might this reanalysis be viewed through cognitive Kuhnian eyes? Comments from here and there will serve as my source for this matter: We need not settle the philosopher's argument about what Kuhn really said and meant (see Lakatos & Musgrave, 1970).

Of course the "anomalous findings" from Brewer's review may be "handled" by the behaviorists, the Kuhnian might reply. They will make *ad hoc* modifications to theory, reject the new cognitive methodology, and fall back upon saving assumptions. And what does it matter? Theories from the two paradigms are really "incommensurable," and experimental observation is much too frail and theory-laden to carry that kind of evidential weight. Eventually we shall forget all about the clash of theories across paradigms as we move on to the solution of theoretical and methodological problems within the new normal science of cognitive psychology. We should now put aside confrontation in favor of justification of the new paradigm on its own merits. Besides, the real moving forces of scientific change, we must recognize, belong less to the dreary rationale of evidence than to the exciting social psychology of science—the attractiveness of new theories, the elegance and persuasion of new presentations, and a rich strain of radical fervor.

But whatever has happened elsewhere, in this reanalysis I have made no modifications of behavior theory, challenged no cognitive methodology, and resorted, I submit, to assumptions no less explicit or plausible than those required by the general cognitive theory. Furthermore, both formulations, with complete "commensurability," address themselves to the same experimental variables—UCS and CS, reinforcer and response, instructions and reports, and a list of various stimulus manipulations long common to the experimental psychology laboratory.

The strength of the empirical warrant we can obtain from experimental observation is certainly a central and high-priority item within the current philosophy of science—nothing less is at stake than our stubborn belief that science really *is* about the real world. But neither Brewer nor I have rejected the minimal legacy of logical empiricism on which the experimental examination of theories still seems worth the candle. If we had, neither of us would have written what he did. And if we must, if experiments are only "exemplars," how could the new normal science solve the theoretical problems *within* the new cognitive psychology?

Finally, I must say that I see less than the advertised grounds for cognitive optimism in the winds of social psychological change. We should not be too parochial to notice the growing strength of radical behaviorism in many other areas of psychology. They have their radical fervor, too — and it may not be terminal euphoria after all. They have a mission and program, and a behavioral technology that are fully understandable to popular magazines, the general public, and politically sensitive granting agencies. How wide and deep would be the determination to pursue a horrendously difficult cognitive psychology with unfunded idealism? It also strikes me, to be blunt, that not everyone with our doctoral union card is smart enough to be a good cognitive psychologist. The radical behaviorist, on the other hand, need not learn much mathematics, experimental design, statistics, computer technology, linguistics, or philosophy at all. The basic problems have been solved for him: Theory, methods, aims are all in the text book. Anyway, when we turn to the teaching of history in our decline, what shall we ever tell our students? That in the Year of Our Lord Nineteen-hundred-and-seventy a group of bright, dedicated, and excellently trained psychologists slipped their S-R bonds—and sniffed the wind?

Whatever the descriptive accuracy of this account, there must be a better way to do science.

ON THE PROBLEM OF HYPOTHETICAL STATES
AND COMPETITIVE SUPPORT

What is the problem of evidential inference set by general cognitive theory and these 11 designs?

Central to general cognitive theory is the postulation of a necessary and causally effective awareness. Awareness of contigency, of E's expectation, of a compliance disposition, all appear within the literature of these designs, but either the distinctions among them are blurred or their interrelations remain unspecified. As the theory is used then, either one form of awareness or a conjunction of two or three is held to be instrumental in conditioning. It functions as a theory with just one hypothetical state—awareness—together with a handful of formal and common-sense antecedents, and a consequent response. Within the 11 designs, the theory maps rather directly onto experimental variables: the particular CS and UCS, or operant and reinforcer, perhaps a commonsense instructional manipulation, and one or two measures. So simple a theory must have a simple experimental representation. In fact, the theory must predict, and can predict no more than, a simple correlation of terminal response with hypothetical manipulations and assessments of awareness. These 11 designs examine that one prediction and no other. But since the same manipulations and assessments can be reconciled with behavior theory—by plausible assumptions of prior conditioning, facilitation or inhibition of conditioning, conditioning of reports, or emergence from the conditioning process—behavior theory may comfortably predict the same simple correlation. The presumed dissociation of awareness and conditioning has vanished and the two formulations are left to predict alike.

What is the more general problem of evidential inference to hypothetical states? We all know that, for any array of experimental findings, there is (in principle, at least) an unlimited set of theoretical interpretations. In actuality, however, the set of explanations available to the research community is finite and usually rather small. We are constrained by limited imaginations, the known structure of laws, antecedent plausibilities, etc. But the central problem arises here: To the degree theoretical explanations are simple—with one-state theories as the limiting, and common, case—both disconfirmation and confirmation are weak. What may be predicted and explained by one of the available theories is readily predictable and explained by available alternatives *in conjunction with credible auxiliary assumptions.* In this way, we saw that behavior theory could be made to comprehend the range of evidence. The general cognitive theory and 11 designs that dominate this literature, I submit, are too simple and improverished to generate strong competitive support for descriptions of hypothetical cognitive events. The method of converging operations requires no greater richness of theoretical and experimental relationships—and fails.

Is there another way? The greater the richness of a network of experimental relationships, the narrower the range of available theories that will predict this network of experimental relationships *without recourse to highly implausible auxiliary assumptions.* Furthermore, the richer the theoretical network, the richer the network of experimental relationships it will generate. Where we ask about hypothetical states and operations, competitive support in the sense of substantial shifts in relative credibility requires the use of a rich network of theoretical and experimental relationships. For competitive support, I believe, we must have (*a*) a theory specifying a fairly rich and precise network of cognitive state variables, together with interrelating cognitive operations of inference and decision, and (*b*) designs examining a fairly rich and precise network of predicted relations among experimental variables—relations going far beyond that simple correlation of instructions or reports with a final response.

But at this point, I'm afraid, I have lapsed into a more dogmatically assertive mood than I would like. I have already tried to develop a method for the use of networks of relationships in obtaining competitive support, a theory of propositional awareness, and supporting experiments (Dulany, 1968), and that is not what I wish to write about here.

Could the problem be still more general than the Grand Paradigm? I know of no agreed upon characterization of cognitive psychology. But common to those inquiries for which I use the term is a concern for the behavior of what we intuit as mental states and operations—*Ss'* states and operations whose behavior at any moment is hypothetical from the point of view of *E*. Furthermore, I find very few experimental designs within that cognitive psychology that would be characterized in any fundamental way differently than the 11 Brewer reviews: One or two manipulations, a response, or a measure or two are all that can be found.

We would do well, I think, to examine the methodological problem of hypothetical states as it arises in other areas of cognitive psychology. The fundamental problem of evidential warrant is the same whether we examine a theory of cognitive states in opposition to either behavior theory or another cognitive theory. If we do not competitively support cognitive theories, what is our claim to a cognitive psychology with a future?

REFERENCES

Brewer, W. F. There is no convincing evidence for operant or classical conditioning in human adults.

Dulany, D. E. Awareness, rules, and propositional control: A confrontation with S-R behavior theory. In T. R. Dixon & D. L. Horton (Eds.), *Verbal behavior and general behavior theory.* Englewood Cliffs, N.J.: Prentice-Hall, 1968.

Garner, W. R., Hake, H. W., & Eriksen, C. W. Operationism and the concept of perception. *Psychological Review,* 1956, **63**, 140-159.

Kuhn, T. S. *The structure of scientific revolutions.* Chicago: University of Chicago Press, 1962.

Lakatos, I., & Musgrave, A. (Eds.) *Criticism and the growth of scientific knowledge.* Cambridge: Cambridge University Press, 1970.

3
BREWER-DULANY DISCUSSION

Brewer: I agree about the desirability of richer theories. But I disagree with Dulany when, playing behaviorist, he talks about the credibility of behaviorist augmenting assumptions. My threshold for a theory's credibility is greater. The whole reason for behaviorism was to enable us to be physicalists. The idea was to have the input be physical quanta coming into the body so that we could ask the physicist to measure it. To deny, as I do, that a physicist can say anything significant about psychological phenomena is to abandon a major prejudice of behaviorism. Dulany does this too, but surreptitiously—as in his account of the masking paradigms. The stimulus was supposed to be physical quanta, but he had to bring in something called "diverting S's attention." The outcome is, as Chomsky's review of Skinner said, to drive the stimulus back into the S's head, violating the assumption the program began with. At this point, my credulity can't be stretched any further: The ball game is over.

Dulany: My argument is that rich theories are *essential.* Because there are so many credible alternative explanations, we must develop a theory able to generate a rich network of experimental relationships that presses its alternatives to extremely implausible saving assumptions. Not that it is good to do this, but that it is absolutely necessary; otherwise, the behaviorist may yet outlive us. It is correct that stimuli have been pushed inside; that is the whole history of the behavioristic retreat, from mediation theory through Hull's pure stimulus acts to Osgood's meaning and the "observing response." But until we have successfully done something *new* the behaviorist can get away with what he is doing.

Halwes: When Brewer finished I said, "Aha, we've won." When Dulany finished I was convinced that we should look again. Now I feel Brewer has shown us that what the behaviorists have done on these problems did not teach us very much. Further, in this domain what is commonly called "cognitive theory" is not a scientific theory at all; it is common sense. Psychology started with common sense before the behaviorist revolution, and then the behaviorists said, "Look, we have this *scientific theory* which will be ever so much better than common sense in explaining these phenomena." Now, not only do we find that the behaviorists have told us nothing of significance, but it also appears that the "cognitive explanations" are just common sense again. I don't think that as cognitive psychologists we know anything more about classical conditioning than my grandmother knows about it. Indeed, neither I nor my grandmother has *studied* it at all. The behaviorists have pretended to study it, and Brewer has kindly pointed out to them that they have failed to do so. Dulany has offered to study it, and that would be kind of him, but at the moment I think it is clear we don't know anything about what's going on. For example, we say that awareness is necessary for conditioning. The behaviorists are telling us awareness does not exist, and we are saying it does, but nobody is finding out what it is or how it works. Then there is that term, "automatic," in the literature. As for as I can tell it means "magical." It means, "I don't have any idea how it works."

To appreciate the cognitive approach we must look at a cognitive theory in a domain where the phenomena have at least been studied from the point of view. Other chapters will outline the kind of theoretical depth that can be provided by cognitive psychologists when they have done their homework. But we are not to be expected to provide *post hoc* explanations for uninformative behaviorist experiments. Everyone should read, for example, Meehl (1967) and Lykken (1968) to see the invidiousness of *post hoc'ing*. From the point of view of granting agencies, tenure and promotions committees, and the like, somebody's research may look like a beautifully integrated research program where everything fits into place; but in fact it is very likely that no theoretical proposition has ever been confronted at all and, if so, has not been supported at all.

Richer theories may be better, but one cannot confuse richness with *post hoc* "explanatory" capability. Behaviorism is extremely "rich" in the latter sense only. Our best argument against the behaviorist is to show that he is a cognitivist too; even so, we have explained nothing yet in these areas, not having gone into the lab and studied the phenomena from our perspective.

Dulany: Again, the point I was trying to make about richness (in the sense of a rich network of interrelations) is that it is absolutely necessary to generate a rich network that can competitively support a theory by stripping away the implausibility of its rival's supporting assumptions. I am not for a moment proposing it as some "objective" standard by which to evaluate theories; rather, I am saying it is a prerequisite to any good theory. My propositional learning theory is rich in the sense that it has been used in classical conditioning, operant motor conditioning, analyzing the "prisoner's dilemma" game, attitude studies, children's probability learning, etc.

My credulity for explanations offered in a given area is inversely related to my familiarity with the area. I am really very pessimistic about our field.

Brewer: Dulany and I look at the history of our field differently. To my mind there *was* a cognitive psychology, that of the Würzburg school, that was doing right-headed work. Then behaviorism came in. Dulany talks of the morass that existed before, implying that it was all as bad as behaviorism. I don't see it that way. The earlier cognitive psychology was much better than it is usually misrepresented to be.

Dulany: I agree that the earlier cognitive psychology was better. But last night I asked McCawley what he felt about the shifts in theory in linguistics. He said, "Well, we go to conventions and meetings and one guy stands up and says 'It's intuitively obvious . . .' and another guy replies 'It's intuitively obvious that it's not . . .' and it ends in an impasse." This is very reminiscent of the old introspectionist controversies, with one theorist maintaining that "It's intuitively obvious that green is an amalgam of blue and yellow" and another one saying "It's prefectly obvious that it's not." Historically, I think their problem was that they lacked a logic and a method of competitive support for competing cognitive theories. And their problem then is our problem now.

Ross: I really question whether Dulany is right in saying science should be so competitive. To me Kuhn's import is that science has been no better in this respect in the past. I don't think it is possible to wipe out a competing theory. We all know that, no matter how long or loudly we argue, Skinner will never become a cognitive psychologist. I say this from personal experience in linguistics, which is now undergoing what might be called a "palace revolution" in generative grammar. I am convinced that the people on the opposite side of the split from me are never going to give up their views, and being honest I will never give up mine. So the question is *"Why* should we compete?" Perhaps the only reasons are economic and political: so that students can write well-motivated dissertations, so that conferences like ours can be held, and so on. I am all for deep theories, but I don't think it is reasonable to expect conclusive demolition of the opposition.

Dulany: That sentiment scares me. Carried to its logical extreme, it leads one to ask, "Why do experiments? Why bother to learn experimental design and control?" I think that Kuhn's analysis of science is reasonably accurate, but that science can be better. I am not suggesting theory demolition as a goal (I agree we will never change Skinner's mind), but there should be specifiable empirical grounds for belief in theories and hypotheses.

Turvey: I think that the older use of the term "cognitive" had to do with conscious experience and awareness. Contemporary cognitive psychology is more concerned with the underlying mechanisms, with what constitutes "tacit knowledge" in Polanyi's sense. We are really trying to find, say, what kinds of operators and routines underlie the processes by which we read, hear speech, or retrieve things in "memory." Thus it is quite appropriate that we should turn our attention to the mechanisms underlying classical conditioning.

McCawley: I would like to refer to a conversation with Dulany last night. What I was talking about was not linguists' intuitions about what is right, but rather their intuitions about what is plausible. It is here that the typical impasse occurs, not in judgments of correctness. But that still leaves the behaviorist in a precarious position. Particularly I remember Brewer mentioning that behaviorists had dismissed objections of the kind Chomsky made on the grounds that they are very complicated, high-powered stuff, and therefore not taken very seriously. But if they are going to attempt an alternative analysis along the lines drawn by Dulany they will have to take Chomsky's objections seriously. To give an account of simple things, like the GSR, their analysis will have to incorporate some kind of treatment of verbal behavior — exactly the sort of thing that Chomsky was objecting to in Skinner's treatment. If their behaviorist analysis of simple things is to work, they will need a behaviorist analysis of the complicated things that can work as well.

Anderson: I would like to make two points. The first one, already emphasized, is that in discussing awareness we are simply talking about our common sense notions. We have gone from common sense notions to behaviorism and then back to our common sense notions with cognitive psychology. I want to remind everyone of Lashley's warning that these subjective common sense concepts probably will not be the ones with which we eventually analyze behavior. The concept of awareness itself will need to be analyzed.

The next point is that cognitive psychologists may not be able to analyze the concept of awareness by the two techniques they commonly use for their analyses: (*a*) introspection of the mental processes, and (*b*) examination of behavior. I think that we can arrive at some of the concomitants of awareness in the brain only by electrophysiological techniques, and that they cannot be made manifest by examining either behavior or introspection.

Dulany: That is a very interesting possibility. However, it is simply the case that at this point we can get private reports of beliefs that not only are qualitatively different, but also can be quantified. We can put these reports into very precise equations that can generate numerical values and have impressively good fit. In all the electrophysiological measures that will tap awareness, there is, as far as I know, no way of distinguishing qualitative differences among the things a subject might believe. In fact, it is probable that electrophysiology as a technique of assessing awareness is 200 years behind private report.

Brewer: I originally set out to study aphasia. I went to medical school and learned about the brain and about neurology. But I left it for the study of psycholinguistics when I came to the conclusion that after I had learned all those things I knew not one thing that constrained me in any way, whatsoever, in learning about language. I still feel the same way (I take that back—we know its in the left hemisphere).

Member of audience: Dr. Brewer: Apparently your conclusion is that a strict incremental, S-R associationistic, physicalistic model of that kind of behavior doesn't really work. That is not really anything new: It has been known for some time. So I don't think that is what you are saying. Your title says there is no evidence of conditioning in adult humans. If you are saying that, I think that is something new and, if true, very interesting. However, I am not sure that you have succeeded in winning me over to that point. First, it doesn't seem to satisfy the operational definition which you describe: There *is* conditioning. So we must go to what you call the theoretical position that there is no conditioning without awareness. But then you turn around in your conclusions, saying it is strange that humans show no unconscious automatic conditioning at all since in fact such conditioning is quite likely to be involved in other aspects of behavior. It seems that you don't really want to maintain completely that there is no conditioning, so what you are saying is unclear to me.

Brewer: The point I was trying to make is that there is no support for automatic or unconscious conditioning. I find it hard to believe that lower organisms like earthworms are using the mechanisms I postulate for cognitive kinds of things. And yet there are parts of our brain that are clearly functioning at a much lower level, so that I wouldn't be shocked to find *some* unconscious automatic conditioning. However, we have to use anecdotal evidence rather than the 10,000 studies in the literature to support it. But clearly I can't believe that we cut off the lower part of our brain.

REFERENCES

Lykken, D. T. Statistical significance in psychological research. *Psychological Bulletin,* 1968, 70, 151-59.

Meehl, P. E. Theory-testing in psychology and physics: A methodological paradox. *Philosophy of Science,* 1967, 34, 103-115.

4

THREE BATONS FOR
COGNITIVE PSYCHOLOGY

John Robert Ross
Massachusetts Institute of Technology

This chapter, written by a linguist, is primarily for cognitive psychologists. It describes three major research areas whose results, I hope, will suggest parallel avenues for psychologists to explore in their investigations of the full set of mental phenomena. The topics of Sections 1–3 are abstract syntax, islands, and non-discrete grammars, respectively.

ABSTRACT SYNTAX

1.1 Syntax, the study of the laws that govern the structure of sentences, which specifies which of the set of all possible sequences of words in a language actually can be used by speakers of the language to communicate, and which specifies how speakers group these words together into constituents—this branch of linguistics was, until the late 1940's, a relatively neglected area.

I think it is accurate to say that the enormous proliferation of syntactic studies in the past decade can ultimately be traced to the work of Zellig Harris, whose previously elaborated theoretical structures, consisting largely of hierarchical groups of such postulated elements as phonemes, morphemes, and constituents, underwent a radical change when Harris attacked the problem of discourse (cf. Harris, 1952, 1963).

The primary problems confronting one who wishes to study discourse are knotty questions like these: Why do some sequences of sentences form paragraphs, while other sequences do not? Why do some sequences of paragraphs form chapters, and others not? Why can only some sequences of chapters form books? And why can sentences and larger units only be formed into cohesive larger units when they occur in a certain order? What are the constraints on possible orders? What kind of formal account can be given of such concepts as "subordination of one idea to another in a given text"?

While attempting to provide answers to such questions, Harris came to the conclusion that the item and arrangement theories which had sufficed for the study of lower units in the speech chain—up to the level of the word, essentially — would have to be enriched by the addition of laws of a fundamentally different type: *syntactic transformations* (cf. Harris, 1957). This type of rule, which provides a formal reconstruction of the notions "related sentence," is typically exemplified by the Grandaddy of Them All, the rule of *Passive*.

(1)   a.   Gordon reviled the committee members.
       b.   The committee members were reviled by Gordon.

By postulating that both of the sentences in (1) are variants of one canonical syntactic form, Harris was able to achieve important results in studying the problem of cohesion in discourse. Put in simple terms, what Harris proposed is stated in (2).

(2)   Big sentences are syntactically made up of little sentences.

These "little sentences" Harris called "kernel sentences."

An example of the factoring of a big sentence into little ones (Harris calls this "kernelization") may prove instructive.

(3)   Having been believed by many fans to have been reviled by Gordon caused the committee members to reconsider their decision not to block his nomination by the Chief.

(4) K_1:   Something (K_2) caused something (K_5).
       K_2:   Many fans believed something (K_3).
       K_3:   Gordon reviled the members.
       K_4:   The members belong to a committee.
       K_5:   Something (K_6) happened again.
       K_6:   The members considered something (K_7)
       K_7:   The members decided on something (K_8).
       K_8:   The members would not block something (K_9).
       K_9:   The Chief will nominate Gordon.

These kernel sentences, in Harris's view, are actually existing sentences of English. The kernels of a language are of a finite length — they are usually quite short — and therefore their number, though large, is also finite.

Since English is infinite, however — that is, since we cannot give an upper bound on the length of an English sentence — these kernels must be combined with one another by processes which can be applied to their own outputs an unbounded number of times — *recursive*, or *iterable*, processes. Such processes would allow the finite number of kernels of any language to be projected into the infinity of its complex, or *surface*, sentences. Harris refers to these processes as *transformations*.

To take an example of a recursive process, let us consider the derivation of the noun *committee member*, which Harris might analyze as proceeding somewhat as in (5).

(5)   a.   Gordon reviled the members who belong to a committee.
      b.   Gordon reviled the members belonging to a committee.
      c.   (*) Gordon reviled the to-a-committee-belonging members.
      d.   (?*) Gordon reviled the committee-belonging members.
      e.   Gordon reviled the committee members.

The derivation would start from the combining of two of the kernels of (3), K_3 and K_4, into the main clause-subordinate clause structure of (5a) by what Harris calls a noun-sharing transformation — both of these kernels contain the noun *member*. Having been formed, the modified noun phrase (NP) of (5a) is then grist for the mills of a number of reduction transformations, the first of which participializes the relative clause [yielding (5b)], the second of which preposes the non-finite modifier [yielding an ungrammatical intermediate step, (5c)], the third of which compresses this modifier still further, yielding the still-awkward (5d), and the last of which gets rid of the predicate of the subordinated kernel, *belonging*.

That such processes must be able to apply to their own outputs, to chase their syntactic tails, as it were, can be seen from the fact that the derived noun *committee member* can itself appear as the first member of a compound like that in (6a), presumably to be derived from something like (6b),

(6)   a.   Committee member committee
      b.   Committee which is for committee members

where (6a) can itself start a compound, as in (7a) [from (7b)],

(7)   a.   Committee member committee member
      b.   Member who belongs to a committee member committee and onward and downward into the bureaucratic night.

It is clear that we need, in addition to the list of kernels given in (4), some means of indicating how they are to be combined, because often there are many combinations of the same set of kernels that will produce different grammatical surface sentences. For instance, if the two kernels underlying (5a) are combined in such a way that K_4 becomes the independent clause, and K_3 the dependent one, then sentence (8) would result.

(8)   The members who Gordon reviled belong to a committee.

I have indicated some of the subordinations which are necessary to convert the unordered set of kernels in (4) into (3) by the expository device of appending to each *something* which will become the site for the embedding of one of the other kernels a parenthesized appositive giving the number of the kernel to be embedded. The hierarchical tree structure of (9), in which triangles are abbreviations for the more detailed structures which could be provided for each individual kernel, is a graphically more perspicuous equivalent of this notation.

(9)

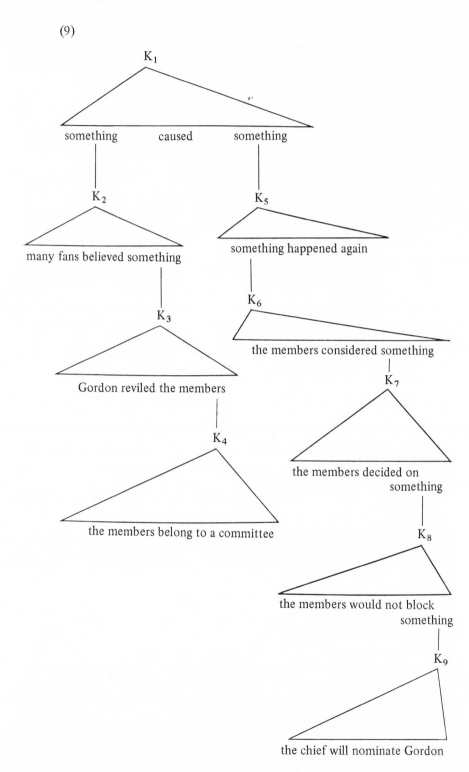

It is easy to adduce evidence for the syntactic correctness of the kernelization sketched in (4)/(9). One example is the fact that if an emphatic reflexive pronoun is inserted before *been reviled* in (3), the pronoun *themselves* produces a grammatical sentence, while the pronoun *himself* does not.

(10) a.   Having been believed by many fans to have $\begin{Bmatrix} \text{themselves} \\ \text{*himself} \end{Bmatrix}$ been

reviled by Gordon caused the committee members to reconsider their decision not to block his nomination by the Chief.

This is easily explicable on the basis of the fact that in the course of deriving (3) from (4), one transformation would passivize K_3, converting (1a) into (1b). And the possibilities for the occurrence of emphatic reflexives in (1b), which are shown in (11), exactly mirror those of (3), the sentence whose derivation (1b) is a part of.

(11) The committee members were $\begin{Bmatrix} \text{themselves} \\ \text{*himself} \end{Bmatrix}$ reviled by Gordon.

In other words, the kernelization of (3) is syntactically justified on the basis of the fact that simple syntactic laws ["emphatic reflexive pronouns follow the noun phrases (hereafter "NP's") they modify"] are statable only in terms of the "little sentences" [and their products — passives like (1b), middles like (12b), datives like (13b), flips like (14b), etc.] which are presupposed by the analysis.

(12) a.   Sophomores can easily translate sonatas.
      b.   Sonatas translate easily for sophomores.
(13) a.   I read 2/3 of my thesis to Harold.
      b.   I read Harold 2/3 of my thesis.
(14) a.   I was lucky that you forgot the password.
      b.   That you forgot the passward was lucky for me.

Let us take the case of the distribution of emphatic reflexives as a down-payment on a full presentation of the evidence which could be given in support of the correctness of (2) and pass on to a second, closely related, insight of Harris's: (15).

(15) Meanings of big sentences are semantically made up of meanings of little sentences.

In other words, kernelization, which is justified on syntactic grounds, provides a semantic, as well as a syntactic, decomposition. This is so obvious, even in the face of the tremendous difficulties posed by any attempt to arrive at a precise formal theory of meaning, as to require almost no comment. To give just one example, it is evident that in whatever kind of formal object one might choose to represent the meaning of (3), the entities designated by the NP *the committee members* must be characterized as bearing the semantic relation of *object* to the past participle *reviled*. But precisely this is also true of the kernelization in (4)/(9).

I will not review here the great strides that have been made in semantics in the past decade, all, I would argue, traceable to Harris's second pioneering insight, (15), but will instead pass on to a third profound insight, (16), which seems to me to be the clear source for the resurgence of interest in questions of universal grammar in recent years.

(16) The grammars for the kernels of any two languages are far more similar than are the grammars of their surfaces.

That is, carrying out transformational analyses of widely divergent languages will yield kernelizations of corresponding sentences[1] whose differences are confined, largely to differences in the order of the elements in the kernels.

Investigation of this hypothesis has also revealed that the transformations needed in any single language to convert a kernelization into a surface sentence of that language will show great similarities to the transformations necessary to produce surface sentences from corresponding kernelizations in other languages. In other words, it is not merely the case that kernelizations of corresponding sentences are highly similar – the same is true of the derivations by which these proceed to their (dissimilar) surface structures. The method of transformational decomposition has led to the discovery of many new and hitherto unperceived axes of similarity among the languages of the world, and has made possible a much more restrictive characterization than could have been attempted before of the notion "possible human language."

1.2 In the renaissance of syntactic and semantic studies that have grown out of Harris's three fundamental insights, a new conception of the nature of language which emerged from the work of Noam Chomsky, a student of Harris', has had an equally potent impact. Chomsky's idea was to regard a natural language as an infinite set of strings on a finite alphabet (of phones, phonemes, morphemes, or words) and to regard a grammar of a language as a rewriting system, a formal device of a general type that was in the process of exploration by mathematicians and logicians, which would generate, or produce, all and only the members of this set in a totally explicit and algorithmic way. Chomsky's theory was, therefore, a kind of synthesis between Harris's transformational analyses and metamathematics. The degree of rigor and precision with which arguments could be framed and concepts defined in Chomsky's theory of generative grammar led to the framing of and discovery of many answers to questions that had not even been clearly formulable

---

[1] By this term, I mean the following. Two synonymous sentences in different languages would be corresponding sentences only if they contained roughly equivalent lexical items. Thus (i) and (iii) would be corresponding sentences, but not (ii) and (iii).

    (i) Fritz is trying to find Michael.
    (ii) Fritz is looking for Michael.
    (iii) Fritz versucht, Michael zu finden.
        tries   to find

Much more could be said about this notion, but I think its intent should be clear enough for the present discussion.

in linguistic discussion prior to the advent of generative grammar. It is impossible, in an article with the limited scope of the present one, to indicate adequately the size of the great leaps in our understanding of linguistic organization – not only in syntax, but also in phonology, semantics, and linguistic change – which were a consequence of this synthesis.

1.3 Of central importance both in Harris's transformational analysis and in Chomsky's generative grammar is the distinction between surface structure, which corresponds more or less directly to articulatory events, and an abstract level of representation, which Harris called the kernelization of a sentence, and which Chomsky called its *deep structure,* which is related to such articulatory events in a complex way. To take one concrete example, in the surface structure of (3), the phonetic sequence [membr], *member,* occurs only once, while the NP corresponding to this sequence occurs in K_3, K_4, K_6, K_7, and K_8 in the deep structure of (3). Clearly, then, these phonetically non-manifested occurrences have to be removed in the passage from deep structure to surface structure, by one or more deletion transformations.

The abstractness of the deep structure of any sentence is measured by the number of transformations in the derivation that starts with that deep structure and ends with the sentence in question. One result of the last 5–10 years of syntactic investigation has been the discovery of evidence for increasingly abstract deep structures. That is, as more research was done on the syntactic organization of classes of sentences, the derivations that had previously been thought adequate for these sentences seemed to require lengthening. Some examples may help to make this point clear.

Consider a causative sentence like (17).

(17) Dr. Grusel is sharpening the spurs.

The deep structure which would, around 1965, the time of Chomsky's *Aspects of the Theory of Syntax,* have generally been assumed to underly (17) is shown in (18).

(18)

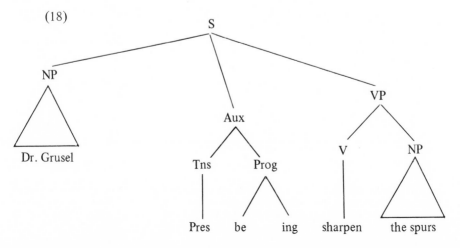

The derivation of (17) from (18) was extremely short — the only transformations were one of agreement, to inflect the tensed part of the sentence with a morpheme indicating the grammatical number of the subject, and one called *Affix Hopping,* which attached the participial suffix-*ing* to *sharpen,* and the present tense morpheme to the auxiliary *be.*

The first step away from surface structure was the reanalysis of causative verbs proposed by Lakoff (cf. Lakoff 1971) shortly after the completion of *Aspects.* Lakoff argued that verbs like *sharpen, harden, redden, break,* etc. had to be syntactically decomposed into (at least) a causative matrix verb and an embedded kernel which contained the non-causative core of the causative verb's meaning[2]. Thus (18) would be split into the two clauses of (19).

(19)

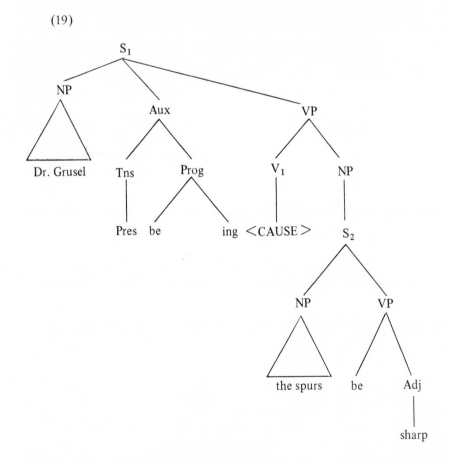

[2] Lakoff also argued that many causatives have to be factored into yet another clause, one whose main verb is an inchoative, with a meaning akin to "come about." That is, a more complete factorization of *sharpenX* would be CAUSE (COME ABOUT (SHARP X)). For our purposes, however, this refinement can be omitted.

The deep structure in (19) would be converted into the now intermediate structure of (18) by a rule Lakoff referred to as *Plugging-In,* which would adjoin the embedded predicate *sharp* to the left of the abstract predicate CAUSE in (19) obliterating all traces of the embedded clause S_2 (by pruning), and making the NP *the spurs* the derived object of the new compound predicate. This compound predicate would later, by morphophonemic rules, be realized as *sharpen.*[3]

One piece of evidence for the correctness of Lakoff's causative analysis concerns the behavior of the pro-form *it,* when it functions as a pro-sentence, as in (20b), which derives from (20a) by the operation of a rule of *S Pronominalization.*[4]

(20) a.

Bill $\left\{ \begin{array}{l} \text{believes} \\ \text{knows} \\ \text{realizes} \\ \text{admitted} \\ \text{etc.} \end{array} \right\}$ *that treason is pleasin',* but

no one else $\left\{ \begin{array}{l} \text{believes} \\ \text{knows} \\ \text{realizes} \\ \text{admitted} \\ \text{etc.} \end{array} \right\}$ *that treason is pleasin'.* $\quad$ *S Pronominalization* $\Longrightarrow$

b. Bill $\left\{ \begin{array}{l} \text{believes} \\ \text{knows} \\ \text{realizes} \\ \text{admitted} \\ \text{etc.} \end{array} \right\}$ that treason is pleasin', but

no one else $\left\{ \begin{array}{l} \text{believes} \\ \text{knows} \\ \text{realizes} \\ \text{admitted} \\ \text{etc.} \end{array} \right\}$ it.

This rule operates to replace the complement objects (or subjects) of certain predicates by *it, when these complements are identical to a sentence elsewhere in*

---

[3] In McCawley (1968), an improved formulation of the rule of *Plugging-In* is given. This rule, rechristened *Predicate Raising,* in also discussed at some length in Postal (1970a).

[4] For a formulation of this rule, cf. Ross (1972b).

the text. Thus, since the italicized object complements in (20a) are identical, this rule can convert the second one to *it.*

Now let us examine how this rule applies to such sentences as (17). Consider (21).

> (21)   Dr. Grusel is sharpening the spurs, but it may take him hours to bring it about.

What is the antecedent of the *it* in (21)? Evidently, it must be some clause like (22),

> (22)   The spurs are sharp.

not the whole of (17). But if this *it* is to result from an application of the rule of *S Pronominalization*, the structure underlying (17) must contain a clausal structure like (22). Since such a clause is not available if (18) is the deepest structure underlying (17), but is if the more abstract (19) is assumed, the *it* of (21) provides support for Lakoff's causative analysis.[5]

(23)

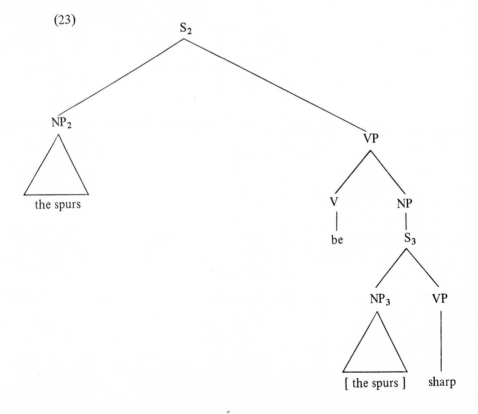

[5] This analysis is not uncontroversial. Cf. Chomsky (1972) and Fodor (1970) for some critical comments, and Lakoff and Ross (1972) and McCawley (1973) for some replies.

The next increase in abstractness was proposed in Ross (1969a). I argued that in deep structures, all adjectives should be analyzed as being the nominal complement objects of a main verb *be,* as suggested in the diagram in (23).

Since the *be* in (23) is an equi-subject verb[6], the rule of *Equi*[7] will obligatorily delete NP_3, under identity with NP_2, and other trivial rules will convert the resulting structure into the structure underlying (22).

Two of the reasons cited in Ross (op. cit.) for assuming that adjectival sentences like S_2 in (19) must be given the more abstract analyses of (23) are the following. First, *S Pronominalization,* and closely related rule, *So Pronominalization,* which also replaces a complement in non-subject position by a pro-form, *so,* under conditions of identity,[8] both treat adjectives as if they were derived from clauses, as can be seen from the conversion of (24a) to (24b).

(24) a.   Parents want one to be *polite,* but being *polite* is often very difficult.

b.   Parents want one to be polite, but being $\left\{ \begin{smallmatrix} so \\ ??it \end{smallmatrix} \right\}$ is often very difficult.

It is still a mystery as to why these processes of proadjectivization are so limited in English. In German and French, for instance, such sentences as those in (25), which have been produced by the operation of *S Pronominalization,*

---

[6] Cf. Perlmutter (1971) for discussion of this term.

[7] This rule is discussed in great detail in Postal (1970b).

[8] This latter rule would thus convert any of the sentences in (i) below the corresponding shortened sentence in (ii).

(i) It is possible *that meat prices will plummet.*

$$\text{but} \left\{ \begin{array}{l} \text{it doesn't seem} \\[1em] \text{they don't} \left\{ \begin{array}{l} \text{think} \\ \text{believe} \\ \text{say} \\ \text{etc.} \end{array} \right. \end{array} \right\} \text{ that meat prices will plummet.}$$

$$\Downarrow \quad \textit{So Pronominalization}$$

(ii) It is possible that meat prices will plummet,

$$\text{but} \left\{ \begin{array}{l} \text{it doesn't seem} \\[1em] \text{they don't} \left\{ \begin{array}{l} \text{think} \\ \text{believe} \\ \text{say} \\ \text{etc.} \end{array} \right. \end{array} \right\} \text{ so.}$$

The operation of this rule is mysterious in various ways (After what predicates can it operate? Why can this *so* not appear in subject position? What relation does this *so* bear to the various other more adverbial *so's* which English abounds with? And so on.), but these need not concern us here.

(25) a.   Hans ist fleissig, aber ich bin *es* nicht.
           Hans is diligent but I   am it not.
           'Hans is diligent, but I'm   not.'

   b.   Jean est paresseux et elles   *le* sont aussi.
           John is lazy   and they (fem) it are also.
           'John is lazy,   and they   are too.'

are flawless, but the corresponding sentences in English, whether involving *S Pronominalization or So Pronominalization,* are hopeless. Cf. (26).

(26) a.   *Hans is diligent, but I'm not $\left\{ \begin{array}{c} \text{it} \\ \text{so} \end{array} \right\}$.

   b.   *Jean is lazy, and I'm $\left\{ \begin{array}{c} \text{it} \\ \text{so} \end{array} \right\}$ too.

Apparently, these pro-forms can never appear after finite forms of *be,* and not even after all non-finite forms, either. Cf. (27).

(27) a.   He's not tall now, but he must have been $\left\{ \begin{array}{c} \text{so} \\ \text{*it} \end{array} \right\}$ earlier.

   b.   I'm not rich, but I will be $\left\{ \begin{array}{c} \text{?*so} \\ \text{**it} \end{array} \right\}$ some day.

Also unexplained is the fact that *it* is so much worse than *so* as a pro-adjective.

Nonetheless, whatever the answers to these questions may turn out to be, the fact that such sentences as (24) exist lends support to the abstract analysis of (23), because only under such an analysis could a maximally general formulation of the two pronominalization rules discussed above be retained.

A second argument for postulating the abstract structure in (23) as the source of adjectival clauses can be derived from the syntactic behavior of appositive clauses. As can be seen from (28), these can be adjoined to NP's,

(28) a.   [The fourth plant]$_{NP}$, which was carnivorous, swayed seductive-
           ly.
   b.   [That martial law will be declared]$_{NP}$, which is a distinct
           possibility, is very disquieting

and as (29) suggests, they cannot be adjoined to such obviously non-nominal constituents as verbs, prepositions, and *not.*[9]

---

[9] The 'ϕ' symbols in (29) are to indicate where the words *resemble, from,* and *not* would have stood in the sources of the appositive clauses in which these symbols appear.

(29) a.   *Tom may resemble, which I ϕ Janet, your geometry teacher.
      b.   *BMW's are from, which Datsuns are ϕ Japan, the Federal
            Republic of Germany.
      c.   *Not, which I did ϕ read your letter, many people like fleas.

Now note that one can find appositive clauses modifying adjective phrases. Cf.
(30).

(30) a.   Marcel is [fond of eating], which Sally is not.
      b.   These facts are [inconsistent with my theory], which I wish they
            weren't.

It should be emphasized that appositives can only modify whole adjective phrases,
not their adjectival heads by themselves. Cf. *(31).

(31) a.   *Marcel is fond, which Sally is ϕ of drinking, of eating.
      b.   *These facts are inconsistent, which I wish they were ϕ with
            your theory, with *my* theory.

Thus I conclude from such sentences as those in (30) that it is necessary that
adjective phrases be dominated in deep structure by an NP for the appositive clause
to modify, as is the case in the abstract analyses shown in (23).

Thus far, I have given two sets of arguments which suggest that (18) should be
replaced by a structure which is more abstract in that it would contain two clauses
which are subordinate to the main verb *sharpen,* or rather to the causative abstract
verb which is contained in *sharpen.* Speaking pictorially, we could say that (32),
which gives the approximate replacement for (18), has been made more abstract
"below" *sharpen.*[10]

(32) [See page 76.]

In the four sets of arguments to follow, I will attempt to demonstrate that (18)
must also be made more abstract "above" *sharpen.*

To this end, consider the behavior of the verb *do* in (33).

(33) Dr. Grusel is sharpening the spurs, and he is panting heavily while he is
      doing $\begin{Bmatrix} \text{it} \\ \text{so} \end{Bmatrix}$.

The fact that *do* can be followed by both the pro-form *it* and the pro-form *so*
suggests that it might be a verb with a complement object, which object had been
pronominalized either by the rule of *S Pronominalization* or by the rule of *So*

---

[10] The reason for the particular choice of subscripts in (32) will become clear by the end of
Section 1.

pronominalization If so, *do* would be like such verbs as *believe, guess, expect, say, imagine,* etc., which also allow either pro-form to replace their objects.

But if these pro-forms in (33) have been produced by a pronominalization transformation, what was the structure of the *while*-clause of (33) before the

(32)

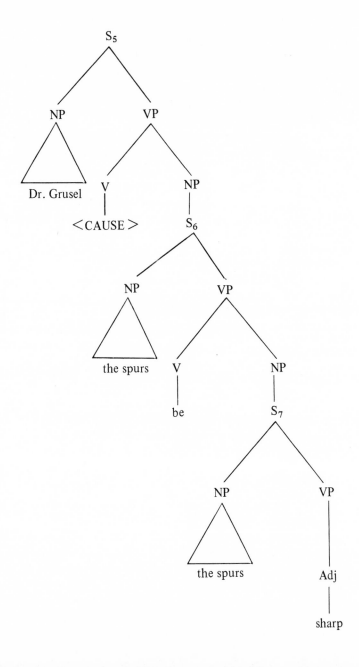

pronominalization took place? Evidently, it must have contained something like the structure shown in (34).

(34)

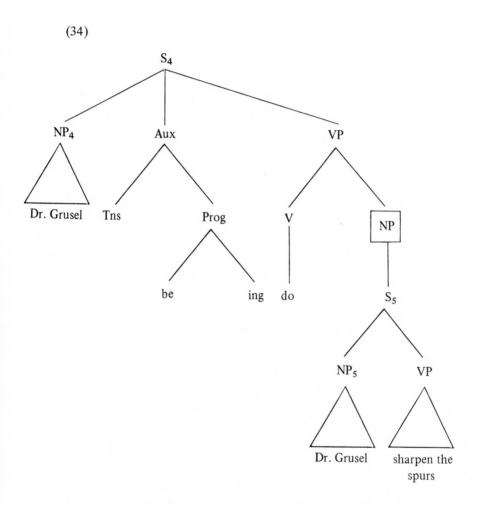

If S_5 in (34) is replaced by *it* or *so,* under identity with a preceding clause, structures like the *while*-clause of (33) will emerge. But what will happen to (34) if no pronominalization can take place?

Obviously, if *do* is a verb which can appear in deep structure with a complement, it will be necessary to specify that it, like the *be* of (23), is an equi-subject verb. Thus *Equi* will always apply to delete the NP in the position of

NP$_5$ under identity with the one in the position of NP$_4$. The structure that would result would, depending on what complementizer had been chosen, be one of the strings in (35).

(35) a.   *Dr. Grusel is doing [sharpening the spurs]$_{NP}$

      b.   *Dr. Grusel is doing [(to) sharpen the spurs]$_{NP}$

While none of these are grammatical, there are independent indications that some such structure is necessary. First of all, the boxed NP of (34) could be the NP to which the appositive clause of (36) has been adjoined.

(36) Dr. Grusel is sharpening the spurs, which he shouldn't be doing.

Secondly, there is a process in English called *Topicalization* which has the effect of moving to the front of a sentence an NP which is being focused on. Thus "regular" NP's, *that*-clauses, and adjective phrases, which I have argued above are all dominated by NP, can all be topicalized, as in the conversion of the sentences in (37) to the corresponding ones in (38).

(37) a.   I've never liked chawing on [*Benson and Hedges*]$_{NP}$.

      b.   We never realized [that Riley was a Rigellian anthroflant in disguise]$_{NP}$.

      c.   Proust was never considered to be [outgoing]$_{NP}$.

(38) a.   [*Benson and Hedges*]$_{NP}$ I've never liked chawing on.

      b.   [That Riley was a Rigellian anthroflant in disguise]$_{NP}$ we never realized.

      c.   [Outgoing]$_{NP}$ Proust was never considered to be.

As we would expect, the nominal object complement of *do* can also, in some dialects, be topicalized, producing such sentences as those in (39).

(39) a.   [Sharpening those spurs]$_{NP}$ I just will not do!

      b.   [Writing thank-you notes]$_{NP}$ most children don't like doing.

One final piece of evidence for the postulation of such structures as (34) is provided by passive sentences like (40a), which would be derived from such ill-formed strings as (40b), which is ungrammatical in the same way as the sentences in (35) are.

(40) a.   Sharpening the spurs should not be done by someone as easily excitable as Dr. Grusel.

     b.   *Someone as easily excitable as Dr. Grusel should not do [sharpening the spurs]$_{NP}$.

Thus we see that there are a number of reasons for postulating that *sharpening the spurs* in (17) derives from the complex verbal structure shown in (34). But how are the structures in (35) converted into the well-formed (17)?

In Ross (1972a), where the above arguments for the existence of a higher *do* are developed more fully, it is suggested that the rule which effects the deletion of this *do* is to be identified with *Predicate Raising*. Whether or not this independently motivated rule can be made use of in converting (35) to (17), the point which is of relevance for the present context is that the syntactic behavior of the verb *do* also requires a more abstract representation of (17) than (18).

The next verb above *do* is *happen*. This is argued for by such pseudo-cleft sentences as (41).

(41)   What is happening is [that Dr. Grusel is sharpening the spurs]$_{.NP}$

The general regularity to be noted about psuedo-cleft sentences is that the clefted constituent, i.e., that constituent which follows the verb *be*, is an NP which would yield a sentence if it were put into the *wh*-clause that is the subject of the pseudo-cleft sentence in the same place that the *wh*-word occupied in deep structure. That is, if we represent the structure of pseudo-cleft sentences by the formula shown in (42),

(42) $\begin{bmatrix} wh \\ pro\text{-}Y \end{bmatrix}$ X ϕ Z be Y

then it must be the case that Y is an NP, and that XYZ would form a sentence.[11]

---

[11] There is a fascinating and little-studied class of counterexamples to this latter claim — so-called amnesties, like the sentences in (i) and (ii) [note the ungrammaticality of the XYZ counterparts in (iii) and (iv)].

(i)   What I want is that he be tickled mercilessly.

(ii)   What he achieved was doubling the voter participation in 3 years.

(iii) * I want that he be tickled mercilessly.

(iv) *He achieved doubling the voter participation in 3 years.

These cases, in which a complementizer selection that would star a string in isolation can be "amnestied" under clefting, do not detract from the importance of the generalization that XYZ in (42) normally constitute a well-formed clause.

That Y can be any of the types of NP that we have investigated thus far —
namely, "regular" NP's, *that*-clauses, adjective phrases, and activity VP's — can be
seen by inspection of the examples in (43), and of their respective XYZ forms in
(44).

(43) a.   What he is peering into is [a cored onion]$_{NP}$.

   b.   What he forgot is [that his creepy-peepy was on when he went to
        the sandbox]$_{NP}$.

   c.   What Mr. Milquetoast never was was [arrogant]$_{NP}$.

   d.   What you should be doing is [shoeing your horse]$_{NP}$.

(44) a.   He is peering into a cored onion.

   b.   He forgot that his creepy-peepy was on when he went to the
        sandbox.

   c.   Mr. Milquetoast never was arrogant.

   d.   *You should be doing shoeing your horse.[12]

Now let us return to the pseudo-cleft sentence in (41). By what I have said
above, its XYZ form, (45), should be grammatical.

(45) *That Dr. Grusel is sharpening the spurs is happening.

Since it is not, we must conclude either that the XYZ generalization above must be
abandoned, or that some process applies to get rid of the *that* and *is happening* in
(45), converting it into (17).

It seems to me that in this case, the latter conclusion is the correct one, because
there is an additional class of sentences that confirms the necessity of postulating a
higher *happen* above all verbs that denote events. These are what I have called[13]
"equative" sentences — such sentences as those in (46).

---

[12]As discussed above, this structure would obligatorialy be converted into (i) by either the
rule of *Predicate Raising* or some equivalent process.
   (i) You should be shoeing your horse.
[13]Cf. Ross (1969a) and Ross (1972b).

(46) He tossed   something interesting   to them:
      X NP_1 Y
     he tossed   a New Hampshire pineapple   to them .
      X NP_2 Y

As suggested by the symbols under the words of (46), such equative sentences may have the form shown in (47).

(47) $X\ NP_1\ Y$: $X\ NP_2\ Y$

Where NP_2 must be "more specific" (whatever formal sense can be given to this intuitively obvious characterization) than NP_1.

In any equative sentence of the form of (47), an optional rule of *Equative Deletion* can delete those parts of the post-colon clause which are identical to parts of the pre-colon clause, namely X and Y. That is, this rule can convert sentences of the form (47) to those of the form shown in (48).

(48) $X\ NP_1\ Y$: NP_2

For example, applying this rule to (46) would cause *he tossed* (= X) and *to them* (= Y) to be deleted, producing (49) as an output.

(49) He tossed something interesting to them: a New Hampshire pineapple.

When we examine the other types of NP_2 that can follow the colon in sentences of the form of (48), we again find the same class of constituents that we have encountered before. Cf. (50).

(50) a.   He said something interesting to us: [that mangoes were tart]$_{NP}$.

      b.   He turned out to be something quite unexpected: [so generous to his subordinates that they loved him]$_{NP}$.

      c.   We may do something quite dangerous: [fry eggs on the Autobahn]$_{NP}$.

Turning our attention now to *happen*-sentences, consider (51).

(51) Something creepy is happening: [(?*that) Dr. Grusel is sharpening the spurs].

I am at present unable to account for the badness of (51) if *that* appears, but there are structures in which the colon is followed by such adverbs as *namely* or *for example,* which I take to have an analysis that is identical in all important respects to that of the equative sentences considered so far,[14] and these structures can manifest a *that*-clause after the colon. Cf. (52).

(52) Something creepy is happening: namely, (that) Dr. Grusel is sharpening the spurs.

The feature of this sentence that makes it of interest in the present context is the fact that *that* can appear in the second clause. Note that this is by no means always true in all two-clause sentences whose clauses are separated by a colon, as (53) shows.

(53) a.   Prices shot up: (*that) the depression began.

b.   Plants must be watered: (*that) they can't survive on love alone.

Nor is it the case that all sentences of the form (48) can have a *that* inserted after the colon, as (49′) and (50′) show.

(49′) *He tossed something interesting to them: that a New Hampshire pineapple.

---

[14] Note, for instance, the fact that all of the sentences of the form (48) — namely, those in (49) and (50) — can have a *namely* inserted immediately to the right of the colon. The same is true, by and large, for adverbs like *for example,* except that with this adverb, some mysterious (semantic?) conditions must be met. Thus observed the contrasts in (i)

(i) I $\left\{ \left\{ \begin{array}{l} \left\{ \begin{array}{l} \text{might} \\ \text{could} \\ \text{should} \\ \text{?*would} \end{array} \right\} \text{have found} \\ \text{*(have) found} \\ \text{* didn't find anything interesting} \\ \text{(have) found some interesting things} \end{array} \right\} \text{something interesting} \right\}$:

for example, a pre-Cambrian walnut.

All sentences of the full form (49) which include either *namely* or *for example* [cf. (ii)],

(ii) ?? He might find something interesting:

$\left\{ \begin{array}{l} \text{namely} \\ \text{for example} \end{array} \right\}$, he might find some used water.

have, to my ear, a distinctly low-faluting ring.

(54)

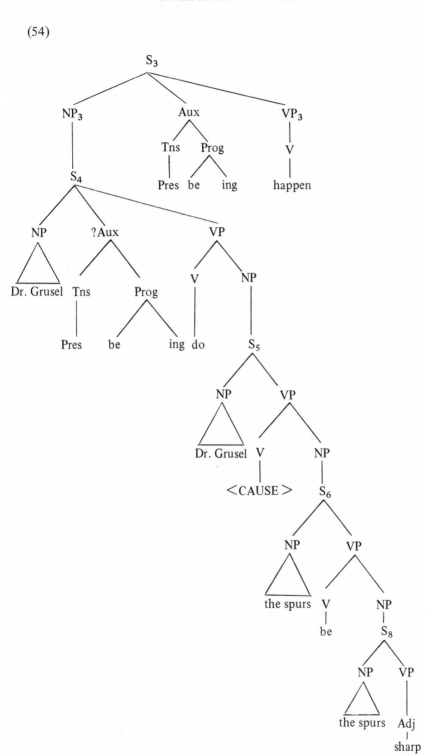

(50') a.   *He said something interesting to us: that that mangoes were tart.

b.   *He turned out to be something quite unexpected: that so generous to his subordinates that they loved him.

c.   *We may do something quite dangerous: that fry eggs on the Autobahn.

The generalization that governs sentences of the form of (48) which contain the complementizer *that* is quite simple: NP_2 in (48) can only start with this complementizer if it is the complement of some predicate in X or Y which takes *that*-clauses.[15] Thus NP_2 in (50a) can start with *that* because this NP is the complement of the verb *said,* which takes this type of complement.

The force of this generalization is quite clear: In order to account for the *that* in (52), we must assume that the predicate in Y of (52), namely *is happening,* can take *that*-clauses, i.e., that such structures as (45) are underlyingly well-formed, as was suggested by the grammaticality of the pseudo-cleft sentence in (41). But if it is underlyingly well-formed, some process must exist which converts it into a well-formed surface structure. I will assume, for the present, that this is a simple rule of deletion, which gets rid of *that* and *is happening,* converting (54), the structure which incorporates all of the abstractness arguments that I have presented to date, into (eventually) (17).

It may turn out that no special deletion rule is necessary — that the rule of *Predicate Raising* can be stated in such a way as to effect the merger of *happen* and *do.* Alternatively, it may turn out that there is no deletion rule at all, but that there is instead a global filter[16] which stars any surface structure in which the node that corresponds to the deep subject to *happen,* NP_3 in (54), for instance, is still a highly sentential[17] complement. If this suggestion proves superior to the postulation of a deletion rule,[18] then, while it would still be correct to claim that such structures as (54) are underlying well-formed, it would not be necessary to postulate the existence of a higher *happen* above every event predicate. Given our present limited understanding of the extremely complex syntax of *happen,* we may continue to regard this as an open question, perhaps, despite the extreme difficulties that the examples discussed in footnote 18 above pose for any deletion analysis.

---

[15] As with pseudo-cleft sentences, this claim must be stated with somewhat greater care, to make allowances for amnesty cases like (i), for those dialects that accept such strings.

(i) ? I want something quite simple: that he be tickled mercilessly.

The general point at issue is unaffected by such sentences, however.

[16] The necessity of expanding linguistic theory to include global, or non-local, processes was first argued for in Lakoff (1970b). For further refinements, cf. Postal (1972).

[17] The need for referring to various types of complements as being ordered with respect to a quantifiable predicate of sententiality (or non-nouniness) is argued for in Ross (in press). Cf. also Section 3 below.

[18] One reason for thinking that a deletion rule may prove to be unfeasible is the possibility of its environment being destroyed by some number of applications of the rule of *Raising* which could have the effect of moving NP_3 and VP_3 in (54) indefinitely far apart, producing

(This footnote continued on page 85.)

I now move to a brief scrutiny of the status of the auxiliary. In Ross (1969b), I presented a number of arguments that suggest that the node *Aux* is not a necessary member of the set of non-terminal phrase nodes admitted in the theory of universal grammar, and that what had previously been classified as auxiliaries should instead be regarded as being main verbs which were defective in a variety of ways (e.g., in that they could not all appear in non-finite contexts, or did not exhibit the full range of verbal inflections). In Ross (1972a), I presented another argument which reinforced this conclusion, especially with respect to the status of the progressive auxiliary *be*.

The evidence in this latter argument turns on the fact that in some cases, a doubl-ing sequence — i.e., one of the form $X + V_1ing + V_2ing + Y$ — is ungrammatical. In (55), some ungrammatical doubl-ing sequences are shown, and in (56), some grammatical ones.

(55) a.   Fritz $\left\{ \begin{array}{l} \text{keeps} \\ \text{*is } keeping \end{array} \right\}$ *looking* at you.

b.   When $\left\{ \begin{array}{l} \text{will you stop} \\ \text{?* are you } stopping \end{array} \right\}$ *seeing* him?

c.   We $\left\{ \begin{array}{l} \text{continued} \\ \text{??are } continuing \end{array} \right\}$ *having* problems with the equine lead.

(56) a.   I can't imagine people who are *sleeping biting* me.
 b.   Your *having quitting* classes to justify is a problem.
 c.   I tried *drinking, running* five miles, and then studying. but nothing cheered me up.

The hypothesis that I advanced for the cause of the ungrammaticalities of (55), in the face of the grammatical sentences of (56) is that *doubl-ing sequences only*

---

such sentences as (i), which are ungrammatical, but which cannot be deleted into grammaticality.

(i) [That Dr. Grusel is sharpening the spur] $_{NP_3}$
      is expected   [to be happening] $_{VP_3}$
      seems
      etc.

These could not be avoided by making the *Happen-Deletion* rule cyclic or pre-cyclic, for the *happen* must remain present until the rule of *Equative Deletion*. This latter rule could not itself be made precyclical, because of the necessity of applying it to cyclically produced sentences, such as passives, so that the passive *by* can appear after the colon in such sentences as (ii).

(ii) The crown was fondled by someone avaricious: by Greta Mingle.

And if *Equative Deletion* is cyclical, a cyclical rule deleting *happen* would apply to the right-hand clause of (52) a cycle before the former rule could apply to save the complementizer *that*.

cause violation when V_2 *is the main verb of the complement of* V_1. [19] If this hypothesis is correct, and I know of no counterexamples to it, then the fact that (57b) is ungrammatical

> (57) a.   That he is goofing off is reprehensible.
>
>   b.   *His *being goofing* off is reprehensible.

implies that the doubl-ing sequence contained in this sentence must be an instance of a verb and its complement both appearing as present participles. That is, *be* must be a main verb. And if it is a main verb here, then it is also one in the source of (17), which would then have to be derived from (58). [20]

> (58) [See page 87.]

The final layer of abstraction that I will argue for in this paper is the performative verb, which I proposed should be at the top of all syntactic deep structures (cf. Ross, 1970). Basically, performative verbs are activity verbs which, when occurring in a first-person non-progressive, non-negative, present tense sentence, can be taken as constituting an instance of the type of speech act that they denote.

For example, the sentences in (59), when uttered in the appropriate circumstances [that is (59a) by a judge to a convicted criminal, (59b) by someone who has the floor in a meeting in which there are no other motions being discussed, (59c) by someone authorized to confer knighthood, etc.] ,

---

[19] In Milsark (1972), a refinement of this condition is suggested, one with which I am basically in agreement, but one which is irrelevant to the conclusions reached here with respect to the main verb status of the progressive *be*.

[20] Note that in (58), I have analyzed the progressive *be* as an intrasitive verb with a subject complement, rather than as a transitive verb with an object complement. The reasons for this decision are gone into some detail in the final section of Ross (1972a), and I will not repeat them here. Actually, I am not sure as to whether it is sufficient to postulate only one occurrence of the progressive *be* in the source of (17). Note that in (41), we find both *happen* and the verb of its complement in the progressive tense. This is not accidental — there is a kind of tense and auxiliary agreement, which has not been studied in the literature, as far as I know, between the matrix and the complement verbs in such constructions. Thus compare (41) with the less than perfect sentences in (i) − (v).

(i) ??What is happening is that Dr. Grusel has sharpened the spurs.

(ii) ??What has happened is that Dr. Grusel is sharpening the spurs.

(iii)?*What will happen is that Dr. Grusel is sharpening the spurs.

(iv) *What happens is that Dr. Grusel is sharpening the spurs.

(v)   What $\left\{ \begin{array}{l} \text{** happened} \\ \text{** was happening} \\ \text{?* must have happened} \\ \text{** had been happening} \\ \text{must have been happening} \end{array} \right\}$ is that Dr. Grusel sharpening the spurs.

(This footnote continued on page 88.)

(58)

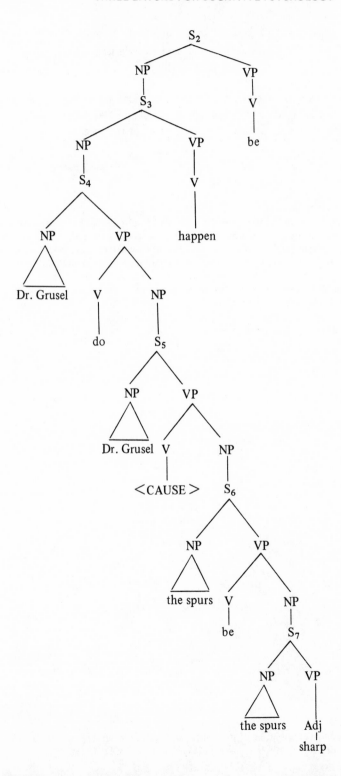

(59) a.   I sentence you to swim in the Rhine.
     b.   I move that we treble our salaries.
     c.   I dub thee Sir Godzilla.

can be taken as a sentencing, a motion, and a knighting, respectively; while the sentences in (60), which contain non-performative verbs, can only be taken as description of habitual activities on the part of the speaker.

Footnote 20 continued –

The facts seem to be quite complex here, and I have not been able to come to a decision as to whether this type of (approximate) agreement could be handled by some form of copying transformation, which I feel to be unlikely, or whether some complex semantic condition involving a matching between two compound auxiliary structures, both of which appear in underlying structure, must be imposed. If the latter is true, as I suspect, then (17) would have not merely one *be* in its source, but two, arrayed in the kind of configuration shown in (vi), which would replace (58).

(vi)

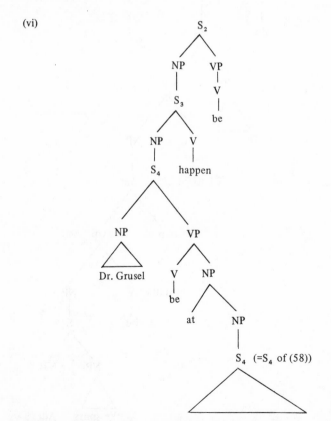

Pending the resolution of the complicated issues surrounding (i) – (v), I have temporized by postulating the slightly less abstract (58) as the source of (17).

(60)　a.　　I insult you.
　　　　b.　　I tickle you because you're such a gloom-pot.
　　　　c.　　I visit the Ozarks.

The claim of Ross (1970) is that every declarative sentence, (17), in particular, comes from a structure containing as its highest predicate a performative verb of saying such as *say, tell, state, declare, assert,* etc. Thus (17) would be derived from (61).[21]

(61)　[See page 90]

Though the performative analysis is not uncontroversial (cf. Anderson, 1970, and Fraser, 1970, for critiques of Ross, 1970), I believe that most of the criticisms of it can be met, and that the weight of the available evidence favors its adoption. Two arguments for it will be reviewed below.

Consider first the behavior of emphatic reflexives in constructions of the schematic form shown in (62).

(62)　Det Adj + *er* N *than* Pro + *self*

One example is the sentence shown in (63).[22]

(63)　Marvin$_i$ thought that your aunt might need a wiser man than himself$_i$ to solve her problem.

The question at issue is this: What are the syntactic conditions which must be met on the NP which is the antecedent of the pronoun in the *than*-phrase in (62)?

First, note that it is a necessary condition for well-formedness that the antecedent NP be in the same sentence as the reflexive pronoun. Such sequences of sentences as those in *(64), in my speech and that of all those I have checked, are ungrammatical: The anaphoric linkage involved in (62)-type constructions cannot extend across sentence boundaries.

(64)*　Marvin$_i$ is brilliant. Your aunt may, however, need a wiser man than himself$_i$ to solve her problems.

---

[21] Note that I have not provided, in this structure, a place for representing the fact that (17) is in the present tense. I will not recapitulate the arguments here, but I would follow McCawley (1971) in hypothesizing that tense morphemes are reflexes of a higher time abverb. The present tense is essentially a copy of *now,* and the past tense is a copy of *then.* This analysis would, of course, entail an even more abstract source for (17).

[22] Identical subscripts on two or more NP's indicate presupposed identity of reference, as discussed in Postal (1970b).

(61)

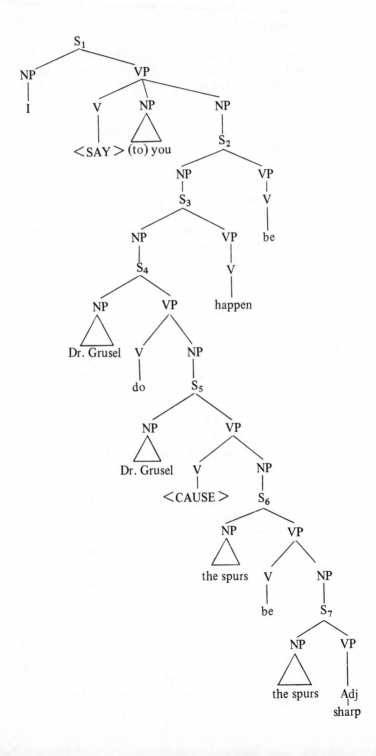

Second, note that while the reflexive pronoun can precede the NP to which it refers, as in (65a), that NP must command the pronoun.[23] In (65b), in which this command condition is not met, no linkage is possible.

(65) a.   That your aunt might need a wiser man than himself$_i$ to solve her problems was distressing to Marvin$_i$,

b.   *That your aunt might need a wiser man than himself$_i$ to solve her problems was distressing to the nurse who was looking after Marvin$_i$.

In (66a) and (66b), I have drawn skeletal diagrams of the sentences in (65a) and (65b), respectively, in order to make the command relationships clearer.

(66) a and b. [See page 92.]

In (66a), since the first S node above *Marvin* is S_1, the top of the tree, *Marvin* commands all the nodes of the tree. But in (66b), the first S node above *Marvin* is S_3, so *Marvin* commands only the elements of that clause.

The situation is exactly similar with respect to the contrast between (63) and *(67).

(67)* The nurse [$_S$who is looking after Marvin$_i$]$_S$ thinks that your aunt might need a wiser man than himself$_i$ to solve her problems.

Again, since *Marvin* is the subject of the main clause in (63), it commands all other nodes in the tree underlying this sentence, in particular *himself*. In *(67), on the other hand, *Marvin* commands only the elements of the bracketed relative clause, so no anaphoric link is possible between *Marvin* and *himself.*

Assuming, thus, that it is only possible to have constructions of the form of (62) when the reflexive form is commanded by the NP which it refers to,[24] what are we to conclude from the grammaticality of (68)?

[23] The important notion of command derives from Langacker (1969). Basically, one node commands a second if the first is a clause-mate of the second or is an element of a clause that dominates the second element. Put in other words, if A commands B in a tree T, then the first S node above A in T will dominate B. For instance, in (i), A and B command each other, and C commands each of them, but is commanded by neither.
(i)

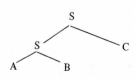

[24] See page 93.

(66) a.

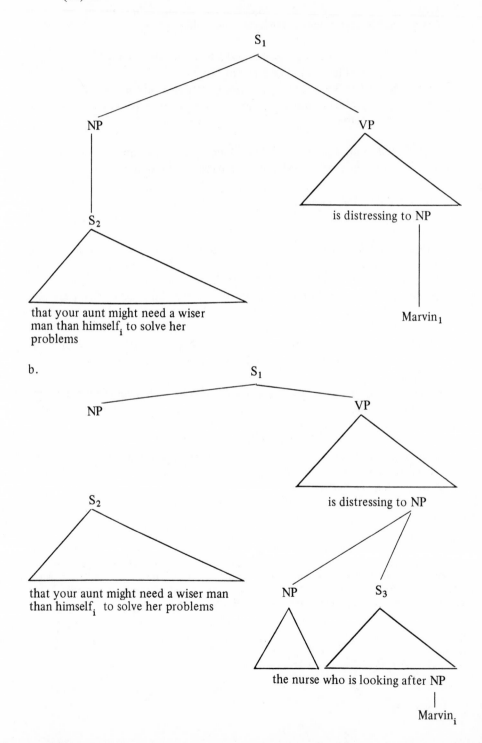

(68)   Your aunt may need a wiser man than myself to solve her problems.

The answer is obvious: (68) must derive from some structure which contains another occurrence of *I*, so that the command law which governs (62)-type constructions is satisfied. Since the performative analysis asserts that all declaratives are embedded as the objects of a higher performative clause of saying, as in (61), the first-person subject of this clause could be the antecedent of the *myself* in (68). Thus this *myself* provides partial support for the performative analysis.

I say "partial" here, because the command condition on (62)-type constructions does not provide any information about how high up in the tree the reflexive antecedent can be — it cannot require it to be a member of the immediately superordinate clause, for we find such grammatical sentences as (69), in which the antecedent is several clauses up.

(69)   Marvin$_i$ thinks [$_S$that many people feel [$_S$that we are of the opinion [$_S$that you should deny the claim [$_S$that your aunt might need a wiser man than himself$_i$ to solve her problems $_S$]$_S$]$_S$]$_S$].

Nor does this command condition specify that the antecedent NP must be a higher subject — if it did, it would incorrectly rule out (70).

(70)   We told Marvin$_i$ that your aunt might need a wiser man than himself$_i$ to solve her problems.

Thus while the *myself* in (68) would be compatible with the source provided by the performative analysis, it does not *require* precisely this source, since the command condition would also be met by any of the following schematically shown sources;

(71)   See page number 94.

(72)   See page number 95.

and indefinitely many others.

---

[24] Note that it is of no consequences how this reflexive pronoun is generated — whether it appears in deep structure in its surface structure form, whether it is derived by a rule of pronominalization from a fully specified NP (like *Marvin*, in the examples discussed above), or whether, a seems most likely to me (though I emphasize that I have no evidence for this opinion), it is derived from a reduction rule that deletes a coreferential pronoun which is followed by an intensifying reflexive, as in the derivations suggested in (i).

(i) $\begin{Bmatrix} \text{he} \\ \text{him} \end{Bmatrix}$ himself $\Rightarrow$ himself

$\begin{Bmatrix} \text{she} \\ \text{her} \end{Bmatrix}$ herself $\Rightarrow$ herself   etc.

(71)

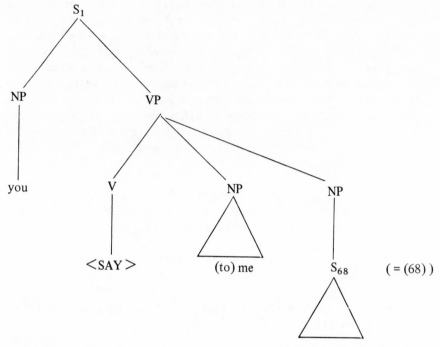

In short, the command condition is a first step along the way, in that it indicates that *something* must be "up there," but it is not specific enough in its requirements to tell us that only the topmost clause of (61) could be the missing something.

The next argument to which we will turn will provide much more detailed information about this "something."

Consider such sentences as (73), in which the verb *believe* occurs with an unstressed direct object, where the combination of verb plus object is used to refer to a clause elsewhere in the discourse.

(73)   Sheila$_i$ said to Jeff$_j$ that termites made great pets, but he$_j$ didn't believe her$_i$.

Here, the clause referred to is *that termites made great pets.* What is of interest is a precise characterization of the conditions under which this particular type of anaphoric linkage is possible.[25]

Notice first that the class of verb that the clausal antecedent functions as the complement of is crucial — cf. (74).

---

[25] Let us exclude from consideration such cases as (i), in which the pronoun following *believe* is anaphoric, but not the verb-object combination as a whole.

(Footnote 25 continued on page 95.)

(72)

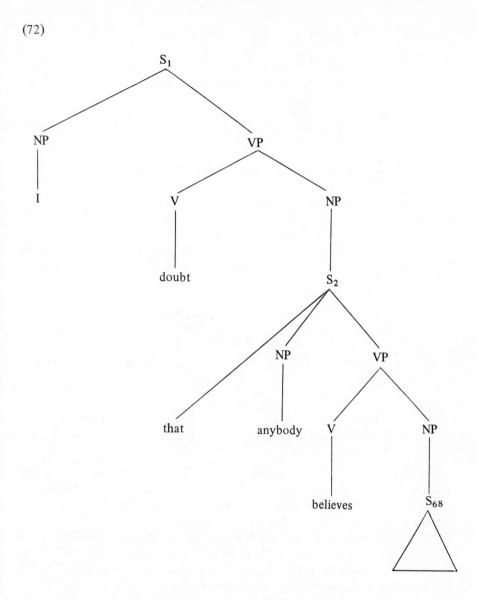

(i) You may believe Senator Quark$_i$, but I don't believe him$_i$.
and such cases as (ii), in which, though the combination is anaphoric, it is not anaphoric to a clause, but rather to a noun like *story, testimony,* etc.

(ii) Bill believed Tom$_i$'s $\left\{ \begin{array}{l} \text{story} \\ \text{testimony} \\ \text{claim} \\ \text{accusation} \\ \text{etc.} \end{array} \right\}$, but we didn't believe him$_i$.

The cases that are relevant for the performative analysis are exclusively cases in which the verb-plus-object combination is anaphoric to a clause.

$$(74) \quad \text{Sheila}_i \left\{ \begin{cases} \text{said} \\ \text{whispered} \\ \text{wrote} \\ \text{wigwagged} \end{cases} \text{to Jeff}_j \\ \text{made it plain without saying a word} \\ \text{*hoped} \\ \text{*doubts} \\ \text{*knew} \\ \text{*thought} \end{array} \right.$$

that termites made great pets, but he$_j$ didn't believe her$_i$.

In general, the only verbs whose objects can be anaphorically linked to *believe + NP* constructions are verbs of linguistic communication — even wigwagging is a little peculiar, for me. Yet as Anderson has pointed out,[26] the object of *make plain* is a viable antecedent. Since, however, such derived nominals as those in (75), which, like the objects of (76), denote emotions, seem unable to function as antecedents,

$$(75) \quad \text{*Sheila}_i \text{ made plain her}_i \left\{ \begin{array}{l} \text{disgust} \\ \text{resentment} \\ \text{enthusiasm} \\ \text{aversion} \\ \text{etc.} \end{array} \right\}, \text{ but no one believed her}_i.$$

$$(76) \quad \text{*Sheila}_i \left\{ \begin{array}{l} \text{shrugged her}_i \text{ indifference} \\ \text{snorted her}_i \text{ impatience} \\ \text{nodded her}_i \text{ assent} \\ \text{glowered her}_i \text{ rage} \end{array} \right\}, \text{ but no one believed her}_i.$$

it seems necessary to impose the condition that this type of anaphora is not only dependent on the semantic properties of the verb whose object is being referred to, but also on the surface clausehood of the antecedent proposition.

The next point to emphasize is that this type of linkage depends on a particular coreference relation obtaining in the sentence. Namely, the object NP in the *believe + NP* construction must be coreferential with the subject of the verb whose complement is being referred to.[27] Thus if *her$_i$* in (73) and (74) is replaced by *me, Ted, us, you,* etc, the sentences become ungrammatical.

---

[26] Cf. Anderson (*op. cit.*).

[27] That this characterization is not quite accurate can be seen from such examples as (i), which were pointed out in Anderson (*op. cit.*)

(i) Jeff$_j$ heard from Sheila$_i$ that termites made great pets, but he$_j$ didn't believe her$_i$.

Examples of this type suggest that the coreference condition should not be stated in terms of the grammatical subject of the antecedent verb, but rather in terms of the actant in its clause which fills the semantic role of agent or source. I will, however, disregard this refinement in the simplified exposition of this paper.

Keeping in mind the two restrictions discussed above, we can see how such sentences as those in (77) support the postulation of a higher verb.

(77)   [Dr. Grusel is sharpening the spurs] $_{S_1}$, but if you don't

believe $\begin{Bmatrix} me \\ *Ted \\ *her \\ us \end{Bmatrix}$, observe him through the peephole yourself.

The fact that this occurrence of *believe me* can be used to refer back to the bracketed clause S_1 of (77) argues that S_1 is the complement of a verb of linguistic communication, and the fact that only *me* (or *us*) can follow *believe* suggests that this verb must have a first-person agent (or source).

Thus (77) provides information of a much more specific nature about what is "up there" than does (68), but both support the postulation of the higher performative clause in (61).

Similar arguments can be developed for postulating a higher performative clause for other types of speech acts as well, but I will not develop them here, for the general conclusion should be clear: Underlying semantactic representations must be inferred to be orders of magnitude more remote from surface structures than was believed to be the case a decade ago.

Though space limitations preclude more than a passing mention of this point here, the type of abstractness arguments I have been outlining here can in fact be pursued much further – so far, in fact, that the line between syntactic deep structure and semantic structure vanishes – hence Georgia Green's term *semantax*. The surface structures of any language are then the result of the repeated application to a universal set of semantic structures of a rather small, largely universal, set of transformations like the ones that have, in the discussion above, been postulated to play a role in the derivation of (17) from (61). The diversity of the surface structures of the world's languages appears not to derive from deep differences, but rather from a number of language-particular restrictions on these general transformations, and in part from the effects of certain language-particular transformations and output conditions.

Under this conception of grammar, which has come to be known as *generative semantics*, [28] we could recode the three basic insights of Zellig Harris which were discussed above in Section 1.1 in the following abbreviated form:

(78)   Big sentences are (semantactically) made up of little meanings – the propositions and open sentences which correspond roughly to the S_i of such structures as (61). And there is one "kernel grammar" for all languages – the rules that specify the set of well-formed semantic structures.

---

[28] For a more detailed exposition of this theoretical framework, cf. Postal (1970a), Lakoff (1972), and McCawley (1967, 1973) and the works cited there.

2. ISLANDS

2.1. The results I will report on in this section concern general constraints on the functioning of transformations. In Section 2.2, I will introduce the notion of *islands,* and show how a particular phrase-structure configuration allows the deduction of a large number of constraints that can be found on various rules in grammars of various languages of the world. And in Section 2.3, I will define and briefly discuss the important notion of *primacy.*

2.2 In Ross (1967), I proposed that the ungrammaticality of the results of topicalizing the NP *these points* in the sentences in (79) [cf. the corresponding bad sentences in *(80)]

(79) a.   She will execute [[anyone]$_{NP}$[who mentions these points$_S$]]$_{NP}$
      b.   We will take up $_{NP}$[either [his proposals$_{NP}$] or [these points$_{NP}$]]$_{NP}$ next
      c.   [[For her to talk about these points$_S$]$_{NP}$] was unexpected.

(80) a.   *These points she will execute anyone who mentions ϕ.
      b.   *These points we will take up either his proposals or ϕ next.
      c.   *These points for her to talk about ϕ was unexpected.

should be accounted for by adding to linguistic theory the following three constraints:

(81) a.   *The Complex NP Constraint*
            No constituent can be chopped[29] out of a sentence modifying a lexical head noun.
      b.   *The Coordinate Structure Constraint*
            No constituent can be chopped out of a coordinate node.
      c.   *The Sentential Subject Constraint*
            No constituent can be chopped out of a clausal subject.

Schematically, what is excluded is moving any constituent along the arrows shown in (82a–c) – therefore, I have x-ed these arrows.

---

[29] In Ross (*op. cit.*), Ch. 6, a distinction is made between "chopping" rules—rules like *Topicalization,* which move a constituent from its original position in a sentence, leaving no trace of where it came from – and "copying" rules – rules which move a constituent, but which leave behind a pro-form to mark the point of departure. One copying rule is *Left Dislocation,* which converts (i) into (ii).
(i) I wish he had soaked the bread longer.
(ii) The bread, I wish he had soaked it longer.
As the sentences in (iii)–(v) show, the rule of *Left Dislocation* is not subject to the three constraints of (81).
(iii) These points, she will execute anyone who mentions them.
(iv) These points, we will take up either his proposals or them next.
(v) These points, for her to talk about them was unexpected.

(82) a.

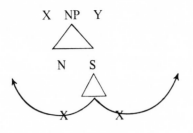

b.

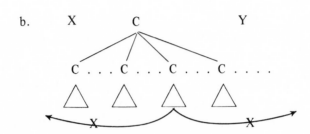

c.

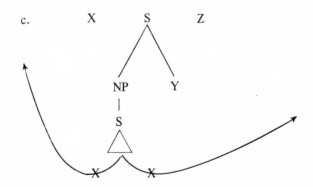

It should be noted that the constraints in (81) are not restricted to the particular rule of *Topicalization* in English — as the examples in (83) suggest, many other chopping rules are affected —

(83) a.   *Tall though I am dating [[a   girl] [who is ϕ]$_{NP}$],
                                          NP
            I am really a midget-head.

      b.   *Not my sock you can't throw [either [his sock$_{NP}$] or ϕ_{NP}]
            into the soup

      c.   *Carefully [[for him to slice the banana ϕ_{S}]$_{NP}$] would be
            expensive

rules which, in happier circumstances can prepose adjective phrases to the front of *though*-clauses, cf. (84a), a copied *not* and an emphasized constituent to the beginning of a sentence, cf. (84b), or an adverb, cf. (84c).

(84) a.   Tall though she is ϕ, I'm a midget-head.

b.   Not my sock you can't throw into the soup.[30]

c.   Carefully, he sliced the banana.

Nor are the constraints intended to be restricted to English. In Ross (*op. cit.*), data from other languages is cited which tends to support the claim that these constraints are universally valid.[31]

Assuming now, with the restrictions noted in footnote 31, that the three constraints of (81) are indeed roughly correct, the question that immediately arises is, why these three? Why is it that elements are forbidden from leaving the sentence of a complex NP, but not the S of a complex VP? And why should it be that elements are forbidden from leaving coordinated elements when they are not forbidden from leaving subordinated ones? And why should it be harder to chop elements out of sentential subjects than out of sentential objects?

While I know of no approach to the last of these three questions that seems promising, it does seem likely that the first two questions might be answered along the following lines.

---

[30] No thanks are due to John Lawler for calling my attention to this ugly class of facts.

[31] Since this work appeared, however, a number of other studies have been made which show that the actual situation with respect to the universality of the constraints is not nearly as simple as I had supposed. In particular, what seems necessary is the postulation of a universal implicational hierarchy of island types, one part of which is shown in (i)

(i) CNPC $\supset$ CSC

That is, any language which has the CNPC will also have the CSC, but not necessarily the reverse. Some languages which appear to have only the CSC are Korean and — notwithstanding what was claimed in Ross (*op. cit.*) — Japanese. In addition, Brazilian Portuguese appears to have a form of the CNPC that is not as general as the version stated in (81a). However, the main point here is not to argue for the particular set of constraints shown in (81), for these are only a first approximation, but rather to call attention to the necessity of attempting to establish some such universal set.

Some important research along these lines is contained in Postal (1971, 1973), Chung (1973), Lakoff (1970a), Witten (1972), Bolinger (1972), Grosu (1972), Neeld (1973), Erteschik (1973), and Chomsky (1973).

Bruce Fraser has pointed out that the word *even,* when attached to a *that*-clause, as in (85b),[32] makes it difficult, if not impossible, to remove elements from the clause. Compare (86a) and *(86b).

(85) a.   He claims that Phil dallied with Andrea.

      b.   He claims even that Phil dallied with Andrea.

(86) a.   Andrea he claims that Phil dallied with.

      b. ?? Andrea he claims even that Phil dallied with.[33]

If we assume that *even* is Chomsky-adjoined[34] to the term it modifies, then the two sentences of (85) would differ from one another in structure as shown in (87).

(87) a.

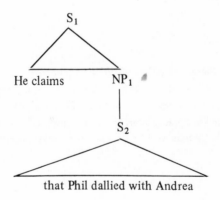

He claims   NP$_1$

S$_2$

that Phil dallied with Andrea

---

[32] Cf. Fraser (1971), in which Fraser uses the term "protected environment" for such *even*-ed clauses.

[33] This sentence is better when *dallied* is contrastively stressed than when it is read with no extra emphasis on this word, which is the reading that I am starring. I have no explanation for this difference.

[34] Cf. Ross (1967) for discussion of this type of adjunction operation.

b.

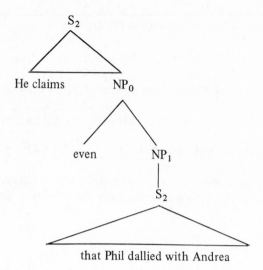

I suggest that the reason that *Andrea* can be topicalized in (87a), but not in (87b), is that in the latter structure, the node NP_0, which was created as a result of the Chomsky-adjunction of *even* to NP_1, is a self-dominating node, that is, a node which immediately dominates another node of the same type[35]. In (88), I propose a principle which would predict the ungrammaticality of ?(86b) as a consequence.

(88). *The Immediate Self-Domination Principle (ISP)*

   a.   No element may be chopped out of a node which immediately dominates another node of the same type.

---

[35] Note that the ungrammaticality of ??(86b) remains if *even* is replaced by *only* or *also*, a fact which suggests the need for the kind of parallel explanation attempted immediately below in the text.

(88) b.

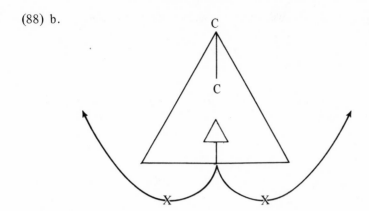

Note that the ISP would subsume as subcases the CNPC[36] and the CSC. In addition, the ISP could be used to provide an explanation of the fact that when a constituent is postposed by *NP Shift*, the rule that converts (89a) to (89b),

(89) a.   She will send a picture of the Waco Post Office to Inspector Smithers

⇓ *NP Shift*

b.   She will send ϕ to Inspector Smithers a picture of the Waco Post Office.

it is more difficult to chop constituents from the shifted constituent than it is to chop them from an unshifted one [compare (90a) and ??(90b)].

---

[36] Only if we assume that the constituent structures of both modified N + relative clause constructions (*the fact which they uncovered*) and sentential N + complement clause constructions (*the fact that they uncovered it*) are to be represented as in (i).

(i)

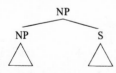

Since relative clauses and noun complements do not conjoin, however, cf. *(ii),

(ii) *The fact(s) which they uncovered and that she uncovered it upset me.

and since there is a systematic difference between the strength of the prohibition on chopping elements inside relative clauses and noun complements, as suggested by the facts from Brazilian Portuguese that were alluded to in footnote 31, this may be an incorrect assumption. If so, then the ISP could only be used to explain the existence of the relative clause part of the CNPC.

(90) a.   The Waco Post Office she will send a picture of ϕ to Inspector Smithers.

  b.   ??The Waco Post Office she will send to Inspector Smithers a picture of.

Under the assumption that *NP Shift* Chomsky-adjoins the shifted NP to the right of the clause [thus the structure of (89b) would be roughly that of (91)],

(91)

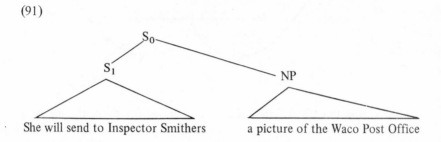

She will send to Inspector Smithers   a picture of the Waco Post Office

an assumption lent support by the fact that the most natural place for parenthetical inserts like *as you know, he felt, to my knowledge,* etc. in (89b) is immediately after *Inspector Smithers*,[37] the awkwardness of ??(90b) would also follow as a consequence from the ISP.

One other process which lends additional support to the ISP is the rule of *Right Node Raising* (cf. Postal, 1974), for details), which optionally converts such coordinate structures as (92a), in which each conjunct contains an occurrence of a coreferential NP (here italicized), into such reduced structures as (92b), in which one copy of this repeated NP has been Chomsky-adjoined to the right of the coordinate node, producing the type of structure indicated schematically in (92c).

(92) a. $[_{S_0} [_{S_1}$ Marcel bought *a picture of the Waco Post Office* from the Costa Rican rebels$_{S_1}$] and $[_{S_2}$ Pedro sent *a picture of the Waco Post Office* to the Monacan underground$_{S_2}$]$_{S_0}$] .

⇓   *Right Node Raising*

  b. $[_{S_1} [_{S_0} [_{S_1}$ Marcel bought ϕ from the Costa Rican rebels$_{S_1}$] and $[_{S_2}$ Pedro sent ϕ to the Monacan underground$_{S_2}$]$_{S_0}$] [a picture of the Waco Post Office]$_{NP}$]$_{S_1}$

---

[37] In Ross (in preparation a), I argue that the basic generalization governing the location of parenthetical inserts like the above is that they do not interrupt constituents, but appear with the greatest naturalness between major constituents of unembedded clauses.

(92) c.

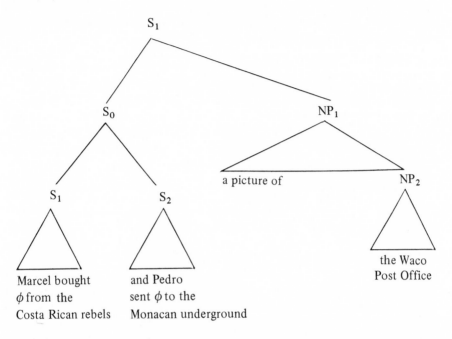

Again, the claim that Chomsky-adjunction is involved in this process can be supported by the observation that the most natural place for parentheticals to be inserted into (92b) is right after *underground,* as would be predicted from the structure shown in (92c) and the generalization of footnote 37.

What is of interest about (92c) for the ISP is the fact that NP_2 is difficult to topicalize out of NP_1, the NP that has been Chomsky-adjoined to S_0, as the awkwardness of ??(93) shows.

(93)   ??The Waco Post Office Marcel bought from the Costa Rican rebels and Pedro sent to the Monacan rebels a picture of ϕ.

Since the ISP would not only subsume (?part of – cf. footnote 36) the CNPC and the CSC as special cases, but would also explain the fact that items may not leave protected environments [cf. ??(86)], and may only leave shifted or right-node-raised NP's with difficulty [cf. ??(90b) and ??(93)], I conclude tentatively that it should be included as a part of the theory of universal grammar.

Of course, if we propose the ISP as a partial explanation for the existence of such constraints as the CNPC and the CSC, we must now deal with a host of thorny questions that sweep in with it. Such as: Why should self-dominating nodes be hard to get things out of, rather than self-non-dominating nodes? Why should some self-dominating nodes be harder to get things out of than others (i.e., why should the CSC be harder to violate than the CNPC, as was pointed out above in footnote

31)? Why should the rules of *NP Shift* and *Right Node Raising*, which Chomsky-adjoin to the right, produce less restricted self-dominating nodes than the process which forms protected environments by Chomsky-adjoining *even, only*, and *also* to the left of a clause? And so on.

Regardless of the answers which future research may provide to these questions, I feel that the ISP can fairly be characterized as an advance over the unhomogeneous set of constraints that were recapitulated in (81).

2.3 The notion of *primacy* is an extension of the important notion of *accessibility*, which was proposed in Keenan and Comrie (1972) and Keenan (1972).[38] Keenan and Comrie show that the various strategies for forming relative clauses which are employed in the widely diverse selection of languages that they survey are all governed by the following hierarchy:

> (94) *The Accessibility Hierarchy*
> Subjects ⩾ Direct Objects ⩾ Indirect Objects ⩾
> Oblique constituents ⩾ Possessors ⩾ Objects of comparative construc-
> tions

The interpretation of the inequality sign is as follows: In any language, if some strategy exists for forming relative clauses in which the shared NP in the constituent sentence is a NP at some given point B on (94), then this strategy will also work for NP's at any other point A on (94), as long as A ⩾ B. Thus any language which can relativize direct objects will also be able to relativize subjects, but there are languages, like Malagasy, which can only relativize subjects. In Keenan and Comrie's terminology, subjects are *more accessible than* direct objects.

The notion of *primacy* is roughly explained in (95).

> (95) *Primacy*
> Node A of a tree *has primacy over* node B ('A→B') if
> (i) A and B are clause-mates, and A is to the left of B, or
> (ii) A is an element of a clause which dominates B.[39].

This definition is coupled with the following constraint:

> (96) *The Primacy Constraint*
> If some process P can operate in a language in such a way as to affect
> or be triggered by some node B, then P will also be able to operate in
> the language in such a way as to affect or be triggered by any node A
> which has primacy over B.

---

[38] An extremely important application of the Keenan-Comrie accessibility hierarchy to the analyses of causative constructions in universal grammar is presented in Comrie (1972).

[39] The notion of primacy is thus closely related to, though not identical with, Langacker's notion of command (cf. footnote 23).

Thus since subjects have primacy over objects, any language which is like English in allowing reflexive pronouns to refer to objects, as in (97a), must also allow reflexives to refer to subjects, as in (97b).

(97) a.　Pete$_i$ talked to Jack$_j$ about himself$_j$.
　　　b.　Pete$_i$ talked to Jack$_j$ about himself$_i$.

However, there are languages, such as German, in which only subjects can be referred to by reflexives. Thus while the German translation of (97b) can make use of the German reflexive pronoun *sich,* as in (98),

(98) Peter$_i$ sprach mit Hans$_j$ uber sich$_i$.
　　　Peter spoke with Jack about self.

the translation of (97a) must use the non-reflexive pronoun *ihn* [cf. (99)] .

(99) Peter$_i$ sprach mit Hans$_j$ uber $\left\{ \begin{array}{l} \text{ihn}_j \\ \text{*sich}_j \end{array} \right\}$.

German thus provides an example of a language which shows that the process of reflexivization is in conformity with (96) and (95i) − the clause-mate part of the definition of primacy. What (95i) − (96) predict is that no language will be found in which only sentences which correspond to (97a) are grammatical.

To see what (95ii) and (96) imply, let us compare the processes of *Reflexivization* in English and Japanese. As is well-known, by and large, English reflexive pronouns can only refer back to an antecedent in the same clause. Thus while (100a) is grammatical in English, *(100b) is not.

(100) a.　Bill$_i$ criticized himself$_i$.
　　　 b.　*Bill$_i$ knows [$_S$ that himself$_i$ is sick$_S$] .

However, in Japanese, sentences corresponding to both of these are grammatical − Japanese has no clause-mate condition on the antecedents of its reflexive pronoun *zibun.*

(101) a.　Biru wa　　zibun o　hihan　　sita
　　　　　Bill (topic) self (acc) criticism did
　　　　　'Bill$_i$ criticized himself$_i$'
　　　 b.　Biru$_i$ wa　　[$_S$ zibun$_i$ ga　byooki da to　iu$_S$] koto o　　sitte iru.
　　　　　Bill (topic)　　self (nom) sick　is that say fact (acc) knowing is
　　　　　"Bill$_i$ knows that he$_i$ is sick"

What (95ii) − (96) predict is that no language will be found which exhibits *only* cross-clause reflexivization.

Another process which conforms with (95) – (96) is *Equi*. While English allows this rule to delete the subjects of lower clauses under identity with either higher subjects [cf. (102a)] or higher objects [cf. (102b)],

(102) a.　　I_i want $[_S$ for me_i to go$]_S$
　　　　　　　　⇓　　*Equi*
　　　　　　　　ϕ

　　　　b.　　He forced me_i $[_S$ for me_i to go$]$
　　　　　　　　　　　　⇓　　*Equi*
　　　　　　　　　　　　ϕ

Serbo-Croatian only permits the former type of deletion [cf. the sentences in (103), which are drawn from Perlmutter (1971)].

(103) a.　　Ja_i zelim [da　ja_i idem$]_S$
　　　　　　I　　want　that I　go
　　　　　　　　　　　　　⇓　　*Equi*
　　　　　　　　　　　　　ϕ

　　　　b.　　Zelim ići
　　　　　　　I want to go

　　　　c.　　Prisilio me je_i [da ja_i idem$]_S$
　　　　　　　forced he　me　that I　go
　　　　　　　　　　　　　⇓　　*Equi*
　　　　　　　　　　　　　ϕ

　　　　d.　　*Prisilio me je ici.
　　　　e.　　Prisilio me je da idem.
　　　　　　　he forced me that I go (=to go)

　　　　　　　He forced me that I go (= to go)

Thus the Serbo-Croatian process of *Equi* can apply to (193a), deleting the second occurrence of *ja* 'I' under identity with the first.[40] Subsequently, a general rule deleting unstressed pronouns applies to delete the subject *ja* of *zelim*, yielding the well-formed string (103b).

However, as the ungrammaticality of (103d) indicates, this process is not applicable in the object of *prisilio*. *Equi* cannot apply to delete the *ja* of (103c) and cause *idem* to be infinitivized. In this case, all that can happen is for the above-mentioned rule of *Pronoun Deletion* to delete this *ja*, leaving the verb *idem* unchanged in the output string (103e).

---

[40]Whether the complementizer *da* "that" is deleted as a part of this process or by a separate one is not germane to the present discussion. Nor is the question as to what process causes the change of the inflected verb *idem* 'I go' to the uninflected infinitive *ici* 'to go.'

Thus we see that Serbo-Croatian provides us with a case that supports (95i) — (96). Essentially, what is excluded is a language which would exhibit the reverse of Serbo-Croatian, as in (104).

(104) a.   I want that I go.

      b.   He forced me to go.

To the best of my knowledge, no such language exists.

The process of *Equi* can also be used to support (95ii), if we assume, following Grinder (1970), that the process which converts (105a) to (105b), which Grinder refers to as *Super Equi,* is to be identified with *Equi.*

(105) a.   [Fred$_i$ knows [that [his$_i$ getting himself$_i$ into trouble]$_{S_3}$ would be inconvenient for me$_{S_2}$]]$_{S_1}$.

      b.   Fred$_i$ knows that getting himself$_i$ into trouble would be inconvenient for me.

In this case, the subject of *getting* has been deleted not by any element of S_2, the clause immediately above it, but rather by *Fred$_i$*, the subject of S_1. Schematically, the deletion has proceeded as in (106).

(106)   [See page 110.]

Under the assumption that the deletions involved in (105) and (102) are in fact parts of the same rule, the Primary Constraint would predict that while a language might exist which exhibited only *Equi*, no language could exist which exhibited only *Super Equi.* In other words, (95)–(96) predicts that while we may find a language which has only sentences produced by *Equi*, like those of (102), and none produced by *Super Equi*, like (105b), we will find no language which has the latter type of sentences unless it also has the former type.[41]

---

[41] I have thus far been unable to find a clear case of a language which has *Equi* but not *Super Equi*, though Japanese may be such a language. Kazuko Inoue has informed me that the following sentence is slightly more acceptable with the reflexive pronoun *zibun* than without it,

(i) Biru$_i$ wa $\left[\left[\left\{\begin{matrix} \text{zibun}_i \\ ?\underline{\quad} \end{matrix}\right\} \text{ ga hayaku kaeru}\right]_{S_1 S_2} \right.$ koto ga$_{S_2}$

      Bill (topic)   self (nom.) early return fact (noun)

      Ann mo   okoraseru daroo to $\left.\right]$ omotta$_{S_1}$

This footnote continued on page 110.

(106)

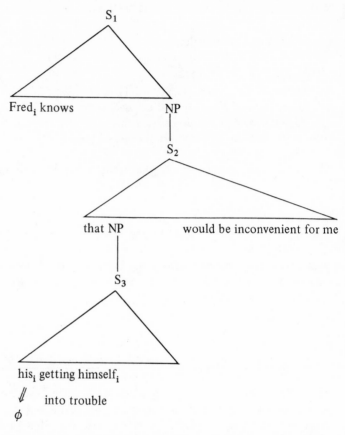

Many other processes could be cited whose operation is in conformance with (95)–(96), but for the present brief survey of the notion of primacy, the ones discussed above should prove sufficient to indicate that the Accessibility Hierarchy must be extended to constrain the operations of other types of rules than those that form relative clauses.

Footnote 41 continued –

Ann even infuriate   would that thought

"Bill$_i$ thought that $\begin{Bmatrix} \text{his} \\ \text{—} \end{Bmatrix}$ returning early would infuriate Ann."

which may indicate that Japanese only has a weak rule of *Super Equi*. On the other hand, Japanese, like Serbo-Croatian, has a rule of *Pronoun Deletion,* and at present, I cannot *demonstrate that the deletion of zibun* in (i) would have to be accomplished by the former rule and not by the latter one. The only other languages that I have been able to check even cursorily – namely German, French, Spanish, Italian, Russian and Czech – all seem to have both kinds of *Equi.* If further investigation should reveal that no language exists which has only *Equi,* then this fact, while not disconfirming (95), could not be explained by it.

3. NON-DISCRETE GRAMMARS

The remaining research I will report on seems to necessitate the introduction into linguistic theory of a formally quite different type of conceptual underpinning than either the theory of generative semantics of Section 1 above or the theory underlying the type of constraints discussed in Section 2. Basically, this research indicates the need for changing the theory of grammar from a discrete theory to a non-discrete one. The logic of the theories discussed in Sections 1—2 contains basically only discrete predicates. For instance, this logic would lead to such claims as the claims that sentences are either well-formed or not; that constituents are either NP's or not; that NP's are either plural or not; that a sentence either does have a certain reading or does not have it; that elements either are or are not elements of different clauses; that groups of morphemes either are or are not idioms; that sentences are or are not related; etc., etc., etc. In other words, the Law of the Excluded Middle has, within the broad framework of generative grammar, always been assumed to hold for most of the predicates used in this theory.

I believe, however, that there are at present extremely cogent reasons for rejecting this law in all of the above disjunctions, and indeed, almost universally within linguistics. That is, I would argue that instead of being viewed as a device for partitioning the set of all strings of words into well-formed and ill-formed strings, a grammar should merely impose a partial ordering upon this set: For example, with respect to grammaticality, the grammar should merely assert that one string A is better than another string B; similarly, that one constituent C is more NP-like than another constituent D; that one constituent E is more plural than another constituent F; that one string M is better on reading Q than another string N is, etc., etc., etc.

While it is beyond the scope of this paper to demonstrate the necessity of such a sweeping reconceptualization of the logic of generative grammar, it is possible to give some indication of the kinds of evidence now available which have led me to this set of conclusions.

In Ross (1972b), I give evidence that suggests that rather than being discrete entities, such categories as N, A, and V are to be arranged in an implicational hierarchy, or cline, or gradient, as shown in (107).

(107)

$$V \; > \; \text{Present} \; > \; \text{Perfect} \; > \; \text{Passive} \; > \; A \; >$$
$$\text{participle} \quad \text{participle} \quad \text{participle}$$

$$\text{Adjectival} \; > \; N$$
$$\text{noun}$$

That is, adjectives are "between" verbs and nouns, as various sorts of participles are "between" verbs and adjectives, and adjectival nouns like *fun* and *snap* are "between" adjectives and nouns. The evidence on which this claim is based is largely of the following form: Some syntactic process applies more to V than to A, and more to A than to N. One example is the rule which allows the epenthesis of the pronoun *it* before the factive complements of certain predicates. There are a fair number of verbs for which this process is possible [cf. (108a)], only one adjective, to the best of my knowledge [cf. (108b)], and no nouns [cf. *(108c)].

(108) a.   I $\left\{\begin{array}{l}\text{resent}\\\text{regret}\\\text{hate}\\\text{dislike}\\\text{appreciate}\\\text{etc.}\end{array}\right\}$ it that /ou used a hanky.

b.   I am aware (of it) that you didn't have to.

c.   Her regret (*of it) that you did was feigned.

Such facts suggest that rather than being assigned to one of some number of discrete categories, words should be given some value (for the present, we can think of the values as being real numbers in the interval [0, 1]) of the feature [αNouny], (equivalently, [αVerby]), and that syntactic processes, such as the rule that inserts *it*, should be assigned threshhold values of this feature, above which they will not operate.

In Ross (1973a), I present a range of arguments to the effect that such constituents as the subjects of the sentences in (109) are less than full NP's.

(109) a.   Some headway was made on this amendment.
b.   There exists a contract.
c.   Accurate tabs were kept on Bingo's expenses.

When we compare the behavior of such subjects with that of such dyed-in-the-wool NP's as *euphoria,* we find that some are more like "true" NP's like *euphoria* than others: They "pass" more of the NP tests than these others do. We can rank them on their "noun-phrasiness," as is done for some of them in (110).

(110) $\longleftarrow$ $\dfrac{\text{'More noun-phrasy'}}{euphoria \;>\; headway \;>\; there \;>\; tabs}$

The inequality sign in (110) is to be interpreted as an implication. For any two items, A and B, if A > B, then if B "passes" some test, A will also pass it. In other words, I am asserting that the mystery items under discussion are *fake* NP's; they only do a subset of what NP's like *euphoria* do. I know of no syntactic processes which are applicable to fake NP's, but not to standard-brand NP's like *euphoria.*

The "tests" for NP-hood — i.e., those syntactic processes which only apply to NP's — can also be hierarchically ordered. An example of the hierarchy formed by three such tests is given in (111).

(111)   ——————————————— Choosier ———————————————→

Tag Formation > *Tough Movement* > *Left Dislocation*

Again, the inequality sign has an implicational interpretation: For any two syntactic processes A and B, if A > B [read: 'A is stronger than B' or 'B is choosier than A'], then whenever B can apply to a given item, A will also be able to.

The direction of the inequality sign is purposely chosen to be the same in (110) and (111): Just as NP's like *euphoria* are found in a wider range of syntactic contexts than NP's like *tabs,* so *Tag Formation* is applicable to a wider class of structures than is *Left Dislocation.*

The two hierarchies above interact to mutually define each other. They form the type of matrix shown schematically in (112), which I will refer to as a *squish.*

(112)

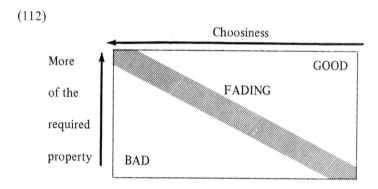

To give a concrete example, the hierarchies in (110 and (111) form the squish shown in (113).

(113)

	Left Dislocation	*Tough Movement*	*Tag Formation*
euphoria	ok	ok	ok
headway	*	?	ok
there	*	*	ok
tabs	*	*	?
	[cf. (114)]	[cf. (115)]	[cf. (116)]

(114) a.   Euphoria, it's greatly overrated.

b.   *Some headway, it was made on this amendment.

*There $\left\{\begin{matrix} \text{there} \\ \text{it} \end{matrix}\right\}$ exists on a contract.

*Accurate tabs, they were kept on Bingo's expenses.

(115) a.   Euphoria is tough to arrange for.

b.   ?Significant headway is tough to make on complex amendments, like this one.

c.   *There is tough to imagine existing a contract.

d.   *Accurate tabs will be tough to keep on Bingo's expenses.

(116) a.   Euphoria should be legalized, shouldn't it?

b.   Significant headway was made on this amendment, wasn't it?

c.   There exists a contract, doesn't there?

d.   ?Accurate tabs were kept on Bingo's expenses, weren't they?

To claim that fake NP's form a squish is to make a quite precise empirical claim. It is to claim that when *all* other fake NP's are "blended into" (113), with as many rows being added as the facts necessitate, and when *all* other processes are "blended into" (113), with as many extra columns being added as there are processes that distinguish themselves, the resulting supermatrix will be well-behaved, as defined in (117).

(117)   A matrix whose cells contain indications of degree of grammaticality is *horizontally well-behaved* if the degrees of grammaticality indicated in the cells of a row increase monotonically (i.e., without changes in direction of increment), or decrease monotonically. If one row has decreasing values, all must; if one row has increasing values, all must. A matrix is *vertically well-behaved* if the degrees of grammaticality indicated in the cells of its columns increase or decrease monotonically in the manner specified above.

A matrix that is both horizontally and vertically well-behaved is *"well-behaved."*

To claim that a body of data forms a squish is to claim that two varying parameters can be found whose pattern of interaction is given by a well-behaved matrix.

In Ross (1973b) I argue that there is a squish of nouniness which has the hierarchy of (117) as one axis.

(117) a.   *that S (that he gave the skunk to me)*

b.   *for NP to V X (for him to give the skunk to me)*

c. $\quad Q \left(\left\{ \begin{array}{l} \textit{where} \\ \textit{when} \\ \textit{how} \\ \textit{how quickly} \\ \textit{etc.} \end{array} \right\} \right.$ $\quad$ *he gave the skunk to me)*

d. $\quad \left[\begin{array}{c} \text{NP} \\ \text{+Acc} \end{array} \right]$ *Ving X* $\quad$ *(him giving the skunk to me)*

e. $\quad$ *NP's Ving X (his giving the skunk to me)*
f. $\quad$ Action Nominal $\quad$ *(his giving of the skunk to me)*
g. $\quad$ Derived Nominal $\quad$ *(his gift of the skunk to me)*
h. $\quad$ Noun *panda*

Except for (117h), the elements of this hierarchy are all complement types. To claim the existence of a squish here is to claim that while there may be syntactic processes that affect just (117a), or just (117a-b) or just (117a-c) or just (117a-d) etc., there will be no processes which affect just (117 a, c, d, g), or any discontinuous range of (117). Some examples of processes which support this claim are the rule of *Preposition Deletion* and the output condition which excludes headless sentence-internal nominal complements. Cf. (118) and (119).

(118) a. $\quad$ I'm amazed (*at) that he gave the skunk to me.
$\quad$ b. $\quad$ I would be amazed (*at) for him to give the skunk to me.
$\quad$ c. $\quad$ I was amazed (at) how quickly he gave the skunk to me.

$\quad$ d. $\quad$ I was amazed *(at) $\left\{ \begin{array}{l} \text{him} \\ \text{his} \end{array} \right\}$ giving the skunk to me.

$\quad$ e. $\quad$ I was amazed *(at) $\left\{ \begin{array}{l} \text{his} \\ \\ \text{the panda} \end{array} \right.$ $\left\{ \begin{array}{l} \text{giving} \\ \text{gift} \end{array} \right\}$ of the skunk to me.$\left. \right\}$

(119) a. $\quad$ *Did that he gave the skunk to me amaze you?
$\quad$ b. $\quad$ *Would for him to give the skunk to me amaze you?
$\quad$ c. $\quad$?*Did how quickly he gave the skunk to me amaze you?
$\quad$ d. $\quad$??Did him giving the skunk to me amaze you?
$\quad$ e. $\quad$?Did his giving the skunk to me amaze you?

$\quad$ f. $\quad$ Did $\left\{ \begin{array}{l} \text{his} \\ \\ \text{the panda} \end{array} \right.$ $\left\{ \begin{array}{l} \text{giving} \\ \text{gift} \end{array} \right\}$ of the skunk to me $\left. \right\}$ amaze you?

Again, what seems to be called for here is some variable feature like [αNouny] (or [αSentential]) with threshhold values indicated on various rules. *Preposition Deletion* must be made obligatory before complements of low nouniness, optional

for embedded questions, and must block before any sufficiently nouny complement. And the output condition which is responsible for the decreasing
awkwardness of the sentences in (119) is obviously sensitive to the value of the
feature [αNouny] possessed by the internal complement. For low values of α,
strings violating the condition are totally excluded, while for high values, no
violations are produced. And for intermediate values, while speakers may disagree
on absolute judgements of such strings as (119c-e), to the best of my knowledge,
speakers will by and large agree on the relative acceptabilities of such strings.

Thus here we see two slightly differing manifestations of the nouniness squish:
The valency of the rule of *Preposition Deletion* assumes the fairly discrete,
categorial, values of OBLIG, OPT, and DNA in accordance with the squish, while
the output condition occasions, for many speakers, no abrupt, categorial, discrete
judgements. It is at present a mystery as to why some manifestations of such
squishes are more categorial than others.

In Ross (in preparation b), I argue that discrete treatments of constraints on
variables, such as the presentation in Section 2.2 above, must be abandoned in favor
of a non-discrete treatment. Basically, what I assert is that it is possible to find a
hierarchy of rule strength [the horizontal dimension of (120)] and a hierarchy of
environment restrictiveness [the vertical dimension of (120)] which interact in the
way shown in the assignment of values to the cells of the matrix.

(120)

			Rule Strength		
		(English) Reflexivization	*Tough Movement*	*Adverb Preposing*	*Topicali- zation*
Restrictive- ness of environment	Within clauses	√	√	√	√
	Into non- finite clauses	x	√	√	√
	Into non- factive *that-* clauses	x	x	√	√
	Into fac- tive *that* clauses	x	x	x	√

As was pointed out in Section 2.3 above English Reflexivization cannot "go
down into" even non-finite clauses [cf. (121)].

(121) Harry promised Mary$_i$ [$_S$ to give her$_i$ (*self) some port$_S$] .

And the rule of *Tough Movement,* while it can extract elements from non-finite clauses [thus (122a) can become (122b)],

(122) a.   It was tough for Jeff to begin $\begin{Bmatrix} \text{to read} \\ \text{reading} \end{Bmatrix}$ this issue of *Zap.*

   b.   This issue of *Zap* was tough for Jeff to begin $\begin{Bmatrix} \text{to read} \\ \text{reading} \end{Bmatrix}$

cannot extract elements from any kind of *that*-clauses, even nonfactive ones, cf. *(123b).

(123) a.   It was tough for Jeff to believe that *Zap* comics could have prurient interest for Judge Fendersnozz.
   b.   *Judge Fendersnozz was tough for Jeff to believe that *Zap* comics could have prurient interest for.

The rule of *Adverb Preposing,* while it is strong enough to extract adverbs from *that*-clauses in the object of non-factive predicates like *believe,* cf. (124),

(124) a.   They believe that Pancho will be tilting this windmill tomorrow.
   b.   Tomorrow they believe that Pancho will be tilting this windmill.

is not strong enough to extract them from factive *that*-clauses, cf. (*125b).

(125) a.   I'm glad that Pancho will be tilting this windmill tomorrow.
   b.   *Tomorrow I'm glad that Pancho will be tilting this windmill.

The fact that *Topicalization can* extract the NP *this windmill* from the object of *be glad* in (125a) [cf. (126)] shows that *Topicalization* is the strongest of all the rules in (120).

(126) This windmill I'm glad that Pancho will be tilting tomorrow.

What is of particular interest about the two hierarchies of (120) is that they appear to be in part universal. That is, for any rule of any grammar, if it cannot work "into" (or "out of") a non-factive *that*-clause, then it will not be able to work "into" (or "out of") a factive clause. Similarly, non-finite clauses are less restrictive than *that*-clauses, for all known languages. And the fact that the possibility of interclausal operations is always implied by the possibility of intraclausal operations is a consequence of (95) and (96). Thus in a way (120) would seem to be a kind of further refinement of the notion of primacy.

In Ross (in preparation c) I show that the hierarchy of rule strengths which was elucidated in connection with (120) implicitly defines a hierarchy of types of open sentences, and that there is a corresponding hierarchy of quantifier strengths, such that they intersect to form a squish highly similar to, and directly related to, the one in (120). Although the complexity of the argument precludes a full discussion here, the submatrix in (127) will give a rough idea of the central idea of this research.

(127)

More restricted ⟶

More in-
clusive ↑

Type of open S \ Quantifier	*several*	*many*	*no*
Quantified NP lower than coref. pronoun	√	x	x
Coref. pronoun inside factive complement	√	√	?
Coref. pronoun inside non-factive complement	√	√	√

To see that *several* is "stronger than" *many* and *no,* compare (128a) with (128b).

(128) a. That several people$_i$ were snubbed angered them$_i$.

b. *That $\left\{ \begin{array}{l} many \\ no \end{array} \right\}$ people$_i$ were snubbed angered them$_i$.

To see that *several* and *many* are "stronger than" *no,* compare (129) with (130).

(129) a. $\left\{ \begin{array}{l} \text{Several} \\ \text{Many} \end{array} \right\}$ people$_i$ believed that they$_i$ were unpopular.

b.   Nobody $_i$ believed that he$_i$ was unpopular.

(130) a. $\left\{ \begin{array}{l} \text{Several} \\ \text{Many} \end{array} \right\}$ people$_i$ were surprised (at the fact) that they$_i$ were unpopular.

b.   ?Nobody$_i$was surprised (*at the fact) that he$_i$ was unpopular.[42]

That is, the schematic phrase structures shown in (131a), (131b), and (131c), which correspond to the rows of (127), are arranged in the following subset relations: (131a), (131b), (131c).

(131)

a.   b.   c.

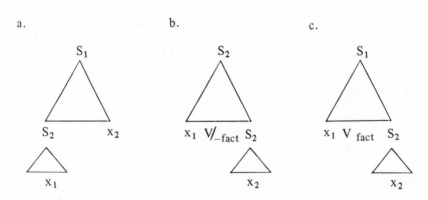

Any quantifier which can, in surface structure, modify x_1 in (131c), with x_2 being a coreferential pronoun, can also modify x_1 in (131a) or (131b), with coreferential pronouns appearing for x_2. And similarly, any quantifier which can appear as a modifier of x_1 in (131b) could also do so in (131a), again with it understood that x_2 contains a coreferential pronoun. The converse is not possible, however, as the sentences of (128)–(130) show. If we view the diagrams in (131) as schematic representations of open sentences, we find that there are syntactic reasons for thinking that some open sentences are more "open" to quantification than others.

Finally, in Ross (in preparation d), I show that there are certain syntactic phenomena which are limited to what we might call "treetops"–the highest islands of trees. All noncyclic fronting rules–rules such as *Adverb Preposing* and *Topicalization*–are limited to occurring in treetops. Thus note that while both (132a) and (132b), which represent the outputs of *Adverb Preposing* and

---

[42]Most speakers that I have checked with do not find that there is any difference in grammaticality between the long and the short versions of (130) – for them, the addition of *at the fact* does not worsen the sentence. However, some speakers share my intuitions, and I have found none with the opposite feelings.

Topicalization, respectively, can appear in isolation, (i.e., in treetops), embedding them in subject clauses, as in (133a) and (133b), respectively, produces rottenness.

(132) a.   Tomorrow we will hire a minority group member.
b.   The overdose of alkaseltzer the DA will probably not even mention.

(133) a.   ??That tomorrow we will hire a minority group member is unlikely.
b.   *That the overdose of alkaseltzer the DA will probably not even mention is unlikely.

Significantly, from the point of view of non-discrete grammar, the embedding of sentences starting with constituents which were preposed by a weak fronting rule produces less ungrammaticality than that which is occasioned by the embedding of sentences starting with constituents that have been preposed by a strong fronting rule. Thus (133a), whose derivation involves *Adverb Preposing,* a relatively weak rule [cf. (125) above], is better than (133b), whose derivation involves the relatively strong [cf. (126)] rule of *Topicalization.* Also significant is the fact that sentences with fronted constituents embed more successfully after non-factive predicates than after factives [cf. (134) and (135)].

(134) They believe that $\begin{cases} \text{tomorrow we will hire a minority group member} \\ \text{?the overdose of alkaseltzer the DA will probably} \\ \text{not even mention} \end{cases}$

(135) They are surprised that $\begin{cases} \text{??tomorrow we will hire a minority} \\ \quad \text{group member} \\ \text{?the overdose of alkaseltzer the} \\ \quad \text{DA will probably not even mention.} \end{cases}$

To sum up, while it is true that research on developing a precise formal theory which would be adequate to the task of describing the many squishes and the intricate interactions among them which can be observed in natural languages is barely underway, it seems to me that the rejection of the Law of the Excluded Middle in favor of some nondiscrete logic, as I have proposed in the works reported on above, has already led to a significant deepening of the understanding of many complex areas of semantax, and is likely to prove to be a fruitful avenue for further explorations in the future.

4. SUMMARY

The three batons of the title of this paper should now have become clear.
In Section 1, a number of arguments were given which pointed to the

conclusion that the underlying structures which previous researchers had assumed to be adequate were too concrete, by orders of magnitude. The question that this suggests for cognitive psychology is this: Does a similar situation obtain with respect to the models that have been proposed for cognitive processes? As an outsider, I cannot point to any areas in which I know existing models to be under-abstract, but it would strike me as odd if two fields as close to one another in content as linguistics and cognitive psychology were to differ markedly in the abstractness of the relations between data and model.

In Section 2, I sketched some preliminary formulations of putatively universal constraints. The questions that I as a linguist have for researchers in cognition are these: Are there analogs to the Immediate Self-Domination Principle or to the Primacy Constraint within psychology? In what areas of psychology must hierarchically ordered structures be assumed? Can the idea of self-dominating nodes be exported from linguistics to be used in describing facets of the types of behavior that are described in such terms? And is the notion of primacy generalizable to such structures? As far as I can see, the prospects for explaining either of the two constraints explored in Section 2 within the bounds of linguistics are not bright. Why, for instance, shouldn't it be precisely those nodes which *do not* immediately dominate other nodes of the same type that prohibit the chopping out of one of their dominees? Or why shouldn't lower elements in a hierarchical structure have primacy over higher ones? While it may yet prove possible to find explanations for some of the particular facets of the universal constraints discussed in Section 2 within linguistics, this seems unlikely to me. Sooner or later, we linguists must hope that it will be demonstrable that the laws of universal grammar that we unearth are special cases of general laws of behavior.

Finally, in Section 3, I have given some indication of the breadth of the range of evidence that suggests that many metalinguistic predicates, such as *is grammatical, is an adjective, is an NP*, etc., etc., should not be thought of as being binary, discrete predicates, but rather as being quantifiable. I have not been able, within the confines of this short paper, to support adequately my contention that this "squishification" of linguistic predicates is necessary almost everywhere, but that is my belief. The question for cognitive psychology is: How's by you? Are there areas of investigation for which discrete systems have traditionally been assumed but for which non-discrete treatment would make more sense? For instance, would it make sense to talk about one subject as having solved a chess problem "more" than another subject? Or of one subject using one scheme for memorization "more" (i.e., more fully, not merely more frequent use) than another subject?

In linguistics, it would seem wise for future researchers to approach any phenomenon under investigation with the beautiful question of Lloyd Anderson – not "Is the phenomenon in question discrete or non-discrete?" but rather "How discrete is the phenomenon?" It may be that this question is as timely for psychology as it is for linguistics.

Acknowledgements

This work was partially supported by a grant from the National Institute of Mental Health (Grant Number 5 PO1 MH 13390-07), whose help I gratefully acknowledge. I would also like to express my appreciation to Kazuko Inoue and Susumu Kuno, for their help in finding Japanese examples, and to Katya Chvany, who tried with me, in vain, to find helpful Russian examples.

I would also like to thank Albert Anonymously, the by now hundreds of students and colleagues who have listened to me talk about the material in Section 1 — abstract syntax — and have then patiently helped me to see that what I did not think was chaff was after all, and whose fault it isn't that so much of it still remains.

And very special thanks go to Jim McCawley, not for any particular comments on this paper, but for being able to be so cheerful at the task of sweeping out the Augean Stables of Meaning, and for just plain being; and to George Lakoff, who and I ([improbably] forthcoming) are said to be writing a book about abstract syntax, and who has taken these first steps towards meaning much farther than I would ever have been able to.

And most specially I am grateful to Paul Postal, whose teaching in the early 60's was the basis of most of abstract syntax and generative semantics.

REFERENCES

Anderson, S. R. Pro-Sentential forms and their implications for English Sentence Structure. In S. Kuno (Ed.), *Mathematical linguistics and automatic translation.* (Report NSF-20 to The National Science Foundation, Harvard Computation Laboratory) Cambridge, Mass., 1968.

Anderson, S. R. On the linguistic status of the performative/constative distraction. In S. Kuno (Ed.), *Mathematical linguistics and automatic translation.* (Report NSF-26, to the National Science Foundation, Harvard Computation Laboratory) Cambridge, Mass., 1970.

Bolinger, D. L. What did John keep the car that was in? *Linguistic Inquiry,* 1972, 3(1), 109-114.

Chomsky, N. A. *Aspects of the theory of syntax.* Cambridge, Mass.: MIT Press, 1965.

Chomsky, N. A. *Studies on semantics in generative grammar.* The Hague: Mouton, 1972.

Chomsky, N. A. Conditions on transformations. In S. R. Anderson & P. Kiparsky (Eds.), *Festschrift for Morris Halle.* New York: Holt, Rinehart and Winston, 1973.

Chung, S. On conjunct splitting in Samoan. *Linguistic Inquiry,* 1973, 3(4), 510-51.

Comrie, B. Causatives and universal grammar. Unpublished manuscript, King's College Research Centre, Cambridge, England, 1972.

Erteschik, N. *On the nature of island constraints.* Unpublished doctoral dissertation MIT, 1973.

Fodor, J. A. Three reasons for not deriving "kill" from "cause to die" *Linguistic Inquiry,* 1970, 1(4), 429-438.

Fraser, J. B. A reply to "on declarative sentences." In S. Kuno (Ed.), *Mathematical linguistics and automatic translation.* (Report NSF-24 to the National Science Foundation, Harvard Computation Laboratory) Cambridge, Mass., 1970.

Fraser, J. B. An analysis of *even* in English. In C. J. Fillmore & D. T. Langendoen (Eds.), *Studies in linguistic semantics.* New York: Holt, Rinehart and Winston, 1971.

Grinder, J. T. Super equi-NP deletion. In M. A. Campbell, J. Davison, W. Fisher, L. Furbee, J. Lindholm. J. Lovins, E. Maxwell, J. Reighard, & S. Straight (Eds.), *Papers from the Sixth Regional Meeting of the Chicago Linguistic Society.* Chicago: Chicago Linguistic Society, 1970.

Grosu, A. The strategic content of island constraints. *Working Papers in Linguistics,* Number 13, 1972, Ohio State University, Columbus, Ohio.

Harris, Z. S., Discourse analysis. *Language,* 1952, 28(1), 1-30.

Harris, Z. S., Coocurrence and transformation in linguistic structure. *Language,* 1957, 33(3), 283-340.

Harris, Z. S., *Discourse analysis reprints.* Papers on formal linguistics No. 2. Mouton: The Hague, 1963.

Keenan, E. L. On semantically based grammar. *Linguistic Inquiry,* 1972, 3(4), 413-462.

Keenan, E. L., & Comrie, B. The NP accessibility hierarchy. Unpublished manuscript, King's College, Research Centre, Cambridge, England, 1972.

Lakoff, G. Repartee, or a reply to "Negation, conjunction and quantifiers."*Foundations of Language.* 1970, 6(3), 389-422.(a)

Lakoff, G. Global rules. *Language,* 1970, 46(3), 627-639.(b)

Lakoff, G. *Irregularity in syntax.* New York: Holt, Rinehart and Winston, 1971.

Lakoff, G. Linguistics and natural logic. In D. Davidson & G. Harman (Eds.), *Semantics of natural language.* Dordrecht: D. Reidel, 1972.

Lakoff, G., & Ross, J. R. A note on anaphoric islands and causatives. *Linguistic Inquiry,* 1972, 3(1), 121-125.

Langacker, R. A. On pronominalization and the chain of command. In D. A. Reibel & S. A. Schane (Eds.), *Modern studies in English,* Englewood Cliffs, N.J.: Prentice-Hall, 1969.

McCawley, J. D. Meaning and the description of language. *Kotoba no uchu,* 1967, No. 9, 10-18, No. 10, 38-48, No. 11, 51-57.

McCawley, J. D. Lexical insertion in a grammar without deep structure. In W. J. Darden, C. J. N. Bailey, & A. Davison (Eds.), *Papers from the Fourth Regional Meeting of the Chicago Linguistic Society* Chicago: Chicago Linguistic Society, 1968.

McCawley, J. D. Tense and time reference in English. In C. J. Fillmore & D. T. Langendoen (Eds.) *Studies in linguistic semantics.* New York: Holt, Rinehart and Winston, 1971.

McCawley, J. D. Review of *Studies on Semantics in Generative Grammar* 1973, to appear.

Milsark, G. Re-Doubl-ing. *Linguistic Inquiry,* 1972, 3(4), 542-549.

Neeld, R. On the variable strength of island constraints. In C. Corum, T. C. Smith-Stark, & A. Weiser (Eds.), *Papers from the Ninth Regional Meeting of the Chicago Linguistic Society.* Chicago: Chicago Linguistic Society, 1973.

Perlmutter, D. M. *Deep and surface structure constraints in syntax.* New York: Holt, Rinehart and Winston, 1971.

Postal, P. M. On the surface verb *remind. Linguistic Inquiry,* 1970, 1(1), 37-120. (a)

Postal, P. M. On coreferential complement subject deletion. *Linguistic Inquiry,* 1970, 1(4), 439-500. (b)

Postal, P. M. *Crossover phenomena.* New York: Holt, Rinehart and Winston, 1971.

Postal, P. M. A global constraint on pronominalization. *Linguistic Inquiry,* 1972, 3(1), 35-60.

Postal, P. M. A paper which some may say is worse than it is. *Linguistic Inquiry,* 1973, in press.

Postal, P. M. *On raising.* Cambridge, Mass.: MIT Press, 1974.

Ross, J. R. *Constraints on variables in syntax,* Unpublished doctoral dissertation, MIT, 1967.

Ross, J. R. Adjectives as noun phrases. In D. A. Reibel & S. A. Schane (Eds.), *Modern studies in English.* Englewood Cliffs, N.J.: Prentice-Hall, 1969. (a)

Ross, J. R. Auxiliaries as main verbs. In W. Todd (Ed.), *Studies in philosophical linguistics: Series one.* Evanston, Ill.: Great Expectations, 1969. (b)

Ross, J. R. On declarative sentences. In R. A. Jacobs & P. S. Rosenbaum (Eds.), *Readings in English transformational grammar.* Waltham, Mass.: Ginn and Company, 1970.

Ross, J. R. Doubl-ing. *Linguistic Inquiry,* 1972, 3(1), 61-86. (a)

Ross, J. R. Act. In D. Davidson & G. Harman (Eds.), *Semantics of natural languages.* Dordrecht: D. Reidel, 1972. (b)

Ross, J. R. Endstation Hauptwort: The category squish. In P. M. Peranteau, J. N. Levi, & G. C. Phares (Eds.), *Papers from the Eighth Regional Meeting of the Chicago Linguistic Society.* Chicago: Chicago Linguistic Society, 1972. (c)

Ross, J. R. A fake NP squish. In Charles-James, N. Bailey & R. Shuy (Eds.), *New ways of analyzing variation in English*. Washington, D. C.: Georgetown University Press, 1973a.

Ross, J. R. Nouniness. In O. Fujimura (Ed.), *Three dimensions of linguistic theory*. Tokyo: The TEC Company, 1973b.

Ross, J. R. Niching. (in preparation a)

Ross, J. R. Variable strength. (in preparation b)

Ross, J. R. Sloppier and sloppier: A hierarchy of linguistically possible open sentences. (in preparation c)

Ross, J. R. Treetops. (in preparation d)

Witten, E. Centrality. In S. Kuno (Ed.), *Mathematical Linguistics and Automatic Translation*, (Report NSF-28 to the National Science Foundation, Harvard Computation Laboratory) Cambridge, Mass., 1972.

5

ON WHAT IS DEEP
ABOUT DEEP STRUCTURES

James D. McCawley
University of Chicago

I'll begin by commenting on the moral that Haj Ross presented at the end of his first section: "We linguists have to have these wildly complicated underlying structures to account for our facts; do you cognitive psychologists need the same sort of machinery to account for your facts?" Personally, I doubt that cognitive psychologists will be able to utilize underlying structures which are abstract in Ross's sense in anything other than the cognitive psychology of language (or more generally, of communication). I note parenthetically that Ross, like most linguists, uses "abstract" in a rather untraditional sense, namely that of "non-patent; far removed from the *surface*"; this is quite distinct from the traditional sense of "abstracted from the specific instances by weeding out inessential characteristics." A surface structure or a phonemic transcription is abstract in the traditional sense but not in Ross's sense.

The underlying structures that Haj talked about do not have the status that transformational grammarians generally ascribe to them. The classical literature (e.g. Chomsky's *Aspects*) and most popularizations state as official doctrine that underlying structures are postulated to explain distributional facts, i.e., the fact that such-and-such a word can occur in such-and-such environments but not others, etc. As he pointed out, the position that Ross and I take is that these underlying structures are not just supposed to explain distributions of words but are intended as some kind of approximation to the meanings of sentences. Sentences have meanings independently of the linguist's desire to account for surface distributions of morphemes, and those surface distributions are heavily influenced by restrictions on how semantic elements can combine into meanings of sentences and how the language allows semantic structures to be expressed; the "intermediate stages" of our derivations are simply our way of representing the interactions of the various linguistic mechanisms that are involved in relating meanings to possible expressions. I thus think that it is only because of a very special property of sentences, namely that they are used to express meanings, that they are amenable to an analysis in terms of underlying structures that are abstract in Ross's sense.

Is there any other kind of linguistic analysis that provides a potentially more fruitful model for possible cognitive psychological analyses? Regardless of its merits in linguistics (where I think it has been pretty well discredited), *structuralism* would seem to me to be more relevant than the approach that Ross talked about today. While there is a wide variety of structuralist conceptions of "phoneme" (for example, those of Saussure, Bloomfield, Sapir, Bloch, and Jakobson), they all constitute attempts to analyze utterances by decomposing them into pieces and identifying those pieces. Structuralist analyses yield things like phonemic represent-ations and surface structures, and my feeling is that it makes more sense for psychologists to look for things like phonemic representations and surface structures manifested in cognitive data than for things like deep structures. To take one concrete example, in the celebrated experiment in which subjects who need string to perform a task fail to perceive as string the string that is holding up a picture, it makes sense to hypothesize some kind of "cognitive map" in which the string is perceived not as string but as some kind of excrescence of the picture, but that cognitive map is related to the physical world as an identification of the pieces of the physical world, albeit an identification in terms of functions and thus more analogous to Sapir's conception of phoneme than to Bloch's.

I should add one point here about structuralist linguistics, namely that among structuralists there is widespread confusion about two distinct questions: that of what is relevant to identifying the units that are postulated and that of what characteristics of the units are distinctive, as opposed to redundant. Many physical phenomena relevant to the identification of some unit are not "distinctive" in the linguist's sense of the term. Let me illustrate this by describing my experience in learning to read and write Chinese characters, which I have been attempting to do since I started studing Japanese 12 years ago. Japanese has a really screwed-up writing system that includes an ungodly number of Chinese characters. I often write characters that to me are perfectly intelligible but which a native writer of Japanese can't decipher. In many cases the thing that I've done wrong is non-distinctive, that is, my mistake doesn't serve as the distinction between some character and another real or imaginable character but still somehow plays a role in the identification of the character. On the other hand, there are enormous differences between ways of writing the same character that native Chinese or Japanese don't notice. (Incidentally, I think that handwriting deserves much more study by linguists and cognitive psychologists than it has received; or is there perhaps work in this area by cognitive psychologists that I just don't know about?)

One area that might constitute a counterexample to my words of pessimism concerning Haj's moral, i.e., an area that might call for analyses that are abstract in Ross's sense, is music. (Have cognitive psychologists done anything on music, for example, on the identification of melodies, harmonies, rhythms, etc.? Again, I don't know.) This is the one area where I was able to come up with something that might fulfill Haj's request (in previous correspondence) for examples of things outside of linguistics that exhibit some analogue to the coordinate structure constraint or the complex NP constraint. The following musical example (from Mozart's C minor piano sonata, K. 457) may illustrate something like the coordinate structure constraint. The sonata begins with a 4-bar phrase that leads

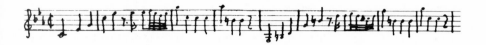

from the tonic to the dominant, followed by a 4-bar phrase that is roughly a repetition of the first 4-bar phrase but which leads from the dominant back to the tonic. Consider the turn that appears in the 2nd and 6th bars. If it were omitted in both bars, the result would still be a perfectly well-formed opening, but if it were present in only one place but absent in the other it would not be:

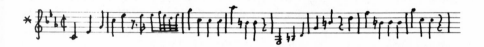

The coordinate structure constraint, stated in its full glory (which is fuller glory than in the statement of it that Ross gave today) says that a transformation may not move material into or out of a conjunct of a conjoined structure unless it does so to all the conjuncts. If it makes sense to regard these parallel 4-bar phrases as making up a conjoined structure (which I am not convinced makes sense), the requirement that the ornament be either present across the boards or absent across the boards might constitute an example of some analogue of the coordinate structure constraint.

Regarding Haj's remarks about "primacy" and universals, he oversimplified the statement of the facts about reflexivization, but if you bring in something closer to the full hairy details you can still argue for something like his implicational hierarchy. Contrary to what Haj said, it is possible to reflexivize into subordinate clauses in English, though under not well-understood conditions, as in Jackendoff's example "The fact that there is a picture of himself in the post office worries Fred." Here *himself* is in a subordinate clause "that there is a picture of himself in the post office," and its antecedent, *Fred,* is in the main clause. But here, contrary to the textbook cases of reflexivization, the use of the reflexive is optional: You can also say "The fact that there's a picture of him hanging in the post office worries Fred," with *him* referring to Fred. This is the same general kind of constraint or applicability which Ross was talking about, i.e., the rule basically applies to clause mates but can be extended to apply into a subordinate clause, with, however, a decrease in the obligatoriness of the rule: It is optional when it applies into a subordinate clause. I would expect the following universal to be true. If a rule is applicable both within a clause and into a subordinate clause, it is possible for it to be obligatory within a clause and optional when it applies into a subordinate clause, but not vice versa.

Regarding the question of the scalarity or non-discreteness of category membership, a sobering question arises: If you accept the claim that there is a scale of membership in various categories, what sense can you make out of linguists' arguments for category membership of specific items, for example, the argument given by Ross (1968) that predicate adjectives (and adjective phrases) are dominated by a node labeled NP? Since the distinction between "sentence," "predicate," and "argument" (= "NP") in semantic structure seems to be absolute, I suspect that the various categorization arguments in existence, if examined critically, will turn out to be either (a) arguments as to the category of the node in semantic structure to which a particular node in surface structure can be traced back, or (b) arguments that show where a particular item fits on one of Ross's scales. Is there any relationship between the scales and the semantic categories? It would be nice if it turned out that there was a one-to-one match between the scales and the semantic categories, with each scale corresponding roughly to a measure of how closely the item in question approximates the "unmarked behavior" of items that are traceable back to the semantic category in question; however, at the moment I have no feeling as to how "nice" things really are.

REFERENCE

Ross, J. R. Adjectives as noun phrases. In D. Reibel & S. Schane (Eds.), *Modern studies in English*. Englewood Cliffs, N. J.: Prentice-Hall, 1969.

6

ROSS-McCAWLEY
DISCUSSION

Ross: I think music is a good case to think about. At Bell Labs in New Jersey there is a melody generator. Researchers there have taken a Japanese folk song and a piece by Shubert (or somebody like that) and, using this melody generator, made a sequence of steps progressing gradually from pure Shubert to pure Japanese folk song with other "steps" being available if you want to make them. I don't know exactly what the constraints are, but they're like Gregorian chants. That is, there are some rules for generating possible sequences, and they can generate possible Japanese folk songs and impossible ones and mark them as impossible. The conclusions I would draw for squishiness here are again that it's like imprinting. That is, the concept of "Japanese folk song" is not an all or nothing, on-off predicate. This even holds for particular Japanese folk songs; that is "Is this particular melody which we have just heard a rendition of Japanese folk song x?"—is not going to be answered yes or no: The answer is going to be "sort of" or "not so much as last time," etc. Now, with respect to this, there's another musicologist whose work I know a tiny bit about. His name is Heinrich Schenker, who lived around the turn of the century in Austria. Schenker (1954) analyzed all tonal music up to roughly Strauss, to around 1900, in terms of what he called an *Ursatz,* which means something like a protoline and a set of rules that apply to expand it. So he would, for instance, derive the entire Jupiter symphony from an *Ursatz* which would be a very simple melody (perhaps with only ten notes in it) and then a set of rules which were supposed to apply to all tonal music or all of tonal music within a particular historical period. This man's work hasn't been studied by any other linguist, to the best of my knowledge. I just happened to know about it incidentially but I'm not enough of a musician to really do a study on it.

I want to say one final thing about the discussions of abstractness: Could it really be that something like that 22-sentence underlying structure for "Floyd broke the glass" is all there? How can it be psychologically real?

Let me stop speculating with this anecdote. We would be doing syntax and out would come this insane, crazy, vastly complicated unstateable fact about a language or language in general and we'd say "Oh, wow, how could that be learned?" I would say, "Look at this, it must be innate: It couldn't possibly be learned." Well, something that really changed my mind was the book by Luria (1968). Since I read about Luria's subject S, I have ceased to say, "How could it be learned?" To be sure the mind of this man was rather like a laser beam trained in the wrong direction: He had a lot of difficulty coming to terms with the so-called real world, and what Luria did was to help him get into a career as a memory specialist. But if that much information can be represented over, in this case, 50 years of a man's life, then just a little bit of that vast amount of power could be used to learn anything. If S had the right kinds of principles, if he had more than associative rules, if *we* really had a learning theory with teeth in it, I think there's a great deal that we have found universal which *could* be learned. In particular, with respect to what McCawley said and to what has often been objected against these terrifically abstract underlying entities (that they are not psychologically plausible), I am not convinced. People say "well, how could somebody be thinking of all these 22 sentences and squish through all these derivations and pack it all into 'Floyd broke the glass' in something under two seconds?" I'm not convinced that we cannot do this, given the existence of this man and this sort of demonstrated power. Luria and his associates tried to find limits on his memory, but they couldn't. They just stopped–they found it was a hopeless undertaking. So now I am perfectly willing to listen to arguments which say that in particular, this linguistic analysis is wrong from a processing view. (That is, that big tree, which I gave you, is wrong.) I think the arguments have to be empirical ones, not arguments to the effect that "well, it couldn't be the case; you just don't have the brain power."

McCawley: Another thing about Schenker which gives further reason for people interested in the kind of structure we have been talking about to look at music is his notion of tonicization, which I think provides a musical analog to the linguist's notion of subordinate clause. In a lot of his musical analysis Schenker will talk about a certain section of the composition as involving subordinate tonality, which is somehow brought into being. Relative to that subordinate tonality, you've got dominant, subdominant, etc., but this is really a subordinate clause so you have to exit from it and get back to the basic tonality of that section of the composition.

Regarding the limits of human memory, and the structures such as Ross's simplified version of "Floyd broke the glass," his choice of words was, I think, unfortunate in a couple of places in talking about it, since it would suggest an extremely common error that turns up in writing about transformational grammar and the human mind and performance, namely the error of supposing that these kinds of underlying structures have to involve mental events of construction of this entire deep structure prior to production of this surface sentence, or even simultaneously with the production of the sentence. I think that an appropriate point of view to take is that you don't necessarily have to have any kind of psychological event or point in time when all of that stuff is simultaneously present in the mind of the speaker that's producing or hearing that sentence. But it makes sense to say that it's there as a representation of the sentence, in the sense that someone who said that sentence could perfectly well correct himself on the basis of his having said a sentence whose semantic structure doesn't correspond exactly to his intentions. Postulating a representation of the sentence is necessary to explain what would go on in a person's choice of sentences. You really have to talk about the interaction between his intentions and extremely complicated structures which his language sets up in correspondence with sentences: the actual sequence of events could perfectly well be that he would say the sentence and only a few seconds later compute the actual total semantic structure which corresponds to it, but it still makes sense to say that that semantic structure is part of the psychological basis of what he does in speaking.

Halwes: First, concerning the business about generative semantics—and especially McCawley's comment that you couldn't expect to find that depth of abstractness in noncommunicative systems: I think that that is very likely *not* to be the case. It may very well be that McCawley's analysis is wrong. It seems to me to be an enormously good bet that whatever kinds of structure are involved in language are also involved in essentially everything that we do. I want to point to a few things which might make that intuitively clear; I don't think I can make the case in any kind of formal way, but I might make it plausible. One of the things that gets avoided in all of the linguistic work from M.I.T. (that I have seen) is what you might call an "aboutness relationship." We all know that communication is somehow supposed to refer to certain states of affairs in the world about which the person is presumably trying to communicate (to another organism). Now that aboutness relationship holds for essentially any kind of act, as far as I can see. Take, for example, walking. Bernstein's (1967) beautiful analysis of motor activity argues that there is what you might call a basic pattern of coordination which goes down any time a person is doing any skilled activity. There's a basic structure to my walking across the floor which you might consider to be analogous to a surface syntax, where you could analyze it into steps and the steps could be put into larger clauses where I have to turn and go this way because that's the way the aisle goes, etc. If you look at the movement as if the person were walking along in the air, you will get what Paul Weiss calls the basic pattern of coordination, which is analogous, I would suggest, to syntax in linguistics. But, in fact, the person's walking along on the ground, and there are various kinds of obstacles that he has to turn to avoid; he has to adjust his steps to the actual terrain so that in a very real sense, the walking is *about* the movement across the actual terrain. First it's about moving from here to there; secondly, at another level, it's about going along a particular pathway which has to be taken to get from here to there. And thirdly, it's about the particular fine adjustments of the basic stepping patterns which have to be made in order that I step *on* this rock instead of kicking it with my foot, etc. So I think that you're going to find that kind of aboutness relationship in any skilled motor activity, not just music and language. Also, you clearly will find that kind of aboutness relationship in perception. And when you start pushing these structures back up into semantics, it looks like what you're doing is pushing them back into an attempt to deal with what we call *knowledge,* that is, what the organism knows about the world, which is what (to use Gibson's term) *affords* all of these fancy things that we do. It seems like an enormously good bet that the knowledge which underlies our communicative acts is essentially the same knowledge which allows us to walk across the room without running into things and which allows us to see the things that we might otherwise run into.

Now about primacy. Somewhere in the middle of Ross's primacy talk the top of my head just blew open and I was ecstatic from then on. Certain things came to me and I would like to point them out as examples. The first examples are not directly concerned with primacy, but rather give some ways of getting yourself into a frame suitable for looking at the implications of Ross's linguistic work for other aspects of psychology. First, when you're dealing with sentences, you're dealing with something like grammaticality and the rejection of non-sentences, and there are certain psychological phenomena which you can use as the same kind of indicator of failure to obey the rules in other domains of behavior. There's one phenomenon called the von Restorff effect where you see a list of words, which you're supposed to remember, and they're all printed in black ink except one that's red. If there's one that's red, then you notice it and you remember it better than the others. That *noticing* phenomenon indicates that the basic structure of your processing of that material has been interrupted by violation of something, which causes noticing. Here you're aware of the material at one level, and all of a sudden you jump down to an awareness of it at another level which, before the jump, was known tacitly. The shift in awareness from one level to another, the noticing, is caused by the violation.

As a second example, there's a beautiful phenomenon that was described to us, when I was a graduate student, by Zoffia Babska, a Polish psychologist who works with children. She told us a story about a time when she presented a kid with a carrot and he took the carrot and put it in his mouth. She presented the child with a plate and he ignored the plate and didn't care much about it. She presented him with a carrot on a plate and he took the plate and put it in his mouth. There's another phenomenon called the Ames room. If you look through that room, the people are seen as different sizes even though they're not. As a fourth example, there's a thing called the Honi phenomenon where essentially if there's somebody that you love put in the Ames room they *don't* change size.

Remember this thing in Fig. 1?

Fig. 1

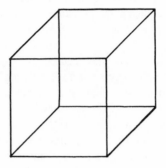

Fig. 2

That's another one. So is the Necker cube portrayed in Fig. 2. These are psychological phenomena you might look at in terms of responses that a subject may make—surprise and eating the plate, etc.—that would tell you that you were dealing with (or in this visual case the inability to construct an integrated experience of that thing which would tell you that you were dealing with) the kind of rule violations the linguists consider when they talk about grammaticality.

Now about squishiness. One of the nice things about music is that there is something analogous to linguistics in the study of music: theory. Theoreticians take Bach and decide what Bach was doing and what rules Bach was obeying when he made his music. So now you have all these rules and can show how Bach's work obeys them. Then you go look at Bach and you find that Bach violated all those rules. But when Bach violates one of these rules, it doesn't sound bad: It adds to the richness of the music. It makes a difference that he uses that particular violation. The presence of a basic structure, of a basic pattern of order in the music, makes it possible for Bach to make violations which do matter. Let me make a very bizarre speculation about the history of the development of language. One of the things that seems to be true about skilled motor acts is that, for example, if I'm going to hit a tennis ball over to the corner, there are essentially an infinite number of ways that I could do it. In fact, I will tend to do it with a certain *style*—my own personal idiosyncratic way. And the more I do it, the more I will drop into a particular style of doing it and the harder it will be for me to do it in one of the other ways that are in principle available to me. Now suppose you have monkeys talking to each other, making these noises, and they gradually drop into a certain style of making noises. You might think about that as the origins of surface syntax if you like. Now once you have a culture in which people have all gradually (through the fact that you learn from your mommy and you don't know whether this particular thing she's doing is crucial or not, as in the case of McCawley's Japanese figures, so you learn all of it that you can including her style) developed a situation wherein everybody in the community is using a particular style in certain respects, then it becomes possible to put an information load on that style. Once you've got a basic pattern structure, you can *violate* it. You can do squishy things with it and use that squishiness, or those violations of that basic pattern of structure, as a way of communicating information.

Ross: Let me say one thing which has come up now in what Halwes said and came up in a comment that McCawley made to Dulany's talk; it's a conceptual idea which is a very good thing to export from linguistics into other fields: the idea of starring things. Ungrammatical sentences are indicated with asterisks or stars. For instance, in cultural anthropology we can view man as generating a set of possible cultures and as refusing to generate ill-formed cultures. The idea of generating an ungrammatical Bach sonata or an ungrammatical culture or an ungrammatical stimulus-response link or an ungrammatical behavior sequence seems very important. For me it's even more important than looking for deep structures and transformations and things like that. The idea of shooting for the stars is a good one.

McCawley: Just a comment on one of the things that Halwes was saying. The example of walking is beautiful and worth much thought, but I'm not convinced that it really leads into anything like the kinds of derivations underlying structures that Ross was talking about. The question is whether these modifications of the basic way of doing things would be analogs to transformations in Chomsky's sense or analogs to transformations in Harris' sense (if they're in fact analogs to either). To the extent that they're analogs to either, they would look to me more like analogs to Harris' transformations, i.e., a relationship between two classes of surface structures. The question I would like to ask is whether whatever you do in walking to avoid stubbing your toe on a rock is analogous to, say, the subject raising transformation or something like that, which is involved in converting Ross's underlying structures into surface structures, or is it analogous to whatever is involved in your, say, speaking in such a way that you don't use a word which would be likely to remind the person you're talking to of some money that you owe him. I think that there are things in the use of language which are analogous to the problem which Halwes was talking about there, but which really would involve some kind of mechanism distinct in nature from grammatical rules in the sense which we've been talking about them.

Brewer: One comment about Luria's *S*. He was clearly abnormal and not representative of human mental ability. Effectively he was a tape recorder and a three-dimensional color camera. This allowed him to do things like memorizing the surface structure of anything he ever heard. Now with all the rest of us poor human beings, when you go away from this conference and someone asks you what was said and you try to recall it, you will not be able to give back surface structure of everything that was said. You will be able to give back to some extent the meanings of some of the talks. *S* couldn't do that very well: He gave back surface structures and whenever he made an error, it was because something was visually similar or sounded the same. He never made mistakes of paraphrase when one word was similar to another in meaning. He was lousy at thinking basically and he couldn't read; he couldn't comprehend paragraphs or science lessons, etc. He could memorize everything, but he couldn't understand it. What is the circumstance of a child who is trying to learn a language? Is he trying to memorize the surface of language? Or is he trying to dig up examples (just like Chomsky says), and he's got to somehow put all this together and come up with abstract structure? It seems to me that what the kid's circumstance requires of him is all those things that Luria's subject was bad at: trying to derive things and put them together and so on.

Ross: Briefly, I wasn't trying to use S for anything other than an existence proof for vast mental capacities, far in excess of what is usually discussed.

Brewer: Ross just mused that from the point of view of cognitive psychology it is hard to know what to do with material like "Floyd broke the glass." The things that look interesting are those places where the language apparatus interacts with the real world, and it does all the time when you really talk. In other words, you relate the knowledge that comes in your eyeball to what you say next. There are even examples in the language where the syntax is manipulated by those things, the classic *reference* phenomena, like "this" and "there" and pronouns—when I say "he left" I have to code it by what isn't there anymore. These kinds of phenomena are the things that look to me like ones that psycholinguists ought to be worried about. Another example occurs in "Floyd broke the glass." The thing that would be interesting would be for someone to give us an analysis, from the syntactic point of view, of a glass. Notice that when we get to glass, suddenly the analysis stops. We don't learn anything about glasses. What is it you know about glasses that makes them different than typewriters? I guess I'd like to have linguists respond to this and to Chafe's (1970) comment that this is all still fundamentally syntactic, even though the name makes it look perhaps another way.

Ross: I'll just say one very brief thing about why we don't analyze glass. The answer is we have to crawl before we can walk. I mean we will; we're getting at it, but so far it's very difficult. Here's the problem in semantic analyses. Some linguist says "Glass" has these four semantic features and they're structured like this: This one applies here, etc. Another guy says "Glass" has these seventeen features and these two apply . . . . What are you going to do? Which one is right? The thing which I think is responsible for the large amount of interest in generative grammar on the part of both psychologists and philosophers is the structures which this kind of argumentation leads linguists to postulate. The first article on generative grammar really is arguably based on simple laws about distribution. "Hit Tom." That's really got a "you" in there: It means "you hit Tom." This is so obvious that it's very hard to distinguish, to point out to people, that generative grammar is really saying something new (because there's all this traditional stuff about the understood subject). Consider a sentence like this: "I wanted a bagel." Just like "I painted a bagel," one could say, and traditional grammarians, I believe, always have said "Wrong!" McCawley and I independently have worked out arguments that "wanted a bagel" really comes from "I wanted to have a bagel." And so "bagel" here is really declausal: It's the last fragment of the old object of want, which is really "I want" – "I have"–or "I will have"–or "I will get a bagel." And one of the syntactic arguments that this in fact is a correct analysis, which was noticed by a Japanese linguist by the name of Masaru Kajita, is this. You can say "by tomorrow" is a future adverb. But it seems to occur in a past-tense clause. Supposedly you can't have that. I mean normally that's impossible so "I wanted a bagel by tomorrow" is starred. But really, i.e., conceptually, what is "by tomorrow" modifying? Well, the thing that's *gone:* It's modifying "have." "I will have a bagel by tomorrow" or something like that. "I wanted—I will have a bagel by tomorrow." Now there are syntactic arguments here like the one I just flashed by in this analysis. My paper argues that really "I wanted a bagel" should differ in underlying structure from "I painted a bagel." In this case "bagel" should be desentential: the last item of a full clause. In "I painted a bagel," no such analysis holds. Now immediately, when a psychologist or a philosopher hears that, he perks up his ears and says "Ha Ha! I understand this simple stuff! This is easy, and it takes us back to structures which are very nice for meaning." Now suppose instead we could show that the following was what we had for "I wanted a bagel", that is, there were a lot of syntactic arguments for this analysis. Suppose there was in fact something *gone* in "I wanted a bagel," and that it was something like this: "I wanted a peanut, which you could put on a bagel." Suppose we could motivate such a structure (which is not logically impossible). Immediately all the philosophers and psychologists go to sleep, because the structures which we would be unearthing would be of no interest to anybody else in any other field. Now what's interesting—and why I would disagree very much with Chafe if you have presented him accurately—is, it seem to me, that syntax, these simple things which are very easy to understand in the basic cases, gives us a way of *justifying* particular semantic analyses for which otherwise there's no justification. As I said, one guy says "this" is a semantic analysis; the other guy says "that" is a semantic analysis; You can't even fight in that case. So as soon as we can find ways of proving what the correct way to unpack "glass" is we'll do it for you, but right now we don't know how.

REFERENCES

Bernstein, N. *The co-ordination and regulation of movements.* Oxford: Pergamon Press. 1967.
Chafe, W. *Meaning and the structure of language.* Chicago: University of Chicago Press, 1970.
Luria, A. R.*The mind of a mnemonist.* New York: Basic Books, 1968.
Schenker, H. *Harmony* (Translated by Borgese). Chicago: University of Chicago Press, 1954.

7

ECOLOGICALLY STIMULATING COGNITIVE PSYCHOLOGY : GIBSONIAN PERSPECTIVES[1]

William M. Mace
Trinity College

STIMULATION AND COGNITIVE PROCESSES

On the face of it, James Gibson's approach to perception is not a likely candidate for concern in a volume devoted to problems in cognitive psychology. There is no need to argue for including perception itself under the heading of cognitive psychology, but Gibson's brand of perception is another matter. His most distinguished research efforts have focused on analyzing stimuli; and the data from his studies have been used to promulgate a theory of *direct* perception—two seemingly very uncognitive enterprises. Gibson, as anyone familiar with him knows, will never present testable processing proposals that could be recognized as normal cognitive psychology. Yet I shall offer his position, and some research on kinetic depth perception guided by it, as not only appropriate for cognitive psychologists to consider but featuring considerations without which cognitive psychology would be certainly incomplete and probably unsuccessful.

In current practice, it is the *processes* associated with a problem which tend to determine its assignment to a psychological category. Sensation, perception, and cognition are labels which suggest a scale of increasingly complex operations performed by the organism on stimuli as they journey from the peripheral receptors to the cortex, and are eventually transformed to a state of "knowledge." Ulric

[1] Research portions reported are based on a dissertation submitted in partial fulfillment of the requirements for the PhD at the University of Minnesota. The author held NIMH Predoctoral traineeship MH06668 awarded through the Institute of Child Development. The computer operations were supported by Program Project grant HDO5027 awarded by NICHD. Special thanks are due Robert Shaw for his enlightened advising and Robert Shear for his lightning programming.

Neisser, whose *Cognitive Psychology* (1967) stands as the closest thing to a manifesto in the field, defines cognition as follows:

> As used here, the term "cognition" refers to all the processes by which the sensory input is transformed, reduced, elaborated, stored, recovered and used. It is concerned with these processes even when they operate in the absence of relevant stimulation, as in images and hallucinations. Such terms as *sensation, perception, imagery, retention, recall, problem-solving,* and *thinking,* among others, refer to hypothetical stages or aspects of cognition [Neisser, 1967, p. 4, my emphasis].

In the developed common usage the inclusion of phenomena under the heading of cognition usually depended on associating them with more or less "complicated" processing concepts. Thus, in showing the role of memory and attention in domains previously counted as more or less "perceptual" (e.g., metacontrast), Neisser could bring new topics into cognitive psychology. Phenomena previously regarded as "sensational," such as pure tones, have been elevated to perceptual or cognitive status as a result of findings which show that the listener must do more integrative work on the input stimulus than previously thought in order to experience what was formerly believed to correspond directly to the excitation of receptors (Creel, Boomsliter, & Powers, 1970). The new cognitive literature shows that relating a topic to memory (and to attentional processes in particular) can guarantee admission into the cognitive empire. The reader may sense that, with processing issues guiding the grouping of phenomena, old topics studied under old categories will soon be carved up properly as the new army of cognitivists cuts through the camouflage of traditional subdivisions to attack the vital centers of information processing. However, the enthusiasm for studying the processes that transform input from the world into perception (or, in the opinion of some, knowledge) of the world has been matched by scorn for the stimulation on which the processing is based.

This dual attitude of exalting the mind's processing power and denigrating the riches of external stimuli unites modern cognitive psychologists with their predecessors in epistemology throughout history, at least since the rejection of the belief that copies of objects emanate from them and "fly" to us for immediate apprehension. This attitude is richly overdetermined (see Gibson, 1960); but, in general, it is a consequence of sharply demarcating man as knower from the things he knows. The division of scientific labor has followed these lines, with geometers and physicists studying the stimulus on one hand; and psychologists, philosophers, physiologists, etc., studying the understanding of stimuli on the other hand. The problem of how man (or any organism) knows his world belongs to the second group, whose representatives take the results achieved by the first group as their starting point – as one should if the division of labor is proper. In the case of less concerned or sophisticated epistemologists, commonsense views of stimuli rather than the views of physics and geometry might be used. In either case, the person asking how knowledge of the world is acquired does not himself ordinarily question the nature of the variables of stimulation available from the world.

The unanimity concerning where to begin work on the problem of knowledge (exemplified by visual perception throughout this chapter) qualifies as one of the more significant achievements of interdisciplinary cooperation in the history of psychology. Geometry was successfully developed and applied by the use of ideal points as basic units; physics found these concepts adequate for optics, and physiology forged the necessary link in the causal chain from world to beast by discovering units that appeared to respond systematically to the physicists' variables (see the work of Bell, Müller, and Volta described in Boring, 1942; Gibson, 1960). These developments reinforced one another sufficiently to leave no doubt that the analysis of the "light to the eye" was in good hands. One might say that the challenges for explaining knowledge of the world really began after the light got into the eye; hence the problems of epistemology were written on the retina.

But these introductory remarks have been vague and assertive. Some representatives of the attitudes toward external stimulation to which I have alluded deserve to be quoted in detail.

In his *New Theory of Vision* of 1709 Bishop Berkeley gave the puzzle of depth its present form on the foundation of Molyneux's Premise (Molyneux, significantly enough, published the first text on optics in English), which obviously takes its givens from perspective geometry: "For distance of itself, is not to be perceived; for 'tis a line (or a length) presented to our eye with its end toward us, which must therefore be only a *point,* and that is invisible [cited by Pastore, 1971, p. 68] ." Pastore compares this initial state to that of a blindfolded man being touched by the end of a pole and asked to judge how long it is. This seems a perfectly adequate place to begin perceptual investigations if we regard the retina as the picture plane onto which the world's light rays are projected. One surely receives only the points of the rays directed endwise toward one's retina. But then the distance that one does experience must come through some means. For Berkeley, these means are primarily association with touch and, secondarily, the sensations of convergence and accommodation of the eyes. Therefore perception is accomplished by adding to and correcting the stimulation so that, in this case, a three-dimensional world can be perceived from a two-dimensional stimulus.

Many modern theorists make similar assumptions about what *cannot* be in stimuli. Koffka asserted that, "Since the mosaic of proximal stimulation possesses no unity, the unity within our behavioral world cannot be explained by a corresponding unity in the proximal stimulation [1935, p. 84] ."

Boring described the function of perception as that of transforming "*chaotic sense experience* into the relative stability of permanent objects ...," then proclaimed that "Perhaps the greatest perceptual achievement of this organism is the way in which it receives on bidimensional retinas optical projections of the tridimensional world, losing, it would seem, all the tridimensionality, and then, taking immediate physiological account of the disparity of binocular parallax and other clues when they are available, instantaneously *puts the solid object together again* in perception, recovering the tridimensionality of the real object which had seemed irrevocably lost [in Leibowitz, 1965, p. 85, my emphasis] ."

A major figure in current perceptual psychology, Richard Gregory, recently described his position as one which supposes

that perceptions are constructed, by complex brain processes, from *fleeting fragmentary scraps* of data signalled by the senses and drawn from the brain's memory banks — themselves constructions from *snippets of the past*. On this view, normal everyday perceptions are not selections of reality but are rather imaginative constructions – fictions – based . . . more on the stored past than on the present. On this view *all perceptions are essentially fictions:* fictions based on past experience selected by present sensory data. Current sensory data (or stimuli) are *simply not adequate* directly to control behavior in familiar situations . . . . The fact is that sensory inputs are not continuously required or available, and so we cannot be dealing with a pure input-output system [Gregory, 1972, p. 707, my emphasis] .

Finally, returning to Neisser, "We have no direct, immediate access to the world, nor to any of its properties. The ancient theory of *eidola,* which supposed that faint copies of objects can enter the mind directly, must be rejected [Neisser, 1967, p. 3] ." And at the end of his introduction he asserted, "No shorter route seems to do justice to the *vicissitudes* of the input, and to the continuously creative processes by which the world of experience is constructed [p. 5, author's emphasis] ."

Whenever one assumes that stimulation is meager but that experience and accomplishment are rich, some rather fancy supplement to the stimulus must be provided. Examples of such supplementation were included in the above quotations. The customary model of supplementation has been logic, which has impressed many thinkers with its power to derive significant conclusions from very simple premises and rules of inference. Thus we have Helmholtz's famous appeal to "unconscious inference." A thinker who hesitates to be as specific as those who appeal to rational inference might settle for a term like "construction," which carries the connotations of building great structures from minor constituents without an early commitment to the type of detail involved. This provides another way of accounting for the inclusion of perceptual problems in the domain of cognitive psychology. Only processes common in discussions of obviously cognitive topics like problem solving and logical inference could possibly "bridge the gap between sensory stimulation and our experience of external objects [Gregory, 1972, p. 707] ."

Boring has been fairly explicit in this regard:

An object can be regarded as an as-if theory of experience. Experience would be as it is if there were permanent objects. And the properties of objects thus become generalizations about experience. So perception, in getting back of experience to the objects, is performing even in primitive man and the animals the same function that science performs in man's civilization. As the purpose of scientific theories is economy of thought, so the purpose of perception is economy of thinking [Boring, 1946, pp. 84-85] .

In the 1950's, Jerome Bruner was advocating the "new look" perception, reflecting his work in cognition, where the essential event was an act of categorization.

The use of cues in inferring the categorical identity of a perceived object . . . is as much a feature of perception as the sensory stuff from which percepts are made. What is interesting about the nature of the inference from cue to identity in perception is that *it is in no sense different from other kinds of categorical inferences based on defining attributes* [Bruner, 1957, p. 123, my emphasis] .

Paul Kolers remarked, "In resolving disparities, the visual system uses mechanisms that seem to be markedly similar to those usually reported only at a more ideational level [Kolers & Pomerantz, 1971, p. 108] ."

Let me close with Gregory's recent echo of Boring's analogy between perception and science:

> The notion of perceptions as predictive hypotheses going beyond available data is alien and suspect to many physiologists. Cognitive concepts appear unnecessary ... but there are surely strong reasons for believing cognitive concepts to be necessary .... More basically, what are essentially cognitive concepts are very familiar in all the sciences, but hidden under a different guise – the method of science.
>
> Generalizations and hypotheses are vital to organized science, for the same reasons they are essential for brains handling data in terms of external objects .... Scientific observations have little or no power without related generalizations and hypotheses. Cognitive concepts are surely not alien to science, when seen as the brain's (relatively crude) strategies for discovering the world from limited data—which is very much the basic problem of all science. Scientific observations without hypotheses are surely as powerless as an eye without a brain's ability to relate data to possible realities – effectively blind [Gregory, 1972, p. 707] .

I would suggest again, then, that the cognitive-constructivist approaches to perception go hand in hand with a commitment to the essential poverty of stimulation, and the belief that the essential features of perception bear no similarity to the available stimulation.

GIBSON'S ALTERNATIVE

Framework. James Gibson has recognized the fundamental reciprocity between characterizations of stimulation and characterizations of processing. For him, perceptual knowledge is first and foremost an adaptive relation between perceived and perceiver. A full understanding of perceptual knowledge requires simultaneously apprehending both terms of the relation. The answer to the question of how perception is possible requires showing how the nature of the perceiver's environment makes it possible, as well as the nature of the perceiver. There *is* an environment to be known, one whose properties determine what there is to be perceived and, indeed, what there has always been to be perceived so far as the evolution of any particular species is concerned. We know, from the varieties of adaptive behavior observed in organisms (as well as from their continued survival as species), that whatever perceptual processes they are using work pretty well to keep individuals in contact with their surroundings.

Gibson claims that geometers and physicists have not provided the analyses of stimuli that are relevant to perception – not from diabolical motives, but because they have never been forced to think about the structure of environments. The usual analyses of stimuli based on geometric points and lines leave a little-noticed gap between these ideal basic entities and the world of perceived surfaces, a gap that is every bit as problematic as the widely discussed one between emotive vocalizations and referential speech. In Gibson's estimation the psychologist who tries to build processing models that do justice to what we know organisms can do in the world is doomed to fail — not because he lacks the cleverness to build brilliant models, but because he is working with the wrong raw materials.

Gibson's significance for cognitive psychology lies not only in his having clearly stated what I have tried to say above, but also in his attempt to construct an alternative approach to the study of stimuli. He has made two key steps. The first is to keep in mind the physical environment to be perceived. A theorist should ask whether or not his own scheme of optical analysis could ever carry the visual information to keep an organism in contact with the significant properties of its environment. The second key step is to realize that a visual "stimulus" (or stimulus in any other modality) could easily be a "higher order." relation defined over spatial and temporal changes of pattern in the appropriate medium. Gibson has shown that when one searches, it does seem possible to discover variables of stimulation which are not only specific to significant environmental properties (e.g., slant of a surface), but also are invariant across normal environmental changes of pattern such as those arising from a change of viewpoint.

Because of the stimulus-processor reciprocity in the perceptual knowledge relation, significant changes in the description of effective stimuli will necessarily require changes in the job description and subsequent modeling of perceptual processing. Such established fields as psychophysics and anatomy would be included in the realms-for-rethinking (see Gibson, 1966). To the extent that stimulus properties which correspond to environmental properties can be found, the character of proposed processes would reasonably change from the intellectualized detective-like inferences described in the first section to the information intake processes Gibson has discussed in so many places.

A further consequence of discovering stimulus properties specific to environmental properties is the justification of Gibson's philosophical direct realism. This position is meant to emphasize the observation that animals are adaptive, rather than fallible beasts. How difficult is it to accept such a position? Admittedly organisms make mistakes sometimes—like traveling an arduous route to drink at a mirage—which could be fatal to an individual—and they could be said to have mistaken appearance for reality. But how wrong was our mistaken drinker? He did not take the sand under his feet to be water. Could he not have been mistaken because the desert heat reflected light in the same way as an oasis? Then perhaps there was no optical basis for any discrimination between mirage and oasis—in which case the "illusion" was a *necessary* consequence of the animal's being attuned to the invariant information specifying water. Furthermore, such events could not be typical in one's life as a whole. Surely there is a long list of properties and events that an organism must perceive accurately and reliably for his species to have survived. This is Gibson's initial stance, and I fail to see how even the staunchest constructivist could quarrel with it. Would the constructivist ever assert that he was seeking "the mechanisms of perception," but that the ones he might find could conceivably be *mal*adaptive mechanisms? But if the mechanisms are held to be adaptive, would not the job description of what they do (which includes a structural description of their input and surely must precede how they work) contain as full a description as possible of the environment to be perceived?

The environment. The first task in Gibson's approach to visual perception is to ask *what there is to be perceived.* His working hypothesis is that there are descriptions of light which do in fact correspond to significant properties of environments. For such correspondences to be possible he must assume (*a*) that organization does exist outside of an organism, both in the physical world of opaque surfaces and in the light structured by multiple reflections from these surfaces in a medium; and (*b*) that environmental properties at a given level of analysis can be uniquely and invariantly specified at a comparable level in this reflected light. Working on (*b*) constitutes the enterprise Gibson calls ecological optics. If fruitful, these assumptions would provide a case for rejecting the more commonly held assumptions of stimulus-environment caprice.

Physical properties of an environment which might have correspondences in light could be suggested endlessly. One could get indefinitely microscopic or macroscopic. Gibson maintains that the levels of analysis of highest priority should be ecological. Atoms and their motion are much too fine-grained an analysis of matter, and photons of light (or the geometric ideal points and lines) are correspondingly too fine-grained for analyzing light. By the same token cosmic properties of the universe's substances and light present far too coarse a level of analysis for one to expect any immediate ecological significance. One should begin, in Gibson's view, to consider the world as a concrete layout of surfaces and events of changing surface arrangement occurring in a medium which contains multiply reflected light (rather than light idealized as emanating from radiant points). Thus the environment to be considered should be the one where organisms perambulate and light reverberates.

The properties of surfaces which are significant for organisms have always made the highest claim on Gibson's classifying and analyzing capabilities. He typically tries to find basic categories which allow one to exhaustively classify all events or properties at that level of analysis. For example, surfaces may be rigid or nonrigid. There is certainly no ready-made analysis coming from any other field that tells us how to discriminate rigid from nonrigid changes in the light structured by such events and objects. It is not an early problem to be tackled with geometry if one is looking to begin with simple problems. In fact the knowledge that there are nonrigid changes in the world which we perceive as rigid (figures in movies) and rigid changes which are seen as nonrigid (ceiling fans seen at eye level; a hardboiled egg rolling endwise; wire cubes under certain strobe conditions) has discouraged people even from considering the possibility of the kind of correspondence Gibson seeks. Nevertheless he would argue that the rigid-nonrigid distinction is fundamental enough in the world to make us keep in mind the possibility that the above countercases are not really countercases, but are instead special cases which actually structure light in the manner specified even though the distal causes are otherwise. After all, the terrain stretching to the horizon is rigid. It is fundamental for all terrestrial animals in the sense that it provides (or "affords," in Gibson's terminology) support for all the animal's activities. Many other obstacles and conveniences in an organism's environment are arrangements of rigid surfaces and are, in fact, obstacles or conveniences by their very rigidity. Besides support, rigid surfaces can afford collision and thus harm organisms when contact is made too forcefully. Animals for their part are nonrigid and surely distinguishable from rigid objects. Thus the distinction is important enough on the face of it, and the evidence of animals' honoring it reliable enough for us to expect that in some way it is always expressed in the light.

The light and information. The key concept relating the structure of light to the structure of an environment for Gibson is optical information. To say that light contains information means that it is structured and that the structure can uniquely specify environmental properties. Structure is defined not over parameters of radiant light rays such as intensity, but over relations of *change* in intensity. Many significant features of an environment, perhaps all if the theory works, may be specified by virtue of their reflecting light in characteristically different patterns, which give rise to corresponding patterns of light transition or contrast. Such features of surfaces include material composition, which determines a specific texture, pattern of pigmentation, and location and orientation relative to other surfaces. Each property gives rise to differential reflection of light. As long as the patterns in light are defined over contrasts—which are determined by the various types of environmental discontinuity—the patterns will certainly be invariant over changes in amount and direction of illumination. And, whenever a relationship can be defined over ordered adjacencies of contrast, the structure will be preserved across changes in point of view since light travels in straight lines in a medium.

Gibson's basic unit of pattern, which he contrasts with the retinal image in other theories, is the optic array. This refers to the pattern of discontinuities in reflected light reverberating in a medium that converges to a potential point of observation. The optic array is the pattern of ordered adjacent contrasts in the full 360° sphere surrounding such potential points of observation. A sphere of light around a point of observation which contains no contrasts is said to contain no structure, hence no information. This would be an ambient array, but not an ambient *optic* array. Gibson argues that the unusual experiences subjects in *Ganzfeld* experiments have reported arise because the subjects have been confronted with an unchanging, homogeneous array which fails to satisfy the necessary conditions for being a stimulus for an eye, i.e., containing abrupt changes in intensity.

The fundamental structure of an ambient optic array should be defined with respect to a moving point of observation. Gibson points out that this is the natural state of any organism relative to his optical environment, and this approach allows us to avoid possible puzzles which could result from trying to relate static analyses to one another in order to synthesize dynamic relations.

The notion of discontinuity constitutes the core of every level of analysis in ecological optics. For example, some type of discontinuity must exist to distinguish surface from *Ganzfeld* (e.g., Gibson, Purdy, & Lawrence, 1955). A regular change of discontinuity may specify a unique surface texture, and can function as a unit on a new level of analysis. The texture itself may in turn change regularly in density and velocity relative to a moving point of observation, thereby specifying a surface at a slant relative to the moving point. In each case a pattern is formed by uniformities of change based on lower-level changes. This is an example of the very important notion of higher-order information. One of Gibson's most significant insights, making his program feasible, was to recognize that structure can be defined over ordered units at many levels. Consequently, failures to discover invariant optical structure corresponding to invariant environmental properties are just as likely to be a result of using the wrong relations to describe the stimulus as of selecting the wrong environmental properties to characterize. For instance, a set of variables might give rise to different outcomes when they are used to compute differences but give rise to invariant outcomes when ratios are computed; or, say, ratios of ratios. In Gibson's view the first requirement for detecting invariant properties of events is the existence of the corresponding invariant structure in the light — but the level of definition required to define the relation which is invariant across overall changes in illumination and point of view is a matter for empirical research. In Gibson's analyses, such relations would be possible wherever systematic changes in environmental properties determine systematic changes in the pattern of light contrasts constituting an optic array. Surely it would be hard to deny that some set of such direct relationships exists. One must realize, moreover, that if this possibility is acknowledged—that certain properties of an environment determine the structure of reflected light—this relationship is by no means analogous to a relation between symbols and symbolized: Rather it is a projective relationship.[2] There is no arbitrary code connecting the two, and no information loss analogous to information theoretic accounts of transmitted communications. It then follows that the optical information is available to any organism which possesses the processing structure required to compute the relational invariants specifying persistent environmental properties and the complementary variants specifying changing properties. But it is the optic array available for exploration, not a retinal image, that is the basis for perception.

Precedents. Perception, seen as an organism-environment relation, surely involves both the processing of information and the information to be processed. When we proceed on this basis, we can be primarily interested in processes if we like, but we should also pay heed to the environmental context to provide helpful constraints for limiting the class of devices we consider. In other words environmental considerations can regulate research in an area where regulation is typically accomplished only by models one is already familiar with. There are some illustrious precedents in science for using a "context of constraint" as an essential tool, if not an explanatory concept.

Invariance principles in physics are one example. Laws of nature which were fairly well understood for many years were later shown to form organized systems in their own right. When the invariance laws were made explicit, many physicists realized that they had been implicitly guided by them for some time. Recognizing

---

[2] Projective, however, here does not mean there are 1-1 correspondences between points at any level of analysis. One should not forget that an optic array may be textured by all the environment's discontinuities at once, e.g., material composition, pigmentation, pattern of illumination (including highlights and shadows), etc. What is "projected" from environment to light is an overall pattern of corresponding relations which are composed of identical nested invariants of ordered discontinuities.

that unknown laws of nature should satisfy appropriate invariance laws has helped guide the selection of hypotheses physicists formulated and experiments they conducted (Wigner, 1970).

Closer to the concerns of evolving, perceiving organisms is the work of Charles Darwin. His best-established scientific competence at the time he was working out the process of evolution was geology. He was, in fact, working actively in geology and more or less founding biogeography during his voyage on the *Beagle*. Michael Ghiselin (1969) assigns a key role to this "context of constraint" in shaping Darwin's evolutionary insights.

Finally, one of the best-loved works in science. D'Arcy Thompson's *On Growth and Form* (1969), showed how homologies across organisms could be established by pointing out that tentatively homologous structures were in fact the result of identical growth processes which had taken place in the framework of differing patterns of stress. Thompson demonstrated that the stress patterns which formed the environments of the morphological structures of interest were far simpler to understand than the relations among the detailed descriptions of features themselves; and in fact such an account proved completely adequate as a type of explanation as well as a tool for discovery.

Much more important, each of these cases is also an example of a very significant unification in its field. Where before there had been a hodge-podge of more or less "understood" local processes, there came to be a comprehensive, unifying system including each of them. Not only was it possible to discover laws of nature to unify observed phenomena, but it was also possible to show that there was another level of higher law which the laws of nature themselves obeyed. This is very much the type of function Gibson's approach could fulfill (see Shaw, McIntyre, & Mace, in press). If there is more unity to be discovered than is currently reflected in perceptual theory, it would seem that a "top-down" strategy such as Gibson's is more likely to discover it than less explicit, more local strategies.

Today investigators are conducting research on processing devices through automata theory. This discipline well recognizes that specifying an appropriate environment is a necessary aspect of defining any computing device. The relationship is integral enough that there is no clear distinction between the processor and its environment.

> The question of where a particular machine ends and its environment begins can be settled only by a convention of definition . . . .When we cannot grasp a system as a whole, we try to find divisions such that we can understand each part separately, and also understand (in that framework) how they interact. When we make such a division for purpose of analysis, each part is treated in turn as the machine of interest and the remainder as its environment. One cannot usefully make such divisions completely arbitrary because an unnatural division of a system into "parts" will not yield to any reasonable analysis [Minsky, 1967, p.19].

With more specifically evolutionary problems in mind, John Holland stresses that

> An adaptive system should seek and exploit environmental regularities–opportunities to depart from enumerative behavior – and should proceed at random only when nothing better is possible. The process of adaptation is essentially that of locating and using such regularities [Holland, 1962, p. 334].

An approach to perception which ignores the structure of environmental stimulation would at best operate under a distinct disadvantage by not searching in every possible place for assistance in making progress toward understanding. At worst it would be condemned to failure.

GIBSON ON "DEPTH"

Contrast between loose organization of "depth cues" and the grammar of ecological optics. Depth perception offers perhaps the best content area in which to highlight the contrast between Gibson and constructive perceptual theorists. Traditionally, the problem of depth, whether in the form of distance of a point from an observer or of solidity of an object, has been a special problem for vision. The Molyneux Premise stated earlier is a representative beginning. Generally it was felt that the flatness of the retinal projection surface was the main obstacle to understanding. How does one extract three dimensions from two? Explanations drew first on the feelings of accommodation and convergence of the eyes as primary cues for the distance of focused objects, but also recognized that depth was perceived at distances too great for the primary cues to be effective, as in pictures. Hence properties of patterns in the light which yielded depth were also considered even if they were regarded as secondary criteria. Pictorial cues were formulated by artists to indicate techniques which could be employed to give a three-dimensional appearance to a two-dimensional canvas. These secondary criteria include superposition, linear perspective, light and shade, aerial perspective, and the seemingly greater length in filled than in empty distance. Motion parallax is often added as a cue which is present in changing three-dimensional patterns, but of course not present in pictures. None of the pictorial cues can be an unambiguous depth index under normal viewing conditions, because we also know that paintings, which use such cues, are really flat (except under very special conditions). In linear perspective, it is known that a single static projection is geometrically ambiguous. Nevertheless these cues ordinarily function well enough for us to judge where the artist has placed all his forms in three-dimensional space. The artist's effects have often been used as evidence of the intermediary enrichment of cognitive-like processes which "add" or "infer" the third dimension.[3]

Interestingly, the pictorial depth cues, formulated as low-level empirical generalizations to assist the practice of art, have received little additional systematic analysis. No one has tried to formulate any higher laws that might be found in them. They seem very much like rules of grammar before the transformationalists,

---

[3] Gestalt psychologists were not stymied by the two-dimensional quality of the retina. They argued that the retina was just one stage of processing the total pattern and could not be divorced from the total field forces, which were three-dimensional. Rather than studying patterns intensively to find all the optical information that might exist among them, however, they studied optical patterns from their role in creating the field forces required to correspond to the perception of three-dimensional objects (see Koffka, 1935). Thus Gestalt theorists were satisfied with having a loosely structured list of cues because the field forces forged the bonds of organization (see the earlier Koffka quotation).

rules which might assert an intuitive connection between types of sentences, such as active and passive, but would search for no formal relation. Depth cues are similar to one another to the extent that they indicate depth. Yet researchers who investigate them imply that the cues just happen to be associated with depth in the world and might as well be otherwise independent. According to this view, a well-defined depth situation is one containing combinations of redundant cues. Ecological optics, on the other hand, would not settle for such a casual state of affairs. Like the transformational grammarian, the ecological optician suspects that "cues" which all yield the same type of judgment share the same higher-order depth information—which would, in turn, relate each cue to the others through an explicit rule system. There is no *a priori* reason why such relations should not exist. Indeed, partial successes in Gibsonian research during the last few years give us much promise of discovering them. Thus following the linguistic analogy, we could think of the ecological optics component of Gibsonian work as a search for the grammar of the light to the eye. This is correct as long as we recognize that the relationships relevant to perception picked up by organisms are not arbitrary (as a linguistic grammar could be), but are uniquely determined by the environment structuring the light. The processing implications are clear. The more elegantly structured and interrelated we can show environmental information to be, the more parsimonious could be the processing strategies evolved in such an environment. The more structure uncovered, the less one needs to posit imagination operating on fragmentary data to explain perception.

Gibson asks that we postpone appealing to abstract spaces which cannot be perceived and to mediational processes akin to translating codes until we have considered the possibility that the question is one of perceiving surfaces and their layout or arrangement; then we should consider very seriously the possibility that different arrangements of surfaces, in *any* direction, determine different patterns in an optic array.

One of Gibson's best-known contributions to perception is his demonstration of the role of texture gradients in depth perception. The fundamental terrain of the earth (which is opaque and textured) determines an optic array gradient of texture which proceeds regularly from a coarse to a fine grain as one describes a visual field from bottom to top. More generally, such texture gradients can specify the slant of any surface relative to a point of observation (although one actually needs more than one optic array sample for this specification). Gibson thought at one time that the gradient concept might prove powerful enough to account for most depth phenomena. For example, since the ground is the usual background against which organisms perceive objects, it was possible to account for "distance" of various objects directly by considering the fundamental background texture occluded by an object on the ground. Solid objects are composed of textured surfaces whose gradients relative to some observer would be particular to their shape and slant. Objects separated in depth from one another as well as from the observer could be specified with reference to the texture gradient of that fundamental frame of reference, the ground, by noticing the regular intervening texture transitions. Thus slant information could also provide separation information. Many ambiguous laboratory situations could be accounted for by the absence of such a specifying background; and where there were biases in the absence of stimulation, the biases tended to be in a direction consistent with the assumption that the ground was still taken as background. For example, objects higher in the visual field tend to look farther away than objects lower in the field in the absence of background texture, as would be the case if the ground were background. On the other hand, against a ceiling, the higher object would be closer.[4]

With texture gradient information, Gibson first showed that one could make strides toward unifying previously disparate types of structure in the light (see Gibson, 1950, for a full account). Although the texture gradient concept is not as comprehensive as once thought, it has provided the insight that depth may be treated as surface layout. Gibson did indicate relations which can be included in more general analyses; for the final result, whatever it looks like, promises to be some form of dynamic transformation on texture—which would surely include velocity gradients specific to the projection of surface texture to moving points of observation and yielding slant. Many common observations (some to be reviewed below) make it clear, however, that gradient information is by no means necessary for perceiving a "three-dimensional" layout of surfaces. Gibson himself maintains that what we must initially consider is a cluttered layout in which a primary fact of kinetic arrays is that textures cover and uncover each other as objects are concealed from and revealed to a point of observation. His earlier mistake, he asserts, was the attempt to formulate optical information for an uncluttered, open layout. The question we want to keep in mind, in looking at a certain class of depth effects, is this: Can we find other ways to describe optical information which approach the comprehensiveness once thought to characterize the gradient concept?

LOOKING FOR MINIMAL INFORMATION FOR SEPARATION OF SURFACES "IN DEPTH"

A research strategy described fully in Mace (1971) addressed the specific problem of finding the minimal optical information capable of specifying separation of surfaces in depth. One could then ask if such a situation contained *necessary* information for depth separation wherever it might occur, and perhaps necessary for all cases where depth is perceived. Thus an empirical groundwork would be laid for a unified theory of surface layout.

The first task was finding a case which the researcher could intuitively judge to contain the least possible known depth information that was, at the same time, analyzable. Such a demonstration would be a focal point for the experimental

---

[4] Explaining the depth cue of height on the picture plane by appealing to an assumptive ground plane might appear to be a constructivist ploy. Gibson would probably not be too disturbed, however, for the kind of experience—based "memory" assumed to be operating here is the entire visual system, developed through the "experience" of evolution to locate objects with reference to the ever-present ground plane. Gibson certainly would deny that the effectiveness of a cue such as height in the picture plane could be accounted for by particular experiences which observers stored on various occasions, then subsequently recalled from their storage-bin memory for reference in an impoverished experimental situation.

analysis required to isolate the effective information in the display. This information might be found to apply to all more complicated situations (if the proper simplification had been performed), and hence could be said to be the minimal necessary and sufficient information for separation in depth.

Principles of simplification and kinetic variable. The first task was to classify the concrete cases that might share the same minimal information for separation but could still be distinguished from one another. Ideally we might find an ordering of cases in which a hierarchy of "depth" qualities is reflected in a concomitant hierarchy of optic array information. One such hierarchy that guided these investigation begins with the *Ganzfeld,* the case of an unstructured ambient array which specifies nothing, or, "no-surface." There is no support for the concrete experience of a surface anywhere (Gibson & Waddell, 1952). With a complication of the *Ganzfeld* providing structure through some contrast, a surface at a distance from the observer can be specified (Gibson & Dibble, 1952). Here one can distinguish two subcases which are always possible in a discussion of separation. First, the perception could be reliable only for the fact of separation itself and not its amount. If could be that additional information is required to allow amount to be perceived reliably, in which case one might call the first case indeterminate and the second determinate distance.

Further possibilities arise if one considers two surfaces, each in the same direction from the point of observation, but at different distances from it. At least two properties might be determinate or indeterminate—the order of the surfaces as well as the amount of their separation already mentioned. Order refers to front-back relations relative to the point of observation. If one knows which is in front and which is behind, order is determinate. If one knows only that there are two surfaces and that they are at different distances, then order is indeterminate. These possible specifications may be applied to cases of opaque surfaces, where the depth relations would be at an occluding edge, and transparent surfaces, where one surface is seen through another. If there are surfaces in a particular environment, and information for them is contained in the optic array, then the surface layout could be said to be completely specified in the light.

Now it becomes clearer what one might be looking for if one declared an interest in finding the minimal information for separation of at least two surfaces in depth. The weakest display to qualify would be one where separation in depth alone was reliably presented in the light without specification of order or degree of separation.

Since it is well known that no pictorial cues for depth, including perspective, can specify a layout unambiguously, only displays that offer more than one sample of an optic array will be considered, i.e., kinetic arrays. (Binocular arrays offer more than one sample, but not all organisms have focusable conjugate binocular systems, whereas all organisms do obtain different samples of the array by actively exploring their environments.)

Now I shall describe the hunt for a minimal case and then some of the initial experimental analyses of the demonstration selected. Like so many enterprises in perception, it can begin with Helmholtz.

In walking along, the objects that are at rest by the wayside stay behind us; that is, they appear to glide past us in our field of view in the opposite direction to that in which we are advancing. More distant objects do the same way, only more slowly, while very remote bodies like the stars maintain their permanent positions in the field of view, provided the direction of the head and body keep in the same directions. Evidently, under these circumstances, the apparent angular velocities of objects in the field of view will be inversely proportional to their real distances away; and, consequently, safe conclusions can be drawn as to the real distance of the body from its apparent angular velocity [Helmholtz, 1962, p. 295].

Thus Helmholtz described the effectiveness of the "depth cue," motion parallax. It is a situation in which the geometry is plain and constitutes a case of potential information in the optic array. Is it detected as such? If organisms determined depth in this manner, they would be computing the differential angular velocities and comparing them for all points (geometrical points?) in their visual field (unless one were to add a filtering device which could select only "strategic" points). This would obviously be a processing hypothesis based on the assumed variable of stimulation. I shall return to the motion parallax cue later.

Two dimensions of change and projective transformations. One of the best-known monocular kinetic depth phenomena is Wallach's kinetic depth effect (Wallach & O'Connell, 1953). This is actually concerned with the perception of rigidly rotating objects rather than separation of surfaces in depth, but it also represents one of the earliest attempts to specify minimally effective information for depth and it does so in a way that would be equally appropriate to Helmholtz's case in the woods. Wallach showed that the shadows of rotating geometric objects (solids, wire figures, and straight rods), when observed on a back-projection screen, provided sufficient optical information for the correct identification of the rotating three-dimensional object. Shadows projected from the same objects when static were not sufficient to specify correctly their three-dimensional shape. Thus the changes in form of the two-dimensional shadow were perceived as projections of rigid rotations of an object rather than elastic changes of form. For Wallach the essential condition for this effect is a change in at least two dimensions. He states that "shadows whose only deformation consists in an expansion and contraction in one dimension will look flat," while "shadows which display contour lines that change their direction and their length will appear as turning solid forms [Wallach & O'Connell, 1953, p. 209]."

In 1934, Metzger (1953) demonstrated that two-dimensional shadows back-projected on a screen from a series of vertical pegs revolving on a turntable provided sufficient information for the perception of their dynamic three-dimensional configuration. Not only were shadows of the top and bottom of the pegs masked from view, but the light source was far enough away from the pegs to approximate an isometric or so-called "parallel" projection. Therefore the shadows of the individual pegs were not seen to undergo perspective changes in either length or width as the pegs revolved from a near to a far position relative to the light source. Since no changes in either size or shape of the shadows were perceived, these cannot be the two variables of optical information responsible for the perceived three-dimensionality. Wallach recognized this problem but dismissed Metzger's case because his interest was in the kinetic depth effect, which he regarded as stronger and more stable than Metzger's phenomenon (Wallach & O'Connell, 1953). White and Meuser (1960) investigated the Metzger rotating bars in some detail; they concluded that it was quite an effective depth situation and used it as evidence that simultaneous changes in two dimensions were not necessary for the perception of depth.

There is, however, still a source of projective information that must be considered as a possible explanation for Wallach's and Metzger's kinetic depth phenomena, namely, harmonic motion. Motion projected from a rotating object onto a plane surface (e.g., shadowgraph of rotating pegs) is called harmonic; i.e., given any projected point on the plane of projection, it periodically moves back and forth on a linear path, accelerating when moving inward from the end-points of its path and decelerating when moving outward from the midpoint of its path. Oscilloscope watchers have known for some years that certain combinations of wave patterns appear to specify rigid surfaces rotating in depth (see, for example, Fisichelli, 1946). These are called Lissajous patterns. All the kinetic depth phenomena discussed so far involve projected harmonic motion. But such motion is not a necessary condition for specifying the separation of surfaces in depth. This becomes clear when we consider still other situations in which kinetic depth effects are obtained, although projective information has been systematically excluded.

Gibson, Gibson, Smith, & Flock (1959) sought to test rigorously the long-accepted idea that *motion parallax* was sufficient information for perceiving depth. Their stimulus display consisted of moving shadows presented to a subject on a back-projection screen. The projected shadows were created by shining a point source of light through two transparent surfaces irregularly covered with talcum powder. These powdered surfaces were rigidly yoked on a common carriage. One surface was directly in front of the other along the observer's line of regard. When the display was static, the projection gave the impression of being a single surface of scattered dark spots. When the carriage was moved on a line perpendicular to the line of regard, however, the shadows projected from each powdered surface moved across the screen at different rates according to the geometry of motion parallax. When the texture motion disparities were large enough to be perceived easily, observers did not judge the order of depth consistently. Sometimes the faster-moving surface was seen as in front and sometimes the slower surface was in front. Thus, an example of an indeterminate order of depth effect was found. If the depth information used had been motion parallax, the faster-moving texture would have been seen in front at all times. Helmholtz was correct about his geometry and thus about the available information, but apparently not about the detected information. Therefore Gibson *et al.* concluded that *Ss* were not informed of the depth through motion parallax.

Gibson suggests that the optical information necessary to specify separation might be what he calls *topological breakage*. This concept refers to the kinetic margin separating two subsets of points which differ in texture elements sharing velocity vectors which are related in some principled way. The principle explaining the perceived coherence of texture elements into a single subset (i.e., an optical whole) was called "the law of common fate" by Gestalt psychologists. Simple examples would be flocks of flying birds, or platoons of marching soldiers. When texture elements sharing common fate are packed with sufficient density and aligned in the proper way, the optical wholes are seen as optical surfaces. Thus, a single optical surface is defined by texture elements having a common kinetic fate (i.e., proportional velocity vectors), while topological breakage, as a higher-order concept, is defined by subsets of texture elements having different kinetic fates. Gibson has also defined topological breakage as a disruption of adjacent order of texture units of one subset by another.

This is an extremely simple but powerful principle, since the information for topological coherence applies to all known cases in which kinetic depth phenomena are perceived. In this concept we seem to have an implicit principle of sufficient generality and logical necessity to account for separation of surfaces not only in three dimensions but in two dimensions as well. For instance, distinct coplanar textured surfaces which move in relatively contrary directions (i.e., that have different velocity vectors) appear to be separated by a margin of topological breakage (e.g., a crack of zero width). Notice that the Gibson *et al.* effect is an instance of transparent depth. One surface is perceived *through* another.

It would appear also that we could reach back and include the Metzger rotating pegs as an instance of the same type of transparent depth. For instance, the shadows from the pegs could just as well be projected from vertical semitransparent stripes painted on a piece of transparent plastic bent around the turntable to form a solid ring. This in turn suggests that harmonic motion might not only be unnecessary for depth in general, but for obtaining Metzger's effect as well.

The Gibson *et al.* experiment provides some very important clues to what might *not* be minimal and/or general conditions for the perception of depth. However, their experiment does not provide enough information to decide what other cases might be counted as instances of topological breakage. That is, we do not know how much or how little a pattern must be transformed for its elements to be considered as changing their adjacent order. Nor is it clear that the crucial information for separation in depth in their case could not be subsumed as a special case of occlusion information, already the most general kind of surface separation information in the literature.

Accretion/deletion of texture as information for occlusion. Whenever an opaque surface moves across another surface in depth it progressively subtracts the optical texture of the rear surface from the optic array. In the same manner, a surface which is uncovered after being behind an opaque surface is specified by the progressive addition of its optical texture to the optic array. Kaplan (1969) has demonstrated the effectiveness of this general type of information, the accretion or deletion of texture at a visual margin, for specifying separation in depth and direction of depth (that is, determinate depth) at an edge.

We know from work done in Michotte's laboratory (Michotte, Thinès, & Crabbé, 1964) that it is unnecessary to have textures on both sides of a margin to perceive determinate depth at an edge. A dark disk whose leading contour suddenly stops at a linear deletion boundary while the trailing contour continues to move is seen to disappear through a slot. Thus an occluding surface is specified in the transformation of the occluded surface alone. Having random texture on both sides of his optical margin gives Kaplan a more dramatic effect, however, for there is no discernible margin of any kind when there is no motion. This buttresses Kaplan's argument for the crucial role of kinetic information.

How could the Gibson *et al.* (1959), results be related to Kaplan's work? He achieved determinately ordered depth judgments, they did not. Fig. 1 suggests a possibility. A horizontally moving version of Fig. 1a is roughly what Kaplan presented, while Fig. 1b is like the Gibson *et al.* case. In the first case, one figure wipes out certain contours of the other; in the second, the figures wipe out one another's contours because there is no brightness difference between the intersecting and nonintersecting portions of the figures. This would almost guarantee indeterminate depth. One could also point out that there was no overall margin defined in the Gibson *et al.* pattern, only an array of mini-margins where each texture clump interacted with others. This lack of an overall margin could have contributed to the indeteminateness of the depth.

If some variation of Kaplan's accretion/deletion transformation were shown to be effective in this indeterminate depth case, it would be a very important finding, because it has already been shown to cover more cases than one might have thought at first glance. For instance, when an object approaches from a distance or we approach it, we see less and less background behind it. We also see less and less of the rear textures of the object itself. When the distance between ourselves and an object increases, background texture is accreted in the same manner that it was deleted in approach. Hence accretion/deletion can also specify approach and recession. Another instance is simply the turning of one's head to look around at the world. The direction we turn can be specified by the addition of texture and the direction we are moving away from by the subtraction of texture at the edges of our eyesockets and nose (Gibson, 1968). This could also be information for distinguishing ourselves from the world (Gibson, 1950).

To stretch his hypothesis further, Kaplan proposed a more general version, which stated that the information specifying depth at an edge is due to the *disparity of rates* of accretion or deletion at an optical margin. The texture with more accretion/deletion is behind. Then the previously described cases form a particular instance of this more general formula. That is, the preserved (occluding) texture has a rate of accretion/deletion equal to zero at the common margin.

a   b

Fig. 1. Two types of occlusion. a. One figure wiping out contours of the other. b. Figures mutually obscuring contours.

Kaplan tested the more general hypothesis by constructing displays with four different rate disparities, ranging from zero to a case where one texture was accreting or deleting at three times the rate of the other. Where accretion (or deletion) occurred simultaneously on both sides of the margin, there was no longer any information for an occluding edge, but rather a stationary margin from which (or into which) the textures were rolling, i.e., a crack.[5] Kaplan had other conditions which had no ready ecological interpretation. Ghostly margins seemed to be specified. Nevertheless there was a strong tendency for *Ss* to report the slower-changing texture as being in front for all conditions with the appropriate disparity. Thus there is a seductive unifying power in a notion as simple as the wiping away and adding of texture.

Limitations of Kaplan's formulations. Powerful as Kaplan's hypotheses appear, however, they work best *post hoc*. The most fundamental difficulty arises when we consider his second, more general hypothesis. To define a *rate* of accretion or deletion in order to calculate a disparity of rates requires that we be able to count texture elements affected per unit time. Kaplan used randomly distributed texture elements on either side of the margin so that any counting method would work, since each side had approximately the same configurations. But imagine that the texture units on one side of the margin are several times longer than on the other side and that the motion at the margin is across this length. Assume also that the distance between elements is identical for both textures, and that the speeds are the same. If the rate of accretion/deletion is defined over the *number* of elements added or subtracted per unit of time then the smaller texture should be seen as behind. But it is easy to imagine a "texture element" whose progressive addition or subtraction is readily apparent; enough so that it would give a Michotte-like "rabbit-hole" effect if seen in isolation. Would we still wish to maintain that accretion/deletion had to be defined over the *number* of whole units which come or go? If not, what would be a unit on this larger texture surface? The rate of accretion/deletion at a margin can be defined only when a general rule relating density of texture, size of texture units, and number of texture units can be defined rigorously.

Thus we should be alert to the possibilities of disambiguating the Gibson *et al.* optical information, for accretion/deletion is not so patent a candidate for expressing the generality of depth information as we might first think. It would be very satisfying if an adequate explanation of the Gibson *et al.* effect might be extended to Kaplan's cases and restore the trend toward unity that was lost when it was only beginning to form.

Relative motion alone. Another result in the Gibson *et al.* paper should receive more attention than it has: The investigators included a condition in which there was just a single opaque spot on each of the parallel transparent surfaces. One spot

---

[5] It should not be assumed that simultaneous accretion or simultaneous deletion at a margin is necessary information for specifying a crack, since a contrary parallel rectilinear translation of texture is also sufficient to determine a margin without depth (i.e., a crack). Such a transformation can be termed a shearing of adjacent texture at a margin whose contour is defined by the direction of contrary translations.

was placed higher than the other, so that there was *no* occlusion information. Nevertheless subjects reported separation in depth when they saw the differential motion. Here, then, is an example of a depth effect carried by something other than the well-known variables that have been discussed. The spots are merely moving relative to one another. They are near each other but they do not intersect. This is an additional reason to suspect that the major effect in Gibson *et al.* does not depend upon occlusion. That possibility will be examined shortly.

Figural conditions for separation in depth. Up to this point the primary emphasis has been on the transformations shown to be sufficient to produce the perception of depth. However, as the difficulties of Kaplan's hypotheses begin to make clear, a truly general formulation of the optical information which specifies depth must take into consideration spatial structure as well as kinetic structure. An acceptable generality (even of a subset of depth cases) must rigorously relate figural and motion properties, just as Kaplan must relate size, number, and density of texture elements to generalize the applicability of the notion of rate of accretion or deletion of texture. Even when not discussing it explicitly, all the aforementioned studies require some specification of the spatial organization to which a transformation of interest will apply to produce depth. For example, some of the displays in Green (1958) showed that certain small, scattered groups of points were insufficient to carry the depth information of a projective transformation.

Some striking instances of the role of figural properties in depth separation were collected by Wallach, Weisz, & Adams (1956). For example, a solid figure-eight shape with no visible discontinuity within its margins appeared to separate into two circles when rotated on a turntable. The circles seemed to revolve independently of one another, one sliding *over* the other. Less symmetric figures such as arrows did not show this effect.

More generally, two types of factors must be considered in any instance of perceptual organization: those which produce coherence and those which produce separation; or information for continuity and discontinuity. For the moment we are most interested in separability or discontinuity in depth. Spatial and kinetic structure may, of course, contribute to either. Hence the necessity of relating the two to define the perceptual information in any event. Johansson (e.g., 1958) has been particularly explicit about specifying both synthesizing and dissociating types of perceptual information.

From speculation to research. We cannot proceed, however, to proposals for the proper segmentation of the optic array into organizing and separating-in-depth factors without certain data. Of all the cases reviewed to this point, the Gibson *et al.* situation stands out as particularly promising. Here a random texture that looks like a single "cloud," when transformed by a mere interpenetrating motion of two subsets of texture, separates perceptually into two noncoplanar surfaces which are not consistently ordered in depth. It appears simple in terms of the information involved as well as with respect to its perceptual consequence from the standpoint of the ecological optics hierarchy presented above; that is, it is an indeterminately ordered depth phenomenon.

What factors are necessary to obtain the perceived separation? Is occlusion required? A random texture was used. Does this contain some necessary spatial structure? The result of the two-spot condition suggests the possibility that neither occlusion nor any spatial structure beyond proximity is needed. But we should be extremely wary of generalizations from two spots to a set of spots or a *texture*. What are the kinetic structural conditions on the separability? Is one pattern of relative motion as good as another as long as one set of spots moves closer to another set? The general question to be posed, then, is: What spatial-kinetic patterns yield separability in depth of the sort obtained by Gibson, *et al.* (1959)?

Pilot demonstrations. The availability of a laboratory computer with an associated cathode ray tube made it possible to artificially structure a large number of patterns of theoretical interest.

The first pattern constructed presented the Gibson *et al.* situation with modifications suggested by the last section. Thus regular, rather than random, patterns were used and there was no occlusion when the two patterns intersected. The patterns are shown in Fig. 2. Each is composed of a lattice of dots all moving with exactly the same motion. Is that sufficient information to specify a surface? When the two patterns intersect without occlusion, would the surface character-istics (if there were any) disappear or maintain their integrity? The intersecting patterns could be considered as somewhat similar to groups of soldiers marching through each other. Then the effect would not be one of depth, for the points would be coplanar.

The actual result was striking and unambiguous. One pattern did indeed appear to be in front of the other. The judgments shifted, thereby indicating that the separation in depth was an indeterminate one, but the basic separation was undeniable. It was extremely difficult to see the points as coplanar. All persons who saw this pattern immediately described it without prompting as one thing moving in front of another and were surprised that there should be any problem, because the phenomenon was so apparent.

Clearly neither occlusion nor a random array is necessary to obtain separation in depth. What is necessary? Can variables be isolated which manipulate the perceived separation? Or will all patterns with *any* detectable motion disparities separate? The investigations to be described explored these possibilities.

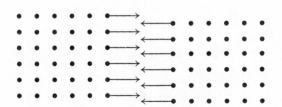

Fig. 2. Schematic representation of pattern used in pilot demonstration. Pattern was small enough relative to the CRT screen that all four margins of each were visible.

EXPERIMENTS

Four ways of modifying the demonstration pattern were selected for experimental analysis.

1. Optical margins or contour. One of the most important types of discontinuity in an optic array is determined by occluding edges in the world (Kaplan, 1969). Kaplan's patterns contained these edge-specifying margins, as did the primary demonstration pattern of Fig. 3. The former was generated by the accretion or deletion of texture, whereas margins in transparency situations result from brightness differences that supposedly could not be described as additions or subtractions of texture. The brightness differences of Fig. 3 are created by changes in texture density. The random textures of Gibson, *et al.* (1959) did not have margins. Hence we ask the question: what is the role of optical margins in the separability of *regular* patterns?

2. Phase. The language of periodic phenomena can be applied conveniently to both the spatial and the kinetic structure of patterns. The lattice patterns used, in these symmetry terms, could be described as the result of two independent translations (Coxeter, 1969). Two types of interaction between identical patterns were of interest. In the first, sections of which are shown in Fig. 3, the rows of one pattern moved directly between the rows of the other pattern. A pattern of this type was called spatially "out-of-phase." In the second type of pattern, naturally called "in-phase," the rows were collinear so that the patterns periodically intersected perfectly.

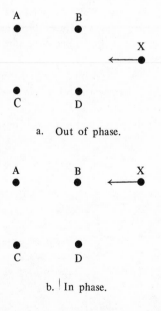

a. Out of phase.

b. In phase.

Fig. 3. Two degrees of "disruption of adjacent order." In a, only one adjacency is disrupted; in b, four adjacencies are disrupted.

The terms referring to phase reflect the frame of reference leading to the use of this variable in the design, but it is certainly not the only frame of reference that would make these patterns interesting. Gibson *et al.* (1959) discussed their separation effect in terms of the disruption of adjacent order of texture elements. If the latter is a proper description of separability information, would it not be plausible to assume that disrupting more adjacent orders would increase the separability effect? Figure 3 shows how "in-phase" and "out-of-phase" patterns disrupt adjacent collinear orders. A point moving "in phase" disrupts only the AB adjacency, while a point moving "out of phase" disrupts BD, AD, BC, and finally AC.

3. Type of motion. Three combinations of motions of the two patterns were selected to compare their depth-inducing capabilities with the other factors on depth-inducing capabilities. In the demonstration pattern, the two patterns moved across the display from opposite directions. Could there be a noticeably different effect if one of the patterns remained static, perhaps as a more stable frame of reference? Patterns of each type were used. The third type of motion was an oscillation of one lattice within another instead of a translation through it.

4. Direction of motion. It was observed in some demonstration patterns that the direction of one pattern's motion across another might make a difference for perceived separation. A lattice moving across an identical static lattice did not necessarily give symmetric perceptions. If the motions were diagonal, separation appeared to be better than with either vertical or horizontal motion.

Shaw (see Shaw *et al.,* in press) has explicitly incorporated the separating-in-depth capacity of diagonally moving rectangular lattices in a symmetry group analysis of these pattern effects. Briefly, he argues that diagonal motion can be viewed as a pattern discontinuity like an optical margin or an "out-of-phase" intersection. The essential assumption is that the spatial arrays are geometric lattices and thus by definition can be thought of as being generated by two independent translations whose basic units of translation are both discrete and proportional in size. Given the directions of these two translations, it can be shown mathematically that in general no motion in the third direction could be generated whose basic unit of translation is either the same size as or even a rational proportion of the bases of the other two—with the exception of a few isolated cases. The same vector basis could be preserved, however, if the display were resolved as a case of transparency, containing patterns at two distances from the observer instead of one. This appears to be a broadly applicable analysis which might be a strong candidate for being a necessary abstract condition that optical structure must satisfy in all cases of perceived depth.

This is a very important empirical juncture. The forms of discontinuity represented could all function as separability factors, but we have no idea how they compare or interact since none of them seems to have ever been manipulated before. The results of these comparisons should tell us a great deal about the direction a comprehensive theory of separability should take; that is, we shall know which instances we must try to include under a common characterization. Of course, the logical necessity for common factors to hold across depth situations cannot be concluded from this or any other set of experiments, since universal claims are only related to a summary of empirical findings. But insofar as common optical conditions can be found to hold across different depth phenomena, to that extent our confidence in the unified depth hypothesis will be strengthened.

Results

To distinguish the effects of each pattern, adults were asked to rate the quality of the separation in depth of each one on a 7-point scale after they had first spontaneously described the whole set of patterns.

Since some depth was reported in most patterns, it was evident that separability information was available. The effects obtained were, like the demonstration pattern, of transparent, indeterminate depth separation.

The most effective separability factor was diagonal motion of the rectangular lattices through one another—a finding consistent with impressions based on the pilot displays. This is the only effect that holds up under repeated experimentation with equal strength, and is the result that has received the most attention in the formulation of new theories (Shaw *et al.*, in press). What was not expected was the striking difference between horizontal and vertical patterns. Horizontal displays were judged better separated in depth than their vertical counterparts. This has been replicated enough to suggest further attention, but since it seems to require somewhat special conditions and since it is not at all clear where to fit it in theoretically it has not received as much attention as the diagonal effect.[6]

Out-of-phase patterns reliably increased the separability achieved by any particular in-phase pattern, but this gain was negligible in the presence of contour or diagonal motion. Type of motion used had no systematic bearing on separability. Contour played a more complicated role in separation, a role which has not been replicated since and, consequently, will be regarded as an ineffective factor.

Despite the fact that depth was reported at least once in all displays, the lattice with no margin which was moving vertically over another lattice in phase was rated by 6 of the 11 observers in the experiment as having *no depth separation at all* (a rating of 0 on the 0–6 scale). Thus mere relative motion of two subsets of dots, micro-accretion/deletion of texture elements, and the disruption of adjacent orders of elements *per se,* are each insufficient to produce depth. To say, then, that the elements of a set are adjacent is not enough to tell what transformations will provide the discontinuity necessary for separation in depth. A truly general

---

[6] All lattices used in these experiments were rectangular, i.e., the vertical and horizontal spacings between points were not equal. A full replication of this 36-pattern study using square lattices (the "second experiment" mentioned above has used rectangular ones) showed that only the diagonal interaction significantly accounted for perceived differences in quality of separation. However, the horizontal patterns were still stronger than the vertical ones and this difference almost reached statistical significance. Hence the horizontal-vertical difference is probably not attributable solely to the rectangularity of the lattices in the experiment being described. The same experiment with the square arrays also failed to replicate the phase effect. There was only a small trend in favor of the out-of-phase patterns. Therefore diagonal interaction must be considered the only reliable effective factor enhancing separation here.

definition of depth information must describe more structure in an array to establish clearly the nature of the continuity relative to which some depth-producing discontinuity can be specified.

Later experiments indicated that the effective "diagonality" must be defined in terms of the pattern's internal structure and not with respect to either an environmental or an observer's frame of reference. This was pointedly demonstrated in the finding that interpenetrating *random* (not lattice) patterns looked well separated regardless of the direction of their interaction. Shaw's analysis shows how certain symmetry considerations might handle these results. The analysis is stated in terms of the regular lattice case; but, since it depends on an interaction between the spatial and the kinetic structures of the display, it could well be generalizable to the finding with random patterns.

SUMMARY AND CONCLUSIONS

Assume it known that animals see surfaces and their layouts, including what have historically been called their depth relations. When proposing how this might be accomplished, from Gibson's point of view, we first try to ascertain the richness of available information; then, if we want to think about the types of processing which might be computing functions of this available information, we seek processes whose structure is compatible with the information putatively used. Theorists like those quoted initially have imagined processes which must produce the known riches of perceptual accomplishment from rather austere stimulation. That is, these theorists need enriching operations. The type of machinery that lends itself to such enriching operations seems to be that which stores what it can in memories, then operates on the stored material with various inferential procedures. This is one type of physical world—stimulus-processor compatibility. However, if the stimulation is thought to be rich and informative, then the structural complexity (which could still be great) of the processes that put one in touch with one's environment might be thought to derive from the necessity for structural compatibility with the available stimulus relations themselves — in the same way that a language processor must be compatible with the structure of the language being processed. The function of having wondrous perceptual processes would then be to find environmental structure rather than to make it up or to assume it on the basis of only suggestive evidence.

Gibson has argued in many places that viewing the function of perceptual processes as one of detecting available information removes the need for appealing to memory-store-plus-inference models of perception. He stresses that memories as such are not required but rather appropriately structured detection devices. Gibson by no means denies the existence of memory functions if we mean by a memory function that an organism's past is very much a part of his present. But Gibson does deny that memories of the sort that might be stored in the bins of a general-purpose storage area play a role in the perception of the significant properties of an organism's environment. In Gibson's detection of pattern invariants over time, the perception of surface layout and events is treated as one might treat the perception of a melody. Recognizing that there is a structure to be detected, in this case the melody, one does not then propose that the individual notes must be remembered in order to compare them with one another and then decide what the melody is on the basis of inferential processes. One must say, however, that the processor can detect structure over time and that this structure is in some sense compatible with the structure of the melody (but this does not commit one to a storage-and-retrieval model of melody detection).

As his alternative conceptualization of processing, Gibson has used the idea of resonance to portray the general type of activity he has in mind. Shaw and McIntyre's chapter in this volume and the recent writing of Karl Pribram on holographic models of memory represent the major progressive elaborations of the resonance model that exist in psychology to date. The resonance concept is one way of capturing what I previously called the structural compatibility between stimulus information and its processors.

The particular research this chapter described was addressed to the problem of specifying the available and used information for separation in depth. It was based on the assumption that certain yet-to-be-discovered abstract conditions are the same across all cases of depth separation. This assumption reflects faith in the unity of the world and of the organisms which have adapted to it. I would argue that for the time being this is heuristically the most fruitful assumption, even though it may be a difficult one to accept. The alternative assumption, that organisms have banks of very specialized detectors for specialized situations, such as one device (or even program) for computing depth from motion parallax, another for superposition, another for perspective, and so on, simply does not seem likely to motivate systematic research.

A selective review of the literature showed that there have been few attempts even to propose a type of depth information available in all instances of perceived separation of surfaces. Of the conditions offered, none was necessary. A demonstration case which did yield depth but apparently involved only the stimulus variable of disruption of adjacent orders of elements (also called topological breakage) in moving lattices was described. However, the insufficiency of topological breakage as an adequate description of separability information was demonstrated in a set of experiments which showed that the disruptions of adjacent order were effective only in certain pattern configurations.

The difficult problem at this point in the program is identical to that encountered in Kaplan's research on depth at occluding edges. It might be stated as the problem of finding a description of the optical events which generalizes the effects of transformations of texture (such as accretion/deletion) across arbitrary textures. It might be that a solution to the current problem would indeed be applicable to other cases of depth separation and hence be a candidate for the necessary and minimal depth information being sought. If these displays were easier to work with than other classes of patterns conceivably bearing the same information, then they would have served their purpose admirably. One might say that they would have proven ecologically relevant after all.

We are not lost in the woods without a compass. The symmetry approach described in Shaw et al. (in press) has the necessary abstract properties that we know a proper analytic scheme needs (e.g., naturally characterizing invariants across transformations and being able to deal with spatial and kinetic structures in a unitary way). In fact, symmetry principles have been proposed there as formal underpinnings for Gibson's work at the level of the basic epistemic relation between organism and environment. The same principles have also been applied to the research described in this paper and other key problems in event perception. In each case the analyses are sketches waiting for much more detail. But the symmetry framework has been fruitful enough to justify concerted efforts to develop it much further.

In general the psychologist must know what the effective stimulus is in a given situation. Contrary to past theory and practice, this is not merely a routine task of manipulating a few isolated stimulus "dimensions" to see which one the organism responds to. It is a task of hypothesizing and verifying stimulus structure which, like the task of writing grammars, demands as much cleverness in imagining possibilities and ways to test them as any processing problem. The particular research efforts described in this paper were meant to dramatize this point. They seem to be as interesting and as fruitful as any strictly process-oriented research being done. A great many problems, new and old, remain, but many seem solvable if we do the concerted theoretical and empirical work required.

REFERENCES

Boring, E. G. *Sensation and perception in the history of psychology.* New York: Appleton-Century-Crofts, 1942.

Boring, E. G. The perception of objects, *American Journal of Physics,* 1946, **14**, 99-107. Reprinted in H. Leibowitz, *Visual Perception.* New York: Macmillan, 1965.

Bruner, J. On perceptual readiness. *Psychological Review,* 1957, **64**, 123-152.

Coxeter, H. S. M. Introduction to geometry (2nd ed.) New York: Wiley, 1969.

Creel, W., Boomsliter, P., & Powers, S. Sensations of tone as perceptual forms. *Psychological Review,* 1970, **77**, 534-545.

Fisichelli, V. R. Effect on rotational axis and dimensional variations on the reversals of apparent movement in Lissajous figures. *American Journal of Psychology,* 1946, **59**, 669-675.

Ghiselin, M. T. *The triumph of the Darwinian method.* Berkeley: University of California Press, 1969.

Gibson, E. J., Gibson, J. J., Smith, O. W., & Flock, H. R. Motion parallax as a determinant of perceived depth. *Journal of Experimental Psychology,* 1959, **58**, 40-51.

Gibson, J. J. *The perception of the visual world.* Boston: Houghton Mifflin, 1966.

Gibson, J. J. The concept of the stimulus in psychology. *American Psychologist,* 1960, **15**, 694-703.

Gibson, J. J. *The senses considered as perceptual systems.* Boston: Houghton Mifflin, 1966.

Gibson, J. J. An outline of experiments on the direct perception of surface layout. Unpublished manuscript, Cornell University, 1968.

Gibson, J. J., & Dibble, F. Exploratory experiments on the stimulus conditions for the perception of a visual surface. *Journal of Experimental Psychology,* 1952, **43**, 414-419.

Gibson, J. J., Purdy, J., & Lawrence, L. A method of controlling stimulation for the study of space perception: The optical tunnel. *Journal of Experimental Psychology,* 1955, **50**, 1-14.

Gibson, J. J., & Waddell, D. Homogeneous retinal stimulation and visual perception. *American Journal of Psychology,* 1952, **65**, 263-270.

Green, B. F., Jr. Some conditions for the occurrence of the kinetic depth effect. *American Psychologist,* 1958, **13**, 406 (Abstract).

Gregory, R. L. Seeing as thinking. An active theory of perception. *London Times Literary Supplement,* June 23, 1972, 707-708.

Helmholtz, H. *Physiological optics.* (Edited by J. P. C. Southall) Vol. 3. New York: Dover, 1962.

Holland, J. Information processing in adaptive systems. *Excerpts Medica International Congress Series* No. 49. Information processing in the nervous systems. Proceedings of the 22nd International Union of Physiological sciences, 1962, 3,

Johansson, G. Rigidity, stability, and motion in perceptual space. *Acta Psychologica,* 1958, 13, 359-370.

Johansson, G. Perception of motion and changing form. *Scandinavian Journal of Psychology,* 1964, 5, 181-208.

Kaplan, G. Kinetic disruption of optical texture: The perception of depth at an edge. *Perception & Psychophysics,* 1969, 6, 193-198.

Koffka, K. *Principles of Gestalt psychology.* New York: Harcourt, Brace, 1935.

Kolers, P. A., & Pomerantz, J. R. Figural change in apparent motion. *Journal of Experimental Psychology,* 1971, 87, 99-108.

Leibowitz, H. *Visual perception.* New York: Macmillan, 1965.

Mace, W. An investigation of spatial and kinetic information for separation in depth using computer generated dot patterns. Unpublished doctoral dissertation, University of Minnesota, 1971.

Metzger, W. *Gesetze des Sehens.* Frankfort: Waldemar Kramer, 1953.

Michotte, A., Thinès, G., & Crabbé, G. Les compléments amodaux des structures perceptives. *Studia Psychologica.* Louvain: Publications Universitaires de Louvain, 1964.

Minsky, M. *Computation: Finite and infinite machines.* Englewood Cliffs, N. J.: Prentice-Hall, 1967.

Neisser, U. *Cognitive psychology,* New York: Appleton-Century-Crofts, 1967.

Pastore, N. *Selective history of theories of visual perception: 1650-1950.* London: Oxford University Press, 1971.

Shaw, R. E., McIntyre, M., & Mace, W. The role of symmetry in event perception. In R. B. MacLeod and H. Pick (Eds.) *Studies in perception: Essays in honor of J. J. Gibson.* Ithaca, New York: Cornell University Press, in press.

Thompson, D. W. *On growth and form.* Cambridge: Cambridge University Press, 1968.

Wallach, H., & O'Connell, D. The kinetic depth effect. *Journal of Experimental Psychology,* 1953, 45, 205-217.

Wallach, H. Weisz, A., & Adams, P. Circles and derived figures in rotation. *American Journal of Psychology,* 1956, 69, 48-59.

White, B. W., & Meuser, G. Accuracy in reconstructing the arrangement of elements generating kinetic depth displays. *Journal of Experimental Psychology,* 1960, 60, 1-11.

Wigner, E. *Symmetries and reflections.* Cambridge: M.I.T. Press, 1970.

8

CONSTRUCTIVE THEORY, PERCEPTUAL SYSTEMS, AND TACIT KNOWLEDGE

M. T. Turvey
University of Connecticut and Haskins Laboratories

In preparing comments on Mace's chapter I found myself in the pleasant position of having nothing to criticize. I am sympathetic to Gibson's theory of perception and I feel that Mace's comments on Gibson and the constructivist alternative are both justified and well put. I will therefore touch upon three topics which are related, if only tangentially, to the issues discussed by Mace. First, I will make additional comments on constructive theory with special reference to the domain of such a theory; second, I will address the idea that "perceptual systems" as defined by Gibson can play several different roles in the perceptual process; and third, I will comment on analysis-by-synthesis to draw a distinction between tacit and explicit identification along the lines suggested by Michael Polanyi (1964, 1966).

CONSTRUCTIVE THEORY AND LINGUISTIC PERCEPTION

Constructive theory assumes that perceptual experience is not a direct response to stimulation. Rather, perceptual experience is constructed or created out of a number of ingredients, only some of which are provided by sensory stimulation. Other ingredients in a perception recipe are provided by our expectation, our biases, and our knowledge of the world in general.

In the extreme constructivist view all perceptual experiences are constructed "from fleeting fragmentary scraps of data signalled by the senses and drawn from the brain's memory banks — themselves constructions from snippets of the past [Gregory, 1972, p. 707]." The extreme constructivist position expressed in this quotation (and criticized by Mace) is conveniently satirized in an analogy drawn by Gilbert Ryle (1949): A prisoner has been held in solitary confinement since birth. His cell has no windows but there are some cracks in the walls through which occasional flickers of light may be seen, and through the stones occasional tappings and scratchings may be heard. On the basis of these snippets of light and sound our prisoner-hero becomes apprised of unobserved happenings outside his cell such as football games, beauty pageants, and the layout of edges and surfaces. In order for our prisoner to perceive these things he must, of course, know something about them in advance. But we should ask how he could ever come to know anything about, say, football games except by having perceived one in the first place.

Ryle's analogy underscores the fact that constructivism in its extreme form takes its departure from traditional image optics rather than Gibson's (1966) ecological optics; it denies richness and variety of stimulation at the receptors and consequently denies the elaborateness of the perceptual apparatus. But if we accept Gibson's arguments for information in stimulation and for perceptual machinery capable of detecting that information then the extreme constructivist view is unnecessary. Thus, for example, given Mace's arguments and demonstration, we need not interpret Wallach and O'Connell's (1953) kinetic depth effect as a perception synthesized out of information collected over a period of time (cf. Neisser, 1968, 1970). That is to say, we do not have to interpret the perceptual experience of a rigid, three-dimensional rotating object as the result of combining successive retinal snapshots of a two-dimensional form. The constructivist interpretation of the kinetic depth effect arises, in part, from the failure to appreciate that transformations of patterns are probably more stimulating and informative than the static patterns themselves.

The main thrust of Gibson's theory, vis-a-vis constructivism, is that complex variables of stimulation specify directly the properties of the world. Perception of the environment corresponds simply and solely to detection of these variables of stimulation, and no intermediary intellectual steps are needed to construct perception out of what is detected. Gibson, of course, does not argue that all perception is of this kind; that is, he does not argue that all experiences called perceptual are a direct function of stimulation. Indeed, he admits that some perceptual experiences are not a function of stimulation at all (Gibson, 1959, p. 466). However, he does believe that perception is exclusively a function of stimulation where conditions of stimulation permit.

One apparent exception to Gibson's principle of direct perception is the perception of either spoken or written language. Given what we know about speech perception in particular (Liberman, Cooper, Shankweiler, & Studdert-Kennedy, 1967), and language perception in general, we can paraphrase Gibson by saying that the conditions of linguistic stimulation do not permit direct perception. The comprehension of linguistic items received by ear and by eye relies heavily on the context in which the items are occuring. Perception of both spoken and written language proceeds faster than it should and it is remarkably unaffected by a variety of omissions and errors. Thus, interpretation of a verbal item in normal spoken or written discourse is in some part dependent on our prediction of what the event might be, and is not simply dependent on the stimulation provided by the item itself. Predictions of—or expectations about—a linguistic event derive from three major sources: our knowledge of what has just been perceived; our internal model of the language, i.e., our knowledge of the various linguistic rules; and our knowledge of the world.

Of course, I have just described the approach to perception known as analysis-by-synthesis, which has assumed a central role in modern constructivist theory (see Neisser, 1967). Yet, while analysis-by-synthesis and constructive theory may prove to be useful to our understanding of the perception of linguistic information by ear and by eye (although it goes without saying that not everybody necessarily agrees; see Corcoran, 1971), they may not prove particularly useful, or even relevant, to other kinds of perception. There are many good reasons for believing that speech perception and reading are special perceptual activities that may not be representative of how perception occurs in general. To begin with, speech perception appears to involve an articulatory model—i.e., a production model (see Liberman *et al.,* 1967). Both experiment (e.g., Corcoran, 1966; Klapp, 1971) and clinical observation (e.g., Geschwind, 1970) suggest that reading is at least in part parasitic upon the mechanisms of speech. No compelling evidence suggests that other forms of perception proceed by reference to a production model. The special character of linguistic perception is further supported by Mattingly's (1972) argument that grammar emerged as an interface between two mismatched nonlinguistic systems which had evolved separately. On the one hand we had mechanisms concerned with transmission—the ear and the vocal apparatus—and on the other we have an intellect which represents, rather amorphously, I suspect, the world of experience (i.e., the mechanism of long-term memory). Grammatical codes, therefore, convert representations of experience into a form suitable for efficient acoustical transmission, or convert phonetic events into suitable form for long-term storage (Liberman, Mattingly, & Turvey, 1972). And surely this kind of radical conversion is at the heart of constructivist theory; both linguistic perception and linguistic memory are restructurings of stimulation. But we should ask, as Liberman (1972) has, whether such radical conversions occur in other perceptual situations.

It is perhaps instructive to note that hemispheric damage which results in the reading impairment generally referred to as word blindness or alexia may leave unimpaired the ability to name objects (Howes, 1962). But more important is the observation that alexic patients generally have no difficulty perceiving the spatial aspects of things such as distance, shape, size, and movement, that is, the properties of stimulation Gibson is primarily concerned with. We should also note a rather perplexing observation reported by Kohler (1951) concerning the Innsbruck investigations on the reversal of the visual world by means of prisms. After weeks or months during which the visual world is seen through prisms which reverse it, the visual world may quite suddenly return to normal. But when this reversal occurs, writing may remain reversed; the perception of written language apparently involves at some level a special visual process. The point is that answers to the question "How do we perceive linguistically?" should not be viewed as answers to the question "How do we perceive?"

PERCEPTUAL SYSTEMS REGISTER MORE THAN INVARIANCES

Traditionally the senses have been conceptualized as passive conduits which transmit imperfect images from the retina to the brain, where they are represented as collections of raw sensations and out of which perception is eventually fashioned. For each kind of sensory experience there is, reputedly, a special sense;

thus, the special sense of vision is the source of visual sensation, the special sense of proprioception is the source of the sensation of one's own movements, and so on. The convention has been to classify the senses by modes of conscious quality.

By contrast, Gibson proposes that the senses are active systems which register the invariant structures of available stimulation furnished at the receptors and which afford the observer direct knowledge of his environment. In this view, the "senses"—which Gibson prefers to call perceptual systems—detect information rather than yield sensations and are classified by modes of activity rather than by modes of consciousness. Thus looking and listening replace, respectively, the having of visual and auditory sensations. Of further importance is the idea that a particular kind of information is not necessarily the special domain of a particular perceptual system, but rather that different systems can detect the same information either singly or in combination.

Gibson's substitution of perceptual systems for the senses is a commendable one, and its far-reaching implications for a general theory of perception have been spelled out by Mace and Shaw & McIntyre in this volume. What I wish to touch upon is the idea that perceptual systems are flexible machineries which can be put to uses other than that of discovering invariants in changing stimulation, although that is their primary function. Thus, in addition to detecting invariances, perceptual systems can be generative devices which construct perceptual experiences of certain kinds. But we should guard against concluding that, just because perceptual systems *can* construct, the everyday perception of the everyday world *is* constructed. In my view, relatively few perceptual experiences are constructed. While there is certainly an intimate and theoretically provocative relation between the workings of a perceptual system as a detector of invariances and the workings of a perceptual system as a generative device, I do not think that the relation is one of identity.

There is certainly nothing novel in the idea that a perceptual system can be generative. Indeed, B. F. Skinner (1963) has elegantly expressed this notion in describing the behaviorist position on conscious experience: "Seeing does not imply something seen." If I understand Skinner, he is saying that seeing is (can be?) a behavior, and therefore seeing a Rolls Royce, for example, is an activity which can be evoked (given the right contingencies) even though no Rolls Royce is present to be seen. Note that the statement which Skinner finds so admirably descriptive of the behaviorist viewpoint is the very kind of statement which expresses the position advanced by constructivists (Gregory, 1972; Kolers, 1968; Neisser, 1967), although I suspect that Skinner and the constructivists find this statement appropriate for different reasons. In any event, the idea that a perceptual system may yield experience in the absence of stimulation has been well recognized. Thus, dreaming, hallucinating, illusioning, and imaging may be considered examples of this characteristic of perceptual systems. But while it is reasonable to propose that a person who is seeing or hearing or smelling things that are not present must be generating them for himself, this need not convince us that the generative mechanisms he uses overlap with the normal mechanisms of seeing, hearing, and smelling. Fortunately there are more solid grounds for inferring the overlap.

In a signal-detection experiment S is asked to image something and to indicate when he has a good image. At that point a signal is either presented or not, and S is required to report whether the signal did or did not occur. If S was entertaining an auditory image and the signal was auditory, then sensitivity is poorer than if a visual image had been entertained. Similarly, detection of a visual signal is impaired more significantly by concurrent visual imagery than by concurrent auditory imagery (Segal & Fusella, 1970, 1971). The interpretation given is that detecting, say, a visual signal and generating a visual image require the services of a common mechanism.

A similar conclusion can be drawn from the work of Brooks (1968). S is required to recall (image) a block F that he has recently studied. With the block F in mind he must signal its corners, signaling those at the bottom and top by "yes," those between by "no," and starting, say, at the bottom right hand corner. The task is far more difficult if he must signal the sequence of yeses and noes by pointing at an array of yeses and noes than if he signals the sequence verbally. The inference is that imaging the block F and pointing at the visually displayed words both depend on the system for seeing. By way of contrast we can ask S to learn a short sentence ("a bird in the hand is not in the bush") and then to go through the sentence mentally, indicating each noun by "yes" and every word that is not a noun by "no." In this case, signaling the yeses and noes by pointing is superior to saying the yeses and noes aloud presumably because the speech imagery required to maintain the sentence and to go through the sentence conflicts with speaking the yeses and noes.

In a similar experiment (Brooks, 1967) S is instructed about the arrangement of digits in a matrix. He is told to image the matrix and then allocate the digits in the matrix according to the instructions, which are presented to him either in a written form or orally. His subsequent recall of digit location in the matrix is poorer in the reading condition than in the listening condition. The inference in this case is that reading a message is antagonistic to the simultaneous representation of spatial relations, whereas listening to a message is not.

Other experiments have pointed to this dependence of memory on the perceptual apparatus relevant to the material to be remembered. Thus Atwood (1971) showed that an irrelevant visual perception interfered more with verbal learning by means of imagery than did an irrelevant auditory task. Den Heyer & Barrett (1971) showed that short-term retention of digits in a matrix was interfered with more by a verbal interpolated task than by a visual interpolated task, while the reverse was true for the retention of the spatial location of the digits.

On this evidence we may conclude that perceiving and imaging engage the same neural apparatus, at least at some level, and that memory-sustaining operations (such as rehearsal) and acts of remembering (such as imaging) are carried out within the perceptual system most related to the memory material. In other words, there is support for the argument that a perceptual system is also a generative system.

It is commonplace to regard imagery, hallucinating experiences, and the like as the arousal of stored representations. The use of nouns such as "image," "hallucination," "dream," etc., commits us to the idea of something — an object or a scene—which is recalled or rearoused or constructed and which then—like a real object or scene—is viewed or experienced by an observer. Alternatively we could argue that the act of imaging or dreaming or hallucinating is experienced, and that (following Skinner, 1963) imaging, dreaming, and hallucinating do not imply things imaged, dreamt or hallucinated. On this argument, which I prefer, it is true to say that I am imaging my grandmother, but it is not true to say that I have an image of my grandmother in my head.

Related to its generative capability is a rather important use for at least one perceptual system, the visual perceptual system; to model or imitate external events. In a sense, all acts of construction carried out by a perceptual system are imitative acts, but what I have in mind here is the idea of the visual perceptual system functioning as an analog spatial model in which orderly, physical operations can be conducted vicariously (cf. Attneave, 1972). This characterization is similar to Craik's (1943) thesis that the brain is essentially a complex machine which can parallel or model physical processes, a capability of neural machinery which Craik views as the fundamental feature of thought and explanation.

Evidence that the visual perceptual system can model physical space, i.e., that it can exhibit processes which have a similar relation structure to physical space (cf. Craik, 1943), is found in experiments conducted by Shepard and his colleagues. In one experiment (Shepard & Metzler, 1971) Ss were shown a pair of two-dimensional portrayals of three-dimensional objects and were asked to decide as quickly as possible whether one of the objects could be rotated into the other. Decision latency was shown to be an increasing linear function of the angular difference in the portrayed orientation of the two objects. At $0°$ difference the latency was 1 sec., while at $180°$ difference the latency was 4 or 5 sec. Each additional degree of rotation added approximately 16 msec. to the latency of recognition, and this was essentially so whether the rotation was in the plane of the picture or in depth. In a further experiment (Shepard & Feng, 1972) Ss were given a picture of one of the patterns of six connected squares produced when the faces of a cube are unfolded and laid out flat. Their task was to decide with minimal delay whether two marked edges of two different squares would meet if the square was folded back into the cube. Time to reach a decision increased linearly with the sum of the number of squares that would have been involved if the folding-up operation were actually performed.

In Shepard's experiments S is apparently imitating covertly the operations which he would perform if he were actually to rotate a physical object or actually to fold up a physical pattern of squares into a cube. Moreover, these convert motor activities parallel actual motor activities in that they are performed in a continuous space and in real time. On the evidence we should argue that the neural spatial representation which is afforded by the visual perceptual system and in which these covert performances occur is a model of, or an analog of, physical space.

From other experiments we can infer an interesting complicity between other perceptual systems and the visual one where spatial properties are involved. Auditory localization (Warren, 1970) has been shown to be better with the eyes open than with the eyes closed; learning responses to tactile stimuli delivered in fixed locations is better with unrestricted than with restricted vision (Attneave & Benson, 1969); and short-term retention of a spatial arrangement of tactile stimulation is impaired significantly more by an irrelevant arithmetic task presented visually than by that same task presented auditorily (Sullivan, 1973). These experiments imply that information about location is mapped into the spatial analog system provided by vision even when the location information is received or detected by other perceptual systems.

KNOWING ABOUT THINGS WE DO NOT KNOW WE KNOW ABOUT

As I have noted, analysis-by-synthesis and constructive theory have much in common. Synthesis is a slippery idea, but we can come to terms with it if we consider the way a blindfolded man might attempt to recognize a solid triangular figure by moving his finger around the outline. (The example is from an early discussion of synthesis by Mackay, 1963). To our blindfolded man the concept of triangularity is defined by and symmetrical with the sequence of elementary responses necessary in the act of replicating the outline of a triangle. Presumably the recognition of any sensory event is in some sense an act of replication of the stimuli received. In other words, replicas of the input are generated until there is a significant degree of resemblance between replica and input. Of course the input which the replicating or synthesizing mechanism is dealing with is in quite a different physical form from the original input to the sensory receptors: probably in neuroelectrical activity of some spatial-temporal specificity. In any event, to identify a triangle I do not have to synthesize triangles; to identify a smell I do not have to synthesize odors.

Analysis-by-synthesis models generally propose that identification lies in the act of achieving a reasonable facsimile of the input. But the constructivist view of perception, at least as I understand it, may wish to ascribe something more than "identification" to the replicative act. The stronger and preferred position is that the perceptual experience of something corresponds to the act of synthesizing that something. Thus, for example, with reference to the spontaneous reversal of perspective during "midflight" of a Necker cube set into oscillating apparent motion, Neisser (1967) comments: "The reversal of perspective at that point emphasizes that figural synthesis is not a matter of cold-blooded inference *but of genuine construction* [p. 144; my emphasis]." The experiences of dreaming, hallucinating, and imaging are especially relevant; as noted earlier, it seems reasonable that a person who is seeing or hearing things that are not present is experiencing his own internal acts of synthesis. But the constructivist view wants to argue, in addition, that the perception of an actual event corresponds to an act of synthesis, and this in my opinion raises a serious and, as far as I know, unanswered question. Is the act of synthesis which underlies the imaging of, say, a capital A or a loved one's face the same kind of operation as that which underlies identification of a capital A or a loved one when they are visually present?

Very little information bears on this question; there are, however, a few hints from case studies of agnosia which suggest that the two operations I have referred to are not of the same kind. A patient who cannot read letters, i.e., cannot identify them when presented visually, may still be able to visualize them and describe their features. Conversely, a patient who can read letters may not be able to image them at all (Nielsen, 1962, pp. 35-40).

Let us hold this somewhat isolated observation in abeyance and turn to a more serious but related problem. If identification occurs in conjunction with the synthesizing of a reasonable match, and if perceptual experience corresponds to that successful act of synthesis, then we should conclude as follows: Conscious perceptual experience of a sensory event is the earliest stage in the processing of that event at which the identification of that event can be said to have occurred. I intend to argue that this conclusion is false and that, at least for certain kinds of linguistic material, identification precedes conscious experience and on occasion can be shown to occur in the absence of any conscious experience whatsoever. If my argument is correct then we should suppose that the processes underlying identification and those underlying conscious experience are quite different. To put this another way, the operations by which identification of a capital A (using our earlier example) proceeds and those by which the conscious experience of a capital A is expressed are not identical. Thus we should not be surprised to find, on occasion, brain-injured patients who cannot identify letters but can easily image them.

Michael Polanyi (1964, 1966) has for some time argued for distinguishing two species of knowledge: tacit knowledge, about which we cannot speak, and explicit knowledge, about which we can. This distinction —adopted here in rather diluted form—will prove fruitful to the ensuing discussion. I will attempt to show that we may know the identity of a verbal event tacitly, but that a further operation— different from that underlying tacit identification—is needed if we are to know the identity of the event explicitly.

A good starting point is provided by the situation in visual masking. When two stimuli are presented to an observer in rapid succession, perceptual impairment may result. Either the first or the second stimulus may be phenomenally obscured, or at least not identifiable. One general principle of masking is especially relevant: When masking is of central origin (under conditions of dichoptic stimulation) the later-arriving stimulus is the one likely to be identified rather than the leading stimulus. In short, masking of central origin is primarily backward, and this, I propose, is an important comment on the nature of central processes (Turvey, 1973). Note also that whether or not a lagging stimulus can centrally mask a leading stimulus is dependent on there being some geometric (and/or perhaps semantic) similarity between the two. By contrast, masking of peripheral origin can occur in the absence of formal similarity; in the peripheral domain the comparative energies of the two stimuli are more important (see Turvey, 1973).

Paul Kolers (1968) offers a useful analogy for backward masking of central origin. The idea is that the central processor may be likened to a clerk who receives customers on an aperiodic schedule. When a customer enters the store the clerk asks a variety of questions in order to determine the customer's dispositions and wants. However, if a second customer enters soon after the first the clerk may be hurried and, therefore, less thorough in his treatment of the first. Consequently, some things may be left undone. But we should note that the clerk has registered and responded to some of the first customer's requests. The analogy emphasizes that, although processing of the first stimulus in a backward masking situation may not be completed and consequently an explicit account of the first may not be forthcoming, something about the first may well be known.

One particular kind of experiment is a rather elegant demonstration of this point. We know that when a stimulus is decreased in physical energy, reaction time to its onset is increased proportionately. However, reaction time to a backwardly masked stimulus, which may appear either phenomenally decreased in brightness or absent altogether, is not so affected (Fehrer & Raab, 1962; Harrison & Fox, 1966; Schiller & Smith, 1966). Thus, we should suppose that in the presence of the masker those operations which determine the phenomenal appearance of the stimulus have been left relatively undone, but those which detect its occurrence and determine its intensity have been completed.

But other experiments are more relevant to the distinction that I seek to draw between tacit and explicit identification. First is an experiment reported by Wickens (1972) which shows that an observer may have some knowledge of the meaning of a masked word even though he might be unable to report the actual identity of the word. In this experiment a word was briefly exposed and followed by a patterned mask. Then S was given one of two possible words and asked to guess whether it was similar in some way to the masked and nonidentified word. This second word was never identical to the masked word but it was, half of the time, similar on some dimension to the masked word. The other half of the time it was dissimilar. For some dimensions at least—the semantic differential, taxonomic categories, and synonymity—S was likely (better than chance) to identify the semantically related word. The conclusion we may draw from this experiment is that one can have tacit knowledge about the meaning of a word in advance of explicit knowledge about its identity. This is also the conclusion I think we should draw from the experiments of Reicher (1969) and Wheeler (1970). Those experiments showed that under identical conditions of backward masking, with careful controls for response-bias effects, a letter could be more accurately recognized if it was part of a word than if it was part of a nonword, or presented singly (cf. Smith & Haviland, 1972). It has always seemed to me that the simplest interpretation of this result is that meaningfulness (and/or familiarity) affects the time taken to process (cf. Eichelman, 1970). But if this is true then we are faced with trying to understand how meaningfulness or familiarity can assist speed and accuracy of identification, since we should argue, on the conventional view, that sensory data have to make contact with long-term storage, i.e., have to be identified, *before* their meaning or familiarity can be ascertained.

This issue is similarly exposed in experiments which demonstrate a direct relation between number of syllables or pronounceable units in a verbal event and time taken to identify it. Thus, for example, Klapp (1971) has shown that the time taken to press a key to indicate that a pair of two-syllable numbers, e.g., 15 and 15, or 80 and 80, were the same was measurably shorter than the time needed to indicate the sameness of a pair of three-syllable numbers, e.g., 28 and 28, or 70 and 70. The question we should ask of this startling result is: How can the number of syllables affect the time to identify, since surely one must first identify an optical pattern such as 15 or 70 before one can know how to pronounce it?

Similarly there is evidence that the category—letter or digit—to which a character belongs can be known before its identity is determined (Brand, 1971; Ingling, 1972; Posner, 1970). In other words, we can know that a character is a letter or a digit before we know which letter or digit it is. On Ingling's (1972) data in particular we should have to argue that determining category membership is not based on any simple or obvious feature analysis. We should also note that these demonstrations are in concert with the special cases of visual alexia reported by Dejerine (1892) and Ettlinger (1967). Here injury to the left hemisphere results in an inability to read letters but leaves unimpaired the ability to read arabic numerals. And it is not that the patient has necessarily forgotten the names, because he might be able to identify letters conveyed to him tactually. Nor is his problem that of being unable to discriminate letter features, since he can sort letters into groups where each group represents one particular letter.

To summarize, there is good reason to propose that with respect to certain events one can be said to know something about the identity of an event before one knows that event's identity. This paradox, alluded to elsewhere by Coltheart (1972a, 1972b), can be resolved if we distinguish between tacit and explicit identification and view the latter as preceded and shaped by the former. An experiment by Worthington (1964) shows that one can have tacit knowledge of the semantic character of an event in the absence of any awareness, i.e., explicit knowledge, of its presence. On the surface, at least, Worthington's experiment had to do with the time course of dark-adaptation. Light-adapted Ss seated in a black room were requested to view a designated area in which would appear a dim white light. Their task was simply that of pressing a button as soon as they saw anything in the specified area. Pressing the button turned the light off and the dependent measure was the time elapsed before the button was pressed. Unbeknown to the Ss, the dim light was a disc with a word printed on it in black. the word could be either obscene or a geometrically similar neutral word. The average buttonpressing latency was determined by the semantic status of the word, with obscene words yielding longer elapsed times. It is important to note that no S ever reported seeing anything in the white light.

Further support for the tacit/explicit distinction is found in the literature on selective attention in audition, particularly in two experiments using the technique of dichotic stimulation with the shadowing of one of the two concurrent messages. The general finding with this paradigm is that S knows little about the unattended message. But I should choose my terms more carefully; the general finding is that very little is known *explicitly* by S about the unattended message. At all events, as Cherry (1953) initially observed and as many have confirmed since (e.g., Triesman & Geffen, 1967) S may be able to give a relatively detailed account of the physical character of the unattended message but may be sorely limited in his ability to report on the semantic content of the message. We shall see, however, that S knows a great deal more about the unattended message than he can tell.

In one experiment (Lewis, 1970) which presented simultaneous pairs of words, the unattended message words were associatively related, semantically related, or unrelated to their partners in the shadowed message. Although Ss were unable to report the words on the unattended channel, shadowing reaction time was slower when the word presented in the nonattended message was synonymous with its pair on the shadowed ear. In short, the unattended words were identified but their identification apparently was not made explicit. Similar evidence is provided in an experiment by Corteen and Wood (1972). Certain words were first associated with shock to establish change of skin conductance to these words alone. The shock-associated words were then embedded in the unattended message along with words from the same class (cities) as the shock-associated words, and with control words. Both the shock-associated and nonshock-associated city names produced a significant number of autonomic responses, even though the subjects (according to the criteria of awareness employed) were not aware of them.

We should suppose, as I did earlier, that there are important distinctions to be drawn between the processes by which we tacitly know and those by which we explicitly know. To begin with, I suspect that the operations of tacit and explicit identification differ in that the former, unlike the latter, do not make demands on our limited processing capacity. Support for this idea can be drawn from several sources: experimental and theoretical analyses of attentional components (Posner & Boies, 1971), attempts to determine the locus of the Stroop effect (Hintzman, Carre, Eskridge, Owens, Shaff, & Sparks, 1972, Keele, 1972), and investigations into the relation between central processing capacity and iconic memory (Doost & Turvey, 1971). Essentially these sources hold that selective attention and limited capacity effects operate after a sensory event has made contact with long-term store (cf. Norman, 1968; Posner & Warren, 1972).

The argument has been made that certain variables which affect identification, such as meaning and familiarity, can only influence the course of perception *after* contact with long-term store. Thus, in an experiment such as Klapp's (1971), contact between an optical pattern, say, "17," and long-term store must precede determination of how that pattern is to be pronounced. Therefore, the number of syllables in the verbalization of the pattern cannot affect the course of tacit identification. On the contrary, number of syllables can only affect the temporal course of explicit identification. By the same token, it is the conversion from tacit to explicit identification rather than the process of contacting long-term store which is sensitive to meaning and familiarity.

A nonlinguistic analog of the Reicher-Wheeler phenomenon has been reported by Biederman (1972). Essentially, the experiment showed that an object was more accurately identified when part of a briefly exposed real-world scene than when it was part of a jumbled version of that scene, exposed equally briefly. And this was true even when S was instructed, before exposure, where to look and what to look for. Biederman's discovery implies that the coherence and symmetry of the real-world scene affected the explicit identification of the particulars of its composition. In a related experiment Eichelman (1970) has shown that a physical match (see Posner & Mitchell, 1967) is made faster between two words than between two nonwords (cf. Kreuger, 1970).

The question we should ask of all these experiments is: How can "higher-order" properties of stimulation, such as symmetry and familiarity and meaning, affect the identification of "lower-order" properties from which the "higher-order" properties are apparently derived? On the present view, the answer to this question is that these higher-order properties are detected by a relatively direct means (analogous, perhaps, to Gibson's idea of "resonance"), and that explicit knowledge about the particulars, and other kinds of information embodied in the stimulation, is accessible only after such tacit identification.

In sum, pattern recognition consists of two rather broadly defined stages. The first is that in which stimulation contacts long-term store, and the second is that in which the tacit identification afforded by the first stage is converted into explicit knowledge. It appears on the evidence that the processes involved in the two stages are quite different. Moreover, it appears that much of what we know about "pattern recognition" is related to the class of operations by which things come out of long-term store, i.e., the tacit-to-explicit conversion, rather than to the manner in which patterns of stimulation contact long-term store in the first place. In short, the "Höffding Step" (Höffding, 1891; Neisser, 1967) remains very much a mystery.

We might also speculate that the *form* of knowledge at the tacit level differs from that at the explicit level. This is, of course, the essence of Polanyi's (1964, 1966) argument. Here we should take it to mean that the explicit account of an event and the tacit account of that same event may look quite different, even radically so. Consider the phenomenon known in the short-term memory literature as release from proactive interference (PI). On successive short-term memory tests of the distractor kind (Brown, 1958; Peterson & Peterson, 1959) S is given short lists of maybe three words to retain, a new list for each test. If the words presented on the successive tests are drawn from the same category, recall performance across the successive tests will decline precipitously. If we now, on a short-term memory test, present words which have been drawn from a category conceptually different from that used in the immediately preceding tests, there is an abrupt recovery in recall performance. For example, if S received three successive tests with digits as the material to be remembered and then on the fourth test he was given letters to retain, performance on the fourth test would be equivalent to that on the first and substantially superior to that on the third. Wickens (1970) has proposed that the PI release procedure identifies "psychological" categories. We can assume that there is a common way of encoding within a class (accounting for the decline in recall) which differs between classes (accounting in turn for the increase in recall with shift in class).

Table 1 shows two distinct classes of material as defined by PI release.

TABLE 1

farm	wife
prevent	burn
uncle	silence
sea	debt
car	sing
play	young
religious	disease
action	box
develop	window

The set of words in the left column consists of a random arrangement of three words drawn from the evaluative dimension, three from the potency dimension and three from the activity dimension of the semantic differential (Osgood, Suci, & Tannenbaum 1957). Each word rates high on one dimension and is relatively neutral on the other two. The right column of words is similarly constructed. The difference between the two columns is that the left-hand column words are drawn from the positive pole of their respective dimensions and the right-hand column words are drawn from the negative pole of their respective dimensions (all words were selected from Heisse, 1965). The experimental evidence is that shifting across dimensions within the same polarity does not yield a release from PI; on the other hand, a highly significant improvement in recall occurs following a change in polarity either within or between dimensions (Turvey & Fertig, 1970; Turvey, Fertig & Kravetz, 1969). In brief, the polarities are orthogonal but the dimensions are not. I should like to argue that this distinction between positive and negative polarity is made only tacitly. In the PI release situation a distinction is obviously being made, and without effort, between the two polarities. But I submit that close examination of Table 1 and careful perusal of the individual words will not lead to the conclusion that the two columns differ in any sensible way. Imagine that the words in the two columns were simply mixed together and one were ignorant of the semantic differential (as were Ss in the experiments). I doubt that one could even begin to sort them into the two categories I have described.

In other words, we can make a distinction tacitly that we cannot readily make explicitly. Quite to the contrary is the situation with nouns and verbs. A shift from nouns to verbs or vice versa does not lead to a release from PI (Wickens, 1970), but one can with some facility distinguish nouns from verbs if asked to do so. In the Lewis (1970) experiment referred to above, synonymity between attended and unattended words exerted a marked effect on the reaction time to attended words, but associative relations based on associative norms did not. We might argue from this result that associative norms reflect explicit distinctions but are themselves not isomorphic with the structure of tacit knowledge. Similarly, we can argue that the structure of tacit knowledge does not incorporate images. On the evidence, a distinction is not made tacitly between high-imagery concrete words and low-imagery abstract words, although such a distinction is clearly made explicitly. Wickens and Engle (1970) failed to find PI release with a shift from concrete to abstract words, and vice versa, even though the imagery variable is known to be important in free-recall and paired-associate learning (Paivio, 1969). Imaging, we might suppose, is constructing from tacit knowledge.

Assuming, therefore, that my interpretation of the PI release situation is not too far off the mark, we may draw the following, highly speculative but intriguing conclusion: One may make distinctions tacitly that cannot be made explicitly, and, conversely, one may make distinctions explicitly that are not furnished tacitly. In the latter case we should assume that such explicit distinctions are constructed.

REFERENCES

Attneave, F. Representation of physical space. In A. W. Melton & E. Martin (Eds.), *Coding processes in human memory*. Washington, D.C.: Winston, 1972.

Attneave, F., & Benson, B. Spatial coding of tactual stimulation. *Journal of Experimental Psychology,* 1969, **81**, 216-222.

Atwood, G. An experimental study of visual imagination and memory. *Cognitive Psychology,* 1971. **2**, 239-289.

Biederman, I. Perceiving real-world scenes. *Science,* 1972, **177**, 77-79.

Brand, J. Classification without identification in visual search. *Quarterly Journal of Experimental Psychology,* 1971, **23**, 178-186.

Brooks, L. R. The suppression of visualization by reading. *Quarterly Journal of Experimental Psychology,* 1967, **19**, 289-299.

Brooks, L. R. Spatial and verbal components of the act of recall. *Canadian Journal of Psychology,* 1968, **22**, 349-368.

Brown, J. Some tests of the decay theory of immediate memory. *Quarterly Journal of Experimental Psychology,* 1958, **10**, 12-21.

Cherry, E. C. Some experiments on the recognition of speech with one and with two ears. *Journal of the Acoustical Society of America,* 1953, **25**, 975-979.

Coltheart, M. Visual information processing. In P. C. Dodwell (Ed.), *New horizons in psychology.* Vol. 2. Harmondsworth: Penguin Books, 1972. (a)

Coltheart, M. *Readings in cognitive psychology.* Toronto: Holt, Rinehart & Winston, 1972. (b)

Corcoran, D. W. J. An acoustic factor in letter cancellation. *Nature,* 1966, **210**, 658.

Corcoran, D. W. J. *Pattern recognition.* Harmondsworth: Penguin Books, 1971.

Corteen, R. S., & Wood, B. Autonomic responses to shock-associated words in an unattended channel. *Journal of Experimental Psychology,* 1972, **94**, 308-313.

Craik, K. J. W. *The nature of explanation.* Cambridge: Cambridge University Press, 1943.

den Heyer, K., & Barrett, B. Selective loss of visual and verbal information in STM by means of visual and verbal interpolated tasks. *Psychonomic Science,* 1971, **25**, 100-102.

Dejerine, J. Contribution a l'ètude anatomo-pathologique et clinique des differentes variétés de cécité verable. *Mémoires de la Société de Biologie,* 1892, **4** 61.

Doost, R., & Turvey, M. T. Iconic memory and central processing capacity. *Perception & Psychophysics,* 1971, **9**, 269-274.

Eichelman, W. H. Familiarity effects in the simultaneous matching task. *Journal of Experimental Psychology,* 1970, **86**, 275-282.

Ettlinger, G. Visual alexia. In W. Wathen-Dunn (Ed.), *Models for the perception of speech and visual form.* Cambridge: MIT Press, 1967.

Fehrer, E., & Raab, D. Reaction time to stimuli masked by metacontrast. *Journal of Experimental Psychology,* 1962, **63**, 143-147.

Geschwind, N. The organization of language and the brain. *Science.* 1970, **170**, 940-944.

Gibson, J. J. Perception as a function of stimulation. In S. Koch (Ed.), *Psychology: A study of a science.* Vol. 1. New York: McGraw-Hill, 1959.

Gibson, J. J. *The senses considered as perceptual systems.* Boston: Houghton Mifflin, 1966.

Gregory, R. Seeing as thinking: An active theory of perception. *London Times Literary Supplement,* June 23, 1972, 707-708.

Heisse, D. R. Semantic differential profiles for 1000 most frequent English words. *Psychological Monographs,* 1965, **79**, (Whole No. 601).

Harrison, K., & Fox, R. Replication of reaction time to stimuli masked by metacontrast. *Journal of Experimental Psychology,* 1966, **71**, 162-163.

Hitzman, D. L., Carre, F. A., Eskridge, V. L., Owens, A. M., Shaff, S. S., & Sparks, M. E. "Stroop" effect: Input or output phenomenon. *Journal of Experimental Psychology,* 1972, **95**, 458-459.

Höffding, H. *Outlines of psychology.* New York: Macmillan, 1891.

Howes, D. An approach to the quantitative analysis of word blindness. In J. Money (Ed.), *Reading disability: Progress and research needs in dyslexia.* Baltimore: Johns Hopkins Press, 1962.

Ingling, N. Categorization: A mechanism for rapid information processing. *Journal of Experimental Psychology,* 1972, **94**, 239-243.

Keele, S. W. Attention demands of memory retrieval. *Journal of Experimental Psychology,* 1972, *93,* 245-248.

Klapp, S. T. Implicit speech inferred from response latencies in same-different decisions. *Journal of Experimental Psychology,* 1971, **91,** 262-267.

Kohler, I. *Uber und Wandlungen der Wahrnehmungswelt.* Vienna: Rudolph M. Rohrer, 1951. (Translated by H. Fiss, The formation and transformation of the perceptual world. *Psychological Issues,* 1964. 3, No. 4.)

Kolers, P. A. Some psychological aspects of pattern recognition. In P. A. Kolers & M. Eden (Eds.), *Recognizing patterns.* Cambridge: MIT Press, 1968.

Kreuger, L. E. Visual comparison in a redundant visual display. *Cognitive Psychology,* 1970, **1,** 341-357.

Lewis, J. L. Semantic processing of unattended messages during dichotic listening. *Journal of Experimental Psychology,* 1970, **85,** 225-228.

Liberman, A. M. The specialization of the language hemisphere. Paper presented at intensive study program of the Neurosciences Research Project, Boulder, Colorado, 1972.

Liberman, A. M. Cooper, F. S., Shankweiler, D. P., & Studdert-Kennely, M. Perception of the speech code. *Psychological Review,* 1967, **74,** 431-461.

Liberman, A. M., Mattingly, I. G., & Turvey, M. T. Language codes and memory codes. In A. W. Melton & E. Martin (Eds.), *Coding processes in human memory.* Washington: Winston, 1972.

Mackay, D. Mindlike behavior in artifacts. In K. M. Sagre & F. J. C. Crosson, (Eds.), *The modeling of mind: Computers and intelligence.* New York: Simon & Schuster, 1963.

Mattingly, I. G. Speech cues and sign stimuli. *American Scientist,* 1972, **60,** 327-337.

Neisser, V. *Cognitive psychology.* New York: Appleton-Century-Crofts, 1967.

Neisser, V. The processes of vision. *Scientific American,* 1968, **218,** 204-214.

Neisser, V. Visual imagery as process and as experience. In J. S. Antrobus (Ed.), *Cognition and affect.* Boston: Little, Brown, 1970.

Nielsen, J. M. *Agnosia, apraxia, aphasia: Their value in cerebral localization.* New York: Hafner, 1962.

Norman, D. A. Toward a theory of memory and attention. *Psychological Review.* 1968, **75,** 722-736.

Osgood, C. E., Suci, G. J., & Tannenbaum, P. H. *The measurement of meaning.* Urbana: University of Illinois Press, 1957.

Paivio, A. Mental imagery in associative learning and memory. *Psychological Review,* 1969, **76,** 241-263.

Peterson, L. R., & Peterson, M. J. Short-Term retention of individual verbal items. *Journal of Experimental Psychology,* 1959, **58,** 193-198.

Polanyi, M. *Personal knowledge: Towards a post-critical philosophy.* New York: Harper, 1964.

Polanyi, M. *The tacit dimension.* Garden City: Doubleday, 1966.

Posner, M. I. On the relationship between letter names and superordinate categories. *Quarterly Journal of Experimental Psychology,* 1970, **22,** 279-287.

Posner, M. I., & Boies, S. J. Components of attention. *Psychological Review,* 1971, 78, 391-408.

Posner, M. I., & Mitchell, R. F. Chronometric analysis of classification. *Psychological Review,* 1967, **74,** 392-409.

Posner, M. I., & Warren, E. Traces, concepts and conscious constructions. In A. W. Melton & E. Martin (Eds.), *Coding processes in human memory.* Washington, D.C.: Winston, 1972.

Reicher, G. M. Perceptual recognition as a function of stimulus material. *Journal of Experimental Psychology,* 1969, **81,** 275-280.

Ryle, G. *The concept of mind.* London: Hutchinson, 1949.

Schiller, P. M., & Smith, M. C. Detection in metacontrast. *Journal of Experimental Psychology,* 1966, **71,** 32-39.

Segal, S. J., Fusella, V. Influence of imaged pictures and sound on detection of visual and auditory signals. *Journal of Experimental Psychology,* 1970, **83,** 458-464.

Segal, S. J., & Fusella, V. Effect of images in six sense modalities on detection of visual signal from noise. *Psychonomic Science,* 1971, *24,* 55-56.

Shepard, R. N., & Metzler, J. Mental rotation of three-dimensional objects. *Science*, 1971, 171, 701-703.

Shepard, R. N., & Feng, C. A chronometric study of mental paper folding. *Cognitive Psychology*, 1972, 3, 288-243.

Skinner, B. F. Behaviorism at fifty. *Science*, 1963, 140, 951-958.

Smith, E. E., & Haviland, S. E. Why words are perceived more accurately than nonwords: Inference versus unitization. *Journal of Experimental Psychology*, 1972, 92, 59-64.

Sullivan, E. V. On the short-term retention of serial tactile stimuli. Unpublished master's thesis, University of Connecticut, 1973.

Triesman, A., & Geffen, G. Selective attention: Perception or response? *Quarterly Journal of Experimental Psychology*, 1967, 19, 1-17.

Turvey, M. T. On peripheral and central processes in vision: Inferences from an information processing analysis of masking with patterned stimuli. *Psychological Review*, 1973, 80, 1-52.

Turvey, M. T., & Fertig, J. Polarity on the semantic differential and release from proactive interference in short-term memory. *Journal of Verbal Learning and Verbal Behavior*, 1970, 9, 439-443.

Turvey, M. T., Fertig, J., & Kravetz, S. Connotative classification and proactive interference in short-term memory. *Psychonomic Science*, 1969, 16, 223-224.

Wallach, H., & O'Connell, D. N. The kinetic depth effect. *Journal of Experimental Psychology*, 1953, 45 205-207.

Warren, D. Intermodality interactions in spatial localization. *Cognitive Psychology*, 1970, 2, 114-133.

Wickens, D. D. Encoding categories of words: An empirical approach to meaning. *Psychological Review*, 1970, 77, 1-15.

Wickens, D. D. Characteristics of word encoding. In A. W. Melton & E. Martin (Eds.), *Coding processes in human memory*. Washington, D.C.: Winston, 1972.

Wickens, D. D., & Engle, R. W. Imagery and abstractness in short-term memory. *Journal of Experimental Psychology*, 1970, 84, 268-272.

Wheeler, D. D. Processes in word recognition. *Cognitive Psychology*, 1970, 1, 59-85.

Worthington, A. G. Differential rates of dark adaptation to "taboo" and "neutral" stimuli. *Canadian Journal of Psychology*, 1964, 18, 757-768.

9

MACE-TURVEY
DISCUSSION

Ross: One question for Turvey: is the tip-of-the-tongue phenomenon an instance of tacit knowledge?

Turvey: Yes, it is a particularly good example.

Halwes: Polanyi explicitly discusses it. We have a feeling that we know something before we become aware of what it is that we know. First we feel that we have solved a problem, and then the solution somehow unfolds in our awareness.

Shaw: Let me develop a point that comes out from phenomena such as Mace presented. Remember that when the dot patterns were crossing each other there was an apparent pause when they were superimposed. This happens despite the fact that the dots are really moving at a linear rate, and there is no actual pause. This phenomenon could be interpreted as a discretization in perception, so that we see an interval before the dots intersect, an interval of intersection, and then one after intersection. In a sense there is a kind of "warping of space" wherever there is an object, and things seem to pour into that sink. (I hate to use the relativistic gravitational metaphor, but I think it is a fair one.) This leads us to assume that there are certain periods, certain kinds of symmetries, involved. If that is the case, we might be able to make a very strong assumption—that in every optical display where we see depth there will be a certain kind of asymmetry. If there is a symmetry possible, say, within a two-dimensional plane that will keep things coplanar, then they will remain coplanar. But if there is a sufficient asymmetry, that is the same as there being a linear independence of the vectors for defining the notion in two planes: we have another vector that has to go somewhere, and that vector throws it into the third dimension. Now we start approaching a very general form of equation for depth. But if we do the analysis at the level of symmetry theory, it doesn't have to be done quantitatively and it doesn't have to be metrical: It is rather in terms of certain kinds of asynchronies, or things being out of phase (or not having the same discrete phase basis), so that discretization takes place in various dimensions of the stimulus. Since they are not all on the same basis, these phase relations force it into a higher dimensional space, because the dimensionality of space is constrained by the number of asymmetries that can be held.

I am doing another experiment now. A screw can be composed in three dimensions out of a rotation and a translation. We are doing it this time with brightness changes, so that a brightness change per unit of rotation may produce a small depth effect, as if the screw were coming out at us as the brightness is increased. But if the brightness change (which is the translatory vector in the third dimension) is made asynchronous with the rotation of the point of light, then the symmetry theory argument would be that, since it takes two vectors to define the circle made by the point of light in the plane, and since there is now an asynchronous vector of brightness change, the visual pattern will now be in the third dimension.

Both phenomena, Mace's depth separation and the 3-D screw, are theorems in group symmetry theory—they were lifted straight out of the book, and both seem to work.

Member of Audience: Is it correct that Turvey has Gibsonian perceptual systems feeding into long-term store, or pattern recognition, without using central processing capacity? And that the output of this pattern recognition then enters into one of two different modalities—either a linear linguistic one, or one for the visual or spatial system that is constructive and consumes central processing capacity?

Turvey: Let us suppose that Gibson is correct when he says that events afford meaning directly. Now, with respect to linguistic events this might be taken to mean that direct contact is possible between the orthographic features of a seen word or the phonetic features of a heard word and its meaning. Donald Norman(1968) has something similar in mind when he suggests that the location of a word in semantic space, i.e., in long-term memory, is specified by the "sensory" properties of that word.

The implication of the term "direct" is that contact with memory is made without recourse to a sequence of discrete intervening operations which consume a portion of the limited processing capacity. However, in my view, contact with memory in the case of linguistic events affords only tacit identification of the event's meaning—another class of operations is needed, whatever they might be, to provide the reader or listener with the meaning explicitly. These latter operations tax the limited processing capacity. Now, I do not think that what I have just described occurs for nonlinguistic perception. For example, I do not think that seeing the layout of surfaces and detecting a gradient of expansion as I move through a normal environment places any great demands on my limited processing capacity, nor do I think that it requires contact with any kind of memory "store." In this respect we should note that Neisser talks of preattentive processes as relatively crude operations that simply segregate the visual field or the acoustic stream into units for the pattern-recognition machinery to work upon. Yet, he also talks of preattention guiding such behavior as driving a car while arguing, say, a moot point from Schopenhauer. The idea is that driving can be preattentively controlled. But driving a car is a very fancy operation; it involves the detection of higher-order variables of stimulation, that is, Gibson's invariances. Preattention, therefore, must be more sophisticated than Neisser supposes since, in actuality, preattention is doing the complex work. And my point is that, paradoxically, this complex work is being performed by relatively "straightforward" (Gibsonian) operations which do not consume central processing capacity.

Halwes: We don't remember preattentive material.

Turvey: In a sense, that is true. Material presented on the unattended channel in a dichotic listening experiment, for example, does not appear to lead to a long-term memory representation. The classic demonstration is Moray's (1959): words presented 35 times to the unattended ear were subsequently neither recalled nor recognized by the subjects. In some iconic memory experiments of my own (Turvey, 1967), reporting the items in a brief visual display presented 54 times was no better than reporting the items in a brief display presented only once. At least for the dichotic listening case we should suppose, on Lewis's (1970) and Corteen and Wood's (1972) evidence, that the "preattentively" processed words in Moray's experiment made contact with long-term storage. The implication, therefore, is that an event may contact tacit knowledge structures and be identified, but that some other operation that uses processing capacity must then occur to ensure that the event is remembered.

Member of Audience: Do you really think that there is a strict dichotomy between a *constructive* perceptual system and something that relates more to stimulus processing?

Turvey: There is some "squishiness" here, but the major point I want to make is this: Perceptual systems can both construct (some) experiences and detect invariances in stimulation, but the two activites are not identical. In my view, most perception is of the kind described by Gibson; that is, most perception does not involve construction. I think that the notions of constructivism are relevant to rather special perceptual activities: namely, those having to do with linguistic experience, and perhaps symbolic activity in general.

Member of Audience: I have been puzzling over a question since Mace asked, "Can we build a thory of perception on the basis of mistakes?" and rhetorically answered, "No." My question is this: What is the conceptual status of inferring, say, coding categories, detection categories, and mapping these into memory categories from errors in recall production? Historically, starting with Bartlett, the procedure has been based upon error data.

Mace: Let me interject one quick point. I emphasized that mistakes should not be fundamental to any theory: they can, however, play an important role. Illusions are of crucial importance, but in many cases there is a sense in which they are not mistakes, at least to the perceptual system. An illusion is such because it shares some of the ecological information that usually occurs in perception.

Turvey: I have given some thought to the question about what error data in memory can tell us. Given the tacit-explicit distinction that I wish to make, we might imagine that the structures of the semantic system need not be specified in error production. Indeed, recall errors may manifest more accurately the *restructuring* of the information from memory to transmission. That is, recall depends upon constructive processes, and perhaps error data reflect the processes of construction but not the structure of memory *per se.* In any event, that is a very interesting and important question.

Halwes: I want to argue first that *all* experience is constructed; and second, that it makes no sense at all to try to decide whether some particular perceptual experience is *either* Gibsonianly invariantly derived *or* constructed.

First, I will give you an analogy: The analogy is to the problem of whether certain behavior traits are innate or learned. Biologists have no particular difficulty with that "problem" since they know that all traits, morphological or behavioral, are both innate and acquired. In fact, all traits are completely innate and completely acquired by experience. It does not make any sense to try to make that distinction about traits or about morphological structures. For example, Kumler's (1971) book *Primate Societies* talks about the adaptive significance of societies. He discusses this "innate versus learned" issue and says that biologists never have to worry about that, because they understand that behavior has to be both, and that it *all* has to be both. He gives an example: Imagine that you are listening to a drummer beating on a drum. Nobody would try to figure out which noises were produced by the drum and which noises were produced by the drummer. You can perfectly well consider, if I change drummers, what the difference in the noises is as a result of my changing drummers. Or I can consider, if I change drums, the problem of the difference in the noises as a result of my having changed drums. But I cannot intelligently consider whether any particular drumbeat results from the drummer or the drum. To extend that analogy to the "innate versus learned" controversy, I can consider whether a particular difference in the behavior of two organisms which have different environments is learned; i.e., is attributable to that difference in environments. I can look at differences in behavior that are attributable to differences in environment, and I can look at differences in behavior that are attributable to differences in innate endowment. But I cannot look at traits as being innate or learned. The conclusion is that it is nonsense to try to decide whether a particular trait (behavioral or morphological) is innate or learned, or what percentage of the trait is innate or learned. Now, instead of using the term "learned," let us use the term "resulting from experience": resulting from the experience of the organism. By the same reasoning we cannot consider whether a particular morphological trait or characteristic of an organism results from innate factors or from experiential factors, nor can we even consider what is the relative contribution of innate and experiential factors. *Every* trait results *entirely* from an interaction of the innate composition of the organism and its experience.

Brewer: How do I account for my feeling that there is some difference in causality between your eye color and the side of your head you part your hair on?

Halwes: You are looking at *differences* between me and other organisms. I did not inherit my eye color: I developed my eye color as a result of particular environmental situations, given the genetic endowment that I had. This is the epigenetic approach. We can regard *differences* between organisms as attributable to innate or environmental factors, but we cannot ask whether a trait, e.g., color, or IQ, is innate or acquired, because the answer is always, "Both."

I want to extend this same principle to the constructive theory of perception. *All* experience is constructed, which means that there are certain active processes underlying experiences. Certain things which we are doing in our head underlie our experiences. Those processes are constrained by all our knowledge (or at least the relevant part of our knowledge, our beliefs, our expectations, our wishes, etc.). They are also constrained by information from the environment which at this point in the history of psychology is best described by Gibson. What we have is an experience which results from the interaction of constructive processes and information which comes into the organism from the world and is well described by Gibson in his program of ecological objects. (The "punctate stimuli" at the basis of classical constructive theories of perception were always posited to come in from the world; it is just that they were not intelligently described.)

Once again, I am not speaking of experience, but rather of the processes which underlie experience. We experience something which we attribute to the external world or something about that world. My experience is not in the world: My experience is in my head. And the experience in my head results from an interaction of input and the information that I already have in my head (about the nature of the world). We know that our knowledge has something to do with our experience, our *perceptual* experience, and that all the experiments and demonstrations the constructivists talk about in perception can be taken as evidence that there are constructive processes going on *at least sometimes* in what we call perception.

Shaw just talked about a *symmetry* between the organism and its environment, between the knowledge of the organism and its environment. I think we can profitably look at a number of symmetries, only one of which is a symmetry between experience and the organism. There is a symmetry between the experience of the organism and its environment; there is a symmetry between the knowledge of the organism and its environment; and there is a symmetry between the organism as a whole and its environment. There is also what we can call the optic array, or the information that comes in from the world; there is a symmetry between the optic array and the environment. The symmetry between the optic array and the environment, interacting with the symmetry between the organism's knowledge and the environment, gives rise to a symmetry between the experience of the organism and the environment which is in certain respects more adaptively useful to the organism than is knowledge alone or the optic array alone (if one can talk of having access to the optic array in some kind of unanalyzed form, which Gibson and I deny). One of the difficulties that Gibson and others have with the notion of construction, which Cassirer (1944) clears up perfectly, is that people think what we get is information coming in from the world, that we then take constructive processes and somehow *distort* the information, and that the result is our experience. What the organism wants—what Gibson wants—is a symmetry between the experience (or whatever term Gibson wants to use) of the organism and the world: that is what ecological perception means. If it is to do one any good to perceive, then there has to be that symmetry. Constructive processes *restore* certain aspects of the structure of the world to the structure of the information which is coming from the optic array. The so-called "distortions" make our experience *more* like the world (in certain respects relevant to our survival) than *either* the optic array *or* our knowledge.

My meaning should now be apparent when I say that there is a strict analogy between the following statements: (*a*) We cannot consider whether a trait either is innate or results from experience, and (*b*) we cannot investigate whether a particular conscious experience in perception results from information coming from the optic array or constructive processes. The argument is more complicated than I have just indicated, because in fact the organism does not always perceive: We sometimes hallucinate, and indeed some people are very much obsessed with the question of whether their experience is hallucination or perception. They are concerned with the problem of the correspondence between their experience and the world. What I will argue is that there is a continuum from perception to hallucinations, and that we have on the one end what could be called very veridical perception and on the other end what could be called pure hallucination. I submit that if you have never had a good hallucination you cannot understand constructive theory, because you do not know (although you may believe) that your constructive processes can produce an experience which is *indistinguishable* from perception. When I say that there is a continuum from perception to hallucination I mean that one could just as well say, "When you are perceiving you are hallucinating what is there" as one could say, "When you are hallucinating you are perceiving what is not there." It does not matter how we use these terms.

Brewer: What about the blind spot? Is that a problem for you? It is *not* language.

Halwes: Gibson's argument about the blind spot is perfectly cogent. He says that what one does is a local analysis of the optic array, and the optic array is not local. He argues that the information in the optic array (as I would say it information somehow Gibsonianly analyzed, going into my constructive processes) specifies this experience.

Turvey: It is again the difference between basing one's theory of perception on ecological optics and image optics.

Mace: You must examine the presuppositions to that kind of thing. If you believe that there is going to be a blind spot, you are obviously starting with the eyeball, tracing information along the retina, saying that there is something there going in. But if you start at the optic array there is always a nicely nested structure of ordered brightness variations organized around any point of observation. Now, what have perceptual systems evolved for? Gibson says it is to pick up that visual information, that perceptual systems are *exploratory* systems, always moving, *necessarily,* in order to sufficiently extract the invariance that can be carried in the transforming optic array. Now you say, "Well, I can do little tricks and find a blind spot. How can I do that?" If we just analyzed the functions of the visual system relative to the *optic array,* we would not immediately expect any blind spots: We would note both the presence of optical information and that the eyeball must be understood as a part of the system for detecting this information. Whether the eyeball has holes in it or not is nothing of consequence, since it is the overall function of the eye relative to the pickup of information that must be elaborated. Concern for the blind spot is an excellent modern instance of the old "constancy hypothesis" (cf. Pastore, 1971). Indeed, there are discrete spaces between the neural receptors. Why is the "non-blind-spot" portion of the visual field not discretely broken up? Is there any reason why the blind spot "problem" should be given special treatment? Gibson typically dismisses such experiments, which apparently demonstrate a blind spot in the visual field, as merely demonstrating another unnatural phenomenon that tells us nothing about the natural functioning of the visual system, since it can be obtained only under highly constrained conditions of observation.

Shaw: If you do retinal image optics, and say that the retinal image moves over the eye, you ask why it doesn't smear, and worry about similar problems; but in ecological optics you say that the eye moves over the optic array, and then there is no reason to worry about why you don't have a blind spot. That is the main point Mace made. If you hold the eye still, fixate it, then you get fractionation, and that doesn't worry you because the eye is not designed to be held in some fixated position. If it is, then all kinds of bizarre things happen. What you are seeing is the information that is available. Your eye is doing something very complicated: your eye is never really still. And you have information in the invariance for the continuity of surfaces. this information is not in any sense filling in a hole, because there is no hole *specified*. Holes have contours—there is no contour on the blind spot.

If I close one eye does that mean I have to fill in half the world? It is the same as asking: If I take out half of my retina do I have to fill it in? I must be filling it in, because I know the floor continues, the wall continues, etc. It is the same argument: that by funneling vision we would have to fill in. But Gibson answers that what we have to do is *sample* more. That's all Gibson would say: You have to sample the three-dimensional optical array.

Halwes: Gibson is not completely innocent: He has systematically ignored processing in his research, and yet makes claims about processing which are infuriating to people who study those processes, because they are naive claims. My favorite one is his argument that somehow it is invalid to do an analysis of a cross section of the momentary experience of the organism, to say something about that, and to conclude something from that about perceptual system; as if somehow—and I think he would actually say something like this — one really meant by this that there isn't any such thing as memory; as if memory were something like history of experience.

Turvey: Gibson doesn't say there is no such thing as memory. He says that when we try to explain perceptual experience we need not assume that the stimulation is handled by a memory system in the sense of having to remember what this thing meant in the past in order to perceive it in the present. Gibson's criticism is directed at *how* the concept of memory is used.

Mace: He is also making the strategic point that, if you can define events over time as units to be detected, then the problem becomes one of accounting for the detection of events. This formulation does not entail an appeal to memory to explain the pickup of events.

Halwes: But that, I submit, is to ignore processing, because certain events like the utterance of a sentence require what can perfectly well be described as memory (in fact people do so describe it), and it seems very well-motivated from the point of view of processing. That whole question about strategy—the claim that ecological optics must precede processing—is not correct: One does it however one can. In vision, Gibson has done a lot of work on ecological optics, and it is persumably very useful to people like Bill Mace and Bob Shaw, who want to do intelligent work on the processing. The work that the Haskins Laboratory group did on the acoustic cues for speech perception might be considered a kind of ecological acoustics, but it was certainly not on the same level of sophistication as the visual analysis of the optical array in visual perception; and yet we are able to make beautiful descriptions of certain aspects of the processing because it happens to be convenient to study certain aspects of the processing in speech perception. We need not finish our ecological analysis of speech stimuli before we can start studying the processes which underlie our experiences.

REFERENCES

Cassirer, E.   The concept of group and the theory of perception. *Philosophy and Phenomenological Research,* 1944, **5**, 1-35.

Corteen, R. S., & Wood, B. Autonomic responses to shock-associated words in an unattended channel. *Journal of Experimental Psychology,* 1972, **94**, 308-313.

Kumler, H. *Primate societies: Group techniques of ecological adaptation.* Chicago: Aldine-Atherton, 1971.

Lewis, J. L. Semantic processing of unattended messages during dichotic listening. *Journal of Experimental Psychology,* 1970, **85**, 225-228.

Moray, N. Attention in dichotic listening: Affective cues and the influence of instructions. *Quarterly Journal of Experimental Psychology,* 1959, **9**, 56-60.

Norman, D. A. Toward a theory of memory and attention. *Psychological Review,* 1968, 75, 722-736.

Pastore, N. *Selective history of theories of visual perception: 1650-1950.* New York: Oxford University Press, 1971.

Turvey, M. T. Repetition and the preperceptual information store. *Journal of Experimental Psychology,* 1967, **74**, 289-293.

10

A SKETCH OF A COGNITIVE APPROACH TO COMPREHENSION: SOME THOUGHTS ABOUT UNDERSTANDING WHAT IT MEANS TO COMPREHEND

John D. Bransford[1] and Nancy S. McCarrell
Vanderbilt University

> *In reading, when I come upon an unfamiliar word or phrase I have a sensation of derailment. Some process that usually flows along smoothly has been interrupted. Some expected click of my mechanism has failed to occur. It has always seemed to be the principal task of psychology to discover the nature of this click. The meaningful linguistic form must set off some characteristic immediate effect in the person who understands. What is the substantial nature of this effect [Brown, 1958, p. 82]?*

Brown describes the question that intrigues us: What happens when we comprehend? Obviously, this question is extremely complex and, as Huey (1908) notes, involves ". . .very many of the most intricate workings of the human mind [p. 6] ." We do not presume to provide an adequate answer, but we do hope to raise particular questions about comprehension that may provoke further discussion and research.

Brown (1958) notes that psychologists' search for the "click of comprehension" led them to ask how linguistic symbols give rise to meanings. Classical accounts generally dealt with individual words and their referents. Words were assumed to acquire meaning by association with their referents. The click of

---

[1] This chapter was written while J. D. Bransford was on leave of absence from S.U.N.Y. at Stony Brook and held a post-doctoral fellowship at the Center for Research in Human Learning, University of Minnesota, Fall, 1972. The Center is supported on grants from the National Institute of Child Health and Human Development (HD-00098 and HD-01136) and the National Science Foundation (GB-17590).

comprehension was assumed to result from arousal of an image of a word's referent (e.g., Titchener, 1909) or from an implicit response to the word that was similar to one's response to the object in the real world (e.g., Osgood, 1953; Watson, 1924). Many problems with referent approaches have been noted (e.g., Brown, 1958; Humphrey, 1963; Slobin, 1971), but we believe the most pervasive ones to be that words were considered the basic units of linguistic analysis (cf. Lyons, 1968, p. 403) and that isolated objects were the units of analysis of "the world." Linguistic communication generally does not involve isolated words, but rather sentences,[2] and a sentence's meaning is not equivalent to the summed meanings of its component words (cf. Miller, 1965; Neisser, 1967). Similarly, our perception of the world is rarely confined to identification of an individual object in isolation, but instead includes perception of an object's role in events. For example, the object in Fig. 1 is usually perceived as a man running (maybe for a touchdown). The same object is perceived as a man chasing in Fig. 1b, and in Fig. 1c (see appendix), the role is again changed.

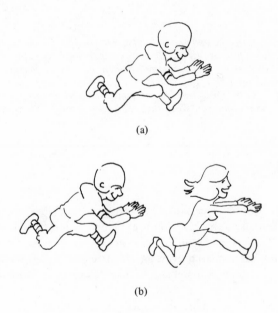

(a)

(b)

Fig. 1. (a) and (b): Object perception as a function of its role in events.

[2] Even isolated words are understood to have propositional or sentential content. For example, the utterance "paper" is understood to mean "there is a paper," "I want some paper," "it's made of paper," "where is some paper," "paper is a word to remember" (if heard in a memory experiment), etc. If someone utters a single word and one cannot understand its propositional significance (e.g., someone runs into your office and yells "paper") one will be puzzled by his act.

Referent approaches were reasonable insofar as they attempted to tie some aspects of meaning to perceptual experience, but they fail because they assume an inadequate analysis of the information available from the perceptual world. Perception affords more than information about the characteristics of individual objects; it affords information about the spatio-temporal *relations* among entities that characterize dynamic perceptual events (cf. E. J. Gibson, 1969; J. J. Gibson, 1966). We shall sketch some implications of an approach to perception that focuses on information about relations rather than isolated entities, and suggest how this orientation yields results that may help us better understand linguistic comprehension.

We shall presuppose all abstract, relational information necessary to detect surfaces and entities, and shall concentrate on relational information among entities that render them meaningful. Mace, Turvey, Shaw, and McIntyre provide excellent discussions of some of the abstract information that specifies surfaces and entities in the perceptual world. We begin by illustrating how relational information is important for understanding entities in our perceptual world.

MEANINGFUL ENTITIES VERSUS BRUTE THINGS

What do we know when an entity is meaningful for us? Dewey (1963) notes that:

> Our chief difficulty in answering this question lies in the thoroughness with which the lesson of familiar things has been learned. Thought can more easily traverse an unexplored region than it can undo what has been so thoroughly done as to be ingrained in unconscious habit. [p. 138].

Fig. 2. (a): An artificial entity.

A simple way to overcome some lessons of the familiar is to begin with unfamiliar entities and ask about the nature of information involved in conferring meaning upon them. This illustrates how meaning arises from perceiving an entity's participation in various events. Figure 2a illustrates an artifical entity. Some *Ss* refer to it as a "bumpy lump" and others as the back of a bear's head. The *Ss* thus attempt to confer meaning upon it (Bartlett's, 1932, "effort after meaning"; Piaget's, 1952, "assimilation"), but their understanding can be manipulated by viewing the entity's role in events. Figure 2b (see appendix) illustrates one sequence of events that gives the entity meaning; Fig. 2c (see appendix) illustrates a different meaning arising from a different sequence of events. Meanings for Figs. 2b and 2c both arise from viewing the entity in different contexts of usage. Figure 2d (see appendix) confers yet a different meaning on the artificial entity. Here the context is not one of usage, but rather specifies information about the entity's genesis from an organism's foot (i.e., it is a footprint). These examples illustrate that information about entities involves knowledge about their relations to other things that we know.

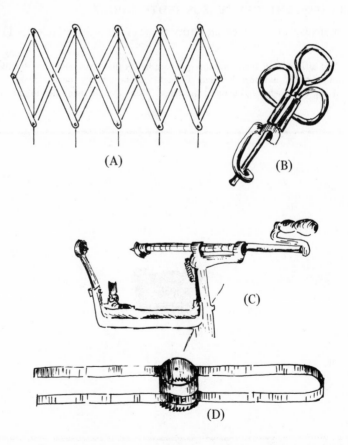

(A)

(B)

(C)

(D)

Fig. 3. (a): Drawings of real "incomprehensible" objects.

Figure 3a illustrates another set of relatively unknown objects. Rather than being artificial, however, they are drawings of real ones. Most people remain puzzled even when presented with the real things. These objects become more meaningful when one understands that they are tools designed to perform special functions. The appropriate functions for each object are provided in Fig. 3b (see appendix). These examples illustrate that information about an isolated object is not sufficient to allow an organism to grasp its meaning. As Dewey (1963) notes:

> To grasp the meaning of a thing, an event or a situation is to see it in its relations to other things; to note how it operates or functions, what consequences follow from it; what causes it, what uses it can be put to. In contrast, what we have called the brute thing, the thing without meaning to us, is something whose relations are not grasped [p. 135].

STRUCTURAL CONSTRAINTS AND MEANINGFULNESS

The claim that objects become meaningful as a function of perceived interrelations with other objects (including ourselves) is not a claim that the relation between the isolated object and its potential meanings is arbitrary. On the contrary, the object's characteristics in isolation (e.g., what it looks like, is made of) constrain the types of events in which it might be involved.

The notion of a nonarbitrary relation between what something looks like and what it means is related to J. J. Gibson's (1966) notion of affordances. Certain objects and their properties provide visual information for the activities and interactions they afford. So, for example, sharp objects afford piercing, certain extensions (e.g., handles) afford grasping, hardness affords pounding, and roundness affords rolling. Even surfaces afford activities since they are "walk-onable," "climbable," and the like. Tolman (1958) presented similar notions in his essay on "sign-gestalts." These are not simply information about the perceived given, described in geometric-technical terms, but include information about "the larger wholes in which the perceived configuration will itself be embedded as one term in a larger means-end proposition [p. 79]." Tolman further introduced the term "manipulanda" which he defines as:

> properties of objects which support (or make possible) motor manipulations of the species ... One and the same environmental object will afford quite different manipulanda to an animal which possesses hands from what it can and will to an animal which possesses only a mouth, or only a bill, or only claws ... grasp-ableness, pick-up-ableness, throw-ableness, heaviness (heave-ableness) and the like—these are manipulanda [p. 82].

Of course, an object's physical form is not only nonarbitrarily related to possible relations with the organism who is the knower, but is also nonarbitrarily related to acts, interactions, and functions involving other objects in its environment. For example, a snake, infant, rabbit, human adult, and toy truck move across a surface in different manners. In each case, the organism's structure and posture provide support for the particular type of movement that takes place. Similarly, an object like a bed affords comfortable reclining, and its structure is clearly nonarbitrarily to its use. Its structure will systematically vary according to the structure of the organisms (e.g., dog vs. human) that use it. And a structure's function may vary according to environmental context. Thus a wire cage supported by a single metal pole attached to a floor would not be a likely candidate for a bed for a human adult because it does not afford comfortable sleeping. However, if the wire frame is presented as a bed for an astronaut free of gravity, its affordance value for sleeping is more readily understood. The unfamiliar objects presented in Fig. 2 provide additional examples of the nonarbitrary relation between structure and function. Their structures place considerable constraints on their possible meanings. None of our informants entertained hypotheses about these objects being edible, sleep-on-able, and the like.

That physical properties may have meaningful implications is important for considerations of perceptual learning, because it suggests that relational information that allows objects to become meaningful also affects what perceptual characteristics are learned. Most researchers in perceptual learning have realized the importance of relations and concentrated on the acquisition of relationally derived distinctive features that serve to differentiate stimuli from other structurally similar ones (e.g., Garner, 1966; Gibson, 1970). But there are other types of relations besides those which occur between structurally similar stimuli, and these too should affect what is learned. For example, one may learn to appreciate unique perceptual character-istics of the different scissors in Fig. 4 by noting how they differ from one another (i.e., by acquiring the perceptual features that differentiate the objects from one another) or,

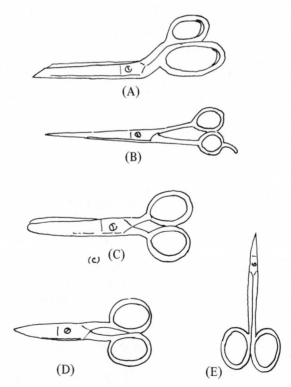

Fig. 4. Scissors: An exercise in structure—function relationships.

each scissor's unique structure can be meaningfully apprehended by better understanding the relations between the structures and the particular functions that each scissors was designed to perform. Table 1 (see appendix) summarizes appropriate functions for the scissors in Fig. 4. This example suggests that not only may physical structures have implications for objects' interrelations with other objects, but also that such interrelations may affect what is noticed about physical structure. Table 2 provides an additional example by listing various contexts of interaction and resulting features that might be noticed about trees.

TABLE 2

Some Structural Properties That Become Important as a
Function of Different Contexts of Usage for Trees

General contextual situation	Important properties
want shade	leaves; relation to the sun
hang a swing	strength and accessability of branch
build a treehouse	strength, closeness of several limbs
use for a bridge	strength, length (i.e., long enough to reach across stream)
put up hammock	closeness to another tree or support
make a snare	suppleness plus strength
escape from a wolf	height, ease of climbing
want fuel	dryness, whether green
want food	whether has fruit
want to hide behind	width, degree of foliage
need overview of land (i.e., lost)	height relative to other trees
need footrest on mountainside	strength

KNOWLEDGE AND RELATIONS

The preceding discussion suggests that knowledge of entities arises from information about their relations to other knowledge, and that knowledge of relations distinguishes a meaningful object from a "brute thing." However, a novel isolated object may nevertheless be meaningful to an organism if its perceptual properties are sufficient to specify what it affords. But note that perceptual characteristics allow us to understand a novel object by their implications for possible interactions in event sequences, hence the relational nature of meaning remains intact.

The importance of relational characterizations of meaning is also emphasized in Burke's (1969) writings. His chapter on antinomies of definition discusses problems involved in thinking of things in terms of substance. He here discusses the etymological origin of the word "substance":

> The word is often used to designate what some thing or agent intrinsically *is* as per these meanings in Webster's "the most important element in any existence; the characteristic and essential components of anything; the main part; essential import; purpose." Yet etymologically "substance" is a scenic [contextual] word. Literally, a person's or a thing's

sub-stance would be something that stands beneath or supports the person or thing . . . The word "substance" used to designate what a thing is, derives from a word designating something that a thing is not. That is, though used to designate something within the thing, intrinsic to it, the word etymologically refers to something outside the thing, extrinsic to it. Or otherwise put: the word in its etymological origins would refer to an attribute of the thing's context, since that which supports or underlies a thing would be a part of the thing's context. And a thing's context, being outside or beyond the thing, would be something that the thing is not . . .

To tell what a thing is, you place it in terms of something else. This idea of locating or placing, is implicit in our very word for definition itself: to define, or determine a thing, is to mark its boundaries, hence to use terms that possess, implicitly at least, contextual reference [pp. 21-24].

Later, Burke discusses the Aristotelian view of substance and contrasts it with Spinoza's ideas:

Starting from the Aristotelian notion that a substance, or being, is to be considered "in itself" . . . Spinoza went on to observe that nothing less than the totality of all the exists can meet this requirement. In Aristotle, each stone, or tree, or man, or animal, could be a substance, capable of being considered "in itself" . . . Thinking contextually, Spinoza held that each single object in the universe is "defined" (determined, limited, bounded) by the other things that surround it. And in calling upon men to see things "in terms of eternity" . . . Spinoza meant precisely that we should consider each thing in terms of its total context, the universal scene as a whole. Only when considering the universe as a whole, and its parts in terms of the whole, would we be making an "intrinsic" statement about substance, since there was but one substance, the universal totality [p. 25].

A relational conception of knowledge has some important implications. First, the meanings of objects may become richer as the environment becomes richer and as one's knowledge increases. Thus, Dewey (1963) remarks that carbon filaments obtained new meaning once electric lights were produced, and that gasoline, once a waste product, secured new meaning when the internal combustion engine was invented. Second, it suggests that just as an object's meaning is acquired through experience with its role in events, so also an isolated event's meaning may depend upon perception or knowledge of a broader event in which it is embedded.

There is a certain picture we have of what constitutes the world and consequently of what constitutes knowledge about the world. The picture is easy to recognize but hard to describe. It is a picture of the world as consisting of brute facts . . . The model for systematic knowledge of this kind is the natural sciences, and the basis for all knowledge of this kind is generally supposed to be simple empirical observation recording sense experiences.

It is obvious that large tracts of apparently fact-stating language do not consist of concepts which are part of this picture . . . Any newspaper records facts of the following sorts: Mr. Smith married Miss Jones; the Dodgers beat the Giants three to two in eleven innings; Green was convicted of larceny; and Congress passed the appropriations bill. There is certainly no easy way that the classical picture can account for facts such as these. That is, there is no simple set of statements about physical or psychological properties of states of affairs to which the statements of facts such as these are reducible. A marriage ceremony, a baseball game, a trial, and a legislative action involve a variety of physical movements, states, and raw feels, but a specification of one of these events only in such terms is not so far a specification of it as a marriage ceremony, baseball game, a trial, or a legislative action. The physical events and raw feels only count as parts of such events given certain other conditions and against a background of certain kinds of institutions . .

. . .it is only given the institution of money that I now have a five dollar bill in my hand. Take away the institution and all I have is a piece of paper with various gray and green markings [Searle, 1969, pp. 50-51].

Isolated objects cannot be taken as the basic unit of analysis when one seeks to understand how they become meaningful. Objects become meaningful by virtue of their interrelations with other objects (including the knowing organism); and objects are not always identified as mere objects. Instead they are understood relative to their roles in events. The information available from perception is therefore considerably richer than information about visual characteristics of individual isolated objects. The next section considers some general classes of perceptually derived information that organisms might acquire.

SOME INFORMATION AVAILABLE FROM PERCEIVING

One aspect of an organism's perceptually derived knowledge should, of course, be knowledge of meaningful entities that populate his environment. This may include information about perceptual properties of entities (including their implications for affordances) as well as information about possible roles the entities may be expected to perform. Thus certain entities may be perceived as capable of self-initiated motion and intent (actors) and hence capable of functioning as agents. Other entities may be perceived as incapable of self-initiated motion and intent, and hence will not be expected to perform self-initiating agent roles. More specific information should be available about particular classes of entities. Some may be perceived as having particular functions (e.g., a kernel cutter, a hat); some as arising from actions of other organisms (e.g., footprints); and some as entities which characteristically perform certain classes of action in the pursuit of certain goals. In short, information about entities places constraints on events in which they are likely to participate and on the roles that they may be expected to perform. Later we shall illustrate how such information may affect organisms' abilities to comprehend novel events.

Besides acquiring relatively stable meanings of classes of entitles from perceiving their interactions in a variety of events, organisms also acquire the counterpart of this information: characteristics of abstract event classes in which a variety of entities may participate. Consider events we might describe as *walking*. Such events can vary in many ways, involving different agents, different speeds (within some limited range), different compass directions, different terrains, etc. Despite all these different particulars the event *walking* is specified by certain invariant information. All instances of walking include information about an agent who does the walking, about some surface on which it walks, about structural support for the walking movement (i.e. appendages that alternately move ahead of one another), and about speed (to differentiate it from *running*). There thus exist abstract invariances characterizing this class of events.

Other events may be more complicated. Events involving surface contact like *touching, hitting, bumping, smashing* entail a minimum of two objects or surfaces (e.g., see Fillmore, 1971). Differentiation among members of the *surface contact* class may involve specification of differential rates of movement (e.g., bumping versus colliding) and may include differential specification of likely outcomes of the events (e.g., boy touches window versus boy smashes window). Events involving breaking provide another example: All involve at least one object (that is broken) and some instigating force responsible. The force may be inanimate (e.g., the wind), of animate nature where the agent itself is the instrument that makes contact, or of animate nature in which an agent uses some outside instrument. Other events are yet more complicated in that they involve interrelations among more objects. So, for example, the event *buying* involves a purchaser, a seller, an object that is bought, and a medium of monetary exchange (cf. Fillmore, 1971).

The invariant descriptions of events also presuppose certain contraints on the classes of objects that participate. Thus events like *walking, jumping,* etc., involve some object capable of self-initiated actions (or has some power source that can instigate such actions) and that has structural features that support the act (e.g., a snake does not walk). Events involving *breaking* require objects composed of classes of substances that can indeed break. In short, just as one's knowledge of entities involves constraints on events in which they may participate, one's knowledge of events includes constraints on the nature of the entities that may participate. Knowledge of abstract events and entities both determine one's ability to comprehend novel aspects of the perceptual world.

COMPREHENSION AS A FUNCTION OF RELATIONS PLUS ENTITIES IN-VOLVED

An organism's knowledge of entities and abstract invariants characteristic of event classes interact to determine its comprehension of novel perceptual phenomena. Consider events involving the movement of some entity. All movements involve some instigating force responsible for them, and the nature of the object undergoing movement will affect one's assumption about the instigating force involved. Thus, imagine that one is sitting at home and that there is a piece of paper on the living room table. Suddenly it flutters upwards a bit and falls to the floor. Such an event is not necessarily puzzling because one can easily think of possible forces that instigated the paper's movements; for example, a sudden breeze. But if one could not postulate a force that instigated the movement he might be puzzled, especially if the event recurred despite efforts to eliminate the suspected cause. Indeed, such circumstances (generally with cups and plates) often cause people to postulate forces such as poltergeists. The inability to isolate possible instigating forces can cause considerable activity designed to understand what is going on. But note that one's interpretation of the event is partly a function of the entity entering into it. Thus if one's pet bird flew off the table in a similar fashion one would not be likely to postulate forces like breezes or poltergeists, since a bird is understood to be capable of self-initiating acts.

As a second example, imagine the following situation: You awake in the morning to find that the dirty dishes left in the sink are now clean, yet you live alone and know you did not wash them yourself. Anomoly arises because one must account for their change from a dirty to clean state. There are a number of ways one might resolve the anomoly. One might remember that he had a houseguest who was very helpful, or that he had indeed washed the dishes after all; or failing all else, he might wonder if he had had a compulsive burglar enter during the night. Any such realizations might result in a click of comprehension, but if they were not reasonable hypotheses, the feeling of anomaly would still persist.

It is instructive to note how the "clean dishes anomoly" arises partly because of one's knowledge of dishes. These are understood as utensils that are designed to perform certain functions (e.g., holding food) and that require certain operations from other organisms if they undergo a change in state or position (e.g., they must be washed, transported, etc., by something other than themselves). Dishes are known to be incapable of self-initiated acts like washing or moving themselves, and events involving such acts must involve some instigating force responsible for the change. This knowledge forces the comprehender to attempt to identify some outside agent that must be involved.

But suppose that one's knowledge of dishes were different, that one knew he owned self-cleaning dishes composed of microscopically thin layers of material such that a single layer peeled over night leaving the dishes clean. Now, despite no agent's having washed them, the sight of clean dishes in the sink would present no anomoly. One would still preserve the invariant information that some instigating force is responsible, but in this case the force could be readily identified as residing in the dishes themselves.

Knowledge of entities and relations also interact to allow the comprehender to understand implicational significances of events which involve more information than is momentarily present. For example, knowledge of footprints includes the information that they are made by an organism's foot, that they are symmetrical to the foot, and so forth. We thus have relatively abstract, relational knowledge of footprints, but the same footprints can have different significances depending on their relation to other things in the world; for example, the situation in which they are found. Thus, if a lost person finds a human footprint in a territory known to be inhabited by friendly people it signifies friends and safety. The same footprint in enemy territory could signify enemies and possible doom. If one thought he were the first person to have landed on the moon, human footprints would signify previous visitors. If one were looking for a lost child, they could signify that he was on the right track. Understanding these different significances presupposes knowledge of footprints. If one thought that they were impressions formed by plant-life, their appearance would not suggest hope in friendly territory, fear in enemy territory, and so forth. Their particular significances would have changed. And of course, if one did not know which environment he was in (e.g., friendly or unfriendly), the footprints would also lose their particular significances, even though their meaning as entities was known. One's knowledge of the meaning of abstract classes of entities and events and perception of their occurrence within particular contexts interact to yield significances. Significances are a joint function of the meanings of entities and the particular contexts in which they occur. As one changes, so generally do the significances as well.

These examples illustrate how relational information about objects and information about abstract invariants characteristic of events interact to affect one's ability to comprehend novel situations. Some events involving certain entities are so readily comprehended that one may hardly notice them. Others require one to seek additional information to adequately understand them, and perhaps to postulate the existence of agents and forces (for examples) which may not be perceptually present. Of course, if people have different conceptions of entities in their world they may understand the same events differently. Thus, an adult from a western culture is likely to understand an echo in the mountains as sound waves bouncing back from particularly shaped surfaces, whereas a person of another culture may understand the same event by assuming a benevolent agent (e.g., a god of the mountain) who is kind enough to return a person's voice. Similarly, whether the wind is considered as an instigating force or an instrument in the hands of a god will depend upon a person's particular world view.

We cannot yet provide a detailed analysis of relational information derived from perception, but we are developing an experimental paradigm that should allow us to study the acquisition of such information and to investigate its effects on organisms' abilities to comprehend novel perceptual events. The basic paradigm is the "ecological niche." It consists simply of a film of a set of artificial entities that can be made meaningful to an organism as a function of his perception of their interactions in the perceptual mini-world. The nature of the organism's knowledge of a particular "world" or niche can be assessed by asking him which of a set of novel perceptual events are probable, improbable, anomolous, and the like. Hopefully this procedure will allow us to study the acquisition of knowledge of objects (including information about affordances and constraints on roles) and abstract invariances characterizing events. Ultimately we would like to study such situations cross-culturally, developmentally, and with adults who may have language deficits, in order to assess the effects of cultural and linguistic knowledge on one's abilities to understand a perceptual world.

To summarize, we have argued that one's knowledge of his environment is considerably richer than knowledge of the perceptual characteristics of isolated objects, and that perceptually derived knowledge entails knowledge of *relations* rather than things. The next section suggests that linguistic comprehension can also be characterized as "the grasping of relations," and that linguistic comprehension depends upon the comprehender's cognitive, alinguistic ability to activate knowledge that will allow relations to be grasped.

LINGUISTIC COMPREHENSION

We have suggested that comprehension of perceptual events often involves assumptions about circumstances (e.g., instigating forces) that may not be immediately perceivable in the environment, and that the comprehender's knowledge of abstract constraints on entities and relations directs the assumptions or cognitive contributions he makes in order to understand. We think that—to an even greater extent than in perceptual comprehension—linguistic comprehension involves cognitive contributions on the part of the comprehender. The remaining sections consider some cognitive contributions that appear to accompany "clicks of comprehension," and argue that the ability to make appropriate contributions depends on the comprehender's currently activated knowledge of his world. In this sense, our approach to language will be similar to one provided some time ago by

Karl Bühler (cf. Blumenthal, 1970) who emphasized the interdependence between linguistic inputs and semantic "fields." According to Blumenthal:

> Bühler's field concept was most important. Given two speakers of the same language, no matter how well one of them structures a sentence his utterance will fail if both parties do not share the same field to some degree ... There are inner aspects of the field, such as an area of knowledge, or outer aspects, such as objects in the environment. Indeed, the field can be analyzed into many aspects. The total field (Umfeld) consists not only of the practical situation (Ziegfeld) in which an utterance occurs, but also the symbol field (Symbolfeld) which is the context of language segments preceding the segment under consideration ... *The structure of any particular language is largely field-independent, being determined by its own particularconventional rules, but the field determines how the rules are applied* (italics added) [p. 56].

We suggest that the "field-independent" aspect of language might be conceptualized as knowledge of cues or instructions for creating meaning, but that the ability to formulate the semantic content of a message, i.e., the ability to achieve a click of comprehension, will also depend upon the comprehender's cognitive contributions. Our arguments will include the following considerations: (*a*) that *Ss* do make cognitive contributions while comprehending; (*b*) that certain contributions are prerequisites for achieving a click or comprehension; (*c*) that knowledge of abstract constraints on entities and relations plays an important role in determining *Ss'* contributions; and (*d*) that meaning is the result of such contributions and is best viewed as something that is "created" rather than stored and retrieved. Following this, we shall consider some implications of the present approach.

SOME CONSIDERATIONS OF THE INFORMATION AVAILABLE WHEN WE COMPREHEND

That linguistic inputs might be viewed as cues or instructions to create meanings implies that semantic descriptions created by *Ss* may not always correspond to the information a sentence "expresses directly." The semantic descriptions created by *Ss* may often include more information than was expressed in a sentence, and the same inputs may result in different semantic descriptions depending on the cognitive contributions that the comprehender makes. This section reviews studies supporting this view.

Consider the following two sentences: (1) *Three turtles rested beside a floating log and a fish swam beneath them.* (2) *Three turtles rested on a floating log and a fish swam beneath them.* Both sentences express a spatial relation between the log and the turtles (either *on* or *beside*) and both express a relation between the fish and the turtles (namely, that the fish swam *beneath* the turtles).

Bransford, Barclay, and Franks (1972) reasoned that although the linguistic propositions underlying the two sentences types were similar, the semantic descriptions constructed by *Ss* might nevertheless differ. Thus, for Sentences (2), *Ss'* knowledge of spatial relations should allow the inference that the fish swam beneath the log as well as the turtles (since the turtles were on the log), but the same inference should be less probable for *Ss* hearing Sentence (1). Memory data supported the hypothesis that sentences like (1) and (2) may result in different semantic descriptions. Subjects hearing sentences like (2) were likely to think that they had actually heard novel sentences that expressed the probable inference (e.g., *Three turtles rested on a floating log and a fish swam beneath it.*); whereas *Ss* hearing sentences like (1) were less likely to think that they had heard its novel counterpart (e.g., *Three turtles rested beside a floating log and a fish swam beneath it.*). These data suggest that *Ss* used the linguistic inputs to create semantic descriptions of situations and that these descriptions often included more information than' the input sentence directly expressed.

An obvious extension of the notion that *Ss* use linguistically communicated information to construct spatial descriptions of situations is that the same sentences may result in different semantic descriptions depending on the contextual information available to each *S*. A pilot study conducted by Bransford, Johnson, and Solomon evaluated this idea. Two groups of *Ss* saw two different pictorial contexts. Group I saw the picture in Fig. 5a, whereas Group II saw the picture in Fig. 5b. All *Ss* were told that these were pictures of a farmhouse and a hill. Both groups were then read the same linguistic passage and asked to try to understand it. In the passage, entities were described in terms of their relation to the farmhouse and the hill. For example, the passage contained the following two sentences: (3) *The pond was to the right of the farmhouse;* (4) *The forest was to the left of the*

Fig. 5. (a) and (b): Two different contexts for farm passage.

hill. Such sentences should have different implications depending upon the intial context from which *Ss* viewed them. Thus *Ss* seeing Picture (b) might assume that anything to the right of the farmhouse was also to the right of the hill, and vice versa, hence they should be likely to think they had heard the novel sentences (5) *The pond was to the right of the hill;* and (6) *The forest was to the left of the farmhouse*. However, *Ss* seeing Picture (a) should be less likely to make such inferences, since for example, the pond could be to the right of the farmhouse and yet in front of the hill.

Recognition data suggested that *Ss* did indeed create different semantic descriptions as a function of the initial context from which they viewed the linguistic passages. The *Ss* seeing Picture (b) were generally unable to differentiate sentences that were actually heard, e.g., (3) (4), from novel but appropriate sentences like (5) and (6). However, *Ss* seeing Picture (a) were able to differentiate such sentences quite well. Note that if only the linguistic input were stored, both groups should have performed in an equivalent manner since the passages they heard were identical. That their performance did differ suggests that the information acquired from the input sentences depended upon the initial contexts from which they were viewed.

Of course, it is likely that *Ss* make assumptions about (and "remember") things other than inferred spatial relations among objects mentioned in the input sentences. For example, they may assume the existence of objects never mentioned in the sentence, or they may elaborate the consequences that particular inputs seem to imply. Johnson, Bransford, and Solomon (in press) showed that *Ss* make assumptions about objects never mentioned in sentences—in this case, the objects were those generally necessary to perform certain acts. The *Ss* were read a series of very short descriptions. Experimental *Ss* were read stories designed to suggest particular inferences about instruments used to carry out the actions. For example:

> John was trying to fix the bird house. He was *pounding the nail* when his father came out to watch him and to help him do the work.
>
> For the control group, the same story frames were used but in each case a verb was changed so that no object was implied or so that the implied object was different:
>
> John was trying to fix the bird house. He was *looking for* the nail when his father came out to watch him and to help him do the work.

At recognition, both groups of *Ss* were presented with the same sentences. The critical instrument-inference item for the above story was:

> John was using the *hammer* to fix the bird house when his father came out to watch him and to help him do the work.

The *Ss* hearing the first version of the story were quite likely to think that they had actually heard the recognition foil, but *Ss* hearing the second version were quite sure that they had not heard it before.

The same study investigated false recognition memory for another class of inferences: those dealing with perceived consequences of input events. Once again, *Ss* were read brief stories. The experimental group heard stories like this:

> The river was narrow. A beaver hit the log that a turtle was sitting on and the log flipped over from the shock. The turtle was very surprised by the event.

If one thinks about this situation for a moment, he will realize that a probable consequence of the log's flipping over is that the turtle would get knocked into the water.

A control group heard the identical story, except that the turtle was *beside* the log rather than on it. After acquisition, both groups heard the same recognition foil: *A beaver hit the log and knocked the turtle into the water.* Once again most *Ss* in the experimental group were quite sure that they had actually heard this sentence whereas *Ss* in the control group felt that they had not heard it before.

These studies suggest that information "directly expressed" by sentences cannot always be equated with the information available to the comprehender. Comprehenders do not simply store the information underlying sentences, but instead use linguistic inputs in conjunction with other information to update their general knowledge of the world. These considerations apply not only to individual sentences but also to sets of sentences. Thus, *Ss* often use information expressed by a number of individual sentences (often ones which are nonadjacent) to form wholistic semantic descriptions containing more information than any particular acquisition sentence expressed (e.g., Barclay, in press; Bransford & Franks, 1971 in press; Potts, 1971). Such studies support arguments made previously by Wundt that "the mind of the hearer is just as active in transforming and creating as the mind of the speaker" (cf. Blumenthal, 1970 p. 37) and that it is the apperceptive constructive processes that organize the input events. We are thereby reminded that an adequate approach to comprehension must consider the cognitive contributions of the comprehender as well as the linguistic characterizations of input sentences. But we need a clearer picture of the role that particular cognitive contributions may play.

COGNITVE CONTRIBUTIONS THAT ARE NECESSARY IN ORDER TO COMPREHEND

A reasonable interpretation might be that *Ss* first comprehend sentences and *then* make cognitive contributions such as elaborating spatial implications, inferring probable consequences, and so forth. One might therefore suppose that cognitive processing takes over *after* something called "linguistic comprehension" take place. But our view of linguistic knowledge as abstract cues or instructions used to create meanings denies that one's knowledge of language incorporates knowledge of meaning—in the sense of meaning sufficient to produce a click a comprehension. Comprehension results only when the comprehender has sufficient alinguistic information to use the cues specified in linguistic input to create some semantic content that allows him to understand. In actuality, there are undoubtedly many levels at which one can understand utterances. Nevertheless, there appears to be some minimum level below which *Ss* will fail to call sentences "comprehensible." This suggests that one may have knowledge of language and yet fail to understand utterances unless one is able to activate appropriate alinguistic knowledge. This section considers some studies that investigate this idea.

Bransford and Johnson (in press a, in press b) sought to manipulate *Ss'* abilities to comprehend by varying the availability of prerequisite information. For example, consider the following passage (which was read to *Ss*) and imagine that you are to try to recall it after it is read:

> If the ballons popped the sound wouldn't be able to carry since everything would be too far away from the correct floor. A closed window would also prevent the sound from carrying, since most buildings tend to be well insulated. Since the whole operation depends upon a steady flow of electricity, a break in the middle of the wire would also cause problems. Of course, the fellow could shout, but the human voice is not loud enough to carry that far. An additional problem is that a string could break on the instrument. Then there could be no accompaniment to the message. It is clear that the best situation would involve less distance. Then there would be fewer potential problems. With face to face contact, the least number of things could go wrong.

One group (No Context *Ss*) heard the passage (read once through) and were then asked to rate it on a 7-point comprehension scale. Following that, they were asked to recall as much as they could. Table 3 indicates that these *Ss* rated the passage as very incomprehensible and showed very poor recall. A second group (Appropriate Context) heard the same tape-recorded passage, but they saw the picture in Fig. 6 for 30 seconds before the passage was read. Note that the passage does not simply describe the picture, but instead specifies events that could happen given the picture as a conceptual base. The *Ss* seeing this picture rated the passage very comprehensible and showed a 100% increase in recall over the no context group (see Table 3). This picture had to be made available to *Ss* *before* they heard the passage, however: A third group (Context After *Ss*) received the appropriate context picture after hearing the passage, and Table 3 shows that this did not appreciably augment their comprehension and recall scores relative to the No Context group. And the ability to comprehend the passage was not simply an effect of mere repetition of information: A fourth group (No Context-2) heard the passage (without context) twice in succession. Nevertheless, they still exhibited poor comprehension and recall scores.

A fifth group was also run in the experiment. These *Ss* (Partial Context *Ss*) saw the picture in Fig. 7 for 30 seconds before the passage was read. Note that the picture contained the same concrete elements as the appropriate context figures, but the relations among the elements were changed. Table 3 shows that *Ss* seeing the second picture did not benefit from it. They still exhibited very low comprehension and recall scores. We shall return to consider why the appropriate

TABLE 3

Mean Comprehension Ratings and Recall Scores
for Experiment on the "Balloon Passage'

	No Context (1)	No Context (2)	Context After	Partial Context	Context Before
Comprehension	2.30	3.60	3.30	3.70	6.10
Recall	3.60	3.80	3.60	4.00	8.00

context helped *Ss* comprehend the passage and why the second picture failed to help them, but first, consider some additional studies that attempt to manipulate *Ss'* ability to comprehend.

The preceding passage referred to a particular situation with which few people were likely to have had contact. However, the importance of prerequisite knowledge is applicable to situations where the semantic prerequisites are available from *Ss'* prior knowledge, but are not activated at the time the passage is heard. Consider the following passage and imagine again that you are to try to recall what you heard.

> The procedure is actually quite simple. First you arrange things into different groups. Of course one pile may be sufficient depending on how much there is to do. If you have to go somewhere else due to lack of facilities that is the next step, otherwise you are pretty well set. It is important not to overdo things. That is, it is better to do too few things at once than too many. In the short run this may not seem important but complications can easily arise. A mistake can be expensive as well. At first the whole procedure will seem complicated. Soon however, it will become just another facet of life. It is difficult to foresee any end to the necessity for this task in the immediate future, but then one never can tell. After the procedure is completed one arranges the materials into different groups again. Then they can be put into their appropriate places. Eventually they will be used once more and the whole cycle will then have to be repeated. However, that is a part of life.

Now read the passage again, but with the knowledge that the topic is *washing clothes*. Results of two such experiments are shown in Table 4. The *Ss* in the No

Fig. 6. Appropriate context for balloon passage.

Fig. 7. Partial context for balloon passage.

TABLE 4

Mean Comprehension Ratings and Recall Scores for
Two Different Experiments on Passages about "Washing Clothes"

| | Experiment 1 | | | Experiment 2 | |
	No topic	Topic after	Topic before	Topic after	Topic before
Comprehension	2.29	2.12	4.50	3.40	5.27
Recall	2.82	2.65	5.83	3.30	7.00

Topic group showed poor comprehension and recall scores, as did *Ss* who received information that the passage was about washing clothes *after* hearing the passage but just before recall. The *Ss* in the Topic Before groups showed higher comprehension and recall scores. Note that prior knowledge is not sufficient to assure comprehension. This knowledge must be activated if one is to understand.

A third experiment by Bransford and Johnson (in press b) is also relevant. *Ss* were read the following passage after informing them that its title was *Watching a peace march from the fortieth floor:*

> The view was breathtaking. From the window one could see the crowd below. Everything looked extremely small from such a distance, but the colorful costumes could still be seen. Everyone seemed to be moving in one direction in an orderly fashion and there seemed to be little children as well as adults. The landing was gentle and luckily the atmosphere was such that no special suits had to be worn. At first there was a great deal of activity. Later, when the speeches started, the crowd quieted down. The man with the television camera took many shots of the setting and the crowd. Everyone was very friendly and seemed to be glad when the music started.

After hearing the passage, *Ss* were asked to recall it. Most sentences were recalled well except for the one about "the landing." There was extremely low recall for this sentence, and *Ss* noted that there was one sentence (i.e., about a landing) that they could not understand. Even when presented with a "cue outline" (e.g., Luckily the landing_____ and the atmosphere_____.), *Ss* exhibited very low ability to remember what this sentence was about.

A second group of *Ss* heard the identical passage but with a different title: *A space trip to an inhabited planet*. These *Ss* showed much better free recall of "the landing" sentence than did the first group, as well as greater ability to fill in the gaps in the cue outline presented above (see Bransford & Johnson, in press b). These results suggest that a sentence that would be comprehensible in isolation (i.e., "the landing" sentence) can become incomprehensible when viewed from an inappropriate context, and that such incomprehensibility has a marked effect on ability to recall. The results also illustrate that the same passage, when viewed from different contexts, can be interpreted as meaning very different things.

EVIDENCE FOR COGNITIVE CONTRIBUTIONS THAT ALLOW ONE TO COMPREHEND

The preceding studies demonstrate that one can have knowledge of language and yet fail to understand utterances if he is unable to activate appropriate knowledge of the world. But it could be argued that these are contrived situations (which they are) and that one's ability to comprehend a multitude of sentences in isolation suggests the existence of other, more natural, linguistic processes that usually take place when one comprehends. We contend that sentences which are and are not comprehensible in isolation differ *not* in terms of necessary cognitive contributions, but rather in terms of the ease with which such contributions can be made. In this section we present evidence suggesting that *Ss* do frequently make cognitive contributions *in order to understand* sentences. Our evidence will still be based on sentences which, although comprehensible in isolation, are still rather difficult and perhaps not "normal." We begin with such sentences for the same reasons that Bühler and his colleagues apparently did (cf. Blumenthal, 1970): They allow an opportunity for otherwise unconscious processes to be observed. In later sections we will consider more "normal" sentences as well.

An experiment by McCarrell, Bransford, and Johnson (in preparation) suggests that *Ss* spontaneously specify certain cognitive conditions while comprehending sentences. Two parallel sets of target sentences were constructed. One set was composed of sentences designed to elicit special assumptions (SA sentences) (e.g., *The floor was dirty because Sally used the mop; The shirt looked terrible because Jane ironed it; John missed the bus because he knew he would have to walk to school).* The second set included similar sentences that were more "self-contained" (SC sentences) in that fewer special assumptions had to be made (e.g., *The floor was dirty so Sally used the mop; The shirt looked terrible so Jane ironed it; John missed the bus so he knew he would have to walk to school).* For the SA sentences, *Ss* are forced into specifying how a state or event (e.g., dirty floor, terrible looking dress, missed bus) could result from a preceding action or idea (e.g., mopping, ironing, knowing about having to walk). Most *Ss* assume that such relations can take place if, for example, the mop was dirty, Sally was a poor ironer, and John wanted to walk to school.

The SA and SC target sentences were embedded in short story frames and read to *Ss*. Either an SA or its SC counterpart was presented in the identical story frame. After hearing the series, *Ss* were asked to recognize which *exact* sentences they had actually heard during acquisition. The question was the degree to which *Ss* would falsely recognize novel sentences that expressed probable assumptions (e.g., *The mop was dirty before Sally washed the floor; John wanted to walk to school so he purposefully missed the bus, etc.*) as a function of whether *Ss* had heard an SA or SC form. The *Ss* hearing an SA form were quite likely to falsely recognize such sentences, whereas those hearing an SC form were not likely to think they had heard them before.

A pilot study has investigated the effects of cognitive contributions on the free recall of sentences. Our reasoning was that if certain sentences (e.g., (1) *The shirt looked terrible because Jane ironed it;* (2) *The mirror shattered because the child grabbed the broom)* require elaborative contributions *(elaboratives)*, they might stand out from other sentences more than their easy counterparts *(easy's)* (e.g., (3) *The shirt looked terrible so Jane ironed it;* (4) *The mirror shattered so the child grabbed the broom).* Hence, *elaboratives* might be more likely to be recalled. Using a within-*Ss* design, we presented *Ss* with sentences such as (1) and (4) and other *Ss* with sentences such as the counterparts (2) and (3). *Elaborative* sentences were recalled more frequently than their *easy* counterparts, hence supporting the notion that there is some psychological reality to cognitive elaborations that take place when we comprehend. Of course, one might argue that the *elaborative* sentences were simply "unusual" and that this accounts for their high recall. But not all "unusual" sentences result in high recall, as the next study shows.

A third experiment (McCarrell, Bransford & Johnson, in preparation) reminds us that certain cognitive contributions may be necessary in order to allow one to comprehend. The immediately preceding study used *elaboratives* and *easy* sentences that were ultimately comprehensible to *Ss* were able to make appropriate cognitive specifications that permitted them to comprehend. In the present study, we designed sentences for which it was unlikely that *Ss* could specify appropriate conditions unless provided with cues from *E*. The study compared recall of these *difficult* sentences with recall of sentences that were *easy* to comprehend. Examples of *easy* and *difficult* sentences are provided below:

Easy: The office was cool because the windows were closed.
          The car was moved because he had no change.
Difficult: The trip was not delayed because the bottle shattered.
          The haystack was important because the cloth ripped.

Note that both the *easy* and *difficult* sentences were constructed by linking easily comprehended, simple sentences by *because*. The differential difficulty of the two sentence sets thus arises from the differential ease with which *Ss* could specify situations in which the *because* relation between the simple sentences could make sense.

Two groups were run: One group (No Context) received a list consisting of eight *easy* and eight *difficult* sentences, randomly intermixed. On the study trials, each sentence was preceded by the subject noun (e.g., the office, the car, the trip, the haystack). On the test trials, the subject nouns were available as retrieval cues. For this condition, *easy* sentences were recalled much better than were *difficult* sentences, with the advantage of the *easy* items persisting over three study-test trials.

The second group (Context) received conditions identical to those of the first except that each sentence was preceded by a context cue rather than a subject noun on the study trials. The contexts for the sentences above were *air-conditioning, parking meter, christening a ship,* and *parachutist,* respectively. They were designed to provide *Ss* with information that would allow them to grasp the *because* relation between the entities mentioned in each clause. The retrieval cues on the recall tests were the subject noun.

Presentation of the context cues eliminated the differential recall for *easy* and *difficult* sentences. The differential difficulty of these sentence classes was therefore not simply a function of the sentences *per se,* but rather of the ease with which *Ss* could specify conditions that would allow the *because* relations to be grasped.

TOWARDS A CHARACTERIZATION OF THE CONSTRAINTS GOVERNING THE SPECIFICATIONS SUBJECTS MUST MAKE

Reasonable evidence suggests that the comprehender must frequently do considerable work to create situations that allow him to grasp the relations specified in input sentences, and that at least some specifications are necessary for the click of comprehension to occur. But such a statement still lacks cognitive content. Why do certain specifications permit comprehension and others result in failure? Do *Ss* randomly make assumptions, or are their assumptions somehow constrained? Do all sentences involve cognitive specifications on the comprehender's part, or are the sentences we have considered merely special cases that are different from those *Ss* normally hear? We cannot completely answer these questions, but in the present section we shall argue that they are worth asking, and we shall speculate on directions one might take in order to determine what adequate answers might be.

CONSTRAINTS ON ENTITIES ENTERING INTO EVENTS

Consider a sentence which most *Ss* find initially anomolous and then comprehensible: *The man put the plane in the envelope.* Most *Ss* assume that the plane must be a toy one; and with this discovery, they comprehend. What is it that forces *Ss* to place special constraints on their interpretation of *plane*?

We have suggested that comprehending involves the grasping of relations, and in the above sentence, an important relation is "*x* is contained by *y*." It seems reasonable that such a relation is known to involve size restrictions between a container and the contained, and that these restrictions force *Ss* to specify certain conditions (i.e. that it is a toy plane) that will allow such a relation to occur. Of course, *Ss* might choose to assume a large envelope rather than a small plane, but the latter is presumably more likely given our knowledge of the world.

This analysis assumes that the relations place the primary constraints on the nature of the entities. Yet, if different entities enter into the same relations, different specifications may emerge. Hence, if the sentence were *The man put the plane in the hanger,* one need not assume that the sentence referred to a toy plane; a hanger is sufficiently large to house a real plane.

If the relation is changed, it can also affect the constraints on size specifications. The sentence *The man saw the plane and the envelope* does not require one to assume a toy airplane since the relations *see* does not involve the same restrictions on size. Nevertheless, *see* does involve *some* size restrictions. Thus, the sentence *The man saw the red blood cells* is usually understood as involving a microscope, whereas the sentence *The man saw the car* is generally understood as involving simply the naked eye.

Size restrictions are, of course, but one of many restrictions on entities entering into events. *Jumping* requires an entity capable of self-initiated movement; hence, the sentence *The lamp jumped* is anomolous because lamps are not capable of self-initiated movement. With a sentence like *it jumped*, the comprehender projects properties of self-initiated movement onto the pronoun *it*. And it would appear that restrictions on *jump* are not restrictions on the lexical items that can occur with it, but rather restrictions on the nature of the entities referred to by the lexical item. Thus if certain characteristics of entities are "suspended" as, for example, in a Walt Disney cartoon, the sentence *The lamp jumped* may be perfectly comprehensible. Such a context may have established that lamps (or trees, or brooms) are capable of self-initiated acts.

INSTIGATING FORCE AS AN ABSTRACT CATEGORY UNDERLYING MANY EVENTS

As another example of the effect of relations (and their participating entities) on comprehension, consider the following sentences: *The wind broke the window; The ball broke the window*. These sentences are comprehended in different ways. In the event section we suggested that changes of state generally involve some instigating force responsible for the situation, and the verb *break* certainly involves a change of state (cf. Fillmore, 1971). Among other things, the comprehender is forced to assign a member of the category *instigating force* to the sentences above.

In the first case, wind can be thought of as both instigator and instrument; but wind is also understood as a force of nature and as incapable of purposefully deciding to break the window (in contrast, for example, with an agent such as *boy*). On the other hand, ball is assumed to be an instrument incapable of acting as an instigator, hence some other instigating force (e.g., gravity, another agent) must be responsible. Thus, if *Ss* hear the sentences *The boy ran home because the ball broke the window* and *The boy ran home because the wind broke the window,* they calculate different reasons for the boy's action. The *Ss* hearing the sentence about the ball generally assume that the boy ran home because he (or a friend) was responsible for breaking the window, but *Ss* hearing the sentence about the wind do not assume that the boy might be responsible. Rather, they may assume that he was scared.

Collins and Quillian (1972) provide another illustration of *instigating force* as an abstract category of information underlying changes of state; in this case, from movement to rest. Consider their sentence *The policeman help up his hand and the cars stopped* (p. 327). The question of interest is whether any specification of the *instigating force* category is tacitly "filled in" when we understand such a sentence (e.g., that an agent, the driver, was responsible for stopping the car).

A method for convincing oneself that such information is tacitly specified is to create a context such that the tacitly assumed agent is no longer available. Collins and Quillian ask the reader to suppose that there had just been an earthquake, and that two cars which had been parked on a hill started to roll down. Now, given the sentence *The policemen held up his hand and the cars stopped,* one is forced to wonder "how did he do that?" When one first read the sentence about the cars and the policeman (without the context), he must have assumed that the drivers caused the car to stop. However, when the context suggested that there were no drivers, one had to look elsewhere for an instigator of the stopping. One was therefore forced to attempt to understand how a policemen's outstretched hand could stop two rolling cars.

Of course, context may not always "subtract" possible assumptions about abstract categories of information (e.g., instigating forces) but may instead supply them; and this too affects one's ability to comprehend. For example, most *Ss* assume that the sentence *The houses moved* is anomalous, The event *movement* involves assumptions about entities entering into it, and *Ss* are forced to specify some instigating force. Since *Ss* understand houses to be incapable of self-initiated movement, and since no instigating force is specified (and none is readily specifiable by the *Ss*), they reject the sentences as anomalous. But if one says *Earthquake: The house moved*, more *Ss* accept the sentence as sensible. An earthquake is a possible instigating force for the movement, hence the sentence is readily understood. The sentence *The stripes expanded* provides a similar example. Initially it appears to be anomalous. But if one says *Balloon: The stripes expanded,* *Ss* are better able to understand it. They not only realize that the stripes could be on the balloon, but also that the balloon could be blown up by some agent and hence the stripes would indeed expand. Notice that *balloon* does not directly specify the instigating force; it does, however, provide sufficient information for *Ss* to specify the force themselves.

The specification of instigating forces can also cause sentences with similar surface structures to be differentially comprehended. In the sentence *The mouse squeaked,* the mouse is understood as the instigator of the event *squeaking*. However, the sentence *The window squeaked* is understood differently, presumably because one knows that windows are not capable of self-initiated acts like squeaking. Windows squeak only if some agent does something to them.

WORDS AS ABSTRACT CONSTRAINTS THAT GUIDE MEANING–MAKING ACTS

As a further example of the cognitive computations involved in grasping meaning, consider the following sentences: *The man used the table to iron the sheet; The man used the iron to iron the sheet.* These sentences specify that table and iron are to enter into a particular relation between man and sheet. The comprehender's *task* is to create conditions that allow appropriate relations to occur. Most *Ss* assume that the man placed the sheet *on* the table and that he used the iron to *do* the ironing. In these examples, the nature of the entities entering into the *use* relation affects the particular nature of the relation that *Ss* compute. And *Ss* must be able to calculate *some* relation between the entities to comprehend the sentence. A sentence like *The man used the jacket to iron the sheet* is incomprehensible to most *Ss* because they are unable to specify situations in which such a relation might occur.

The previously discussed sentences *The man put the plane in the envelope* and *The man put the plane in the hanger* provide an additional example of differential interpretations of a relation as a function of the participating entities. We noted that specification of the container as either envelope or hanger placed constraints on *Ss'* interpretation of *plane*; however, this specification also had additional implications in that it further affected one's interpretation of the word *put*. Putting a toy plane into an envelope presumably involves the use of hands, whereas putting a real airplane into a hanger necessitates a very different understanding of the word *put*. It appears reasonable to suggest that words and sentences specify some abstract conditions concerning the nature of the relations and the participating entities to be considered, and that it is the comprehender's ability to think (i.e., create situations such that the relations can be realized) that allows him to understand what the sentence might mean.

The conception of words as abstract constraints that guide meaning creation may help us understand how words can have so many different senses of meanings. If meaning results from *Ss'* creations of situations that permit the occurrence of certain relations specified in a sentence, a word should be interpreted differently as a function of its context. Consider, for example, the word *use*. One can use a rope, knife, box, etc., and in each case what one understands by *use* depends on the nature of the entities involved in the event *using*. Furthermore, the same entity can be used for different functions. Thus, to use a wooden box to carry books is different from using it to reach the ceiling; to use a rope to tie a package is different from using it to climb down from the third floor. And one uses a knife to cut bread in a different manner from using it to drive a screw into the wall. In each case the word *use* imposes abstract constraints on the nature of the event considered, but the entities involved affect the semantic content of the relation that comprehenders create.

The verb *escape* provides another example. To escape from an airplane may involve a parachute; to escape from a sinking boat may involve getting wet. And to escape from a lion may involve climbing a tree or running very fast. The linguistic characterization of *escape* must be something very abstract like "make x get away from an undesirable situation y"; but the comprehender's understanding of the *escape* relation will be a function of the entities involved. And note that certain contexts make it difficult to calculate a meaning. The sentence *The man escaped from the ice cream cone* is initially difficult to comprehend—despite the fact that one can use the word *escape* in other contexts without any problem. If *Ss* generate or are supplied with information that allows them to specify conditions that permit an *escape* relation (e.g., the cone fell from a second story window and the man moved away from its fall), they are better able to comprehend. Another example of cognitive specification is illustrated by the verb *fly:* The sentence *The bird flew through the air* is usually assumed to involve wings; the sentence *The Saucer flew through the air* is usually assumed to involve some human or Martian agent; the sentence *The house flew through the air* is generally assumed to involve strong winds such as a tornado; and the sentence *The pilot flew through the air* is generally assumed to involve a plane. In each case, comprehension requires that one must have a feeling of knowing some possible manner in which flying could occur, and the most probable manner is a function of the entity that enters into the event.[3]

---

[3]The notion of "feeling of knowing" is, of course, quite slippery, but nevertheless important to consider for sentence comprehension. It seems unlikely that *Ss* must make
Footnote continued on page 214

Of course, not only may a word be interpreted differently as a function of its sentence context, but a whole sentence may also be understood differently as a function of the larger context in which it is heard. The following passage, read at normal speed, illustrates how overall context can affect Ss' understanding of the relations specified in a sentence:

> The man was worried. His car came to a halt and he was all alone. It was extremely dark and cold. The man took off his overcoat, rolled down the window, and got out of the car as quickly as possible. Then he used all his strength to move as fast as he could. He was relieved when he finally saw the lights of the city, even though they were far away.

Immediately after hearing this passage, Ss were asked to answer two questions as quickly as possible: (1) Why did he take off his overcoat? (2) Why did he roll down the window? For both sentences the results were rather striking. The Ss generally took a very long time to answer (10−20 seconds), and they were unsure of the answers they gave (e.g., "maybe he rolled down the window to check for oncoming traffic").

A second group of Ss was also run in the study. They heard the identical passage except that it contained one additional adjective which told them that the car was submerged (i.e., *His submerged car came to a halt . . . .*). These Ss could answer the questions about the coat and the window very rapidly, and were quite certain of the answers they gave.

Evidently, the first group understood the relations between the man, coat, and window as one of temporal succession, and did not process the relations beyond that. The second group however, understood these relations at a richer level than one of mere temporal succession, and hence could readily answer why the coat was removed (so he could swim more easily) and why he opened the window (to swim out). The same abstract constraints can therefore result in different meanings as a function of the contributions made by the S.

As a final example of abstract constraints that direct the comprehender to specify certain situations, consider relations such as *if . . .then* and *because*. These words direct Ss to attempt to specify situations in which one thing could follow from another, and this is often a difficult task. In sentences like *The mirror shattered because the child grabbed the broom,* Ss can assume that the child hit the mirror with the broom and broke it. But if Ss are presented with a sentence like *The haystack was important because the cloth ripped,* they have a much more difficult time specifying conditions that could permit the relation—unless a cue such as *parachute* is provided by E. Even with the cue, Ss must presumably make some additional cognitive specifications: that the parachute was *above* the haystack when it ripped, etc.

Footnote continued from page 213

particular specifications in order to understand all sentences. For example, the sentence *The boy broke the window* is easily understood because one knows that there are many particular ways he could specify this event. And comprehension of the sentence *The man fixed the car* does not require that the listener be a car mechanic. Nevertheless there is some minimal level of feeling a possibility for a specification that is a prerequisite to comprehension.

We think that the *because* and *if . . .then* relations make it difficult to comprehend the balloon passage presented earlier. For example, the sentence *If the balloon, popped, the sound could not carry . . . .* was difficult to comprehend in isolation. One problem was that *Ss* had to decide what *sound* referred to, and the most likely candidate was that sound was something made by the ballons when they popped. But given this interpretation, it became difficult to understand why the sound could not carry. The *Ss* were forced to imagine some situation in which the relation made sense. They reported that they did come up with some conditions that allowed some sentences in the balloon passage to be comprehended, but that these situations then failed to specify conditions necessary for understanding subsequent sentences.

The *Ss* seeing the partial context picture were in a similar predicament. They knew that the balloons were being held by the boy, but again *sound* seemed to refer to the result of the balloons popping and therefore the question of why the sound did not carry had to be resolved. Some of these *Ss* also remarked that they could specify conditions allowing the comprehension of some sentences, but that they could not create an overall situation in which all the sentences of the passage made sense.

The *Ss* seeing the appropriate picture were in a different situation. They could understand that an implication of the balloons' popping would be that the speakers would fall and that *sound* referred to the noise from the speakers and not from the balloons. The picture also allowed them to calculate why the sound could not carry; namely, because the speakers would be too far away from the girl if they fell to the ground. In short, *Ss* seeing the appropriate context picture before hearing the passage were able to specify how the relations referred to in the utterances could be realized. The appropriate context picture was, therefore, not a static set of retrieval cues nor a mnemonic device into which *Ss* could "plug" the input sentences; rather, it communicated information that allowed *Ss* to specify how certain relations could occur.

QUESTIONS RAISED BY THE PRESENT APPROACH

We have proposed that knowledge of language might fruitfully be conceptualized as knowledge of abstract cues or instructions that guide the comprehender. The semantic content of a particular linguistic message is created only as the comprehender, guided by the linguistic cues, specifies conditions under which the abstract relations can be realized given his knowledge of the world. A person may therefore have knowledge of a language and yet fail to comprehend an utterance because he is unable to make the necessary cognitive contributions. And the same sentences may be understood differently as a function of the cognitive contributions that different listeners make.

If the present approach is to be fruitful, an important future problem is the characterization of the abstract information specified by lexical items (plus certain rules of syntax), and the investigation of the manner by which this information is utilized by the comprehender to achieve the click of comprehension to which Brown (1958) referred. Some of our information about certain lexical items undoubtedly derives from information about events that they may refer to, or from information about the relations that a class of entities has to other aspects of the world. For example, we have suggested that events involve restrictions on the nature of the entities that enter into them and may require certain "categories of information" (e.g., an instigating force, an instrument to carry out an action, etc.) that the comprehender must "fill in." Linguistic symbols that refer to such events or entities should activate information about such abstract specifications, and the symbols will differ in terms of the degree of specificity implied (e.g., a toy truck, a snake, and a human can move across a room, but only a human can walk).

We have concentrated on arguing *why* one should characterize abstract constraints specified by lexical items rather than attempt an explicit analysis of them. The latter analysis, of course, must eventually be achieved for the present approach to work. Fillmore's (1971) work characterizing conceptually inherent arguments which underly verbs should be particularly valuable in this endeavor. Of course, not all perceptual relations will have single lexical equivalents. But Fillmore's work nevertheless promises to yield insight into possible abstract categories of information that must be specified by the comprehender, and into presupposed constraints on the nature of entities that can participate in certain events. It is important, however, to distinguish between an analysis of verbs in terms of their conceptually inherent arguments and an analysis of verbs in terms of the minimum number of arguments that they must take to form an acceptable surface structure utterance. As an example, Fillmore (1971) notes that the sentence *She bought it* is acceptable and contains two surface structure arguments (i.e., *she* and *it*) but that conceptually, the event *buy* also involves information about a seller and some medium of exchange (e.g., money). If one of these categories of information can not be tacitly "filled in" by the comprehender, he remains puzzled by the utterance (e.g., a penniless man announced his plans to buy a Cadillac—medium of exchange?; a trapper, the supposed sole winter inhabitant of a backwoods area, says that he bought supplementary provisions last January—a seller?). From our present orientation, a characterization of verbs in terms of conceptually inherent arguments is of more immediate concern than a characterization of constraints on their surface structure acceptability. The latter problem is, of course, also important, and surface structure acceptability is undoubtedly related to the number and type of conceptually inherent arguments required of various verbs. But we should also be prepared to find that surface structure acceptability is subject to many relatively arbitrary, conventional linguistic constraints.

Analysis of constraints on classes of entities and events must also be supplemented by a consideration of more basically syntactic knowledge. There are many different linguistic devices that various languages use to cue the comprehender to create meaning, and these devices must be known for adequate comprehension to occur. At present, we are in no better position to characterize abstract syntactic knowledge than we are to specify one's knowledge of lexical items. Nevertheless, it seems fruitful to consider some problems which seem more solvable if one assumes that knowledge of language is knowledge of abstract syntactic and semantic cues used to create meaning, and if a characterization of such cues could be eventually achieved.

First, an obvious implication is that we might begin to understand why individual word perception is not the primary element in sentence comprehension. Thus Stahlin, who studied and elaborated some of Bühler's introspective techniques (cf. Blumenthal, 1970) wrote:

As for the question of cognitive representation of word-meanings, we meet an insurmountable obstacle. The question is put the wrong way to be relevant to our experiments or similar ones, for when a sentence rather than single words are presented a subject does not, under normal circumstances, arrive at a "word perception" (*Wortauffassung*) that is distinct and different from sentence comprehension . . .It hardly needs to be said that individual words must be understood before the sentence-thought can be comprehended. But the important fact is that the reverse relationship also exists: With the majority of words we do not at all arrive at a recognition and assimilation of word meaning separate from sentence comprehension. As soon as the sentence thought is assimilated in consciousness—and the tendency to do this as soon as possible is always there—then sentence comprehension determines the manner in which the individual words are assimilated as parts of the sentence context [pp. 52-53].

If the relations direct *Ss* to specify appropriate situations to create some semantic content, then we might expect sentence comprehension to take precedence over word comprehension. For example, we cannot make an appropriate specification of the meaning of something like *plane* until we know the event it enters into. The event will place constraints on whether it is a real plane, a toy plane, a plane in the air or on the ground, and so forth. Words provide abstract constraints that govern the possible interpretation, but the interpretation is a function of the total event. Of course, at times we may make specifications before a total sentence is completed (as in classic garden path sentences), but the eventual appropriate specification is determined by the total event.

A second implication is that we might better understand how the same word can have so many different senses as a function of context, and how metaphorical sentences can often be so readily understood. If semantic content is created rather than stored, we should expect variation depending upon context. And if *Ss* have to specify situations that allow them to grasp relations in order to understand literal sentences, the processes involved in comprehending metaphor should not be different in kind from other comprehension. Thus, the literal sentence *The mirror shattered because the child grabbed the broom* requires one to specify how grasping a broom could result in a mirror shattering, and the metaphorical sentence *Redwood trees are the skyscrapers of the forest* (cf. Verbrugge & McCarrell, in preparation) requires one to specify how redwoods and skyscrapers could be similar in some way. Of course, the comprehender knows that redwoods are not really skyscrapers (hence its metaphorical status), but the basic problems of specifying conditions that allow certain relations is no different from the problem of comprehending literal strings.

A third implication is related to comprehension of metaphorical sentences that involve relations or similarity. The comprehender must discover some basis for similarity—a "feature" shared by both entities. Yet shared "features" differ as a function of the sentence in which entities appear. Our approach may provide some insight into the reasons why certain "features" of entities or concepts are differentially salient as a function of different contexts. As Olson (1970) noted, the feature *terrestrial* becomes salient when one is comparing a horse to a whale, despite the fact the *terrestrial* is not included in the list of features appearing in a dictionary meaning of *horse*. Yet a feature like *domesticated,* which does appear in the dictionary definition, may become salient when one is comparing a horse to a mountain goat. We have considered many types of relations (besides that of similarity) between entities, and have noted that the nature of the relation and its participating entities constrain the types of assumptions that one must make. The sentence *The man put the plane in the envelope* requires most *Ss* to assign the feature *toy* to *plane*. The sentence *The man lifted the piano* makes most *Ss* think of the fact that pianos are heavy in a sense in which the sentence *The man played the piano* does not. And the sentence *The man cooked the meat over the fire* may make one assume that fire is "good," but the sentence *The boy burned his hand in the fire* may cause one to assume that fire is "bad." The features which appear salient about an entity will be a function of the event in which it participates. And the analysis of perceptual knowledge in the event section suggests that what we call features are really labels for relations, and not primitive elements that entities "have" (and which can be exhaustively listed in one's "mental dictionary").

Fourth, if the preceding implications deny that an isolated word can be considered the basic unit for an analysis of comprehension processes, does it therefore follow that an isolated sentence is the basic unit? Are sentences which are comprehensible in isolation somehow a "purer form" of sentences than those which are comprehensible only in context? Katz and Fodor (1963) claim that the sentence in isolation should be the basic object of analysis. They state:

> But a theory of settings must contain a theory of semantic interpretation as a proper part because the readings that a speaker attributes to a sentence in a setting are a selection from among those that the sentence has in isolation . . .a theory of semantic interpretation is logically prior to a theory of the selective effect of setting [p. 405].

In short, the sentence in isolation has many readings, and a context simply helps the listener select a particular one.

Our approach suggests a different view of this problem. First, knowledge of language would include information about cues to be used to create meaning, and in this sense the cues could be available prior to any effect of setting or context. But the act of creating meaning sufficient for a click of comprehension would require the comprehender to specify situations that allow him to grasp the abstract relations mentioned in the input sentences. Sentences which are comprehensible in isolation would be those for which such specifications were possible; sentences which are context-bound would be those for which the comprehender needed assistance to specify what the situations might be. And ambiguous sentences would be those for which two or more specifications were possible, thereby allowing the sentence to be understood in different ways. Accordingly, context might not only constrain situations so that one rather than many meanings are possible for a sentence (as is emphasized by Katz and Fodor), but it might also provide information so that sentences which received *no* adequate readings when presented in isolation could be understood.

Finally, (and most generally) we might gain some insight into the relation between a formal competence model of language and a psychological performance model (e.g., see Fillenbaun, 1971; Fodor & Garrett, 1966; Garrett & Fodor, 1968). Such a relation has been conceived in many ways. One might, for instance, assume that performance equals competence plus psychological constraints (e.g., memory limitations), and that the rules of grammer are thus somehow in the head. One might then assume that *Ss* comprehend sentences by "running the rules backward," and that such rules are psychologically real. On the other hand, one might assume that there is no psychological reality to the rules of transformational grammar, but that there is psychological reality to the structural descriptions that these rules assign. But even here there are a number of options. Does one assume that *Ss* first find a syntactic deep structure and *then* assign a meaning to a sentence, or might the relations we find characterized in deep structural relations be the *result* of *Ss* knowledge of the constraints on the entities and relations represented in the linguistic string?

Our approach to comprehension suggests that it may be fruitful to pursue the latter alternative. It seems reasonable to assume that the surface-structurally similar sentences *The mouse squeaked* and *The window squeaked* are understood differently *not* because one first discovers a deep structure and then interprets the meaning of the lexical items, but because one's knowledge of the entities and events in the sentence forces different semantic interpretations to be made (e.g., windows are not capable of self-initiated acts like squeaking, hence some other force or agent must have been involved). And the sentence *They are chanting vespers* and *They are chanting monks* seem to be understood differently because of semantic information available about vespers and monks. Similarily, the ambiguous sentence *The boy was found by the nog* can be disambiguated as a function of our knowledge of *nogs*. If *nog* is assumed to refer to a monument in Central Park the sentence will be understood as a paraphrase of *The boy was found near the nog;* but if it refers to a furry animal with a good nose for tracking, the sentence will be understood to be a paraphrase of *The nog found the boy.*

We do not mean to suggest that there are *no* syntactic cues that affect semantic interpretation. It is obvious that surface structure syntax, for example, is extremely important; otherwise we could not differentiate sentences like *Paul saw Mary* and *Mary saw Paul.* And it seems probable that one's knowledge of lexical items may include grammatical specifications as well as semantic ones. But we would like to suggest that semantic constraints also play an extremely important role in determining the nature of semantic representations, and that the types of relations summarized in deep structural characterization may often be the result of semantic constraints rather than a prerequisite way station that must be discovered before any semantic processing takes place. (The present characterization—if viable—would in no way invalidate Chomsky's *formal* approach to language, since his is not meant to be a performance model.) In short, the present approach suggests that we might not only consider surface structure cues to syntactic structure, but also semantic cues to cognitive structure. Thus the sentences *The man put the toy plane in the envelope* and *The man escaped from the falling ice cream cone* are reported by *Ss* to be easier to comprehend than their counterparts with the word *toy* and *falling* deleted. These cues apparently help specify situations that *Ss* would have to discover anyway; they help *Ss* create the cognitive structures that they need. These examples also seem to illustrate situations (in addition to those provided by Fodor & Garrett, 1967; Hakes, 1972) where increases in syntactic complexity actually facilitate comprehension, since the addition of *toy* and *falling* increases the syntactic complexity of the sentence *Ss* hear.

SUMMARY

Our approach to comprehension focuses on the comprehender's ability to use his general knowledge to create situations that permit the relations specified in input sentences to be realized, or to postulate situations (e.g., instigating forces) that allow perceptual events to be understood. In short, the ability to create some level of semantic content sufficient to achieve a click of comprehension depends upon the comprehender's ability to think. This leads us to attempt to characterize the abstract relational knowledge derived from perceptual experience, and to study how this information places cognitive constraints on one's ability to understand linguistic strings.

It is painfully obvious that the present chapter has barely scratched the surface of the problem of comprehension. In fact, the more we study the area the more we discover what we do not know. In particular, we need to determine how our approach resembles and differs from those proposed by Clark, (in press) Collins and Quillian, (1972) Kintsch, (1972) Rumelhart, Lindsay, and Norman, (1972) Shank, (1972), Trabasso, (1972), and Winograd (1972). Besides having the advantage of formal characterizations of their concepts, these authors raise many important questions that we have not considered here. We have no illusions about having answered how one achieves a click of comprehension. Our purpose has been to sketch a general orientation towards this problem, and to present some experimental paradigms that may help us study it in greater detail.

ADDENDUM ON COMPREHENSION AND IMAGERY

In recent years imagery has played an increasingly important role in accounts of language processing and memory (e.g. Bower, in press; Paivio, 1969, 1971). Begg and Paivio (1969), for example, have argued that linguistic inputs are treated in two different manners, with concrete sentences being stored as images and abstract sentences as linear, acoustic strings. We shall consider some questions about the role of imagery as it relates to our approach.

First, organisms have considerable information available from perceptual experience with their environment, and this information provides a basis for understanding linguistic strings. But we would not want to conclude that knowledge derived from perception is anything like a "storehouse of images." The information available from perception is abstract and relational in nature (and includes constraints on roles entities may assume, abstract invariants characteristic of events, etc.), just as the information necessary for detection of perceptual information is abstract (e.g., see Mace Turvey and Shaw and McIntyre, in this volume). Even studies on abstraction that utilize visual stimuli (e.g., Franks & Bransford, 1971; Posner, 1969) show clearly that *Ss* do not simply store snapshots of individual configurations. Instead they perceive relations among various configurations, and these relations form an abstract system which determines *Ss'* performance in subsequent recognition tasks. In short, the importance of abstract, relational information is not emphasized in a "storehouse of images" view.

A related point is that information about the perceptual characteristics of isolated objects is not necessarily assumed to be sufficient to grasp their meanings. Organisms must have information about an entity's relations to other aspects of his knowledge system to understand it. It follows that an image of a word's referent cannot be equated with its meaning, and similarly, the meaning of a whole sentence like *The man made a touchdown* cannot be equated with an image of a man crossing the goal line. One must have additional knowledge in order to understand what a touchdown means. Indeed, as Dewey (1963) noted:

> An idea, logically speaking, is not a faded perception of an object, nor is it a compound of a number of sensations. You would not get the peculiar meaning attached to, say, "chair" by having a mental picture of one. A savage (sic) might be able to form an image of poles and wires, and a layman of a complex scientific diagram. But unless the savage knew something about telegraphy, he would have no idea, or at least no correct idea, of the poles and wires, while the most accurate mental reproduction of the diagram would leave the layman totally without understanding of its meaning, and hence without an idea of it, even though he could list all *its* qualities one by one [p. 235].

Third, our approach questions Begg and Paivio's (1969) hypothesis that concrete sentences are stored as images and abstract sentences as linear, acoustic strings. The storage of auditory and visual images could not account for *Ss'* abilities to understand and remember sentence meanings, and the data used to support the notion of differential storage of concrete verus abstract sentences can be interpreted differently.

Begg and Paivio found that *Ss* who heard concrete sentences were later more likely to detect changes in meaning (subject-object reversals) than changes in wording (synonym substitutions). Conversely, *Ss* who heard abstract sentences were more likely to detect changes in wording than changes in meaning. Begg and Paivio concluded that this differential memory for aspects of the sentences (meaning vs. exact words) reflects differential forms of coding of abstract and concrete sentences at input. Concrete sentences were assumed to be coded in an imaginal-spatial manner, and abstract sentences were assumed to be coded in a verbal-sequential form.

It is important to note that Begg and Paivio assumed that their abstract and concrete sentences were equally comprehensible. Their evidence was the finding that the overall sensitivity to change (detection of subject-object reversals plus detection of synonym substitutions) was about the same in abstract and concrete groups. Yet it seems clear that adding these two performance measures together yields a questionable index of comprehension. If the sentences do in fact differ in comprehensibility, the results may have been due to this factor rather than the fact that the sentences were "stored in different modes."

Johnson, Bransford, Nyberg, and McCleary (in press) sought to determine whether Begg and Paivio's results did in fact arise from differences in comprehensibility of abstract versus concrete sentences. First, using Begg and Paivio's original sentences, they sought a more direct measure of comprehension by asking *Ss not* whether they had actually heard a sentence during acquisition, but whether a test sentence *meant* the same thing as a sentence heard before. Regardless of how *S* processed the original, if he understood the original and retained its meaning he would be expected to accept a synonym substitution which preserved the meaning, and to reject a subject object reversal which destroyed the meaning. For concrete sentences, *Ss* did pick "meaning-preserving" test sentences. For the abstract sentences, however, *Ss* were unable to distinguish between sentences that were in fact meaning preserving and those that were meaning distorting but contained the same words. These data are consonant with the notion that *Ss* did not in fact adequately understand the abstract strings.

Subsequent studies removed the study from an investigation of memory to one of an investigation of comprehension. The *Ss* were simply presented with Begg and Paivio's abstract and concrete sentences and asked to rate their comprehensibility. Results confirmed our expections: *Ss* rated the abstract sentences as significantly less comprehensible than the concrete.

We suspect that "meaning-distorting" errors arise more from *Ss* inabilities to adequately understand input sentences than it does from the concreteness or abstractness of the words comprising such sentences. Hence if abstract sentences are readily understood, they too should result in meaning preserving paraphrases by *S*. In normal communication situations, abstract sentences are generally spoken in contexts were *Ss* can specify situations that permit their adequate comprehension. When abstract sentences are removed from context, *Ss* may have no choice but to attempt to remember individual strings of words. But, of course, the same situation can occur with sentences composed of concrete words. If *Ss* are unable to make the cognitive contributions necessary for adequate comprehension, they also should be expected to make meaning distorting errors.

Fourth, the present approach emphasizes the importance of the question *"Where do images come from?"* In particular, how are the unbounded number of novel compound images that result from sentences formed? Surely images are not simply conditioned sensations. The semantic content of words changes as a function of their contexts, and so do *Ss'* images as well. Compound images must result from constructive processes on the part of comprehenders, and *Ss* must be able to specify situations where particular relations among entities might occur. Of course, with two concrete words (e.g., chicken, hat) *Ss* can almost always specify some figurative relations that will permit a composite image. But with more complex situations, *Ss* should sometimes have difficulty realizing permissible relations and hence should be unable to image even when a sentence is composed of concrete words. In short, there should be cognitive prerequisites for images to be formed.

In conjunction with Jeffery Franks, we conducted a pilot study to investigate constraints on image formation. The 20 sentences to be learned were the incomprehensible sentences used in some of our previous studies (e.g., *The notes were sour because the seam split, The streak blocked the light,* etc.). Each sentence was read to *Ss* and was preceded by a concrete cue (e.g., bagpipes, window). The *Ss* were instructed to form an image of each concrete cue and then image some relation between this and the sentence with which it was paired at acquisition.

They were told they would later be read the cues and were to recall the sentences paired with them.

Two groups were run in the experiment. For Group 1, cues and sentences were appropriately paired such that the cues allowed *Ss* to specify situations permitting appropriate relations to be realized. For Group 2, cues and sentences were randomly paired with the constraint that no appropriate pairings occurred. In cued recall, the *Ss* in Group 1 recalled 95% of the sentences (scored for paraphrase). Group 2 *Ss* exhibited extremely low cued recall with only 3% correct. Of course, these results are not surprising, and perhaps essentially trivial. But they do demonstrate constraints on image formation. The *Ss* must be able to specify appropriate relations between entities. If they are unable to do this, *Ss* report that the sentences are not adequately imageable and are difficult to recall.[4]

The notion of cognitive constraints on image formation suggests an additional consideration. Most studies of imagery and paired-associate learning (cf. Paivio, 1967, 1971) have found that concrete words are better stimuli than abstract words in that they result in faster learning. Paivio (1969) suggests that concrete words may act as "conceptual pegs" that are easily retrieved and to which appropriate response items may be hooked. But are the results of such studies a function of the fact that the stimulus words are inherently concrete or abstract, or are they a function of the fact that *Ss* have a more difficult time finding appropriate relations among abstract stimuli and their respective responses? One way to distinguish between these two questions is to create situations where relations among abstract stimuli and their subsequent response items are readily perceivable, and investigate the effects on *Ss'* ability to learn. In short, one can ask whether there could exist conditions such that an abstract stimulus would be as good as or better than one which is concrete.

At Stony Brook, Elizabeth Cole is currently completing a project designed to answer this question. Her preliminary results indicate that abstract stimuli can indeed be better than stimuli which are concrete. Cole used stimulus-response, response (S-RR) sets as her to-be-learned items. The RR items were kept constant across three groups, but the stimulus items were varied. Group 1 received stimulus items that were concrete according to Paivio's norms. Groups 2 and 3 received stimuli that were abstract. In Group 2 the stimulus items were randomly paired with RR items. In Group 3, pairings were set up so that the RR items could be meaningfully related to the stimulus items (e.g., *decree: King-messenger; enterprise: sidewalk-lemonade; hindrance: wheelchair-stairway;* etc.). Pairings were controlled so that the RR items were no more frequent associates to the abstract stimuli than they were to the concrete stimuli.

---

[4] The nature of information available to the comprehender can also affect the speed with which appropriate relations are discovered. For example, Carol Ray, at Stony Brook, has presented *Ss* with three successive lists like the following: Mailman, box plastic, room, hose, sheet, cigarette, flood. Subjects given mnemonic training (e.g., method of loci) showed high recall scores at a slow rate of presentation (5 seconds per item) but their performance declined at a faster rate of presentation (1.5 seconds per item). In contrast, *Ss* given a theme for each list (e.g., new waterbed) exhibited much less decline in recall at the fast acquisition rate.

Results for Group 1 and 2 replicated the usual findings in imagery studies: Concrete stimuli resulted in faster learning than did abstract stimuli. Group 3, however, performed better than both Groups 1 and 2. In short, abstract stimuli were better than concrete. It appears that when abstract words are taken out of their normal contexts and randomly paired with response items it is very difficult to find some way in which they relate. When conditions are set up so that meaningful relations can be found, however, abstract stimuli can do as well as, or even better than, concrete.

Similar results were found in an experiment conducted by Peterson (1972). In this study, all *Ss* learned the same stimulus triads, but were provided with either concrete or abstract members of each triad as retrieval cues. The members of each triad could be interrelated by a theme (which was not to be recalled) that preceded each triad (e.g., *laboratory:* research, scale, beaker; *holdup:* arm, crime, man), and stimuli were constructed such that abstract members of each triad (e.g., research, crime) had a more direct semantic relationship to the theme than did items which were concrete (e.g., scale, arm). The abstract retrieval cues resulted in nearly 100% greater recall for stimuli than did their concrete counterparts, regardless of whether one scored for correct recall of both of the remaining members of the triad (e.g., the cue *research* yields *scale, breaker;* the cue *scale* yields *research breaker*) or whether one scored only for the recall of the single remaining word in the triad that the common to both cue groups (e.g., the word *breaker* is a target work irrespective of whether *Ss* received the cue *research* or *scale*).

The preceding studies suggest that meaningful relations among items may be a more important variable for memory than concreteness and abstractness ratings for isolated words. Indeed, the notion that the semantic content of words is created in context suggests that it should be difficult to predict from individual word norms to interword contexts, and the above mentioned studies support this idea. Of course, the motion that the ability to form cohesive relations among concrete stimuli is important for recall has been emphasized by others (e.g., Asch, 1962; Bower, in press; Rohwer, 1966), and the previous studies are in agreement with their views. However, most investigators have nevertheless concentrated on cohesive *figurative* relations that bind *concrete* entities. The present approach suggests that we might ask whether the broader class of semantic relations that are meaningful yet may be less cohesive figuratively (e.g., the woman stood by a tent, saw a wolf, looked for a tree and wished for a gun) might also be important for effective recall, and reminds us that the semantic content of words in isolation might be different from their context-bound form. It appears that we cannot effectively predict learning ability by using individual word norms. If we can also find that figurative relations are only a subset of relations that produce effective recall, then we might further ask whether imagery really holds any special claim on memory, or whether imaging is merely one of many ways to interrelate stimuli and thereby achieve better recall.

APPENDIX

TABLE 1

Scissors: An Exercise in Structure-Function Relationships

	Structure	Function
(a)	Dressmaker shears	
	heavy	because of heavy use.
	one hole larger than other	so that two or three fingers will fit in larger hole – allows greater steadiness as one cuts cloth on flat surface.
	blades off-centered and aligned with finger hole edge.	so that blade can rest on table surface as cloth is cut – again, greater steadiness.
(b)	Barber shears	
	very sharp	to cut thin material; i.e., hair.
	pointed	permits blades to snip close to scalp and to snip very small strands of hair.
	hook on finger hole	a rest for one finger which allows scissors to be supported when held at various angles–hence greater manueverability.
(c)	Pocket or children's scissors	
	blunt ends	so scissors can be carried in pocket without cutting through cloth; so children can handle without poking themselves or others.
	short blades	allows greater control by the gross motor movements of the child just learning to cut.
(d)	Nail scissors	
	wide and thick at pivot point	to withstand pressure from cutting thick and rigid materials; i.e., nails.
	slightly curved blades	to cut slightly curved nails.
(e)	Cuticles scissors	
	very sharp blade	to cut semi-elastic materials; i.e., skin of cuticles
	small, curved blades	to allow manueverability necessary to cut small curved area.
	long extension from finger holes to joint	as compensation for short blades, necessary for holding.

Fig. 1. (c): Object perception as a function of its role in events.

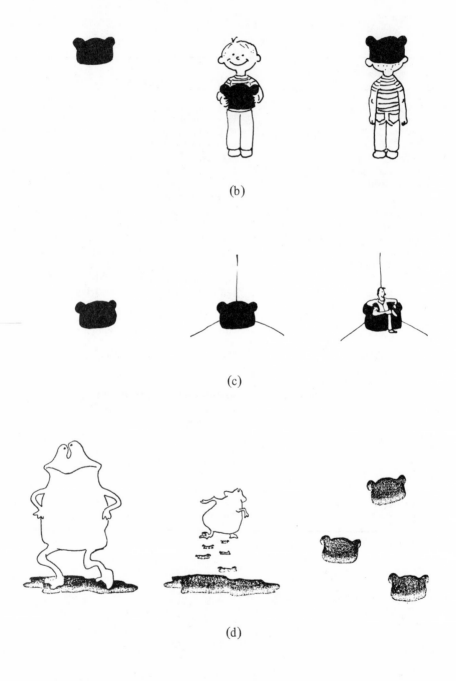

Fig. 2. (b), (c) and (d): Meaning as a function of entities'
relations to other aspects of the world.

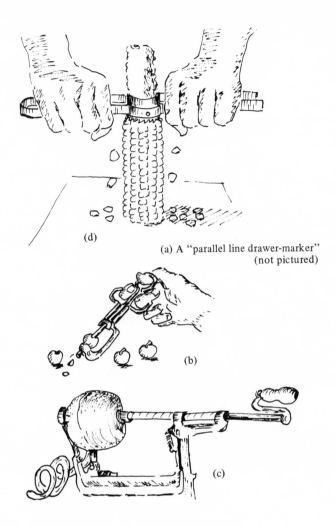

(a) A "parallel line drawer-marker"
(not pictured)

Fig. 3. (b): Contexts for objects in Figure 3(a).

REFERENCES

Asch, S. E. A problem in the theory of associations. *Psychological Beitrage,* 1962, **6,** 558-563.

Begg, I., & Paivio, A. Concreteness and imagery in sentence memory. *Journal of Verbal Learning and Verbal Behavior.* 1969, 8, 821-827.

Barclay, J. R. The role of comprehension in remembering sentences. *Cognitive Psychology,* in press.

Blumenthal, A. L. *Language and psychology.* New York: Wiley, 1970.

Bower, G. H. Mental imagery and associative learning. In L. Gregg (Ed.), *Cognition in learning and memory.* New York: Wiley, in press.

Bransford, J. D., Barclay, J. R., & Franks, J. J. Sentence memory: A constructive versus interpretive approach. *Cognitive Psychology,* 1972, 3, 193-209.

Bransford, J. D., & Franks, J. J. The abstraction of linguistic ideas. *Cognitive Psychology,* 1971, **2,** 331-350.

Bransford, J. D., & Franks, J. J. The abstraction of linguistic ideas: A review. *Cognition: An International Journal of Psychology,* in press.

Bransford, J. D., & Johnson, M. K. Contextual prerequisites for understanding: Some investigations of comprehension and recall. *Journal of Verbal Learning and Verbal Behavior,* in press. (a)

Bransford, J. D. & Johnson, M. K. Considerations of some problems of comprehension. Paper presented at the 8th Carnegie conference on cognition, May 1971. In press. (b)

Brown, R. *Words and things.* New York: Free Press, 1968.

Burke, K. *A grammar of motives.* Berkeley: University of California Press, 1969.

Clark, H. H. Semantics and comprehension. In T. A. Sebeok (Ed.), *Current trends in linguistics,* Vol. 12, *Linguistics and adjacent arts and sciences.* The Hague: Mouton, in press.

Collins, A. M., & Quillian, M. R. How to make a language user. In E. Tulving & W. Donaldson (Eds.), *Organization of memory.* New York: Academic Press, 1972.

Dewey, J. *How we think.* Portions published in R. M. Hutchins & M. J. Adler (Eds.), *Gateway to the great books.* Vol. 10. Chicago: Encyclopedia Britannica, Inc., 1963. (Originally published by Heath, 1933, 1961.)

Fillenbaum, S. Psycholinguistics. *Annual review of psychology,* 1971, **22,** 251-308.

Fillmore, C. J. Types of lexical information. In D. D. Steinberg & L. A. Jakobovits (Eds.), *Semantics: An interdisciplinary reader in philosophy, linguistics and psychology.* Cambridge: Cambridge University Press, 1971.

Fodor, J., & Garrett, M. Some reflections on competence and performance. In J. Lyons & R. J. Wales (Eds.), *Psycholinguistic papers,* Edinburgh: Edinburgh University Press, 1966.

Fodor, J., & Garrett, M. Some syntactic determinants of sentential complexity. *Perception & Psychophysics,* 1967, **2,** 289-296.

Franks, J. J., & Bransford, J. D. Abstraction of visual patterns. *Journal of Experimental Psychology.* 1971, **90,** No. 1, 65-74.

Garner, W. R. To perceive is to know. *American Psychologist.* 1966, **21,** 11-19.

Garrett, M., & Fodor, J. Psychological theories and linguistic constructs. In T. R. Dixon & D. L. Horton (Eds.), *Verbal behavior and general behavior theory.* Englewood Cliffs, N.J.: Prentice Hall, 1968.

Gibson, E. J. *Principles of perceptual learning and development.* New York: Appleton-Century-Crofts, 1969.

Gibson, J. J. *The senses considered as perceptual systems.* New York: Houghton Mifflin, 1966.

Hakes, D. Effects of reducing complement constructions on sentence comprehension. *Journal of Verbal Learning and Verbal Behavior,* 1972, **11,** 278-286.

Huey, E. B. *The psychology and pedagogy of reading.* Cambridge, Mass.: M.I.T. Press, 1908 (1968).

Humphrey, G. *Thinking.* New York: Wiley, 1963.

Johnson, M. K., Bransford, J. D., Nyberg, S., Cleary, J. Comprehension factors in interpreting memory for abstract and concrete sentences. *Journal of Verbal Learning Behavior,* 1972, **11,** 451-454.

Johnson, M. K., Bransford, J. D., & Solomon, S. Memory for tacit implications of sentences. *Journal of Experimental Psychology,* in press.

Katz, J. J., & Fodor, J. A. The structure of a semantic theory. In L. A. Jakobovitz & M. S. Miron (Eds.), *Reading in the psychology of language.* Englewood Cliffs, N. J.: Prentice-Hall, 1967.

Kintsch, W. Notes on the structure of semantic memory. In E. Tulving & W. Donaldson (Eds.), *Organization of memory.* New York: Academic Press, 1972.

Lyons, J. *Introduction to theoretical linguistics.* New York: Cambridge University Press, 1968.

McCarrell, N., Bransford, J., & Johnson, M. *Problem-solving components of comprehension,* in preparation.

Miller, G. A. Some preliminaries to psycholinguistics. *American Psychologist,* 1965, **20,** 15-20.

Neisser, U. *Cognitive psychology.* New York: Appleton-Century-Crofts, 1967.

Olson, D. R. Language and thought: Aspects of a cognitive theory of semantics. *Psychological Review,* 1970, **77,** 257-273.

Osgood, C. E. *Method and theory in experimental psychology.* New York: Oxford University Press, 1953.

Paivio, A. Mental imagery in associative learning and memory. *Psychological Review,* 1969, 76, 241-263.

Paivio, A. *Imagery and verbal processes.* New York: Holt, Rinehart & Winston, 1971.

Paiget, J. *The origins of intelligence in children.* New York: W. W. Horton, 1963.

Peterson, R. C. A cognitive approach to imagery. Unpublished doctoral dissertation, University of Minnesota, 1972.

Potts, G. A cognitive approach to the encoding of meaningful verbal material. Unpublished doctoral dissertation, University of Indiana, 1971.

Rohwer, W. D., Jr. Images and pictures in children's learning. In H. W. Reese (Chm), Imagery in children's learning: A symposium. *Psychological Bulletin,* 1966, 57, 271-278.

Rummelhart, D. E., Lindsay, P. H., & Norman, D. A. A process model for long-term memory. In E. Tulving & W. Donaldson (Eds.), *Organization of memory.* New York: Academic Press, 1972.

Searle, J. R. *Speech acts: An essay in the philosophy of language.* London: Cambridge University Press, 1969.

Schank, R. C. Conceptual dependency: A theory of natural language understanding. *Cognitive Psychology,* 1972, 3, 552-631.

Slobin, D. I. *Psycholinguistics.* Glenview Ill.: Scott, Foresman, 1971.

Tichener, E. B. *Lectures on the experimental psychology of the thought processes.* New York: Macmillan, 1909.

Tolman, E. C. *Behavior and psychological man.* Berkeley: University of California Press, 1958.

Trabasso, T. Mental operations in language comprehension. In J. B. Carroll & R. O. Freedle (Eds.), *Language comprehension and the acquisition of knowledge.* Washington: Winston, 1972.

Watson, J. B. *Behaviorism.* New York: People's Institute, 1924.

Winograd, T. Understanding natural language. *Cognitive Psychology,* 1972 3, 1-191.

11

TOWARD UNDERSTANDING UNDERSTANDING

Jeffery J. Franks[1]
Vanderbilt University

On Science:

> *"the union of passionate interest in the detailed facts with equal devotion to abstract generalization."*
>
> —*Whitehead*

> *"When human beings acquired the powers of conscious attention and rational thought they became so fascinated with these new tools that they forgot all else."*
>
> —*Watts*

Bransford and McCarrell have discussed a contextual approach to the problem of understanding. Their chapter considers what is involved when people understand perceptual and linguistic events. It outlines a possible theoretical approach to the processes of understanding we go through in everyday contacts with the world. I would like to step back a few paces to consider not the problem of understanding *per se*, but rather the problem of understanding understanding. I will discuss some of the assumptions we hold (as psychologists, linguists, philosophers, etc.) that influence our thinking and theorizing about understanding. I shall use "understanding" as a cover term that involves all aspects of cognition—including memory, meaning, language, perception, etc. This usage involves all the problems considered above by Bransford and McCarrell.

To start with, consider the following problem: "Why are psychologists, linguists, philosophers, etc. so dumb when it comes to the problem of meaning?" We have been investigating, and thinking about, the nature of meaning and knowledge for

[1]This chapter was prepared in collaboration with John D. Bransford and Nancy S. McCarrell; however, errors or misconceptions are solely mine. Although separate, it remains an attempt to supplement and develop their ideas. This research was supported in part by NIMH Grant No. MH-22366.

thousands of years, but have not gotten very far. Our lack of progress is especially surprising in view of children's developing in just a few years an adequate "theory of meaning and knowledge[2] — adequate in that the child can use language and interact with the environment effectively. The difference between the child and us, as psychologists, is that the child is acquiring the knowledge system itself, while we are attempting to acquire a theory, or formal understanding, of this knowledge system. But what is this difference? How do the child's acquisition processes differ from the theorist's? The methods, procedures, and analytic and logical processes that theorists use are not obviously the same as the investigatory techniques the child uses in acquiring knowledge about his interactions in the world. If they were, we could have formulated a theory of knowledge and meaning in a few years, just as the child does.

This example points out a fundamental problem that cognitive psychology must grapple with. The gap between the child and the theorist exemplifies the gap between tacit knowledge (as Polanyi, 1966, uses the term) and phenomenal, conscious experience. This gap, or maybe chasm, stands in the way of our understanding of understanding. This chapter considers the relation between tacit knowledge and experience, and raises some possible implications for cognitive psychology.

THE RELATION BETWEEN TACIT KNOWLEDGE AND EXPERIENCE

The basic thesis I will develop is the following: All events that we consider to be psychological phenomena presuppose relational structures in an underlying tacit knowledge system. Psychological phenomena includes both overt responding and conscious or phenomenal experiencing. Tacit knowledge refers to knowledge of which we normally are not (and probably cannot be) directly aware. Hayek (1969) argues similarly, asserting that phenomenal experiences and responses are determined by abstract relations. I shall not attempt to prove this general thesis; rather, my purpose is to present examples and arguments which lend plausibility to this view of how our heads work. Then I will consider possible implications for methods and theories in cognitive psychology.

Everyday examples demonstrate that tacit knowledge relations must underlie our overt responding, our imaginal experience, and our language usage. Consider first the obvious case of motor responses, taking as typical the example of riding a bicycle. Once we have acquired this ability we can ride with facility, but this does not mean that we can tell someone how we are accomplishing the task. We are not aware of the relations that compose our knowledge of bicycle riding. We must be processing information in highly complex ways during this motor performance, but these relations are not available to our mind's eye. We are aware of performing the

---

[2] Knowledge, meaning, and understanding will be understood as follows: "Knowledge" refers essentially to static, semi-permanent long-term memory relationships. "Meaning" refers to relations activated or generated as a function of knowledge relations and the particular present enivronmental context. "Understanding" is a function of the extent to which adequate (coherent, complete) meanings have been generated in a particular context.

act but not of the knowledge that allows us to do it: That knowledge is tacit. Our use of language may allow us to cue or direct someone else to respond in such a way as to similarly learn to perform the act. But we cannot communicate to that person the knowledge relations that we have learned.

Acts of recognition illustrate the same point. For example, we can all recognize a dog as a dog. But we cannot introspectively observe the structural relations in our knowledge that form the basis for this recognition. We are not, and probably cannot be, directly aware of the set of relations that specify the mapping between the physical stimulus (the object dog) and the conceptual system that forms our knowledge of (the concept) dog. This is the problem of pattern recognition: How is it that we are able to classify events as members of one category rather than of another? If we had direct awareness of knowledge relations that form the basis of pattern recognition, the problem would not be a problem. With direct awareness of the underlying relations, we could symbolize them, splice together a model of the processes, and feed it into a computer which would be as efficient as we in recognizing and classifying objects. But this is not the way it is; pattern recognition remains one of psychology's sticky problems. Obviously knowledge contains the relations that allow and determine such recognition (since we continually do it), but this knowledge is tacit: Its nature does not appear in the mind's eye.

The same thing occurs with language. Consider words: What is the meaning of a word? Or, in other words, what is the nature of that knowledge by which we use and understand words appropriately? Again, the knowledge structures that determine meaning are unavailable to consciousness. If we could be directly aware of these structures the problem of semantics and meaning would not puzzle us. If direct introspection were possible, we could formulate a theory of meaning by overtly symbolizing the contents of our awareness. The very fact that the problem of meaning remains one of the most difficult in psychology is strong evidence that tacit knowledge structures underlie and determine the phenomena of consciousness and overt responses.

Chomsky often makes a similar point in discussing grammatical relations. He has argued that we must be "using" such relations in language usage, but that we cannot directly observe or report what they are. That is, we cannot simply introspect and read out the grammar of English. In the context of Chomsky's view, it may be pertinent to refer to a point that will be considered below. Although we are not directly aware of the grammatical relations that we know tacitly, Chomsky argues that we do have awareness of these relations in another way: We *are* aware of impressions of relatedness. Chomsky terms these impressions of relatedness intuitions. Intuitions form the basic data for linguistics; they form the basis for inferences about the nature of the tacit knowledge relations that underlie them. A linguistic intuition is our awareness that a relation exists, but not an awareness of what the relation is. I will consider later the place of intuitions in cognitive psychology.

The examples just discussed support the thesis that tacit knowledge structures underlie all psychological phenomena. Turvey's chapter discusses experimental evidence which indicates the importance of tacit knowledge in dealing with psychological phenomena and which also provides support for the thesis. I will henceforth assume the validity of the thesis and now sketch in more detail the nature of the relationship between tacit knowledge and psychological phenomena. To do this I must distinguish two aspects of cognition.

One aspect is our complete long-term memory structure, that is, everything we know about the world. I will refer to this as "knowledge." This is our semipermanent, relatively static knowledge; Hayek (1952) uses the term "map" to refer to this structure. The second aspect of cognition comprises those relations activated at any point as a function of environmental context and "stored" knowledge relations. I will refer to these activated relations as "meanings"; Hayek uses the term "model." Psychological phenomena, including overt responses, imagery, and language usage or speech (both overt and covert) are functions of these activated relations or meanings.

Now, where does the notion of tacit knowledge fit in? What I labeled "knowledge" above is tacit in an obvious and trivial way. A person cannot be aware of, or respond on the basis of, static nonactivated knowledge relations. At a particular time, a person cannot be aware of all that he knows simultaneously. However, the examples mentioned above point to a more interesting aspect of cognition that is tacit. They indicate that aspects of "meanings" are also tacit. That is, we are not directly aware of the activated knowledge relations that underlie and determine phenomenal experiences and responses. Thus meanings have overt manifestations in the form of images, language, and responses, as well as tacit aspects that determine the overt manifestations (i.e., tacit meaning). A rewording of my basic thesis then is: *All overt responses and phenomenal experiences presuppose underlying tacit meaning structures.*

The relationship being proposed may be clarified by analogy to transformational grammar. The system of knowledge relations is like a grammar: it is a system of generative relations, having the capacity to characterize (and thus be the basis of our coping with) both novel and previously experienced events. Particular meanings are like particular sentences. Specific sentences are generated by the grammar. Likewise, meanings are particular derivations generated by the knowledge system. The structure of meanings is determined by knowledge[3] just as the structure of sentences is determined by grammar.

Let us extend our linguistics analogy further and discuss the relation between tacit meanings and their overt manifestations. The analogy here is to surface versus deep or underlying structure: Overt manifestations of meaning (imagery, overt and covert speech, and responses) are analogous to surface structure sentences. Tacit meanings are like the underlying structures of sentences. Of great importance (as in the case of sentences), is the fact that the forms or structures of overt

---

[3] I am focusing attention on the knowledge system. I do not mean to de-emphasize environmental, contextual factors as discussed by Bransford and McCarrell. I think the view developed by Shaw and McIntyre, that knowledge is a set of relations between organism and environment, is the most heuristic way to approach cognition. Since elaboration in these directions would complicate the present discussion, I have chosen to emphasize the organism aspect of this relationship.

manifestations (the surface structures) of meaning do not necessarily directly reflect the form of the underlying tacit meaning structures.

IMPLICATIONS OF TACIT KNOWLEDGE

The behaviorist orientation has led psychology to concentrate on observables: stimulus events in the environment and overt responses. With the development of cognitive psychology there has been less avoidance of mentalistic concepts: Knowledge or memory structures have been proposed which are based on linguistic terms and relations (e.g., Katz & Fodor, 1963; Kintsch, 1971; Collins & Quillian, 1970), and on combinations of linguistic structures and imagery (e.g., Paivio, 1971). This return to postulation of structures in the head has been partly due to researchers' decision that to limit psychological constructs to overtly observable stimuli and responses placed undue restrictions on theory development. From a broader perspective, however, this same argument can be applied to the cognitive positions. I will argue that cognitive psychology, like behaviorism, is too much concerned with observables, and that this orientation may be limiting our theorizing. Cognitive psychology has expanded the set of observables to include phenomenal experiences like images and covert speech (e.g., covert hypotheses that *Ss'* are postulated to form) as well as overt responses and stimuli. Mentalistic constructs are observables in exactly the same way that overt stimuli and responses are; we are consciously aware of them. But note these observables presuppose tacit (unobservable) knowledge relations, and the structure of these observable phenomena does not directly reflect the structure of the tacit knowledge/meaning relations that determine them. This implies that present cognitive theories are formulated in terms of constructs that are not adequate to account for our meaningful interactions in the world. In the following sections, four current issues in cognitive psychology will be discussed: I will indicate how orientation to observables may limit theorizing, and how reexamining the issues on the basis of the proposed relation between tacit knowledge and experience may reorient our thinking.

CONCEPTUAL VERSUS SPECIFIC MEMORY

The issue is whether long-term memory (knowledge) is best considered a generative conceptual system or a storehouse of specific memories of past experiences. The storehouse view has been dominant since at least the time of the British associationists. It continues to exert a major influence on theoretical positions and dominates the methodology of most experimentation within cognitive psychology. Views stressing storage of specific input items as memory units dominate the theoretical and experimental endeavors not only in psycholinguistics but also in more traditional verbal learning and memory. Bransford and McCarrell have questioned the utility of such views which emphasize memory for particular words or sentences actually presented at input, and which formulate memory models using particular input items as units of storage.

An alternative view, of memory structures as generative systems (represented, for example, by Bartlett, 1932), is far less popular than the specific memory position. It seems obvious that both views must have some validity. We all experience specific recollections of past events; this supports some form of the specific memory view. Just as clearly, we must know (remember) past events in such a way that they allow us to cope with novelty. Thus, at least part of our long-term memory must be in the form of generative conceptual functions that can specify the structure of novel events. Our discussion above can help conceptualize these alternative modes of memory.

Our *static tacit knowledge* system corresponds to the generative conceptual system required for coping with novelty. Much learning must consist of restructurings of the relations in this system. On the other hand, the specific derivations (meanings) generated from knowledge can be considered the basis for specific memories or recollections. Specific memories amount to maintaining some specific record of previously generated derivations.

What I want to consider is this question: If both types of memory have validity, then why have psychological theorists spent so much time on specific memory (i.e., recollecting) and ignored conceptual memory (i.e., knowing)? This question reflects something about the limitations on us as theorists, i.e., it is related to the problems of understanding understanding.

I proposed above that conscious experiences and overt responses can be considered to be "overt" manifestations of specific derivations from generative tacit knowledge relations. Thus both imagery and particular language outputs (whether overt or "inner speech") reflect individual derivations specific to the particular environmental context present at that moment. But all that we are aware of are particular derivations, not the tacit knowledge relations that generate them. We are not directly aware of underlying generative structures; we are aware of generated specific products. I suggest that this is why we are so preoccupied with specific memories. The mental structures we can introspect upon are specific, and phenomenally, thinking processes appear as manipulations of these specifics. We cannot image a generative relation, nor does labeling with a word (or string of words or symbols) make us any more directly aware of our tacit generative knowledge: labels are just labels, not the relations themselves. We can only be indirectly aware that knowledge must be generative: We can infer this from our ability to cope (consciously and behaviorally) with novel events, but this does not make us directly aware of the nature of these underlying relations. The tendency to theorize and experiment on specific memories, then, may reflect a general tendency to work with observables (whether overt or conscious).

My point here is that, first, we are only aware of aspects of specific derivations and, second, because of a general preference for working with observables, we have tended to concentrate on specific memories related to these observable derivations. This argument is merely a special case of a more general case: Psychologists (as well as people in general) rely too much on observables in constructing their theories and experiments. In the case of specific versus conceptual memory, this penchant for observables has led us to ignore not only a very pervasive and important characteristic of knowledge (i.e., the ability to cope with novelty), but also corresponding theoretical mechanisms necessary to account for this. I am not arguing that we consciously assert this stress on observables; rather, this orientation toward observables is a general tendency that occurs automatically due to limitations on our direct awareness. Below I shall indicate further cases where this "natural" stress on observables may be limiting, in an epistemological sense, our conceptualization of problems such as imagery, pattern recognition, and the nature of semantic memory. The restriction upon thinking is that because of this emphasis we can't, or at least usually don't, question it.

Actually, the gap between generative tacit knowledge and the derivations that form the basis of our phenomenal events is wider than I have portrayed it in discussing specific versus conceptual memory. The generative relations that form our passive tacit knowledge are in a sense two steps removed from direct conscious experience, as may be seen by returning to the grammar analogy. I proposed that the events of consciousness (as well as overt responses) can be likened to the surface structures of sentences. As in grammatical theory, full characterization of responses and phenomenal experiences (e.g., imagery as well as "inner language") must include a specification of deep structure relations, i.e., tacit meanings. These tacit meanings are specific to a particular derivation from the generative knowledge system. They are activated knowledge relations that underlie and determine the nature of the surface structure-like events in the mind's eye. But because these activated underlying relations are tacit, we are not directly aware of these deep structures. Thus, in order to get some notion of the relations composing static tacit knowledge, we must first infer the deep structure relations that underlie specific conscious events or responses. From these formulations of particular derivations, we must then try to infer the nature of the system of tacit knowledge relations that generated them. And our formulations of these different levels must always be characterized in surface structure terms, since these are the only entities we can be aware and think in terms of.

This situation (if our analogies are valid) makes a mess of theory and experimentation, because there is no reason to believe that the relationships charactering the structure of events in awareness are the same as, or even obviously related to, the tacit relations that underlie them. As in linguistics, surface structure relations are not necessarily the same as underlying deep structure relations. These deep structural aspects (as well as their conscious surface structure manifestations) are inherent parts of particular derivations from tacit knowledge. We must make some progress in specifying these deep structures before we can hope to infer the tacit relations from which they were generated. The contextual theory of meaning discussed by Bransford and McCarrell can be considered an effort to clarify the nature of the deep structure relations underlying images and language strings.

Imagery and Memory. After its banishment from experimental psychology by behaviorism, imagery is again a popular research area. Paivio (e.g., 1971) and others have demonstrated the predictive value of imagery in memory research, and it is invoked as an explanatory construct in many discussions of comprehension (e.g., Collins & Quillian, 1970). Let us consider the nature of imagery from the present perspective. First, I am using the term "imagery" to refer to that "picture," or "sound" or other phenomenal event in the mind's eye that we consciously experience. In this usage, "unconscious image" is a contradiction of terms. Also, I am distinguishing between imagery and those events or structures which we might label "perceptual knowledge of the world" or "abstract schemata." The latter terms fall under the heading of tacit knowledge. This usage of imagery should cause no problems: It is the ordinary language use of the term. It is also, presumably, the usage *Ss* are working with when making imagery ratings which are used as predictors in recent experimentation (e.g., Paivio, 1971). *Ss* are not instructed to rate the abstract perceptual structure or schemata of words. As discussed above, images are consciously experienced aspects of particular derivations generated from tacit knowledge: The structure of an image is determined by tacit knowledge structures. Particular meanings are generated from tacit knowledge, and sometimes these derivations are manifested in imagery. But all images have underlying tacit meanings. Images are not units of storage: They are products. In process terms, images are outputs of underlying tacit structures just as overt responses are usually considered to be outputs of mediating knowledge structures.

This makes apparent an alternative to thinking about imagery as a mediator of behavior. Images are not necessarily causal links (e.g., as memory engrams) between input events and overt responses. Given a particular situation, imagery and overt responses may be alternative derivations (i.e., different surface structures) generated from a common set of activated tacit knowledge relations (tacit meanings). They are alternative surface structures (observable manifestations) derived from tacit knowledge, but the structure of the imagery does not directly determine overt responding. Figure 1 depicts these contrasting views of imagery.

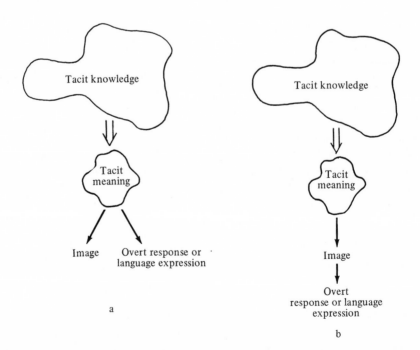

Fig. 1. Two views of imagery.

Figure 1-a illustrates imagery as an alternative surface structure to overt responses. Both are manifestations of underlying relations, but they are not *causally* related to each other. Figure 1-b shows imagery as a mediator of overt responses: Here the structure of the image determines (either completely or partially) the structure of the response. To clarify these views let us extend our analogy with grammars.

In both cases a set of activated tacit knowledge relations underlie the observable images and responses. This set of relations is similar to the deep or underlying structure of a sentence: Like "deep structures," they are not relations that appear in awareness. Alternatively, for imagery as a mediator, the image is analogous to the surface structure of a sentence, and overt responses are analogous to the phonological instantiation of the surface structure. The structure of the image determines the structure of the overt response, as surface structure relations determine phonological instantiations.

But for the position that imagery and responses are alternative derivations another analogy is appropriate. We can consider the image and the overt response to be two alternative surface structures related through a common deep structure. However, these surface structures are not directly determined by each other. In this analogy, images and responses are like paraphrases, alternate expressions of a common underlying tacit meaning. The demonstration of which, if either, view is more valid will rest on a much deeper characterization of the structure both of tacit knowledge and of images and responses than is now available. (My preference is for the common deep structure view.)

Bransford and McCarrell have argued that it is heuristic to consider imagery an indicant of comprehension. When a word or a sentence has been processed within tacit knowledge to a sufficient extent, we say we have understood its meaning. The argument is that if an image occurs, then we have comprehended the word or sentence. But it is the fact of comprehension, and not the imagery, that is crucial to the effectiveness of memory for items. On this view, imagery ratings may be predictors of effectiveness of memory, but it is the processes of comprehension within tacit knowledge that causally lead to both imagery and the effectiveness of memory: The images themselves do not determine memory efficiency. This argument is a special case of the general position that imagery and responses are alternative derivations from tacit knowledge.

At a more general level, no matter which analogy (1-a or 1-b) is closer to the conceptualization that directs one's research and theorizing, the analogies are useful to emphasize the need for structural accounts of imagery and its role. A particularly important point that follows is, as Bransford and McCarrell have argued, that it is not appropriate to think about images as stored, unanalyzed copies of previously experienced events. Thinking of images and responses as alternative outputs leads one (actually forces one) to devote one's major attention to considerations of the nature and structure of tacit knowledge. This is probably the basic issue in cognitive psychology, and it is an issue which has not received sufficient thought. Research on imagery such as that of Paivio (1971) has tended to treat images as units of memory storage and as causal mediators between input and responses. This treatment, like the orientation toward specific memories, is due to too much theoretical orientation toward observables. Actually, images as units of memory are a particular version of the specific memory position. Although Paivio (1971) discusses imagery as generative to handle novelty, he seems to be referring to tacit abstract perceptual knowledge or schemata and not to images as specific phenomenal experiences as rated by *Ss* and as used in his experiments. Specific images don't provide generativity. The problem is that imagery is seductive. It correlates with, or is concomitant to, so much of our memorial and comprehension processes that it is easy to fall into treating an image as a thing (a specific unanalyzed engram) and ignore the structural relations that must underlie the particular image generated. However, to account for effects other than gross correlations between imagery and, say, memory, we must consider the tacit meaning structure underlying the image. Such structural analyses will be needed, for example, to account for effects correlated with the "vividness" or the "dynamism" of imagery. Such structural analyses wait, however, as researchers prefer to deal with observables, with the conscious image, and formulate memory structures with observable images as units of storage.[4]

COGNITIVE STRUCTURALISM

The next two sections sketch two additional areas of investigation in cognitive psychology: the problems of pattern recognition and theories of semantics. In each case I will argue that an orientation to the observable surface structures of psychological events limits our conceptualization. Theorizing in these areas reflects a renewed interest in structural problems in psychology. Although these "new" structuralist views differ from the "old" structuralism of Wundt and Titchener (cf. Boring, 1950), the conceptualizations remain very similar in general form: Both are compositional. Certain elements are postulated as pieces or units of knowledge, and these elements are put together with relations or rules to form more complex structures. The theories constitute efforts to characterize what we know, i.e., the structure of our knowledge. I will indicate possible inadequacies inherent in this general approach to knowledge structures, and argue that this compositional orientation is due to overreliance on observable surface structure manifestations of perceptual and linguistic events.

Pattern Recognition

Pattern recognition involves the problem of classifying a particular input into its appropriate perceptual/conceptual class. Solution of the pattern recognition

---

[4] I should make clear that I am arguing against an overemphasis on observables in formulating theories of memory structure and knowledge, and *not* against an emphasis on observables in research. An experimental orientation demands "objective" communicable methods and specification of variables. Also, thinking about problems and formulation of hypotheses appears in our awareness (as researchers) in terms of imagery and covert and overt speech. But this does not imply that the underlying memory or knowledge structures have any isomorphism with the units and relations that we consciously experience. This will be further discussed when symbol systems are considered below.

problem will require theoretically specifying the structure of our perceptual knowledge systems. A typical approach to pattern recognition makes an appeal to common elements or features (e.g., Neisser, 1967; Uhr, 1966): That is, the proposed theoretical structures involve specification of a list of properties common to members or instances of the class. For example, the common features composing "capital A's" might be line segments; the common elements of "chair" might be legs, backs, seats, etc. Of course, unordered sets or lists of common features by themselves do not form an adequate basis to account for our abilities to identify and classify events. The features must be appropriately interrelated. The proposed knowledge structure of a perceptual class consists of a set of elements or features plus a set of relations or rules for combining these elements.

What is involved in our ability to identify and classify events also leads us to emphasize a further aspect of any pattern recognition theory with claims to empirical adequacy: the facility with which we can identify and cope with novel instances of a class. Just as in the case of language (see Chomsky, 1970), novelty in perception has important implications for pattern recognition. Environmental events rarely, if ever, are exact copies of previously experienced events. Every "A" (or "chair") we encounter probably differs in greater or lesser degree from previously experienced instances. In pattern recognition, as in language, there is essentially an infinitude of possible instances of any perceptual/conceptual class. Grammars are formulated as generative recursive systems to characterize the unbounded set of potential sentences. Likewise, in pattern recognition, an adequate characterization of our knowledge would seem to involve some sort of generative recursive structures.

Thus, in outline, we have a theoretical approach that can characterize the nature of the perceptual knowledge which provides the basis for our pattern recognition capacities. Our knowledge of perceptual classes is a set of generative structures, each consisting of a set of features and a set of relations for combining these features, and at least some of these relations are recursive. These structures generate all the instances of each class. These generative perceptual structures form our tacit perceptual knowledge. Our perceptual and memorial images of class instances, verbal descriptions of these instances, and overt responses to them are overt manifestations of particular derivations (instances) generated by the knowledge structures.

Is this the general nature of perceptual knowledge? I think the answer is "No." The arguments against this element composition approach are extensions of earlier arguments by Cassirer (1923) and the Gestaltists (e.g., Kohler, 1947). The usual application of Gestalt ideas is to the figural aspects of objects, that is, to the spatial-temporal form of an object. The Gestaltists argued that perception of figural aspects cannot be accounted for by combining elements (in their arguments, the elements were sensations). They stressed the wholistic character of figures and the maxim that the whole is greater than the sum of its parts. Boring (1950) proposes that Gestalt psychology died of its success. The Wholism principle was absorbed into and became part of psychology's general theoretical conceptions. I do not think Boring is right about this. Current theorizing about the structure of knowledge has in general ignored Gestalt arguments and their implications. To support this claim, let us overview the Gestalt argument with respect to the element composition view of perceptual knowledge.

The point here is largely captured in the adage "A picture is worth a thousand words," or, in the present discussion, "An image (perceptual or memorial) is worth an infinitude of words." If perceptual experiences and underlying perceptual knowledge structures were composed of sets of elements (features) and compositional relations, then we could label each element and each relation. The symbol system so specified would be isomorphic with perceptual knowledge, and the adage would not apply. But the adage does seem applicable and this implies a nonelemental basis for perceptual knowledge.

As the Gestatists argued, perceptions are wholistic, as are phenomenal experiences of perceptual and memory imagery. No listing of symbols and relations can exhaust the content of these experiences. These images are derivative surface structure representations generated by our perceptual knowledge. Thus, perceptual knowledge structures must also be wholistic to generate such wholistic derivations.[5] It will not do to postulate a tacit perceptual knowledge system of interrelated elements or features and expect to recursively generate the wholistic structures of imagery. Quantitatively increasing the complexity of a structure by recursively adding additional elements into relationships with other symbols cannot characterize the qualitatively nonsymbolic nature of perceptual structures. With symbol manipulation systems we can generate an infinitude of products, but only by quantitatively adding more elements from some finite set, not by making qualitative distinctions. The qualitative distinctions involved in perceptual information would necessitate making up an infinite set of discrete elements.

An important distinction here is that a structured relation among elements is not equal to a wholistic Gestalt. There seems to be some tendency to equate the notions (e.g., see Neisser, 1967, on the relationship between Gestalt psychology and transformational linguistics). The Gestaltist use of the metaphor of "fields" in contrast to structures of interrelated (associated) elements is one way to highlight this distinction. The notion of "fields" allows us to conceptualize perceptual processes without needing to posit elemental parts and relations. Perhaps psychology too quickly rejected the explanatory usefulness of "fields." (This is not to argue for the particular physiologizing of the Gestalters with respect to fields, but rather for the heuristic value of fields as a metaphor for conceptualizing tacit perceptual structures.)

In addition to the figural aspects of perception, an adequate theory must account for identity of forms under transformation, and contextual aspects of recognition and meaning. Gibson's (1966) theory of perception deals with the first of these aspects, while Bransford and McCarrell discuss the importance of context.

---

[5] The term "analog" may help convey my meaning here. A discrete system can simulate an analog system but it remains a simulation. Before we can piece together a discrete simulation we must "understand" the analog relations we are simulating. We must know, in a wholistic, overall way, the analog relation we are modeling before we can "approximate" it with a nonwholistic symbolization.

Gibson's approach to perception seems to be a promising alternative to "substantive" element composition views of pattern recognition. Gibson's notions of detection of invariants under groups of transformations, and the concept of resonance, can be considered an approach to characterizing tacit perceptual structures. We are not phenomenally aware of the invariant relations and transformation groups *per se:* We must ferret those out by inferring and then describing ecologically valid environmental structures "meaningful" to the organism.

However, if I understand the Gibsonian approach, it too has limitations. Transformation groups characterize invariant properties of some structure. In perception these structures are the forms, the figural structures or patterns in the environment. The figural Gestalts are not dealt with in Gibson's theory. But if invariants are what we detect or resonate to in "identification" of environmental contexts, then these invariants must be invariants of "something," i.e., of some figural structure. These figural structures seem to be determinants of actions: For example, our actions must negotiate paths over, under, around, and through specific "objects" in the environment, and not just detect the invariants that "classify" the objects as events of a particular kind. Our actions are specific to particulars. The constructive contextual approach can be considered part of the approach to dealing with particulars. Bransford & McCarrell deal with meanings and significances specific to particular contexts, although they do not attempt to account for figural properties *per se.* To stretch some words a bit, we might say Gibsonian invariants afford identification, but the figural particulars afford action.

If tacit perceptual knowledge is not a set or elements or features plus relations, then what are these features and relations that we are so prone to posit as knowledge structures? In considering this question we are again led to the basic issue of this chapter, the relation between tacit knowledge and experience. The features and relations among these elements are aspects of conscious experience: They are aspects (not elements) of our tacit knowledge that have been "abstracted" into focal attention and labeled with symbols or words. Following our earlier analogies, features and relations are "pieces" of surface structures generated by tacit knowledge. To take a previous example, identification of alphanumeric characters is often thought about in terms of matching up lists of features composed of differently shaped lines, in different orientations, when the characters are hooked together in particular ways. But the present argument is that these lines and interrelations are pieces abstracted from surface structure awareness. The tacit knowledge structures are wholistic Gestalt/Gibsonian structures. However, since we are not directly aware of these tacit structures, we regularly are led into attempts to solve the problem by appealing only to aspects of surface structure derivations from tacit knowledge (e.g., features of particular images). By analogy to language, this is like trying to solve the problems of paraphrase by listing the words that are common to a set of paraphrasic sentences (and maybe, in addition, listing observable relations among words that are common to the set: for example, pairs involving words which follow other words in the sentence). Actually, pattern recognition may even be worse than the language paraphrase case, since in language words *may* be units both of surface and of tacit knowledge structures. To think adequately about pattern recognition we will have to eschew our predilection for equating aspects of observable experiences with pieces of underlying knowledge. The basis for recognition of similarity and identification of events lies in the relations in our tacit generative knowledge, not in the surface structures of particular derivations.

My argument is that particular features are consciously abstracted from underlying wholistic structures or patterns, but that these features presuppose the wholes. Tacit wholes determine experiential pieces; the pieces do not determine or compose the wholes. This is what "The whole is greater than the sum of its parts" means. A piece or feature is only an aspect of experience which has relevance for sequential conscious thought or communication thanks to its "place" in the wholistic underlying knowledge. The particular aspects or features abstracted at any given time will be determined by the underlying figural and invariance relations and the particular context of the event.[6]

The present conception of tacit perceptual knowledge and its relations to experience obviates what may be a major problem in the "features" approach, i.e., the question of what are the atoms, the basic units, of knowledge from which perceptual events are composed. To take the example of chairs, it might be argued that, for instance, a "seat" is a feature. But this feature itself is a concept, or class, and obliges us to ask what are the features of a seat. This leads to a regression in search of basic features (i.e., a finite list of "atoms" of perceptual knowledge). Attempts to formulate such lists of atoms lead to infinite lists (see, e.g., Titchener's attempt to compose such a list of atomic sensations, in Herrnstein & Boring, 1966). Under the present conceptualization, we would in fact *expect* an infinite list, since features are particular aspects abstracted from a wholistic derivation generated by tacit knowledge, given a particular context. The particular aspects we choose to abstract and label are a function of the essentially infinite set of particular contexts of occurrences (see Bransford & McCarrell), and thus we would expect an essentially unbounded set of such features. We can cope with an infinitude of features, but tacit perceptual knowledge is not composed of these features.

In summary, our basic problem in perceptual knowledge seems to be that we cannot consciously think or conceptualize in terms of wholistic generative relations. To think about and work with a relation we first label it (give it a symbol) to make it a substantive entity. Then we think about it as a relation (a thing) between X and Y (two or more other things). It seems that we cannot consider a relation as just that, a relation, rather than as a relation between things. However, that appears to be just what our tacit perceptual knowledge system is, i.e., a set, or even better, a pattern of relations. This seems to be what Lashley (1950) and Gibson (1966) have in mind with the notion of resonance, and also it is implicit in the "fields" of the Gestaltists: Tacit perceptual knowledge is a generative, recursive, Gestalt pattern. Even these words don't seem to make much sense, but that is because we cannot

---

[6] Note that a particular experiment defines a particular context. An experiment can direct people to respond to particular aspects or features of events, without necessarily supporting these features as compositional elements of perceptual knowledge.

easily think in terms (even the words "in terms" indicate our penchant for, or even limitation to, elementistic symbolic thinking, cf., Watts, 1958) of a wholistic pattern that is generative and recursive. Somehow perceptual knowledge is a structure that tunes itself to (or resonates with) the unbounded variety of stimulus patterns from the environment. In some recursive but wholistic way, it can generate all the distinctions and nuances in events while at the same time "recognizing" or "assigning" to the event the general classifications that have utility for functioning in the world. My basic thesis is that to have conscious understanding of our perceptual knowledge systems we must learn to think about, or at least feel, wholistic generative recursive thoughts, in contrast to our usual thinking in discrete, symbolic, recursive thoughts. To formally theorize and communicate about perceptual knowledge, we must use symbols and relations among symbols. But we must be careful not to let this limitation mislead us into thinking that perceptual knowledge is such a symbol manipulation system, involving elements ("symbols") and relations among these symbols.

Theories of Semantics.

A second line of psychological theorizing about knowledge structures is found in recent theories of semantics. Such theories are proposed to account for understanding of language strings (words, sentences, etc.), and have been proposed in linguistics (e.g., Katz & Fodor, 1963; Katz & Postal, 1964), computer simulation (e.g., Quillian, 1969), and psychology (e.g., Kintsch, 1971). These theories are attempts to characterize aspects of our knowledge systems which are used in the comprehension of language. The general form of these theories may be characterized as symbol manipulation systems (SMS); that is, the proposed semantic structures are composed of symbols (words) and relations among these symbols. This section will consider the potential adequacy of such symbol manipulation theories as accounts of semantic knowledge. In outline, the discussion will proceed as follows: I will argue that symbol manipulation theories of semantics are feature theories or element composition theories. Certain problems with such approaches will be indicated, and a possible alternative conceptualization invoking perceptual knowledge structures will be offered. Finally, I will consider the relationship of tacit knowledge and experience to the present problem of semantic theories, and propose that symbol manipulation approaches are a further instance of too great an orientation toward observables.

Semantic Structure as a Symbol Manipulation System (SMS). Let us briefly sketch the Katz-Fodor-Postal (KFP) system (1963, 1964) as an example of an SMS approach to semantics. The KFP theory portrays semantic knowledge as composed of a dictionary plus projection rules. The dictionary specifies semantic properties of lexical items (words in terms of distinctive features (animate inanimate, human nonhuman, etc.), some orderings among these features, and a distinguisher which carries those nuances of meaning not captured in the features. The projection rules combine feature plus distinguishers for particular lexical items to form a greater set of features plus distinguishers that is the reading of a sentence. Words (symbols) play three roles in this system. The lexical items defined in the dictionary are words. The features composing these items are words, and the distinguishers, which are generally propositional structures, are composed of interrelated words. In addition to these words or symbols, the system has rules for manipulating or relating the symbols, including the ordering relations among features, the projection rules, and the syntactic (or other) relations that are used in specifying distinguishers in terms of propositional structures. Thus, in overview, the KFP theory is an SMS with words as elements and relations for combining these elements to form semantic readings of words, sentences, and presumably extended discourse.[7]

Notice that the KFP approach is (and I will argue below that all SMS's of semantics are) a form of element composition theory. The features proposed by KFP are basic elements (semantic atoms) from which the meanings of other words are composed. Ideally, the distinguishers in the KFP theory would ultimately be decomposed into feature structures. The problem is: "What is the basic set of features or elements from which the meanings of words and longer language strings are composed?" This is the problem since no finite (much less, small) set of features will do. Bollinger (1965) points out many nuances in meaning that a particular word can take as a function of the sentential contexts in which it appears and each nuance apparently requires the positing of an additional feature. Since the set of possible sentential contexts of a word is very large, the set of necessary features becomes immense, effectively infinite. Characterizing the elements of semantic knowledge as an essentially infinite list of features makes little psychological sense. Adding an additional knowledge element for each particular situation we encounter allows facile postdiction but aids us little in prediction and understanding of semantics and processes involving semantics, like comprehension.

How might we get around such problems with feature lists? The apparent alternative in the KFP system is to rely on the distinguishers. Instead of trying to decompose distinguishers into features, we might leave them as propositional structures − that is, as sets of words tied together by relations. Then these propositional structures can characterize the nuances in meaning neglected by the feature list. Now we need an infinite propositional structure for each distinguisher to capture the potentially infinite nuances of meaning. Obviously we need some recursive relations somewhere in this account to handle these infinite nuances with finite means. What is needed is some finite set of symbols (features) and some relations (some of which are recursive) that interrelate them.

So let us recompose an SMS theory of semantics. The semantic structure of a lexical item or word consists of a finite set of symbols (words) interrelated by a recursive structure like a grammar (or some alternative set of recursive rules). This recursive structure can then generate the set of specific propositional structures

[7] As another example of an SMS, consider the systems proposed in Quillian (1969) and Collins and Quillian (1970), which are quite similar in form to KFP. Their systems consist of words interrelated by relations (e.g., hierarchical relations among nouns, and inference rules defined across these hierarchical structures). The semantics of nouns are elaborated by listings of features or properties which themselves are specified in terms of words or, perhaps better, simple propositions, (e.g., "is yellow" as a property of "canary") or more elaborate propositional structures (e.g., "has long, think legs" as a property of ostrich").

constituting the semantics or meaning of that word which is appropriate to any particular context. Of course, in addition to generative structures for the semantics of words, we will need further relations or rules that interrelate or combine the generated word structures to form the larger propositional structures of sentences and extended discourse.

Now we can eliminate the KFP distinction between features and distinguishers. KFP features are merely symbols (words), like any of the other symbols (words) in the theory. The generative systems that form the semantic structures of words will contain symbols, and some may be the KFP features. The particular symbols chosen as features by KFP may be more general in that they form part of the particular generated propositional structures of a word in a greater number of (or possibly all) the potential contexts of occurrence of that word, while other symbols (words) will be part of these generated structures in a lesser number of cases. However, this is a relative distinction and not a distinction in kind. The frequencies of occurrence of these symbols in the set of particular propositional structures derived from the generative semantic system as a function of context will form a continuum: What we tend to call features of a word are merely those symbols that occur most frequently in the derived semantic structures of the word.

This characterization of semantic structure is compatible with extant symbol manipulation theories of semantics: It is merely an extension of the KFP system. The approach of generative semanticists (e.g., Ross & McCawley, Lakoff, 1971), appears quite similar to the position just developed, in that it elaborates the underlying structure of words and sentences in propositional structures. Kintsch's (1971) approach is quite similar. Likewise, "associative net" theories of semantics from a computer orientation (e.g., Quillian, 1969) treat the semantic structure of a particular word as the set of all its potential interrelationships with other words.

In summary, all current semantic theories are element composition theories. The basic elements are any or all the words (symbols) a person knows. Semantic knowledge consists of generative relational systems defined across subsets of words to form the semantic structures of particular words, and further generative rules specifying the potential interrelations among the semantic structures of words that can compose language strings. The particular context of occurrence of a word determines the particular propositional structure (meaning) that is derived from the generative semantic knowledge structure of that word, and this holds also for sentences and extended discourse.)

Adequacy of SMS approaches to semantics. Now consider the potential adequacy of SMS theories to account for semantic knowledge and language comprehension. There is no denying that the form of the SMS theory I sketched above *can* potentially generate a distinctive propositional structure for each and every possible meaning of words, sentences, and extended discourse: This is due simply to the inclusion of recursive rules. For each contextual meaning nuance we come across, we can merely add in additional structuring among the symbols so the derived propositional structure will be different (in terms of included symbols and relations) from all other nuances. This by itself is not very interesting. The utility of the model will come in providing a more specific structuring of the theory in terms of more general symbols and relations that can significantly simplify semantic theory so we can understand its general properties.

But the search for more general symbols would return us to the task of discovering features a′ la KFP, and this does not appear viable. It seems, then, that more general relations are needed to give us a simplified picture of semantics. Thus, although we end up with an immense set of symbols, at least we can understand semantics in general in terms of the overall structuring principles. Apparently this latter alternative is the task accepted by the generative semanticists, computer-oriented investigators, and others, such as Searle (1969). The problem of the "intrinsic" semantic structure of words is in general avoided. Words, as needed, are treated as units of structure, and the search turns to the seemingly more viable task of formulating general rules or relations for structuring these units.

I suggest that this search is misdirected, for the following reasons: First, the intrinsic semantic structure of words cannot be ignored. Words, as we use them in everyday language, are not homogeneous, identical particles, like elementary particles in physics. In physics, general functions or structures can be specified across the units because the nature of the particular units involved in a specific "context" does not interact with and change the nature of the general functions (see Elsasser, 1966). In contrast, the "meanings" of words *do* interact and, in a sense, uniquely specify the relations among words in language. This is one of the basic points of Bollinger's arguments and is the point elaborated by Bransford and McCarrell in discussing the importance of context. The search for general relations is much the same as the search for general features; the semantics of relations, like those of symbols, are contextually determined. If these arguments hold, they indicate that to *find general semantic relations we should be attempting to form a theory of contexts* and not a theory of general relations among words.

This point relates to a second misgiving I have about SMS approaches to semantics. Where might we look for a theory of contexts? Two obvious possibilities present themselves: linguistic contexts and perceptual contexts. Linguistic contexts are the specific sets of words (symbols) and relations among them instantiated in a particular discourse. The search for principles of linguistic context (of which Searle's, 1969, speech acts might be an example) implies that words and relations among words are part of tacit semantic knowledge since the principles of linguistic context are to be specified as structures across words and their interrelationships. But what sense does it make to say that knowledge (and hence the derived meanings) of words (and extended discourse) consists of their interrelationship with other words? Words are merely arbitrary acoustic-articulatory images.[8] It does not seem that the derived meaning(and hence, tacit knowledge structure) of a word (an arbitrary symbol) can be accounted for by the composition of its interrelations with other arbitrary symbols. But this is exactly what SMS theories propose.

SMS theories are tautologies: The semantics of symbols are characterized in terms of relations among other symbols, but the symbols and relations are not hooked to perceptual knowledge. This seems rather strange, since we may

---

[8] Of course, these images have motoric or auditory structures that underlie them, but these underlying structures are not semantic or meaning-related (with the possible exception of phonetic symbolism, if that principle ever proves valid).

reasonably suppose that *one of the basic functions of language is to communicate information about events in the world.*

Actually I have somewhat overstated the aim of SMS theories. They are not proposed to account for all the meaning of particular language strings. Rather, they propose that certain aspects of meaning, traditionally delimited as semantics, can be captured in terms of interrelations among symbols, and that these aspects can be separated from those aspects that relate to the perceptual world (e.g., see Katz & Fodor, 1963, pp. 403-408, and the introduction of imagery structures by Collins & Quillian, 1970). Thus, in essence, a "dual code" structure of knowledge is hypothesized. The knowledge structures that are the basis for generation of meanings consist of both relational structures among symbols (semantics) and perceptual knowledge structures, with some further relations between semantics and perceptual knowledge. The study of contexts for language usage can then proceed as two semi-independent enterprises, corresponding to the investigation of linguistic context and perceptual context. Bransford and McCarrell present arguments stressing the importance of perceptual events and perceptual contexts in language comprehension. In addition they go further and question the positing of *any* specifically linguistic structures in accounting for language comprehension. They ask, "Can the separate aspect of semantic knowledge that consists of symbols and their interrelations be eliminated, and can the meaning structures underlying language comprehension be attributed to perceptual knowledge?" A number of reasons might lead one to make this assumption. If these reasons are valid, the value of the assumption lies in redirection of our thinking about where to look for general regularities and relations that can characterize meanings communicated through language.

Language and perceptual knowledge. To discuss reasons for the assumption that no symbolic linguistic relations are involved in meaning structures, let us sketch a possible relationship between language and perceptual knowledge. Language is basically a communication system, and not a medium for "storage" of knowledge. Language is a symbol manipulation system which consists of arbitrary units (symbols) and symbol manipulation rules. Theories of phonology and syntax are theories concerning the structuring of arbitrary words and relations among words for purposes of communication. Thus, *aspects* of our knowledge do consist of SMS's, but this knowledge (phonology and syntax) is of an arbitrary, conventionalized communication system and not a knowledge structure that underlies the meaning of what is communicated.[9] The knowledge structure that underlies meaning is tacit perceptual knowledge, as discussed above. Words are labels for perceptual classes (see, e.g., Lenneberg, 1967). Syntactic relations are established conventions for cuing off integrations of perceptual events.

Looked at from the comprehension side, the linguistic symbols (words) "communicate" what perceptual classes are to be activated, and the linguistic

---

[9] Thus the often held position in linguistics that meaning is not a linguistic concern (see Chomsky, 1957; Lyons, 1970).

relations among the symbols "communicate" how the derivations (meanings) in these perceptual classes are to be integrated. The meaning of a sentence is not captured by linguistic symbols and relations; rather, meaning is in the integrated tacit perceptual meaning structure. The linguistic structures form a communication device for directing meaning formation. In this sense, words and relations act as a sort of catalyst for the formation of the meaning structure, but themselves are not part of it.[10]

Now consider the evidence that might lead one to hold this conception of the relation between language and perceptual meaning. The most general kind concerns the utility of language; it facilitates our interactions in the world. In everyday communication, words, sentences, and extended discourse are useful because they "refer" to environmental events and our interactions with these events — they "refer" to actions, feelings, and perceptual events.[11]

This does not prove that there are not linguistic semantic relations between words as units. But it does indicate that, if such knowledge relations exist, they too have "reference" to environmental relations, or more specifically to perceptual knowledge structures. If not, they are meaningless knowledge relations, meaningless in the sense that they have no effect on perceptions, actions, and feelings. If such relations are posited to exist and to have no reference to meaning, then why call them semantic? They are syntactic relations in the usual sense of the term, as "syntactic" is used in linguistics. They are structural relations between arbitrary symbols (words). Nonarbitrariness comes with reference to meaning.

Here the reader may feel that I am playing with words, and that it doesn't matter what we call such relations. If such relations among symbols are part of our

---

[10] From a knowledge acquisition perspective, linguistic structures may indeed influence the nature of the perceptual knowledge that is acquired. Words and sentences can be used to direct "attention" to the environmental events that are instances of perceptual classes, thus directing what is acquired. However, the linguistic structures do *not* form part of this acquired structure. Again, it must be emphasized that we are separating knowledge of the communication device that is language from the knowledge underlying meanings.

[11] Note that the present scheme is not the "classical" notion of reference discussed, for example, by Rosenberg and Travis (1971). Words (and relations among words, for that matter) do not *refer* to objects, actions, etc., in the environment, nor do they refer to images (as defined above). They "refer" to generated meanings derived from perceptual knowledge. But "reference" here may be the wrong word. There is not an association, or hook, between the word and a thing called a perceptual knowledge class. Such substantive treatment of perceptual knowledge as a thing is misleading. Perceptual knowledge is a wholistic generative structure or pattern which generates particular wholistic patterns or meanings as a function of environmental contexts or events. With the activation of a particular meaning, the articulatory (phonological) and syntactic knowledge systems may be activated, leading to a language expression (one of many that might be appropriate) that can communicate meaning by cuing off a similar meaning derivation in a listener. But there is no unique association, or reference, between things (words and perceptual classes). Language expressions (words, sentences, etc.) and perceptual (or motoric, or affective) meanings are correlated derivations generated as a function of perceptual contexts (where in many cases of verbal interaction the perceptual contexts will be perceptual patterns cued off by previous language expressions). The nature of the correlations awaits further specification of perceptual knowledge and perceptual contexts (see Bransford & McCarrell).

knowledge, and if they cue off perceptual structures leading to integrated meanings, then why not call them semantic?

I choose not to call them semantic because the term is misleading. The distinction in terminology is important for several reasons: First, calling these relations syntactic reminds us that accounting for the relationships between such syntactic relations and the perceptual meaning they cue off remains one of our major problems. Second, referring to these relations as semantic seems to lead us to posit as knowledge relations more and more relations among symbols in an attempt to capture more and more of the meanings of words and sentences. As will be argued below, because meanings are wholistic, contextually determined structures, this positing of intersymbolic relations can go on forever. On the other hand, calling such relations syntactic may make us more discrete and lead us to look elsewhere for general relations appropriate for characterizing meanings.

A third point is related to these: Since these proposed semantic relations cue off perceptual relations in *any* case, these symbolic semantic relations may be *redundant* and more appropriately characterized in terms of the perceptual structures themselves. For an illustration, consider a strong candidate for a semantic relation among symbols: the inference rule that applies to the noun hierarchies in the Collins and Quillian model (1970). This rule allows us to infer, for example, that since a bird has wings and a canary is a bird, therefore a canary has wings. The rule is specified in terms of the symbols (in this case the words "bird," "Canary," and "wing") and the symbolic relations among them in the semantic network. Is this inference rule a knowledge relation among symbols? it can be argued otherwise. To illustrate, let us perform a hypothetical experiment.

Condition a chimp to make a particular response to a class of objects, e.g., birds. During conditioning present many different kinds of birds, but never a canary. Following this conditioning present a canary and, low and behold, the chimp "generalizes" and responds to the canary. Has not the chimp made a Collins and Quillian inference, although in this case we might rather call it generalization? I do not think we would want to call this inference a symbolic relationship. The inference was due to perceptual similarities captured in the chimp's perceptual knowledge.[12] The point is that we too have perceptual knowledge systems in which similarity relations hold. These relations provide a basis for inferring or generalizing "novel" relations in the generation of perceptual meanings. Do we in addition *redundantly* code these perceptual relations as relations among symbols? Maybe, but not necessarily.

How does this relate to the terms "semantic" and "syntactic"? I hope it indicates that many relations we posit as semantic may be redundant with relations derivable from perceptual knowledge, and it may be appropriate to eliminate the redundancy and concentrate on understanding the perceptual structures. I do not mean to imply that we have no knowledge of logical inference rules and relations

---

[12] One might argue that the chimp does not really know the class of birds, but rather was generalizing from particular acquisition stimuli. This strategy would not obviate my argument. It would merely say that the relevant perceptual class involved in the similarity relation was narrower than the full class of birds, but the same general point would still hold.

with which we can manipulate arbitary symbols. Rather, the question is: Do we ordinarily use such rules and relations in everyday language comprehension? Besides these general considerations of reference, what evidence might support my sketch of the relation between language and perceptual knowledge? The experiments and demonstrations of the importance of perceptual contexts in language comprehension discussed by Bransford and McCarrell lead these authors to a position very similar to mine. A further line of evidence is found in the literature on imagery (e.g., Paivio, 1971).

Although Paivio's dual code theory conflicts in certain ways with the present position, the experiments demonstrating the importance of imagery (and thus perceptual structures) support the present approach and highlight the importance of investigations of perceptual knowledge.

When someone says a word and an image appears in awareness, this cannot be accounted for by relations between the word and other symbols. As stated in the discussion of pattern recognition, the image is an integrated whole that is the conscious manifestation of tacit wholistic meanings derived from perceptual knowledge. The same holds for sentences. For example, say you were presented with the sentence "The dog bit the bone," and you have an image of a dog biting a bone. The image will 'contain' not only particular derivations or instances (images) of the perceptual classes "dog," "bit" and "bone," but also certain perceptual relations among these derivations: for example, the dog opening his mouth and closing it around the bone. This integration of perceptual information cannot be captured by symbolic relations which interrelate the symbols "dog," "bit," "bone." The structure of the image is a wholistic analog representation, formed by direct perceptual integration of the different aspects of meaning cued by the words and syntactic relations in the sentence. But whether a particular sentence is consciously imaged or not, its meaning (and our understanding of it) must often be accounted for by perceptual relations. For example, the meaning (and our understanding) of the sentence "The stripes expanded" is not very clear. By itself, the sentence has weird construction. Yet if it is preceded by "The man blew up the striped balloon," the meaning of "The stripes expanded" crystallizes. Our understanding of "The stripes expanded" is determined by integration of the perceptual information for the man blowing up the balloon. The meaning of the sentence is contingent on perceptual knowledge of a balloon inflating and of what happens as it stretches. Such information is not captured in a set of interrelated symbols. Many examples and demonstrations discussed by Bransford and McCarrell make a similar point. Not only imagery, but language comprehension itself is contingent on perceptually integrated meanings. In all such cases the lack of a conscious image does not mean perceptual knowledge is not activated. Comprehension still involves a perceptual meaning structure.

The imagery evoked by the utterances above is positive evidence for the present position, but all the expressions were concrete. What about abstract expressions? Are these not a countercase to the present position? The meanings of abstract words seem best characterized as interrelations with other words. Even Paivio, who stresses imagery, accounts for knowledge (or memory) of abstract words and sentences in terms of symbols and relations among symbols. But even the meaning (and understanding) of abstract expressions can be handled by perceptual knowledge. Abstract words, like concrete words, to be meaningful (see my discussion of "reference") must ultimately be tied to the environment and our interactions with it. In the case of abstract words like "freedom," the perceptual meanings cued off may be manifested as images of complex integrated "scenes" rather than as images of objects. For example, images of freedom might include "a convict climbing over a prison wall" or "a woman unencumbered by a bra." The environmental events captured in perceptual knowledge correlated with an abstract word may be quite varied and complex, but the meanings cued off by such terms are perceptual structures. Again, the absence of an image in some, or even many, cases does not imply the absence of tacit perceptual meanings in these cases.[13]

The final evidence we will consider, which lends support to the present position concerning language and perception, comes from recent developments in linguistics: Ross's discussion of the notion of a category "squish." He suggests that certain syntactic distinctions which have been traditionally considered discrete categories (e.g., verbs, adjectives, and nouns) are better seen as merely aspects of a "quasi-continuum," i.e., a squish. These categories fade into one another; they are squishy. If Ross's arguments are correct, it would seem that some of the most obvious candidates for knowledge in terms of discrete symbols and relations among symbols are in fact not that; rather, the knowledge structures are a continuum. This development in linguistics would be compatible with and could be taken as support for the present position, which stresses wholistic, "continuous" underlying knowledge/meaning structures.

Lakoff's [14] discussion of "fuzzy logic" leads to a similar conclusion. Lakoff states that "natural language concepts have vague boundaries and fuzzy edges," and that 'the phenomena ... are beyond the bounds of classical set theory and the logics based on it.' Thus he argues that many aspects of our knowledge of language are not appropriately considered to be what I have termed SMS's. These aspects cannot be characterized in terms of discrete entities (symbols) and relations among them. Rather, our knowledge of categories is fuzzy (squishy, to use Ross's term), and the relations that apply are those of a fuzzy logic. Again, words are more like labels for aspects of continua, and these aspects trail off into each other. Here, then, is another case from linguistic theory which can support the present position advocating wholistic, nondiscrete underlying meanings and knowledge structures.

---

[13] As an aside note that, in everyday conversations, abstract words and sentences seem to be used in the context of some specific environmental event or in the context of previous expressions which have cued off perceptual meanings of specific events. Such contexts provide the basis for generation of specific meaning derivations of these abstract terms and thus facilitate their comprehension.   In experimental settings these contexts are rarely provided, and to comprehend the abstract expressions Ss must generate their own (typically under time constraints). Failure to generate an adequate perceptual meaning, and thus failure to comprehend, could at least partially account for results like those of Begg and Paivio (1969), which seem to show memory for abstract expressions in terms of the specific words presented.

[14] As in Hedges: A study in meaning criteria and the logic of fuzzy concepts. (Unpublished manuscript, University of Michigan, 1972.)

The final linguistic evidence I will consider concerns generative semanticist characterizations of the underlying structure of sentences. Ross has presented a possible candidate for the underlying structure of "Floyd broke the glass." The underlying representation he sketched contained about 19 distinct propositions but also included a number of cover markers indicating terms that remained to be expanded into propositional structures. This seems like a lot of underlying propositional structure for such a simple sentence. In addition, if one continued such an analysis it is not clear that the list of underlying propositions would ever end. Ross, in fact, alluded to this possibility. Such potentially unbounded elaboration of underlying propositions seems neither parsimonious nor facilitative of our understanding of knowledge/meaning structures, and tends to indicate that a search for alternative characterizations is needed.   The present proposal of underlying wholistic perceptual structures is, I hope, such an alternative. As a matter of fact, if the underlying meaning structures are indeed wholistic representations, then a potentially infinite elaboration of propositional structures underlying sentences is exactly what would be expected. Let us illustrate this metaphorically. If the underlying meaning of a sentence is a representation of a wholistic environmental/perceptual event or context (or, let us say, if this representation can be characterized as a continuous n-dimensional space), then this space can be "sliced" in an infinite number of ways. We can express each slice as a proposition. Since we can keep slicing forever, we can list propositions forever and never succeed in characterizing the meaning underlying the sentence. The same metaphor holds for features. In this case we just call a slice a feature and label it with some symbol. If so, then we should search for new metaphors to express our meaning knowledge structures (perhaps like those alluded to in the discussion of pattern recognition), and we should be wary of positing symbolic knowledge relations.[15]

Obviously, none of the evidence discussed in this section disproves the existence of symbolic relations that underlie the meanings (and our comprehension) of language expressions in everyday communication. However, as a group, this evidence provide a plausible argument that psychology needs a new metaphors and principles for understanding the meanings communicated through language, i.e., some alternatives to the current SMS conceptions. The present conceptualization of the relation between language and perceptual knowledge is one possible avenue to follow in the search for these alternatives.

Before leaving this discussion I should mention some seeming exceptions, where knowledge structures do in fact appear to be relational structures among symbols.

[15]Metaphors themselves support the above sketch of language and perceptual knowledge. Imagery seems to correlate highly with metaphorical expressions. However, in this case even the particular imagery cued by the metaphor (and thus the corresponding tacit perceptual meaning) seems grossly different from what is meant. The information communicated seems to involve very general tacit perceptual structures, which remain invariant across the metaphorical event and the event for which it is a metaphor. If this is the case, the study of metaphors would be a fruitful line of investigation in the search for general relations of perceptual knowledge and perceptual contexts.

An obvious example is our knowledge of mathematics. One might argue for an empiricistic perceptual basis for this knowledge, but I think that in pure mathematics we now can and do in fact manipulate and relate arbitrary symbols (see Cassirer, 1969). Although mathematics is an SMS knowledge structure, it is only tangentially involved in meaning structures that underlie everyday language communication: When numbers are used in everyday conversations, they refer to something.

I have already mentioned that the syntax and phonology of language seem to be a case of an SMS in knowledge. Given arguments like those of Ross and Lakoff above, we need to work out which aspects are to be characterized as relations among symbols.

A final potential counterexample is rote memory. Suppose I present you with the expression "Tylum migto szan," and you memorize it for later recall. Your knowledge (memory) of the expression will be an arbitrary relation among arbitrary symbols. We *can* rote-memorize meaningless strings of symbols and thus have knowledge structures consisting of relations among symbols, but it seems rather awkward to term the activation of this knowledge structure "a meaning." My position is that such rote-memorized symbolic relations do not play a role in ordinary language communication, except in a context like that of my asking you to recall the above expression verbatim, and your doing so, in which case the situation or context is already providing some aspects of meaning for the expression.[16]

Tacit knowledge and language. I have presented an extensive argument against symbol manipulation systems as theories of language meaning. By now the reader may wonder what other kinds of theories there are besides what I have characterized as 'symbol manipulation' theories. What theory is *not* a set of symbols structured by relations? As far as I know, all theories, whether formulated in terms of mathematics, logics, or even ordinary language, are symbol manipulation systems. However, we must distinguish between a theory as a model, a theory as a communication device, and that which it models (in the present instance, the underlying knowledge structure). My argument above questioned the efficacy of treating SMS's as an instantiation of (not a model of) underlying knowledge. It seems necessary to use symbols and relations among symbols as a medium for structuring theories and communicating knowledge. However, we must be wary of letting the symbolic nature of our theories misguide thinking about the nature of underlying tacit knowledge meaning structures.

This brings us back to the basic theme, the relationship between tacit knowledge and psychological phenomena, and its implications for cognitive psychology. In language comprehension, tacit knowledge is perceptual knowledge and the tacit meanings which are derived from it. One form in which activated tacit meanings are consciously manifested is in language expressions (words and strings

---

[16]Even in cases of memorized strings of meaningless symbols it is misleading to characterize such knowledge as "things." The representation, if it exists, will rather be some derived structure within the generative phonological–syntactic knowledge system.

of words). The discussion above proposes that surface structure phenomenal experiences of words are radically different from the tacit meanings that underlie them. To understand meanings we must look (or infer) beyond the contents of awareness. SMS theories of semantics are a prime example of how our "natural" preoccupation with observables (conscious or overt) can misdirect our conceptualizations of the problems of psychology. If images are seductive, then words are insidious. The ever-present play of words in awareness, on paper, and in speech seems to make it well-nigh impossible for us to resist inserting them as units of our meaning knowledge structures. If my arguments hold, we must forego this temptation.

INTUITIONS AS CLUES TO TACIT KNOWLEDGE

My general theme has been that all observable psychological phenomena presuppose underlying tacit knowledge structures. My argument has been that the structures of tacit meanings cannot be understood in terms of their observable surface structure manifestations. If this is the case, then the question becomes, "How can we study this tacit nonobservable knowledge system?" A partial answer may be found in transformational linguistics. The distinction between tacit knowledge and surface structure manifestations is an important aspect of the transformational linguist's approach to the study of language. The speaker-hearer's knowledge of the grammar of a language, as well as of many aspects of particular derivations' underlying structure, is tacit. Speakers are not directly aware of the grammatical relations of their language, that is, they do not experience "grammar" or even the underlying structures of particular derivations: They experience "surface structures." Yet the linguistic enterprise takes as its task specification of underlying relationships and the inference from those relationships back to the grammar that could generate them. It is at this point that the notion of "intuitions" becomes very important: Intuitions about relations (for example, among sentences) form the basis from which the linguist constructs his formal specification of the grammatical rules. For the linguist, intuitions are a window to tacit knowledge of language. In a sense, the linguist's job can be characterized as one of formally specifying why he has his intuitions. He attempts to construct a system of rules that can generate an explicit relational basis for his intuitions.

With the rise of transformational grammar, examples of linguistic intuition have become familiar. For example, we have the intuition that "The boy hit the ball" and "The ball was hit by the boy" are related or similar in meaning. The average speaker-hearer surely has this intuition, but he is unable to spell out the basis for it. He cannot tell someone the relationships in his knowledge system that are the basis for this impression of relatedness. The linguist assumes the task of spelling out the knowledge basis for the intuition. For example, Chomsky (1965) accounts for the intuition in this case by assigning similar deep structures to the two surface structures. Whether such a formulation of its basis is valid or not, an important point is that the formalization comes after the intuition.

I have proposed that the knowledge structures forming our understanding and responding to both perceptual and linguistic events are tacit relations. If our knowledge structures are largely tacit, then how are we to theorize about them? The answer in linguistics is: through our intuitions. Can we adopt a similar strategy in cognitive psychology? Actually the question is behind the actual case. We already rely heavily on intuitions as data in psychology (as I will discuss below).

If intuitions are important, what exactly are they? As Chomsky uses the term (e.g., 1965), an intuition seems to be an impression of relatedness, without one's necessarily and usually being able to immediately state the basis for the relation. Let us elaborate this notion of "impression of relatedness." I have proposed that conscious, phenomenal experiences are surface structure manifestations of tacit knowledge relations. Two modes of phenomenal experience that I have discussed are imagery and language (word strings). Extending Chomsky's use of the term, we can regard intuitions as a third mode of awareness deriving from tacit knowledge. Relations are activated within tacit knowledge, and we phenomenally experience these activated relations as intuitions.[17]

The use of intuitions carries over into psycholinguistic research, but where do intuitions come into psychology, besides psycholinguistics? It seems that the answer is, "Everywhere." For example, we might well say that the two forms in Fig. 2 look similar. We have an impression of relatedness, in this case of similarity of form, but probably cannot spell out the structural relations in our tacit knowledge

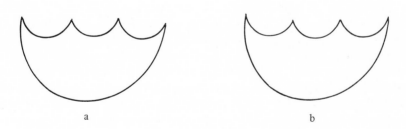

Fig. 2. Two similar forms.

[17] Following my general thesis, I do not consider intuitions to be a *causal* link between tacit knowledge structures and overt responding. Rather, I consider intuitions another output of tacit knowledge manifested in parallel with other surface structures like language, images, and motor responses. This use of the term "intuition" is somewhat different from some of its philosophical uses, in which intuition contrasts with reasoning as an alternative active mode of knowing (cf. Langer, 1951), and which seem to treat intuition as if it were some "mechanism" for processing information. In our usage intuitions are not functions for processing information; rather, they are phenomenal indicants that relations are activated (i.e., information is being processed) in tacit knowledge.

that form its basis. If we could, we would be well on the way to solving the problems of perception. One might try to tell someone else how these two forms are alike in ordinary language terms: For example, one might say they both have four points on top of a rounded bottom. However, these "reasons" for similarity are not the tacit perceptual relations that form the basis for recognizing similarity, for the reasons noted in the discussion of pattern recognition. Also, note that the intuition (the impression of similarity in form) does not require such verbalizations: The intuition is phenomenally given, independently of any verbalized reasons for it. As in linguistics, the symbolized reason comes after the intuition and is a "formalized" account for it. This is just one example of an intuition outside the area of language. This intuition of similarity of form and the related impression of difference or dissimilarity are basic data for theories of form perception. The task of the psychologist becomes one of theoretically specifying a set of knowledge relations that can account for the intuition.

The above, of course, is not simply an isolated case of use of intuitions in psychology. On the contrary, intuitions may be the major source of data for psychology. For example, we have impressions of familarity or recognition. We recognize an event as something experienced before, or at least something similar to what we previously experienced. We cannot specify the knowledge relations that form the basis for this recognition response. This phenomenal response is an intuition, an impression that the present experience is related to a previous one. Again, getting overt responses does not alter the intuitional basis of the responding. Our theories of recognition are formal attempts to account for properties of this intuition of familiarity.

Consider the problem of pattern recognition—for example, our classification of a particular dog as a "dog." We have relatedness between the particular event being experienced and a knowledge class. Should we refer to this as an intuition? We have an impression of relatedness which we can label. Because we can label it, e.g., "That perceptual event is a dog," it seems rather odd to call it an intuition. But where did the classification come from in the first place? It is reasonable that at some point in history (or prehistory) there was no label for the class "dog," and that someone had the intuition, the impression, that the set of events that are dogs were related, and then labeled the class. The notion that the label came before the class is rather nonsensical. This may seem a rather farfetched example, but isn't this how classifications in science, for example (i.e., labels of classes of more recent origin), come about? In creating taxonomic classifications in biology, for example, isn't it reasonable to suppose that the biologist had an intuition of the relatedness among the members within a classification before labeling it? It makes little sense to say the scientist creates a label and then goes out and finds a set of events for which he can use the label. The relatedness in tacit knowledge structures comes first, with intuition as a manifestation of this relatedness. Then, if the tacit knowledge relation has sufficient utility, the relation is labeled with a word or symbol so it can be communicated. Words may just be labels for what we would once have experienced only as intuitions.

The point I want to make about intuitions—though I may be stretching it a bit in the pattern recognition case—is quite simple: Intuitions are not some ghostly mentalistic bugbears that threaten the empirical enterprise of psychology. We use intuitions all the time—in specifying the events in stimulus and response classes, in choosing operational definitions, and in using measures like ratings of recognition and similarity. It is an interesting task to try listing different general classes of intuition, e.g., impressions of novelty, familiarity, similarity, difference, anomaly. Can psychology be characterized as the science of explaining intuitions?

Intuitions are clues to tacit knowledge relations — not clues in that they tell us the structural nature of a relation, but rather clues that a relation exists. But are intuitions really unique psychological phenomena in this respect? Don't we use other psychological phenomena in the same way? Are not images, language expressions, and motor responses also clues that tacit knowledge relations exist, and is it not our task to form theoretical expressions characterizing these underlying relations? The answer is, "yes, these phenomena are also clues, but the special importance of intuitions is in the kinds of tacit relations they are clues for." Images, language expressions, and responses are clues to properties of particular derived meanings. In contrast, intuitions seem to be clues to more general relations in tacit knowledge. Intuitions of similarity and difference, of novelty, familiarity, anomaly, etc., are impressions of general, more global, structural relationships among events. For example, my intuition that visual images are wholistic Gestalts or patterns led me to propose as a general property of tacit perceptual knowledge that it is a wholistic generative pattern. A task that remains is to formulate a more theoretically useful symbolic expression of this intuition.[18]

If intuitions are as important to the psychological enterprise as they appear to be, then a promising area of investigation would seem to be the study of intuitions themselves: that is, not just using them as tools in investigating other phenomena like language or perception, but rather searching for the general principles of structure and "usage" of intuitions as we do for words and images.[19]

In closing, let us consider whether, or to what extent, intuitions form a golden road to tacit knowledge. Are intuitions somehow undistorted clues to tacit knowledge relations? In thinking about this question, remember the distinction between tacit knowledge and events in awareness. Imagery, language, and overt responses all are based on (i.e., are outputs of) underlying tacit knowledge structures. In none of these cases is a characterization of the structure of the conscious or overt event a direct representation of the tacit relations which generated it. An image, a language string, or a response is a surface structure, and each of them has a tacit underlying structure. Then we have intuitions as another sort of event in consciousness. How do they fit in?

---

[18]Note that the intuition is not "part of" the visual image itself. The intuition is a separate, distinct phenomenal experience, just as in linguistics the intuition of the grammaticality of a sentence is not 'part of' the sentence itself.

[19]Halwes discusses below a possible distinction between two modes of perceiving. One mode is our usual way of thinking about perception, which seems to involve sequential decision processes. Halwes portrays a second mode as more nondirective and wholistic. He gives the perceptual processing involved in Neisser's (1967) scanning task as an instance of this second mode. One way of characterizing this second mode may be to say it is "perceiving" by intuitions.

Is an intuition a direct impression of tacit underlying relations or is it, too, "distorted" or altered like other conscious experiences? Do intuitions also have underlying tacit structures that determine our surface structure impressions of relatedness? Are there deep structures of intuitions that directly relate to the underlying tacit knowledge relations? Are conscious impressions some sort of transformed surface structure? If so, can we use our intuitions to look back on the tacit structures of other intuitions (or themselves, for that matter)? Let me leave you with these questions and with the hope that my speculations have helped to clarify someone else's thinking besides my own.

REFERENCES

Bartlett, F. C. *Remembering.* Cambridge: Cambridge University Press, 1932.

Begg, I., & Paivio, A. Concreteness and imagery in sentence memory. *Journal of Verbal Learning and Verbal Behavior,* 1969, 8, 821-827.

Bergmann, G. The problem of relations in classical psychology. *Philosophical Quarterly,* 1952, 2, 140-152.

Bollinger, D. The atomization of meaning. *Language,* 1965, 41, 555-573.

Boring, E. G. *A history of experimental psychology.* New York: Appleton, 1950.

Cassirer, E. *Substance and function.* New York: Dover, 1923.

Cassirer, E. The concept of group and the theory of perception. In P. Tibbits (Ed.), *Perception.* Chicago: Quadrangle, 1969.

Chomsky, N. *Syntactic structures.* The Hague: Mouton, 1957.

Chomsky, N. *Aspects of the theory of syntax.* Cambridge, Mass.: MIT Press, 1965.

Chomsky, N. *Language and mind.* (Rev. ed.) New York: Harcourt, Brace, 1970.

Chomsky, N. Deep structure, surface structure, and semantic interpretation. In D. D. Steinberg & L. A. Jakobovits (Eds.), *Semantics: An interdisciplinary reader.* Cambridge University Press, 1971.

Collins, A., & Quillian, M. R. Experiments on semantic memory and language comprehension. In L. W. Gregg (Ed.), *Cognition in learning and memory.* New York: Wiley, 1970.

Craik, K. J. W. *The nature of explanation.* Cambridge: Cambridge University Press, 1943.

Elsasser, W. M. *Atom and organism.* Princeton: Princeton University Press, 1966.

Gibson, J. J. *The senses considered as perceptual systems.* Boston: Houghton Mifflin, 1966.

Hayek, F. A. *The sensory order.* Chicago: University of Chicago Press, 1952.

Hayek, F. A. The primacy of the abstract. In A. Koestler and J. R. Smythies (Eds.), *Beyond reductionism.* London: Hutchinson, 1969.

Herrnstein, R. & Boring, E. G. (Eds.), *A source book in the history of psychology.* Cambridge, Mass.: Harvard University Press, 1966.

Katz, J. J., & Fodor, J. A. The structure of a semantic theory. In L. A. Jakobovits & M. S. Miron (Eds.), *Readings in the psychology of language.* Englewood Cliffs, N.J.: Prentice-Hall, 1963.

Katz, J; J., & Postal, P. M. *An integrated theory of linguistic descriptions.* Cambridge, Mass: MIT Press, 1964.

Kintsch, W. Notes on the structure of semantic memory. (Technical Report, Department of Psychology) Boulder: University of Colorado, 1971.

Kohler, W. *Gestalt psychology.* New York: Liveright, 1947.

Kuhn, T. S. *The structure of scientific revolutions.* (Rev. ed.) Chicago: University of Chicago Press, 1970.

Langer, S. K. *Philosophy in a new key.* New York: Mentor, 1951.

Lakoff, G. On generative semantics. In D. D. Steinberg & L. A. Jakobovits (Eds.), *Semantics: An interdisciplinary reader.* London: Cambridge University Press, 1971.

Lashley, K. S. In search of the engram. In *Physiological mechanisms in animal behavior.* (Symposium No. 4, Society for Experimental Biology) Cambridge: Cambridge University Press, 1950.

Lenneberg, E. H. *Biological foundations of language.* New York: Wiley, 1967.

Lyons, J. *Noam Chomsky.* New York: Viking Press, 1970.

Neisser, U. *Cognitive psychology.* New York: Appleton, 1967.

Paivio, A. *Imagery and verbal processes.* New York: Holt, Rinehart & Winston, 1971.

Polanyi, M. *The tacit dimension.* Garden City: Doubleday, 1966.

Quillian, M. R. The teachable language comprehender: A simulation program and theory of language. *Communications of the ACM,* 1969, **12**, (8), 459-476.

Rosenberg, J. F., & Travis, C. *Readings in the philosophy of language.* Englewood Cliffs, N.J.: Prentice-Hall, 1971.

Searle, J. R. *Speech acts: An essay in the philosophy of language.* London: Cambridge University Press, 1969.

Uhr, L. (Ed.) *Pattern recognition.* New York: Wiley, 1966.

Watts, A. W. *Nature, man and woman.* New York: Vintage Books, 1958.

12

THE PROBLEM OF MEANING AND THE INTERRELATIONS OF THE HIGHER MENTAL PROCESSES

William F. Brewer[1]
University of Illinois at Urbana-Champaign

This chapter attempts to place the work of Bransford, McCarrell, and Franks (hereafter BMF) in the larger context of investigations of mind, and to extend their analysis to broader issues. To understand how mind works one must take very seriously the fact that the higher mental processes are intimately interrelated. An analysis of these interrelations leads to a natural solution to the problem of meaning. This solution shows that theories which deal with meaning in terms of an isolated higher mental process cannot be correct, and thus that theories of meaning as images (British Empiricism, Paivio) and meaning as language (Transformational Linguistics, Psycholinguistics) must be in error.

THE INTERRELATIONS OF THE HIGHER MENTAL PROCESSES

To say that perception, imagery, language, memory, and thought are interrelated may not seem of great theoretical import, but understanding of this issue could have the same systematic impact on theorizing in cognitive psychology as did Chomsky's "common sense" observation that a human being can understand and produce an indefinitely large number of sentences. The interaction of the higher mental processes is clearly demonstrated by: (*a*) our ability to image some portion of what we have seen, heard, remembered, or thought; (*b*) our ability to speak about what we have seen, imaged, remembered, or thought; (*c*) our ability to remember what we have seen, imaged, heard, or thought; (*d*) our ability to think about what we have seen, imaged, heard, or remembered. These armchair facts show that information can flow from one higher mental process to another, but do not tell

[1] Some of the thoughts in this chapter were developed in discussion with Roger Chaffin, Dick Harris, Tom Leahey, Charles Osgood, Kay Bock, and Chris Tanz.

Higher Mental Process Being Influenced

	Perception	Language	Memory	Thought
Perception	//////	Yes	Yes	Yes
Imagery	?	?	Yes	Yes
Language	Yes	//////	Yes	Yes
Thought	Yes	Yes	Yes	//////

Influencing Higher Mental Process

Fig. 1   A "periodic table" of higher mental processes

the exact nature of the interrelations. To work out the full theoretical implications it is necessary to develop a deeper analysis of the interactions of the higher mental processes.

These interactions can be examined through the development of a "periodic table" of higher mental processes (see Fig. 1). Each entry in the table represents the action of one process on another. The data to be filled in is of two different types: (a) evidence that the particular higher mental process does influence the operation of the other higher mental process; (b) the exact nature of the interaction of the two higher mental processes.

Language on perception. The classic argument for the effect on language of perception was, of course, Whorf's hypothesis that characteristics of a particular language (such as the grammatical categories) have a strong effect on the speaker's perception of the world (Carroll, 1956). Recent work casts doubt on the stronger forms of this hypothesis (Lenneberg, 1967, Ch. 8). However, there is evidence for the influence of language on perception.

Bergson (1911) used evidence from speech perception to show the influence of language on perception:

> I listen to two people speaking in a language which is unknown to me. Do I therefore hear them talk? The vibrations which reach my ears are the same as those which strike theirs. Yet I perceive only confused noise, in which all sounds are alike. I distinguish nothing, and could not repeat anything. In this same sonorous mass, however, the two interlocutors distinguish consonants, vowels and syllables which are not at all alike, in short, separate words. Between them and me where is the difference? The question is, how can the knowledge of a language, which is only memory, modify the material content of a present perception, and cause some listeners actually to hear what others, in the same physical conditions, do not hear [p. 134].

Pillsbury and Meader (1928) also noted the interaction of the language system with the incoming speech signal. They state, "The process and laws of supplementing also hold for listening. The sound must supply relatively little, as can be seen from the small amount that can be detected in an unknown tongue. One cannot repeat sentences. One cannot even recognize as the same a sentence from a foreign language when it is repeated in close succession [p. 146]."

Recent work on speech perception has supported Bergson, and Pillsbury and Meader, showing that perception of spoken language is dependent upon language-specific mechanisms which drastically restructure the incoming physical stimuli (Liberman, Cooper, Shankweiler, & Studdert-Kennedy, 1967). Miller and Isard (1963) found that syntactic but anomalous sentences are perceived better under auditory masking than are word strings, thus showing an effect of language (syntax) on perception. Additional evidence for the influence of syntax on perception was obtained in Garrett, Bever, and Fodor's experiment (1966) showing that the locations of clicks superimposed on a sentence are misperceived and heard as occurring at the syntactic breaks of the sentence.

Reading is another good example of the influence of language on perception. Huey (1908) showed that subjects report seeing more at a given exposure duration if the stimulus material is linguistic. More recently Reicher (1969) and Wheeler (1970) have shown that forced-choice letter recognition is better for words than for nonwords. Thus, there is good evidence for the effects of language on both auditory and visual perception, though the nature of the interaction remains obscure (see Brewer, 1972).

Thought on perception. Many writers have argued that thought can have a strong effect on perception. For example, Kuhn (1970, Ch. 10) has stated that scientists working in different paradigms see the world in different ways. However, the evidence usually used to support this position seems to confuse the effects of thought on perception with the effects of perception on thought. In other words, when someone with a Copernican world view looks at the sun, he doesn't perceive the earth moving around the sun; he still sees the sun moving across the sky, but this perceptual input enters his knowledge network and is analyzed in terms of the earth moving around the sun (see Gregory, 1970, Ch. 8).

In a weaker form, however, thought may affect perception. For example Bugelski and Alampay (1961) have shown that the perception of an ambiguous figure (rat-man) can be biased toward one of the possible perceptions by the set established by a preceding series of pictures. Thus, the expectation that the pictures were pictures of animals biased the subjects towards perceiving the rat form of the ambiguous figure.

Perception on language. If one holds that language serves as a vehicle to express thought and that perceptual information is available to the other higher mental processes, then it is obvious that perception will affect language. However, these assumptions are not shared by many linguists and psycholinguists, and so it is necessary to examine them in some detail.

In 1751 the English linguist James Harris made the following insightful observation about the use of articles in English: "[when we see something—is it] *Known, or unknown?* Seen now *for the first time,* or *seen before,* and now remembered? — 'Tis here we shall discover the use of the two Articles (A) and (THE). (A) respects our *primary* Perception, and denotes Individuals as *unknown;* (THE) respects our *secondary* Perception, and denotes Individuals as *known.* To explain by an example — I see an object pass by, which I never saw till then. What do I say? — *There goes A Beggar, with A long Beard.* The Man departs, and returns a week after. What do I say then? — *There goes THE Beggar with THE long Beard* [pp. 215-216]."

More recently the linguist Hermann Paul (1891) made the argument for the influence of perception on language to account for the logical structure of "sentence fragments." He stated, "In other cases, it is the object of perception common to speaker and hearer alike—the *situation*—that forms the logical subject, to which the attention may be still more pointedly directed by gestures. This object of perception may be the speaker or the person accosted; *cf. your servant, most obedient servant; all right, welcome; so sad! why so sad?* Besides these we have many exclamations of astonishment and alarm and appeals for aid, like *fire!— thieves!—murder!—help!* and challenges, like *Friend or foe?* We have questions, too, like *Odd or even?— Right or left?* [p. 118]."

Even more recently a few psychologists have understood the theoretical significance of these points and have made them respectable by carrying out demonstration experiments. For example, Wales (1970) showed Ss a movie in which an actor came into the scene, left, and came back. Ss were asked to write what they saw. Wales found that upon first mention an unknown person or object was referred to as "an X," but on second mention the same person or object was referred to as "the X."

Osgood (1971) has shown the same effect of perceptual knowledge on selection of definite and indefinite articles. Osgood also used experimental manipulations to show the effects of perception on a wide variety of other linguistic phenomena. For example, he showed that upon first view Ss typically described a particular scene as "A green cup is on the table." However, if in the immediately previous demonstration they had seen a man holding a red cup, they would typically write something like "The cup on the table is green," for the same scene. In similar fashion Osgood showed the effects of perceptual input on tense and pronouns.

Olson (1970) carried out experiments in which Ss were asked to tell a listener where to find a hidden object. If the object was placed under a round white block near a round black block, Ss tended to say that "It's under the white one." However, if the object was hidden under the same round white block when a white square block was near by, Ss tended to say, "It's under the round one."

R. J. Harris (in press) has shown the effect of perception on language by having two groups of Ss describe a cartoon. One group was told to write a description of the cartoon for someone who had never seen it. The other was told to write a description for someone who was looking at the picture, but did not understand the humor. The second group, who could assume common perceptual knowledge, used more definite articles, more pronouns, and mentioned fewer concrete objects.

Note that these investigations are properly classified as studies of the effects of perception on language only because the relevant knowledge was obtained through visual perception. A deeper analysis of the results would show that the perceptual information entered the *Ss'* knowledge network and the resulting thoughts (a linguistic knowledge) were expressed in language. Both Olson (1970) and Osgood (1971) seem to argue that visual perception operates directly on language. Thus, Olson hypothesizes that linguistic choices are made to differentiate a referent from a perceived set of alternatives, and Osgood refers to the perceptual information as "driving" the linguistic output. Franks, in the present volume, also leans toward visual perception as underlying language. For example, see the section "Language and perceptual knowledge," and on another issue, "abstract words, like concrete words, to be meaningful . . . must ultimately be tied to the environment and our interactions with it [p. 253]."

The difficulty with using visual perceptual information to underlie language is that visual perception is too inflexible to account for the facts. Thus, Olson's account of meaning in terms of the differentiation of a set of perceived alternatives falls apart when applied to any sentence taken at random from this chapter. Osgood's discussion of perception "driving" language is subject to Chomsky's (1959) classic demonstration that language is not stimulus bound. In fact Osgood's own data (1971, Table 2) show the force of Chomsky's argument, since of 26 *Ss* viewing the same scene, not one describes it with the same sentence. Franks' hypothesis of development of the meaning of abstract words and sentences from perceptual knowledge likewise faces the difficulty of producing a plausible account, in perceptual terms, of the meaning of abstract words or sentences.

The general difficulties with the perceptual approach to meaning were nicely pointed out by Husserl: "Let us consider an example. I have just looked out into the garden and now given expression to my percept in the words: 'There flies a blackbird!' *What is here the act in which my meaning resides?* I think we may say . . . that it does not reside in perception, at least not in perception alone . . . For we could base different statements on the *same percept,* and thereby unfold *quite different senses.* I could, e.g., have remarked: "That is black!,' 'That is a black bird!,' 'There flies that black bird!,' 'There it soars!,' and so forth [1913, p. 680]."

Another difficulty for perception-based theories of meaning is that similar shifts in articles and pronouns can be obtained through previous linguistic mention of something or shared memory, thus suggesting a more general underlying system. A final difficulty is that congenital blindness appears to have little or no effect on the development of language.

All these difficulties can be avoided by taking the position that perceptual information enters into the knowledge network formed by the interconnected higher mental processes, and is expressed in language via the thought system. Thus we can agree with Jespersen's (1924) analysis of the determinants of the definite article, "In *the rose, rose* is restricted to that one definite rose which is at this very moment in my thought and must be in yours, too, because we have just mentioned it, or because everything in the situation points towards that particular rose [p. 109]."

Thought on language. To understand the relationship between thought and language, the crucial question is the one in the title of Osgood's 1971 paper,

"Where do sentences come from?" A succinct answer is given by B&M: from "the a-linguistic knowledge system."

One of the earliest discussions of the relation between thought and language is in Aristotle, who stated that, "Spoken words are the symbols of mental experience and written words are the symbols of spoken words. Just as all men have not the same writing, so all men have not the same speech sounds, but the mental experiences, which these directly symbolize, are the same [335 B.C., p. 25]." Since theories of the higher mental processes were then in their earliest stage of development, it is hard to know what Aristotle took to be the nature of the mental experiences expressed as words—some commentators think he considered them to be images.

Descartes (1641) took a firm position on the separation of language and thought. He stated, "Moreover, in reasoning we unite not names but the things signified by the names; and I marvel that the opposite can occur to anyone. For who doubts whether a Frenchman and a German are able to reason in exactly the same way about the same things, though they yet conceive the words in an entirely diverse way [p. 137]?"

Locke (1690) held a view similar to Descartes', but was more explicit about the mental process hypothesized to underlie language. He stated, "The use of words then being to stand as outward marks of our internal ideas, and those ideas being taken from particular things, if every particular idea that we take in should have a distinct name, names must be endless. To prevent this, the mind makes the particular ideas received from particular objects to become general [p. 145]." Thus, the position that language is the expression of thought has a distinguished philosophical pedigree, and it is interesting to note that on this issue (conceptualism) Locke and the Continental philosophers are in agreement (see Aune, 1967).

William James' famous chapter on the stream of thought gives some of the strongest introspective evidence yet brought to bear on this problem.

> And has the reader never asked himself what kind of a mental fact is his *intention of saying a thing* before he has said it? It is an entirely definite intention, distinct from all other intentions, an absolutely distinct state of consciousness, therefore; and yet how much of it consists of definite sensorial images, either of words or of things? Hardly anything! Linger, and the words and things come into the mind; the anticipatory intention, the divination is there no more. But as the words that replace it arrive, it welcomes them successively and calls them right if they agree with it, it rejects them and calls them wrong if they do not [1890, Vol. I, p. 253].

In addition to introspective evidence on word finding, James used the logical relations expressed by certain words to make the point in a different fashion.

> When we read such phrases as "naught but," "either one or the other," "*a* is *b*, but," "although it is, nevertheless," "it is an excluded middle, there is no *tertium quid*," and a host of other verbal skeletons of logical relation, is it true that there is nothing more in our minds than the words themselves as they pass? What then is the meaning of the words which we think we understand as we read? What makes that meaning different in one phrase from what it is in the other? "Who?" "When?" "Where?" Is the difference of felt meaning in these interrogatives nothing more than their difference of sound? . . . The truth is that large tracts of human speech are nothing but *signs of direction* in thought [1890, Vol. I, pp. 252-253].

Stout also presented a number of powerful arguments: In 1896 Stout had a perfectly clear understanding of Chomskian creativity in language. In arguing against an associative view of language Stout pointed out that, "In general, Campbell's doctrine rests on a false estimate of the amount and kind of verbal repetition which is to be found in ordinary discourse. Let any one pick out at random a sentence from a book, and then let him look for another exactly like it: it is a hundred to one that he will fail in finding one even by a long and diligent search [1896, Vol. I, p.91]." Stout, however, realized that this implied a similar creativity of thought; "language shares the plasticity of thought itself; it is being incessantly adapted to new occasions in the most delicate way, new combinations of words accompanying new combinations of meaning [p. 87]." That human beings have both creativity of thought and creativity of language has been noted in more recent times by Langacker (1968, p. 88). Stout attacked linguistic association theories by pointing out that without a level of thought behind language they couldn't account for "our ability to reproduce the substance of what we have heard or read in language of our own differing from that in which it was originally conveyed [1896, Vol. I, p. 87]."

Binet and Simon (1908) used evidence from the language of mentally retarded patients to argue for the separation of language and thought. They report the following interchange with a 25-year-old, severely retarded patient.

> We asked her, "Who gave you that pretty ring?" Without hesitation she replied, "Mama." Let us weigh this word. Let us note that in order for the thought contained in this reply to be completely developed in language, it would be necessary that Denise had replied to us or had simply thought to herself the following sentence, "It was mama who gave me this ring." But she cannot articulate even mentally this sentence, which is very evident, since her vocabulary is reduced to five or six words and her mental level does not permit her to make sentences. We are therefore very certain that, in this case, her thought has no corresponding series of necessary words; it is indeed a thought without sufficient words and consequently there is in her a thought without words [p.212].

Binet and Simon also argued that Denise's use of single word imperatives to make complex requests is evidence for underlying thoughts, not underlying words.

The careful work of the Würzburg psychologists gave much information about thinking and language. Most important, perhaps, was their discovery that much complex cognitive processing (thinking) required to carry out cognitive tasks is not available to the conscious mind. For example Ach (1905) pointed out that Ss given 6/2 as a stimulus would respond 8, 4, or 3 depending on whether they were instructed to add, subtract, or divide; and yet Ss didn't report any conscious correlate for the different operations. Selz (1913) made similar arguments for finding the superordinate or coordinate of a given stimulus word. Karl Bühler (1908a) found that even in more complex tasks (e.g., understanding aphorisms such as, "We depreciate everything that can be explained.") much of the mental processing was not available to the conscious mind. In summarizing the work of the Würzburg school, Humphrey (1951) concluded that their research established that *"We may . . .think a proposition, or (draw) an inference . . .in such a way that the activity in question falls within none of the sensory modalities* [p. 129]." Franks is making the same point when he argues that knowledge structures consciousness but does not appear in it.

Butler (1925) pointed out the lack of language in complex motor tasks. He asked, "Do we think in words, again, when we wind up our watches, put on our clothes, or eat our breakfasts? If we do, it is generally about something else. We do these things almost as much without the help of words as we wink or yawn, or perform any of those other actions that we call reflex, as it would almost seem because they are done without reflection. They are not, however, the less reasonable because wordless [p. 32]."

The philosopher Blanshard (1939) pointed out the implication of the process of visual recognition for the language-thought issue. He argued that "not even a behaviourist would say that whenever we recognize a road or building, or identify our own hat in a collection, the process consists of *sotto voce* speech. It is useless to insist that this might be proved by further experimentation. Experimentation will never prove that when I walk into a room and recognize at a glance three or four of my friends who are present, my vocal organs are naming them all simultaneously, or that when a lecturer in mid-course perceives an acquaintance in the crowd, his vocal mechanism can perform at once two incompatible tasks [1939, Vol. I, p. 322]." Shepard (1967) carried out a study of recognition memory for pictures that provides experimental support for Blanshard's argument.

H. H. Price's important book *Thinking and Experience* (1969) provides much evidence for the separation of language and thought. For example, he shows the import of the underlying direction of thought in prose.

> Now let us consider some long and complicated piece of verbal thinking ... Let us suppose that this piece of thinking requires a whole paragraph, say three hundred words, to formulate it ... Clearly the whole three hundred words are not before our minds at the same time. In any one specious present five or six of them might be there, subvocally spoken or in the form of verbal imagery. But what about the others? By the time we get to the middle of the paragraph, we may indeed be recollecting *some* of the earlier ones, and possibly anticipating *some* of the later ones. But even if we bring in recollection, and anticipation too, it is quite clear that the whole three hundred are never before our minds all at once. Our consciousness would be crowded out if they were. How then do we manage to keep our heads throughout the whole process? How do we know which word to say next, and how do we fit the later ones on to the earlier ones (which have dropped out of consciousness by then) so that the whole series of words make one coherent discourse? The obvious answer is that the "general sense" or "general drift" of the whole paragraph is before our minds throughout [p. 310].

The arguments thus far presented have used evidence from human beings with language. The separation of language and thought can also be supported by evidence from a variety of nonlinguistic organisms.

Clearly lower organisms can think. The evidence is particularly unambiguous with higher primates, such as the chimpanzee. For example Hayes and Nissen (1971) report that Viki, a home-reared chimpanzee, was able to sort pictures of animals (mammals, birds, insects) from pictures of inanimate objects with 85% accuracy. She was able to sort pictures of children from pictures of adult humans with 89% accuracy. Records of home-reared chimps are full of evidence for higher-level cognitive processing. For example, the Kelloggs (1933, p. 248) report the following observation. Gua had been told to remain seated on a stool some distance from her adopted parent. She became anxious about the separation and attempted to get down, but was told she had to stay on the stool. After a period of increasing anxiety she climbed down, slid the stool over to her adopted parent, and then quickly jumped back up on the stool, thus obeying the letter of the law, if not the spirit. Such evidence makes it obvious that animals without language can carry out complex cognitive operations that would be called thinking if observed in human beings. Human preverbal children are at least as smart as chimpanzees and thus also provide evidence for thought without language (for example, Piaget, 1952).

Human adults with aphasia also show thought without language. In general severely aphasic patients exhibit some deficits on (overtly) nonlanguage tests, but this is to be expected, since a severely aphasic patient has considerable brain damage. Of interest for the language-thought issue is that some patients with little or no remaining language are able to score in the normal range on nonlanguage tests (Meyers, 1948; Weisenburg & McBride, 1935; Zangwill, 1964). Deaf children show little verbal language and provide another source of evidence. Furth (1966) has compared deaf children to normal children on a variety of cognitive tasks and found evidence for intact thought processes in deaf children.

Therefore evidence from a variety of nonverbal organisms supports the position that complex cognitive processing can be carried out in the absence of language, and hence thought must be separate from language.

In the framework of the present chapter, many phenomena used in current linguistics as evidence for the deep versus surface structure distinction are actually evidence for the thought-language distinction. Thus, ambiguous sentences, such as "They are feeding her dog biscuits," are sentences whose linguistic structure in isolation can be interpreted as expressing two different thoughts. Semantically anomalous sentences, such as "The stone is embarrassed," do not violate linguistic rules; they express "unthinkable" thoughts (Brewer, 1974b; Drange, 1966). Finally, that one can use language to lie implies that there is something behind language that is separate from the linguistic utterance itself.

To summarize, in developing a theory of the higher mental processes, thought must be separated from language and must in fact underlie language, for the following reasons: (a) language can differ while thoughts remain the same (synonyms); (b) thoughts can differ while language remains the same (ambiguity); (c) word-finding difficulty shows thought behind language; (d) linguistic paraphrases must be united by underlying thought; (e) one-word utterances can express a very complex thought; (f) complex motor tasks don't require language; (g) the process of visual recognition does not require language; (h) the theme of discourse requires an underlying thought scheme; (i) nonverbal organisms, such as animals, young children, aphasics, and the deaf, all show evidence of thought; (j) the concept of lying requires a level of thought behind language.

On the experimental side, the effect of thought on language can be seen in a series of studies by Bransford and Johnson (1972, 1973), Dooling and Lachman (1971), and Dooling and Mullet (1973). In these studies Ss were given linguistic input designed to be hard to grasp in isolation. Then some Ss were given knowledge about the theme of the story through pictures, titles, or key concepts. All of these experiments found that the groups with the additional knowledge were able to use that knowledge to interpret the linguistic input, and thus showed higher comprehension and memory for the stories than did *Ss* who didn't have thematic clues. These studies thus provide evidence that having an appropriate conceptual framework facilitates linguistic comprehension.

Perception on memory. If the higher mental processes are interconnected, it should be possible to show an effect of perception on memory. In practice it is hard to find experiments supporting this interrelation, but it is not hard to design a study that would qualify. Bransford and Johnson (1972) have shown that *Ss* memorizing a (deliberately) vague passage have superior recall if they are shown a picture giving the essential relations missing in the story. In this study the picture was taken away before *Ss* heard the story, and so they used the knowledge obtained from the picture to help structure the story. If the picture had been placed before them at the beginning of the story and left there for the duration of the story, the perceptual information immediately available to *Ss* would have facilitated story recall.

Imagery on memory. With the loosening of the methodological and epistemological constraints of Behaviorism in the last decade, imagery has come back into its own in psychology. One technique that has been used to show the effects of imagery on memory has been the manipulation of the character of the linguistic material to be memorized. Paivio (1969, 1971b, 1972) has shown that high-imagery (concrete) words are remembered better than low-imagery (abstract) words in standard experimental learning tasks (paired-associate learning, free recall, serial learning, etc.). Yuille and Paivio (1969) have also shown that high-imagery discourse is easier to recall than low-imagery discourse, but there may be a problem in this study with the comprehensibility of the abstract passages (see Johnson, Bransford, Nyberg, & Cleary, 1972). Thus, at least for isolated concrete words, there is convincing evidence that linguistic input supplies information to *S's* imagery system and that images produced by this system facilitate recall.

The other basic technique used to show effects of imagery on memory is to give instructions designed to make *S* actively use the imagery system in the memory task. Bower (1970, 1972) showed that, for a noun-noun paired-associate task, asking *S* to form a visual image of the two referents interacting in some way produces enormous facilitation of memory compared to a verbal repetition control group. Ross and Lawrence (1968) taught *Ss* to learn a list by taking a mental walk through the university campus and placing the images of the words to be memorized at various places along the walk. *Ss* using this *loci et res* technique showed almost perfect immediate recall of 40-item lists and fairly good recall for successive 40-item lists over a number of days. Meudell (1971) has produced intriguing evidence for the effects of imagery on memory. He asked each *S* to tell him how many window panes there were in his living room. All *Ss* reported using imagery to carry out the task, and the time taken to answer was an increasing function of the number of panes reported. Thus, there is good evidence that many verbal memory tasks activate the visual imagery network and that the images produced facilitate *S's* recall of verbal material.

Language on memory. The fact that language can have a powerful effect on memory has been known since the first experimental investigations. Ebbinghaus (1885) compared the number of trials he took to memorize prose with the number of trials he took to memorize an equivalent amount of nonsense syllables. He found that it took 10 times as many trials to memorize the nonsense syllables. Ebbinghaus' finding has been replicated many times with similar results (see Welborn & English, 1937, for a review). Marks and Miller (1964) have shown that word lists and semantically anomalous sentences are harder to memorize than normal sentences.

Thus the degree to which stimulus materials approximate natural language has a strong facilitory effect on memory. However, in these studies it is difficult to distinguish between the effect due to language *per se* and that due to information conveyed by language entering *S's* knowledge network and then interacting with other higher mental processes.

For example, Brewer (1974b) argued that semantically anomalous sentences are not anomalous because they violate linguistic rules, but because they express unthinkable concepts. He showed that within the traditional class of semantically anomalous sentences there are thinkable-imageable sentences (The man was eating the clock) and unthinkable sentences (The health was rolled up). A study of recall memory for these sentence types was carried out, showing that there were no significant differences in recall scores for normal sentences and thinkable-imageable anomalous sentences, while recall scores for unthinkable anomalous sentences were significantly below those for the other two sentence types. Thus, it appears that much difficulty in memorizing scrambled or anomalous sentences is not due to language *per se,* but to the fact that these sentences do not lead to a coherent thought or image which can be used to recall the original linguistic input. Bransford and McCarrell make a similar point: "One can have knowledge of language and yet fail to understand utterances if one is unable to activate appropriate alinguistic knowledge of the world [p. 204]."

A totally different technique was used to show an effect of language on memory in the classic study of Carmichael, Hogan, and Walter (1932) on the effects of verbal labels on memory for forms. This study and a later replication (Herman, Lawless, & Marshall, 1957) asked different groups of *Ss* to remember ambiguous visual figures. For one group a figure would be labeled with one word (eyeglasses), while for the other group it would be labeled with another word (dumbbells). In both studies *Ss'* drawings tended to be distorted to look more like the referent of the label presented. There is a possible difficulty with these studies, in that the experimental situation might have contained subtle demand characteristics (Orne, 1962) and these could have produced the resulting distortions. However, if the studies can be taken at face value, they are like the prose recall studies in that the effect is not due to language *per se,* but to the fact that the language input allowed access to *S's* knowledge network where he has information about the visual shapes of the referents of the verbal labels.

While it is hard to separate language, thought, and imagery in memory studies, there are techniques to show the effects of language itself on memory. In color memory tasks it appears to be very difficult to develop a good internal representation of a particular shade of color. Thus, Lantz and Stefflre (1964) suggest that *Ss* in a color recognition task use language to encode the color and then use their knowledge of the relation between their language and the colors in the recognition task to enable them to pick the correct color. These authors proposed that the accuracy with which one individual is able to communicate the information about a stimulus to another would be closely related to the accuracy with which an individual is able to encode the information for his own use. They obtained measures of communication accuracy for a set of colors from one group of *Ss* and showed that these correlated highly with color recognition memory scores of another group.

Glanzer and Clark (1962, 1964), also working with a linguistic encoding hypothesis, demonstrated that length of verbal description of an array of designs showed high correlation with memory for the designs. (A moderately easy array would be: "eight designs, every other one black.") Thus there is fairly good evidence that perceptual information can be taken in, encoded into linguistic form, and then used to facilitate recall of the initial perceptual information.

Another way to study the effects of language on memory with minimal interaction from thought and imagery is to deal with phonological characteristics. In a massive investigation to find the variables underlying memory for nonsense syllables, Underwood and Schulz (1960) discovered that pronunciability of nonsense syllables was the best predictor of response learning. In other words, an item that was easy to pronounce, like "BAL," was easier to remember than a hard item, like "RZQ." However, even this study is not a clear demonstration of the effects of language alone on memory, since in 1971 the members of the Ebbinghaus empire discovered that the sneaky introductory psychology *Ss* have been cheating all along, and have been turning many nonsense syllables into words to remember them (Prytulak, 1971). To the extent that *Ss* are able to use this strategy, the effect of pronunciability on memory is mixed with components from the thinking and imagery systems.

A study that gives fairly clean evidence for the effect of language on memory is the rhyme study of Bower and Bolton (1969). These researchers found that paired-associate items that rhymed were easier to learn than items that didn't rhyme, and thus, by showing an effect on memory through purely phonological characteristics, have provided a demonstration of a language-specific effect on memory.

Bock and Brewer (in press) did a study that can be interpreted as showing the effects of syntax on memory. The experimental sentences used each contained one of the standard English optional surface transformations (particle movement, indirect-object inversion, adverb preposing, *that*-deletion). These investigators hypothesized that if *Ss* in a sentence-recall study are remembering the underlying ideas and reclothing the thoughts with words on recall, then sentences with optional transformations ought to give *Ss* particular difficulty in recall. For example, an *S* hearing a particle-movement sentence like "The hi-fi fanatic turned the volume up," should find on recall that he has two perfectly acceptable linguistic structures which fit the same idea (the original sentence or "The hi-fi fanatic turned up the volume"). Results were as predicted; when scored for exact recall, the sentences with optional transformations showed many more errors, and these "errors" consisted of writing down the underlying idea in the wrong form. Thus this study shows an effect on memory due to the existence of a certain class of syntactic rules in English.

It is possible to show an effect of language *per se* on memory, but the effect doesn't seem overwhelmingly impressive. The importance of language for humans is in culture memory. Language gives us the ability to express thoughts in overt form and then pass them along through oral tradition or in written form.

Thought on memory. Discussion of the interaction of thought and memory can be separated into two parts: (*a*) the argument that memory for linguistic material actually involves memory for ideas which underlie language; (*b*) the argument that memory of new material interacts with the rest of S's knowledge.

This chapter's section dealing with the influence of thought on language gave a variety of evidence leading to the conclusion that thought must underlie language. Given that this is the case, then memory for linguistic material may actually consist of the parallel memory of both words and ideas, and there might be differential loss of information contained in one of the two systems. While it is clear that there can be specific linguistic memory (as in repeating a sentence in an unknown language), this section argues that to a large extent memory for linguistic material is actually memory for ideas.

The position that human memory is really memory for ideas goes back a long way. For example, John Locke stated that memory was the "storehouse of our ideas [1690, p. 141]." It should be remembered that Locke was a conceptualist, not an imagist, and therefore the ideas in memory are not simply images, as the later British Empiricists would have it (see Aune, 1967; Price, 1969).

In the early stages of the development of psychology, William James made an insightful observation on the issue. He pointed out that, "When we have uttered a proposition, we are rarely able a moment afterwards to recall our exact words, though we can express it in different words easily enough. The practical upshot of a book we read remains with us, though we may not recall one of its sentences [1890, Vol. I, p. 260]."

Gustaf Stern also understood this point. "In all ordinary discourse our attention is directed towards the topic, the referents; our mind goes on at once from the words to the referents, from the symbol to that which it symbolizes, and promptly forgets all about the symbols [1931, p. 32]."

Pillsbury and Meader also argued for the idea theory of memory. "Frequently, too, the process of interpretation goes still farther and one remembers only the general thought that has been expressed and not the shade of expression or the particular words that were used. This is not due to the forgetting merely, but to the fact that the words heard are translated into thoughts or into one's own words, while the spoken words in and of themselves neither make nor leave any distinct impression on the mind [1928, p. 130]."

The first empirical work to support the memory for ideas approach was the early paper of Binet and Henri (1894) titled "La mémoire des phrases (mémoire des idées)." This was an extraordinarily thoughtful paper, but due to the associationist-behaviorist trend of memory research, it dropped into obscurity. Binet and Henri distinguished between memory for words and memory for the ideas that underlie them. They pointed out that for short passages words are frequently recalled exactly, showing accurate memory for words. However, with longer passages the number of synonym substitutions goes up drastically. They argued that the increased number of synonym substitutions is due to the fact that Ss have forgotten the exact words used, but have retained the correct underlying ideas, and then during recall express the ideas with the wrong words, thus giving the substitutions.

Karl Bühler (1908b) also carried out an early study to distinguish between memory for words (sensory memory) and memory for ideas. Bühler read Ss a list of 20 proverbs, such as "When the calf is stolen, the farmer repairs the stall." Then Ss received a second series of proverbs including a number of items expressing ideas similar to one of the items on the original list, e.g., "One looks to the cask when the wine escapes into the cellar." Ss were able to indicate with almost complete accuracy which proverbs in the second list were similar to items in the first list. However, when asked to recall the original proverbs they often made changes in wording. Bühler used this to argue that thoughts could be "clothed" in different words and that memory for thoughts was different from memory for exact words. That Bühler was using recognition memory to test for ideas and recall to test for words weakens the specific comparison of word memory versus ideas memory, but the fact that Ss could pick out proverbs expressing similar ideas where there were no words or syntax in common does lend support to his general theoretical conception. It is interesting to note that these proverbs even differ at the level of semantic interpretation used in current transformational linguistics, e.g., the first sentence is about a calf, and the second, about wine.

During the Dark Ages of memory research (1913-1962) there were no advances beyond the early work of Binet and Bühler. However, several iconoclasts did keep the tradition alive. Bartlett (1932) used the method of repeated reproduction of prose passages to qualitatively investigate the types of changes that occur in memory for linguistic material, From these experiments Bartlett concluded that "The form, plan, type, or scheme of a story seems, in fact, for the ordinary, educated adult to be the most dominant and persistent factor in [structured prose] material [p. 83]." Gomulicki (1956) also studied the changes Ss made during prose recall and argued for memory as an abstractive process.

One of the first studies in recent cognitive psychology that attempted to bring back the memory for ideas approach was the work of Jacqueline Sachs (1967). In some respects Sachs made an explicit attempt to update the earlier work of Bühler. Ss listened to a paragraph of prose and then were given a sentence and asked to indicate if it occurred in the passage or not. Some of the recognition sentences contained semantic changes; some contained stylistic syntactic changes. Immediately after hearing a sentence, Ss could detect both types of changes at a high level of accuracy. However, when the recognition test came after 80 syllables of intervening material, performance on stylistic changes dropped to near chance, while performance on semantic changes remained at a high level. Thus, like Bühler's work, this study suggests that one must separate memory for ideas from memory for words.

Another study in this tradition is that of Bransford and Franks (1971) on the abstraction of linguistic ideas. Bransford and Franks used the massive interference effects produced by presenting successive fragments of a long sentence to show that

Ss retained only the basic complex ideas, and not the specific words used to express that idea. This study was replicated by Franks and Bransford (1972) with abstract sentences to show that the information was not being retained in the form of images.

Brewer has recently carried out a series of studies on memory for ideas using recall techniques. In one of these studies (1974a), following the work of Binet, I have argued that if the memory for ideas approach is correct then even when *Ss* recall the words of a sentence completely accurately they may have accomplished this by transforming the original linguistic material into ideas, retained the ideas, and then transformed the ideas back into words for recall. To test this hypothesis sentences were developed, each containing one word that has a very close synonym in English (e.g., "The Indian was hiding below [under] the bridge"). I argued that *Ss* hearing the version containing the word "below" would transform the sentence into idea form and retain this information while losing the exact words. Then, for recall, *Ss* would have to transform the ideas back into words. If these complex transformations actually go on, then during recall *Ss* should frequently fall into the trap set for them, by lexicalizing the underlying idea with the wrong word. If no information was retained about the exact words used and the two synonyms were exactly equivalent expressions of the underlying idea, then the synonyms should shift exactly half the time. In practice, there are strong biases toward particular realizations of an underlying idea, so that by giving the nonpreferred form it is possible to show enormous shifts in recall. For example, when the sentence above was heard in the version using "below," it was recalled correctly by only 6% of *Ss,* transformed into "under" by 71%, with 23% making other errors. Results similar to this were also found for both abstract and concrete sentences, under rote memory or gist memory instructions and for time periods of 5 minutes to 2 days. These results provide strong support for the idea theory of memory at the level of single words.

Brewer and Shedletsky (1974) have investigated the theory of idea memory at the sentence level. They had *Ss* memorize sentences such as "The cat jumped over the wall and the dog jumped over it too." With sentences of this form there is parallel structure for the underlying ideas, and so many words can be deleted without changing the underlying ideas (e.g., "The cat jumped over the wall and the dog jumped over too"; "The cat jumped over the wall and the dog jumped too"; "The cat jumped over the wall and the dog did too"; etc.). We predicted that *Ss* given one of the sentences from this set would have great difficulty in recall, since they would have remembered an idea which could be expressed in words in at least five different ways. The results supported the memory for ideas position: 52% of the sentences were recalled as presented, while 48% of the sentences recalled were sentences not presented, but members of the set of alternative realizations of the original idea. Thus, overall there is considerable evidence to support the position that natural language material is typically remembered in terms of underlying ideas.

The second point for this section is the implication for memory of the interconnection of the higher mental processes. When something is remembered, it is not just remembered in isolation—it interacts with the knowledge network formed by the interconnections between the higher mental processes. In the early years of psychology this was known as apperception, and the knowledge network was referred to as the "apperceptive mass." Boring (1957) attributes the concept to Herbart and explains Herbart's usage as follows: "The apperceiving of an idea is therefore not only the making of it conscious, but also its assimilation to a totality of conscious ideas, which Herbart called the 'apperceiving mass' [p. 257] ."

Wundt (1907) developed a similar concept to deal with nonassociative mental phenomena.

> Finally, in the apperceptive functions and in the activities of imagination and understanding, this principle finds expression in a clearly recognized form. Not only do the elements united by apperceptive synthesis gain, in the aggregate idea which results from their combination, a new significance which they did not have in their isolated state, but what is of still greater importance, the aggregate idea itself is a new psychical content made possible, to be sure, by the elements, but by no means contained in these elements. This appears most strikingly in the more complex productions of apperceptive synthesis, as for example in a work of art or a train of logical thought [p. 369].

Experimental investigation of the interaction of memory with the *S's* knowledge network appears to have begun with the 1894 paper by Binet and Henri. Their discussion of the results of the prose recall errors of the children in this study mentions a class of errors called errors through imagination. Among these errors are shifts such as recalling "her herd" as "her sheep." This type of error would appear to show that *S* is not just a passive receptor of ideas, but actively integrates new information with his knowledge. B&M made this point at the conference by stating that "A sentence that would seemingly be comprehensible in isolation . . . can become incomprehensible when viewed from an inappropriate context . . . the same passage, when viewed from different contexts, can be interpreted as meaning very different things [Manuscript version of chapter 12] ."

Bartlett's analysis of *Ss'* successive reproduction of stories led him to emphasize the interrelation of memory and knowledge: "Remembering is not the re-excitation of innumerable fixed, lifeless and fragmentary traces. It is an imaginative reconstruction, or construction, built out of the relation of our attitude towards a whole active mass of organized past reactions or experience [1932, p. 213] ."

BMF and their colleagues have reintroduced the apperceptive mass into current cognitive psychology. The first experiment on this topic was Bransford, Barclay, and Franks' classic study (1972) showing that *Ss* hearing a sentence such as "Three turtles rested on a floating log, and a fish swam beneath them," gave many false recognitions of "Three turtles rested on a floating log, and a fish swam beneath it." This, of course, showed that *Ss* were not able to discriminate the ideas explicitly expressed in the original sentence from their own inferences.

Johnson, Bransford, and Solomon (1973) demonstrated the effect with a different set of inferences. They showed that *Ss* in a recognition task could not distinguish between actual sentences they had heard and the same sentence plus an implied instrument or consequence (e.g., "He was pounding the nail [with a hammer] ").

Brewer (1974c) has shown the interaction of memory and knowledge in a recall task. A series of sentences were designed to imply something that was not literally expressed in the isolated sentence. For example, the sentence "The safe-cracker put the match to the fuse" implies that the safe-cracker lit the fuse, as can be seen by the "but not" test for implication. When a sentence implies another sentence the sentences can be conjoined with "but not," e.g., "The safe-cracker put the match to the fuse, but it did not light." For many of the implication sentences in this study over half the Ss wrote not what they heard, but what was implied by the sentence.

A final and quite different example of the action of the apperceptive mass in memory is found in the work of de Groot (1966). He found that chess masters do not differ from weak chess players in their general visual memory, but that if both groups are given 5 seconds to look at a chess board containing an actual game and then asked to reproduce the positions of the pieces, there is little or no overlap between the performance of the two groups. In this case, the chess master's knowledge of chess interacts with the new information to produce an enormous memory advantage for the chess master.

All these studies argue that memory for ideas must underlie memory for verbal material and that memory interacts in a very intimate and complex fashion with S's knowledge network.

Perception on thought. If the higher mental processes are interconnected, it should be possible to show that perception interacts with thought. Scheerer (1963) may have shown the faciliatory effect of visual perceptual information on thought. Scheerer's Ss were to carry out a task that required two sticks to be tied together. The problem was easy when the necessary string was hanging on a nail in the wall, but was quite difficult when the string was holding a mirror or sign.

The experiments of Bruner, Olver, and Greenfield (1966) on conservation of volume appear to give an example of perception inhibiting thought. Five-year-old children saw two equal beakers of water. The water from one was poured into a tall thin beaker behind a screen, and the children, when asked which had more water, said they were equal. However, the children said there was more water in the tall thin beaker when the same procedures were carried out with the screen removed so that they could see the higher level of water in the tall thin breaker. Thus perceptual information interacted with the children's ability to conserve volume.

Bransford and McCarrell give a variety of pictures which show that in different contexts the same perceptual input can be thought about in quite different ways. One final illustration of the effect of perception on thought is the fact that most of us are better chess players when allowed to see the chess board than when blindfolded.

Imagery on thought. Currently there is a debate over whether imagery is used to carry out verbal syllogisms (Clark, 1971, 1972; Huttenlocher & Higgins, 1971, 1972). Instead of becoming involved in this argument it seems wiser to find evidence of a more clear-cut nature.

Shepard and Metzler (1971) have investigated the speed with which Ss can indicate that two different perspective drawings are representations of the same three-dimensional object. The response time was a linear function of the amount of actual physical rotation that would be required to bring the two objects into the same orientation. Shepard and Metzler use this data plus introspective reports of their Ss to argue that Ss were carrying out the task by mentally rotating the objects at a constant 60 degrees a second. Shepard and Feng (1972) show similar results for a mental paperfolding task. Thus, there is evidence that mental imagery plays a part in thinking.

Language on thought. If one conceptualizes language as the expression of thought, it becomes hard to find clear cases of the influence of language on thought. Bever (1970), Slobin (1971), and Osgood (1972) have argued that the degree of difficulty of linguistic structures is determined, in part, by the discrepancy between a language's surface structure and underlying cognitive structure. Thus, one can argue that the difficulty produced by a particular linguistic structure in comprehension or acquisition is at least an indirect effect of language on thought.

Another argument for the effect of language on thought is the common observation that vague thoughts on some topic are clarified by putting them in overt linguistic form, particularly written form. One of the obvious beneficial characteristics of writing down a complex train of thought is that it helps overcome the difficulties of memory limitation. Thus, it is possible to find limited evidence for the impact of language on thought, but, as would be expected, the effect is not very impressive.

Overall, examination of the interactions of the higher mental processes lends strong support to the position that these interrelations must be taken into account in the development of an adequate theory of mind.

THE PROBLEM OF MEANING

Thus far, I have carefully tried to avoid using the word "meaning." This is because I intend to define the word in terms of the interrelations of the higher mental processes.

The problem of meaning has taken many forms; for our purposes it is to give an adequate psychological account of "meaning" in instances such as the following: (*a*) The world "big" means the same as the word "large." (*b*) The French word "cheval" means the same as the English word "horse." (*c*) The word "date" has a number of different meanings. (*d*) "Qztx" doesn't mean anything in English. (*e*) The sentence "The psycholinguist gave the behaviorist a copy of *Syntactic Structures*" means the same as "The psycholinguist gave a copy of *Syntactic Structures* to the behaviorist." (*f*) If one doesn't realize that the sentence "Nixon's the one" is being spoken with irony, then one hasn't understood the speaker's meaning. (*g*) It sometimes takes a few seconds to understand the meaning of a political cartoon.

Post-Watsonian psychology has a painfully bad record in attempting to deal with meaning. Watson (1920) stated that "The question of meaning is an abstraction, a rationalization and a speculation serving no useful scientific purpose [p. 103]." Miller and Selfridge (1950) suggested that meaning could be looked at as "degree of contextual constraint [p. 183]." Noble (1952) operationalized meaning in terms of number of associations elicited by a word in one minute. Skinner (1957) concluded a discussion of meaning with the statement, "The only solution is to reject the traditional formulation of verbal behavior in terms of meaning [p. 10]." Deese (1962) proposed replacing the traditional concept of meaning with "associative meaning," defined in terms of associative overlap on a free association task. Clearly none of these approaches gives any help in developing an account of the problems listed above.

In the last decade many cognitive psychologists have borrowed the solution to the problem of meaning provided by transformational linguistics, the hypothesis that meanings are semantically interpreted deep structures (Chomsky, 1965; Katz & Fodor, 1963). While this definition in terms of abstract entities is a vast improvement over the behavioristic approaches taken earlier, it is still insufficient.

The meaning of meaning. Broadly, the meaning of a word, sentence, object, or event for an individual can be taken to be the entire knowledge relating to the word, sentence, object, or event available to that individual through the interrelated higher mental processes. This broad usage is necessary to handle the traditional problem of the meaning of objects, i.e., how I know that red thing is an apple, that it grew on a tree, that it is good to eat, etc. While B&M never give an explicit definition of meaning, they appear to hold something very close to this position.

However, this sense of meaning is too broad to handle the meaning of symbols in communication. When a chemist uses the word "iron" in conversation with a non-chemist, he doesn't usually use the word expecting that his hearer will know about the electron shell structure of the element. Thus, we need a narrower usage for the meaning of the symbols used in ordinary conversation.

In this narrow sense, the meaning of a word can be taken as the subset of knowledge indicated by the word that a speaker can assume will be shared by his hearer. The meaning of a sentence is the knowledge structure derived through the interaction of the meanings of the words and the deep syntactic relations of the language. In keeping with the previous analysis of the higher mental processes, most of the knowledge will be in the form of ideas without sensory accompaniment.

The fact that meaning has been defined in terms of the knowledge of the speaker-hearer thus accounts for why a speaker of English knows that a dog is animate. There is no need to postulate semantic hierarchies or linguistic definitions to account for this knowledge. With this approach anomalous sentences, such as "The stone was thinking of Vienna," are odd because they clash with the hearer's knowledge of the world, not because they violate linguistic selection restrictions. Defining meaning in terms of knowledge also accounts for the fact that when someone is told that "The rock is inside the box," he knows that the rock is smaller than the box. Since the meaning of a word is relative to the knowledge of the speaker-hearer, this approach provides a framework to handle actual conversations. For example: "[W.F.B.'s office on a weekday—W.F.B. speaking] That sounds like my son coming down the hall." "[reply by hearer who knows my son] Is John's school in session today?" "[reply by hearer who doesn't know my son] Is his school in session today?" "My son" means different things to these two people, and this is reflected in the fact that the first speaker's reply included my son's name. Note that both speakers share the knowledge that children should be in school on weekdays, thus accounting for their questions.

Defining meaning in terms of knowledge avoids the impossible theoretical difficulties that develop for a theory which defines meaning in terms of a single isolated higher mental process such as imagery or language. However, the present definition only sketches the direction for a successful definition of meaning. To produce a richer definition it will be necessary to provide an adequate account of the knowledge structure assumed in this definition.

ISOLATION THEORIES OF MEANING: IMAGES

If meaning must be defined in terms of the interaction of the higher mental processes, it follows that any theory of meaning that tries to solve the problem within an isolated higher mental process must be in error.

One classic isolation theory of meaning is the hypothesis that mental images are the underlying meanings of words. The image approach goes back to the Greeks but it took hold with a vengeance after Berkeley's famous attack on Locke's theory of abstract ideas. Berkeley argued that "I find indeed I have a faculty of imagining, or representing to myself, the ideas of those particular things I have perceived . . . But then whatever hand or eye I imagine, it must have some particular shape and colour. Likewise the idea of man that I frame to myself must be either of a white, or a black, or a tawny, a straight, or a crooked, a tall, or a low, or a middle-sized man [1710, p. 407]." Thus, Berkeley held that images are particular and used images to handle the problem of meaning. The imagist tradition flowed from Berkeley to James Mill to John Stuart Mill, and finally down to the psychologist Titchener. With the advent of Behaviorism, this particular isolation theory of meaning came to an abrupt end in psychology, to be replaced with the even less adequate behavioristic theories.

However, as the behavioristic paradigm has begun to crumble over the last decade, a number of psychologists (Bugelski, 1970; Paivio, 1969) have attempted to handle the problem of meaning by going back to the image theory. Begg and Paivio (1969) have extended the image theory to handle sentence meaning. They argue that the meaning of a concrete sentence is represented as a complex visual mental image, while the meaning of an abstract sentence is represented as a sequence of words.

The image theory of meaning can be shown to be wrong on both logical and empirical grounds. The classic logical arguments against imagism can be found in Humphrey (1951), Mandler and Mandler (1964), and Price (1969). One fundamental difficulty is that meaning cannot be derived from images. For example, in the sentence, "I imaged a purple platypus and Berkeley imaged a pink one," it is necessary to know the syntactic relations of the language to derive the appropriate image. Thus, one needs to know the particular syntactic rules of English in order to know that "purple" applies to "platypus," and not to "Berkeley." It is also necessary to know that "one" is the sign for parallel structure in this case, to know that Berkeley imaged a platypus. It is necessary to understand the abstract and nonimageable syntactic relations of a sentence to produce the appropriate image.

Another way to see the difficulty is to examine the meaning of different types of words in terms of image theory. What are the images of syntactic words like "therefore" and "if"? William James correctly pointed out that these words are verbal skeletons of logical relations. The image theory can't handle abstract words. What are the images of words such as "difficult" or "infinity"? The image theory doesn't even work for supposedly concrete nouns. Thus, if one images a St.Bernard to stand for the meaning of "dog," how does one keep from confusing the meaning of "St. Bernard" and "dog"?

Experimental evidence also provides grounds for rejecting image theory. One difficulty with the image theory is that the introspective data of the Würzburg psychologists showed that much cognitive processing goes on without obvious conscious correlates. Thus, Bühler concluded from his careful research on thinking that "Something as fragmentary, sporadic, and as accidental in consciousness as the presentations in our experience of thinking cannot be the carriers of solid and continuous thought-contents [1908a, pp. 39-40]."

T. V. Moore (1919) showed that latencies for the meaning of words are shorter than latencies for images of words. Paivio (1971a) has also sometimes found this relationship. If the meaning comes before the image, how can the image be the meaning?

Paivio (1969, 1971b) has shown that concrete words and sentences are easier to remember than abstract words and sentences. This finding must be dealt with (see below), but it should not be taken as evidence for the image theory of meaning.

Begg and Paivio (1969) have presented data from a memory study of abstract and concrete sentences which they consider strong evidence for the image theory. They hypothesize that concrete sentences are remembered as mental images and report data to show that *Ss* make many errors in recognizing synonym substitutions in the original passages. They argue that since *Ss* have remembered an image, and not the words, they can't tell which particular word was used, e.g., "hostage" or "captive." However, for the abstract sentences *Ss* have remembered the words, and for these sentences the *Es* report data showing that *Ss* do recognize synonym shifts, but don't recognize changes in meaning. Again Begg and Paivio argue that this finding supports their hypothesis, since abstract sentences have no image (meaning?) and are remembered as a string of particular words.

While the interaction of error type and sentence type has been taken as strong support for image theories of meaning, Johnson *et al.* (1972) have shown severe difficulties with this experiment. These investigators have shown that the abstract sentences used in the Begg and Paivio study were much more difficult to comprehend, thus accounting for the fact that *Ss* had more difficulty in recognizing a change in meaning for the abstract sentences. This finding would seem to invalidate this particular experiment, though not the image theory in general.

B & M present a variety of experiments as evidence against the image theory. They show that sentences that are understood are better remembered than sentences that are not understood, and that it is possible to write abstract sentences that are easy to remember. And finally they report several studies (one by Cole) showing that by using the logical relations between words it is possible to make abstract words function as better recall cues than concrete words, e.g., "research" is a better cue for "scale" and "beaker" than is "beaker" for "research" and "scale." As used by B & M it appears to me that none of these experiments have any logical force against Paivio's theory. They simply show that it is possible to use various mnemonic devices to make abstract words easy to remember. If used in a slightly different fashion, these studies can prove awkward for image theory. These experiments show that logical relations can have a powerful effect on memory, yet what is the status of such things as logical relations between words in an image theory?

Brewer (1974a) has carried out a study which would seem to cause fundamental difficulty for the image theory. Begg and Paivio argue that *Ss* recode concrete sentences into images and thus make errors in recognizing synonym substitutions; abstract sentences are not recoded into images and are supposed to be remembered in terms of the words themselves. Brewer argued, therefore, that abstract sentences can be used to make a crucial comparison between the memory for ideas approach and the memory for images approach. If abstract sentences are remembered in terms of underlying ideas, then *Ss* in recall should make synonym substitution errors on these sentences, just as they do on concrete sentences. However, if abstract sentences are remembered as sequences of words, they should not show synonym substitutions. Brewer found that abstract sentences each written to contain a potential synonym show large numbers of synonym shifts in recall, just as concrete sentences do. This finding supports the memory for ideas position that abstract sentences are transformed into ideas for storage.

Thus on both logical and empirical grounds, the hypothesis that images are the meanings of words has been shown to be inadequate. B & M occasionally seem to argue that the general superiority of concrete linguistic material over abstract linguistic material is an artifact. The view that the higher mental processes are interrelated suggests a different interpretation. When one understands the meaning of a concrete sentence, that information is available to the imagery system; and so, one may form a mental image in addition to grasping the meaning. Thus, the interrelation hypothesis suggests that the parallel information available for concrete words and sentences accounts for the superiority of these words and sentences in memory.

ISOLATION THEORIES OF MEANING: LANGUAGE

Linguistics. Over the past two decades the work of Noam Chomsky (1957, 1965) has revolutionized linguistics and had considerable impact on psychology and philosophy. Chomsky's 1957 monograph was an enormous achievement; it made explanation the goal of linguistics, proposed that linguistic intuition be the data base for linguistics, reintroduced abstract entities into linguistic theory, and provided specific proposals to deal with English syntax.

However, in retrospect it seems clear that Chomsky was not able to break away from all the assumptions of American structural linguistics. In particular, he has had severe difficulty in dealing with the problem of meaning.

The most important figure in American structural linguistics was Leonard Bloomfield. In his 1914 book Bloomfield took a mentalistic position on language; however, by 1936, under the influence of behaviorists in psychology (Max Meyer, Albert Weiss) and in philosophy (R. Carnap, O. Neurath), Bloomfield explicitly rejected the position taken in this chapter. He stated, "It remains for linguists to show, in detail, that the speaker has no 'ideas,' and that the noise is sufficient—for the speaker's words act with a trigger-effect upon the nervous systems of his speech-fellows [1936, p. 93]."

Chomsky inherited much of Bloomfield's attitude toward meaning. In one of his first papers Chomsky stated that "semantic notions are really quite irrelevant to the problem of describing formal structure [1955, p. 141]." In this paper he gave the reason he was suspicious of meaning: Meaning is a notoriously difficult notion to pin down. If it can be shown that meaning and related notions do play a central role in linguistic analysis, then its results and conclusions become subject to all the doubts and obscurities that plague the study of meaning, and a serious blow is struck at the foundations of linguistic theory [p. 141]." In *Syntactic Structures* Chomsky continued to hold the view that syntax and semantics were independent and attempted to use syntactic devices to deal with problems of meaning. Thus, he argued that the difference between "John admires sincerity" and "Sincerity admires John" could be accounted for by the difference between the syntactic class "proper nouns" and the syntactic class "abstract nouns." It is interesting to note that Lees, in his 1957 review of *Syntactic Structures,* tried to give the problem of meaning away by suggesting that the solution to the problem of meaning was likely to come from psychology, not linguistics (p. 393).

The work of Katz and Fodor (1963) was the first explicit attempt to deal with meaning within the generative transformational framework. Katz and Fodor raised the question of the necessity of including information about the world in a semantic theory, but decided that this is an impossible task, and so rejected the possibility. Thus, Katz and Fodor explored the possibility of treating meaning as it has been treated in this chapter but chose instead to develop an isolation view in which linguistic meaning was handled in terms of semantic markers, selection restrictions, and projection rules.

Chomsky's *Aspects of the Theory of Syntax* (1965) summarized the first stage of the development of transformational linguistic theory. Sentences were derived from a base component which consisted of phrase-structure trees and basic syntactic categories. The Katz-Fodor semantic theory was included as a semantic component which interpreted the information from the base component.

If the higher mental processes are interrelated, then it should be possible to show that the attempt to deal with meaning at a purely linguistic level has severe difficulties. For ease of discussion the theories of Katz and Fodor (1963) and Chomsky (1965) will be referred to as "the transformational theory."

In the transformational theory, semantic anomaly is dealt with through the interaction of selection restrictions and semantic markers on the lexical items. This seems to ignore the obvious fact that the reason we find the sentence "My typewriter is embarrassed" odd is that the ideas expressed in this utterance are incompatible with our knowledge of the world.

The transformational theory attempts to handle semantic facts by providing an appropriate set of semantic features for each lexical entry. However, since thought processes are creative, there will be an infinite amount of knowledge that must be incorporated in sets of semantic features. Thus, after the transformational theory has provided a set of features for the lexical item "rubber ball," we can use the deviance of the sentence, "The rubber ball fell to the floor and shattered into a thousand pieces," to force the transformational theory to add the feature "non-shatterable" to its analysis of "rubber ball" This game could go on endlessly. As soon as the transformational theory gives an account of a semantic fact in terms of semantic features, the cognitive theorist can produce a sentence using some aspect of his knowledge of the world to force the addition of another semantic feature.

If semantic anomaly is really due to knowledge of the world, then changes in knowledge of the world should produce changes in the deviance or nondeviance of given sentences. Thus if we know that a rubber ball has been dipped in liquid oxygen, then the sentence about the rubber ball shattering should no longer be deviant; and in fact, if we make that assumption, it becomes nondeviant.

The position that ideas underlie words also has implications for the transformational theory. In this theory transformations are frequently used to delete certain linguistic entities. For example, in imperative sentences the "you" is deleted (Jacobs & Rosenbaum, 1968; Postal, 1964). In comparative sentences such as "Kwakiutl is harder than English," there is a deleted "is hard" (Lester, 1971). In the case of transitive verbs that can have or not have an object, the object is deleted in the latter case. Thus, "I smoke" is the deleted form of "I smoke cigars" (Cattell, 1969). In other cases certain semantic and syntactic facts about sentences are accounted for by postulating an underlying linguistic entity and then deleting it. Thus the use of articles in English has been accounted for by postulating an underlying "one" (Perlmutter, 1970). The force of declarative sentences has been accounted for by an underlying "I say X to you," which is then deleted (Ross, 1970). Sadock (1969) has added a second underlying sentence to Ross's analysis, which he refers to as the "unpronounced higher structure," and he is concerned because he is not sure what the verb is in his "superhypersentence."

Because the transformational theory is an isolation theory of meaning, it has had to postulate linguistic entities where an interaction theory would postulate some nonlinguistic knowledge. For instance, in the imperative the speaker knows who he is giving the command to, and thus there is no need to postulate an underlying linguistic entity, just an underlying knowledge of the situation in the mind of the speaker. Actual conversations are full of the interaction of language and knowledge. If one gets on an elevator and looks at the person nearest the buttons, he might say, "Which floor?" Is there any need to postulate an underlying linguistic entity?

Generative transformational linguists have frequently pointed out that they have resurrected the older structural linguistics that preceded discriptive linguistics. However, in holding the linguistic isolation theory of meaning the transformational linguists have diverged from the interaction approach that was actually taken by many of the earlier linguists.

For example, Jespersen (1924) made a clear attack on the postulation of underlying *linguistic* entities. "An old-fashioned grammarian will feel a certain repugnance to this theory of one-member sentences, and will be inclined to explain them by his panacea, ellipsis. In 'Come!' he will say that the subject 'you' is understood, and in 'Splendid!' and 'A capital idea!' not only the subject ('this'), but also the verb 'is' is understood. In many exclamations we may thus look upon what is said as the adnex, the subject (primary) being either the whole situation or something implied by the situation [p. 306]." The quote from Paul (1891) in the earlier section about the effect of perception on language makes a similar point.

Stern (1931) also attacked the linguistic isolation theory:

> The theory embraced by many writers ... concerning so-called supplementation, rests on the assumption that the *words* are the only basis for comprehension and the mental processes involved therein. According to the theory adopted in the present work, a clipped symbol may adequately perform its function of referring to a certain referent, and the *referent* then becomes the basis of the further mental processes, leading to the actualization of relevant items of the hearer's knowledge with regard to it. Similarly in the case of omissions, only with the difference that the reference to the item originally denoted by the word now left out, must always be supplied by context, including inference [p. 247].

And finally, this issue was not missed by the acute introspective eye of William James (1884), who pointed out that "whether I say 'I write with steel pens,' having such a pen in my hand, and seeing it move over the paper; or whether I say 'I write with them,' in a conversation whose general topic is steel-pens; or whether I say 'Quills are better'; or whether I simply *intend* to say any one of these things, but no image verbal or other arises, because my attention is suddenly diverted;–whichever of these facts occur, most people would describe my mental state as 'thought about steel-pens' [p. 22]."

These quotations lend considerable support to the position that transformational linguistics retained some of the positivistic bias of structural linguistics and thus was not able to adopt the truly mentalistic approach represented by earlier linguists and by the interaction theory proposed in this chapter.

Another area where transformational theory's isolation approach causes great difficulty is with deictic elements of language (Lyons, 1968, pp. 275-281; Weinreich, 1966, pp. 154-158). Deictic elements are the formal structures that can only have meaning with respect to the spatio-temporal orientation of a sentence in its linguistic and nonlinguistic context. Among the clear deictic elements of English are demonstrative adjectives such as "this" and "that," personal pronouns, articles, verb tense, and time adverbs such as "yesterday." The information necessary to speak or understand a deictic word is typically nonlinguistic, and thus cannot be dealt with by an isolation theory of linguistic meaning. For example, in the sentence "I want this one," the hearer interprets "this" in terms of the spatial orientation of the objects being discussed with respect to the speaker. The discussion of perception on language reviewed theoretical and empirical evidence showing that the definite determiner "the" is used when the speaker assumes the hearer has knowledge about the object referred to, and argued that this knowledge is frequently in nonlinguistic form.

The use of pronouns is another good example of deixis. In transformational theory pronouns are derived from a co-referential noun that appears elsewhere in the sentence, thus accounting for the pronoun in sentences such as "Hermann Paul may have been an old fashioned linguist, but he knew about deixis." However, transformational theory cannot deal with pronouns in the case where we are looking at Hermann Paul's grave and one of us says to the other, "He may have been an old fashioned linguist, but he knew about deixis." The isolation approach to pronominalization forces linguists to commit a linguistic cardinal sin–they must use two different theoretical mechanisms to handle what is clearly the same phenomenon. The way out of this dilemma is to assume that the information that specifies the form of the pronoun in all cases comes from the speaker's nonlinguistic knowledge of who or what he is talking about. This hypothesis is, of course, not original: William James (1884) gave a similar analysis for "I write with them," when spoken in a conversation about steel pens.

The problems of deictic words for the transformational theory are particularly interesting, since these words have typically been considered part of the syntax, which is, according to this theory, independent of semantics. However, the origin of the content words in a sentence poses equally grave problems for an isolation theory. In the sentence "I write with steel pens," where did the words "steel pens" come from?

Another serious problem for an isolation theory of meaning is sentence implication. Frequently much information available to the hearer is obtained through the interaction of the linguistic input and his knowledge network. Thus, in the sentence "The getaway car headed north and then made two right turns," the hearer knows that the car was heading south. Such information is simply not linguistic in character and therefore cannot be dealt with by an isolation theory of meaning. Sometimes the syntax gives inferential information. Thus in the sentence "He is a behaviorist, but smart," the use of "but" strongly implies something about the speaker's beliefs about behaviorists.

If these arguments about the transformational theory are correct, they raise an interesting problem. What is the status of the "purely syntactic" evidence that has been used to support the linguistic isolation approach? I am uncertain about the implications, but think that some if not all syntactic arguments can be reinterpreted in terms of the knowledge of the speaker.

In the framework of the interaction approach, syntax is a linguistic device used to communicate knowledge from a speaker to a hearer. In some ways the syntactic system *is* an isolated system. The syntactic classes must originally have had a semantic base (nouns represent things, verbs express actions, adjectives refer to attributes). However, at some point the syntactic system becomes crystallized as a rule system, so that speakers of English are forced to treat the word "toast" syntactically as a mass noun, even though it clearly refers to a countable object. Thus, we must say "I would like some toast," instead of "I would like a toast."

Recently a number of linguists have taken a position opposed to the isolation theory of meaning and similar to the one taken in this paper. While some of these linguists are loosely grouped together in the school called "generative semantics," it is not the case that all work in generative semantics is compatible with the interaction position. In fact, some theorizing in generative semantics assumes a syntactic, isolation theory of meaning. Many papers in this tradition (see recent issues of *Linguistic Inquiry*) postulate underlying sentences to handle facts better dealt with as underlying nonlinguistic knowledge.

However, much recent linguistic theorizing is consistent with the interaction position. McCawley (1968) has argued that semantic anomaly is best treated as due to violations of the hearer's knowledge of the world. In the same paper he argues that pronominalization should be dealt with in terms of the speaker's intended referent. Langacker's (1968) introductory text treats sentences as having an underlying "conceptual structure." Robin Lakoff (1972, 1973) has made strong arguments for the necessity of including contextual information and other types of knowledge of the world in linguistic theory. Chafe's book (1970) is in some ways consistent with the approach of this chapter, and his recent thinking (Chafe, 1973, 1974) is almost completely in keeping with the position of this chapter.

Psycholinguistics. The early work of Chomsky (1957) was the major impetus leading psychologists interested in language out of the wasteland of S-R theory. Psychologists coming from a behavioristic tradition simply were not accustomed to dealing with serious problems, and so had no conceptual framework to bring to bear on the issues of language. Thus, the first generation psycholinguists took Chomsky's theory as a psychological theory. This can be seen in its clearest form in Miller, Galanter, and Pribram (1960), which, in the discussion of how sentences are spoken, presents a diagram from Chomsky showing everything starting from the initial symbol "S." Early empirical work in this area (e.g., Miller, 1962) was a refreshing change from the previous S-R approaches to language, but the isolation theory of meaning and emphasis on syntax inherited from transformational linguistics made that approach inconsistent with the interaction theory. In many ways the work of BMF and the present chapter can be looked upon as attempts to expand the early paradigm into a truly mentalistic account of language and the other higher mental processes.

Language acquisition. Early work on language acquisition (Chomsky, 1965; McNeill, 1966) also took an isolation approach to meaning. It often seemed to treat language as a formal system that could be learned in isolation from the child's knowledge of the world. For example, in a paper given in 1960, Chomsky conceded that semantic information might be required to learn a language, but proposed that this information might serve only as a "motivation for language learning, while playing no necessary part in its mechanism [1962, p. 531]."

If the purpose of language is to express thought, then it must be the case that a major part of acquiring language is learning what knowledge is being expressed in the language that is heard, and conversely how to express knowledge in linguistic form. Thus, learning language must be intimately bound up with the child's knowledge of the world. The area of language acquisition has recently begun to leave the isolation approach, and appears to be moving in directions compatible with the interaction position (see Macnamara, 1972, for a review).

Artificial intelligence. Recently, investigators in artificial intelligence have attempted to build programs to understand natural language (Schank, 1972; Winograd, 1972). In trying to deal with language in the explicit fashion required for actual programming, these researchers have had to incorporate conceptual knowledge of the world into their programs. Thus, in many ways these programs are compatible with the interaction framework.

Philosophy of language. Most philosophy of language still appears to be wandering around in the wastelands of Behaviorism. A recent book on the philosophy of language by Alston (1964) explicitly rejects the idea theory of meaning and warns the student to avoid the "basic mistake" of assuming that meanings are "entities of a sort that are otherwise specifiable [p. 21]." Norman Malcolm (1971) has also pointed out that attempts to develop psychological theories of the higher mental processes are useless:

> The mistake here is easy to state but profoundly difficult to grasp. Recognizing someone is not an act or process, over and above, or behind, the expression of recognition in behavior ...Thus, it is the facts, the circumstances surrounding that behavior, that give it the property of expressing recognition. This property is not due to something that goes on inside. It seems to me that if this point were understood by philosophers and psychologists, they would no longer have a motive for constructing theories and models for recognition, memory, thinking, problem solving, understanding, and other "cognitive processes" [p. 387].

While philosophy of language as a whole has not made much progress in going back to its rich heritage, there have been exceptions. H. H. Price (1969) takes a point of view very close to that expressed in this chapter. Bar-Hillel (1954, 1969) has pointed out the importance of indexical (deictic) expressions and the pragmatic aspects of language, and thus supported the interaction view. Searle's work on speech acts (1969) and Grice's work on conversational implicature (n.d.) seem to represent breaks away from the isolation view of meaning toward the position of this chapter.

In summary, it would appear that the isolation view of linguistic meaning has severe difficulties and that there has been movement away from it in the last few years on a broad front covering many disciplines.

OBJECTS IN ISOLATION

The interaction approach helps resolve the traditional problem of the meaning of objects. Berkeley (1709) gave a classic description of the problem: "Sitting in my study I hear a coach drive along the street; I look through the casement and see it; I walk out and enter into it; thus, common speech would incline one to think, I heard, saw, and touched the same thing, to wit, the coach. It is nevertheless certain, the ideas intromitted by each sense are widely different, and distinct from each other; but having been observed constantly to go together, they are spoken of as one and the same thing [p. 33]." Thus, Berkeley understood the problem, but gave the standard associationist solution. However, as B & M point out, "perception affords ... information about the spatio-temporal *relations* among entities [p. 191]." A number of writers have agreed with B & M in pointing out that one has many kinds of knowledge about objects. Thus, Bergson (1911) stated. "To recognize a common object is mainly to know how to use it [p. 111]." Stern (1931) makes a similar point: "A door has meaning for us because we know what it can be used for [p. 26]."

Thus, a better solution to the problem of the meaning of objects would appear to be the one given by B & M: "Knowledge of entities arises from information about their relations to other knowledge, and that knowledge of relations distinguishes a meaningful object from a brute thing [p. 195]."

SENTENCES IN ISOLATION

Almost all current research in linguistics and psycholinguistics uses sentences isolated from linguistic and nonlinguistic context. However, if meaning really interacts with the total knowledge network of the hearer, then treating sentences in isolation may produce severe methodological artifacts. This is an old argument. For example Stern (1931) made the point insightfully:

> A full context has the same consequences as previous knowledge—or the latter may be regarded as context; it renders a complete *verbal* expression unnecessary; incomplete, allusive phrases are typical of the conversation between intimates who are familiar with each other and with each other's affairs and points of view, and of utterances concerning the situation perceptually present to the interlocutors . . . Words, gestures (symbols and signals), and the perception of the situation, perhaps also of the speaker's actions, collaborate to demonstrate his meaning to the hearer. The proportion of words may, on occasion, sink to a minimum without giving us the right to regard the expressions actually used as defective: they duly fulfill their part in the communication and are perfectly adequate to it [pp. 125-126].

Uhlenbeck (1963) pointed out the problem in reviewing the early work of Chomsky: "Every sentence needs to be interpreted in the light of various extra-linguistic data. These data are (1) the situation in which the sentence is spoken (2) the preceding sentences, if any (3) the hearer's knowledge of the speaker and the topics which might be discussed by him; in other words the hearer must know the frame of reference of the speaker in order to arrive at the correct interpretation, that is the interpretation intended by the speaker [p. 11]."

Garfinkel (1967) has made a strong argument for context from the viewpoint of ethnomethodology. He stated that in real conversations "Many of its expressions are such that their sense cannot be decided by an auditor unless he knows or assumes something about the biography and the purposes of the speaker, the circumstances of the utterance, the previous course of the conversation, or the particular relationship of actual or potential interaction that exists between user and auditor. The expressions do not have a sense that remains identical through the changing occasions of their use [p. 40]."

Rommetveit has also given many examples of the importance of context in his 1968 book.

The reason for emphasizing context is not to argue that one can't study sentences in isolation, but to point out that natural language doesn't consist of sentences or words in isolation, and that the study of sentences out of context should be carried out with the realization that it is a very artificial situation.

Harris and Brewer (in press) have given an experimental demonstration of this methodological difficulty. They reported that, in a recall task for sentences in isolation, 45% of the sentences showed shifts in tense. They argued that this was caused by the fact that tense is a deictic element, and thus relatively meaningless in isolated sentences. In a second experiment temporal adverbs were added to the same sentences to supply a partial temporal framework, and there was a drastic reduction in tense shifts.

Thus in dealing with sentences in isolation the investigator must realize he is dealing with an unnatural situation, and that *Ss* will be attempting to deal with the lack of context by imposing the best framework they can bring to bear on the situation.

COMPREHENSION

B & M give a variety of evidence to support the position that comprehension is an active process which uses the entire knowledge of the hearer. It appears that in understanding a linguistic utterance the relevant information is brought to bear spontaneously and without conscious concomitants. A number of earlier researchers in this area have emphasized this point.

Stout (1896) stated that:

> All specification of meaning by context or circumstances is due to the competition and co-operation of apperceptive systems. The dominant system which corresponds to the universe of discourse suppresses the activity of those components of the meaning of a word which it is unable to apperceive; and in like manner the meanings of different words limit each other by mutual apperception. In this process not only does what precedes limit and determines what follows, but what follows also limits and determines what precedes [Vol. II, pp. 217-218].

Bühler asked "What is the process of comprehending words or sentences? It is obvious and undisputed that something in the subject meets halfway whatever is to be comprehended, and enters some kind of connection with it. Herbart and his school were particularly interested in this process, and gave the precious name apperception precisely to that variety of apprehension phenomena which includes comprehension [1908a, p. 48]."

Stern gave a number of arguments for the active nature of comprehension: "The comprehension of an utterance demands incessant activity on the part of the listener, and the effect of the utterance is perhaps best described as a regulating of the receiver's own mental processes [1931, p. 20]." And in another place he pointed out that "A listener, too, does not merely receive and passively register the meanings of the words he hears, but proceeds at once to combine them with what he previously knows or has heard of the topic [p. 34]." The interrelation of the higher mental processes must be considered an active system.

CONCLUSION

There is strong evidence that the higher mental processes are intimately interrelated. This interrelation appears to require that meaning be defined in terms of the interconnected knowledge of the speaker-hearer and therefore that any theory that attempts to deal with meaning in terms of an isolated higher mental process, such as imagery or language, is inadequate.

REFERENCES

Ach, N. *Ueber die Willenstaetigkeit und das Denken.* Goettingen: Vandenhoeck und Ruprecht, 1905. (Partially translated as: Determining tendencies: Awareness. In D. Rapaport (Ed.), *Organization and pathology of thought: Selected sources.* New York: Columbia University Press, 1951.)

Alston, W. P. *Philosophy of language.* Englewood Cliffs, N.J.: Prentice-Hall, 1964.

Aristotle. *On interpretation. ca.* 335 B.C. In R.M. Hutchins (Ed.), *Great books of the western world.* Vol. 8. Chicago: Encyclopaedia Britannica, 1952.

Aune, B. Thinking. In P. Edwards (Ed.), *The encyclopedia of philosophy.* Vol. 8, New York: Macmillan, 1967.

Bar-Hillel, Y. Indexical expressions. *Mind,* 1954, **63**, 359-379.

Bar-Hillel, Y. Universal semantics and philosophy of language: Quandaries and prospects. In J. Puhvel (Ed.), *Substance and structure of language.* Berkeley: University of California Press, 1969.

Bartlett, F. C. *Remembering: A study in experimental and social psychology.* London: Cambridge University Press, 1932.

Begg, I., & Paivio, A. Concreteness and imagery in sentence meaning. *Journal of Verbal Learning and Verbal Behavior,* 1969, 8, 821-827.

Bergson, H. *Matter and memory.* London: Allen & Unwin, 1911.

Berkeley, G. *A new theory of vision.* 1709. London: Dent, 1910.

Berkeley, G. *The principles of human knowledge.* 1710. In R. M. Hutchins (Ed.), *Great books of the western world.* Vol. 35. Chicago: Encyclopaedia Britannica, 1952.

Bever, T. G. The cognitive basis for linguistic structures. In J. R. Hayes (Ed.), *Cognition and the development of language.* New York: Wiley, 1970.

Binet, A., & Henri, V. La mémoire des phrases (Mémoire des idées). *L'Année Psychologique,* 1894, 1, 24-59.

Binet, A., & Simon, T. Langage et pensée. *L'Année Psychologique,* 1908, **14**, 284-339. (Translated in: A. Binet & T. Simon, *The intelligence of the feeble-minded.* Baltimore: William & Wilkins, 1916).

Blanshard, B. *The nature of thought.* 2 vols. London: Allen & Unwin, 1939.

Bloomfield, L. *An introduction to the study of language.* New York: Holt, 1914.

Bloomfield, L. Language or ideas? *Language,* 1936, **12**, 89-95.

Bock, J. K., & Brewer, W. F. Reconstructive recall in sentences with alternative surface structures. *Journal of Experimental Psychology,* in press.

Boring, E. G. *A history of experimental psychology.* (2nd ed.) New York: Appleton, 1957.

Bower, G. H. Imagery as a relational organizer in associative learning. *Journal of Verbal Learning and Verbal Behavior,* 1970, 9, 529-533.

Bower, G. H. Mental imagery and associative learning. In L. W. Gregg (Ed.), *Cognition in learning and memory.* New York: Wiley, 1972.

Bower, G. H., & Bolton, L. S. Why are rhymes easy to learn? *Journal of Experimental Psychology,* 1969, 82, 453-461.

Bransford, J. D., Barclay, J. R., & Franks, J. J. Sentence memory: A constructive versus interpretive approach. *Cognitive Psychology,* 1972, 3, 193-209.

Bransford, J. D., & Franks, J. J. The abstraction of linguistic ideas. *Cognitive Psychology,* 1971, 2, 331-350.

Bransford, J. D., & Johnson, M. K. Contextual prerequisites for understanding: Some investigations of comprehension and recall. *Journal of Verbal Learning and Verbal Behavior,* 1972, 11, 717-726.

Bransford, J.D., & Johnson, M. K. Considerations of some problems of comprehension. In W. G. Case (Ed.), *Visual information processing.* New York: Academic Press, 1973.

Brewer, W. F. Is reading a letter-by-letter process? In J. F. Kavanagh & J. G. Mattingly (Eds.), *Language by ear and by eye: The relationships between speech and reading.* Cambridge: MIT Press, 1972.

Brewer, W. F. Memory for ideas: Synonym subsitutions. Unpublished manuscript, University of Illinois, 1974.(a)

Brewer, W. F. Memory for imageable and nonimageable anomalous sentences. Unpublished manuscript, University of Illinois, 1974. (b)

Brewer, W. F. Memory for the pragmatic implications of sentences. Unpublished manuscript, University of Illinois, 1974. (c)

Brewer, W. F., & Shedletsky, L. J. Reconstructive recall: Verb-phrase deletion and pronominalization. Unpublished manuscript, University of Illinois, 1974.

Bruner, J. S., Olver, R. R., & Greenfield, P. M. *Studies in cognitive growth.* New York: Wiley, 1966.

Bugelski, B. R. Words and things and images. *American Psychologist,* 1970, **25,** 1001-1012.

Bugelski, B. R., & Alampay, D. A. The role of frequency in developing perceptual sets. *Canadian Journal of Psychology,* 1961, **15,** 205-211.

Bühler, K. Tatsachen und Probleme zu einer Psychologie der Denkvorgänge. *II. Uber* Gedankenzusammenhaenge. *Archiv für die Gesamte Psychologie.* 1908, **12,** 1623. (Translated as: On thought connections. In D. Rapaport (Ed.), *Organization and pathology of thought: Selected sources.* New York: Columbia University Press, 1951. (a)

Bühler, K. Tatsachen und Problem zu einer Psychologie der Denkvorgänge. III. Über Gedankenerinnerungen. *Archiv für die Gesamte Psychologie,* 1908, **12,** 24-92. (b)

Butler, S. Thought and language. In *The Shrewsbury edition of the works of Samuel Butler.* Vol. 2. New York: E. P. Dutton, 1925. (Reprinted in: M Black (Ed.), *The importance of language.* Ithaca: Cornell University Press, 1962.)

Carmichael, L., Hogan, H. P., & Walter, A. A. An experimental study of the effect of language on the reproduction of visually perceived form. *Journal of Experimental Psychology,* 1932, **15,** 73-86.

Carroll, J. B. (Ed.) *Language, thought, and reality: Selected writings of Benjamin Lee Whorf.* Cambridge, Mass.: MIT Press 1956.

Cattell, N. R. *The new English grammar: A descriptive introduction.* Cambridge, Mass.: MIT Press, 1969.

Chafe, W. L. *Meaning and the structure of language.* Chicago: University of Chicago Press, 1970.

Chafe, W. L. Language and consciousness. unpublished manuscript, University of California, Berkeley, 1972.

Chafe, W. L. Language and memory, *Language,* 1973, **49,** 261-281.

Chomsky, N. Semantic considerations in grammar. *Georgetown Monograph Series in Languages and Linguistics,* 1955, **8,** 141-158.

Chomsky, N. *Syntactic structures.* The Hague: Mouton, 1957.

Chomsky, N. Review of B. F. Skinner, *Verbal behavior. Language,*1959, **35,** 26-58.

Chomsky, N. Explanatory models in linguistics. In E. Nagel, P. Suppes, & A. Tarski (Eds.), *Logic, methodology and philosophy of science.* Stanford, Cal.: Stanford University Press, 1962.

Chomsky, N. *Aspects of the theory of syntax.* Cambridge, Mass.: MIT Press, 1965.

Clark, H. H. More about "Adjectives, comparatives, and syllogisms": A reply to Huttenlocher and Higgins. *Psychological Review,* 1971, **78,** 505-514.

Clark, H. H. On the evidence concerning J. Huttenlocher and E. T. Higgins' theory of reasoning: A second reply. *Psychological Review,* 1972, **79,** 428-432.

Deese, J. On the structure of associative meaning. *Psychological Review,* 1962, **69,** 161-175.

de Groot, A. D. Perception and memory versus thought: Some old ideas and recent findings. In B. Kleinmuntz (Ed.), *Problem solving: Research, method, and theory.* New York: Wiley, 1966.

Descartes, R. *Meditations on the first philosophy: Third objection and reply.* 1641. In R. M. Hutchins (Ed.), *Great books of the western world.* Vol. 31. Chicago: Encyclopaedia Britannica, 1952.

Dooling, D. J., & Lachman, R. Effects of comprehension on retention of prose. *Journal of Experimental Psychology,* 1971, **88,** 216-222.

Dooling, D. J., & Mullet, R. I. Locus of thematic effects in retention of prose. *Journal of Experimental Psychology,*1973, **97,** 404-406.

Drange, T. *Type crossings: Sentential meaninglessness in the border area of linguistics and philosophy.* The Hague: Mouton, 1966.

Ebbinghaus, H. *Über das Gedächtnis.* Leipzig: Duncker & Humblot, 1885. *(Memory: A contribution to experimental psychology.* New York: Dover, 1964.)

Franks, J. J., & Bransford, J. D. The acquisition of abstract ideas. *Journal of Verbal Learning and Verbal Behavior,* 1972, 11, 311-315.

Furth, H. G. *Thinking without language.* New York: Free Press, 1966.

Garfinkel, H. *Studies in ethnomethodology.* Englewood Cliffs, N.J: Prentice-Hall, 1967.

Garrett, M., Bever, T., & Fodor, J. The active use of grammar in speech perception. *Perception & Psychophysics,* 1966, 1, 30-32.

Glanzer, M., & Clark, W. H. Accuracy of perceptual recall: An analysis of organization. *Journal of Verbal Learning and Verbal Behavior,* 1962, 1, 289-299.

Glanzer, M., & Clark, W. H. The verbal-loop hypothesis: Conventional figures. *American Journal of Psychology,* 1964, 77, 621-626.

Gomulicki, B. R. Recall as an abstractive process. *Acta Psychologica,* 1956, 12, 77-94.

Gregory, R. L. *The intelligent eye.* New York: McGraw-Hill, 1970.

Grice, H. P. Logic and conversation. Unpublished manuscript, n.d.

Harris, J. *Hermes: Or a philosophical inquiry concerning language and universal grammar.* London: Bolas, 1751. (Reprinted: Menston: Scholar Press, 1968).

Harris, R. J. Effects of nonlinguistic knowledge on language production. *Journal of Psycholinguistic Research,* in press.

Harris, R. J., & Brewer, W. F. Deixis in memory for verb tense. *Journal of Verbal Learning and Verbal Behavior,* in press.

Hayes, K. J., & Nissen, C. H. Higher mental functions of a home-raised chimpanzee. In A.M. Schrier & F. Stollnitz (Eds.), *Behavior of nonhuman primates: Modern research trends.* Vol. 4. New York: Academic Press, 1971.

Herman, D. T., Lawless, R. H., & Marshall, R. W. Variables in the effect of language on the reproduction of visually perceived forms. *Perceptual and Motor Skills,* 1957, 7 (Mono. Suppl. 2), 171-186.

Huey, E. B. *The psychology and pedagogy of reading.* New York: Macmillan, 1908. (Reprinted: Cambridge, Mass.: MIT Press, 1968.)

Humphrey, G. *Thinking: An introduction to its experimental psychology.* New York: Wiley, 1951.

Husserl, E. *Logische Untersuchungen* (2nd ed.) Halle: M. Niemeyer, 1913. (*Logical investigations.* New York: Humanities Press, 1970. 2 vols.)

Huttenlocher, J., & Higgins, E. T. Adjectives, comparatives, and syllogisms. *Psychological Review,* 1971, 78, 487-504.

Huttenlocher, J., & Higgins, E. T. On reasoning, congruence, and other matters. *Psychological Review,* 1972, 79, 420-427.

Jacobs, R. A., & Rosenbaum, P. S. *English transformational grammar.* Waltham, Mass.: Blaisdell, 1968.

James, W. On some omissions of introspective psychology. *Mind,* 1884, 9, 1-26.

James, W. *The principles of psychology.* 2 vols. London: Macmillan, 1890.

Jespersen, O. *The philosophy of grammar.* London: Allen & Unwin, 1924. (Reprinted: New York: Norton, 1965.)

Johnson, M. K., Bransford, J. D., Nyberg, S. E., & Cleary, J. J. Comprehension factors in interpreting memory for abstract and concrete sentences. *Journal of Verbal Learning and Verbal Behavior,* 1972, 11, 451-454.

Johnson, M. K., Bransford, J. D., & Solomon, S. K. Memory for tacit implications of sentences. *Journal of Experimental Psychology,* 1973, 98, 203-205.

Katz, J. J., & Fodor, J. A. The structure of a semantic theory. *Language,* 1963, 39, 170-210.

Kellogg, W. N., & Kellogg, L. A. *The ape and the child.* New York: McGraw-Hill, 1933.

Kuhn, T. S. *The structure of scientific revolutions.* (2nd ed.) Chicago, Ill.: University of Chicago Press, 1970.

Lakoff, R. Language in context. *Language,* 1972, 48, 907-927.

Lakoff, R. Social context. Unpublished lectures, University of Illinois, April, 1973.

Langacker, R. W. *Language and its structure.* New York: Harcourt, Brace & World, 1968.

Lantz, D., & Stefflre, V. Language and cognition revisited. *Journal of Abnormal and Social Psychology,* 1964, **69,** 472-481.

Lees, R. B. Review of N. Chomsky, *Syntactic structures. Language,* 1957, **33,** 375-408.

Lenneberg, E. H. *Biological foundations of language.* New York: Wiley, 1967.

Lester, M. *Introductory transformational grammar of English.* New York: Holt, Rinehart & Winston, 1971.

Liberman, A. M., Cooper, F. S., Shankweiler, D. P., & Studdert-Kennedy, M. Perception of the speech code. *Psychological Review,* 1967, **74,** 431-461.

Locke, J. *An essay concerning human understanding.* 1690. In R. M. Hutchins (Ed.), *Great books of the western world.* Vol. 35. Chicago: Encyclopaedia Britannica, 1952.

Lyons, J. *Introduction to theoretical linguistics.* London: Cambridge University Press, 1968.

Macnamara, J. Cognitive basis of language learning in infants. *Psychological Review,* 1972, **79,** 1-13.

Malcolm, N. The myth of cognitive processes and structures. In T. Mischel (Ed.), *Cognitive development and epistemology.* New York: Academic Press, 1971.

Mandler, J. M., & Mandler, G. *Thinking: From association to gestalt.* New York: Wiley, 1964.

Marks, L. E., & Miller, G. A. The role of semantic and syntactic constraints in the memorization of English sentences. *Journal of Verbal Learning and Verbal Behavior,* 1964, **3,** 1-5.

McCawley, J. D. Concerning the base component of a transformational grammar. *Foundations of Language,* 1968, **4,** 243-269.

McNeill, D. Developmental psycholinguistics. In F. Smith & G. A. Miller (Ed.), *The genesis of language.* Cambridge, Mass.: MIT Press, 1966.

Meudell, P. R. Retrieval and representations in long-term memory. *Psychonomic Science,* 1971, **23,** 295-296.

Meyers, R. Relation of "thinking" and language: An experimental approach, using dysphasic patients. *Archives of Neurology and Psychiatry,* 1948, **60,** 119-139.

Miller, G. A.   Some psychological studies of grammar. *American Psychologist,* 1962, **17,** 748-762.

Miller, G. A., Galanter, E., & Pribram, K. H. *Plans and the structure of behavior.* New York: Holt, 1960.

Miller, G. A., & Isard, S. Some perceptual consequences of linguistic rules. *Journal of Verbal Learning and Verbal Behavior,* 1963, **2,** 217-228.

Miller, G. A., & Selfridge, J. A. Verbal context and the recall of meaningful material. *American Journal of Psychology,* 1950, **63,** 176-185.

Moore, T. V. Image and meaning in memory and perception. *Psychological Monographs,* 1919, **28,** (Whole No. 119), 67-296.

Noble, C. E. An analysis of meaning. *Psychological Review,* 1952, **59,** 421-430.

Olson, D. R. Language and thought: Aspects of a cognitive theory of semantics. *Psychological Review,* 1970, **77,** 257-273.

Orne, M. T. On the social psychology of the psychological experiment: With particular reference to demand characteristics and their implications. *American Psychologist,* 1962, **17,** 776-783.

Osgood, C. E. Where do sentences come from? In D. D. Steinberg & L. A. Jakobovits (Eds.), *Semantics: An interdisciplinary reader in philosophy, linguistics and psychology.* London: Cambridge University Press, 1971.

Osgood, C. E. Cognitive and sentential complexity. Unpublished manuscript, 1972.

Paivio, A. Mental imagery in associative learning and memory. *Psychological Review,* 1969, **76,** 241-263.

Paivio, A. Imagery and language. In S. J. Segal (Ed.), *Imagery: Current cognitive approaches.* New York: Academic Press, 1971. (a)

Paivio, A. *Imagery and verbal processes.* New York: Holt, Rinehart & Winston, 1971. (b)

Paivio, A. A theoretical analysis of the role of imagery in learning and memory. In P. W. Sheehan (Ed.), *The function and nature of imagery.* New York: Academic Press, 1972.

Paul, H. *Principles of the history of language.* (Rev. ed.) London: Longmans, Green, 1891.

Perlmutter, D. M. On the article in English. In M. Bierwisch & K. E. Heidolph (Eds.), *Progress in linguistics: A collection of papers.* The Hague: Mouton, 1970.

Piaget, J. *The origins of intelligence in children.* New York: International Universities Press, 1952.

Pillsbury, W. B., & Meader, C. L. *The psychology of language.* New York: Appleton, 1928.

Postal, P. M. Underlying and superficial linguistic structure. *Harvard Educational Review,* 1964, **34,** 246-266.

Price, H. H. *Thinking and experience.* (2nd ed.) London: Hutchinson, 1969.

Prytulak, L. S. Natural language mediation. *Cognitive Psychology,* 1971, **2,** 1-56.

Reicher, G. M. Perceptual recognition as a function of meaningfulness of stimulus material. *Journal of Experimental Psychology,* 1969, **81,** 275-280.

Rommetveit, R. *Words, meanings, and messages.* New York: Academic Press, 1968.

Ross, J. R. On declarative sentences. In R. A. Jacobs & P. S. Rosenbaum (Eds.), *Readings in English transformational grammar.* Waltham, Mass.: Ginn, 1970.

Ross, J., & Lawrence, K. A. Some observations on memory artifice. *Psychonomic Science,* 1968, **13,** 107-108.

Sachs, J. S. Recognition memory for syntactic and semantic aspects of connected discourse. *Perception & Psychophysics,* 1967, **2,** 437-442.

Sadock, J. M. Super-hypersentences. *Papers in Linguisics,* 1969, **1,** 1-15.

Schank, R. C. Conceptual dependency: A theory of natural language understanding. *Cognitive Psychology,* 1972, **3,** 552-631.

Scheerer, M. Problem-solving. *Scientific American,* 1963, **208,** 118-128.

Searle, J. R. *Speech acts: An essay in the philosophy of language.* London: Cambridge University Press, 1969.

Selz, O. *Ueber die Gesetze des geordneten Denkverlaufs.* Bonn: Coehn, 1913. (Partially translated in: G. Humphrey, *Thinking: An introduction to its experimental psychology.* New York: Wiley, 1951.)

Shepard, R. N. Recognition memory for words, sentences, and pictures. *Journal of Verbal Learning and Verbal Behavior,* 1967, **6,** 156-163.

Shepard, R. N., & Feng, C. A chronometric study of mental paper folding. *Cognitive Psychology,* 1972, **3,** 228-243.

Shepard, R. N., & Metzler, J. Mental rotation of three-dimensional objects, *Science,* 1971, **171,** 701-703.

Skinner, B. F. *Verbal behavior.* New York: Appleton, 1957.

Slobin, D. I. Developmental psycholinguistics. In W. O. Dingwall (Ed.), *A survey of linguistic science.* College Park, Md.: Linguistics Department, University of Maryland, 1971.

Stern, G. *Meaning and change of meaning.* Göteborg: Elánders Boktrycken Aktiebolag, 1931. (Reprinted: Bloomington: Indiana University Press, 1964.)

Stout, G. F. *Analytic psychology.* 2 vols. London: Swan Sonnenschein, 1896.

Uhlenbeck, E. M. An appraisal of transformation theory. *Lingua,* 1963, **12,** 1-18.

Underwood, B. J. & Schulz, R. W. *Meaningfulness and verbal learning.* Chicago: Lippincott, 1960.

Wales, R. Comparing and contrasting. In J. Morton (Ed.), *Biological and social factors in psycholinguistics.* Urbana: University of Illinois Press, 1970.

Watson, J. B. Is thinking merely the action of language mechanisms? *British Journal of Psychology,* 1920, **11,** 87-104.

Weinreich, U. On the semantic structure of language. In J. H. Greenberg (Ed.), *Universals of language.* (2nd ed.) Cambridge, Mass.: MIT Press, 1966.

Weisenburg, T., & McBride, K. E. *Aphasia: A clinical and psychological study.* New York: Commonwealth Fund, 1935. (Reprinted: New York: Hafner, 1964.)

Welborn, E. L., & English, H. Logical learning and retention: A general review of experiments with meaningful verbal materials. *Psychological Bulletin,* 1937, **34,** 1-20.

Wheeler, D. E. Processes in word recognition. *Cognitive Psychology,* 1970, **1,** 59-85.

Winograd, T. Understanding natural language. *Cognitive Psychology*, 1972, **3**, 1-191.

Wundt, W. *Outlines of psychology*. (3rd ed.) Leipzig: Engelmann, 1907.

Yuille, J. C., & Paivio, A. Abstractness and recall of connected discourse. *Journal of Experimental Psychology*, 1969, **82**, 467-471.

Zangwill, O. L. Intelligence in aphasia. In A.V.S. de Reuck & M. O'Connor (Eds.), *Disorders of language*. Boston: Little, Brown, 1964.

13
BRANSFORD-McCARRELL-
FRANKS DISCUSSION

Bransford: I would like to ask Brewer why he feels that when we set up conditions to give abstract words a chance, so to speak, that it cannot dent the Paivio approach.

Brewer: Because one must get at the logic of the experiments and not simply have a variable that can outweigh their variable. In one section you argue that abstract words are necessarily different: that they must have particular kinds of contacts to have meaning. At that point you begin to get at the issue, but basically your studies simply use cute cognitive strategies to show that one can make abstract words easier to remember than concrete words. That seems interesting, but the same effect could be shown with word frequencies. Suppose the same technique shows that low frequency words are easier to remember than higher frequency ones. Would we want to conclude something about some theoretical position?

Bransford: Words are interpreted as a function of their role in various contexts. What one really finds in ratings of isolated words (e.g., such as imagability, salient features, etc.) is the modal context that people bring to bear on them in the first place. But when words appear in a *particular* context, they may act differently. If one manipulates (or controls) the context brought to bear on them, then frequency effects may change, imagery value may change, their most salient features may change, etc.

In addition, we are concerned with the question of whether imagery *per se* is really the most powerful variable in memory, as Paivio suggests. Perhaps imagery only *seems* to be the most powerful variable because it has been compared with inferior alternatives.

Brewer: You haven't really taken a position on the function of imagery. The way I view a concrete sentence (as distinct from an abstract sentence) is that there is an abstract level of meaning one must go through to get to the meaning of both types of sentence. Our heads have another system that allows a picture of the concrete sentence to be made, and that gives certain advantages; this also holds for words in isolation. The old Würzburg work found that the majority of people have a big red apple that pops into their head when someone says "apple." If someone says "virtue," all kinds of things happen in our heads, but the percent that are images is much smaller. So I believe that the Paivio ratings of words in isolation actually do get at something.

Bransford: We question whether ratings of individual words tell anything about the intrinsic properties of such words. We suggested that one cannot predict from ratings of individual words in isolation to words in context. Since words generally occur in an explicit or assumed context, it seems important to attempt to understand how context can affect the ways in which words "act."

It might be valuable to determine what it means for a word to be concrete or abstract. If one looks at the Paivio norms, a word like "collie" may be concrete but so may a word like "dog." Why should this be so? Perhaps what seems concrete to a person is largely a function of his familiarity with invariances in a certain area of knowledge. For example, it may be that "taxes" seem concrete to us, and yet the meaning of this word involves many abstract relations to other things that we know. On the other hand, the word "exponent" may seem very abstract: We have to work to find some particular context in which it might make sense. But to a mathematician, "exponent" may seem rather concrete (not "imagable," but concrete). If one can show that different words are abstract or concrete as a function of the general knowledge available to the listener, then one can more readily assume that these ratings are not so much a function of the perceptual characteristics of the word's referent as they are a function of one's familiarity with the invariances in the contexts to which the words may apply.

Turvey: If we assume that something like PI release might tell us something about underlying organization, it is interesting to note that imagery does *not* produce PI release.

Halwes: The heart of the BMF Chapters is the notion that sentences don't carry their meanings. We have a conceptual schema of what is going on when we want to say something to somebody; we have some "imaginary" representation of some state of affairs in the world, and to communicate that means that we get a representation of that state of affairs in the world into their head. The sentence serves as an input which is dealt with by constructive processes in principally the same way Gibsonian stimulus information is dealt with by constructive processes when coming up with perceptual experience.

But when BMF say that all meaning arises from the nonlinguistic system, I don't quite believe that. If the meaning of sentences is an experience of some state of affairs, generated by our imagining or cognitive processes, then the nonlinguistic system can *by itself* without any linguistic input give rise to those "imaginary" representations.

But one reason for thinking that the BMF claim is not quite true is that the nonlinguistic system develops at the same time (in the same head) as the linguistic system, and the developmental tendency of the child is presumably influenced by his use of the language (among other things).

Franks: I am not clear: Are you arguing for some linguistic meaning over and above it, or talking about *a*linguistic meaning?

Halwes: I am saying that if we try to distinguish linguistic meaning from alinguistic meaning we are doing something incorrect, because meaning is our internal representation of what is going on, and it is conditioned by the fact that we are a language-speaking organism.

Franks: We are not denying that language, since it directs us to environmental events, obviously *constrains* knowledge. But that doesn't mean that the units that structure knowledge *is* language.

Halwes: I agree strongly with your basic point. I think it clear that in the head, knowledge is not fundamentally propositional. It may be that there is no conscious knowledge at all. The term "conscious knowledge" is merely two words juxtaposed, and we pretend that that means something. We have conscious experience, but there is nothing to which we might be referring when we use the words "conscious knowledge." Certainly tacit knowledge is not in propositional form. But when you say that what occurs in your experiments is *more* than ambiguity, you are giving away a useful term, ambiguity, to people who do not actually understand it. The processes that we are discussing go on *anytime*: What's called disambiguation is a myth. What really is going on in "disambiguation" is *comprehension,* which means coming up with a reading for the input.

Bransford: We don't use the term because linguists, e.g., Katz and Postal, have a particular meaning for it. K & P say that all context does is help one select the correct reading from all those that the sentence or word has in isolation. We are saying that there need be *no* readings at all that are isolated from context.

Halwes: I would like to recover the term "ambiguity" for our use. From the perspective you have been proposing, essentially *every* input is ambiguous, and the problem of understanding *any* input is the problem of "disambiguating" it. What we mean when we say "ambiguity" is that there is an example of an input which is ambiguous in an interesting way, which is easy to see, and that can be used to show something about the way our heads work.

Dulany: When you say you doubt the existence of conscious knowledge, are you also doubting the existence of conscious beliefs? Is your doubt an epistemological one connected with the certainty of beliefs?

Halwes: Anything that becomes conscious, in the experience of adult western enculturated people, is a construction. It can be in whatever modality we like. In an abstract sense all constructions can be thought of as images: To simplify the argument, consider all constructions (some kind of) images. Now the knowledge which is "stored in memory," what we call knowledge, is *not any kind of image,* including whatever experience it is that we construct which we call our "conscious knowledge that X," or our "conscious beliefs that X." If I consciously am aware that "tables are hard," that means I have constructed some kind of experience which I use to represent to myself or others my knowledge that tables are hard. I have not captured my knowledge that tables are hard in that utterance, or'in that other constructed experience. I wouldn't want to argue that there is no isomorphism between experience and knowledge, but experience and knowledge are not the same kind of thing, and it is confusing to conflate those notions.

Dulany: Why couldn't one say that in expressing a proposition we are expressing a piece of knowledge?

Halwes: In saying that, you expressed the belief that knowledge comes in propositional form. But knowledge does not come in propositional form: Propositions are built out of knowledge (if you like), knowledge is required to make propositions, but it is inconceivable that one could take propositions which are our knowledge and put them together somehow and make some other propositions which are the ones we want to say. At some point we run out of propositions and we still need some knowledge to express the propositions which we are going to say are our assumptions.

Dulany: We agree that propositions are abstractions, but they are the most useful form of abstraction for representing knowledge and experience in science.

Halwes: Do you feel that knowledge is represented in propositions in your memory?

Dulany: I don't know.

Halwes: That's the heart of the problem. That's the question.

Turvey: Let me ask the BMF group a simple question: What is remembered?

Franks: Beyond the actual input, what we remember is that input coming in, and getting processed inside of our knowledge system. What we remember will be some modification of our knowledge system that is a function of what we have activated as a function of that input.

Turvey: How then do we chronologically recover the order of events?

Franks: In some sense, time-line information is "built-in" as part of the entire knowledge system. But in no case does one remember all the details in chronological order (except in pathology, like Luria's patient *S*). Normal people have a highly abstract, schematized, constructive memory.

Weimer: What has become of the concept of schema in the BMF "schema"?

Franks: The whole tacit knowledge system is one grand schema.

Brewer: The history of this issue is consistent; people ask the question Turvey asked: "What form is it stored in as it comes in?" What makes most people comfortable is to find something: let it be images, let it be words, let it be *something*. But every time someone takes that position they find they can't handle what goes on and then they take the position called conceptualism. BMF and I hold the position of conceptualism. When conceptualists are asked what it is or in what form is the thing stored, they usually come back with "It's very abstract." Another thing BMF left unsolved was that they never gave a definition of meaning.

Bransford: For years philosophers have said that we can't ask what *the* meaning of X is, and recently theorists have argued that all we can ask is the conditions of its use. One thing we are trying as an alternative approach is to say "We can't tell you what meaning is, but we can give some notions of the information involved when we know something, and how it is that that information is acquired." The point is that meaning is not a "thing."

Brewer: Is it that in comprehending we are updating our apperceptive mass? When I heard your sentence I absorbed it into my knowledge system. Clearly we don't want to talk about it as a thing, but rather as the state we are in.

Bransford: In the event section we argue that the *only* way we know something is in terms of its relation to something else. Knowledge is not a state, but an activity of relatedness.

Weimer: What is the relationship between meaning and knowledge?

Bransford: Knowledge is broader!

Franks: The way we use the term, knowledge is a long-term structure, a long-term memory: It's that tacit knowledge structure that has some permanent basis and which structures how one operates on any given input at any given time.

Meaning is that activated part of tacit knowledge that's a function of the present inquiry. Meaning as we use it is a transfer of information.

Halwes: Would you object to saying that meaning is the experience given rise to by the input? I think you are distinguishing conscious from tacit knowledge, and the activated part of our knowledge is not necessarily conscious in the sense of experiencing it. Meaning should be carried both tacitly *and* consciously.

Turvey: I have a horrible thought for a Gibsonian. Seeing doesn't imply something seen (that's a nice constructivist comment). By the same token, remembering doesn't imply something remembered. Also, knowing doesn't imply something known.

Bransford: Weimer asked about the relationship between meaning and knowledge. But an equally important one is between memory and knowledge. Tulving recently wrote a paper on episodic versus semantic memory that brings out some important points. Work with aphasics in Britain suggests that they clearly have knowledge, and yet lack memories as we think of them. The kinds of theories of memory we tend to build are all ones that assume we store some kind of engram or a "thing" and that we go back and find "things" in remembering. But then it's not clear what it means to remember something versus to know it. But one knows rather than remembers that there are 12 inches in a foot. It would take considerable information reactivating the actual context of learning to call that a memory. In short, it may take *more* information to agree that something is a memory than to say that it is something we know.

Related to this is the fact that many approaches to comprehension have tried to treat comprehension in terms of some kind of stored "things" that we match to or check against. The problem of comprehension has thus been treated as the problem of how we find some "match". One of the things that Johnson and I reported (Bransford & Johnson, in preparation) is that one does different things depending on whether one is trying to check the current status of his knowledge system versus attempting to use current knowledge (and modify it) to understand what someone says. One may hear the sentence "Canaries eat cigarettes" and claim that it is false. On the other hand, one may hear "The canaries ate the cigarettes" and attempt to understand the particular situation that the speaker had in mind. In short, whether one is checking the current status of his knowledge system or attempting to understand a speaker can have an important effect on the nature of the information that he understands.

14
ALGORISTIC FOUNDATIONS TO COGNITIVE PSYCHOLOGY[1]

Robert Shaw and Michael McIntyre
Center for Research in Human Learning,
University of Minnesota

> *"It is a curious fact ... that as reasoning improves, its claims to the power of proving facts grow less and less. Logic used to be thought to teach us how to draw inferences; now it teaches us rather how not to draw inferences."*
>
> *—Bertrand Russell*

> *"The specialist is one who learns more and more about less and less and thus ends up knowing everything about nothing."*
>
> *—attributed to George Bernard Shaw*

What is known and *how* it is known are relative questions that make no sense independent of the question of *who* knows. Indeed, our opinion is that the central question of cognitive psychology concerns the essential nature of a knowing-agent, rather than just what is known or even how what is known *is* known. Only a certain kind of sceptic can hold that all things are relative without falling into the absurdity that if *everything* were relative, there would of course be nothing for it to be relative *to*.

In the past decade or so psychology has relinquished its obsessive concern for the question of how organisms behave, or can be made to behave, in favor of a broader set of questions. It is now popular to assume that *what* people process is

[1] Preparation of this paper was supported, in part, by a Career Development Award to Robert Shaw from the National Institute of Child Health and Human Development (1 KO4-HD24010) and by grants to the University of Minnesota, Center of Research in Human Learning, from the National Science Foundation (GB-35703X), the National Institute of Child Health and Human Development (HD-01136 and HD-00098), and the Graduate School of the University of Minnesota.

information, where for some theorists information is a pure mathematical measure of the uncertainty conveyed by disjunctive decision possibilities, and for others it is a semantic measure of the ecological significance of structured stimulation for a particular class of organisms. *How* information is processed is sometimes said to be by rules, procedures, algorithms, or some other functional analogue to computer programs. And, finally, the clinician reminds us that people are somehow the thinking, planning, dreaming, loving, hating, and behaving agents in whom the above processes reside, and for whom information is valuable. Unfortunately, we have so far failed to reach a consensus about the interrelationship of the *what, how* and *who* questions, much less how they might be answered.

This chapter discusses the concepts and principles by which these three problems might be related and attempts to specify the metatheoretical criteria by which answers to each might be recognized. Our intent is to provide a cogent rebuttal to reductionistic claims that theoretical solutions to any one of them alone will suffice for them all. We also hope to demonstrate that the inadequate interest shown thus far by cognitive psychologists in the nature of the epistemic-*who* (the knowing agent) has been a chief stumbling block in our attempts to understand the nature of what information is, and how it is processed. It is, of course, both trite and tiresome to argue merely that psychologists should study the *whole* man without explaining how this might be done. A more adequate approach must at least discuss the theoretical principles and methodological tools by which a start can be made.

The first section provides a theory-sketch of the class of dynamic systems to which knowing-agents belong, and tries to suggest why a study of man and other organisms at this level has dividends for the study of the other two questions. Section two discusses a new and admittedly radical approach to theory construction and evaluation which is especially tailored to the needs of cognitive psychology. The final section attempts to apply principles and concepts introduced in the earlier sections. Thus, to a great extent, the cogency and relevance of the arguments presented in the earlier sections must be judged in the light of the success of the final one.

I. ALGORISTIC BASES TO THE EPISTEMIC-WHO

Warren S. McCulloch, one of the founders of the cybernetic movement in the early 1940's, was an intellectual catalyst of the highest magnitude. His seminal papers seeded the minds of many students and colleagues, which he cultivated by periodic trips to the world's major life science laboratories. The titles of his papers tell us much, not only about the man, but about the loftiest aspirations psychobiologists and cognitive psychologists might entertain: "What's in the brain that ink might character?"; "Machines that think and want?"; *"Mysterium Iniquitatis:* Of sinful man aspiring into the place of God"; "Why the mind is in the head"; and many others. What we have called the question of the "epistemic-who," or knowing agent, is meant to be synonymous with the question so elegantly suggested by his title, *The Embodiments of Mind* (McCulloch, 1965).

John von Neumann, the mathematician and close friend of McCulloch, once argued that the real challenge for psychology and biology was not merely describing the behaviors of man, nor the topography of the brain, but of discovering logical methods by which we might determine what purposive activities (what he called "effectivities") a system might support as its structural complication approached that of the human brain. He was afraid that the usual hypothetico-deductive techniques and modelling procedures might fail when applied to living systems of great structural complexity (Shaw, 1971). He speculated, moreover, that the problem might ultimately arise from the fact that new effectivities emerged in quantal jumps as the systems become more complex.

In the light of von Neumann's arguments the task of cognitive psychology is not so much to describe what behaviors man might emit, nor even what stimulus conditions might evoke them, but to determine what is in the nature of man that requires and supports the need and purpose of such activities—whether they be physical or mental. Again the marvelous balance of poet, mathematician, physiologist, psychologist, and theologian in McCulloch expressed the issue more eloquently than most.

When as a young student at a Quaker college McCulloch was asked by his advisor what he wanted out of life, he replied; "I have no idea; but there is one question I would like to answer: What is number that man may know it, and a man, that he may know number." His Quaker advisor smiled thoughtfully and replied, "Friend, thee will be busy as long as thee lives."

McCulloch and Pitts (1953), by providing an abstract neural model, did not intend primarily to give an accurate description of real neurons, for they chose to leave out of the design of their modules important properties such as refractory periods. Nor did they merely intend to simulate behaviors, nor even to demonstrate that at limit extremely complex finite neural nets approached the computational power of Turing machines (i.e., the most powerful class of computing machines), as many reviewers have claimed. Rather they were after a far deeper question: How can a complex system of neurons, a living brain, come to know the world and to perform adaptively in it?

McCulloch (1951), like James J. Gibson, believed that what best characterizes the effectivities of living brains is their ability to detect and use invariant aspects of sensory stimulation, which reliably specify environmental "universals" such as shape, distance, size, position, and time. Gibson pushes us even deeper into the question of *what* is perceived, and hence might be learned, by arguing that what is directly perceived is the value or functional utility (affordances") of objects and events for the organism. The nature of such value as afforded by the organism's pick up of the invariants of sensory information, Gibson tells us, is both "formless and timeless" — a statement that echos the tenor, if not the substance, of McCulloch's concern for how a neural brain can be a knower of universals.

How might we, however, avoid getting lost in the rarefied atmosphere of platonic ideals, if we pursue this question? Can this question be pursued empirically as well as theoretically? We believe these issues can be favorably resolved by an approach which provides an integral attack on the *what* and *how* questions by using the *who* question as a theoretical fulcrum. If we can even roughly decide on the nature of the epistemic-who we will, at the same time, *have* to take a stand on the nature of the information processed from and about the environment, as well as on the nature of the psychological processes required to do so.

Who? What? and How?: A Closed Class of Questions

It is often the case that methodologies of sufficient precision to study one fundamental question are inadequate for the study of others. Controls required to rid experimental designs of confounding factors may at the same time rule out inferences that go beyond the single question posed by the theorist. For instance, if one is studying the effects of a drug on learning one must control any effects due to individual differences. In this way the study of the effects of *what* on *how* is only interpretable when the *who* variable has been controlled.

In a deeper theoretical sense, it may be the case that theoretical assumptions about the fundamental nature of certain psychological processes (e.g., that they are *serial* rather than *parallel, discrete* rather than *continuous, probabilistic* rather than *deterministic, learned* rather than *innate, voluntary* rather than *automatic, conscious* rather than *unconscious,* etc.), impose such logical restrictions as to make inferences to other views of the same processes impossible, since by definition they lead to contradiction. When this is the case, many fruitless and interminable controversies arise (witness the "nature-nurture" controversy earlier this century and reviewed in the Chomsky (1959) and Skinner (1957) debates, the "structuralist-functionalist" arguments between Lashley (1950) and the Gestaltists over the status of the memory trace; or the Neisser-Sternberg arguments over visual processing as parallel or serial, respectively).

A classic case took place in the 1930s between Einstein and Heisenberg over the issue of whether physical reality is fundamentally based on chance or deterministic laws. "God does not play at dice!" proclaimed Einstein, "But he does!" countered Heisenberg. Who is right?

"Both and neither," suggested Niels Bohr, for whether a significant degree of arbitrariness can be imputed to the nature of physical events depends not so much on what is true as on the way one asks the question.

Different questions may require such radically different experimental methodologies and theoretical contexts that the answers they yield are complementary. To achieve an answer to one question one necessarily sacrifices any claim to the other (a veritable "you can't have your cake and eat it too" limitation on the techniques science can use in its interrogation of nature). Thus, Bohr's principle of complementarity suggests a deeper epistemological insight than either of the stubborn positions adopted by Einstein or Heisenberg, since it provides a reason for the methodological chasm that exists between relativistic and quantum physics.

Similarly, complementary relations exist in fields other than physics. Consider, for instance, the conflict in goals that arises when one anatomist wishes to base the theory of brain functions on the dissection of "dead" brains while another insists that the proper approach is implantation of electrodes into the living brain. Clearly, the anatomical scope of "dead" anatomy may be broader than that of "living" anatomy, while the latter may be able to peer deeper into brain functions than the former. The two approaches can not even in principle be integrated since an attempt to increase the scope of surveillance by simultaneously implanting more and more electrodes would destroy the normal functioning of the living brain as surely as any attempt to dissect it by scapel.

Consequently, we see such a complementarity holding between current approaches that seek to study the *what* of perception, as opposed to those seeking to explain the *how* of perception. The former view is exemplified by James J. Gibson's (1966) investigations into the direct sources of information pickup by the visual system, which he terms "ecological optics," as opposed to the more Helmholtzean approaches which assume preconscious constructive processes, say as exemplified by the information-processing theories of Sperling (1960), Neisser (1967), Gregory (1966), Kolers (1968), Norman (1969), Broadbent (1958), and Haber (1969).

These constructive theories, as compared to Gibson's, do not really qualify as theoretically commensurable alternative explanations of the same phenomena, as might seem at first glance. Rather, they differ so radically in their definition of perception as to begin from contradictory assumptions which lead to quite different theoretical goals. Gibson defines perception as the direct pick-up of informational invariants by the senses operating as a perceptual system, while the other theorists (although often at odds on many secondary issues), seem to agree that perception is not a direct psychological process but involves the mediation of memory, learning, or cognitive subprocesses. Gibson's concept of information is dependent on the genetic preattunement of the species, and the education of attention for the individual organism, in the detection of certain fundamental invariants of stimulation from the terrestial environment (e.g., gravity, sky-above and ground-below, horizon, texture gradient of the ground plane, texture-flow field properties of the optic array, etc.). Such informational invariants specify important properties of the organism's environment, to which it must adapt to survive and maintain its health and well-being; hence, the perceptual information can be said to specify "affordances" of great ecological significance.

On the other hand, the so-called "dynamic" perceptual theorists rarely discuss the ecological significance of perceptual information and often ignore or denounce the concept of invariance. Instead, they discuss the ordered stages of processing and the rules or procedures used by each stage. Their approach essentially assumes that perceptual processing can be analyzed into discrete temporal cross-sections, perpendicular to the flow of information.

In contradistinction to this approach, Gibson assumes that perceptual processing of information is a continuous interactive relation between the organism and its environment. The all-important invariant relationships exist *not* in the discrete cross sections of the information flow, but in the constant longitudinal relations picked-up over time by an "afferent-efferent-re-afferent" continuous process loop.

If, as Gibson claims, ecologically significant informational invariants exist only over time, then it is not surprising that theorists who study discrete cross sectional segments of the information processes fail to find them, and therefore deem them to be of little theoretical importance. Thus, the claim that the two approaches are complementary is not so far-fetched as might first be thought.

It is fair to conclude that the major difference between Gibson's ecological approach to perception and the dynamic approach is that Gibson is really asking the *what* question while the other theorists are asking the *how* one. Where Gibson emphasizes the study of information as determined by the organism-environment interaction, the other theorists emphasize the study of the information-processing capabilities of organisms after they are presented with any information — whether of ecological value or not.

However, only the *what* and *how* questions are touched by the union of these two approaches. Unfortunately, this leaves virgin the question regarding the nature of the perceiver *qua* agent that processes what the environment has to offer and hence knows how to survive. Since the intersection of the *what* and *how* questions is in the nature of the epistemic-*who*, we might hope that due consideration of this third side of the issue will help integrate the two approaches discussed above and weld the three together into a coherent account of "knowing" organisms.

The question of the epistemic-who should not be confused with the claim that the concept of a knowing agent refers to an unanalyzable metaphysical "spook" or ghost in the biological machine. On the contrary, we will attempt to analyze the class of systems to which knowing-systems might belong. Nor does the proposed analysis degenerate into descriptive phenomenology, nor become a virtual sink-hole of introspective analysis. Rather we shall attempt to relate the class of systems that best describe knowing-agents to various classes of well-defined abstract automata (i.e., "machine" theory).

There is a major distinction between the so-called "algorithmic" approach, which attempts to characterize psychological processes in terms of input (stimulus) — output (response) functions, and what we will call the "algoristic" approach. The algorithmic approach fails to prescribe the intrinsic requirements which must be satisfied by complex systems which evolve, grow, develop, and function under the dominion of natural law.

Clearly, cognitive psychology must offer a description of agents more precise than that provided by the description of algorithms which psychological processes might follow in satisfying observed input-output functions. The class of abstract machines that may be competent to process such algorithms is obviously much larger than the class of machines that may be physically realized by construction as artifacts or by natural evolution. In fact, mathematics as such does not address this narrower question of what natural constraints must be satisfied by abstractly competent machines for them to be as effective as humans when functioning under real time and real space constraints imposed by the conservation of energy and work laws. (Exactly what these constraints might be will be discussed later.)

Moreover, there is considerable reason to suppose we have not yet defined the nature of "machine" with sufficient precision or abstraction to characterize how a neural brain might also be a "knowing" brain. Since, we believe, this is the question of the abstract *who* rather than of the *what* or *how* of knowing, a new set of assumptions about analysis may be needed to move toward the required theoretical basis for cognitive psychology. If we are lucky, or nature should be benevolent, we may be able to discover a *closed* set of variables which allow us to express the complementarity relation holding among the three primary analytic concepts of psychology (i.e., the *who, what* and *how* concepts). If so, then whatever properties we discover about one of these factors will imply the existence of a compatible set of properties with regard to the other mutually dependent ones. As a concrete illustration of how these concepts may belong to a closed set consider the following: The degree of hardness of a sheet of metal tells us something about the nature of the saw we must use to cut it (i.e., something about *what* is to be done); a blueprint or pattern must be selected in the light of what can be cut from the materials with a given degree of tolerance (i.e., *how* it is to be done); while both of these factors must enter into our equations to determine the amount of work that must be done to complete the job within a reasonable amount of time. This latter information provides a job description that hopefully gets an equivalence class of existing machines rather than a class that might accomplish the feat in principle but not in practice (i.e., implies the nature of the *who* or *what* required to do the task).

The value of seeking closure to our set of analytic concepts lies in the hope that we will succeed in discovering a logic of co-implication on which to build the laws of cognitive psychology. Only by making a cogent case for the possibility of such a logic of closed concepts can we justify introducing additional variables into our science in defiance of Occam's wise admonition not to multiply entities beyond necessity.

Now we must attempt to clarify the claim that the intuitive meaning of the concept of a knowing-agent is not exhausted by a description of what he does or how he does it. We will also argue that the "logic" of instantiating abstractly competent systems requires that the functions carried out by the device be supported at the physical, biological, and psychological levels; that is, the components of the system must be defined to satisfy natural constraints imposed by each of these levels of analysis. The multilevel support requirement rules out the possibility that some levels can be reduced to others. This is the only "metaphysical" postulate required and is asserted more for its pragmatic value as a working hypothesis than as a necessary truth. For instance, one immediate consequence of the multilevel support postulate is that it provides an hypothesis which accounts for the spurious evidence favoring reductionistic theories, say those that argue that psychological phenomena are epiphenomena of, or identical to, biological ones, or that biological phenomena can be totally explained by physical laws. From this postulate we can argue that the evidence presumed to support reductionistic arguments is due to the theorist mistaking co-implicative relations among the closed set of variables for an identity relation among them. Thus in order to lay the foundations for a truly general cognitive psychology we must both distinguish and relate the concept of information to the physical energy distributions which manifest it, the biological processes which preserve informational invariants, and the psychological processes which detect and use them. Our claim is that each of these levels constrains and supports the others. Thus, since none can be functionally independent of the others, reductionism is ruled out.

Toward a Rigorous Definition of Algorist

In the ninth century A.D. Al-Khuwarizimi wrote a book on procedures for arithmetic calculation. After his book became know to European scholars his name was latinized to 'Al-Gorism.' Later any procedure for calculation came to be an "algorism," while the man who executed the procedures was known as an "algorist." Our current term "algorithm" is a later corruption of this earlier term. But what became of the term "algorist?"

Often, when a word disappears from technical discourse, it is because the concept referred to has been discovered to be useless or fallacious and therefore abandoned (for instance, such terms as "aether" in reference to a medium which supports electromagnetic propogation, or "phlogiston" as the substance liberated when a material burns). More recently the usefulness of the terms "force" and "causation" have been seriously questioned by physicists and philosophers of science (Russell, 1945).

There are other cases, however, in which terms disappear from use that are more difficult to account for. For instance, the concept of vitalism (*elan vital*) served no useful purpose in biology although this is not due to the fact that current definitions of life or organism are sufficiently precise to disallow application of the term. Consider as evidence that this is still an open issue the fact that although we are willing to call ourselves, as well as animals, insects, paramecia, and even plants, "organisms," we do not know what to call viruses. It could be that we just do not know enough about them; or it could be that there is something fundamentally wrong with our intuitive conception of "organism" which guides our use of the term.

Such slippage in our technical vocabularies must be taken very seriously since it often indicates significant conceptual problems at the basis of a science. Many philosophers continue to agonize over the definition of such words as "life," "consciousness," "free-will," and "value," for this very reason. We submit that the passing from usage of the term "algorist" is similar evidence that no science, psychology the least, has successfully formulated a technically useful term for agent, not because the concept is itself intuitively barren (the way "force" has become in theoretical physics), but because of the dramatic advances in physics and more recently in computer science, that psychology as a science has been encouraged to press more toward *what* and *how* questions than *who* questions. Assuming that co-implication holds among the variables involved in this closed set, we should not be surprised that no major breakthroughs in cognitive psychology have yet occurred. If we fail to ask *who* is conscious or living, or *who* has free will, or for *whom* something has value, but only how he might be conscious, living, free, or served by value, or of what he is conscious, by what means he is living, free, or served by value, then we should not be surprised that our experiments uncover more phenomena than they explain, that our theories raise more questions than they answer. By concentrating too much on a few of the questions, we have given up whatever logical leverage we might have on all the questions. Whitehead once observed that if you wish to understand truly the conceptual framework of a historical period, ask not what answers they give to the questions they raise, but what questions they *fail* to raise.

In order to illustrate our underlying confusion regarding the distinction between *how* and *who* questions, consider the development of the field of computer science. Parallel to the etymological development of the term "algorithm" was the concept of calculator. In ancient time the calculator was merely a mechanical aid to calculation by a human agent, (e.g., a set of counting beads, measuring sticks, or vessels), while an algorithm was considered a procedural aid to calculations by algorists. A clear-cut intuitive distinction existed between algorithms as procedures, calculators as mechanical aids, and algorists (or agents) who used the two.

Now notice what has become of the precise distinction among these terms due to the spectacular developments of computer science: Ask yourself, "Is the programmer of a modern multipurpose digital computer or the machine itself most appropriately consider the algorist?" If this question poses no difficulty, consider how fuzzy the distinction becomes as we progress toward the construction of truly intelligent autonomous devices capable of dynamic self-programming when but provided an initial program and presented suitable data to work on. A closer analogy between such machines and humans can be seen than might be obvious since there is good reason to believe humans are not born *tabula rasa,* and that perceptual equipment may be genetically pre-attuned to the perceptual information of our terrestrial world.

Not only is our concept of living agent semantically "squishy" but so is our concept of machine or calculator. If we assume that the technological development of machines continues unabated, there is the realistic possibility that the dividing line between nonliving machine and living system might become increasingly obscured. Consider, for instance, the malevolent and egotistical computer named Hal on the space ship in the Stanley Kubrick movie *2001* which took over the ship and began killing the crew. Here is a hypothetical case of a machine that was more than just a mechanical aid to calculation. Hal surely had autonomous agent-like properties and thus qualified as an algorist. Many philosophers of science have unsuccessfully agonized over the question of what criteria, if any, are sufficient for deciding when a complex machine with human effectivities ceases being nonliving and nonhuman (MacKay, 1952; Putnam, 1960; Scriven, 1953). At what point would it be necessary to give machines like Hal, or even machines that are developmentally his intellectual inferiors, civil rights? When would we consider pulling the plug on such machines (as was eventually Hal's fate in the movie) as homocide and therefore punishable by law? Would we want to argue that such advance machines are not really algorists since they did not naturally evolve? Or, would it be more rational to argue that there are two kinds of living agents—those that are born of woman and those that are constructed by man?

Not only does the concept of intelligent agent shade off into that of calculator when considering sophisticated machines, but so does the notion of calculator merge with that of an algorist when a man is sufficiently competent to eschew mechanical aids and executes all the algorithmic steps mentally. As Wittgenstein so well knew, this kettle of logical worms is a simulation theorist's nightmare. Very strong assumptions about the nature of cognitive processes are required to disentangle the notions of "rules involved in behavior," "rules entailed by behavior," and "behavior entailed by rules." No wonder that many of us find the phrase "rule governed behavior" difficult to use in a technically precise way. Yet however we decide this issue, the solution will contribute only indirectly to a clear intuitive account of algorists. For at best an analysis of the algorithmic, or heuristic, procedures which approximate them tells us only *how* what is done *is done,* and does not address either the question of what information presented to the senses might specify about the environment, nor what significance it may have for any class of algorists. Moreover, no one should be surprised that attempts to provide a logical analysis of scientific phenomena often (or perhaps always) require *ad hoc* augmentation by extralogical principles to be adequate.

A classic example of this was Bertrand Russell's attempt to characterize physical events so that the results of quantum and relativity physics might be incorporated into our commonsense belief system about physical phenomena (Russell, 1948). One troublesome result of advances in these fields was to bring into question the causal analysis of physical events due to the recognition by most logicians of science that a *ceteris paribus* clause (i.e., other things being equal) must be included among the antecedent premises of such analysis (Lakatos, 1970) to render the condition for causal interaction sufficient. Russell provided the following extralogical postulates which he believed sufficient (although not necessary) to render highly probable the conditions for causal interaction among physical events (an object itself being an event). They are (*a*) quasi-permanence, (*b*) separable causal lines, (*c*) spatio-temporal continuity, (*d*) a structural postulate, and (*e*) the postulate of analogy.

Similarly, one might ask what extralogical assumptions must be entertained regarding the epistemic-who, if both information and cognitive processes are to be adequately characterized. To arrive at the metatheoretical postulates of a truly general cognitive theory which incorporates all three questions, we must first determine where the field is at the moment.

Paradigm Shift? When Descartes wrote "On the automation of Brutes," spring-wound mechanical toys were the highest development of scientific models for men and other animals. When telephone switchboards were considered an engineering triumph (at the turn of the 20th century), Sherrington's switchboard-based reflexology provided a theoretical mechanism popularly received by behaviorists. By midcentury, feedback mechanisms and servomechanisms had been developed to provide a goal-directed, quasi-purposive, control system for anti-air-craft artillery and to steer ships and missles. Consequently, homeostatic principles gained popularity in both biology and psychology. Currently, programmable, multipurpose computers epitomize man's technological development. Hence, we are not surprised to find concepts borrowed from computer science, and its cognate disciplines of mathematical linguistics and automata theory gaining popularity among psychological theorists. New terms like "psychological competence," "rule-governed behavior," and "simulation model," are replacing more shop worn terms such as "habit structure," "associative network," and "stimulus-response model."

It is ironic, if not surprising, that such innovative concepts derive from theorists whose training was in fields other than psychology. Theorists such as Piaget, a biologist, Simon, a chemist, Minsky, a computer scientist, and Chomsky, a linguist, have had a vitalizing and lasting influence. Where probability theory was once the dominant method for formalizing psychological phenomena, algebraic structure theory (that part of mathematics which includes the theory of formal languages and grammars, abstract automata, switching theory, semi-groups, groups, lattices and categories) is gaining prominence (Arbib, 1969a; Chomsky, 1963; Clowes, 1967; Ernst & Newell, 1969; Norman, 1970; Pylyshyn, 1972; Quillian, 1967; Scandura, 1973; Selfridge, 1959; Suppes, 1968; Winograd, 1972).

Although it is difficult to give a general characterization fair to all these views, and probably impossible to cite a single set of premises and principles commonly assumed by such new and diverse approaches to the study of cognition, they nevertheless seem to embody a common ideal; namely, they attempt to provide a rigorous, detailed formal analysis of cognitive processes. (For the sake of generality, we are incorporating the various modes of processing involved in perception, thinking, communication, memory, etc., under the single term "cognition.")

If we follow the suggestion by metamathematicians to consider algebraic functions (or equivalently, relations) to be well-defined (in the finitistic sense) when an algorithm is constructed by which they might be computed (or generated), then all the above approaches can be said to be attempts to discover the *algorithmic* bases of cognitive processes. The intuitive notion of an *algorithm* for a computable function is that of an *effective* procedure which consists of a sequence of instructions so simple, discrete, deterministic, and finite that a noncreative agent (a machine) can execute them to find the values of the functions without guesswork or inference.[2] Thus, the attempt to discover the algorithmic bases of cognitive functions is the attempt to define the algorithms by which neurological mechanisms might compute them.[3]

We can all agree it is too soon to decide the ultimate validity of any of these algorithmic approaches to psychological theory, but it is by no means premature to ask whether theoretical efforts should be focused solely on this level of analysis and whether investigations at this level alone are even potentially capable of providing adequate explanations. This is not to argue against the importance of algorithmic analysis, since we feel it to be a necessary part of any approach. Rather, our contention is that the algorithmic bases of cognitive processes can only be defined relative to what we wish to call their *algoristic* bases.

Earlier we discussed how slippery the distinction between the concepts of algorithm and algorist has become due to their converging etymological heritage

---

[2] The fact that some of the theorists mentioned above may prefer to think of psychological processes as heuristic and probabilistic, rather than as algorithmic and deterministic, does not invalidate their inclusion under the rubric of the algorithmic approach. It can be argued that for all finite devices the probabilistic success of heuristic procedures executed by them can only be rigorously defined relative to the ideal limits prescribed by algorithms which they most closely approximate. Recognition of this fact seems to be the primary motivation of Chomsky's *competence-performance* distinction.

[3] A word of caution: The desire for formal precision characteristic of these contemporary algorithmic approaches should not be confused with the now *passé* attempts by earlier psychologists, such as Hull and Lewin, to axiomatize various aspects of psychology. Axiomatization is not the issue: Rather the substantive issue concerns what *ideal* goals cognitive theory should strive toward to achieve the most adequate forms of explanations for significant psychological phenomena. The issue then is primarily one of the pragmatic utility of the theoretical focus prescribed by the algorithmic presuppositions of these approaches.

and the fact that the notion of mechanical execution of computational procedures has been easier to describe rigorously than has the intentionality of agents. The reason for this difficulty is that just as the intuitive notion of function rests conceptually on the intuitive notion of an *effective* procedure, or algorithm, so the intuitive notion of algorithm rests ultimately on what is meant by an epistemic agent, or algorist.

The history of contemporary American psychology can be viewed as falling into three major periods which embody the distinctions we wish to make: The first period, running from the early 1920's until the mid 1950's, was characterized by attempts to discover the behavioral bases of psychological phenomena. The second period, from the 1950's until now, has been characterized by attempts to discover the algorithmic bases of behavior.

Currently, however, we seem to be on the threshold of a third period, in which theorists attempt to discover the algoristic bases of the "algorithms" of mind. Although many earlier theorists have anticipated the goals of this third period, no clear formulation of what constitutes an algoristic basis has yet been given. Disenchantment with the pure syntactic approach to psycholinguistic theory and the rebirth of interest in its semantic foundations, the growing concern over the bases of human intentional behaviors and the desire for reintroducing "value" into perception by assuming an ecological approach, the bankruptcy of computer models for psychoneural processes, the limited success of simulation models for cognitive and perceptual processes, as well as the renewed interest by contemporary philosophers in the mind-body problem in the guise of the "man-machine" analogy, all seem to argue strongly that the field is once again in transition.

Consequently, a first and necessary step to reformulating the goals of cognitive theory is to clarify the distinction between the algorithmic and algoristic bases of psychological phenomena. We turn now to this problem.

Algoristic bases to algorithms. The intuitive notion of an algorithm, or computation procedure, can only be made formally rigorous when the class of mathematical functions that are mechanically computable can be distinguished from those that are not. To understand what this means consider a simple case: There is no known algorithm for trisecting an angle using just a straight-edge and compass. Since early Greek geometers first began searching for such algorithms, many hours have been squandered on this problem by holiday mathematicians. It can now be shown that this particular function—the "trisection-of-angle-by-compass-and-straight-edge" function—is not computable. The question of the existence of an algorithm for computing this particular "trisection" function could be settled because its intuitive content was precisely understood by everyone.

It is generally agreed that the meaning of the assertion, "X is a function computable by an algorithm" or less redundantly "X is a computable function" was exhausted when definition of the total class of such functions was provided by Church (1936) and Kleene (1936) in 1935 (Kleene, 1967). Church proposed that the intuitive class of all computable functions was identical to a well-defined class of functions he and Kleene independently showed to be computable by a system of simple logical rules termed the "lambda calculus."

A little later A. M. Turing independently demonstrated that a very simple hypothetical computing machine consisting only of symbols on a linear tape, a reading and writing head, and an alphabet, could be "programmed" to compute any function computable in the manner of the lambda-calculus. This hypothetical device became known as the universal Turing machine since Turing made the same claim for it as Church did for his calculus; namely, that what is meant intuitively by a function being "computable by an algorithm" was identical to it being computable by this abstract machine. This conjecture, often called the Church-Turing thesis, is not capable of mathematical proof in the strict sense because it asserts the equivalence between the concept of a formally precise object, a Turing machine, and one that is merely intuitive, an algorithm.

However, it should be pointed out that the thesis does seem to be true on grounds of inductive generalization (although it has its detractors, e.g., Kalamar, 1957) since each time a universal device, say an abstract neural-net, Post or Wang-machine has been designed that appears *prima facie* different from a Turing machine, it turns out to be formally equivalent in that it can execute no new algorithms.

Does this mean then that the universal Turing machine and the class of abstract automata equivalent to it provide a rigorous instantiation of what we intuitively mean by an algorist? The answer is "No," because such abstract automata do not satisfy the natural constraints that must be satisfied by any real agent. For instance, Turing machines are assumed to possess infinite memory capacity, to be perfectly reliable, and to compute as fast as you please—all ideal properties not representative of any organism or actual machine. Furthermore, if we take into account the constraints placed on the working of organisms by the laws of physics and biology, many *cost* variables other than *amount of storage space* and *reliability* become relevant to the concept of an actual agent of computation. For example, due to the very general design required to insure its universality, the Turing machine would be a very inefficient computing machine if actually constructed. A special-purpose machine constructed to compute just a small class of functions would be far superior in efficiency to the multipurpose universal Turing machine, as regard the cost of the computation.

As algorists, such special purpose devices are quite different from Turing machines since the *ideal* limits on the "cost" of computation must be determined by variables that play no essential role in our intuitive concept of algorithm—variables such as the *material composition* of components (e.g., How much speed or heat can they withstand?), their *geometric configuration* (e.g., Are they large or small? Numerous? Do they maximize adjacency relationships?) as well as the resultant effects of the environmental conditions surrounding the machine (e.g., temperature, gravity, atmosphere, humidity, etc.). There can be no doubt that determination of appropriate cost variables involve extralogical principles that go beyond the logical variables required to describe the algorithms the machine may be capable of executing. It goes without saying that humans and other organisms are subject to a wide range of such cost variables including psychological cost variables, the capricious functioning of faulty components, and even design errors due to the logical slack in evolutionary principles (Wistar Institute, 1967).

A final reason why a completely rigorous understanding of the concept of algorithm gets us no closer to our goal of an explicit theory of algorists is the observation that *the notion of algorist is in fact presupposed in the very concept of algorithm,* as the ancients well knew. A little discussed condition that must be satisfied by any procedure that can be deemed "effectively" rigorous is that it be stated in a "natural" way—that is, it must be described in terms of "self-evident" primitive concepts and stated in terms of an elementary notation system that is truly easy to understand by whatever algorist is selected to execute the algorithm. By an algorithm we mean a procedure whose first step as well as each subsequent step can be unequivocally understoood by the user. A procedure that is not self-evident in this sense must either be potentially analyzable into steps that are, or it is not an algorithm. Similarly, if its instructions are couched in a language too vague or too complicated to be clearly understood by the potential user, then it fails to qualify as an algorithm since the rationalistic criterion for it being a natural or clear intuition is also violated.

But clearly this is a *cognitive* assumption about the ability of the human algorist to understand some things better than others. In this sense, the concept of algorithm can only be unabiguously understood when that of the algorist is. It is quite perplexing to those who wish to keep the foundations of mathematics logically pure to admit that underneath it all lies a truly cognitive assumption; but here is the concept of the algorist, like the legendary Atlas, bearing the world of mathematics on its shoulders. Moreover, to Bertrand Russell's famous witticism regarding the nature of mathematics that "mathematics may be defined as the subject in which we never know what we are talking about, nor whether what we are saying is true. . ." we must add, "nor to whom we speak."

Therefore, if the primary evidence for an algoristic level of analysis is the *a priori* need for an agent which naturally "compiles" certain algorithms more efficiently than others, then the intuitive concept needs to be rigorized in the following way: First, the cost parameters must be shown to follow intrinsically from the logic by which the system is designed, and secondly, the cost parameters must be shown to be compatible with the *intentionality* requirements of the system (i.e., the cost of computing a behavioral or mental function must not be so dear as to preclude successful adaptation to the exigencies of its environment, nor so lenient as to allow unrealistic achievements).

Thus, the cost of appropriate functioning for a *natural* system derives from both an *intrinsic* and an *extrinsic* source, while that of an *abstract* system derives merely from an intrinsic one. Regarding intrinsic cost constraints, neither type of system can achieve a level of computational efficiency which surpasses that permitted by the most economical algorithms that can be shown to be logically possible. However, the natural system if further restricted to levels of functional efficiency dictated by the mechanical efficiency of its material components, which must labor under the space-time restrictions imposed by natural law. This leads us to expect that the class of algorithms that can be defined which are *in principle* capable of computing well defined psychological functions will be spuriously larger than the class that can actually be executed on the neurological machinery with its *real* time/*real* space processing limitations.

Moreover, the logically possible algorithmic bases to cognitive processes must be shrunk still further to accommodate the particular properties of the energy distributions which carry the information required for an organism's adaptive responding.For all these reasons, as argued earlier, the algorist or epistemic-who can be considered to be the logical intersection of the algorithmic basis (the *how*) of cognitive processes and the informational sources (the *what*) of the environment.

Of course, Chomsky, Simon, and other theorists characterized earlier as proponents of the algorithmic approach to theory construction in psychology recognize the need for an approach that incorporates cost parameters into models of cognitive processes. In fact both Chomsky (1965) and Simon (1969) have discussed the problem. Moreover, both express optimism regarding the possibility of introducing cost parameters as adjunct adjustments to algorithmic (competence) models. At times this optimism seems tantamount to the reductionistic belief that the algoristic basis of cognitive processes can be 'mapped' onto the algorithmic ones. So far such direct augmentation of algorithmic models by cost parameters has not proven systematically possible. However, Chomsky's admonition to theorists that a formal grammar is not to be taken as a "process" model, but to consider it neutral with respect to the processes of both speaking and comprehending, seems to be evidence that he recognizes the incommensurability that exists between cost and competence.

Two current areas of research in algebraic structure theory seem especially cognizant of the problem of determining the cost parameters of algorithms and machines which compute functions of the considerable complexity required of living systems. The first is the exciting work being pursued in the new branch of recursive function theory known as the theory of computation, especially that part called the theory of computational complexity (Blum, 1967; Hartmanis & Stearns, 1965; Minsky & Papert, 1968). A second source of relevant techniques may issue from attempts to model systems that perform biologically significant functions, such as self-reproduction and regeneration or reparation of parts (Arbib, 1969). This work is ultimately aimed at the explanation of evolution of species and the growth of individuals. The most dramatic result in this area is von Neumann's proof of the existence of a universal constructor machine which can reproduce any other machine, analogous to the ability of the universal Turing machine for computing any function. This proof is of special interest because for the first time it suggests that mathematicians, and not just physicists or biologists, must interest themselves in the idealization of structural rather than just algorithmic properties of machines. Such work can be thought of as pointing toward a geometry of machines. In order to have a machine that will reproduce itself, or another machine, there must, in addition to the program providing the 'blueprint' which guides construction, also be formally described an available stockpile of compatible parts and a suitable space in which these parts can be retrieved and assembled. Consequently, if the parts are to be assembled into a machine, they must be structurally compatible with the manipulative organs of the parent machine. The material composition as well as intrinsic geometry of both parts and manipulative organs must be "naturally" designed for one another. For instance, it would be impossible for a parent machine with mechanical manipulators to reproduce itself if the stockpile was liquid. Clearly, the parts must be discretizable, suitably rigid, etc., if they are to be naturally suitable for the desired construction. Discretizability and rigidity are intuitive mathematical concepts whose idealization have played a prominent role in set theory and geometry respectively.

To interpret the intuitive notion of a "natural" medium for the instantiation of a given algorithm, we need to gather up into a coherent theory all such idealized properties of media which are required as support for the computation of various kinds of functions. Consider, for instance, the abstract properties of materials in which analogs to digital conversion can and cannot take place, or in which serial simulation of parallel processes would be impossible, etc.

The discovery of the appropriate idealizations of the structural properties of materials that form a suitable stockpile of parts and assembler organs, as well as the discovery of proofs regarding which of these properties define a *universal* stockpile, are problems whose solution would shed light on what we mean by agent-like machines. A universal stockpile of parts would require the abstract specification of all properties which all types of materials must satisfy if they are to be mutually compatible as components of a system which has a *natural* algorithmic basis, i.e., which computes functions satisfying both the natural cost parameters and intentionality of physically, biologically, and psychologically realizable systems.

Unfortunately, such proofs may not be possible so long as we assume the laws governing such materials to be abstractly equivalent to the laws of physics. The properties of algorists as psychological agents may transcend even those prescribed by current biological theory. If so, what might we expect to be the nature of such algoristic laws? In the next section we explore a possible answer to this question.

Mind: A Higher Phase of Matter

Since Thales of Miletus in the fifth century B.C. asked, "What is matter?", many diverse and immense answers have been given. It has been suggested that the science of the ordinary phases of matter, e.g., gas, liquid and solid, was adequately accounted for by the classical physics of the 19th century. Recently, however, a new and most predominant phase of matter was discovered—the so-called "plasma" phase—whose properties were found to transcend the laws of classical physics and to require explanation in terms of the new physics of quantum mechanics.

Since Driesch and other vitalists debated the biological mechanists, there have been perennial claims that living systems consist of a phase of matter not adequately covered by the laws of physics, classical or otherwise. Several contemporary scientists have argued that in living systems we encounter matter in the 'protoplasmic' phase that is governed by 'biotonic' rather than physical laws (Elsasser, 1958; Wigner, 1970). In support of this claim, Wigner, a Nobel laureate in physics, has provided a proof that quantum mechanical laws do not provide a sufficient account of explaining the logic of biological reproduction—a property many theorists believe criterial for distinguishing living from nonliving matter (Ashby, 1962; von Neumann, 1966). Claims by some mathematicians (Arbib, 1969; Block, 1967) to the contrary do not refute this, since as yet no one has been able to show that their models are able to satisfy the stringent "cost" requirements of reliability and real-time and real-space development set by natural evolution.

If it is indeed true that the laws for lower phases of matter discovered by classical physics can no more explain the higher phase of matter dealt with by quantum mechanics than the latter laws can explain the biotonic phase of matter, then still higher phases of matter might exist that are beyond the province of even biotonic law. Such speculation that intemperately proliferates levels of analyses understandably is apt to send reductionists and nonreductionists alike away to sharpen Occam's razor.

There does seem to exist dramatic, if not precise, evidence for the existence of a still higher phase of matter than even the protoplasmic. We refer, of course, to the "psychological" phase and to "consciousness" as it crucial property. Many plants and lower organisms presumably reproduce and, thus, are governed by "biotonic" law, but do so with no wit of consciousness, just as many physical systems exist which possess plasmic properties but no biotonic ones.

Whatever might be meant by the intuitive concept of algorist, we suggest that an essential part of its theory must account for that aspect of man, organism, or machine that both expends the cost of executing algorithms as well as constrains the selection of processing goals. Furthermore, the concept of the algorist seems to play as fundamental a role in physics as we have argued it does in mathematics. Many of the greatest theorists in physics agree that it does.

In 1912 a group of scientists met in Berlin to co-author a manifesto to "oppose all metaphysical undertakings" and to champion the view that a better philosophy "should grow in a natural manner out of the facts and problems of natural science" (Clark, 1971). The manifesto continued:

> In the theory of relativity [physics] touches the most searching question thus far of episteomology: is absolute or is only relative knowledge attainable? Indeed: Is absolute knowledge conceivable? It comes here directly upon the question of man's place in the world, the question of the connection of thought with the brain. What is thought? What are concepts? What are laws? In psychological problems, physics and biology come together. [p. 197].

Among the three dozen signatures endorsing this document are those of Mach, Einstein, and Sigmund Freud.

Just a few years ago Wigner (1970) cautiously reiterated this view that psychology has a key role to play in the unification of science:

> One is less inclined to optimism if one considers the question of whether the physical sciences will remain separate and distinct from the biological sciences and, in particular, the sciences of the mind. There are many signs which portend that a more profound understanding of the phenomena of observation and cognition, together with an appreciation of the limits of our ability to understand, is not too distant a future step. At any rate, it should be the next decisive step toward a more integrated understanding of the world... That a higher integration of science is needed is perhaps best demonstrated by the observation that the basic entities of intuitionistic mathematics are physical objects (e.g., models), that the basic concept in the epistemological structure of physics is the concept of observation, and that psychology is not yet ready for providing concepts and idealizations of such precision as are expected in mathematics or even physics. Thus this passing of responsibility from mathematics to physics, and hence to the science of cognition ends nowhere [pp. 36-37].

We believe that cognitive psychology buttressed by the concept of the algorist, can at last begin assuming its full responsibility in the efforts to find a unitary basis for all science.

Unfortunately, Wigner's pessimism seems warranted at the present since no precise theory of algorists yet exists. In the next section we want to discuss the metalogical principles required of all sciences which desire to rigorize the algoristic foundations we are admonished to seek by the poet Dylan Thomas when he says, "Man be my metaphor!"

II. TOWARD INVARIANCE LAWS IN PSYCHOLOGY

We have argued that the concept of algorithm as an *effective* procedure depends upon the notion of an agent, or algorist, who computes the procedure. What is meant by the intuitive term "effective" is always relative to the context of constraint within which the algorist must function. Hence some knowledge of the capabilities of the agent, or class of agents for whom the algorithm is intended, is a necessary prerequisite for providing a truly effective definition of algorithm. For this reason it follows that the true meaning of 'effective' entails the extralogical requirement that the algorithmic basis be compatible with the algoristic one.

Often the dependency of the effectivity of algorithms on algoristic factors is evidenced by the fact that the algorithm, as stated, leaves unspecified some formally inessential choices which must be left to the volition of the algorist, (e.g., the mathematician executing the algorithm or the programmer who programs the machine to do so). For instance, if several numbers are to be multiplied together, it may be left to the algorist to choose the order in which they are combined. Of course, in all cases determinate choices must be made or the algorithm will not execute properly. Exactly how such choices are made is logically arbitrary, since the numbers can be selected in various ways and combined in different orders. That many equivalent alternative choices exist follows from the fact that multiplication is both associative and commutative.

As the functions to be computed increase in complexity, the number of arbitrary choices that must be made to execute the algorithms effectively increase proportionally. Under such circumstances, the algoristic bases for some machines may prove to be more compatible with certain strategies for choosing than others. That is, the extralogical requirements for executing the algorithm may be more costly for some machines than others.

Consequently, there seems to be no universal form for algorithms which will guarantee *a priori* that they can be compiled or executed with equivalent ease by all algorists. Mathematical knowledge, like all knowledge, has no absolute form, but seems to be relative to the processing capabilities of the agents which use it.

To summarize, there are at least two ways the realization of algorithms tacitly depends on the concept of the algorist: first, in their *definition,* since whether a procedure is deemed "effective" depends on the existence of some class of agents competent to follow the procedure without creative intervention. This extralogical constraint defines a lower limit on the precise application of even the simplest algorithms. Secondly, the actual implementation of algorithms requires that the agent be provided with a strategy by which to interpolate the formally arbitrary choices needed to render the procedure practically effective. The fact that cost requirements for doing so may exceed the performance capabilities of the algorist, when the algorithm becomes complex, suggests an upper limit on implementation exists. Although this upper limit may appear to be only practical, it is, in fact, a theoretical limit, for there exists no algorithm for predicting *a priori* exactly where in the execution of complex procedures a given algorist may have to interpolate logically arbitrary decisions. Moreover, whenever a complex algorithm is implemented by a new algorist, it must be checked *post hoc* to see if it actually executes. But who or what does the checking?

Any new algorist competent to check whether the previous algorist is able to execute the algorithm effectively, must possess knowledge of that algorist's cost factors, structural design, etc., to determine its compatibility with the bases of the algorithm. But the checking procedure must also be an algorithm. Therefore, who checks the checker to determine if it can actually execute the checking algorithm? Since cost factors, intentionality, and other properties of actual machines which limit and direct its computational abilities can not be algorithmatized, no *a priori* solution can be found to circumvent the regress.

Granting the above argument, then the nature of the algoristic bases for machines is a topic worthy of study. The concept of a knowing agent seems to be what Whitehead called "a recalcitrant fact." It simply will not dissolve under algorithmic analysis. Instead, there seem to exist algoristic limits on the rigorous definition and effective application of algorithms. In this way cognitive variables not only enter into the foundations of pure mathematics, but into their application as well. Consequently, it is a mistake to identify the concept of algorist with what machines can do, or how they can do it.

On the other hand, there must be some lawful relationship among the three bases of support for natural phenomena that renders them naturally compatible, or they could not coexist. This is as true for man-made machines as it is for organisms. The designer of computers must satisfy mutual compatibility relations among the informational, algorithmic and algoristic bases or else, (*a*) the information may not be compilable by the machine, (*b*) the programs may not execute, or (*c*) the machine will not satisfy the intentions of the user.

How nature achieves similar ends through evolution, with a minimum of arbitrary contrivance, is one of the most perplexing problems of science. This process can be seen as either marvelous or inevitable. For Leibniz the process was inevitable.

Compatibility and existence. To Leibniz should go the credit for recognizing the importance of developing a logic of synergistic relations among natural systems. Although his metaphysical doctrines have been ignored, we would not be wise to dismiss lightly the work of the co-inventor of the calculus and a thinker who has been acclaimed as "one of the supreme intellects of all time [Russell, 1945, p. 581]."

Leibniz held that substances can not interact. Moreover, he believed there were an infinite number of them, which he called "monads." No causal relation could hold between them. What seems to be an action of one body on another in physics is not a true causal interaction. Rather he assumed there existed a "pre-established harmony" between the changes of state in one monad and those in another that produced the appearance of interaction. Thus, what passes for causal interaction among substances is but a parallel coordination of state changes.

Leibniz also explained perception in terms of a harmonious change in the state of the observer on the occasion of a change in state of the event. Coordination of state changes was not itself considered miraculous, but rather due to the inexorable unfolding of natural laws according to a primitive harmony or symmetry among substances. Consequently, this is the best of all possible worlds because it alone is inevitable.

Leibniz, as a consummate logician and rationalist, refused to leave anything to chance. He endorsed a "principle of sufficient reason" according to which nothing happens without a reason. What then is the reason for the preestablished harmony of natural events? To this question he gave the following argument:

Only those things may coexist which satisfy certain fundamental compatibility relations. Thus, it may be possible that some Structure A should exist, and also possible that some Structure B should exist, but not possible that both A and B should exist; that is, they may be logically incompatible. For instance, ice can exist and fire can exist but ice may not be compatible with a universal conflagration, nor fire with a frigid, energy-dead universe. Two or more things are only "compossible" when it is possible for all of them to coexist.

Leibniz made compatibility relations among logically possible structures the defining criterion for existence. He argued: "The existent may be defined as that which is compatible with more things than is anything incompatible with itself." That is to say, if A is incompatible with B, while A is compatible with C and D and E, but B is only compatible with F and G, then A, but not B, exists *by definition*. Hence, to exist is to be mutually compatible with the most things.

Notice how Leibniz's argument inverts the usual evolutionary argument for the "struggle of things to exist." The mechanism of natural selection proposed by Darwin provides a means for weeding out those species of organisms that are not sufficiently compatible with their environments to continue to exist. Leibniz, on the other hand, claims an even more central role for compatibility relations; namely, that only those things can coexist to compete which are sufficiently compatible to do so.

Darwin's theory addresses the question of the algorithmic mechanism by which nature selects from among existing species those that might continue to evolve. By contrast, Leibniz's theory addresses the deeper question of how the existence of such systems might be explained. This question is aimed at clarifying the algoristic basis of life as well as all natural phenomena. Perhaps this is the reason it has proven considerably more difficult to investigate.

As we shall see, Leibniz's insights, as curious and radical as they may seem, have been partially vindicated by contemporary science. Causal interaction among substances has been brought into question in physics by Heisenberg's principle of indeterminacy and Boltzmann's law; it has been questioned in biology by Weiss (1969), Elsasser (1958) and others; and has never really gained a strong foothold in psychology due to the intractability of the mind-body problem.

The compatibility relation that is assumed to hold among the different phases of matter hints at a notion of preestablished harmony not unlike that proposed by Leibniz. This may seem quite far-fetched and an unwarranted metaphysical assumption; yet it is neither, as we will argue in the next section.

Laws of Nature and Invariance Laws

By a *natural* law we mean a law which explains *intraphasic* interactions, that is, the interactions among phenomena instantiated in the same phase of matter. There can then be physical laws of at least two varieties as well as biological laws and psychological laws, corresponding to the mechanistic, plasmic, biotonic, and psychological phases of matter, respectively. The nature of interactions between different phases, however, is not causal in the usual sense at all. We will explore this claim in a moment.

The coimplicative relationship among the questions concerning the bases of natural phenomena, as well as the transitive closure of the phases of matter, suggests that sufficient compatibility holds among the various phases of phenomena to permit some kind of *interphasic* interaction as well. Whereas in quantum physics one primarily studies *monophasic* phenomena (i.e., one phase of matter), psychology is by its very nature more complex (This, of course, is not a novel claim). In psychology we must ask what effect physics has on biology such that psychological experiences of a certain sort result. This means that psychology essentially deals with *"polyphasic"* phenomena. Thus, it is the laws of interphasic interactions that must be captured. In physics such laws are called *invariance* laws, since they refer to the structure cf the interaction of natural laws.

The conclusion we will argue for in this section can now be stated: *The laws of psychology must be invariance laws; the explicit form of such laws is mnemic rather than causal; the polyphasic interactions are macro-deterministic rather than micro-deterministic; the nature of scientific theorizing is assertive (adjunctive) rather than hypotheticodeductive;* and, finally, *symmetry group theory provides a meaningful analysis of invariance laws.*

We assert that all the above conclusions can be supported by scientific argument, rather than by metaphysical speculation. Indeed, it is a matter of record that theorists in other fields have already reached a consensus on most, if not all, of the above points. We fully expect that as the field of psychology matures and greater precision is achieved, similar conclusions will be pressed upon us.

A final point, that is a methodological corollary of those above, is the claim that the concept of algorist plays a central role in all sciences (as it apparently does in mathematics). Thus, as Wigner, Einstein, Mach, and Freud all seem to agree, cognitive psychology may prove to be the study of variables intrinsic to all sciences. We will now discuss each of these points in turn.

Knowledge of the Physical World

Creatio ex nihlo is the cosmological principle, entertained by some scholastic philosophers, that the world was created from nothing. The astronomer Hoyle, when asked to defend his use of this principle in astronomy, replied that it is often necessary in science to tolerate bizarre and exceptional assumptions to preserve more fundamental ones, such as the conservation laws and the consistency of mathematics. Contemporary theoretical physicists have had to be extremely tolerant in this regard with the advent of such concepts as antimatter, time reversals, ephemeral particles, curved space, and complementarity conditions (e.g., wave and particle aspects of light).

Recently, some theorists in quantum mechanics have reached the exceptional conclusion that cognitive variables enter directly into the wave equations describing physical events. If this turns out to be a "recalcitrant fact," major repercussions will be felt throughout all sciences.

Most people have little trouble accepting the premise that physical events can somehow act upon the "mind" to produce changes in psychological states. But they balk, and feel common sense is violated, by the inverse claim that mental states may somehow directly affect physical states, (psychosomatic effects, perhaps, being a "gray" case).

As bizarre as the inverse assumption may seem, there now seems to be evidence for it.

Postulates of scientific knowledge: What are the general conditions that make knowledge of physical events possible? First, if the world consisted of an unstructured chaos then no knowledge would be possible. Even if the world consisted of a plurality of uncorrelated events, the exigencies of life (assuming it were possible) would be totally arbitrary, thus precluding adaptation by any living creature. For knowledge to be possible, then, we must assume uniformity of structure at some level of analysis across all classes of events, and assume that such structure is preserved to some significant extent by the knowledge-gathering processes of organisms.

In addition to structural uniformity across events, there must exist natural laws which can be learned so that similar responses are adaptive across families of event classes. However, the assumption that natural laws exist is not alone sufficient to guarantee continued adaptation by the species. We must also assume that the natural laws governing each phase of matter remain globally invariant, i.e., do not change arbitrarily with the passage of time or change of locale.

Consider what would happen if the laws of physics were variant from moment to moment, or from place to place. Objects would have no relatively permanent shape, hence food and mates would be unrecognizable and dangerous situations unavoidable. If the laws of biology were not invariant, then mating would not guarantee the survival of the species, vital functions might cease to support life, and information-processing capabilities of the sensory systems might not permit interpretable perceptions. The lack of invariance of psychological laws might preclude learning, memory would be unreliable, and problem solving impossible. Moreover, adaptive responses emitted by an organism would be accidental.

It is not even enough to assume events exhibit higher order structural uniformities, or that monophasic natural laws are relatively unchangeable with respect to each other. A final assumption is required, if knowledge of the world is to be possible, and this assumption brings us to the highest abstraction in all of science. We must somehow guarantee the compatibility of the various sets of natural laws; they must not only be invariant within their particular phase, but must exhibit conjoint invariance across phase boundaries. This highest order of structure among phases constitutes an invariance law or symmetry postulate.

Thus, for knowledge of the physical world to be a possible achievement of knowing-agents, there must be four levels of structure to experience: (a) events must be structured; (b) families of events must be lawful; (c) natural laws must be globally invariant; and (d) invariance laws must hold over phases of matter.

Wigner (1970) calls the progression from events to natural laws, and from natural laws to invariance laws, "the hierarchy of our knowledge of the world around us." Although the progression seems to provide an accurate account of the foundations of scientific epistemology, it does not actually seem to be hierarchical.

In a hierarchy, categories at the same nodal level do not interact. However, there is ample evidence that the various phases of matter, all of which have the same level in the classificatory schema, do in fact interact—although not in a causal manner. If this is the case, then either the assumption that the phases of matter are at the same level in the hierarchy is false, or else scientific knowledge of the world is not strictly ordered in a hierarchical fashion.

Types of invariance laws.[4] Physics distinguishes two types of invariance laws: the classical laws, which had their most precise formulation in the Special Theory of Relativity, and the newer type (not so well understood) that the General Theory of Relativity provides. Theoretical physicists have now shown that laws of nature must be derived from invariance laws rather than vice-versa.

In fact, the structure among the natural laws, which is what we mean by invariance laws, has proven so symmetrical that in some cases new laws of nature have been inferred from the presumption that they were needed to complete the symmetry of that structure. The existence of antimatter, the symmetry of chemical properties as captured by Mendeleev in the periodic table, chemical steroids, the law of parity, and other discoveries have been progeny of this principle. What more dramatic testimony could Leibniz have wanted in support of his postulate of preestablished harmony than this evidence of a higher order symmetry in nature?

As Wigner points out, and Einstein heartily emphasized, neither type of invariance law is an *a priori* category of pure reason, nor are they speculative results of metaphysical theory. Rather, both are products of careful observation in science and a conservative evalutation of experimental data. There are cases where invariance laws have been found wanting in these regards and were subsequently abandoned.

Fourier's principle of similitude is an example. It was abandoned, not because it lacked theoretical plausibility, but because it was inconsistent with empirical results. The principle claimed that the absolute magnitude of objects was irrelevant with respect to their behavior on the proper scale. The discovery that atoms possessed elementary charges, and that light was the limiting velocity in the universe, were serious anomalies that led to the principle being discarded.

The first type of invariance laws were based on geometric symmetries that hold over the space-time continuum. These are analogous to Klein's symmetry group

---

[4] Wigner (1970) is the main source for much in this section. We refer the reader to this collection, especially pp. 3-51, 153-200, for an authoritative discussion of many of the topics overviewed here.

representations for various types of geometric spaces (more will be made of this analogy in Section III). These geometric invariance laws are formulated in terms of structural symmetries among events themselves, such as objects remaining rigid when displaced (i.e., preserving their shape), or the so-called "constant radius of curvature" which holds throughout space.

The second type, the newer invariance laws, are dynamic in the sense that they apply to laws of nature, rather than events. These provide a formulation of types of interactions which can exist among events. In doing so dynamical laws, however, do not apply to events or correlations among events, but to types of interactions. Mathematically, the laws of geometric symmetry can be characterized by a single group while the dynamical laws of interaction symmetries can only be characterized by a different group for each type of interaction. Currently, we have no knowledge of the exact relationship that holds among the interaction groups or how they relate to the geometric symmetry group.

It is exactly these differences between phenomena governed by geometric laws of invariance and dynamical laws of invariance which specify the differences between phenomena instantiated in the first "mechanistic" phase of matter and the second "plasmic" phase of matter, respectively. Thus, the necessity of distinguishing the first two phases of matter follows naturally from the fact that distinct types of laws exist which are currently irreducible to a common law. The argument, however, for the necessity of postulating the third or "biotonic" phase of matter is more difficult to make than that for the first two phases of matter.

What must be shown is that the laws governing physical phenomena, instantiated in either of the first two phases of matter, are insufficient for explaining biological phenomena. In other words, it must be shown that biological laws can not even in principle be reduced to physical laws. Three major arguments have been offered:

1. Evidence is provided to demonstrate that the principles of biological evolution and reproduction cannot be adequately explained by physical law. Theorists of this persuasion point out that life is characterized by a change from a more homogeneous form of matter to a more heterogeneous form. Thus, this increase in structured complexities, or "negentropic" tendency in nature, violate the conservation laws. This means that neither the mechanistic laws of classical physics nor the quantum law are able to predict biological events (e.g. life) because, being negentropic, their probability is essentially *nil* (Elsasser, 1958; Quastler, 1953).

2. A second viewpoint respects the claim that physical laws (especially those of quantum mechanics) apply everywhere in nature and are sufficient to predict all significant events. Their failure, however, to explain the origin of life, biological evolution, or reproduction is due to the practical inability of any agent (e.g., his mortality) to execute the astronomically complex computations required of such complicated events (Shaw, 1971; von Neumann, 1966; Wigner, 1970).

3. Still another argument, and one that seems most cogent to us, argues from the circularity of the logical interaction of the three bases of reality support for any phenomenon—physical, biological or psychological. The argument goes as follows:

It is generally recognized that the quantum mechanical theory of energy propagation (i.e., energetic events) provides a necessary, if not sufficient, description of the informational bases of all knowable phenomena. Furthermore, one can argue that, in principle, the laws of biology provide a necessary description of the 'machinery' for modulating the environmental information. In this way, biological laws provide the logical interface between physical laws and psychological laws.

As argued earlier, most theorists agree that psychosomatic interactions occur, so that mental states (e.g., fear, worry, excitement, etc.) may produce changes in physiological states (e.g., perspiration, blood pressure, pilo-erection, ulceration, heart palpitation, etc.). It is even more obvious that biological manipulation of physical states is possible, (e.g., the displacement of objects by hand, reduction of oxygen to carbon dioxide, vocalic sound productions, energy storage, etc.)

These mutual interactions among the phases of matter can be illustrated diagramatically: physical phase ↔ biological phase ↔ psychological phase. But can there be a mutual interaction between the psychological and physical phases of matter, i.e., can mind affect matter? Parapsychology calls this phenomenal possibility "telekinesis." If such an interaction were in any sense possible, then the hierarchical model of scientific knowledge breaks down, and we must consider some other structure to be a more appropriate model for our epistemology than a hierarchy.

In other words, if we could show that the following schema holds for the polyphasic interactions, then the type of invariance law we need would have a different characterization than might be otherwise sought.

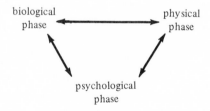

If this state of affairs actually is the case, then it would follow that:
(a) reduction of biological law to physical law is logically impossible;
(b) reduction of psychological law to biological law is also impossible;
(c) there would exist a *transitive closure* to the phases of matter; and
(d) the co-implicative relationship imputed to hold among the informational, algorithmic, and algoristic bases of phenomena, would thereby possess existential reality (i.e., be instanced by the transitive closure of the phases of matter).

Not only would the verification of these four hypotheses rule out the hierarchical ordering of natural phenomena (as claimed incidentally by Wigner and more emphatically by Simon, 1969) but it would require a new conception of the relationship of mutual interdependence of these phenomena. A term suggested by von Foerster (1962) and Shaw (1971) for the mutual interdependence of the complex interactive structures is "coalition." A *coalition* consists of polyphasic laws, a symmetry of acausal interactions among all components, and super-additivity of effects (i.e., emergent properties) to which natural laws apply nonlinearly, since they must be applied across phase boundaries.

Still further important implications would follow from the validity of the above hypotheses. Claims by epiphenomenalists that life 'emerges' from 'dead' matter, or that sentient and conscious states emerge from torporic matter would be invalidated. Rather, a Leibnizean view of mutually compatible phases of matter would be more reasonable; where physical, biotonic, and psychological phenomana would be in all ways compossible actualities of equal existential rank.

The symmetry of the relations among the different phases of existence would be an invariance law of the highest degree. Such a law would constitute a unitary law common to all sciences. Einstein once explained that he had discovered Relativity theory because he had been "so firmly convinced of the harmony of the universe" (Clark, 1971, p. 343). This is but one example of the implicit faith in symmetry, as the highest law of nature, that guides most scientists as it did Leibniz.

The role of the epistemic-who in physics. Heisenberg (1958), in characterizing the current state of physics, observed: 'The laws of nature which we formulate mathematically in quantum theory deal no longer with particles themselves but with our knowledge of the elementary particles." The laws of quantum mechanics can not be formulated in a fully consistent way without reference to what is consciously experienced by the observer. The indispensable role of conscious experience in formulating our ultimate conception of physical events can be illustrated in the following way:

It is assumed that given any event, all possible knowledge about the event can be given in its wave function. The exact form of such equations need not concern us. The mathematical language of quantum mechanics provides a means by which the probabilities that an event will be perceived to be in various possible states can be precisely determined within certain practical limitations (Bohm, 1951). For instance, if the event is a pulsing radiation field, its wave function will provide an estimate of the likelihood it will be experienced by an observer who looks in a certain direction, or that it will leave an impression on a photographic plate.

Although complete knowledge of the wave function does not always permit exact predictions of what will be experienced by an observer interacting with the system, in most cases it does permit one to predict later experiences with increased certainty. Thus, one may be sure that, if a flash is not experienced from one direction at a certain time, then one will surely experience the flash from another direction at some later time.

The important point is that the wave function is a way of predicting what will be experienced given that something else has been experienced. What is meant by the future behavior of a natural system or event is ultimately based on what has been directly experienced by a conscious observer in the immediate past. In this way the information based on the environment, described in terms of physical laws, consists of probability connections between subsequent perceptual impressions that it makes on the observer, if the observer *interacts* with it repeatedly. Thus, the result of an observation mathematically modifies the wave function of the perceived system. Wigner summarizes the argument this way:

> The modified wave function is, furthermore, in general unpredictable before the impression gained at the interaction has entered our consciousness: it is the entering of an impression into our consciousness which alters the wave function because it modifies our appraisal of the probabilities for different impressions which we expect to receive in the future. It is at this point that consciousness enters the theory unavoidably and unalterable. If one speaks in terms of the wave function, its changes are coupled with the entering of impressions into our consciousness. If one formulates the laws of quantum mechanics in terms of probabilities of impressions, these are *ipso facto* the primary concepts with which one deals [pp. 175-176].

Hence, at this point the theoretical physicist is operating *de facto* as a cognitive theorist.

The natural question to raise is whether or not the wave function describing an event is the same when a conscious observer interacts with the event as when an inanimate measuring device does. It is extremely surprising to find that, according to Wigner, the wave function describing the event is actually quite different in the two cases. One consequence of this fact is that a new postulate must be introduced into physics which says that the laws of motion of quantum mechanics become grossly nonlinear if conscious beings enter the picture.

Thus it seems proper to argue that mind affects body (in the above sense). This of course is not the dramatic interpretation usually given to the term "telekinesis" by science fiction writers, but it is a legitimate one nevertheless. This is really not so surprising a conclusion when one considers that we know of no phenomena in nature in which one component of an interaction affects another component without the second also affecting the first—although the strength of the reciprocal counter effect may be very, very small.

Recall that the mechanical effects on light are easily measured, while the measurement of the effects of light on the mechanical motions of bodies are much more difficult to make. Indeed, as Wigner points out, it is unlikely that the latter effects would have been detected at all, if theory had not first shown the necessity for their existence.

Invariably, one of the main functions of theory is to alert us to the great significance of small effects which might otherwise go unnoticed. This is amply illustrated in the fact that although Newtonian mechanics and Relativistic mechanics make essentially the same predictions with respect to gravitational attraction in weak or moderately strong fields, they differ by small but measurable amount in strong gravitational fields.

The most precise test of the difference predicted by the two theories had to do with whether or not a shift of the wavelength of light occurred as a function of gravitational attraction. The direct test of this hypothesis did not take place until nearly half a century after Einstein's original paper. Robert Oppenheimer (in Clark, 1971) wrote of the test of the proposed Einstein shift:

> The most precise and, I think, by far the most beautiful example of this is a recent experiment conducted at Harvard in which light was simply allowed to fall down from the third floor to the basement of the Physics Building. One could see how much bluer it had become; one part in 10^{14}; not very much [p. 261].

It is ironic that in science so much so often rests on such little differences between competing theories. Consequently, it is likely that definitive psychological theory will require a comparable level of precision. Thus, there is little wonder that current theoretical descriptions of psychological processes are insufficiently precise to significantly constrain the selection of neural functions that might support those processes.

There is evidence then that the phases of matter constitute a closed set, since the psychological phase may indeed interact directly with the physical phase *vis à vis* the wave function. The conclusion that the phases of matter represent a closed set of concepts is important for two reasons: First, it precludes a regress to higher and higher phases of matter, since the various phases have transitive closure, i.e., A implicates B, B implicates C, and C implicates A. Secondly, transitive closure to the phases provides additional evidence for the claim that the co-implicative relation holds among the *what, how* and *who* questions, and that this reflects the compatibility condition which must hold among the informational, algorithmic, and algoristic bases.

The Logic of Invariance Laws

The preceding section attempted to show that although the different phases of matter interact, they do so in a nonlinear fashion, i.e., in some higher order way than mere linear, causal interaction. By demonstrating their transitive closure, we at the same time invalidated certain logical argument forms that might otherwise be applied to model them.

Normally, one can argue that if A implies B, B implies C, then by transitivity, A implies C. But given that cognitive variables, instantiated at the psychological phase, must be assumed to be primitives for the physical phase, such transitive arguments no longer hold. von Neumann (1966) and McCulloch (1965) both suspected that such logical problems might emerge whenever biotonic considerations were introduced into mathematical formulations of natural law.

To see this, consider the following case: Let $(x > y)$ represent the relation "founded upon" in the sense of furnishing necessary conditions (Read: x is founded upon y). As argued earlier, it is reasonable to assume that physical laws provide the necessary bases for the information processed by organisms, and that biological laws provide the necessary bases for the algorithms computed by organisms in processing the information. This can be expressed as:

algoristic bases $>$ algorithmic bases $>$ informational bases,

and, thus, by transitivity:

algoristic bases $>$ information bases.

But by the argument for the co-implication of these bases we also have:

informational bases $>$ algoristic bases.

Transitive closure introduces a symmetry of relationships among the bases of phenomena which destroys the asymmetry required for a valid interpretation of the dominance relation. Moreover, we cannot assume that the above propositions have the logical form of the hypothetical conditional, since the co-implication relation among the bases would have to be represented as a set of biconditionals, i.e., " if x then y" and "if y then x." The biconditional form is inappropriate since it implies that the bases are formally equivalent. This is obviously an invalid interpretation of the compatibility relation among the bases of phenomena, since their natural laws are monophasic and nonlinear across phase boundaries. Laws for each phase are quite different and not generalizable given our current tenets of science. Thus, the hypothetical propositional schema is an invalid model for the invariance laws which are needed to bridge the gap between phases.

Is there another propositional form that might provide a more adequate model? Before attacking this question, let us explore in more detail the properties that such a propositional interpretation of invariance laws must possess.

One of the chief properties of invariance laws is that they must be *polyphasic*. They must capture the compatibility relations holding among the different phases which explain the nature of the symmetry of natural laws across phase boundaries. In this sense invariance laws can be said to describe all possible *interphasic* interactions. It follows that a causal interpretation is not applicable to invariance laws since all natural laws, (including causal ones if they exist), become nonlinear when so applied.

Intuitively, we recognize this when we question the simplistic causal argument that there exists an unbroken causal sequence from events in the environment to events in the central nervous system to changes in psychological states. Cornsweet (1970) cogently illustrates why such functions, what he calls "modular transfer functions," often become nonlinear. The nonlinearity of such modular transfer functions has long been recognized in psychophysics in the concepts of thresholds and adaptation levels. We deal next with the polyphasic property of psychological laws.

Invariance Laws as Mnemic Relations

Bertrand Russell in *The Analysis of Mind* (1921) suggested that there is an important difference between the traditional mechanistic interpretation of causal laws and those required for psychology. Although he did not explicitly recognize the polyphasic property of psychological laws (i.e., that they must be invariance laws), he provided a logical analysis which fits nicely with this interpretation.

Traditionally, a causal law in physics is one which expresses the results of micro-deterministic (i.e., point-by-point) interactions among physically contiguous events. Two events are said to be physically contiguous, if they have neighboring values on the space-time continuum; that is, they must be spatially and temporally adjacent. Indirect causal interactions may take place between noncontiguous events if and only if they are connected by an interpolated sequence of events which interact in a direct causal manner. Such a causal sequence can be said to form a *reduction chain* that causally links the non-contiguous events by a well-defined series of linear micro-deterministic relations.

Of course, everyone is aware of Hume's criticism that contiguity alone is not sufficient to guarantee that a causal interaction takes place between events. Similarly, we have been repeatedly admonished that a mere correlation between the changes in state of the contiguous events, even when perfect, does not logically imply that a causal relation holds. Some extralogical assumptions are needed to supplement the contiguity assumption.

Intuitively, causal relations between events must satisfy the same abstract requirements for simple and immediate conceptual dependence as do adjacent steps in an algorithm. As argued in Section I, a procedure is effective (algorithmic) when the agent, by a process of immediate rational assessment, is able to move mechanically from each antecedent step to each subsequent step without recourse to *ad hoc* inferences or guesswork.

In the physical situation, causal interactions must satisfy similar criteria to be equally effective. A sequence of interactions among a chain of contiguous events is effectively linear and mechanistically causal when, (*a*) the relation between each event is microdeterministic in the sense that no simpler relations can be interpolated between them, and (*b*) there is a direct transference of energy from one event to the next exhibited by a measurable complementary change in the state vectors of the events involved.

Unfortunately, the above situation does not provide an adequate model for explaining what transactions take place between *heterophasic* events that are not only separated in space-time, but which also involve several phases of matter. Under such circumstances single natural laws become grossly nonlinear when applied across phase boundaries. The difficulty of providing a causal interpretation for interphasic interactions is compounded by the tendency of unspecified cognitive variables to creep into the interaction. Russell termed the relation between such noncontiguous, psychologically dependent events, *mnemic.*

Mnemic relations can be shown to play a necessary role in the description of all psychological phenomena: Let A be an event which reliably evokes an experience B in some conscious organism O when presented. Consequently, we say O perceives A at time t_k whenever experience B occurs. Now let a be a distinctive element of A, such that under appropriate conditions if a is presented to O, then either experience B, or some close correlate experience B' is evoked, (i.e., where B' is in the equivalence class of B). Under such circumstances we will say that A *specifies* the event A by redintegrating the original experience of A.

The above formulation has the virtue of not favoring any particular theoretical interpretation of psychological phenomena, while, at the same time, providing a minimal description for what counts as a psychological phenomenon. Thus, it provides the following logical schema for psychological phenomena:

If $A \rightarrow B$ at t_1 and $a \rightarrow A$, then $(a \rightarrow A) \Rightarrow B$ at t_k
(or B', as the case may be).

We can now define a *mnemic relation* as that transitive relation which holds between a and B (or B'), i.e., $a \Rightarrow B$ (or B').

Traditionally, the relations $A \rightarrow B$ has been given a mechanistic causal interpretation on the grounds that A and B are events linked by a reduction chain of biological events, while the relation $a \rightarrow A$ was said to be an associative relation and was treated in the usual behavioristic way. However, given the possibility that cognitive variables may ultimately be needed to provide precise physical description of events (e.g., A or a), the $A \rightarrow B$ relation can hardly be said to be mechanistically causal.

The claim that $A \rightarrow B$ is causal in the classical mechanical sense also ignores the fact that such relations defined over physical, biological, and psychological events are interphasic. This means that the function mapping A onto B is nonlinear and that any law explaining how this mapping occurs must be polyphasic. It follows, of course, that such explanatory laws for psychological phenomena must be invariance laws rather than natural laws (in the sense defined earlier).

Similarly, the relation $a \rightarrow A$ can not be adequately explained in terms of associative laws, since cognitive variables also enter irreducibly into the precise physical description of the events to be associated. This follows directly from the fact that a and A are contiguous physical events whose wave functions, when observed by a conscious agent, necessarily interact to produce a nonlinear mixture (Wigner, 1970). Hence relations $A \rightarrow B$ and $a \rightarrow A$ like $a \Rightarrow B$ are mnemic rather than mechanistically causal (i.e., linearly micro-deterministic). We will call such polyphasic interactions *macro*-deterministic instead of micro-deterministic for these reasons.

Hence, since psychological phenomena always involve menmic relations, they cannot be explained by mechanistic causal law. Rather they must be explained by invariance laws, since such laws are needed to coordinate macro-deterministic interactions that take place across phase boundaries. Luckily, there already exists laws for macro-deterministic interactions in science. By studying the form of such laws we might discover exemplars for psychological laws.

Boltzmann's law. Strict micro-deterministic laws demand that the degree to which each element of a complex structure contributes to the interaction with another complex structure be precisely specifiable (in principle). We have already seen how this is not possible in quantum physics when cognitive states are involved, nor when attempts are made to apply quantum laws to biological phenomena (e.g., biological reproduction), nor to psychological phenomena which are mnemic. One begins to wonder whether there are any nontrivial interactions to which micro-deterministic laws apply.

Weiss (1969) has argued that nearly all significant biological interactions fail to yield to micro-deterministic analysis. He suggests that this is due to the fact that Boltzmann's law applies equally well to biology as to thermodynamics, celestial mechanics, statistical mechanics, information theory, and quantum mechanics (and now we might add psychology to the list).

The significance of Boltzmann's law is best explained by means of a simile: In an economy not everyone can be the most wealthy. Only a few people can be most wealthy. Either everyone has the same amount of money, and in that sense nobody is wealthy, or some people must have more money than others, Now assume that money is continuously changing hands. To apply the simile to Boltzmann's law simply interchange the words "energy" for "wealth," "particle" for "person," and "population" for "economy": In a population not every particle can have the most energy. Only a few particles can be most energetic. Either every particle has the same amount of energy, and in that sense there is entropy, or some particles must have more energy than others. Now assume that the energy states of the particles are continuously changing.

This bears on the possibility of micro-deterministic analysis as follows: When two complex populations come into proximity, any interaction that transacts energy is going to be primarily due to very few particles at any given moment. This is due to the fact that only a small percentage have sufficient energy to break away from the others. At some later moment, after the initial interactions, the previous small subset of particles will have dissipated their energy, and a new subset must take over if the interaction is to continue.

Therefore, at any given moment the probability that a particular sample of particles, small enough to be analyzed, contains all those particles responsible for the interaction is very, very small. Since it is not practically possible to track the individual particles over time and change of position (to determine their individual contribution to the overall interaction, micro-deterministic analysis is not scientifically feasible.

Weiss argues that for similar reasons, although you may have a transaction going on between large cell populations in biology (what he calls a "macro-deterministic interaction"), micro-deterministic analysis is practically impossible. This is due to the fact that the cell by cell communication lines seem to be coaxial, with considerable time-sharing of the same neural fibers and chemical messengers by a large number of noncontiguous cell assemblies. In this respect, biotonic law proves to be nonlinear also. Thus, biotonic law, like psychological law, is not reducible to physical law nor is it modelled by strictly linear causal law.

For all the above reasons, there is ample support for the claim that phenomena of different phases may interact at a macro-deterministic level but not at micro-deterministic one. The laws governing interactions among various phases of matter seem invariably to assume a mnemic form which is manifested in their nonlinearity when applied across phase boundaries.

The question remains, however, whether there actually exists an invariance structure to the natural laws applying to the different phases of matter, so that macro-deterministic, interphasic interactions might be explained. If we could determine the propositional form of these laws, we would have taken an important step toward that goal. This is our last question before considering the applicability of invariance laws to psychology in Section III.

The adjunctive logic of invariance laws. Whatever the laws of psychology, they must explain mnemic relations, since causal relations cannot be said to hold. Such laws must also explain the macro-determinism that apparently holds across the different components of polyphasic phenomena.

If the distinct natural laws peculiar to each phase of matter were incompatible and totally asymmetric, psychology as a science would not be possible, since it deals essentially with polyphasic phenomena. Consequently, the laws of physics would remain unelucidated because cognitive variables would not be well-defined in the wave function equations.

For such reasons, study of the logical structure of scientific theories which invoke invariance laws, or symmetry postulates, is worthwhile. For this study to be successful, however, the relationship between natural and invariance laws must be clarified. We must also consider how invariance laws can be given empirical support.

Finally, if causal interactions do not hold, then we must show how macro-deterministic ones can explain mnemic relations.

The Stoic philosophers distinguished several kinds of logical propositions, among them the *hypothetical, causal,* and *adjunctive.* The hypothetical or conditional proposition take the form, "*If x,* then *y.*" This can be constrasted with the causal proposition, "*Because* x, then *y,"* and the adjunctive proposition, "*Since x,* then *y.*"

The hypothetical proposition is invalid whenever the premise is true and the conclusion is false, and valid otherwise. It can be said to be conditionally true or *correct,* if the opposite of its conclusion contradicts its premise (i.e., by *modus tollens*). However, the opposite of the conclusion (e.g., not *y*) is not necessarily inconsistent with the premise (e.g., *x*). For instance, "If this is Monday, I go to work." However, I may not go to work because it is Labor Day. This does not, of course, imply that it is not Monday. To argue so is to commit the fallacy of affirming the consequent.

Hypothetical propositions make a poor model for natural laws, since there are too many ways in which they can be invalid. They also fail to provide a necessary relationship between premises and conclusions. The reason why these limitations make the hypothetical proposition an inappropriate model for either natural laws or invariance laws becomes apparent as soon as one attempts to fit these laws to this propositional schema.

Let the initial and auxilliary conditions that define the domain of application of the natural law correspond to the premise of the proposition. The valid outcome predicted by the natural law will then correspond to the consequent of the proposition. A principle is considered to be a natural law (*a*) if the denial of its prediction or consequent is necessarily inconsistent with the premises and (*b*) when its premise can be shown to be true (i.e., when its initial and auxilliary conditions can be shown to be satisfied). This is to say, a natural law is a principle that predicts true outcomes whenever it can be shown to validly apply.

It clearly violates what we mean by a natural law to say the law validly applies but does not predict the outcome. In such a case, either we would not accept the principle in its stated form as being a valid law, or else we would deny that the conditions for its application had actually been satisfied.

This is not the case for hypothetical propositions: Where a law cannot be validly applied to any situation where its premises are not true, a hypothetical proposition is valid by definition even when its premises are false. Attempts to interpret laws as hypothetical propositions have also led to paradoxes in what we all accept to be the function of scientific theory but which cannot be formally shown to be the case.

Popper (1959) and others have shown that neither natural laws nor theories are logically verified, when stated in hypothetico-deductive form, simply because their predictions are confirmed. Affirming the consequent of a hypothetical proposition does not affirm the premise: Hence, if law *x* predicts outcome *y,* given that *y* is true does not imply that *x* is true.

Unfortunately, Popper's attempt to find an alternative way to evaluate scientific laws and theories does not work either. Popper argues that even though we cannot verify laws or theories directly, we can evaluate them by attempting to falsify them, that is, by showing that their predictions do not hold. The falsifiability procedure is based on the valid argument schema known since antiquity as the *modus tollens:* If law x, then outcome y, but not y, therefore, not x.

It has been argued (Lakatos, 1970), however, that falsifiability is never achieved in practice, since the premises for a law or theory are such a complex of variables that it is not possible to determine which one has been falsified. This allows the theorist to choose at his discretion whether a major or a minor assumption of his theory is at fault. Given this choice, we would not reject the core of the theory or law that had been so arduously developed.

When Einstein was told that Eddington's measurement of light bending around the eclipsed sun agreed with the predictions of his theory, he replied: "But I knew that the theory is correct." When asked what if there had been no confirmation of his prediction, he candidly countered: "Then I would have been sorry for the dear Lord—the theory *is* correct [Clark, 1971, p. 369]." Theories, like laws, seem logically inaccessible. It is not, however, the case that logic makes no difference in theory evaluation (and a law is, of course, just an accepted consequence of a theory), but that logic makes *so little* difference. The fruitfulness of a theory in explaining anomalies and bringing general consistency into science are more important than either logical verification or falsification. In other words, the degree to which a new law applies symmetrically across a wide domain of natural phenomena and relates other laws is the highest criterion of its worth. It is also a realistic measure of the resistence scientists will show in abdicating it.

What other logical forms than the hypothetical proposition might be better for representing these facts about theory evaluation? Let us consider the Stoics' conception of causal propositions.

A causal proposition begins with a true premise and ends with a necessary consequence, e.g., "Because it is day, it is light." This way is more appropriate to expressing the form of laws, since the hypothetical form is still valid if its premises are assumed false. For instance consider the following hypothetical: "If it is night, it is light"; given "It is night," then it follows that "It is light"—a valid logical argument but scientifically false.

It is not possible, however, to perform such a trick on our scientific intuition with causal propositions. A causal proposition is incorrect (by definition) if it begins with a false premise or ends with a conclusion which does not follow from it. Thus, unlike hypothetical forms, the causal interpretation demands that the premise and conclusion correspond.

Although the schema for natural laws seems to be satisfied by causal propositions, the intuitive notion of causal relation cannot be effectively captured in formal statements. Moreover, as argued earlier, invariance laws which character- ize the symmetry relations existing among natural laws do not seem to fit the schema for causal propositions.

The mutual compatibility of the various phases of matter, which permits some kind of macro-determinism to hold among their distinct phenomena, does not permit (nor does it require) the micro-deterministic relations necessary to the concept of causal interaction. The adjunctive propositional form offered by the Stoics, although essentially ignored by history, seems more promising.

An adjunctive proposition begins with a true premise and ends with a necessary consequence; e.g., "Since it is day, then the sun is shining." This proposition is incorrect when it either begins with a false premise or ends with a consequence which need not follow. The adjunctive proposition professes both that the second member follows from the first and that the first member is true. It is this propositional schema which, we believe, best fits the sense of both mnemic and macro-deterministic relations expressed by natural laws, as well as by invariance laws.

If we analyze the adjunctive proposition, "Since x then y," in terms of truthtables, it is the case that in order for the adjunctive relation to hold both x and y must be true. The adjunctive relation is false otherwise. Now this looks suspiciously like the truth functional definition of a conjunctive relation (e.g., x and y). It differs, however, in one important way: Where conjunctive relations are commutative (i.e., "x and y" is equivalent to "y and x"), adjunctive relations are not; hence "Since x, then y" does not imply "Since y, then x."

The adjunctive formulation also seems to capture the sense that laws of nature apply in an inexorable manner to grind out reality. This is expressed simply as the adjunctive proposition that "Since the law applies, the observed outcome *must* follow (necessarily)." If the outcome does not follow invariantly upon correct application of the law, we have grounds for falsifying the whole proposition, since in an adjunctive proposition the truth of the conclusion follows necessarily from the truth of the premises. Thus, in this special sense, the falsifiability criterion is preserved.

The verification criterion, however, does not hold for adjunctive propositions at the level of natural law. The observation (y) that some event (x) occurs as predicted by physical laws x does not verify that x is a law.

Thus, given y, it is fallacious to affirm x. Although natural laws apply to predict outcomes, no number of observed outcomes can be used logically to verify the law. This fact is expressed in the noncommutativity of the adjunctive propositional form of the natural law [i.e., $(x{>}y) \not\equiv (y \cdot (y \rightarrow x))$].

One might even question the utility of the verification procedure, since natural laws are postulated on more general grounds than observations. The major grounds for accepting or rejecting principles as natural laws is whether or not they fit into the invariance structure of a science and clear up anomalies and relate other principles.

The accuracy with which natural laws predict effects is not so important as the degree to which they contribute to the coherence of explanations for natural phenomena. Since one might predict what one does not understand, prediction alone is an insufficient criterion of the explanatory worth of either theories, hypotheses, or laws. Scientific theories or natural laws which help simplify a field will never be abdicated solely on the grounds that they are not predictive. Indeed, they should not be, since the conditional logic of verification does not apply.

At the higher level of invariance law, however, the postulated symmetry of interaction among the phases of matter lends a special validity to the verificationist's argument that cannot be found at the level of events and natural laws. In a sense the successful application of laws to phenomena in one phase implies the existence of similar laws that apply to correlated phenomena in other phases.

Due to the symmetry relation that must hold among phenomena in various phases (if they are to be compatible), it follows that there must exist some degree of reciprocity between the laws of observation which hold in the psychological phase and the laws of physics. Hence, perception of an event is due to psychological laws which must have some invariant relationship with the physical laws that determine the event. This invariance law can be expressed adjunctively as $X \diamond Y$ where X stands for the laws of physics and Y for those of psychology. The invariance relation "$\diamond$" can be defined as: $(X \diamond Y) \equiv [(X > Y) . (Y > X)]$. In words, the laws of physics adjunctively imply the laws of psychology and vice-versa. Of course, the other phases of matter can be included in a similar fashion. But let us see if adjunctive logic is sufficiently powerful to express some of the conclusions argued for earlier regarding the interpenetration of psychological variables into the description of physical events.

By the definition of natural law we have $X > x$, where x is the physical event or set of events predicted by X, as well as $Y > y$, where y is the experience of observing x. We can now prove the following: Given $X \diamond Y$, $X > x$, and $Y > y$, we derive $X \cdot (X \rightarrow Y)$ from the definition of the invariance law and $Y \cdot (Y \rightarrow y)$ from the definition of natural law. By simplification we have $X > Y$ and $Y \rightarrow y$. Then by transitivity we derive $x \rightarrow y$. Since X is given, by conjunction we have $X \cdot (X \rightarrow y)$ and by the definition of the adjunctive we finally derive $X > y$. By a similar line of proof we can also derive $Y > x$.

In words, we can prove that since the laws of physics are what they are, the perceptual experience y is what it is. This is in agreement with the view that the laws of physics determine the informational bases for perception. Indeed, we would be disturbed if adjunctive logic could not express this assumption. More importantly, however, we have also demonstrated that the laws of psychology enter into the determination of physical events, that is, $Y > x$. This is a nontrivial conclusion which generalizes the earlier claim by Wigner that pyschological laws determine the nature of the algoristic bases of physical events. This is exactly the conclusion one expects to be the case if the adjunctive analysis of the invariance law of physics and psychology is valid.

The final conclusion which needs to be expressed adjunctively is $x \diamond y$. This expression asserts that a mnemic relation holds between a physical event and the perceptual experience of it. As argued earlier, a mnemic relation is symmetrical and captures what is meant by a macro-deterministic interaction existing between a physical event and its psychological correlate. Consequently, it follows directly from the definition of the invariance relation presumed to hold whenever there is a veridical perception of a physical event, that $x > y$ and $y > x$.

The adequacy of the adjunctive analysis of macro-deterministic interactions is further supported by the fact that, given $X > x$ and $Y > y$, as well as $x > y$ and $y > x$, we can again derive transitively the earlier conclusions, $X > y$ and $Y > x$. This completes the adjunctive analysis of natural and invariance laws. Moreover, we have shown what we set out to do in this section (as outlined on p.325).

In Section III, we provide some concrete illustrations of how symmetry postulates allow us to derive specific invariance laws in psychology.

III. INVARIANCE LAWS FOR PSYCHOLOGY

Our primary goal in Section III is to provide a tentative theory of cognition based on invariance laws which relate the three bases of support. Such a theory must explain polyphasic phenomena that arise primarily from the interaction of psychological laws with physical and biological laws.

More specifically, a theory of cognition should explain the nature of information by which events are known, what is contributed individually by physical, biological and psychological factors (i.e., how the algorist interacts with the information made available by the environment), and, finally, it should describe the mechanism by which cognitive capacities are acquired. Unfortunately, such a large order is beyond our scope. We will, however, sketch the framework we feel such a theory must ultimately fill.

Cognitive Symmetry: The Fundamental Invariance Law for Psychology

A theory of cognitive functions should explain the invariant relationship which must exist between what an agent truly knows and what can be known. Ultimately, this would be nothing less than a theory of the exact algorithmic relationship that must exist between the informational bases of events and the algoristic bases of the knowing agent. It must explain how organisms select and process the information made available by environmental events to satisfy intentions necessary to the achievement of adaptive goals.

A precise theory will provide mathematical characterization of those cognitive functions which map informational structures onto decision states of the agent. Before the proper mathematical formulations of the algorithmic bases can be discovered, the cognitive principles governing the knowledge transaction must be made intuitively clear.

Eventually, due to the polyphasic nature of psychological phenomena, even the biological processes which support these cognitive functions must also be rigorously defined. We concur, however, in the popular belief that a solution to the physical and psychological problem will greatly enhance the possibility of solving the biological one, since a precise "job" description is likely to provide an important source of constraint for selecting among competing biological models.

The fundamental problem of cognitive theory. The basic problem of cognitive psychology can be expressed schematically in terms of the adjunctive analysis of invariance laws proposed earlier: Let ϕ refer to the physical states of sources of information in the environment and ψ to those cognitive states resulting from the processing of that information. The expression $(\phi \diamondsuit \psi) = [(\phi > \psi) \cdot (\psi > \phi)]$ denotes the adjunctive relationships that must be preserved by the biopsychological processes if the organism's knowledge of its world is to be sufficiently true to be adaptive. Recall that since these are mnemic relations, no micro-deterministic interaction can hold between the variables designated.

A theoretical explanation of the left side of the adjunctive expression, $(\phi > \psi)$, would answer the question of how the information determined by the environment macro-deterministically interacts with the psychological states of the organism. Conversely, a theoretical explanation of the right side ($\Psi \gtrless \Phi$), would answer the question of how psychological processes macro-deterministically interact with informational states (e.g., events) of the environment. The expression $\Phi \diamondsuit \Psi$ signifies that this reciprocal interaction is symmetrical, such that some invariant relations (properties) in Φ are preserved in Ψ and *vice-versa*.

Consequently, the expression $\phi > \psi$, (i.e., since the structure of the environment is what it is, then psychological experiences are what they are), is an elegant statement of the problem of how organisms perceive their worlds. With respect to this issue, we side with J. J. Gibson (1966), who should be given credit for emphasizing the importance of the invariance concept for perceptual theory.

Gibson argues that perception is logically a *direct* process by which invariants of energy distributions (i.e., physical information) are detected by organisms. The hypothesis that perception is direct means that no other psychological processes mediate the detection of information. Neither memory, inference, nor images play a necessary role in the pick-up of information which invariantly specifies an event, although these secondary processes may all be accompaniments or byproducts of the perceptual process. Since this is admittedly a radical hypothesis, we will return later to defend it.

The expression $\Psi \gtrless \Phi$, (i.e., since psychological processes are what they are, then the nature of information is what it is), is essentially an elegant statement of the problem of how psychological states interact with physical events to determine new states of information beyond those determined by physical factors alone. It addresses the issue of what informational aspects of energy distributions exist because organisms perceptually interact with their world.

Although we also view this interactive process as being direct and in no sense psychologically mediated, we feel it has received less emphasis than it deserves by Gibson and his students. This view is not, however, inconsistent with Gibson's fundamental theory. Indeed, it is implicit in his theory of the ecological foundations of perception.

To recapitulate, two main concepts must be explained by any cognitive theory: first, the nature of invariant physical information that is intrinsic to energy distributions that need only be directly modulated by the organism; and, secondly, the nature of invariant psychological information that is a direct product of the biological processes which modulate physical information.

This formulation of the problem of cognitive theory allows two different interpretations of the concept of psychological information. The most obvious interpretation is that perceptual systems differentiate physical information in the course of modulating it. For instance, it is known that the lens and macula region of the human eye are slightly yellow in color. This has the effect of filtering out those wavelengths toward the blue end of the spectrum that contribute most to chromatic aberration. Similarly, the shift from rods to ones in bright light displaces vision toward red wavelengths that cause less trouble (Wald, 1950).

Still more dramatic is the ability of the perceptual systems to track, focus, and attend to subtle aspects of physical information while ignoring others. In spite of the ambient flux of multiply reflected light in a well-lighted environment even a single eye is able to detect the optical invariants for edges of objects, and texture, size, shape, and brightness gradients which yield the precise layout of complex environments. Different voices and other distinct sounds can be readily identified in spite of their being nested simultaneously within complex ambient noise, say as experienced in the hub-bub of traffic or a cocktail party.

The psychological enhancement of specific dimensions of physical information is a "negentropic" process, since attentional processes objectify partitions of complex energy fields that often exceed mere intensity level differences (e.g., by pick-up of phase differences). The main function of the perceptual systems seems to be not only the discovery of objective "seams" in energy distribution, but the insertion of them when it is ecologically adaptive to do so.

Thus, a second interpretation of the expression $\Psi \succ \Phi$ is this apparent ability of the cognitive system to exceed mere differentiation of given structural contours of ambient energy, as specified by what we have called physical information. Although this ability of the cognitive systems to "broadcast" structure is admittedly problematic and surely requires more precise empirical evidence than yet exists, it is nevertheless predicted by the symmetrical form of the invariance law. If such a claim can be experimentally validated, then Wigner's (1970) observation that natural laws are often conjectured on the grounds that they are needed to fulfill the symmetrical structure of invariance laws would again be supported.

The above adjunctive statement of the invariance law holding between psychology, biology, and physics, specifies the complete content of the field of cognitive psychology and demarcates it from other sciences.

Adaptation as the dynamic expression of symmetry. How might invariants of energy distributions be detected by organisms? How might adaptive states of organisms be conditioned by informational invariants? There is considerable evidence that energetic systems have a natural tendency to reorganize their states to symmetrically balance those forces tending to disturb their equilibrium. Mach (1902) observed, "In every symmetrical system every deformation that tends to destroy the symmetry is complemented by an equal and opposite deformation that tends to restore it.

One might generalize this symmetry postulate from single systems to interacting systems in the following way: What is meant by *equilibration* of one system to another is that a symmetry exists between the energy states of the two systems such that a change in the state configuration of one system invariantly induces a corresponding change in the other. We would like to generalize this symmetry postulate still further to incorporate the symmetry of states that might be induced across phase boundaries (i.e., by the invariance laws) to account for macro-deterministic interactions.

The basic postulate of cognitive theory envisioned here must accord with the adjunctive analysis of the proposed invariance law, $\phi \diamond \psi$, given above. Here is a tentative statement of the required symmetry postulate: *An organism achieves the highest degree of equilibration with its environment (i.e., has ecologically relevant knowledge of it), when there exists a persistent symmetry between its psychological states and the informational states of the environment.* This postulate is called *the principle of cognitive symmetry* (for a detailed discussion of this principle see Shaw, McIntyre, & Mace, 1973).

Whenever, in the ensuing discussion, we invoke this principle, it should serve as a reminder of all conditions governing the applicability of invariance laws to psychology argued for earlier (e.g. macro-determinism, mnemic relations, and adjunctive analysis). There are many reasons why little progress has been made toward the study of the invariance laws of psychology.

Problems of the ecological approach to psychology. There are two essential aspects to an ecological approach: First, the effects of the environment on the organism must be determined, and secondly, the effects of the organism on the environment must be determined. An ecological approach to psychology emphasizes the effects of physical information, made available by the environment, on the cognitive states of the organism, and the reciprocal effect of these states, *vis à vis* the modulatory activities, on that information. Hence an ecological approach to cognitive psychology could naturally be founded upon the principle of cognitive symmetry.

The further assumption that the perceptual mode is a direct pick-up of invariant information poses several problems. Invariant information consists of structural relations in energy distribution which remain the same although other structural relations may undergo change. That organisms can come to know their worlds by means of perceived invariants, and thereby interact adaptively with it, requires the validity of two assumptions: First, the ecologically significant properties of the environment must determine invariant physical information. This is properly a problem of physics. However, since there is at present no well demarcated macrolevel, ecological physics, the solution to this problem falls by default to the cognitive psychologist. Lack of training in fundamental techniques of physics perhaps explains to some extent the lack of interest shown by most psychologists in pursuing an ecological approach.

A second assumption that must be justified is that given the first assumption, the invariants of perceived information must be shown to logically specify the ecologically relevant environmental sources of that information. This is essentially a problem for ecologically applied mathematics, a field not yet developed. Some examples, however, of what such applied mathematical techniques may look like can be found in Gibson, Olum, and Rosenblatt (1948), where optical expansion patterns and motion perspectives are analyzed; in Purdy (1958), where a mathematical theory of planar texture gradients is given; and in Hay (1966), where rotations and translations of rigid objects are studied.

Thus what the complete application of the ecological approach to psychology requires is considerable sophistication in mathematics, physics, and psychology, a combination of interests not often found in those qualified to undertake the approach, and a combination of qualifications not often found in those interested in doing so.

There is, of course, much ground work on the problem to be laid by experimental psychologists. The study of the first half of the invariance law, $\Phi \gtrless \Psi$, must be accomplished before a serious study can begin on the second half, $\Psi \gtrless \Phi$, which is more central to the task of cognitive psychology. In the next section we sketch some of the problems that need to be investigated.

The Discovery of Physical and Psychological Invariants

Let us assume that a quantum mechanical description can in principle be provided for all significant aspects of the environment. As argued earlier, although such a description may provide a necessary basis to information, it will not provide one sufficient to account for the psychological experience of such information. That is, it might establish the basis for $\phi > \psi$ but it would not adequately characterize what is meant by $\psi > \phi$.

It is very important, however, that as much be explained in terms of physical law as possible, to lessen the task of psychological explanation. Thus we need to assay the extent of applicability of physical law to delimit the proper domain of psychological law. A systematic survey of the various types of information invariants will aid the attainment of this goal.

Types of invariants. Four types of invariant information seem evident: *global* and *local physical* invariants, as well as *global* and *local psychological* invariants. Although these invariants should be rigorously defined, for the purposes of this chapter they can be comprehended best by illustration.

The physical invariants are objective in that they do not depend on algoristic bases and exist in spite of the sentient properties of organisms. Global physical invariants specify properties of the environment that are *coordinate-free*, in that they are conveyed by information which is available everywhere, at all times, independently of organisms. Examples of ecologically significant environmental properties of this type are the terrestrial horizon, the direction and strength of gravitational attraction, the range of terrestrial temperatures, the texture gradient of the ground plane, the refractive index of air, the perspective information from objects distributed over the ground plane, the course of the sun that determines the day-night schedule, as well as the changing patterns of shading and shadows. Since these properties of the environment are ubiquitous and perpetual, they do not depend on the point of view of the organism.

By contrast, local physical invariants are only conveyed by information that is specified for a particular point of view of an organism. Where the above properties are globally available throughout the terrestrial environment, and constitute permanent relations between organisms and their world, local physical invariants are determined by temporary relationships an organism may have with his environment. Examples of these are fixed-point properties and kinetic invariants of flow fields determined by an organism's locomotion through his world, or by objects in the world moving relative to the organism.

Whereas global invariants specify properties by which organisms orient to their world, local invariants specify properties by which they might orient to objects in the world. While global properties are coordinate-free, and structurally defined properties, local ones are coordinate-dependent and functionally defined. This difference can best be appreciated by considering in detail ecologically significant examples of each type of physical invariant for humans.

Globally Invariant Physical Information

The orientation systems of higher animals depend upon information which specifies the terrestrial horizon, the direction of gravity, and the slant of the ground plane. Due to the perpetual and ubiquitous nature of the perceptual universals and their significance for orientation, it is likely that species evolved a selective attunement to them. The genetic pre-attunement of organisms to global invariants would render unnecessary learning to perceive them. Presumably, pre-attunement can be due to the evolution of specialized sensory organs or to the natural propensity to be functionally adept at detecting their existence.

The horizon as a global invariant. In humans, as well as most animals, the vestibular sense is operative at birth and responds efficiently to changes in body posture from the upright postion. Thus, direct perception of the direction and strength of gravity provides one of the three axes required for a perceptual reference system, say the y axis. Direct perception of the horizon and the extent and slant of the ground plane would provide the other two orthogonal axes needed to complete the system, say the x axis and z axis, respectively.

Although it is not known whether there is any anatomical specialization in the visual system of humans or most animals which might account for the direct pick-up of the optical invariants specifying the horizon or the texture gradient of the ground plane, there is abundant evidence that the ability to do so emerges in great strength at very early ages (Gibson & Walk, 1960). The functional development of the spatial reference system in children has been studied extensively by Piaget and Inhelder (1956) and Piaget, Inhelder, and Szeminska (1960). The chief evidence for the functional specialization of the human perceptual system with respect to each axis of spatial orientation comes from experiments demonstrating the child's differential ability to discriminate and use them at various stages of development (Pufall & Shaw, 1973).

It is interesting to note, however, the existence of the so-called "visual stripe" in the pidgeon: A set of cells on its retinae appear to be especially senstive to horizontal lines. It is quite conceivable that this specialized structure evolved to facilitate the bird's orientation to the horizon while in flight. That this is a reasonably effective way to achieve level flight patterns is indicated by the fact that few airplanes today are built without an instrument which shows the orientation of the wings to the horizon.

The horizon also provides a globally invariant reference axis by which to judge the relative height of objects distributed over the ground plane at various distances from the stationary observer. The angular distance from the top of objects of equal height to the horizon divides the angular length of the object into an invariant proportion. By simple trignometric calculations it is possible to show that this invariant relationship provides a precise perceptual yardstick by which to judge directly the relative sizes of objects, even those with which the observer has no previous experience. In other words, neither familiarity, memory, nor intellectual inference is required to mediate the direct perception of relative size. This is a fact well-known to artists (see for instance the discussion of perspective by Paul Klee, 1953).

Although the mathematical formulation of other global invariants may not be so obvious, there is every reason to believe equal rigor is obtainable. Consider another less obvious global invariant of physical information: We see the shapes of stationary objects (e.g., trees and rocks) and protuberants and concavities of the ground plane (e.g., hills and dales) by means of light contrasts. If the light reflected from them were homogeneous (i.e., a Ganzfeld), then the layout of the environment would be optically unspecified.

Light contrasts originate because sunlight is differentially reflected by surfaces as a function of their orientation, as governed by the law of reflection and the nature of their material composition (i.e., their matte or specular quality). In spite of the variability of sunlight due to change in weather conditions, the same light contrast relations are defined over the relatively permanent surfaces of the environment.

One global optical invariant which exists is the relationship between highlights (regions of greatest reflectance) and accents (regions of deepest shading). For instance, if a coin is illuminated, the crescent shaped highlights on the side nearest the sun will always be balanced by an inverted crescent shaped accent. Thus, it will always be the case that the shape of regular objects will be optically specified by an invariant relationship between highlights and accents — what mathematicians call an enantiomorphic symmetry (i.e., a bilateral symmetry between structures of opposite contrast value).

If this enantiomorphic symmetry is truly a global physical invariant (as argued earlier with respect to the horizon), the principle of cognitive symmetry predicts that the visual system might be genetically pre-attuned to directly perceive it. There is evidence that this is so.

A picture of an object drawn by using only accents usually appears to be more than a mere jumble of disconnected black lines. Instead, the observer often sees the complete object. More importantly, he will report seeing highlights symmetrically opposed to the accents, that complete the contour, even though they are not actually in the drawing. Highly embossed lettering on a white matte surface, strongly illuminated from one side in such a way that only accents are visible, will nevertheless be easily readable. Many introductory psychological textbooks use illustrations of this type to demonstrate how familiar figures might be intellectually completed. However, if the above hypothesis is correct, direct perception of the contrast symmetry due to genetic pre-attunement of the visual system is a more viable explanation than the mediation hypothesis.

Our summary hypothesis can be stated adjunctively as follows: *Since global physical invariants are invariant over the terrestrial portion of the space-time continuum, the orientation system of organisms must be genetically pre-attuned to directly perceive them.* We now turn to a corollary of the principle of cognitive symmetry to explain the role of experience.

Locally Invariant Physical Information

If direct perception of globally invariant physical information is due to the evolutionary attunement of the biological systems supporting cognitive processes, then, by contrast, direct perception of local invariants is due to attunement of the modulatory states of those biological systems by the experience of the organism with its world. According to the principle of cognitive symmetry this attumement arises from the symmetrical rearrangement of states of the biological system with respect to the invariant structure of the events perceived.

Presumably, the attunement is accomplished through what Gibson has called the "education of attention"; that is, organisms learn to differentiate physical information such that the invariants specifying various classes of events are preserved. Such a process can be thought of as an efferent analogy to the afferent synthesis of neuro-motor synergisms, say as required to account for the smooth intergration of complex motor acts involved in learning to speak, to play the piano, to dance, or drive a car (Lenneberg, 1967). (For a detailed development of this view applied to cognition see Jenkins, Jiménez-Pabón, Shaw, and Sefer, 1974.)

Local invariants for motions and movements. Examples of local physical invariants are plentiful. A simple one explains how organisms coordinate their actions with respect to objects in the environment. The principle of cognitive symmetry requires that an organism's attunement to these less permanent aspects of its environment be achieved through modulatory activities. The recognition of an event (up to determination of class equivalence) is achieved by the induction of a unique modulatory state configuration which is invariant with the informational invariants determined by the event and which specify the event. To be explained, of course, is the process by which the symmetrical modulatory state configuration is induced by the informational invariants of the event. However, let us first consider some detailed examples of local invariants of physical information.

A textured object that looms toward a stationary observer determines optical information specifying both its shape and its approach velocity (i.e., speed and direction). If the object is on a collision course with the observer, a symmetrically expanding radial flow field will be kinetically defined over its texture. The shape of the object will be specified projectively by the invariant termini of the lines of flow (e.g., its contour). The speed of approach will be specified by the rate of texture flow along these radial lines, as well as by the apparent increase in projected perimeter size. The direction of travel of the object will be specified by the relatively invariant center of the flow pattern defined by the intersection of the radial flow lines. This center of the flow field is mathematically termed a *fixed-point property*. So long as this property exists in the flow field, all velocities of texture units along the radial lines of flow will be equal, and the shape of the perimeter contour will only alter ever so slightly (i.e., since on-line projections of three-dimensional objects at different distances are not strictly speaking simply similarity transformations or magnifications).

On the other hand, if the center of the expanding radial flow pattern is not a fixed-point property, then the velocities of individual lines of texture flow will not be equal. The asymmetrical pattern of flow defines the direction of travel of the object relative to the point of observation. Thus, if the center of the flow translates laterally, say to the observer's right, then the object will pass by the observer on his right. On the other hand, if it has an upward translation, this specifies that the trajectory of the object will pass overhead.

The important point to note is that fixed-point properties of flow fields are, mathematically speaking, the simplest possible invariants. But they only exist for observers situated at the proper relative point of observation (i.e., on a line defined by the flight path of the object). For this reason they are called local perspectival invariants.

Notice that the intentions of the observer determine whether he wants to maximize or minimize the lateral velocity component of the center of the object's flow field. If the object is a missle to be dodged, he will want to move in such a way as to maximize the lateral velocity vector. On the other hand, if he is a baseball player and wishes to catch the missle, he will want to minimize the lateral flow vector with respect to the position of his glove. In such cases consideration of the intentions of the epistemic-who are logically prior to the informational or algorithmic analyses.

Note also that for a locomoting organism wishing to steer toward or away from objects in the environment, the same analysis holds with but minor modifications. Similarly, it can be shown that the perspective invariants determined in the light from a rotating object, sufficient to specify its shape for a static observer, are also available in the light picked up by an observer who orbits around a static object. Thus, there is a symmetry of information for the shape of an object between what can be picked up by a static observer and what can be picked up by a moving observer.

All relative displacements between observers and objects or locales in the environment can be composed from a combination of rotations and translations (i.e., the set of displacements is closed). The symmetry relationship between observers and parts of the environment means that, in principle, for every displacement of objects in the environment, a complementary displacement can be carried out by the observer (i.e., all displacements have inverses).

This means that the possible locomotions of an observer relative to the environment are a mathematical group, just as the possible displacements of objects are a group. These groups are symmetrical or isomorphic groups. Each is a *dual* representation of what might be called the *modulatory group*. Moreover, the possible complementary motions of objects and observers means that each group contains abstractly equivalent inverses of the operations performable in the companion group. In other words, the group of motions, like the group of movements, are concrete instances of the abstract modulatory group. What are the perceptual consequences of the abstract symmetry of these two groups?

The most subtle aspect of the group theory analysis of cognitive activities is that symmetry groups, such as these dual representations of the modulatory group, are but special applications of the principle of cognitive symmetry to a restricted domain of phenomena. In this case, the domain is the perception of local physical invariants. Furthermore, if the principle of cognitive symmetry is a necessary postulate, violation of it should have empirical consequences. Thus if the group symmetry relation between the algoristic bases and the informational basis is destroyed, successful cognition of the world should be disrupted. Evidence that this is the case exists.

When the perspective information specifying the shape of an object is modified to violate the necessary symmetry relationship between an observer and the object, the object no longer can be recognized for what it is. One way of demonstrating this is to stroboscopically illuminate a rotating wire cube (Shaw et al., 1974). If the rotating object is strobed so that the observer glimpses nonadjacent discrete perspective projections in rapid succession, the cube is no longer recognizable, but is seen as a complex disconnected figure with more than six sides. Moreover the faces not only appear to rotate in contrary directions but appear to be elastic rather than rigid. Thus, when the structure of the modulatory group is destroyed, the cognition of shape is disrupted.

The modulatory group also includes the finer adjustments of the perceptual systems as well. In addition to gross locomotions and postural changes, modulatory activities of the visual system include vergence and accomodative adjustments of the conjugate binocular system. A transformation of optical information so that local invariants are either destroyed or greatly modified distorts veridical perception. For instance, by means of a "pseudo-scope" (an arrangement of mirrors) the eyes can be made to converge on distant objects as if they were much closer. In such cases the size of the objects appears greatly diminished and their distance much closer.

A reciprocal effect can be achieved by presenting the visual system with erroneous perspective information, as in the Ames' distorted room demonstration. Here a room was constructed whose floor, walls, and windows do not have perpendicular corners but which appear so when viewed appropriately. An object placed in one corner of the room appears much smaller than when placed in another corner.

Additional evidence in support of the necessity of satisfying the symmetry between the attuned modulatory states of the perceptual system and the local invariants of the environment is provided by stabilized retinal image demonstrations (Pritchard, 1961). When, by the use of a corneal attached lens device, an image is made to remain stationary relative to the movements of the eye, it fractionates and finally disappears altogether. This demonstrates that the destruction of the inverse symmetry relationship between the motions of objects in the world relative to the movements of the observer destroys the structure of the modulatory group, hence preventing cognition.

Another source of evidence for this claim derives from experiments in which observers wear spectacles that optically transform the world (Kohler, 1964). Spectacles can be worn which color the world, turn it upside down, reverse it, or shift the location of objects systematically to the right or left. In all these cases, the visual system recalibrates itself with the orientation system so that after several days the visual world no longer appears transformed. Dramatic evidence that the state configuration of the modulatory system has been systematically transformed to compensate for the transformation of optical information is provided when at last the spectacles are removed. Incredibly, the world now viewed without the spectacles looks transformed opposite to what was seen while wearing the spectacles.

What better evidence could one ask for in support of the claim that the modulatory activities must form a group? The inverse relationships induced on the visual system by a systematic transformation of optical information is also consistent with the claim that the modulatory group is instantiated in the two symmetrical dual groups defined over the informational bases of the world and the algroistic bases of the organism. Mathematically, it is well-known that a systematic transformation of a group does not necessarily destroy its structure.

Still stronger evidence of the validity of the symmetry group analysis of cognition, as required by the principle of cognitive symmetry, would be to show that certain arbitrary systematic transformation of information can not be adapted to. Again such evidence exists.

If prismatic spectacles are worn where each eye looks through a wedge prism whose base is oriented in a temporal direction, what is called the *color-stereo* effect is experienced (Kohler, 1962). Due to the differential refraction of light of different wavelengths, the observer with these spectacles will see colored objects proportionally displaced. Thus, a woman wearing a red blouse might be seen walking across the street with her red blouse following a few feet behind her, mysteriously moving in perfect synchrony with her movements. Even after wearing such spectacles for almost two months, Kohler reports that the visual system failed to adapt to the color-stereo effect.

Similarily, deep sea divers who spend many hours every day under water never succeed in adapting to the effects of the refractive power of water. Since the refractive index of water is greater than that of air, all objects are made to look larger and, therefore, appear closer. Although experienced divers learn to intellectually correct for this in judging distances, their visual systems do not: The magnification is always seen.

Both the color-stereo and the water magnification effects provide evidence that not all systematic transformations of physical information can be offset by recalibrations of the modulatory system. In other words, the operation by which these optical devices transform information is not a member of the modulatory group and, hence, has no inverse. Why might this be so?

The color-stereo effect presents the visual system with a random assortment of displaced images. An observer looking around his world is just as likely to encounter objects of one color as another. As light of various wavelengths is picked-up, the amount of displacement of the images is nearly unpredictable. With no invariance in the transformations presented there is no possibility of a systematic inverse transformation of the modulatory system that might compensate for the arbitrary change in the state of the world.

As Kohler (1962) points out, there is good reason to believe that the visual system has been genetically pre-attuned to utilize a natural color-stereo effect caused by design of the eyes. It has perplexed biologists that the fovea of most animals, including man, lies to one side of the optical axis of the lens system. This misalignment, combined with the eye's natural degree of chromatic aberration, may produce prismatic effects that give rise to a weak color-stereo effect. The functional utility of this effect, however, is not yet understood.

The failure of underwater observers to adapt to the refractive index of water is also probably due to genetic pre-attunement. After millions of years of living in an air filled environment, it seems reasonable to conclude that the evolutionary design of the visual system has been specifically attuned to the refractive index of air—a global physical invariant like the refractability of light according to wavelength. The visual system can no more adapt to these global physical invariants than it can to the horizon, day-night schedule, terrestrial thermal conditions, texture gradient of the ground plane, or gravity. Therefore, at all levels of analysis, from gross to fine modulatory activities, the principle of cognitive symmetry must be satisfied if normal cognition is to be possible.

The Principle of Perceptual Transitions

A very important hypothesis emerges from close examination of the question regarding how the modulatory states of organisms become attuned to local physical invariants through experience. The principle of cognitive symmetry states the necessary conditions for such attunement but does not provide a sufficient mechanism for explaining how the attunement is accomplished. The basis for the principle by which local physical invariants condition symmetrical modulatory states is Mach's (1902) conjecture that "symmetry carries over into equilibria."

One of the most difficult problems in psychology, and one which approaches the difficulty of the so-called "many-body" problem in physics, is explaining the perceptual analysis of complex events. Why do people see complex events in specific ways when often the information determined by them is ambiguous, and thus specifies many different events? What minimal information is needed to specify adequately the nature of an event? When is such information redundant?

An answer to each question hinges on whether we can predict the structural components of complex events to which observers are most likely to attend. In other words, we must be able to explain how invariant structures in the event induce a symmetry, or equilibrium, of modulatory states in the organism.

Let us say that components with the greatest probability of being attended to (i.e., highest cognitive saliency) possess the greatest *attensity* value. If we had some principle by which we could determine the relative attensity value for each structural component of an event, then we might predict which structures of the event are most likely to be seen first. The structural component with the greatest attensity value that is seen first would be a likely candidate for the anchor or reference point around which less attensive structures might be organized.

Such a principle would allow us to predict the perceptual transitions among modulatory states as a function of the structural development of the event over time. Furthermore, such a principle could be interpreted as providing an explanation of the modulatory "program" by which the perceptual system becomes attuned to invariant information through experience. Discovery of such a principle of perceptual transitions would provide another instance of the successful application of the principle of cognitive symmetry—this time to the domain of "event" perception.

The world is full of various classes of events—events where the symmetry period is degenerative, as in the case of a bouncing rubber ball; events whose symmetry period is repetitive, as when a wheel rolls or a person walks; reversible events, as in opening and closing a door, or the swinging pendulum of a clock; irreversible events, as in burning a forest or bursting a balloon; and "slow" events, such as evolution, growth, and aging. The symmetry period of an event is specified by all the nonredundant information presented within some region of space-time values. All events have such periods, even non-repeatable and irreversible ones, because the symmetry description is abstract (i.e., a class description) rather than specific to a particular event.

In many cases the symmetry period must be discovered for events which are not spatially or temporally contiguous, and which are, therefore, mnemically rather than causally related. For instance, although we can not see the same egg broken twice in succession, we learn to recognize the symmetry period of the event class by seeing different eggs broken. Similarly, we learn the symmetry period of the human aging process by synchronic examples (i.e., by seeing people of different age levels). In order for such concepts to be learned, we must be able to perceive the invariants of the transformations by which the changes take place.

Local invariants can be distinguished by their dimensionality. The simplest local invariant is a fixed-point property. Since such invariants are defined over points they have a dimensionality of zero. An invariant relation defined over two relatively fixed points determines a fixed line and thus is one dimensional; an invariant area or plane surface is determined by three points and is said to be three dimensional, and so on. The *degree* of an invariant property is simply one more than its number of dimensions (e.g., a fixed-point property is a first-degree invariant).

We are now in a position to formulate *the principle of perceptual transitions* needed to explain event perception: *Global physical invariants have greater attensity than local ones. The attensity of local invariants is inversely proportional to their degree. Thus, the perceptual organization of an event proceeds from globally invariant properties to locally invariant properties according to their degree. In the case of invariant structures of the same degree, the structure most consistent with lower degree invariants will have the greatest attensity.*

Let us now apply the principle of perceptual transitions to predict a well-known perceptual phenomenon. If you place a light on a wheel and roll it laterally across the floor of a darkroom, observers report seeing the light trace out a continuous, scallop-shaped curve called a *cycloid*. A cycloid is an open curve symmetrical around a perpendicular bisector. The termini for the cycloid traced out by the light lie on the ground plane at a distance apart equal to the circumference of the wheel. The height of the cycloid is the diameter of the wheel.

A dramatically different phenomenon, however, is reported when a second light is placed at the center of the wheel. The rolling wheel is now seen to trace out a complex event consisting of two distinct components: The rim light is seen to be orbiting around the hub light while this rotary system translates rectilinearly across the floor.

The puzzle to be explained is why the mere addition of one light can make such a dramatic change in what is seen. Geometrically, the rim light still traces out the same curve as before, but is now seen to trace out a circle when the context of the second light is added. Furthermore, a circular trace is radically different from a cycloid trace: Where a cycloid is an open curve, a circle is closed; where a cycloid has but a single axis of symmetry, a circle has an infinite number of them. Instead of the translating orbiting system, why isn't a cycloid with a straight line trace through it seen?

In the case with a single rim light, the wheel is seen to trace out a cycloid because that curve is the lowest degree invariant optically specified. A static cycloid is a third-degree invariant, while a kinetic one is a fourth-degree invariant, since it has the added dimension of time. The direction in which the event unfolds and its orientation to the observer is defined within the framework of the observer's spatial reference system. This spatial reference system is defined over the global physical invariants. This is as expected by the principle, since local invariants are always oriented within the system of global invariants which have the greatest attensity.

Now consider how new, lower-degree local invariants are introduced when the hub light is added to the display. The hub light traces a straight line over time, a third-degree invariant. This invariant, according to the principle, has greater attensity than the cycloid, since it is of lower degree. The hub light then becomes the anchor or reference point around which the other components of the event are organized.

The next invariant of greatest attensity is the fixed radial distance between the hub light and the rim light which sweeps out a circular area. The areal invariant (e.g., the circle) is a third degree invariant. Since this curve is one degree lower than the fourth degree invariant specifying the cycloid, it is seen next. And finally, a translating rotary system is a fourth-degree invariant. But since it is consistent with more of the lower-degree invariants (e.g. the circle and the line of translation) than the fourth-degree cycloid, it is seen while the cycloid is not. Thus, a translating rotary system is the event of greater resultant attensity than a repeating cycloid. If valid, this analysis solves the Gestaltists' problem of what is meant by "good" form (Prägnanz).

We contend that the principle of perceptual transitions will apply algorithmically to predict the perceptual organization of any event, regardless of its intrinsic complexity.

It is important to point out that this principle, although algorithmic in its application by the human perceptual systems, nevertheless has an algoristic basis. The role of the epistemic-who enters, as expected, in the form of a cost variable—what might be called the psychological analog to the principles of "least effort." This principle asserts that natural phenomena develop along lines of least resistance. Without the assumption of this algoristic principle at the basis of cognition, invariants of lesser degree would have no logical priority over those of greater degree. Hence the principle of perceptual transitions would not be derivable from the principle of cognitive symmetry.

The principle of perceptual transitions, if it continues to prove its mettle, may qualify as the first precise example of an invariance law in cognitive psychology. This is only half the story. An explanation must also be given for the second half of the adjunctive expression for invariance laws in psychology, $\psi \!>\! \phi$. The algoristic basis also imposes structure on physical information, to produce local and global invariants over and beyond those that can be explained by physical law alone.

LOCAL AND GLOBAL INVARIANTS OF PSYCHOLOGICAL INFORMATION

Currently, little that is precise can be offered regarding the manner and extent to which psychological states directly impose structure on physical information (i.e., about $\psi > \phi$). Consequently, in an attempt to round out the chief problems faced by cognitive theorists, we shall offer a few tentative speculations.

Finding Seams in the World of Energy Flux

A person who has dropped a gold coin in his yard one evening returns the next morning to search for it among the glistening, dew laden grass. By selectively attending to all yellow glitterings he easily finds it. A copy editor rapidly scans through pages of print, scarcely comprehending what is read, but accurately circles in red mistakes in spelling and punctuation. A ballet master comments critically on minute flaws in the performance of his prima ballerina that go unnoticed by the admiring audience. An eminent guest conductor kindly chides the slightly off-key, off-tempo performance of the home orchestra and directs them to the performance of their life. The trained linguist detects the subtle accent of a well-schooled emigrant who has been told by other natives that he speaks with no accent. The disembarking passenger sees his wife's face within the large crowd.

In all such examples, none of the properties detected are in any way specially noted within their context of ambient physical information. We see or hear better what we notice, whether or not it is set apart by any obvious energy accents.

The perceptual partitioning of energy distributions by highly selective modulatory activities attuned by experience is what Gibson (1966) has called "the education of attention." As argued earlier, the objectification of either phase or amplitudinal characteristics of ambient energy distributions is a negentropic process, requiring information producing processes. It requires cognitive processes that raise the attensity level of a particular property of physical information over and above the average attensity level of the total available information.

Normally, the probability of an individual property being attended to over its background energy level is a function of the "signal-to-noise" ratio. The apparent function of selective attention is to enhance the signal-to-noise ratio of certain properties through selective modulation. There are only two ways this might be achieved: Either the information must be directly modulated at the energy source, or the transmitted information must be differentially modulated on reception. The latter case requires no unusual assumptions beyond the hypothesis that cognitive processes detect, filter, and, perhaps, amplify information. The former case, however, apparently strains scientific credulity by suggesting a bizarre conclusion, namely, that cognitive processes somehow act directly upon the physical sources of information—a hypothesis apparently invoking a mysterious mental force that acts at a distance.

Must we affirm the "modulation-upon-reception" view and reject out of hand the "action-at-a-distance" view? Or can the two views be reconciled under the scope of a theory of a higher order invariance law which succeeds in banishing mysterious forces from psychology, as Einstein's relativistic space-time invariance law banished from physics Newton's mysterious gravitational force without banishing gravity as a useful concept? Perhaps the direct cognitive modulation of events can be preserved as a useful concept in a similar manner. Such a notion might prove useful in explaining several puzzling psychological phenomena.

Psychological Information

A person who speaks English can hear pauses and breaks in the acoustic stream of speech signals that clearly separate phoneme, morpheme, phrase, and sentence boundaries. A foreigner who speaks no English will not be able to hear where these same boundaries occur. For a native speaker the segmentation problem for English speech is solved perceptually, while for a non-English speaking person the problem is not solvable at all, no matter how carefully he listens. Consequently, whatever allows a native speaker to solve perceptually the segmentation problem can not be attributed solely to discontinuities specified in the acoustic stream.

This is a good example of the distinction between psychological information and physical information. The fact that as the foreign speaker learns English he also comes to perceive the speech segments indicates that whatever acoustic invariants signify their existence, their modulation requires attunement through experience. Hence they are local invariants and probably not due to genetic preattunement of the species. By contrast, however, if it is true that young infants require no learning in order to perceive the distinction between speech and nonspeech sounds, then one might expect the acoustic invariant for speech to be due to genetic pre-attunement, i.e., to be a global psychological invariant.

The crucial question for cognitive theory is how acoustical contours become nonlinearly modulated to create perceptual boundaries where none exist in the physical information. Similar processes seem to be operative in visual perception as well.

Usually we think of the world as composed of rigid objects and sharp edges. A wave function characterization of the ambient optical energy available over a given period of time provides only a probability distribution of continuous energy spectra. Due to the diffraction of light by rough corners of objects, reflection by many faceted, multicolored surfaces, and refraction by a dust filled, gaseous medium, no sharp optical contours truly exist. Like acoustic waves, optical waves interfere in both additive and subtractive ways to create standing as well as kinetic four-dimensional convolutional waveforms.

The fact that so-called "optical illusions" exist confounds any claim that what humans see is directly based on the available optical information. In the Herring illusion, parallel straight lines are seen to warp curvilinearly away from each other over a fan-like pattern of straight lines; in the Müller-Lyer illusion, lines of equal length appear to be different in length; and in the Necker cube illusion, a three dimensional cube is seen to reverse, although it is well known that a single perspective is not sufficient to specify a unique solid shape.

Perhaps what is in the light, as in the speech signal, is something *more* than the laws of physics place there. But what and how? There seems to be a real possibility that many geometric illusions can be explained by the fact that the perceptual systems of organisms have been designed by evolution to function discretely and with finite capacity.

Machines that "see" illusions. The claim that the retinal image contains all the information necessary for vision can be shown to be false on many accounts. The existence of the geometric iilusions mentioned above provides one obvious source of evidence that no simple relationship holds between the optical information projected into the visual system and what is in fact seen.

Moore and Parker (1972) have designed a machine in the form of a computer program which "sees" the Müller-Lyer illusion in the sense that it computes approximately the same discrepancies in length between the two figures as reported by human observers. The fact that such illusions of length have been shown to hold for other species (e.g., the Jastrow illusion on chickens by Révész, 1934), suggests that they may be due to a very general property of nervous systems (e.g., their discrete functioning).

Although we cannot go into the mathematical details of Moore's model here, it can easily be shown that such geometric illusions as the Müller-Lyer do not occur if the model is provided an infinite number of continuous computational states. However, in order to implement the model on a digital computer with a finite number of discrete states, the perceptual function by which the figure is processed by the model had to be both finitized and discretized. It was found that the strength of the illusion varies directly with the coarseness of the samples of the figure taken, and inversely with the number of samples processed. Thus it seems likely that the illusions arise for humans and other animals for precisely the same reason, namely, the finite discreteness of their perceptual processes.

Another important property of Moore's model is that it is able to analyze complex figures into their structural components. By assigning a weight to types of discrete samples it is possible to enhance various levels of substructure in a complex figure. In this way, various attensity values can be differentially assigned by a very general principle to all significant properties of a figure. Thus the model is able to attend differentially to various parts of a complex figure. At Minnesota we are currently elaborating these features of this model to test the application of the principle of perceptual transitions to see if the model will "see" simple events as human observers do.

Thus, there does seem to be evidence that perceptual modulation of physical information might create new information that has psychological significance. Just as invariant physical information comes in two varieties—local and global—so does invariant psychological information. The invariance law relating physics and psychology has closure. In closing we would like to discuss the consistency we feel this view of cognitive theory has with Gibson's theory of direct perception.

THE ADVANCING SIEVE OF TIME

An impression may have been conveyed by our claim that since to some extent cognition, no less than physics, structures what is known, then natural phenomena must be subjective rather than objective. This is in no way a necessary interpretation. Since the fundamental view of this chapter rests on an epistemo-logical assumption that whatever is known is known directly, we favor a "direct" realism as argued for by Gibson (1967). This is not to argue, however, that what is known is everything, but only that in so far as knowledge is possible at all, it is neither constructed by subjective processes nor merely passively imposed upon the knower by physical processes. Instead, to summarize, what is known is a complex interaction of what is, how it is known, and who knows it. A simple analogy may provide a concrete illustration of the relation among these things.

A radio is constructed to tune in certain wavelengths and not others. To pick-up a particular station, its tuner must be in an appropriate state-configuration. The station's transmitter induces a voltage change in its antenna which propagates through the air and induces a voltage change in the receiver's antenna. The receiver then amplifies the received signal.

When you consider the fact that a large number of stations are broadcasting at once and that each induces a complex pattern of voltage changes in the receiver's antenna, it is amazing that the radio can be tuned to detect just one of them. Although the selective attention of the human perceptual system may be more precise, it may not operate much differently.

What "direct" pick-up means in the case of the radio is that the entire active circuit of the radio is in a resonant state. There is a direct transduction of invariant wave form characteristics of the energy transmitted (say from the voice of the announcer) that is preserved in the resonant state of the receiver. By terming this process a *transduction* we mean to distinguish it from a *translation* which necessarily involves "coding" steps. Such coding steps mediate the reception of information by interpolating symbolic representations of the energy forms somewhere between the event and the final detection state of the receiver. At the United Nations a human interpreter performs such a "coding" step for the foreign representatives. In computers this is done by a compiler.

Neisser (1967) speaks of the problem of the Höffding step in perception: how an input gets together with a stored trace. If perception, however, is a direct transduction by the perceptual systems as Gibson suggests, no such problem need be solved. Moreover, if no coding steps mediate the modulation of perceptual information, then no recoding of stored traces or retrieving of information is required; again, no Höffding step necessarily occurs. This difference between a theory of direct perception and a theory of mediated perception is exactly the difference between semantic directed processing and syntactic directed processing (Jenkins et al., 1974).

The evolution and maturation of the cognitive systems can be likened to the process of designing a radio to pick up certain stations and not others. The effect of experience on the cognitive systems is analogous to tuning in a particular station at a particular time. Now, if we make the radio portable and move it through the environment, stations at different locations with similar wave-lengths fall into equivalence classes, so that the setting on the tuner begins to take on the abstract properties of a concept. (It is instructive to attempt to elaborate the analogy to see when or if it breaks down.)

Various significant properties of the environment "broadcast" invariant wave forms which are directly transduced by the cognitive system, if it is properly tuned to modulate them. How the attunement process is adaptive, whether genetic or through experience, presumably is explained by the law of cognitive symmetry. It is important to emphasize that the invariants of information do not need to be "symbolically represented," "stored," or "imaged" in the cognitive structures of the organism before, during, or after this processing. If they are, it is for reasons beyond those that need be satisfied for perception. Rather, the invariants of information that relate the sources in the environment with the knowing organism are the same invariants throughout the transduction; otherwise they would not be "invariants."

It is accurate to say that the event perceived is "spread" out over that portion of the space-time continuum in the neighborhood of the observer (Russell, 1948). In no sense does an event exist independently of the invariant information which identifies it. The two concepts are logically co-extensive and spatio-temporally coterminus. The invariants are directly modulated (i.e., transduced); hence that portion of the event defined over those invariants must be also.

The wave function characteristic of a modulated event is different from that of an unmodulated event, since from the standpoint of physics the event in each state is defined by a different probability distribution predicting what information is potential. This view of events as probability distributions over a certain region of space-time poses a philosophical paradox for the direct realist; perceived or known events present actual rather than merely probable information to an appropriately attuned knowing agent.

If knowledge is assumed to be probable then science becomes hypothetical rather than adjunctive. Given the earlier arguments for an adjunctive logic of natural and invariance laws, the view one holds regarding knowledge is not a question of abstract metaphysics, but a pragmatic question of choosing the most appropriate logic in which to express one's commitment to one's ideals. Since we hold both scientific and personal knowledge to be obtainable, and concur with Leibniz in postulating an underlying symmetry to nature, the very existence of events adjunctively implies the existence of knowledge that is compatible with them. And as we tried to show, this compatibility relationship, due to the invariance postulate, implies that knowledge is obtainable. But how can the concepts of potential information and actual knowledge be theoretically reconciled within the manifest scientific framework?

The argument we wish to make is analogous to the hypothesis proposed by Sir Lawrence Bragg, who hoped to reconcile wave and particle views in physics. He suggested, "Everything that has already happened is particles, everything in the future is waves. The advancing sieve of time coagulates waves into particles at the moment 'now' [in Clark, 1971, p. 420] ."

It is not just the advancing sieve of disembodied time which distills from potential physical information actualized events, but the embodiment of mind which modulates invariant knowledge from these events. It may just be that neither the speech segments in the acoustic stream, nor the hard optical edges which define the shapes of objects, nor the attensified objects enhanced during a search, nor the subtlest ecologically significant nuances of any event, have any existence until carved out of the energy distributions by a goal-directed algorist.

The greatest difficulty in accepting the above notion derives from the commonsense assumption that events are somehow "out there" while knowledge of them (e.g., concepts, percepts, images, etc.) is somehow "in the head." The line between the experience of objective and subjective phenomena is held sacrosanct. But this dualism is no longer supported by physics, psychology, or even mathematics.

Percepts, concepts, memories, ideas, and other contents of mind usually considered private and subjective, are in fact as much "out there" as particles, stones, tables,.and stars. Acceptance of invariance laws for psychology means the placing of psychological, physical, and biological phenomena on equal footing, within a framework of an objective reality that favors none of them, but accommodates them all. The challenge for cognitive theory is to grasp the full implications of the statement that ideas are not in the mind, nor objects in the world, but that both are in the meeting of mind and matter.

But surely the direct effect of "thoughts" on "matter" is an exceptional conclusion to say the least. However, if the above arguments are valid, then the search for invariance laws that govern psychological phenomena leads to the first "bizarre" conclusion of our science. The wise theoretician will suspend judgment on this issue since there are no valid *a priori* grounds on which hypotheses can be rejected just because they shock scientific sensibilities. To reject them out of hand by ignoring the need for invariance laws in psychology may jeapordize the hope of discovering the polyphasic laws required for the science.

Indeed, the direct interaction of cognitive variables with the wave functional character of events may prove in the long run to be one of those "very small effects," like the effect of light on matter, upon which new sciences are founded.

REFERENCES

Arbib, M. A simple self-reproducing model. In C. H. Waddington, (Ed.), *Towards a theoretical biology.* Edinburgh: Edinburgh University Press, 1969. (a)

Arbib, M. *Theories of abstract automata.* Englewood Cliffs, N.J.: Prentice-Hall, 1969. (b)

Ashby, W. R. The self-reproducing system, *Symposium on self-organizing systems.* London: Pergamon Press, 1962.

Block, H. D. Simulation of statistically composite systems. In G. Shapiro and M. Rogers (Eds.), *Prospects for simulation and simulators of dynamic systems.* New York: Macmillan, 1967.

Blum, M. A machine independent theory of the complexity of recursive functions. *Journal of the A.C.M.,* 1967, **14**, (2), 322-336.

Bohm, D. *Quantum theory.* Englewood Cliffs, N.J.: Prentice-Hall, 1951.

Broadbent, D. E. *Perception and communication.* London: Pergamon Press, 1958.

Chomsky, N. A review of B. F. Skinner's *Verbal Behavior. Language, 1959,* **35,** 26-58.

Chomsky, N. Formal properties of grammars. In R. D. Luce, R. Buch, & E. Galanter (Eds.), *Handbook of mathematical psychology.* Vol. 2. New York: Wiley, 1963.

Chomsky, N. *Aspects of the theory of syntax.* Cambridge: MIT Press, 1965.

Church, A. An unsolvable problem of elementary number theory. *American Journal of Mathematics,* 1936, **58,** 345-363.

Clark R. *Einstein: The life and times.* New York: Avon Books, 1971.

Clowes, M. B. A hierarchical model of form perception. In W. Wathen-Dunn, (Ed.), *Models for the perception of speech and visual form.* Cambridge: MIT Press, 1967.

Cornsweet, T. N. *Visual perception.* New York: Academic Press, 1970.

Elsasser, W. *The physical foundations of biology.* London: Pergamon Press, 1958.

Ernst, G. W. & Newell, A. *GPS: A case study in generality and problem solving.* New York: Academic Press, 1969.

Gibson, E. J. & Walk, R. D. The "visual cliff." *Scientific American,* 1960, **202,** 64-71.

Gibson, J. J. *The senses considered as perceptual systems.* Boston: Houghton Mifflin, 1966.

Gibson, J. J. New reasons for realism. *Synthese,* 1967, **17**, 162-172.

Gibson, J. J., Olum, P., & Rosenblatt, F. Parallax and perspective during aircraft landings. *American Journal of Psychology,* 1948, **61**, 119-123.

Gregory, R. L. *Eye and brain: The psychology of seeing.* New York: McGraw-Hill, 1966.

Haber, R. N. (Ed.) *Information-processing approaches to visual perception.* New York: Holt, Rinehart & Winston, 1969.

Hartmanis, J., & Stearns, R. E. On the computational complexity of algorithms. *Transactions of the American Mathematical Society,* 1965, **117**, 285-306.

Hay, J. C. Optical motions and space perception: An extension of Gibson's analysis. Psychological Review, 1966, **73**, 550-565.

Heisenberg, W. The representation of nature in contemporary physics. *Daedalus,* 1958, 87, 95.

Jenkins, J. J., Jimenez-Pabon, E., Shaw, R. E. & Sefer, J. *Schuell's aphasia in adults.* New York: Harper & Row, 1974.

Kalamar, L. An argument against the plausibility of Church's thesis. In A. Heyting (Ed.), *Constructivity in mathematics,* (Proceedings of colloquium held at Amsterdam August 26-31, 1957) Amsterdam: North-Holland, 1957.

Klee P. *Pedagogical sketchbook.* New York: Praeger, 1953.

Kleene, S. C. λ-definability and recursiveness. *Duke Mathematical Journal,* 1936, **2** 340-353.

Kleene, S. C. *Mathematical logic.* New York: Wiley, 1967.

Kohler, I. Experiments with goggles. *Scientific American,* 1962, **206**, 62-72.

Kohler, I. The formation and transformation of the visual world. *Psychological Issues,* 1964, **3**, 28-46, 116-133.

Kolers, P. Some psychological aspects of pattern recognition. In P. Kolers, & M. Eden (Eds.), *Recognizing patterns: Studies in living and automatic systems.* Cambridge: MIT Press, 1968.

Lakatos, I. Falsification and the methodology of scientific research programmes. In I. Lakatos & A. Musgrave (Eds.), *Criticism and the growth of knowledge.* Cambridge: University Press, 1970.

Lashley, K. In search of the engram. *Proceedings of the Society of Experimental Biology,* 1950, **4**, 454-482.

Lenneberg, E. *Biological foundations of language.* New York: Wiley, 1967.

Mach, E. *Science of mechanics: A critical and historical account of its development.* Chicago: Open Court, 1902.

MacKay, D. M. Mentality in machines. *Proceedings of the Aristolelian Society,* 1952, **26**, (Suppl.) 61-86.

McCulloch, W. S. Why the mind is in the head. In L. A. Jeffress, (Ed.), *Cerebral mechanisms in behavior, behavior.* New York: Wiley, 1951.

McCulloch, W. S. *The embodiments of mind.* Cambridge: MIT Press, 1965.

McCulloch, W. S., & Pitts, W. H. A logical calculus of the ideas immanent in nervous activity. *Bulletin of Mathematical Biophysics,* 1943, **5**, 115-133.

Minsky, M., & Papert, S. *Perceptrons.* Cambridge: MIT Press, 1968.

Moore, D. J. H., & Parker, D. J. Machine Preception. *Australian Telecommunication Research,* 1972, **6**, 3-11.

Neisser, U. *Cognitive psychology.* New York: Appleton, 1967.

Norman, D. *Memory and attention: An introduction to human information processing.* New York: Wiley, 1969.

Norman, D. *Models of human memory.* New York: Academic Press, 1970.

Piaget, J., & Inhelder, B. The child's conception of space. London: Routledge and Kegan Paul, 1956.

Piaget, J., Inhelder, B., & Szeminska, A. *The child's conception of geometry.* New York: Harper Torch Books, 1960.

Popper, K. R. *The logic of scientific discovery.* New York: Harper & Row, 1959.

Pritchard, R. M. Stabilized images on the retina. *Scientific American,* 1961, **204**, 72-78.

Pufall, P., & Shaw R. E. Analysis of the development of children's spatial reference systems. *Journal of Cognitive Psychology,* 1973, **5**, 151-175.

Purdy, W. C. *The hypothesis of psychophysical correspondence in space perception.* (Doctoral dissertation, Cornell University) Ann Arbor, University Microfilms, 1958, No. 58-5594. (Reproduced in part as Report No. R60ELC56 of the General Electric Technical Information Series.)

Putnam, H. Minds and machines. In Sidney Hook (Ed.), *Dimensions of mind: A symposium.* New York: New York University Press, 1960.

Pylyshyn, Z. W. The problem of cognitive representation. (Research Bulletin No. 227, March, 1972) London, Ontario, Department of Psychology, University of Western Ontario.

Quastler, H. (Ed.) *Essays on the use of information theory in biology.* Urbana: University of Illinois Press, 1953.

Quillian, M. R. Semantic memory. In M. Minsky (Ed)., *Semantic information processing.* Cambridge: MIT Press, 1968.

Révész, G. System der optischen und haptischen Raumtauschungen. *Zeitschrift fur Psychologie,* 1934, **131,** 296-375.

Russell, B. *The analysis of mind.* London: Allen and Unwin, 1921.

Russell, B. *The ABC of relativity.* London: Allen and Unwin, 1925.

Russell, B. *A history of western philosophy.* New York: Simon and Schuster, 1945.

Russell, B. *Human knowledge: Its scope and limits.* New York: Simon and Schuster, 1948.

Scandura, J. *Structural learning: I. Theory and research.* New York: Gordon and Breach, 1973.

Scriven, M. The mechanical concept of mind. *Mind,* 1953, **62** (246), 230-240.

Selfridge, O. G. Pandemonium: A paradigm for learning. In, *The mechanisation of thought processes.* London: H. M. Stationery Office, 1959.

Shaw, R. E. Cognition, simulation, and the problem of complexity. *Journal of Structural Learning,* 1971, **2** (4), 31-44.

Shaw, R. E., McIntyre, M., & Mace, W. The role of symmetry in event perception. In R. B. MacLeod & H. Pick (Eds.), *Studies in perception: Essays in honor of J. J. Gibson.* New York: Cornell University Press, 1974.

Simon, H. A. *The sciences of the artificial.* Cambridge: MIT Press, 1969.

Skinner, B. F. *Verbal behavior.* New York: Appleton, 1957.

Sperling, G. The information available in brief visual presentations. *Psychology Monographs,* 1960, **74** (11, Whole No. 498).

Suppes, P. Stimulus-response theory of finite automata. (Tech. Rep. No. 13, Psychology Series) Stanford: Institute for Mathematical Studies in Social Science, Stanford University, 1968.

Von Foerster, H. Biologic. In E. E. Bernard & M. R. Care (Eds.), *Biological prototypes and synthetic systems.* Vol. 1. New York: Plenum Press, 1962.

von Neumann, J. *Theory of self-reproducing automata.* A. W. Burks (Ed.), Urbana: University of Illinois Press, 1966.

Wald, G. Eye and camera. *Scientific American,* August, 1950, **183,** 32-41.

Weiss, P. A. The living system: Determinism stratified. In A. Koestler & J. R. Smythies (Eds.), *Beyond reductionism: New perspectives in the life sciences.* London: Hutchinson, 1969.

Wigner, E. P. *Symmetries and reflections: Scientific essays in honor of Eugene P. Wigner.* (In W. Moore & M. Scriven (Eds.)) Cambridge: MIT Press, 1970.

Winograd, T. Procedures and a representation for data in a computer program for understanding natural language. (MAC TR-48, Project Mac,) Cambridge: MIT, 1971.

15
SHAW-McINTYRE DISCUSSION

Halwes: What's the origin of the term coalition?

Shaw: I got it from Von Foerster. Intuitively we think of a coalition – like a coalition among companies or people – as an organization where the "components" are operating toward some end because they're compatible with each other and they've come together in a coalition because together the whole has greater power than the sum of the parts. One of the properties that you find true of, say, populations, (that Von Foerster, 1962, talks about) is that, from a mathematical standpoint, as populations of cells (or organisms or whatever—it's completely abstract) begin growing, there is a point at which they reach a critical mass and become self-supporting. At this point they can be said to form a coalition. There's another point where, if a population keeps growing, the supply lines break down because they get too over worked and it begins decomposing again. The interdependency relationships are critical to a certain size: It has to be very complex to begin with, too complex to analyze in a microdeterministic way, but if it gets too big then it becomes unwieldy and won't function at all. If it's too small, it won't have self-reproducing powers of reparation for things that disappear.

Consider the human body, where approximately every seven years the cells are replaced. Things are continually being brought back into a sub-coalition. There's a certain symmetry among the cells, but they're not the *same* cells. It's as if the position they have in terms of their interaction or interdependence with the rest of the cells in the coalition determines the support of the whole system.

One of the important transformations that can be defined over a coalition which can't be defined over a hierarchy (or anything else) is what anatomists have called remodeling. For instance, when a face grows and a person becomes older, his whole body remodels. It doesn't just get larger, and things don't get arbitrarily moved around and disconnected or distorted. Changes happen because of determinate interaction, but the sources of control have never been understood on a micro-level. According to Donald Enlow (1968) people doing vector analytic work in dynamic anatomy (as opposed to dead anatomy) do not yet know how the face retains its identifiable properties as belonging to a particular species rather than being the face of a monster or some other species. We know that individual faces do retain their individual identity in spite of growth changes, but nobody understands the controls on the growth process that allow the invariants to persist over time. We might naively think "Well, the skin is pliable and soft; it's moldable by the skull and just sits on top of the skull and as the skull grows, it moves the skin around." Right? Wrong! That's not the way it seems to work at all. In fact, the skull has inadequate centralized growth control as far as can be determined: Control probably comes from soft parts of the anatomy. Or if one wants to take the weaker position, there's joint control, both in the bone marrow and in the soft parts. But it's not truly a localized control: There appear to be control factors for global transformations. One of the examples of a global transformation would be the remodeling transformation involved in an artist's caricature of a face.

So how can coalitions be changed? How do coalitions develop and what is the symmetry operation that retains their invariant structure, whatever that might be? I suggest that it's a remodeling transformation; and when we understand what this group is like then we will be able to apply it to various kinds of objects and determine whether our intuitive concept of coalitions applies or not. Moreover, we will be able to determine what the properties of coalitions are, just the way we would apply cyclical groups to rotated objects to determine what the invariant properties are for a rotatable object. Here it's not rotatable objects; it's growing systems. I see the problem of coalitions to be what Piaget in *Biology and Knowledge* (1971) called "homeoretic" logic. How do we deomonstrate at any particular point in a system which is changing over time that it retains enough invariants to be identified as one over-all process? The analogy of a homeostatic model won't do it.

Homeostasis seems to be a product of homeorhesis. Homeostasis is an adaptive set of relationship around some central value. It's like a thermostat that fluctuates positively and negatively around some point. However, if someone is to drive from here to Pittsburgh and he is being homeostatic, he will require a directing line that will take him there. A homeostatic mechanism will allow one to stay on the yellow line, or to stay on a compass direction. But what if one doesn't have anything that simple, what if there are no initial compass readings, and what if there are no yellow lines down the road—in other words, what if there is no local information for a goal? How would one solve that problem? Consider the homeorhetic versus the homeostatic solution; by a hemeorhetic solution one would mean the homing problem is solved by the system knowing how to get back on course once it has gotten-off. If I take a detour for a while, I can get back on the path to the goal further down the line. But I do not return necessarily to an old compass reading. I may have to circle around the goal and come in on a new heading. Hence no single-valued reading will do it; I can't be merely homeostatic. Migrating animals do this: They fly around storms or swim around obstacles. Evolving species or growing animals "remodel" but still retain their goal-invariance, i.e., their identity. Homeorhesis is the key to how coalitions change locally but remain globally the same.

The abstract machine model that I would try to fit to the notion of coalitions is an iterative array of finite automata, submersed in a medium so that the resonance properties of the medium condition certain kinds of activities (or depress certain activities) in the individual automata. This means an essentially parallel propagation of control can emanate from any single point in the array, that it need not be serially propagated. It also means that when a control signal is sent out it becomes decentralized.

Von Foerster gives a definition, but it's essentially the Gestalt notion that the whole is greater than the sum of the parts: There are global properties supported by all the components operating together that one can't find invariant at a lower level of analysis. An example would be something like connectivity. If we have, say, a fishnet and want to know "Is every strand connected with every other strand?" we've got to run connectivity tests that have a complexity factor of n based on the size of the net. One of the properties of true super-additive coalitions is that when one wants to run a set of tests to determine if they have some invariant properties, we will find that the number of test to run increases proportionately with the size of the coalition, maybe exponentially. If we try to do a theory of coalitions the way we normally do, we would end up adjuncting in our premises a set of provisos to meet — well, we'll use the word "complexity" problems—we would probably end up with a list of adjunctive provisions that would be more complicated than the properties of the coalition we're trying to explain, or more numerous than the rules we would have to use to describe the coalition in the first place.

This view relates to von Neumann's argument that there may be in nature things that we don't know how to capture yet in the way we use mathematics (I don't want to say that it's too powerful for mathematics). Up to some degree of complexity, we can give a recursive description of the phenomenon that is simpler than the phenomenon itself; but when things reach a point of becoming sufficiently complicated to be self-supporting, in the way of being a coalition, von Neumann argues that they may become so complicated that any symbolic description of them will turn out to be less elegant than the object itself. That means that if I'm trying to simulate the human brain, and it is a coalition, that the simplest model for the human brain *is* the human brain. Any attempt to reduce it to simple simulation procedures by saying, "Look, I know how to construct a human brain, or I know how to give the algorithmic basis to the human brain," will turn out to be as complicated as any other description we want to give — it just won't be as elegant as the brain itself. If we want to talk about its functioning, we must recognize that it has super-additive properties, that more and more things begin being supported globally as it gets more complicated than all the local features you can describe.

But the issue here is really not whether one can come up with a class of machines that does what the organism does, but whether one can *know* what that function is. Nobody expects that anyway: We don't expect a strong simulation. But I am arguing that there is no algorithm for recognition of a good simulation because we're not really instantiating a machine according to the same laws that the human body's instantiated by. I can see one tacking on provisos to get around that problem, but it may be hopeless. I'm saying a better solution is not to involute on the algorithmic analysis to the point where we depend on fault-finding algorithms. If we don't know how it works, if we can't trace its operation, then the model is usless. To say that because one knows rudimentary instructions and formulation rules and composition rules, that we *understand* how things function, is a fallacy to my mind. That's not the nature of determining what the effectivity of a machine is in terms of its goal direction or purposes, behavior, etc. Those are not formal algorithmic problems: They've not even defined solely over the algorithmic basis. They're defined over the instantiability of that machine under natural law , so that the argument would be equivalent to postulating the unknown planet, or postulating anti-matter, or the existence of the missing elements in the periodic table. The adjunctive approach is to grab the bull by the horns and say, "Let's change the context of constraint in which we're building our algorithmic analysis and build different kinds of algorithmic analyses, that are more compatible with things we must adjunctively assert." It's not just the computer scientist's problem. It's up to the *psychologist*. It's a problem of understanding the natural space in which things get instantiated, an *algoristic* problem, and it has to be solved in a particular field by whoever the experts are.

REFERENCES

Enlow, D. *The human face: An account of the postnatal growth and development of the cranofacial skeleton.* New York: Harper & Row, 1968.

Piaget, J. *Biology and knowledge.* Chicago: University of Chicago Press, 1971.

Von Foerster, H. Biologic. In E. E. Bernard & M. R. Cave (Eds.), *Biological prototypes and synthetic systems.* Vol. 1. New York: Plenum Press, 1962.

16

STRUCTURAL REALISM, COALITIONS, AND THE RELATIONSHIP OF GIBSONIAN, CONSTRUCTIVIST, AND BUDDHIST THEORIES OF PERCEPTION

Terry Halwes
University of Connecticut

My presentation has two sections: The first is parallel to what Shaw and McIntyre have presented. I will give an inelegant presentation of what they said, so that the full value of the elegance of their presentation will be clear. In the second section, I will speak about perception—perception by individual organisms and perception by sciences (if science is conceived of as a coalition which perceives its environment in some sense). But first I want to give a few examples of coalitions, which will help our understanding of the concept. One example of something that might be viewed as a coalition is an organism. Simple organisms like amoebas seem to have the properties that Shaw and McIntyre described. The difference between a coalition and a near facsimile becomes clearer when we examine the difference between a true culture, such as a tribe of American Indians, the Pygmies as described by Turnbull, or the Eskimos, in all of which people coexist (in the sense of cooperatively living together and helping each other to survive), and that which we call a nation, in which people not only do not coexist, but cooperatively help each other to die, and be sick and insane. Another example is a language community: all the people who speak French, for example. This has the coalitional properties of fuzziness of boundaries, decentralization of control, and internal communication. If such a structure gets too big, it splits up into smaller communities.

PART I

Let me begin by explicating the thesis of *structural realism.* (Structural realism does not conflict with Gibson's position of direct realism, and direct realism is one way of doing a structural realism.) I will try to put some boundary conditions on realism, and on what one could conceivably mean by *truth* in science. These conditions are, to me at least, intuitively obvious.

In *The Nature of Explanation* Kenneth Craik (1943) has a chapter, reprinted extensively, called "Hypothesis on the Nature of Thought." There Craik argues that to understand intelligence—to understand thought—we must view the problem in a new, although fairly obvious way. First Craik makes an assumption which, although intuitive, is not normally made by philosophers, namely, that reality exists and that one does not have to worry about whether an external reality exists or not. He also assumes that human beings *do* have knowledge: He puts the burden of proof on those who would argue that we do not have knowledge or that reality doesn't exist and says, in effect, "Let's just assume that it's all right to suppose that reality exists and see where we can go from that assumption." Then he adds, "*The mind embodies a model of the world.*" Next he qualifies what he means by a model, such as, "This model is not a static model; it's a working model which enables the organism to simulate various real events and processes." That's exactly what he meant: The model enables the organism to parallel various real processes. It is by virtue of this capacity of the organism to parallel real processes with its internal model of those processes that the organism is able to do all the things that we call cognition. What Craik was saying was, "If you want to be able to make any progress on the problem of knowledge, that is how you have to look at it." That is the way to look at the problem, and the other ways (which I won't even mention) are misleading and not helpful.

Bertrand Russell (1948) came to a similar position. If one considers the problem of truth, one must ask what it is that makes knowledge of any use to anyone. The only thing about knowledge that could conceivably correspond to our intuitive notion of truth (or "goodness" of knowledge, or usefulness of knowledge, or whatever) is *correspondence* between that knowledge and the world.

As an aside, in the history of arguments about the nature of knowledge and truth in philosophy there have been two major positions: One of them is the correspondence theory of truth or meaning; the other, the coherence theory of truth or meaning. The correspondence theory says knowledge exists because it corresponds with the world. The arguments against the correspondence position take this form: "That can't be right—if it were true, then there would be no way we could know whether knowledge were true or not because we would have to know what the state of the world was in order to evaluate knowledge, which would mean that we needed to have *perfect* knowledge of the world in order to evaluate our *partial* knowledge. If we did have it, then we could say, 'Oh, we don't really need the partial knowledge. Let's just have perfect knowledge and be done with it.' " The opponents of this position proposed what is called the coherence theory of truth, which holds that truth is a matter of consistency. In Shaw's terminology, "It's true if it's compatible," or, if it fits together and works, then it's true. Cognitively, if this new bit of putative knowledge fits well with what I already believe, then it's true.

I wish to argue that to understand knowledge we have to make a separation. We must separate the problem of *what is knowledge* from the problem of *how we know we've got it:* that is, separate the problem of the nature of knowledge from the problem of the evaluation of knowledge. If we do that (and I submit that that separation has not been made by most philosophers) it becomes clear that one can have a correspondence theory of the *nature* of knowledge and the *nature* of truth and a coherence theory of *how we know* we have it or not. Let's look for a moment at the nature of knowledge independently of how we know if we have it or not.

Russell argues (this is the end of my aside) that our knowledge could conceivably correspond with the world in its *structure* only, and in no other way. That is the only possibility: There are no alternatives. Rather than repeat his argument, I will make the point more simply. If we don't have a structural correspondence, that means we have a real, a material correspondence. If there were a material correspondence between our models and reality, then if I perceive apples, that means that I've got apples in my head—not structures that are a lot like apples, but apples. They may not be the same apples as the apples out in the world, but I have an internal copy of them. There's an apple "out there" and I have an apple "in here." That, I submit, would give us who perceive apples a headache, and since we demonstrably do not always have a headache in that situation, it follows that we do not have apples in our heads. The knowledge *in my head,* therefore, can conceivably correspond with the world only in its structure.

But we still have the concept of structure and "structural correspondence." N. R. Hanson (1970) has clarified the concept of structure. What do we mean by structure? Consider a melody. Suppose somebody thinks of a melody, and then plays it on a flute. The melody goes rippling through the air and is heard by me. If I decide to record it, I will bring engineers and equipment, and ask the flute-player to play the melody again. I will then record it, take it to a factory, make records of it, sell the records, etc. If you hear it and decide that you like it, you may make a recording of it on your home tape recorder; and if you're a musician you may decide that it has a very interesting structure and write it down in musical notation and make a fugue out of it. These things are all very different; the wiggling of your eardrum is very different from the black marks on the paper. But there is one aspect, the structural one, in which the wiggling of your eardrum and the black marks on the paper are the same. That aspect of structure which is common to all the examples (including a neurological representation of the melody in the human head) *is* the melody. That is what we *mean* by the melody. The melody is that structure.

Someone might say, "Well, aha, melody is an abstract structure which ...." No. *There are no abstract structures:* All structures are embodied structures. All structures are manifested structures. Every one of the things just described, including the black marks on the paper, is a real "physical" structure. It is a real manifestation or embodiment of that structure (or instantiation of that structure), and certain conventions tell us that certain other aspects of the real situation in which the structure is manifest are irrelevant (e.g., the fact that it's flat, and it's on a piece of paper made of 40% used rags and 60% dead trees, that the notes are black instead of green, that they are this thick, etc.). Such aspects of structure are known to be irrelevant because we understand the convention of musical notation, which lets us look at that way of embodying that structure and pick out of it those aspects which are the melody and manifest them on, say, the piano.

Suppose you say, "But what about thought?" Craik contends that thought is just the same: In thought, structures are manifested; there's real "stuff" going on in your head which has the same structure as the "stuff" in the world which it represents or which it *models*. Certain aspects of the structure of the world are embodied in our internal model of the world, and it is the correspondence between those structures which is the basis of intelligence.

One thing might be confusing, namely, that we can *refer* to a structure; we can indicate a structure without embodying it. If I say, "Mary had a little lamb," I refer to a structure which is the melody "Mary had a little lamb," and my reference to it is done with a symbol, "Mary had a little lamb," that has no structural relationship to that melody. It's an arbitrary symbol that is assigned to that structure as a name. Now I can present that name and thereby (as demonstrated by Bransford and Franks) under the right conditions bring about in someone's head that structure, but the name "Mary had a little lamb" does not *carry* its meaning. *A symbol does not carry its meaning.* There are abstract representations of structure, but there still are no abstract structures. "Michael Turvey" is an abstract representation of a certain structure in the universe. The words "Michael Turvey" as an abstract representation of the real object which we call Michael Turvey do not correspond to him in structure in any way. There is no structural correspondence between the real Michael Turvey and the name: The evidence is that if, for example, I say, "Would the real Michael Turvey stand up," and if Michael is being cooperative, *he* will stand up and the symbol will not. (That test doesn't work for melodies. It's not an infallible test of whether we have an abstract or an embodied structure, but it shows the difference between indicated and embodied structures.)

Let's look at some conclusions that can be drawn from this analysis. What can be done with this conceptual framework? Craik does a beautiful thing with it: He says, "Look, if all our knowledge is our internal model of the world, then it doesn't matter how we embody those structures and in fact we can expect that they will be embodied in many different ways." Let me give an example. Consider the problem of how we know the principle of causality. (Assume for the moment that the principle of causality is real, and that we have knowledge of that principle: perhaps not perfect knowledge, but some knowledge—enough that we can bring that principle to bear on our simulations of various real events and processes. If the principle of causality is false, then whatever real principle is true will follow this argument in the same way. This argument holds for *whatever* principle happens to be true of the world, whether causality or synchronicity or something totally unknown). Craik argues that the way we know causality is not through some notes in our memory that say, "Hey, don't forget about the principle of causality." Rather, the principle has to be applied whenever there is an internal simulation. That is, the principle of causality is represented in our memory (or our mind, or internal model of the world) thus: Our minds are made out of matter and thereby obey all the physical laws that matter obeys. We know the principle of causality by virtue of our heads being made out of matter. Presumably, we know many other physical laws by virtue of our heads being made out of matter. Certain other things—which could be called biological laws—are known, we might suppose, through the cells that make up our heads: Things that are true of all cells are true of the cells in our heads; and when they do what they do, they do it according to those laws. Since all heads are made of cells, we thereby know a great deal about organisms.

What we have been talking about is all that is needed to enable anyone to do some of the things that organisms do with their "knowledge." All we need (to be able to do the things that we do) is something going on in our nervous systems which corresponds with reality in structure in relevant respects. I don't have to know the ultimate nature of a table to keep from running into it, or to put something on it and have it stay there. All I have to have is sufficient structural correspondence between the relevant aspects of the structure of the table and relevant aspects of the structure of my internal model of it. The embodiments of those structures do not in any sense have to be the same or similar: The material need not be the same. Now consider the principle of causality again. There is a place in the nervous system where causality occurs: Presumably synaptic transmission occurs according to the principle of causality (if that is really the principle). Nerve A fires and it makes nerve B fire, so that every time neural transmission occurs there is a *representation* of the principle of causality.

Now I want to consider squishiness (I will be eternally grateful to Haj Ross for introducing that term). I want to propose a neural instantiation of squishiness. Karl Pribram, in *Languages of the Brain* (1971), has several chapters describing the holographic theory of memory. Pribram talks about some properties of nervous tissue. Everybody, he says, has thought that nervous tissue works like synaptic relays. But if we look at a single nerve we see other things going on which have been called dendritic potentials or slow potentials. Looking at a single nerve we can only say something weird is happening; we don't really know what it is—some change in the electrical potential around certain parts of the neuron. Looking at the slow potentials we have a field, a sort of "wiggliness." If we look at the global properties of the brain in this respect there are waves and interference patterns. If we look at the individual neuron and its individual slow potentials, we can't see that; but many of them together show a complex pattern continually changing over time, in a regular and orderly but very complicated way. Presumably these regular and orderly changes in the slow potential field regulate whether the nerve fires or not. Neural firing is discrete, an all-or-none process. But now we find that the causal relations controlling that firing are continuous rather than discrete. The situation is exactly analogous to that in linguistics which led Ross to abandon all-or-none categories for a "category squish," and the holographic conception of memory that Pribram proposes is built upon this neural squishiness.

Historically, psychologists have held a machine model of the way mind works, and now theorists from several fields come along and say, "Nope, it's squishy. There are coalitions and we can't think about it as discrete . . ." But either the nerves fire or they do not. Either you did kick the person or you did not. Either I did say "cat" or I did not. How are we going to reconcile these squishy, holographic, dendritic potential, coalitional properties which seem to be present (in what we might call active, or semantic, memory) with all the hard, solid, discrete "lumps" coming out in behavior? I think we can see a resolution in the individual neuron. At the neural level there are slow potential activities on the dendritic side and actual "yes or no" firings on the other. But let's suppose with Pribram that active memory is squishy and holographic and coalitional and, as Carl Jung would say, synchronistic, and that acts, on the other hand, have "edges." Look for a moment at some other kinds of coalitions. One property of coalitions is that of lacking distinct boundaries. The anthropologists Berlin and Kay wrote a book called *Basic Color Terms: Their Universality and Evolution* (1969), which talks about the ways different languages use what are called *basic color* terms. Everyone thinks that the color spectrum is continuous, that one can cut it up however one likes: Indeed, we find earlier anthropologists claiming that how it is cut up is completely arbitrary. Berlin and Kay show that it is not at all arbitrary, and that in fact certain languages (or classes or languages) always cut it up in essentially the same way. Moreover, there is an ordering principle over those classes of languages: In a language in which there are only basic color terms for black and for white, if one names one color in addition to black and white, it will be red. If two colors are named in addition to black and white, the colors named will be red and either blue or yellow. If three colors are named—red, blue, and yellow. If our—red, blue, yellow, and either orange or green. If five—red, blue, yellow, orange, and green. The English language is as sophisticated as a language has ever been found to be in this respect.

Now consider all the languages of a particular type. Berlin and Kay did experiments with Munsell color chips presented in a regular array with spectral hue going across one way and saturation going another and asked people, "Show me the best red." Everybody in their sample from a particular culture would show them the best red, and Ss would make their marks on a chart of the color chips. Then they did that task with another culture that has the same color categories. Also, with the same Ss, they said, "Draw a line around the category red." They found that within a given culture there was much greater agreement about the best red than about the edge of the category. But they also found, looking across cultures that have the same basic pattern of color names (and these are mainly languages which before the transformational revolution would have been called "unrelated"), less variance across the means of the cultures than across the means of the individuals within a particular culture. Naming color, deciding whether something is, say, red or not, is not done by seeing a color fall within a certain boundary—it's done by seeing how close it comes to a prototype.

Another familiar example of squishiness and discrete categorization is the behavior of lateral inhibitory analyzers (or Hubel and Wiesel cells) for property detectors in sensory systems. Suppose we have a line detector for which there is a prototypic stimulus to which that cell will fire maximally. If we change it in any way, tilt it, make it shorter, longer, darker, fatter, or curvier, the cell will not fire as much and we'll get an inverted U-shaped function for each of those dimensions; and there may be dimensions which the cell doesn't respond to, and if it is changed in those ways it still fires just as much. One could say that the properties of the cell were invariant with respect to that change. But the point is that here is another example of the organism looking for the *best* instance of a category and finding it in a squishy way. What the organism does is not squishy. Either the cell fires or it doesn't. Either it says red or it doesn't, but it can say either "That sort of seems like red" or "Oh, boy! RED!"

Now I have noted that active memory is squishy and acts are not so squishy. But the parallels to the history of linguistics need to be emphasized, to show how much this has changed our theorizing. In 1957 or so, we had surface structures derived from deep structures which were considered to be the heart of the matter, and they were interpretively related to meanings. Now let's identify meanings with memory and tacit knowledge, and let's identify surface structures with acts. As we go through history to what Ross called abstract syntax, where we gradually pushed our rules back toward the meanings so that they were not just interpretative, we finally reach a point called "generative semantics"–at which point we can't tell where the semantics ends and the syntax starts. We don't know how to discretely cut up the list of rules that maps memory onto behavior–memory onto an act, onto a description of behavioral structure. We start with a description of the structure of the act and map back into a description of the structure of what is going on in memory that underlies that act. As we do that, suddenly there is evidence that the kinds of categories that are relevant, the kinds of categories that are in our logical description, are squishy. As our analysis moves back into semantic memory we have to deal with squishy categories. I believe that this aspect of tacit knowledge is inherently squishy. At the deep structural level we have squishy, coalitional, holographic memory, but at behavior we have discrete acts with edges; and as we finally get rules to start mapping from squishy memory to discrete acts, we start having squishiness in our categories and our rules.

DISCUSSION

Member of Audience: How do you relate tacit knowledge, as inherently "squishy," to our feeling of certainty that we know something?

Halwes: Consider an analogy: There's no way for me to tell where the edge of a hill is. Here's a valley and there is a hill and nobody can identify the boundary with certainty. With a precise mathematical function I might be able to take some higher-order derivative to tell where the inflection point is, i.e., where the hill starts. I know for certain that there's a hill there, but I don't know where the hill separates from the valley.

One of the convenient things about knowledge in its relation to the world is that the world has certain aspects which are *not* squishy. There are tables that do have edges; there are prime numbers that do have certain properties and are discretely different from the other numbers. Inasmuch as my knowledge does in fact correspond in structure with the world, it will have edges in it: It will be discrete. There will be discrete structures within my knowledge, or at least representation of the discreteness of those structures. That doesn't mean that the representations themselves are discrete: I can have a hologram in which I take a picture of two cubes, and in the hologram at every point is the information specifying those two cubes, and their discreteness, their relative position, and so on.

Member of the Audience: How do you decide what are the psychologically relevant aspects of structure?

Halwes: There are several answers to that. One of them, which Gibson might give, is that the organism evolved to pick up just those invariances which afford the kinds of interactions with the environment that the organism must make to survive or adapt to it, so that in some real sense we don't have to cognitively decide what's relevant in the structure. For example, in the work on speech perception done at Haskins Labs, even though the speech signal in some acoustical representation is very messy, we are quite good at picking out just those aspects of the signal that are needed to understand speech. But the machinery in our heads for doing that evolved at the same time that the machinery in our mouths evolved for making speech noises. Philip Lieberman's (Lieberman, 1968; Lieberman, Klatt, & Wilson, 1969) work on the evolution of the human vocal tract shows that the reason monkeys can't talk is not that they're dumb, but rather that they can't make such noises with their mouths; their mouths are not constructed correctly. He shows that the human vocal tract has evolved in such a way as to enable man to speak, and that the selection pressure to do that was so strong that it was able to develop in the face of changes such as the dropping of our larynx (which means that we now have two cavities that are separable by the inflection of our tongue and the proximity of it to the roof of our mouth, which allows variation of the relative size of those two cavities, which gives formant structure, which is what carries most of the segmental information in speech). Now dropping the larynx, which makes speech possible, also makes it possible for us to choke to death. Monkeys presumably don't choke to death when food falls on top of the larynx and they gasp it in; they can choke to death if they get a bone stuck in their throat, but not by inhaling food (at least it's very much harder). So we have an evolutionary change in the morphological structure of the human vocal tract which makes it adaptive for speaking and maladaptive for breathing and eating. There must have been a staggering selection pressure to make it so. Now, whenever a morphological change has taken place in an organism through evolution, there always has been an accompanying change in the neurological wiring or structure of the organism, making it possible and easy for the organism to use that morphological structure. If a duck has big blue patches on the bottom of its wings that it uses to attract its mate, it also has some programs wired into its head that make it tend to display when its hormonal level is high. Speech is a special case, because the organism produces the same thing that it wants to pick up. But all that Gibson and Shaw emphasize—the senses considered as perceptual systems—can be handled on an evolutionary model. With regard to psychological decisions about relevance of structure, there is the problem of attention, and I will discuss that in Part II.

Member of Audience: My question is whether causality is contradictory to what Shaw said about particular neurologies supporting the algoristic and information model. Your comment was that the structure of a melody exists even on the paper, as well as in the head. It seems that by the same reasoning the characteristics of the paper should have an influence on the melody, that the ink on the paper should have an influence on the songs.

Halwes: I think that you're misunderstanding what I said. A basic point of Russell's structural realism is that it doesn't matter *how* we structurally represent certain aspects of reality as long as we do so if it's relevant. So assume that there really is a squishy memory, which is how we represent what we commonly think of ourselves as "knowing." In some sense we need to know about causality if we want a simulation that we make with our internal model to work. But we don't have to know it in the sense of having it stored in squishy memory in an interference pattern, because no matter what kind of memory we have, we can't build a memory which will not "know" the principle of causality. That doesn't mean that one couldn't build a memory which would pretend that the principle of causality wasn't true; nor does it mean that one couldn't come to know—know in the squishy sense, in the sense of tacit knowledge—that the principle of causality was true. Witness the fact that we're talking about it: The basis of my talking about the principle of causality is not that my mind is made out of matter; it is rather that I have indirectly learned some things about causality by paying attention to certain aspects of reality, so not only do I have the fundamental representation of causality in the structure of my brain by virtue of its being made out of matter, but I also have some tacit knowledge about causality by virtue of my having paid attention to certain relevant aspects of the world.

I will make a distinction at this point. Up to now we've been discussing tacit knowledge as if it were homogeneous, but I think we will have to distinugish at least two kinds of tacit knowledge, if not more. Tacit knowledge is knowledge that we don't know that we have, or that we are not at the moment that we are using it aware that we have. So let's suppose that we have squishy, holographic tacit knowledge. But we also have some knowledge which, while perhaps not now present in the holographic matrix, could be retrieved from more permanent memory. One could learn that the organism had that kind of knowledge by doing certain experiments, and ascertain the properties of that kind of knowledge. This knowledge is like the organism's knowledge of causality—we would learn that we had it by doing physics, discovering the principle, and then noticing that the organism behaves in accordance with it. There is other knowledge, about biological things, which the organism has by virtue of the fact that its brain is made of cells, which we would learn about by doing cell physiology. It might be a little clearer if we made up some terms, e.g., material knowledge, which we have because our brain is made out of matter, organismic knowledge, which we have because our brain is made of cells, and tacit knowledge, which is squishy holographic coalitional knowledge.

Member of Audience: Wouldn't we then have to say that the table has tacit knowledge of causality?

Halwes: The table *embodies* the structural relationships that we call causality: It would be silly to call it knowledge. I think that way of putting it is not unnatural if Craik's definition of the problem of understanding the way the mind works is taken seriously. As I said, there are different kinds of knowledge. There is some which we would easily call knowledge, and there is the "other" aspect of our internal model of the world, embodied in the very stuff it's made of, which one presumably has in order that one's internal simulations of the world will be correct. We don't have to call it knowledge, but if somebody asks, "How do you know the principle of causality?" or, "How does your dog know the principle of causality?" the answer is as I've described. We don't have to call it knowledge if we don't want to call it knowledge. But the internal model of the world is primary, is prior to and more important than the different ways of representing it. The fundamental problem is to see the symmetries between the environment and optic array (or the information coming into the organism from the environment), and the internal model of the environment, the experience of the organism, and what the organism does. We may want to partition those symmetries, and maybe we can; probably it's interesting and useful to do so. But before we can partition them, before we can start deciding how various aspects of the symmetrical structure are embodied in the organism, we must first be able to see it *as* a symmetry. The knowledge relationship, which is fundamentally the relationship between the organism's model and the environment, is that symmetry.

PART II

G. Spencer Brown, who might be called a logician, wrote a book called *Laws of Form* (1969). He is mentioned briefly in Bertrand Russell's autobiography. In effect Russell wrote that he was feeling out of touch with modern logical work, that he didn't have anything to contribute, and then Spencer Brown came to see him and explained a new way of dealing with logic which Russell found fascinating. It opened him up and he felt as if he were involved again in the things he had been studying when he was younger. What Spencer Brown told Russell is in *Laws of Form*. The book's starting point is Boolean algebra: Spencer Brown noticed that Boole and others, in making up algebras of logic, made an error. The error was to *interpret* the algebra before deriving the theorems. At the beginning, when one first starts to do Boolean algebra one *decides* that 1 means true and 0 means false: The symbols have been interpreted. They are no longer abstract symbols; they are interpreted symbols. Spencer Brown said, in effect, let's not do that; let's start with an uninterpreted algebra and then see what we can do about proving the theorems in the full generality of the thing. What he developed was a logical calculus which is both elegant and powerful in comparison to Boolean algebra. It enabled him to do amazing things, such as resolving Gödel's dilemma. He has also been able to derive a logical arithmetic. We can see what this arithmetic does by taking, for example, one of Lewis Carroll's logic problems in which the cow is sitting on my lap, all aardvarks prefer snaps, no graduate student at the University of Connecticut understands constructive theory, etc. When all those eighty premises are put together in an argument we come up with a conclusion such as "It is unholy to eat bricks." But we can solve the problem by simply writing it out in the notation of Spencer Brown's algebra: Do cancellation and it's solved. (Of course there are more powerful operations than simple cancellation.) In addition to such problems of logic, the book also has several passages of more general interest. This is one of them:

> Discoveries of any great moment in mathematics and other disciplines, once they are discovered, are seen to be extremely simple and obvious, and make everybody, including their discoverer, appear foolish for not having discovered them before. It is all too often forgotten that the ancient symbol for the prenascence of the world is a fool, and that foolishness, being a divine state, is not a condition to be either proud or ashamed of.

> Unfortunately we find systems of education today which have departed so far from the plain truth, that they now teach us to be proud of what we know and ashamed of ignorance.

This is doubly corrupt. It is corrupt not only because pride is in itself a mortal sin, but also because to teach pride in knowledge is to put up an effective barrier against any advance upon what is already known, since it makes one ashamed to look beyond the bounds imposed by one's ignorance.

To any person prepared to enter with respect into the realm of his great and universal ignorance, the secrets of being will eventually unfold, and they will do so in a measure according to his freedom from natural and indoctrinated shame in his respect of their revelation.

In the face of the strong, and indeed violent, social pressures against it, few people have been prepared to take this simple and satisfying course towards sanity. And in a society where a prominent psychiatrist can advertise that, given the chance, he would have treated Newton to electric shock therapy, who can blame any person for being afraid to do so?

To arrive at the simplest truth, as Newton knew and practiced, requires *years* of *contemplation*. Not activity. Not reasoning. Not calculating. Not busy behavior of any kind. Not reading. Not talking. Not making an effort. Not thinking. Simply *bearing in mind* what it is one needs to know. And yet those with the courage to tread this path to real discovery are not only offered practically no guidance on how to do so, they are actively discouraged and have to set about it in secret, pretending meanwhile to be diligently engaged in the frantic diversions and to conform with the deadening personal opinions which are being continually thrust upon them.

In these circumstances, the discoveries that any person is able to undertake represent the places where, in the face of induced psychosis, he has, by his own faltering and unaided efforts, returned to sanity. Painfully, and even dangerously, maybe. But nonetheless returned, however furtively [Spencer Brown, 1969, pp. 109-110].

I want to try to tell you something of what G. Spencer Brown meant when he wrote that. I will start with an example from an experiment done by Ulric Neisser. Neisser (1967) did some experiments called scanning experiments. He started by studying people who look for items to clip in newspapers. There are clipping-finding firms which say, "If you hire us, we will find for you all the places in all the newspapers (that you tell us to look in) where anybody said anything with your name in it, or whatever you ask us to look for." These "spotters," usually women, go through the papers and find all these things; it is done with about 80% accuracy and incredibly fast. At least it appears fast to people using their heads in what we consider a normal way. Neisser also found that it didn't matter how many things had to be spotted: 30 items could be spotted just as fast as 2 could. Neisser found that people can *learn* to do it. People can learn to scan a list and find an item that they have been instructed to look for, and they can do it very fast, no matter how many items they are looking for.

Anyone who wants to develop that skill can do so. We can call it "finding." In order to learn to do "finding," we have to learn how to experience—say, if we do it visually—*experience* a visual array *without constructing* our experience. We must learn how to scan a visual field. As my best example, this is how I learned that I could do it: I was in a field with a group of people wandering around looking for a girl's bracelet. It was a big field, and the bracelet was somewhere in the field. About fifteen people were looking for it, and I was sitting there because I assumed that fifteen people could find it. But I got tired of waiting, so I decided that I would help. I decided that instead of looking for the bracelet I would just scan over the field, and sure enough, about a minute later I found the bracelet. When we do this,

Neisser says, it seems that we don't even see what we're looking at. We don't see the blades of grass, or the words on the list, except that we do *see* them and know they're there, but we don't see them in the way that we normally see them. We can't say what any of those words are. I couldn't tell where the individual blades of grass were, though in some sense I knew that there were blades of grass there. Somehow the object emerges from the background and we do see *it.* We scan the array, and there, if we encounter it, is the thing we're looking for.

If one were doing that task without using Neisser's strategy, one would look at every single thing encountered—one would look at every blade of grass, decide that it was not a bracelet, go on and look at the next blade of grass, etc. In terms of constructive theory, we would construct an experience of that blade of grass, decide that it wasn't (reject it as a recognition of) the desired object, and go on with the search strategy. In the finding strategy, we scan the field and when we pass over the area where the object is, we construct that, and there it is. There is data relevant to this. Sperling (1960) presents an array of, say, letters tachistoscopically. Some of them are yellow, some are red, and some green, for example. Then, after the display has gone away, he gives the *S* a cue which tells him which color he's supposed to see and then the *S* tells *E* which ones were of that color. This is Sperling's evidence that there is not, apparently, the same kind of limit on what we might call tacit knowledge (or what Neisser calls preattentive processing) that there is on central processing. Somehow we can take in an enormous amount of information if we don't have to report it. But Sperling's experiment shows that doing this is not as simple as we might expect: We can't just walk in and sit down in front of the T-scope and do it. We have to learn *not so see* what he shows us: to learn *not* to look at it in the way that is normal to us. We have to learn to sit there and let it happen: Then the cue comes and—*Boom!*—we see exactly what we were supposed to see.

I might construct an experience of only, say, the yellow letters. Again: Red cue comes up and I see only the red letters. If I attempted the task without any practice at learning how to do it, how not to automatically construct what comes up on the screen, I would not succeed. I would see the first five letters in the line, or this letter over here and that letter over there, etc., but I would not be able to manifest the Sperling phenomenon.

There is, then, a mode of perception available to us which we do not normally use, which is very similar to what G. Spencer Brown described. Remember what he said: "To any person prepared to enter with respect into the realm of his great and universal ignorance, the secrets of being will eventually unfold"—not thinking, not reading, not talking, not making an effort, not busy behavior of any kind, not activity, not reasoning, not calculating—simply *"bearing in mind* what it is one needs to know." If we try to do the Sperling or Neisser tasks and don't really know what we're looking for, we won't succeed.

The key is simply to bear in mind what it is one needs to know. Neisser talks about focal attention as if it were an act, and Skinner talks about perception as if it were an act. I often talk about experience as if it were an act, an act of construction. I want to sharpen my earlier remark—that all experience is both constructive and Gibsonian. I said that there is an exception to that generalization in the phenomenon of hallucination, which is more or less purely constructive. And now I would add that there is a class of exceptions on the other side—a mode of experience in which the Gibsonian information is experienced relatively directly. Let me step back and give an analogy that is not really an analogy: goal seeking.

Organisms seem capable of taking on any number of forms to manifest themselves in any number of ways. An organism apparently can turn itself into any of a number of "tools." By "tool" I mean a way of organization that may enable the organism, because it is thus organized, to get this job done. We decide what needs to be done to achieve a goal, then we turn ourselves into a machine for doing that, and then we start doing it; when we get to the goal, we notice that we've gotten there and we stop. That strategy is what social psychologists talk about in role theory, and constructing our experience is what we talk about in perception.

One of the general characteristics of roles in social interaction, strategies of construction in perception, etc., is that the organism, turning itself into a machine for doing something, becomes more sensitive to certain aspects of the information coming in from the environment which it has determined, in its definition of the task, to be relevant. In driving my car, I may become more sensitive to feedback that I get from my arms about what the steering wheel is doing; I may become more sensitive to certain aspects of the visual array which tell me whether the car is on the road or not; but I also become *less* sensitive to everything else—everything that is not in the definition of the "machine" that I have become. Here the organism becomes more efficient in doing what it has decided to do. But in certain kinds of situations this strategy doesn't work, namely when one has turned oneself into the wrong machine. That would be the case, for example, if I happened to turn myself into the wrong kind of machine while trying to establish a relationship with a person of the opposite sex. If I had not turned myself into the wrong kind of machine, i.e., if I had not made myself insensitive to everything except what I expected to need to do, then I would have been able to notice that person's negative response to what my machine was doing. But that information did not get into the definition of our machine: Perhaps we assumed that it would work, which is why we're shocked when it doesn't. If the definition of our machine has omitted something relevant to the accomplishment of our task, it's likely that we will make an error.

Another kind of thing can happen as well: We may actually go through a goal state which is abstractly equivalent to the goal specified, and leave it because it's not what we decided we wanted. Having made ourselves insensitive to everything which would tell us anything except what we expected to need to know, we didn't notice that we had gotten there, because we were defining "there" in terms of surface structure instead of deep structure.

As shown by Neisser's experiments and Spencer Brown's book (and by various other things going on in the world), we don't have to do it that way. We don't have to turn ourselves into machines to do some thing; it's just that people do, in fact, usually turn themselves into machines for doing various things. We don't have to construct our experience in perception; it's just that we do in fact usually construct our experience in perception. It's not that the organism cannot be Gibsonianly aware of the environment; it's just that we—as almost every adult human does—construct our perceptual experience almost all the time. We may not even have an experiential basis for knowing what is meant by saying that we do not *have* to construct experience. "Almost all the time" means literally that.

There have been many attempts to make people aware that they don't have to turn themselves into machines and that, in fact, if they didn't they would be better off—happier, stronger, more able to do the things they must do to survive or to achieve whatever they want. All the mystics that ever lived have made such attempts. For example, the Zen Buddhists claim that the way to know about something is to sit and look—not because we couldn't learn anything about it by turning ourselves into machines for learning about it, but because if we do that we have already constrained what we can possibly learn about it. We have assumed that we know what is needed to know and turned ourselves into machines for learning that. If we're lucky and good at turning ourselves into machines, we will learn that, but we will not learn anything else. Similarly, asking a very wise person who knows all about the world for the answer to a particular question would be different from asking, "Please tell me what would be most interesting and useful for me to know at this time." We get much more interesting, much richer answers with the second strategy.

In psychology, we pretend an interest in other people; but most of us are interested in ourselves, and maybe in the people that we interact with every day. We have a personal interest in the things that we learn in psychology, so the problem of the algorist in psychology is very much like the question "Who am I?" Socrates' answer is "Know thyself." But in trying to know ourselves we've turned ourselves into machines for knowing ourselves according to the methodological principles that were laid down by behavioristic psychology, western philosophy, and so forth. Now these principles do demonstrably work: People who believe them can learn *some* things about who they are. Although many have argued that we haven't learned very much about who we are, we have learned something about what we are doing and we have learned something about how we do it. Even so, we can't go very much farther in the direction of learning about what we are doing or how we do it without learning something more about who we are.

When I say we construct our experience—we normally construct all our experience— that includes our experience of our self. In doing so we use our tacit knowledge. The Zen Buddhists (and their predecessors) have been talking about it for 3,000 years. Freud tried to talk about it and called it the unconscious. The unconscious is what holds all the information about how to construct our experience of our self, as well as all our other experience, as well as everything else we do. When the Buddhists, Freud, and others talk about the unconscious, they also talk about what is called the ego. Today the ego has a poor reputation: People have a tendency to think that egos are bad. Let me quote a passage about the badness of egos by George Santayana, at the beginning of Erving Goffman's *The Presentation of Self in Everyday Life (1959).* Santayana says:

> Masks are arrested expressions and admirable echoes of feeling, at once faithful, discrete, and superlative. Living things in contact with the air must acquire a cuticle, and it is not urged against cuticles that they are not hearts; yet some philosophers seem to be angry with images for not being things and with words for not being feelings. Words and images are like

shells, no less integral parts of nature than are the substances they cover, but better addressed to the eye and more open to observation. I would not say that substance exists for the sake of appearance, or faces for the sake of masks, or the passions for the sake of poetry and virtue. Nothing arises in nature for the sake of anything else; all these phases and products are involved equally in the round of existence . . .[Goffman, p. vii] .

The question, then, is not so much whether the ego is bad or not; nevertheless we do have egos, and it is, I submit, a relevant part of the problem of understanding who we are to look at the problems they pose.

Let's relate this to perception (we are in fact speaking of perception here). We're speaking of our perception of ourselves: How do you or I experience ourselves? But let's look at ordinary perception again, at the problem of how to put Gibsonian theory together with constructive theory, in the narrow sense. I submit that all construction in perception is *based on* Gibsonian direct realism; that what constrains it is the tacit knowledge of the group of invariants which are introjected in the sense of Gibson. (We might call the narrow sense of constructive theory which is supposedly at odds with Gibsonian direct realism "classical constructive theory," and call the theory which I'm describing here, which says that the two are not opposed but rather indispensable parts of an integrated theory of perception, coalitional constructive theory.)

Our constructions are also constrained by our beliefs, our knowledge, etc., about what we might see. In experiencing the world, just as in experiencing ourself, we have a theory of the way the world will be; we construct an experience of the world based both on the information coming in (as Gibson has described), and on what we believe is supposed to be there. Don Juan, talking to Carlos Castaneda (1969) says, "You talk too much. You talk to yourself all the time." And what happens when we talk to ourselves is that things come to us—information comes to us, and we talk to ourselves about it, and when we talk about it we make the world be stable. We make the world continue to look the way we believe that it ought to look. But if we would stop talking to ourselves about what happens to us, then eventually we would see the world the way it really is. While it's true that we can experience the Gibsonian invariants directly, we do not *normally* do so. We do not normally let ourselves simply resonate with reality at the place where we are.

I think that this conception of turning ourselves into a tool is much deeper, much more pervasive, and has a much greater effect on our lives, on our experience of ourselves, on our ability to learn things about our world, than might be imagined. A friend once told me a story: One day he was sitting around thinking about thinking, and said, "Now, it seems to me that I usually think in words and that sometimes I think in images." Then he considered the question, "Is it possible to think without using either images or words?" What happened when he asked himself that question was that it "blew the top of his head off." While I don't expect that I've blown the top of the reader's head off, I do think it useful to consider that the way we all normally think is by using tools, such as our ability to talk, our ability to talk to ourselves, our ability to make or construct pictures, etc., and that we somehow try to use these tools for cutting up the world, into snippets if you like, that are going to be useful for the goals we perceive. Here we are, "snippeting" away, holding the top of our heads on with both hands. I suggest that we don't have to do that: If we stop, life will become more interesting and we will presumably become better psychologists, i.e., scientists who understand how the mind works.

Let me close with an allegory that makes this point. *The Once and Future King* by White (1966) tells a beautiful story about Merlin and Arthur. Merlin teaches Arthur by turning him into various animals; Arthur lives with the animals for a while, and they teach him how they live. In his last lesson Arthur is turned into a badger. He lives with a badger, and the badger reads him his thesis (in White's book, writing a dissertation is a symbol of wisdom). The badger explains why all animals are under the dominion of man, why all animals love man when man gives them a chance (as in the case of St. Francis): There are all these embryos "up there," says the badger, and God and his people are working to get them ready. What the embryos have in common is that they all look alike. In fact, they all look like a little human being with an enormous head. God says, "All right, each of you is allowed to choose two or three tools which will be useful in your life." And so some embryos choose to have their body be like a boat and to use their mouths as scissors; some choose to have their arms be wings and their feet clamps and their bills knives. The badger chooses to have his fur to be a shield and his front paws be digging tools and his mouth be a weapon. Now we come to the last embryo, which is man. And God says, "You're the last one, man. What do you want?" And man says, "I have thought about it very carefully and decided that since You made us in this form, You must have had a good reason, and so I choose to keep what You have given me already. I will not take on any new tools and I will try to get along with whatever tools I can pick up in my world."

As a human organism grows, it has to learn how to pick up the tools, how to make them, and use them, to do the things that other animals do with their fur, their bills, their beaks, their claws, their wings, etc. If I want to fly, I must build an airplane. However, a time comes in the life of a human organism when it realizes that it has done all it can do in developing tools and learning to use them, and it looks for something else to occupy its time. Nicoll (1957) writes about something taking place in the early phase of life which he calls a growth of essence, the essence of the organism. Later pain and boredom start impinging on the organism and it starts building a shell around it, a shell of the things we might call tools. That shell, which is the personality, with time grows thicker and better able to deal with various aspects of the world, to protect the essence of the organism from being damaged, hurt, bored, or whatever, by its environment. A time comes when the personality has developed so much that it seems nothing else could be added to it. At some point we reach the decision that all the things we could do if we decided to will not give us, once we get them, what we thought they would give us. At some point the organism decides that it's tired of all that development of personality; and if it stops, and if it has the right kind of guidance (which it does if it really stops; then the guidance just comes, by a principle which Jung called synchronicity), then the personality starts collapsing back in on the essence, which grows again using the personality as food. The organism becomes able to do the things it was able to do with its tools, but now it does them with its essence, with its tacit knowledge, and it can also do the things it was not able to do because it had not developed those tools. The organism stops experimenting with particular tools and begins to rely on the raw intelligence of a truly general purpose intellect. That, I submit, is what we must do if we are ever to understand the problems (and the promises) of cognitive psychology. It is time to let go of the top of our heads.

REFERENCES

Berlin, B., & Kay, P. *Basic color terms: Their universality and evolution.* Berkeley: University of California Press, 1969.

Castaneda, C. *The teachings of Don Juan: A Yaqui way of knowledge.* New York: Ballantine, 1969.

Craik, K. J. W. *The nature of explanation.* Cambridge: Cambridge University Press, 1943.

Goffman, E. *The presentation of self in everyday life.* New York: Doubleday, 1959.

Hanson, N. R. A picture theory of theory meaning. In R. G. Colodny (Ed.), *The nature and function of scientific theories.* Pittsburgh: University of Pittsburgh Press, 1970.

Lieberman, P. Primate vocalizations and human linguistic ability. *Journal of the Acoustical Society of America,* 1968, **44,** 1574-1584.

Lieberman, P., Klatt, D. H., & Wilson, W. A. Vocal tract limitations on the vowel repertoires of rhesus monkeys and other nonhuman primates. *Science,* 1969, **164,** 1185-1187.

Neisser, U. *Cognitive psychology.* New York: Appleton-Century-Crofts,1967.

Nicoll, M. *Psychological commentaries on the teaching of G. I. Gurdjieff and P. D. Ouspensky.* Vol. 1. London: Vincent Stuart, 1957

Pribram, K. *Languages of the brain.* Englewood Cliffs, N. J.: Prentice-Hall, 1971.

Russell B. *Human knowledge: Its scope and limits.* New York: Simon & Schuster, 1948.

Spencer Brown, G. *Laws of form.* London: Allen & Unwin, 1969.

Sperling, G. The information available in brief visual presentations. *Psychological Monographs,* 1960, **74** (Whole No. 498).

White, T. H. *The once and future king.* New York: Berkeley, 1966.

17
A POSSIBLE SOLUTION TO THE PATTERN RECOGNITION PROBLEM IN THE SPEECH MODALITY

Terry Halwes and Bobbette Wire
University of Connecticut

On the way home from the conference we generated a conceptual synthesis which may lead to an understanding of how a person knows what someone is saying. This brief description is not intended to be comprehensive, but may allow people who are really interested (and willing to read the background material cited at the end of the chapter) to make the necessary connections.

This note consists of two sections: The first describes where things stood at the time of the conference—this part of the theory is fairly well substantiated by experimental evidence, only some of which will be referred to. The second section deals with our extension of the theory. This aspect of the theory is speculative, and there is still no direct experimental support for certain important claims. However, it is the first conceptual analysis of the pattern recognition problem, at this level of detail, which could conceivably be correct, given our present knowledge.

OUTLINE OF A CONSTRUCTIVE MOTOR THEORY OF PHONOLOGICAL EXPERIENCE

Our normal experience of language consists of at least three distinct, quasi-independent modes of construction. If we concern ourselves with spoken language, from the point of view of the listener, the three are: (*a*) a semantic mode, corresponding to the processes that underlie what is called comprehension and imagination, whereby we experience the "meaning" of what we hear; (*b*) a phonological mode, fundamentally an articulatory process, whereby we experience *what* has been said to us, distinct from what it means (this is the mode of experience that lets us quote a nonsense sequence like "jor gexle fubbed rel" without having any idea of what it might mean); (*c*) an acoustic mode, which corresponds to our normal manner of experiencing non-speech sounds, and whereby we experience certain non-linguistic aspects of speech, as well as the acoustic basis of the linguistically relevant aspects of speech (though this latter does not generally play a very large role in our direct experience of a speech situation, except under the conditions of certain laboratory experiments).

These three modes of construction are, as we emphasized, quasi-independent. Each can proceed without the others, as in one's hearing synthetic speech without hearing it *as* speech, hearing nonsense syllables without understanding them, saying nonsense syllables to oneself without either hearing or understanding them, or imagining some state of affairs in the world without any use of language (either internal or external). We say *quasi*-independent because the three modes normally influence each other, as in Warren's (1970) experiments where listeners, presented with a sentencce in which noise has replaced a highly redundant word (a word strongly determined by the surrounding semantic context, like "to" in "going to the store"), *hear* the missing word as if it had not been replaced by noise.

Here we are specifically concerned with the phonological-articulatory mode of constructing experience. This mode plays a role in many different cognitive skills: It is involved in perceiving, remembering, imagining, hallucinating, and producing speech, and is also used in reading and writing.

Concerning the nature of this mode of experience, called the "speech mode" by Liberman, Cooper, Shankweiller & Studdert-Kennedy (1967), we may say this with some confidence:

Underlying the experience of language at the phonological level, in every form of language use, are processes which are basically identical to the motor coordination processes involved in speaking, with the motor commands being in some way inhibited in all cases but that of overt speech.

That phonological experience is fundamentally articulatory in nature is apparent from a vast range of experimental and theoretical work. Among the best sources are the papers by Liberman *et al.* (1967) and Warren (1970), cited earlier, and a paper by Galunov and Chistovic (1966).

For the basic motor coordination processes of speech to be involved in the articulatory basis of phonological experience is *prima facie* plausible, especially under a general constructive theory. Experimental support comes from electromyographic and other studies of activity in the articulatory muscles during speaking, imagining speech, listening to speech, reading, etc. (McGuigan, 1966, is the easiest introduction to this work.)

This account can presumably be extended to deal with experiencing any skilled motor act which one can perform oneself (e.g., watching someone walk across the room). Festinger (Festinger, Burnham, Ono, & Bamber, 1967) has a theory, somewhat related to ours, which attempts to deal with visual shape experience (although it is considerably more speculative than the above account). But we must warn of the likelihood that there must be some sorts of experience that cannot be accounted for with motor construction at all: the perception of color, for example.

The heart of the "pattern recognition problem" has usually been considered to be the problem of the "Höffding step": How does one get from an analysis, however sophisticated, of the input information (in the case of speech, an analysis of the acoustic signal) to an identification of the perceptual object, as demonstrated by naming the object, for example? The theories described above do not, in themselves, provide *any* way of dealing with the problem of the Höffding step, though less explicit "motor theories" have often been proposed to do so. However, none of these theories has ever made explicit how the supposed motor involvement in perception was to accomplish the jump from analyzed information to recognition. Here we sketch an account which conceivably can do so.

AN ECOLOGICALLY VALID SYMMETRY THEORETIC, COALITIONAL CONSTRUCTIVE MOTOR THEORY OF SPEECH RECOGNITION

In addition to the theory of phonological experience sketched above, several other conceptualizations, most of which have been discussed in this volume, form the basis of our theory of speech recognition:

1. The epistemology of structural realism, specifically Gibsonian direct realism discussed in terms of symmetry, à la Shaw and McIntyre, and Mace, and by Cassirer (1944). Briefly, this is a view of the basic situation of perception as one in which the organism is building up internal cognitive structures that are symmetrical with certain aspects of the "external" world. These structures are the basis for constructive processes that give rise to other cognitive structures, which processes underlie (or *are*) the organism's experience.

2. Coalitional resonance models of active memory—see discussions in this volume by Shaw and by Halwes, as well as Pribram's *Languages of the Brain* (1971). These models show how the structures mentioned in (1) above may be manifested in the brain.

3. Pribram's account, again in *Languages of the Brain,* specifically in Chapters 12 and 13, of the basic mechanisms of motor coordination. It is essential to read his presentation of the theory in the original, but we will quote a few of the most crucial aspects here.

> The results of these experiments and observations showed that the motor regions of the cortex were critically involved in the control of neither individual muscles nor specific movements. Rather, the motor cortex seemed to play some higher order role in directing action—action defined not in terms of muscles, but of the achievement of an external representation of a psychological set, or plan [p. 241].

> The ready answer to the question of how movement becomes transformed into action is that a sort of Imaging process must occur in the motor cortex and that the Image is a momentary Image-of-Achievement which contains all the input and outcome information necessary to the next step of that achievement [p. 243].

> Finally, the conception of the functions of the cerebral motor cortex of the precentral gyrus has radically changed. This part of the brain cortex has been shown to be the *sensory cortex for action.* A momentary Image-of-Achievement is constructed and continuously updated through a neural holographic process much as is the perceptual Image. The Image-of-Achievement is, however, composed of learned *anticipations of the force and changes in force required to perform a task* [p. 250; emphasis added].

With the relevant background information thus outlined, let us sketch the theory itself:

Assume that the auditory system extracts certain structures from the input acoustic signal—the very structures it has been evolutionarily "designed" to extract in order to permit the recognition of speech. Now, on Pribram's analysis of the nature of the motor cortex, it is at least possible that the Höffding step problem simply disappears. Presumably those invariant structures which are linguistically relevant on the input side are the same as the structures which are linguistically relevant on the output side, in the coordination of the articulatory muscles; for there is a strict isomorphism between the linguistically relevant aspects of the acoustic signal and the linguistically relevant aspects of the articulatory gestures, the former being produced directly by the latter. Moreover, the neural machinery for processing the acoustic signal evolved together with the neural machinery for controlling articulation. So the recoding problem—the problem of getting from acoustic signal to articulation — dissolves, and we are left with the relatively simple task of moving the information specifying the input structures into the motor cortex.

So at least in this admittedly limited case, the problem of the Höffding step would seem to have vanished. And this is what Gibson has suggested all along.

REFERENCES

Cassirer, E.   The concept of group and the theory of perception. *Philosophy and Phenomenological Research,* 1944, 5, 1-35.

Festinger, L., Burnham, C. A., Ono, H., & Bamber, D. Efference and the conscious experience of perception. *Journal of Experimental Psychology,* Monograph Supplement, 1967, 74 (Whole No. 637).

Galunov, V. I., & Chistovic, L. A. Relationship of motor theory to the general problem of speech recognition. *Soviet Physics-Acoustics,* 1966, 11, 357-365.

Liberman, A. M., Cooper, F. S., Shankweiller, D. P., & Studdert-Kennedy, M. Perception of the speech code. *Psychological Review,* 1967, 74, 431-461.

McGuigan, F. J. *Thinking: Studies of covert language processes.* New York: Appleton-Century-Crofts, 1966.

Pribram, K. *Languages of the brain.* Englewood Cliffs, N.J.: Prentice Hall, 1971.

Warren, R. M. Perceptual restoration of missing speech sounds. *Science,* 1970, 167, 392-393.

18
WHOLISTIC AND PARTICULATE
APPROACHES IN NEUROPSYCHOLOGY[1]

Robert M. Anderson, Jr.
Stanford University Medical School

> *Bertie says that I am muddle-headed,*
> *but I think that Bertie is simple-minded.*
> *—Alfred North Whitehead*[2]
> *(speaking of Bertrand Russell)*

Intellectual enterprises have often behaved as if they were manifestations of the Hegelian Spirit oscillating about the Absolute. A concept comes into existence and with it its opposite. For a time the original conception occupies the fancy of the intellectual community. But sooner or later its opposite captures the imagination of the scientist-philosopher and grows—feeding on the popularity of the original concept. But after a time the original idea . . . *ad infinitum?*

The dialectic manifests itself on all levels of theory—in struggles within metaphysics, in research programs, and in puzzles within research programs. In the theory of light there were Cartesian pulses (waves), then Newton's corpuscles, then in the 18th century waves again, and then quanta (particles). In the theory of the organization of psychological functions in the brain, the oscillation went: Gall (localized)—Flourens (distributed)—Fritsch and Hitzig (localized)— Lashley (distributed). The dialectical process of science is also at work in the rivalry between wholism and atomism. In biology an ancient vitalism was banished by a severe mechanism, but a specter remained crying for justice—the dynamic organization of some units is something more than those units alone. Of course, the mechanists

[1] This paper has been written while receiving support as a Biological Sciences Training Fellow on a grant from the National Institute of Mental Health: MH 8304-09. I have profited from the suggestions of Karl H. Pribram, D. N. Spinelli, and Thomas H. Brown, none of whom shares any of the blame.

[2] I have been assured by John Goheen, Professor Emeritus of Philosophy at Stanford University, that Whitehead said this, but have been unable to find it in print.

never wished to deny this. The distinction between wholistic and atomists is a matter of emphasis. The atomist is primarily interested in the unit itself and in simple interactions between a few units. He thinks that if he examines the units closely enough, he will be able to figure out how to build, say, a living, experiencing brain. The wholist, on the hother hand, is primarily concerned with complex (and often global) interrelations and patterns of the unit. Emphasis is placed on the context or environment of a unit. The wholist works down to the arrangement of the units from their overall organization.

The specter of vitalism will have its revenge. A new wave is cresting with the demise of positivism and reductionism: It is evidenced by contemporary thought in the philosophy of science (Feyerabend, 1962; Kuhn, 1970) and in the philosophy of biology (Koestler & Smythies, 1969). This volume, with its emphasis on context, decentralization of control, and coalitions as important in cognitive processes, in contrast to the accepted, more atomistic mechanisms of feature analyzers and hierarchies, adds a substantial ripple to the waxing suprareductionist oscillation. Perhaps unknown to most cognitive psychologists, however, is a similar wholistic-atomistic rivalry in neuropsychology.

The wholistic-atomistic controversy in neuropsychology has its roots in the seesaw debates over the localization of psychological function in the context (Boring, 1950; Luria, 1966; Yong, 1970). Gall speculated in 1825 that certain psychological functions are precisely located. Flourens lesioned birds, found that abilities were recovered, and concluded that functions are not localized. The discovery of Broca's "speech area" and Fritsch and Hitzig's stimulation work with dogs argued for localization.

In the early 20th century the swings of the pendulum were damped a bit when the strict localization-nonlocalization dichotomy was rejected. In correspondence to the behavioristic revolution in psychology, some workers emphasized fairly specific in-out connections (reflexes) in their accounts of the workings of the nervous system (Pavlov, 1927; Sherrington, 1906). Also on the localization side was the discovery that loss of certain large portions of the cortex resulted in irreparable impairment of relatively specific abilities (Jacobsen, 1935; Klüver & Bucy, 1937). Parts of the sensory-motor cortex were even correlated with particular parts of the body (Marshall, Woolsey & Bard, 1941). At the same time, an opposite trend was represented in the work of the Gestalt psychologists and Karl Lashley. Köhler inferred from numerous perception experiments, via the principle of isomorphism, that brain processes underlying perceptual processes must be global, DC neuro-electric friends rather than the interaction of punctate neural (Köhler & Held, 1949). Lashley attempted to refute Köhler's hypothesis by implanting gold pins in the cortex to disrupt the fields, and then determining whether behavior was altered (Lashley, Chow, & Semmes, 1951). He found no change. Lashley, however, was not unsympathetic with the wholistic approach. Among his most famous contributions is his disproof of the idea that engrams or memory traces are localized in particular places in the cortex (Lashley, 1950). Learning and memory appeared to depend not so much on what particular cortical area was available but on how much cortex was spared by a lesion. To explain how memories are distributed over the cortex and account for stimulus and behavioral equivalence. Lashley hypothesized the existence of standing wave patterns set up by the interference of volleys of neural firing (Lashley, 1942). Lashley was never clear, however, on how such wave patterns could distribute a retrievable memory.

D. O. Hebb in his landmark work, *The Organization of Behavior* (1949), agreed with both Lashley and Köhler in their disenchantment with switchboard or connectionist theories and in their emphasis on the problem of perceptual generalization. He believed, however, that they had gone too far in their total denial that the same cells need to be excited to arouse the same perceptions. He thought that the truth must lie somewhere between the extremes of Lashley and Köhler's configuration theories and the connectionist theories. Thus he proposed his cell-assembly theory: Pattern recognition is slowly learned through the repeated excitement by particular stimulus patterns of assemblies of neurons and their consequent association. The distribution of perceptual memory is accounted for by the assumption that after a time cell assemblies will be laid down all over the cortex.

In the later fifties and early sixties, the atomistic approach to neuropsychology reached a peak with Mountcastle's (1957) discovery of the columnar organization of the somatosensory cortex and with Hubel and Wiesel's work on the visual system. Hubel and Wiesel undertook to map the receptive fields (areas of the retina which when stimulated excite or inhibit the activity in particular neurons—see Hartline, 1938) of cells in the primary and secondary visual areas in the cat by tapping individual cells with tiny microelectrodes. They found that receptive fields became progressively more complex and specialized as one ascended the visual system. The fields at the lateral geniculate nuclei were circular with an excitatory or inhibitory center and a complementary surround (Hubel & Wiesel, 1961). It appeared that they might function for the organism as dot detectors. At the striate cortex, Hubel and Wiesel found a predominance of neurons which responded to a line of stimulation at a particular place on the retina (line detectors). In the striate cortex they also found, besides these "simple" cells, "complex" cells that responded most strongly to lines of one orientation projected over an area of the retina (moving lines). From these results they inferred a neuronal wiring diagram: The visual system was organized in a hierarchical fashion with lines of retinal ganglion cells feeding into single cortical simple cells via the geniculate nuclei (Hubel & Wiesel, 1962). Simple cells whose receptive fields have the same orientation converge in turn on a single complex cell, and so on through the lower and higher order hypercomplex cells that reside in areas 18 and 19 (Hubel & Wiesel, 1967). Gross (Gross, Bender & Rocha-Miranda,1969) has extended the investigation to the inferotemporal cortex in the monkey. The cells Gross studied had large and complex fields, and one controversial cell appeared to respond maximally to a cutout of a monkey hand. (The final stage in the process heirarchy?) Thus we have an atomistic physiological account of pattern recognition.

Hubel and Wiesel's feature detector account (i.e., account in terms of finely tuned, single cells whose receptive field properties are innate) followed close on the heels of McCulloch's similar account of the visual system of the frog (supported experimentally by Lettvin, Maturana, McCulloch, & Pitts, 1959) and with it captivated the scientific mind. The feature detector explanation of perception was elegant and simple, and "felt" familiar since it fit in with the artificial intelligence work that had been done on pattern recognition. The feature detector account makes four important claims:

1. The single cell is the functional unit in perception. It stands at the nodes in the processing hierarchy,

2. The processing is serial: ganglion cell—simple cell—complex cell—hyper-complex cell.

3. Processing involves the serial activation of anatomically distinct regions in the brain (Mishkin, 1966, 1972).

4. Levels of cell type in the processing hierarchy correspond to serially activated regions in the brain. In the cat, ganglion cells are in the retina, simple cells in area 17, complex cells in areas 17 and 18, hypercomplex in 18 and 19, and finally the mythical "grandmother" cell in the inferotemporal cortex in the monkey (and man?).

Although the feature detector account has many appealing characteristics and has stimulated a great deal of fruitful research, in the later 1960's and early 1970's many anomalies have been surfacing. Hoffmann and Stone (1971) have discovered, by measuring latencies of response on stimulation of the optic nerve, that complex-field cells are connected monosynaptically to the optic radiations—thus opening up the possibility that cells with complex fields process information in parallel rather than serially via simple cells. Even more problematic is the fact that Spinelli (1967), by using a computer to pass a dot through the visual field, found cells with incredibly complex fields in the retina of the cat. This suggests the unpleasant possibility that Hubel and Wiesel's geometrization of the visual system might be an artifact of their choice of stimulus shapes to be waved about in front of the animal. Further evidence that questions the Hubel and Wiesel hierarchical model lies in Spinelli's finding of a large percentage of cells with disc-shaped fields in the visual cortex of both cat (Spinelli & Barrett, 1969) and monkey (Spinelli, Pribram & Bridgeman, 1970).

Hubel and Wiesel have themselves refuted the hypothesized correlation between levels in the processing hierarchy and regions in the brain. Many hypercomplex cells have been found in area 17 (Hubel & Wiesel, 1968). A finding by Hubel and Wiesel that is even more devastating for the feature detector account lies in their visual deprivation experiments. When cats were deprived of visual experience with one eye, important changes took place in a number of cells that could be driven by that eye and in the fields of the cells that could be driven. After deprivation the cat eventually learned discriminations with the deprived eye, but *the properties of and number of feature detectors did not change* (Hubel & Wiesel, 1970). A dissociation between feature detectors is thus shown (Creutzfeldt & Sakmann, 1969; Ganz, 1971).

These anomalies suggest that feature detector theory, simple and familiar though it may be, might have little to do with how we perceive. Perhaps the physiology of the perceptual process cannot be captured by an analysis in terms of smaller and smaller units; a wholistic approach may be required. Adey (1965) has proposed a field theory similar to Köhler's. Other wholistic theories seem to generally agree in their denial of the single cell as the functional unit in perception and in their substitution of groups or ensembles of cells. E. Roy John, for example, hypothesizes that information is coded in the cortex in temporal patterns of firing of cells in ensembles (John, 1967, 1972).

The most completely worked out wholistic theory, however, is that of Karl Pribram (1971). Pribram, like Lashley, postulates that memories are laid down as interference patterns. However, unlike Lashley, he has a well-defined mechanism in mind for how this can be accomplished (Pribram, 1966, 1969, 1973). Pribram places the locus of interaction at junctions (synapses) between neurons. Neural junctions simultaneously activated form a "wavefront" which can interfere with other such "wavefronts" in the same ensemble but originating in other parts of the nervous system. Pribram further points out that interference phenomena are the basis of optical information processing (or holography), and that holograms, due to their distributed information storage mechanisms, have many of the properties which the brain possesses and that have puzzled neuroscientists for so long. (For a simple explanation of the optical hologram see Kock, 1969.) For example, a holographic memory trace distributed over part of the cortex would allow the retrieval of all the original information even if parts of the trace were destroyed. It also solves the Köhler and Lashley problem of perceptual generalization. Pribram does not, however, attribute all psychological functions or even all perception to the neural holographic process. Feature detectors do play a limited role.

> Along with other mechanisms, they are thought to provide the essential reference, the backdrop against which other more labile configurations of neural events transpire. They are the wired-in parts of the screen, the warp across which the woof of experientially sensitive neural microstructure is woven. At any given moment the fabric of the screen processes the neural events impinging on it—pre-processes them on the way to subsequent cell stations. The warp of the screen is unaffected by the processing, but a residue is left on the woof, another thread has been woven into the fabric [Pribram, 1971, p. 325].

Of prime significance are the feature detectors sensitive to spatial frequencies or environmental textures (Campbell, 1973; Pollen & Taylor, 1973). Cells are organized in cortical columns which serve as feature analyzers (ensembles of cells which have been broadly tuned by experience, e.g., Spinelli's, 1970, OCCAM units). The feature analyzers are laid down holographically, and the neural processes are holographic at the synaptic junctures within columns. Each column acts as a TOTE unit which is in turn organized with other columns into higher level TOTES (Miller, Galanter, & Pribram, 1960).

For Pribram, contra Hubel and Wiesel, a good deal of perceptual processing is parallel. Lateral inhibition serves to sharpen and transform input to the cortex (Phelps, 1972) and acts as a mechanism for producing wavefronts. The infero-temporal cortex acts in parallel to filter input to the visual cortex and thus assist in pattern recognition (Gerbrandt, Spinelli & Pribram, 1970; Pribram, Spinelli & Reitz, 1969).

Atomistic feature detector theory has difficulties giving an account of pattern recognition, but it doesn't even get off the ground as an explanation of the richness of visual experience. Although I may recognize that two script "f"s are both "f"s, I will also notice differences in the hand in which they are written. Such richnesses of texture are not accounted for by feature detector theory. Pribram locates the process of visual imagery in the visual cortex. Visual awareness is produced by the playing of input patterns over the dendritic feltwork of the striate area. (Pribram emphasizes the more wholistic analog processes occurring in the junctional microstructure as opposed to the digital, on-off character of the axonal impulse; see Hebb, 1949; McCulloch, 1965.) The input patterns contain information about spatial frequencies or textures in the environment, thus lending richness to the visual experience.

The atomistic feature detector view also fails to explain the richness of color experience. Recordings of individual neural units have revealed that only about 10% of the cells in the cortex are responsive to color. A problem arises: The visual field appears to be full of color, not just 10% colored. Feature detector theory has no answer. If, however, we assume that the important units for color experience are ensembles of cells rather than single cells, the problem vanishes. Single cells could participate in more than one ensemble, and their participation not be discoverable by means of single-cell, microelectrode techniques. For example, if a cell participated in the firing of an ensemble that responded to green light and an ensemble that responded to red light equally, recording from the cell would reveal only a lack of change on presentation of red light and then green light to the animal, and the conclusion would be that the cell had nothing to do with color—yet *ex hypothesis* it would (Anderson, 1972; Hayek, 1952). This suggests that the beautiful single-cell nodal hierarchy of Hubel and Wiesel may be due (in part) to a methodological bias. By recording only from single cells they may be missing important intercell relations. The haunting possibility is that trying to discover the "units of perception" by single-cell technique may be almost as hopeless (to use an exaggerated analogy) as trying to find how a car works by bombarding it with alpha particles in a cloud chamber. Atomistic explorations on the microlevel may not yield the higher-order organization. This problem is recognized by some advocates of the atomistic approach (Kandel & Spencer, 1968) but has not appreciably changed laboratory practice.

The dialectic sometimes must struggle to achieve its end. In the oscillation of ideas the particulate approach to the psychological functions of the brain has peaked. In its excess, its deficiencies are revealed, and the scientific mind is pulled back again—toward the wholistic approach.

REFERENCES

Adey, W. R. Electrophysiological patterns and cerebral independence characteristics in orienting and discriminative behavior. *Proceedings of the International Congress of Physiological Sciences,* Tokyo, 1965, 324-339.

Anderson, R. M. *An essay in neuroepistemology.* Unpublished doctoral dissertation, University of Minnesota, 1972.

Boring, E. G. *A history of experimental psychology.* New York: Appleton-Century-Crofts, 1950.

Campbell, F. The transmission of spatial information through the visual system. In *The Neurosciences: Third Study Program.* Cambridge, Mass.; MIT Press, 1974.

Creutzfeldt, O., & Sakmann, B. Neurophysiology of vision. *Annual Review of Physiology,* 1969, 31, 499-544.

Feyerabend, P. K. Explanation, reduction, and empiricism. In H. Feigl & G. Maxwell (Eds.), *Scientific explanation, space and time.* (Minnesota Studies in the Philosophy of Science, Vol. 3) Minneapolis: University of Minnesota Press, 1962.

Ganz, L. Sensory deprivation and visual discrimination. In H. L. Teuber (Ed.), *Handbook of sensory physiology.* Vol. 8. New York: Springer-Verlag, 1971.

Gerbrandt, L. K., Spinelli, D. N., & Pribram, K. H. The interaction of visual attention and temporal cortex stimulation on electrical activity evoked in the striate cortex. *Electroencephalography and Clincal Neurophysiology,* 1970, **29,** 146-155.

Gross, C. G., Bender, D. B., & Rocha-Miranda, C. E. Visual receptive fields of neurons in inferotemporal cortex of the monkey. *Science,* 1969, **166,** 1303-1306.

Hartline, H. K. The response of single optic nerve fibres of the vertebrate eye to illumination of the retina. *American Journal of Physiology,* 1938, **121,** 400-415.

Hayek, F. A. *The sensory order.* Chicago: University of Chicago Press, 1952.

Hebb, D. O. *The organization of behavior.* New York: Wiley, 1949.

Hoffmann, K.-P., & Stone, J. Conduction velocity of afferents to cat visual cortex. *Brain Research,* 1971, **32,** 460-466.

Hubel, D. H., & Wiesel, T. N. Integrative action in the cat's lateral geniculate body. *Journal of Physiology,* 1961, **155,** 385-398.

Hubel, D. H., & Wiesel, T. N. Receptive fields, binocular interaction and functional architecture in the cat's visual cortex. *Journal of Physiology,* 1962, **160,** 106-154.

Hubel, D. H., & Wiesel, T. N. Receptive fields and functional architecture in two non-striate visual areas (18 and 19) of the cat. *Journal of Neurophysiology,* 1967, **30,** 1561-1573.

Hubel, D. H., & Wiesel, T. N. Receptive fields and functional architecture of monkey striate cortex. *Journal of Physiology,* 1968, **195,** 215-243.

Hubel, D. H., & Wiesel, T. N. The period of susceptibility to the physiological effects of unilateral eye closure in kittens. *Journal of Physiology,* 1970, **206,** 419-436.

Jacobsen, C. F. Functions of the frontal association area in primates. *Archives of Neurology and Psychiatry,* 1935, **33,** 558-569.

John, E. R. *Mechanisms of memory.* New York: Academic Press, 1967.

John, E. R. Switchboard versus statistical theories of learning and memory. *Science,* 1972, **177,** 850-864.

Kandel, E. R., & Spencer, W. A. Cellular neurophysiological approaches in the study of learning. *Physiological Review,* 1968, **48,** 65-134.

Klüver, H., & Bucy, P. C. "Psychic blindness" and other symptoms following bilateral temporal lobectomy in rhesus monkeys. *American Journal of Psychology,* 1937, **119,** 352-353.

Kock, W. E. *Lasers and holography.* Garden City, N. Y.: Doubleday, 1969.

Koestler, A., & Smythies, J. R. (Eds.) *Beyond reductionism.* New York: Macmillan, 1969.

Köhler, W., & Held, R. The cortical correlate of pattern vision. *Science,* 1949, **110,** 414-419.

Kuhn, T. S. *The structure of scientific revolutions.* Chicago: University of Chicago Press, 1970.

Lashley, K. S. The problem of cerebral organization in vision. In *Biological symposia: Visual Mechanisms.* Vol. 1. Lancaster: Jacques Cattell Press, 1942.

Lashley, K. S. In search of the engram. In Society for Experimental Biology *Physiological mechanisms in animal behavior.* New York: Academic Press, 1950.

Lashely, K. S., Chow, K. L., & Semmes, J. An examination of the electrical field theory of cerebral integration. *Psychological Review,* 1951, **58,** 123-136.

Lettvin, J. Y., Maturana, H. R., McCulloch, W. J., & Pitts, W. H. What the frog's eye tells the frog's brain. *Proceedings of the Institute of Radio Engineering,* 1959, **47,** 1940-1959.

Luria, A. R. *Higher cortical functions in man.* New York: Basic Books, 1966.

McCulloch, W. S. *Embodiments of mind.* Cambridge, Mass.: MIT Press, 1965.

Marshall, W. H., Woolsey, C. N., & Bard, P. Observations on cortical sensory mechanisms of cat and monkey. *Journal of Neurophysiology,* 1941, **4,** 1-24.

Miller, G. A., Galanter, E. H., & Pribram, K. H. *Plans and the structure of behavior.* New York: Holt, Rinehart & Winston, 1960.

Mishkin, M. Visual mechanisms beyond the striate cortex. In R. W. Russell (Ed.), *Frontiers in physiological psychology.* New York: Academic Press, 1966.

Mishkin, M. Cortical visual areas and their interaction. In A. G. Karczmar & J. C. Eccles (Eds.), *Brain and human behavior.* New York: Springer-Verlag, 1972.

Mountcastle, V. B. Modality and topographic properties of single neurons of cat's somatic sensory cortex. *Journal of Neurophysiology,* 1957, **20,** 408-434.

Pavlov, I. P. *Conditioned reflexes.* Oxford: Humphrey Milford, 1927.

Phelps, R. W. *Inhibitory interactions in the visual cortex of the cat.* Unpublished doctoral dissertation, Stanford University, 1972.

Pollen, D. A., & Taylor, J. H. The striate cortex and the spatial analysis of visual space. *In The neurosciences: Third Study Program.* Cambridge, Mass.: MIT Press, 1974.

Pribram, K. H. Some dimensions of remembering. In J. Gaito (Ed.), *Macromolecules and behavior.* New York: Plenum, 1966.

Pribram, K. H. The neurophysiology of remembering. *Scientific American,* 1969, 73-86.

Pribram, K. H. *Languages of the brain.* Englewood Cliffs, N.J.: Prentice-Hall, 1971.

Pribram, K. H. How is it that sensing so much we can do so little? In *The neurosciences: Third Study Program.* Cambridge, Mass.: MIT Press, 1974.

Pribram, K. H., Spinelli, D.N., & Reitz, S. L. Effects of radical disconnection of occipital and temporal cortex on visual behavior of monkeys. *Brain,* 1969, **92,** 301-312.

Sherrington, C. S. *The integrative action of the nervous system.* New Haven: Yale University Press, 1906.

Spinelli, D. N. Receptive field organization of ganglion cells in the cat's retina. *Experimental Neurology,* 1967, **19,** 291-315.

Spinelli, D. N. OCCAM: A computer model for a content addressable memory in the central nervous system. In K. H. Pribram & D. Broadbent (Eds.), *Biology of memory.* New York: Academic Press, 1970.

Spinelli, D. N., & Barrett, T. W. Visual receptive field organization of single units in cat's visual cortex. *Experimental Neurology,* 1969, **24,** 76-98.

Spinelli, D. N., Pribram, K. H., & Bridgeman, B. Visual receptive field organization of single units in the visual cortex of monkey. *International Journal of Neuroscience,* 1970, 1, 67-74.

Young, R. M. *Mind, brain and adaptation in the nineteenth century.* London: Oxford University Press, 1970.

19
TOWARD A THIRD METAPHOR
FOR PSYCHOLINGUISTICS[1]

George A. Miller
Rockefeller University and The Institute for Advanced Study

Once "the growth of vocabulary" was an active field of research in American psychology, but in recent years little has been written about it. What happened? Were all our questions answered, so that further work became unnecessary? Or is vocabulary growth a problem temporarily neglected, but soon to be rediscovered? Or is it possible that studies of vocabulary growth did not dry up, but that old questions were reformulated in a new way under a different name?

A case can be made for each explanation. It is doubtful that any service would be rendered by deciding whether the problem has been solved, neglected, or transformed. The reason for raising the question is that our fluctuating interest in vocabulary growth provides a striking example of fashions in theory and research. Not only can a review of this topic provide a perspective on recent trends in psycholinguistics, but, given the obvious importance of vocabulary for any balanced account of linguistic proficiency, it can suggest problems for future theory and research.

PHASE ONE

The history of vocabulary studies has not been carefully analyzed, but it is generally agreed that developmental studies of vocabulary began long ago with parental diaries of children's speech, became more representative and methodologically sophisticated in this century, and culminated in the extensive surveys of the

[1] The preparation of this paper was supported in part by USPHS Grant No. GM 16735 from the National Institute for General Medical Sciences to Rockefeller University, and by a grant from the Sloan Foundation to The Institute for Advance Study.

I am indebted to Michael Cole. Stephen Isard, Philip N. Johnson-Laird, Aravind Joshi, and Stanley Peters for many profitable discussions of the ideas and opinions underlying this paper; they are not responsible, however, for any errors of conception or detail.

1930s and '40s. Once a data base had accumulated, however, enthusiasm cooled. This initial period of investigation can be referred to as Phase One.

The typical Phase One study of vocabulary growth estimated the number of different words that children knew, and expressed the results as a function of the children's ages or school grades. Results accumulated during Phase One show that about 35% of variance in the Stanford-Binet intelligence scores of eight-year-old children can be accounted for by differences in vocabulary size (Templin, 1957). Or, again, the recognition vocabulary of an eight-year-old child of average intelligence increases by about 29 words (or about 16 morphemes) every day (Smith, 1941; Templin, 1957). These facts are undeniably interesting. It is not obvious, however, what use should be made of them; the empirical data outrun any available psychological interpretation. Once such estimates had been made as rigorously and intelligently as possible, the problem of vocabulary growth seemed to be solved. Psychologists interested in child language turned to other things.

There were many things to turn to. While vocabulary was becoming unfashionable, grammar was becoming all the rage. Young psychologists who in earlier decades might have studied the acquisition of vocabulary were now captivated by the arcane intricacies of grammar acquisition. One index of this shift is provided by chapters on child language in handbooks. In 1954 McCarthy devoted ten pages of her chapter in the second edition of Carmichael's *Manual of Child Psychology* to an excellent summary of work on vocabulary growth. In 1966 Ervin-Tripp devoted only two pages of Hoffman and Hoffman's *Review of Child Development Research* to some critical comments on the same subject. And in 1970 McNeill did not mention vocabulary growth in the third edition of *Carmichael's Manual.* Pages thus saved were devoted to detailed analyses of successive grammatical stages. This comparison is not intended to disparage these chapters; it can be assumed that these distinguished authors reflected accurately the research interests in child language at the time of writing.

So, what happened to vocabulary growth? One might claim that it became abstract and changed its name to "semantic development." In Ervin-Tripp's and McNeill's chapters, for example, vocabulary is discussed in terms of universal semantic features (or markers) that are thought to be packaged in various combinations in the particular words of particular languages. This level of abstraction is only loosely tied to those lists of words that so many parents lovingly compiled for their growing children.

Theories about semantic markers are still programmatic; we don't even know what the markers are, much less how to record their occurrences in child language. So now the tables are turned; the interpretations outrun any available psychological data. As Ervin-Tripp remarks, "Changes in the semantic system have, in fact, been only sketchily studied [p. 63]," and Dale (1972) introduces an excellent chapter on semantic development with the observation that, "In the competition for least understood aspect of language acquisition, semantic development is surely the winner [p. 131]." In response to any claim that work continued under this new name, therefore, one is tempted to reply that students of child language saw their duty and didn't do it.

Those discussions of "The Growth of Vocabulary" that for many years contributed an indispensable section to any serious survey of child language found no place in the formulations of the 1960s—formulations that, by and large, accepted the primacy of grammar as a basic axiom. Research on child language changed, reflecting our changing conception of what language is. No one inclined to mourn the passing of vocabulary studies, however, should resent the birth of syntactic studies; grammar acquisition is an essential part of language development.

We must remember, however, that vocabulary acquisition is also essential. A child who knows no words in a language can scarcely exhibit grammatical competence in it. A psycholinguist's preference for studying syntax does not abolish a child's need for lexical knowledge. Faced with this stubborn truth, we can predict that vocabulary development will not be indefinitely ignored; there will surely be a Phase Two. Indeed, there are already signs of renewed interest in lexical mastery among developmental psycholinguists who suspect that syntactic competence cannot be the whole story (see, for example, Anglin, 1970).

HOPES FOR PHASE TWO

When vocabulary becomes fashionable again we will have to ask about much more than its size. In the light of subsequent events, one is struck by the oddity of equating so complicated a cognitive process as vocabulary growth with so superficial a psychometric method as estimation of vocabulary size. One supposes that the early preoccupation with size must have been related to the emergence of intelligence testing and to the discovery that vocabulary tests are the most useful indicators of verbal intelligence. In the intervening years, however, our theories about the nature of intelligence have been considerably enriched as psychometric definitions have been supplemented by theories more analytic of intelligent thought and action. Since there is a connection between intelligence and vocabulary, our psychometric definitions of vocabulary growth should undergo a corresponding transformation. Phase Two can hope for a redefinition of vocabulary growth comparable in spirit and intent to the redefinition of intelligence that resulted from the work of Piaget, Werner, Bruner, and other cognitive psychologists.

In Phase Two we can hope to see, in addition to greater respect for the syntactic functions that words serve, a more careful analysis of the cognitive basis for vocabulary growth. In particular, we can hope for better definitions of what a word is and what it means to know one. Such problems of definition arose during Phase One; McCarthy comments that among the basic difficulties contributing to the confused state of the early literature on children's vocabularies was the lack of proper criteria for knowing a word, and failure to define precisely what the unit of measurement was. By the close of Phase One it had been possible to agree on definitions satisfactory for psychometric testing, but these agreements were merely convenient methodological standardizations, not the fruits of better linguistic or psychological theories. In Phase Two, psycholinguists will have to find a better way to think about what a word is, and cognitive psychologists will have to provide a better notion of what knowing is. Our new studies of vocabulary growth should be equipped from the outset with better definitions for both "vocabulary" and "growth."

When we look at vocabulary in the context of current theories of cognitive growth, it is obvious that we must consider qualitative as well as quantitative changes. If we take qualitative changes seriously, however, it becomes difficult to see where a child's conceptual development leaves off and his lexical development begins. Indeed, it is possible to construe many of Piaget's studies as attempts to assess a child's understanding of such words as "space," "time," "more," "all," "brother," "dead" (see Berko & Brown, 1960). One might argue that a child who says there is more liquid when it is poured from one shape of container into another simply does not know what "more" means. If this interpretation were accepted, then any claim that interest in the growth of vocabulary had declined in recent years would have to be rejected; probing children's concepts was even more popular during the 1960s than was the analysis of children's grammar.

Students of cognitive development, however, resist any narrowly lexicographic interpretation of Piaget's work. Flavell (1963), for example, regards the claim that Piaget has studied what children think certain words mean as a criticism—an undeserved criticism—of Piaget's intentions and results. There is much more to cognitive development than merely learning the meanings of words. Flavell claims that "in most of Piaget's studies, whatever vocabulary change occurs is in large measure a consequence, reflection, or symptomatic expression of an underlying and more fundamental cognitive change [p. 434]." Vocabulary growth is a surface manifestation of prior developments at a deeper and more conceptual level of understanding.

It would seem, therefore, that we can study cognitive development without considering vocabulary. On the other hand, it is much less plausible that we could study vocabulary growth in a psychologically interesting way without placing conceptual development near the center of our investigation. If we are to add qualitative dimensions to the quantitative studies of Phase One, we must incorporate the point of view and results of conceptual studies into our formulations.

This integration of conceptual and linguistic theories is far easier to demand than to provide. Attempts to achieve such a unification have so far succeeded only in lending support to the claim that conceptual advances precede lexical advances, a claim that might be caricatured as meaning that nobody (not even a child who utters words he does not yet understand) can express ideas he doesn't have. The logic of this position must be respected, but it is hardly a conclusion that demonstrates the unique value of psychological research. It does little to dispel our ignorance of how conceptual advances are represented in language—to illuminate in any detail precisely how cognitive developments can lead to linguistic developments.

Moreover, too much satisfaction with the conclusion that concepts precede words could tempt us to ignore the fact, eloquently expressed some time ago by Vygotsky (1962), that linguistic communication is a social process. It is through language that each society puts its own peculiar stamp on conceptual development. The lexicon is our treasurehouse of socially shared concepts, concepts that all our children are expected to master. To ignore that fact would be to abandon valuable guidance as to which conceptual developments are important and deserving of study. It may be possible to study some aspects of conceptual development as if they were inevitable results of imposing our kind of physical environment on our kind of nervous system, but the peculiarly human concepts to which our languages have assigned lexical forms cannot be analyzed in any serious way without taking into account the social conventions they incorporate.

In brief, Phase Two must exploit insights achieved through the study of cognitive development, but those qualitative dimensions of growth must be embedded in a framework provided by a better definition of what a vocabulary is. The vocabulary that a child must learn presupposes mastery of a large variety of concepts that society has found to be important; before we can study his growing mastery of those concepts in any detail, we must ourselves have a better, more self-conscious conception of what they are.

If Phase Two will depend on a more sophisticated notion of vocabulary, then the next question must be: Where are we to find a better theory of vocabulary? It seems unlikely that we could evolve a better theory of vocabulary outside of a better general theory of language, so the answer to this question should be sought from linguistic theory. Psychologists who turn in this direction, however, are likely to find more help than they know how to use. The current scene in theoretical linguistics is rich with rival hypotheses concerning the proper way to incorporate lexical and semantic rules into generative grammar; one could spend an educational year just reading the proposals that have been advanced.

There is reason to think that the proliferation of polemics in this lively branch of linguistics is a symptom of conceptual difficulties, not an orderly extension of accepted theories into novel territories. Rather than review this debate, it might help to stand back from it and look instead at the larger historical context.

TWO METAPHORS

Historians of science find it helpful to characterize successive stages in a science in terms of root metaphors (or paradigms) accepted by the majority of scientists during each stage. Two such metaphors can be recognized in the history of studies of the psychological foundations of language. At present we seem to be testing the limits of the second metaphor and desperately in need of a third.

Until about 1950 the metaphor accepted by most American students of the psychology of language was "association." For those who accept the association metaphor, the psychology of language is a special chapter in the psychology of learning. The nervous system is man's great connecting machine; learning is the process of establishing new connections; to learn a language is to learn connections between words and things. During its heyday most linguists were content (for reasons of their own; see, for example, Bloomfield, 1933, Ch. 2) to make as few additional assumptions as possible about the psychological implications of their work. Given this frame of reference, the flowering of vocabulary studies during Phase One was no accident; the growth of vocabulary was of central importance for associationistic theories of language.

A major weakness of this approach is its inability to deal adequately with combinatorial aspects of language. It may be possible to think of a word as a learned association between a perceptual referent and a phonological shape, but linguistic communication uses sentences. There are far too many different sentences for anyone to believe that they are learned associations between states of affairs and strings of words. So the need for a combinatorial theory—for a grammar—eventually became obvious. Attempts were made to formulate combinatorial theories of an associationistic kind as stochastic processes, and some people still hold to such versions of the associationistic paradigm (see, for example, Suppes, 1969).

During the 1950s, however, a new metaphor captured the imaginations of the current generation of workers. The new metaphor was "communication." As formulated by mathematical theorists (e.g., Shannon, 1948), a communication system has a source, a channel, and a receiver; correlations between source and receiver are established by signals sent over the channel between them. These signals encode messages; the rate at which messages can be sent depends on the variety of different signals that the channel can carry per unit time.

The communication metaphor focuses attention on the set of alternative signals. Thus, the communication metaphor is strongest just where the association metaphor is weakest. For human language, grammatical sentences are the signals to be analyzed, and Chomsky in 1956 accepted the communication metaphor as the basis for his generative theory of grammar. A generative grammar is a set of rules that characterizes all and only the admissible signals—the sentences—that can be communicated over a linguistic channel. Thus, the communication metaphor called for a better theory of syntax, and generative grammar answered that call in an elegant and exciting way.

When psychologists shifted their attention from words to sentences, the inadequacy of the association metaphor became obvious. The meaning of a sentence is not the linear sum of the meanings of the words it contains. If it were, then "Brutus killed Caesar" and "Caesar killed Brutus" would be synonymous; all blind Venetians would be Venetian blinds; all ambiguous sentences would be puns. Moreover, those ubiquitous little words – the *if*'s, *and*'s, and *but*'s – that play such a critically important role in syntax would have to be learned by associating them with some kind of referential object or image.

Those who adopted the communication metaphor had little interest in the growth of vocabulary. Words are merely the formal atoms combined in grammatical sentences; it is the rules of combination, not the atomic elements, that capture the center of the theoretical stage. The communication metaphor has little to say about vocabulary growth.

Indeed, it has little to say about meaning, and therein lies a weakness. Within the communication metaphor, meaning is that ineffable something that should remain invariant under different encodings of the same message. It may be acceptable for a communication engineer to concentrate exclusively on the signals his equipment must transmit, but that is not a useful approach for a psychologist. People look right through the linguistic signal they receive to discover the message it encodes; a theory that has no central place for meaningful messages can scarcely satisfy a psychologist. Because of this weakness, some linguists and psychologists refused to abandon the association metaphor, but for the majority who accepted the communication metaphor there was no turning back. Somehow, meaningful aspects of grammatical sentences had to be incorporated into the theory.

Precisely how semantic rules should be incorporated into a framework of syntactic rules became a central dispute among linguistic theorists. In response to such considerations, Chomsky in 1965 revised his position to make room for both phonological and semantic aspects of language. A fundamental distinction was drawn between the surface structure of a sentence and its deep structure. Surface structure could be converted into a phonological signal for transmission; deep structure could be semantically interpreted; the grammar provided rules of transformation for deriving the surface signal from the deep, semantically interpretable structure of the sentence. But syntax, which characterizes the set of admissible sentences, remained primary; phonology and semantics were merely realizations of the underlying syntactic abstractions.

The 1965 revision of Chomsky's theory was scarcely announced before alternative proposals began to appear. Many denied the reality of deep syntactic structure and suggested that distinctions between syntactic and semantic rules should be abandoned. The argument between "interpretive semanticists" and "generative semanticists" continues, with little indication that either side will ultimately persuade the other.

At present, therefore, a psychologist interested in vocabulary growth will not find among linguistic theorists the kind of agreement about lexical and semantic questions that would encourage him to stake any considerable investment of time and energy on one or another particular theory of vocabulary. Of course, theoretical anarchy is nothing new to psychologists; some brave souls have already planted their pennants in one camp or the other. But the possibility should be considered that the metaphor on which this theoretical development rests is somehow inadequate for psychological purposes. Despite all its advantages over the association metaphor, the communication metaphor has no natural place for semantics, and must treat meaning in terms of coding theory, transformations, translations, or other ways of mapping one set of well-formed signals into another. It is not that anything is wrong with such formulations, but that something vital is missing from them.

The difficulty of incorporating meaning into the communication metaphor makes it particularly difficult to give a coherent account of language development. As Sinclair-de-Zwart (1969) has pointed out, a child does not regard language as an autonomous object to be known, but as a representation of what is known. Meaning plays a critical role in determining what a child learns to do with linguistic structures. The nature of this dependence on meaning does not lie in some immature incompetence of the infant; it can be clearly demonstrated with adults. For example, if we ask college students to discover syntactic rules for an artificial language that has no semantic interpretation, they will go about it stupidly, make many mistakes, and, most significantly, have no clear idea whether they have mastered the entire language or only some subset of it. If sentences in the artificial language are given an interpretation as, say, commands executed by a computer, then the behavior of the computer provides a criterion for judging one's level of mastery (Miller, 1967, Ch. 7). In order to know that one knows a language, it is necessary to have some use for it. But pure syntax, devoid of semantic interpretation, is useless. The primacy of syntax may be a valuable axiom for linguistics, but the primacy of semantics is a better axiom for psychology.

What we need is a new root metaphor, one that incorporates the best of earlier metaphors, but gives a more central role to semantics. If such a metaphor were available, it might provide a more adequate theory of vocabulary. Then we could hope to see studies of vocabulary growth flower again in the predicted Phase Two.

TOWARD A THIRD METAPHOR

It is not very helpful to call for new metaphors. To tell a scientist struggling with an overwhelmingly difficult problem that he needs a better metaphor is like telling a discouraged freshman that he needs 20 more IQ points, Even when you are right, it is not obvious what to do about it. There would be little point in making a case for the exhaustion of the communication metaphor if alternatives were inconceivable. Fortunately, recent conceptual advances point in a new direction for theory and research in psycholinguistics.

If our diagnosis is correct, a third metaphor should characterize what a person *is doing* when he produces or understands linguistic signals. Within the standard version of the communication metaphor it has been convenient to relegate what a language user does to a realm called "performance," sharply distinguished from the realm of "competence" that linguistic theory is supposed to characterize in some abstract way. We certainly should not join those who suggest that this is an improper or unimportant distinction. Most cognitive psychologists would, for general reasons having little to do with language studies, insist on a clear distinction between what organisms *can* do and what they *do* do; it is a cornerstone of their resistance to radical behaviorism. But to accept the distinction need not commit us to abandoning descriptions of performance.

To focus on what people are doing helps narrow our search for a new metaphor. Whereas the first metaphor led us to look for *connections* between words and things, and the second led us to look for *rules* characterizing acceptable signals, the third should lead us to look for *procedures* involved in using language. When we add to this procedural criterion a stipulation that the new metaphor should enable us to describe semantic aspects of language, the black hole we are trying to fill begins to assume a rough shape.

The proposal that we should put the *use* of language foremost is not novel. Wittgenstein (1953) and a whole school of linguistic philosophers have helped to light the way. But Wittgenstein's proposal for a metaphor was *ein Spiel,* which, when translated as *a game,* does not immediately suggest the kind of theories linguists need; the theory of games is a branch of economics, not of linguistics or psychology (however, cf. Lewis, 1969). Nevertheless, linguistic philosophers have kept alive an alternative view that should encourage us to view an emphasis on use as not an entirely fruitless undertaking if only we can find a better root metaphor on which to base our theories.

Harrison (1972), writing within a frame of reference he attributes to Wittgenstein and Chomsky, has provided a version of linguistic philosophy better suited to our psychological purposes. One part of Harrison's philosophy that deserves careful attention from psychologists is his description of what he calls "linguistic devices." He illustrates what he means by a linguistic device by stating some explicit procedures a child might learn to carry out in the course of learning to use the English verb "bring." It is not necessary to review the half-dozen different linguistic devices that Harrison describes—his description is psychologically naive and intended to be merely illustrative—except to say that each of them resembles a program of instructions for the discriminations, computations, and actions involved in using "bring" in particular situations. The critical point is that as the uses of "bring" become more complicated, simple linguistic devices are incorporated into complex ones as subdevices. Harrison's thesis is that when a child learns to use language he learns many such related linguistic devices, and it is in terms of these linguistic devices that his basic linguistic competence should be described. (Syntactic rules are abstractions that a linguist can draw from this basic competence.)

Harrison comes as close an any linguistic philosopher to providing an explicit psychological hypothesis about what a person is doing when he learns and uses language. Each linguistic device can be described as a bit of programming that must be learned, a routine that must be internalized and that can be called as a subroutine in other routines.

Harrison's linguistic devices direct our attention to a difference between the traditional philosophical approach and the emerging mathematical approach to semantics. Most philosophers place verification somewhere near the heart of their semantic theories; some have even gone so far as to claim that knowing the meaning of a sentence is equivalent to knowing the conditions under which the propositions that it expresses would be true. Although this verificational approach encounters insuperable difficulties when applied to natural language, Tarski's (1956) formulation of a theory of truth in formalized languages is usually taken as the model for what a satisfactory semantic theory should look like. By contrast, Harrison implies that procedures, rather than truth values, should be the atomic elements of any semantic analysis of natural languages.

The theory of computation may provide an alternative semantics more compatible with the procedural emphasis that Harrison espouses. Of particular interest is the semantic theory of computer languages. The meaning of a computer program is what it does; the meaning of the instruction "Add x,y," for example, is what the computer is supposed to do when it receives such an instruction. A semantic description of a computer language enables us to characterize what any program written in that language does. A general semantics for programming languages is a theory that enables us to characterize abstractly what any program in any language could do. The task of such a theory can be characterized more explicitly as follows: When a computer program is written to perform some particular function, how do we decide it actually does what it was intended to do? It will not suffice to run the program and see, for the result of running it must be compared with some characterization of what it was intended to do. How to characterize what programs are intended to do is the subject of the semantic theory of computer languages. How the intended procedures are actually implemented, either by computers or by a nervous system, is of secondary importance in this theory.

There have been several attempts to formulate such a theory; the most general is that of Scott and Strachey (1971). Semantic theories formulated along these lines decompose the meanings of compound expressions into simpler expressions describing performable operations, thus contrasting with Tarskian theories that decompose the meanings of compound expressions into simpler expressions of determinable truth value. The goals are similar, but the ultimate elements of the theory are different. If such a theory were achieved in full generality, it might give cognitive psychologists a formal language in which to describe the procedures that a language user must be able to carry out.

Let us, therefore, consider "computation" as our candidate for a third metaphor. There is a considerable technological foundation for this metaphor, just as there was for the communication metaphor before it. Harrison was not the first to explore in this direction; many analogies have been drawn between information processing by machines and by nervous systems. What we need is someone to do for the computation metaphor what Chomsky did for the communication metaphor. That is to say, we need a coherent, explicit, formal statement that can transform this general metaphor into a specific psycholinguistic theory. Harrison is merely one of several workers struggling toward that formulation. Other suggestions for a procedural semantics have come more directly from computational linguistics and artificial intelligence. With regard to details, there is at least as much disagreement among procedural semanticists as among generative grammarians, so the crystal ball is anything but clear. Nevertheless, some general outlines can be discerned.

PROCEDURAL SEMANTICS

Consider how computers are used. The machines themselves operate on patterns of electrical pulses. Different instructions are represented by different patterns. Each make of machine comes equipped with its own list of instructions, most of which are closely tied to the detailed electronic operations the machine can perform. Human programmers cannot think clearly about complicated problems when they must be translated into such detailed instructions, so "higher-level languages" have been invented to provide commands more closely related to the problems to be solved. In order for some particular machine to carry out those commands, of course, they must first be translated into the machine language of that particular computer. This translation is usually performed by the machine itself operating under a translating program called (generically) a "compiler." A compiler for FORTRAN, for example, takes instructions written in the FORTRAN language and translates them into instructions in the language of whatever machine is to make the computation. Once a program has been compiled, it can then be run on the machine. So there is a two-stage process involved, first compiling the program, then running it.

Programming languages have both syntactic and semantic aspects. Their syntax—their rules for writing commands that the compiler will accept—is usually quite rigid; anyone who has misplaced a comma or misspelled an expression knows how rigidly these rules are enforced. The methods used to specify the syntax of programming languages are much the same as those used to describe the syntax of any formalized language (e.g., formal logic); they are, in fact, the same methods that mathematical linguists, under the communication metaphor, have applied to the syntax of natural languages.

On the other hand, the semantics of higher-level programming languages—their rules for assigning performable operations to syntactically well-formed commands—differs from the semantics of logical languages, which assigns truth values to well-formed formulas. Assigning "true" or "false" to a particular expression is merely one kind of procedure that a programming semantics must include. In turning to computation as a third metaphor, therefore, we are proposing that a procedural semantics is more appropriate for describing natural languages than is a propositional semantics. The question is how this general proposal can be applied to the specific case of linguistic communication between human speakers and listeners.

If we think of a human nervous system as some kind of computer, we can ask whether there is anything analogous to higher-level programming languages. An obvious suggestion is that natural languages might be so regarded. Woods (1968), for example, noted that in the design of question-answering programs for computers, an input question must be treated as if it were a program for the computer to execute; interpreting a question is directly comparable to compiling a program for answering it. Davies and Isard (1972) have carried the analogy further; they suggest that all sentences can be regarded as bits of higher-level programming, and that understanding any sentence is analogous to compiling the program it encodes.

Once compiled, of course, a program may or may not be run. One obvious advantage of the Davies-Isard suggestion is that it provides a natural way to disconnect the understanding of a sentence from any actions it might entail, thus dissolving a bond that has always bedevilled associationistic theories of language and that has led to the invention of such ill-defined intervening variables as "dispositions to respond" (Morris, 1946), or "representational mediation processes" (Osgood, 1952). Davies and Isard suggest that the compilation and execution processes can be separated by the earliest possible "point of refusal." Neither man nor machine can *refuse to obey* a command until the command has been understood. Thus, compilation must occur automatically without conscious control by the listener; he cannot consciously *refuse to understand* a command. Davies and Isard suggest that loss of conscious control over one's compiler corresponds to "knowing" a language.

According to this version of the computation metaphor, the source produces programs, the channel carries these programs to the destination, and at the destination they are compiled. Since compiling a program is much better understood than writing one, this approach offers more insight into the listener than the talker. We are led, therefore, to consider the nature of compilers and their suitability as analogs for the human process of interpreting grammatical sentences. If we imagine that the "listener-compiler" takes spoken words a few at a time and stores them in some kind of auditory buffer memory until they can be translated into a program of instructions to operate the neural computer, then there must be available in long-term memory a set of subroutines for each word. If no program can be compiled, the input sentence is not understood. If more than one can be compiled, the input sentence is ambiguous.

In terms of our present context, set by psychological studies of vocabulary, knowing a word is defined as being able to compile well-formed programs when that word is part of the input signal. This definition implies the existence of something like a lexicon—a set of subroutines that can be called when different words are used—but this procedural lexicon would be very different from the dictionaries of everyday use, and the subroutines called by a particular word would not resemble a familiar dictionary entry. At present we have little idea how these subroutines should be written; deciding on an appropriate formulation is a critical task for any psycholinguistic theory that adopts the computation metaphor. But the obvious implication is that knowledge about a word need not be compacted and deposited in any single place corresponding to *the* lexical (or encyclopedic) entry for that word; procedures can be composed and related more freely and flexibly than, say, lists of semantic markers. The theoretical problem is how best to exploit that freedom.

The output of the compiler would be a program in the sense made most explicit by Newell and Simon (1972). Newell and Simon have proposed an extensive theory of human problem solving based on the computer metaphor; to simplify their task, they deliberately ignore the perceptual inputs and behavioral outputs of their hypothetical information-processing system. The general nature of their enterprise, however, makes it implicit that the perceptual processes involved in hearing and understanding a sentence must translate it into some notation usable by the programs involved in thinking. The Davies-Isard proposal, therefore, is compatible, in spirit if not in detail, with the Newell-Simon proposal, and might be regarded as filling a gap left in the more general theory. One senses, therefore, an impending convergence on a psycholinguistic theory based on the computer metaphor.

One impressive application of this kind of thinking to the understanding of natural languages has been the work of Winograd (1971), who programmed a hypothetical robot to move blocks in response to commands given in English. Such applications do much to clarify what a semantic theory must be and do to describe such information processing. If "procedural semantics" is to be our new theory, then Winograd's work is the clearest glimpse yet of what the future holds.

Consider some advantages of this theory. In addition to separating compilation from execution, a procedural approach does not suffer from the old embarrassments about the meanings of little words—the *if*'s, *and*'s, and *but*'s—for these are critically important signals as to the order in which subroutines must be compiled. Nor is there any reluctance to deal with sentences, rather than isolated words; the verb will be recognized as the basic operator in any clause, for it organizes the roles of the various nouns that can serve as its arguments. Rules of syntax will be seen as abstractions from, not as components of, the user's knowledge of his language. Syntactic rules are not rules that children must discover and learn, but generalizations about what children learn, generalizations against which a psycholinguistic theorist can test more specific procedural hypotheses. The computation metaphor is potentially able to encompass all that was previously formulated in the association and communication metaphors, but without their weaknesses.

These hints should suffice to indicate that something exciting is going on in the theory of computational semantics. To what extent psycholinguists stand to benefit is still not clear; we must be prepared to discover that how people understand sentences has nothing to do with how computers compile programs. Even if that were all we learned, however, we would know a lot more about how people understand sentences than we know now.

ON KNOWING WORDS

We should try to relate the shape-of-things-to-come (as here envisioned) to the questions of vocabulary growth with which we began. If, as Davies and Isard imply, words are bits of programs, then knowing them is a matter of "knowing how," not "knowing that." This observation immediately suggests a parallel with certain passages in Piaget (1962), who argues that "The first use of language is mainly in the form of orders and expressions of desire.... the act of giving a name to an object is not merely that and nothing more, but the statement of a possible action [p. 222]." To think of words not as names for concepts, but as programs for action, fits well with Piaget's insistence that the basic structures of intelligence rest on sensory-motor foundations acquired during the earliest years of life. At this level the reconciliation in Phase Two of our theories of conceptual and of linguistic development should not be difficult.

In order to put empirical flesh on the bare bones of this metaphor, however, psychologists will be obliged to take the detailed structure of lexical concepts more seriously than they have in the past. It will no longer suffice to say that a person—either child or adult—knows what a word means and to assume that this claim requires no further explication for speakers of English. A scientific account will entail an explicit hypothesis about the routines that a language user has learned to compile for using the word, along with, perhaps, a comparison with routines compiled for this word by other people. And that, in turn, will require us to develop techniques for discovering and testing such hypotheses. How this should be done is by no means clear, but just to indicate the kind of hypothesis about linguistic routines that might be involved we can elaborate on Harrison's example for "bring."

A first step in describing the compiler might be to describe its output. What operations should the compiled program have under its control? Probably the most exhaustively studied instances involve verificational operations. A person who knows how to verify the sentence "Bill brought a book" must be able to construct from it a routine that includes (among other things) the following five tests for determining whether the sentence is true or false. The verification routine he compiles must determine that :

(a) Bill and the book are together from time t to time t';
(b) Bill is moving from t to t';
(c) the book is moving from t to t';
(d) what Bill does causes what the book does; and
(e) Bill is in the region of the speaker at time t'.

A listener may not wish or may not be able to run a routine incorporating all these tests, but to verify the sentence he must be able to compile it, i.e., form a program that contains pointers to previously stored subroutines for performing these tests.

Each of these five tests could also be a component of some verb other than "bring." For example, (a) would be included in "Bill had a book," (b) in "Bill moved," (c) in "A book moved," (d) in "Bill threw a book," and (e) in "Bill came." Hence, there is a sufficient basis for expecting the various motion verbs to be related or, as we used to say, associated.

All the tests in this verification routine are perceptual tests, as are the assumed recognition routines for "Bill" and "a book." This peculiarity of the verb "bring" would not be shared by such other verbs as "owned," "understood," "remembered," etc. They are, however, *generalized* perceptual tests, in the sense that the exact manner of moving, the precise way of being together, the actual causative relation, etc., are not specified. What this generality implies about the relation between perceptions and lexical meanings is significant, especially if one is still tempted by some varieties of associationistic theory.

Even "bring," however, will be compiled with nonperceptual operations if some procedure other than verification is involved. A declarative sentence may simply be accepted, in which case the compiler produces a program for updating the listener's information. For the question "Did Bill bring a book?" a vocal response, the utterance "Yes," "No," or "I don't know," is contingent on the outcome of the perceptual tests. For the questions "Who brought the book?" or "What did Bill bring?" still different programs are required from the compiler. For the command "Bring a book" the compiled program would indicate that the person addressed should perform the indicated actions. The form of the sentence—declarative, interrogative, imperative—must be reflected in the particular routine that is compiled (Davies & Isard, 1972). The alternative outputs as a function of mode will be similar for many different verbs, and so will provide a basis for the kinds of generalizations that grammarians are expected to draw. To compile these routines correctly, however, a language user need not know the grammatical rules in anything like the abstract form that linguists state them.

Constructing appropriate routines for different English sentences is not easy work, especially when one tries to make the construction plausible and consistent over a reasonable sample of the lexicon. It is obvious that our analysis of lexical concepts cannot stop with the consideration of a single word, for we know that words are related in groups that serve to cover various aspects of any given conceptual domain. An analysis of "bring" must be supplemented by a similar analysis of other verbs that describe how objects can change location (Miller, 1972). Such analyses will force us to pay close attention to the conceptual content of language, not merely to the processes by which it is acquired; Piaget's epistemological explorations of space, time, motion, number, etc., should provide much needed assistance in this kind of analysis.

Some of this work has already been done—or at least begun—by linguists and ethnologists who describe lexical relations in terms of semantic components, features, or markers; these meaning elements should provide valuable clues as to shared subroutines. If the compiler analogy is correct, however, describing shared subroutines is but a small part of the task. The more challenging part is to describe how these subroutines should be assembled for different sentences to reflect the different uses to which sentences can be put.

Although the theoretical task is formidable, the general strategy is sufficiently clear to support an intelligent attack on it. How we are to test such formulations by observing the behavior of language users is not so clear. Some methods of psychological scaling are available, but they should be supplemented with coordinate observations of other kinds. Comparison of semantic structures in widely different languages may provide useful information for separating what is psychologically universal from what is culturally specific, but such evidence is better gathered by linguists and anthropologists than by psychologists. The growth of these semantic structures in children also offers an opportunity to study the problem from a different vantage point, and it is not implausible to speculate that studies of child semantics may play an important role in the exploitation of the computer metaphor.

The predictions that emerge, therefore, are that "the growth of vocabulary" will become "semantic development," that the problem will again become a focus for intense investigation, but that the construction of new hypotheses and new techniques of investigation will place more severe demands on the skills and imagination of psychologists than they have been accustomed to in the past.

CONCLUDING CAVEAT

A period of consolidation, of "normal science," is required between "paradigm shifts" (Kuhn, 1970). When a new paradigm is first adopted it is not possible to distinguish between difficulties that can be resolved by natural extensions of paradigmatic research and difficulties that will eventually outrun it and lead to the next "scientific revolution." A critic of a new view, therefore, can do little more than list problems it must face. Which, if any, of his criticisms may prove to be fatal weaknesses must remain an open question until the range of applicability of the new metaphor has been explored.

There has been enough debate about *l'homme machine,* however, to provide a challenging list of problems for the computation metaphor. We know, for example, that whatever a human brain may be, it is certainly not a high-speed digital computer. This objection, however, is beside the point. The claim is not that the human brain is a computer, but that there are generalizations valid for any device that performs certain types of information processing. The information processing common to brains and computers does not exhaust the variety and function of brain processes. The computation metaphor serves best as a basis for cognitive theories, and has little place for the affective components of language or thought. Whether the emotional connotations of words and sentences can be incorporated into such an extravagantly cognitive theory is an important question.

It is reasonably obvious that, in addition to subroutines needed to compile a program for grammatical sentences, an adequate theory will eventually have to allow for the use of considerable nonlinguistic information, for the organization of lexical concepts into semantic domains, for the setting of goals and the construction of plans, for the use of imagery and metaphor. These are matters that outrun even a broad definition of the scope of psycholinguistics, but they serve to remind us that the success of the computation metaphor in psycholinguistics will depend on its success elsewhere in psychology.

As formulated by Davies and Isard, the new view is obviously weakest in its characterization of a speaker. The speaker is a generator of programs; presumably he can compile and execute his own programs through a kind of inner speech that constitutes one form of thinking. Thus, boundaries between psycholinguistic theory and general cognitive theory will be most difficult to draw when we try to characterize what a speaker is doing. It is here that a productive period of normal science seems most needed.

Whatever the eventual fate of the computation metaphor, however, we obviously need some new formulation that will provide a more central role for semantics in general and for semantic development in particular.

REFERENCES

Anglin, J. M. *The growth of word meaning.* Cambridge, Mass.: MIT Press, 1970.

Berko, J. & Brown, R. Psycholinguistic research methods. In P. H. Mussen (Ed.), *Handbook of research methods in child development.* New York: Wiley, 1960.

Bloomfield, L. *Language.* New York: Holt, Rinehart & Winston, 1933.

Chomsky, N. Three models for the description of language. *IRE Transaction on Information Theory,* 1956, IT-2, 113-124.

Chomsky, N. *Aspects of the theory of syntax.* Cambridge, Mass.: MIT Press, 1965.

Dale, P. S. *Language development: Structure and function.* Hinsdale, Ill.: Dryden, 1972.

Davies, D. & Isard, S. D. Utterances as programs. In D. Michie (Ed.), *Machine Intelligence 7.* Edinburgh: Edinburgh University Press, 1972.

Ervin-Tripp. S. Language development. In L. W. Hoffman & M. L. Hoffman (Eds.), *Review of child development research.* Vol. 2. New York: Russell Sage Foundation, 1966.

Flavell, J. H. *The developmental psychology of Jean Piaget.* Princeton, N.J.: Van Nostrand, 1963.

Harrison, B. *Meaning and structure.* New York: Harper & Row, 1972.

Kuhn, T. S. *The structure of scientific revolutions.* (2nd ed.) Chicago: University of Chicago Press, 1970.

Lewis, D. K. *Convention: A philosophical study.* Cambridge, Mass.: Harvard University Press, 1969.

McCarthy, D. Language development in children. In L. Carmichael (Ed.), *Manual of child psychology.* (2nd ed.) New York: Wiley, 1954.

McNeill, D. The development of language. In P. H. Mussen (Ed.), *Carmichael's manual of child psychology.* (3rd ed.) New York: Wiley, 1970.

Miller, G. A. *The psychology of communication: Seven essays.* New York: Basic Books, 1967.

Miller, G. A. English verbs of motion: A case study in semantics and lexical memory. In A. W. Melton & E. Martin (Eds.), *Coding processes in human memory.* Washington, D.C.: Winston, 1972.

Morris, C. W. *Signs, language, and behavior.* Englewood Cliffs, N.J.: Prentice-Hall, 1946.

Newell, A. & Simon, H. A. *Human problem solving.* Englewood Cliffs, N.J.: Prentice-Hall, 1972.

Osgood, C. E. The nature and measurement of meaning. *Psychological Bulletin,* 1952, 49, 197-237.

Piaget, J. *Play, dreams, and imitation in childhood.* (Trans. by C. Gattegno and F. M. Hodgson) New York: Norton, 1962.

Scott, D. & Strachey, C. *Toward a mathematical semantics for computer languages.* (Technical Monograph PRG-6) Oxford: Oxford Computing Laboratory, 1971.

Shannon, C. E. A mathematical theory of communication. *Bell System Technical Journal,* 1948, **27**, 379-423.

Sinclair-de-Zwart, H. Developmental psycholinguistics. In D. Elkind & J. H. Flavell (Eds.), *Studies in cognitive development: Essays in honor of Jean Piaget.* New York: Oxford University Press, 1969.

Smith, M. K. Measurement of the size of general English vocabulary through the elementary grades and high school. *Genetic Psychology Monographs,* 1941, **24**, 311-345.

Suppes, P. Stimulus-response theory of finite automata. *Journal of Mathematical Psychology,* 1969, **6**, 327-355.

Tarski, A. The concept of truth in formalized languages. In A. Tarski (Ed.), *Logic, semantics, metamathematics: Papers from 1923-1938.* (Translated by J. H. Woodger) Oxford: Oxford University Press, 1956.

Templin, M. C. Certain language skills in children: Their development and interrelationships. *Institute of child welfare monographs.* (Serial No. 26) Minneapolis: University of Minnesota Press, 1957.

Vygotsky, L. S. *Thought and language.* (Trans. by E. Hanfmann and G. Vakar) Cambridge, Mass.: MIT Press, 1962.

Winograd, T. *Procedures as a representation for data in a computer program for understanding natural language.* (Report AI TR-17) MIT Artificial Intelligence Laboratory, 1971.

Wittgenstein, L. *Philosophical investigations.* (Trans. by G. E. M. Anscombe) New York: Macmillan, 1953.

Woods, W. A. Procedural semantics for a question-answering machine. *Proceedings of the AFIPS 1968 Fall Joint Computer Conference,* 1968, **33**, 457-471.

20
OVERVIEW OF A
COGNITIVE CONSPIRACY:
REFLECTIONS ON THE VOLUME

Walter B. Weimer
Pennsylvania State University

A reflection contains all the information present in the original perspective from which an object or event is viewed. When the original object is as rich in information content as this volume, "reflections on the volume" must be interpreted more modestly. Instead of summarizing or paraphrasing what has been said (in which case reflection means, at best, "reminiscence"), I will try to add some new meaning to the preceding papers by putting the issues discussed in a larger, or at least a more explicit, context. If successful, my remarks will enrich rather than merely reflect the book. Throughout I shall attempt to be *critical* of the preceding papers: In a sense the only failing of the conference that generated this book has been that where we have had discussants they have been too much in agreement with the positions of the chapters commented upon. An air of self-congratulation permeates many of the preceding pages, and some brief remarks on the enormous problems facing cognitive psychology should serve to temper our naive optimism at the meager strides made up to this point. In a very real sense the major contribution of this volume has been to make us clearly aware of the nature and enormity of the problems facing any cognitive psychology worth of the name: What we have learned is a feeling for what we don't know about the higher mental processes. Ideally these comments will temper our optimism about present achievements without dampening our enthusiasm for the work yet to be done.

THE FOREST LOST IN THE TREES: LEARNING THEORY, BEHAVIORISM, AND COGNITIVE PSYCHOLOGY

Despite the excellence of their chapters, I believe both Brewer and Dulany have lost sight (albeit for different reasons) of the paradigmatic (in Kuhn's sense) import of the transition from behavioristic learning theory to cognitive theory. Having sunk to the level of behaviorism (to deal with it on its own terms) they have become mired in issues and details whose importance is greatly lessened if not trivialized entirely when viewed from another perspective. This point emerges clearly when considering the context in which each author's chapter is embedded. In Brewer's case, the overriding context concerns the question of how to best fight the revolutionary battle (between behaviorism and cognitive psychology) and win; in Dulany's case the over-arching question concerns the methodology of scientific research necessary to do genuinely scientific cognitive psychology. Let us consider these in turn.

Brewer and the revolution in psychological theory. In his oral presentation, Brewer alluded to a seminar at Minnesota about five years ago in which I attempted to convince the "rat running" learning theorists that Chomsky's revolution in linguistics could not be stopped at the borderlands of psycholinguistics: that if the arguments were accepted *anywhere* in psychology, they had to be accepted everywhere (this was a period in which a common learning theory response was that "since rats don't talk, Chomsky has nothing to say to me, and therefore I'm not impressed"). Both Brewer and I are concerned to make the same point: that the revolution requires a radical reformulation (from the cognitive point of view) of the domain of learning. We both want to say that learning theory has nothing to say to cognitive psychology, but that cognitive psychology has everything to say to learning theory. But we have chosen very different strategies to try to "get through" to the rat runner. Brewer remarked that I used all the "high-powered" arguments—meaning those from linguistics and the philosophy of science—and he felt that, although impressive, they didn't really "get through" to hit the learning theorist "where his theoretical heart is." To do that, Brewer felt, it is necessary to meet behaviorism on its own home ground and show the learning theorist that *his* phenomena are actually cognitive in nature. That reasoning, in simplified overview, is what lies behind his painstaking demolition of the traditional interpretation of Pavlovian and operant conditioning in humans.

Although I share his interest, and consider his review a valuable addition to cognitive psychology, I remain unconvinced that his strategy is effective in converting (or even in scaring) the learning theorist. Behaviorists are an enterprising lot, and their surivial to this late date is largely due to their ability to give plausible *post hoc* accounts of other theorists' data. Indeed, there is nothing in any of the data base of cognitive psychology that a determined learning theorist cannot "explain" on a *post hoc* basis in a manner congruent with behavioristic principles (as Dulany points out so clearly). I think it likely that the learning theorist's most common response to Brewer's paper will be, "So what's new? Until you provide a completely worked out cognitive theory that explains conditioning, I am not going to change." And, as we must all (Dulany perhaps excepted) admit, there is no cognitive theory, even on the horizon, that can do that. What Brewer has shown is the ineffectiveness of behaviorism to deal with its own domain, not the superiority of the cognitive approach. This will certainly embarrass the behaviorist who believes that holding a falsified theory is "unscientific," but it will not convert him to the cognitive point of view. As Kuhn has convincingly argued, one paradigm will not win over the residual practitioners of a rival unless it is perceived to offer *more* than the rival.

If there is any possiblity of conversion, or to say the same thing, arguing for the superiority of cognitive over behavioristic theory, it will lie in showing that there are *obvious* phenomena, found *throughout* the psychological domain, that can be given a principled explanation by cognitive theory and that cannot be handled by the learning theorist except in an *ad hoc,* concept-distorting manner. Against Brewer I believe that the "big" arguments, transferring the linguistic examples to the *entire* psychological domain, are the best way to go. In short, it does not matter that (as Dulany emphasizes) learning as a domain is a presently undecided area— the devastating arguments against behaviorism are the linguistic and philosophical ones, and he who understands these arguments will opt out of behaviorism *despite* the fact that behaviorism can still rationalize the domain of learning very effectively.

To see this, consider in overview the following half-dozen arguments that the transformational grammarian introduced to psychology:

1. The very existence of genuine novelty in behavior was denied by behaviorism, because (as I have argued in detail elsewhere; Weimer, 1969, 1973) all learning theories are common element transfer theories incapable of handling genuine novelty (See Dollard & Miller, 1950, p. 37, on what novelty is for the behaviorist). In contrast, creativity or productivity is the rule rather than the exception in language and all skilled behaviors. Thus there are indefinitely many "behaviors" that learning theory cannot address at all.

2. An analogous argument follows from the existence of deep structure ambiguity (and hence for the necessity of a deep structural level underlying behavior). This entire class of behaviors, in which one and the same surface structure has two (or more) deep structure "meanings" (as in "praising professors can be platitudinous"), simply did not exist for the behaviorist, because he did not make the surface-deep distinction. Despite its continual presence, this kind of ambiguity just did not exist as a scientific datum until transformational grammar came along. And yet this ambiguity is inherent in *all* behavior, as the ambiguity of human action (consider the textbook ethics example: "Was behavior A an act of type X or Y?") and the problem of what response is "learned" in transfer of training make clear.

3. The hierarchical control of movement, as in the difference between the "S" in articulating "Stra" versus "Stro," the Lashley (1951) examples of serial ordering, etc., are all incapable of being handled by a linear or chaining mechanism of the mind, such as associationism. Learning theory explanations of behavior, because they are associationistic, cannot handle the vast majority of behaviors.

4. Equally devastating for theories that account for learning in terms of copying identical elements is the problem of prose recall. There is just no way to understand why subjects will be very certain that they heard you say "Here come da judge" when what was actually said concerned the eminent arrival of a magistrate. The Bransford, McCarrell, and Franks papers bring this argument strategy to a very high state of development.

5. The inherent ambiguity of functionally specified behavior plagues behaviorism. As Brewer noted, learning theory was supposed to be "scientific" because stimuli and responses could be defined in physically specifiable terms. Yet in practice all learning theorists lapsed into functional specification of behaviors (such

as "leaping the barrier" as a response: See Hull, 1943, p. 25). But functional specification *alone* is inherently ambiguous: Without a concomitant structural specification of behavior (a grammar of behavior, if you will) to show the derivational history of the "mere movements" that constitute a behavior, one cannot unambiguously specify which behavior those movements instantiated. This is the *primacy* of structural analysis over functional specification: It is the only way known to disambiguate otherwise inherently ambiguous performances (see Weimer, in press b).

This latter point is worth expanding. Just as it is necessary to have available the information provided by the derivational history underlying an utterance (the structure of its generation) to disambiguate it, it is necessary to have a precise specification of the syntax of action to answer the question "What is learned?" (or "What response occurred?"). This "disambiguation" of behavior is really not a matter of ambiguity, but rather of explanation. For just as the disambiguation of an utterance is actually its *comprehension,* the disambiguation of behavioral action is actually its *explanation.* The behaviorist, with an inherently ambiguous account of the generation of behavior (because it is purely functionally specified), actually doesn't *understand* it at all; that is, he cannot *explain* the generation of behavior at all. In order for learning theory to even get off the ground, it must have an account of the genesis of behavior from deep conceptual structures to observed surface responses. Such an account will have to be a structural determination of behavior analogous to the structural determination provided by a grammar in linguistics.

6. Perhaps the key to all these arguments against behaviorism can be found in the indispensability of abstract entities in *theoretical* science. Advanced sciences explain the phenomena of their domains by postulating abstract, often in principle unobservable, entities as causally responsible for appearances. Behaviorism, committed to "objectivity" and "observability" at the molar level of phenomenal appearances, as touchstones of scientific sophistication, can countenance no abstract entities.

When faced with the problem of creativity of productivity in language, as well as deep structure ambiguity, the linguist has no choice, if he wants an explanatorily adequate theory, but to postulate control systems that range over fundamentally abstract entities at a deep conceptual level. Faced with the same problems in the remainder of the psychological domain, the psychologist will have to do likewise. When he does, he will *ipso facto* no longer be a behaviorist, and Brewer's review will find its significance in pointing out that behaviorism couldn't handle its own domain, not in converting behaviorists to cognitive psychology.

Dulany and the methodology of scientific research. Because of his continued interest in the area, Dulany's approach to cognitive psychology gravitates to issues in the philosophy of science. While he has long denied the adequacy of behavior theoretic formulations to cognition, Dulany still regards behaviorism as a formidable foe, one that will survive the resurgence of cognitive psychology unless it can be attacked on methodological grounds. His goal is to defend cognitive "learning" theory (his propositional learning theory) by attempting to make it methodologically more secure than behaviorism. At present Dulany sees no methodological criteria that decide the issue, and this is his chief problem: He reasons that, unless cognitive psychology can become more methodologically sophisticated than behaviorism, behaviorism may yet win the day.

Again I must demur. I believe that there are *philosophical* criteria that dictate choice of the cognitive paradigm over behaviorism, but I think that recent work in the methodology of scientific research, due principally to Thomas Kuhn (1970) and Imre Lakatos (1970, 1972), has made it quite clear that no methodological criteria can ever decide between competing "paradigms." Since I have dealt with these issues extensively elsewhere, I shall resist detailed analysis and summarize a few salient points.

Consider these arguments against behaviorism: By indicating the limitations of the behaviorist approach, and demonstrating its lack of awareness of problems and issues of paramount importance, these arguments, although "merely" philosophical, still mitigate against behaviorism.

(a) The indispensability of abstract entities in scientific theory construction, mentioned above, is an inherently philosophical consideration. Recent analyses of the nature and function of scientific theory have devastated the conception of theory upon which behaviorism rests. For example, Körner (1966) has shown that the disconnection between theory and experience is total and complete, i.e., that all scientific propositions and entities, even the so-called "observational" ones, are abstract. The "foundations" picture of knowledge, implicit in logical empiricism and behaviorism (and responsible for the concern with concrete and particular observables) has been annihilated by Popper (1959) and his students (e.g., Agassi, 1966; Feyerabend, 1962, 1965).

(b) Simultaneously, the nature of *evidence* has changed. It has become quite obvious that no scientist has ever been persuaded to or dissuaded from a theory by "data." Theories determine data, not vice versa: Indeed there would be no data at all without prior theoretical specification of what, in the flux of experience, constituted *significant* observation. Facts, far from being the data base upon which theory rests, are the end products of theory (see Popper, 1959). Thus the behaviorist's "facts" carry no weight except within his own theoretical framework, and, when examined from an *external* framework, they may not be facts at all. Indeed, this is exactly what Brewer's review argues: The "facts" of human conditioning, so sanctified within behaviorism, are not at all what they are said to be. Looked at in this perspective, the broad "data base" that the behaviorist so loudly proclaims as the basis of his "scientific" status evaporates.

(c) Our understanding of scientific *inference* has thoroughly discredited the naive inductivist methodology that behaviorism endorses. Since there is no data base that is "firm" enough to serve as a foundation upon which to erect a science, the cautious induction-from-particulars model of scientific progress that the behaviorist defends as the epitome of scientific sophistication turns out to be "unscientific." The tenability of building-block methodology was destroyed eons ago, and behaviorists are among the last holdouts who have not acknowledged the failure of this Baconian ideal of science (see Agassi, 1966).

(d) In a more substantive vein, the program of dispositional analysis of the psychological domain, an integral tenet of behaviorism, is severely limited. As I have argued (Weimer, in press a), to insist that psychology be understood in terms of "dispositions to respond" is to insist that the science be incomplete, descriptive rather than explanatory, incapable of causal specification, unable to treat phenomenal experience, and totally incapable of accounting for creativity or productivity in behavior. Should that list of specifications not look appetizing, the only hope is to abandon behaviorism. But this again, rather than just a "methodological" consideration, is primarily a consideration of the nature and role of psychology as a theoretical science, and of the expectations that are reasonable for a science of the psychological domain.

Should one wish to shift focus from general philosophy of science considerations which militate against behaviorism to the better-delimited area of "scientific method," one can consider Shaw's analysis of scientific inference as a case in which cognitive psychology can improve upon traditional philosophical views. Analyzing the "logic of science" in terms of adjunctive logic is more accurate historically, with regard to how science has actually been done, and is simultaneously consonant with the cognitive approaches to perception and concept formation discussed in this volume. Thus the cognitive theorist's reply to Dulany's quest for methodological criteria of choice is to point out that (a) recent philosophial analyses of methodology indicate that no such criteria exist, and (b) cognitive psychology can provide an account of scientific concept formation that can explain how science "gets done" in the absence of such criteria.

A role for Brewer's review. There is still a definite and invaluable role for Brewer's review of the cognitive nature of human conditioning: It will enable the cognitive theorist to *use* conditioning as an experimental device to answer questions within the new paradigm. A doctoral thesis at Penn State illustrates this point. Frank Faile (1972) wanted to see what the subjective unit of speech production is, to see whether any of the extant linguistic theories have psychological validity. To consider only extremes, some approaches say that the speaker plans his utterance (and then produces it) in units of words, while others suggest sentences are planned as units. Faile thought that what is planned is more likely to be the phonological phrase, an "intermediate" sized unit, than either of the other extremes. But how can one ascertain the size of the production unit experimentally? Faile's technique utilizes the Ivanov-Smolensky "anticipatory instructed conditioning" procedure: S is told to jerk his arm the moment he becomes aware that a given word is going to occur in his utterance. When the location of anticipatory jerks is correlated with production of the utterance, it appears that the phonological phrase, rather than either the word or the sentence, is indeed the subjective unit: Jerks appear at the beginning (or boundary) of the phonological phrase in which the key word occurs rather than at the word before or at the beginning of the sentence.

Had it not been for Brewer's review, this research would have been damned from both sides. The behaviorist would have ignored it because anticipatory instructed conditioning is "obviously" not true (i.e., unconscious and automatic) conditioning. Brewer's reinterpretation obviates such an interpretation, as it does the cognitive theorist's suggestion that "conditioning" is irrelevant to the higher mental processes. By legitimating conditioning techniques as experimental paradigms *within cognitive psychology,* Brewer has performed an invaluable service. Now it is incumbent upon cognitive psychology to experimentally "takeover" this domain and generate experiments within its point of view. This will provide the sort of "competitive support" that Dulany rightly points out we have yet to deliver.

THE CART BEFORE THE HORSE: LINGUISTICS AND ITS ROLE IN COGNITIVE PSYCHOLOGY

Since the transformational or generative grammar revolution occasioned the resurgence of psycholinguistics, the relationship between linguistics and psychology has been one-sided and unidirectional: Linguistics has led the way and psychology has followed meekly behind. Throughout the last decade, psycholinguistic research has consisted of borrowing the latest linguistic formulation for an area to "experiment" upon it. Psycholinguistics has depended for its impetus and direction upon the more highly developed "state of the art" in linguistics: Linguistics has been the *de facto* parent discipline. Yet Chomsky himself has clearly and repeatedly pointed out (e.g., in *Language and Mind*, p. 1) that linguistics is but one branch of cognitive psychology. This being so, cognitive psychology ought to constrain developments in linguistics as much as vice versa. The psychologist ought to be able to tell the linguist where to go in his future research as often, if not more often, than the other way around.

The primacy of cognitive psychology. Perhaps the really unique (and promising) aspect of this conference is that for the first time the linguists listened more than they talked. The psychologists dominated the focus and set the topics for discussion, even in traditionally "purely linguistic" matters. For the first time, as one wit remarked, it was the linguist whose mouth was in the fly-catching position, rather than the psychologist. This reversal is of monumental import for cognitive psychology: It marks the first time in the (recent) history of the discipline that the substantive theory and research has caught up with, and perhaps outpaced, the "state of the art" in linguistics. It means, in a nutshell, that cognitive psychology may at last be ready to stand on its own feet as an independent discipline.

Granting this reversal, the relationship between linguistic and psychological theory must be rethought. The once straightforward questions, "What can the psychologist learn from the linguist?" and "What is the relationship between the two disciplines?" can no longer be given pat answers. There now appears to be (to use Ross's admirable term, which instantly became the catchword of the conference), a considerable amount of "squishiness" here. Indeed, the development of generative semantics from the standard syntactic theory, and the change in the conceptualization of the nature and role of meaning in that development, indicate some of the squishy problems facing us.

One thing to note in Ross's outline of the development of generative semantics is the uniform and seemingly inexorable progression from the purely syntactic conception of deep structure in the standard theory of Chomsky (1965) through a quasi-semantic position in abstract syntax (Ross, 1967) to a purely semantic conception in generative semantics *circa* 1969. This developmental progression was instrumental in removing one of the favorite retreats of the embattled neobehaviorist, who saw in Chomsky's dismissal of meaning to the nether regions of interpretative semantics a reason for ignoring transformational grammar and its arguments against behaviorism. (Osgood's comments of 1963 and 1968 to the effect that psychology is on its home ground when dealing with meaning, are a case in point.) Generative semantics removed this line of retreat by the simple expedient of putting meaning, the psychological concept *par excellence,* in the driver's seat in linguistics, i.e., in the deep structure.

Although generative semantics has been successful, up to a point, in dealing with the abstract semantic relationships underlying sentences, its very success has pointed out what is, for the psychologist, the most severe limitation of all current linguistic formulations: the inability to deal with larger conceptual units of analysis than the sentence. By looking at the nature and role of meaning within the sentence the linguist has ignored the cognitive constraints that are operative across sentences in connected discourse. Just as it was once a telling argument against earlier conceptions to point out that people speak sentences rather than words, it is equally telling to point out that sentences only mean what they do in fact mean because they are embedded in the complex web of cognitive relations that constitute human knowledge and understanding. In a sense, the transition from traditional psycholinguistics to cognitive psychology is that from Ross's paper to the work of the BMF group. The generative semanticists have made the case within linguistics for the semantic nature of the deep conceptual structures underlying sentences, while Bransford and his collaborators have made the case that meaning can only be understood, if at all, within the larger context of the intentional framework of human knowledge and conceptual discourse. Unless cognitive psychology can deliver an analysis of the nature and richness of human understanding, the generative semanticist will not be able to complete his analysis, or to show how it relates to other aspects of the psychological sciences (recall Ross's remarks about the semantics of "glass").

The semantic nature of deep conceptual structures. Let us back up to examine two issues before looking at the problems posed by the BMF papers. The first concerns the sharp split between the cognitive psychologists represented in this volume and the views of Jim McCawley. Recall that Ross asked whether psychologists had found any areas, other than the psychology of language, in which it was necessary to postulate abstract underlying structures as causal determinants of phenomena. McCawley, responding to the intrinsic *semantic* nature of the generative semanticist's deep structures, found himself unable to imagine any area except music in which there could be underlying cognitive structures that were abstract in Ross's (semantic) sense. In discussion afterward, Terry Halwes took sharp exception to McCawley's position, arguing for the indispensability of the surface-deep distinction in all of psychology. I think that the vast majority of psychologists would side with Halwes against McCawley, and that the evidence Halwes cited can be elaborated indefinitely. But the important point is that, as in the case of language, the deep conceptual structures Halwes was emphasizing are semantic in nature. Human action and knowledge are intrinsically intentional and meaningful, and the entire psychological domain will require the same kind of abstract entities as language. The separation between linguistics and psychology will not be based upon the intrinsic nature of the abstract entities causally responsible for surface structure phenomena (both will be equally "cognitive" and "semantic"), but ultimately will be due to pragmatic factors concerning the domains of inquiry. The linguist must come to realize that meaning is first and foremost the province of psychology, and not a special feature of language.

History of science and the importance of "notational variants." The second point concerns the syntax-semantics feud raging between the neoorthodoxy—Chomsky and the syntacticians promulgating the "extended standard theory" (EST) through its successive revisions—and the young heretics in the semantics camp (Ross mentioned the "palace revolution" in his talk; he modestly neglected to mention his firing some of the first shots). The psychologist cannot (especially speaking from his armchair) presume to legislate theoretical issues within linguistics, even though he may have reasons for preferring one position to another. But speaking as a part-time historian and philosopher of science, I can easily show one defense of the EST to be no defense at all: the so-called "notational variant" argument that Chomsky (e.g., 1971, p. 188 *ff*) has employed to dismiss his opposition. Briefly, Chomsky has argued that, *formally* speaking, the choice between abstract syntactic entities and abstract semantic ones is of no consequence, and that the generative semantics position is "merely" a notational variant of the EST. Since it is only a notational variant, Chomsky has reasoned, generative semantics cannot be seriously considered an alternative to his theory. The crucial point is taken to be the purely formal equivalence of the two approaches—since the same uninterpreted calculus could equally represent both, there must be no difference between them.

But the history of science provides numerous examples of the theoretical inutility of one approach despite the purely formal equivalence of two systems. Let me remind you of a few examples. First recall that Newton and Leibniz both "invented" the calculus. But Newton's system, "fluxions," as he called it, while formally equivalent to Leibniz's calculus of infinitesimals, was so esoteric as to be virtually unusable. The calculus we learn today is directly related to Leibniz's system, and Newton's is a historical curiosity. Despite their formal equivalence, no one could *use* Newton's notation. As a second example, consider the history of the "rational mechanics" of Newton's successors. Joseph Louis Lagrange and William Rowan Hamilton developed mathematical functions formulating the state description of mechanical systems. With the aid of Hamilton's insight James Clerk Maxwell was able to develop electromagnetic field theory, but only after discarding his unworkable notation. The Lagrangian function is actually a more restricted form than Hamilton's, but the science of mechanics advanced further with it, until Maxwell had the insight to use Hamilton's reasoning but not his notation. Thus, even though Hamilton's formalism was in a sense more powerful than Lagrange's, it was less useful to the science of mechanics.

Perhaps the above examples seem too remote and too dependent upon the practical utility of a given formalism in comparison to a rival. If so, we might consider a contemporary controversy. The point of this, as in the other examples, is that it *must* always be logically possible for two theories to be equally powerful in predictive and explantory ability yet wholly dissimilar with regard to the understanding of their given subject matter. Wave mechanics and matrix mechanics were shown by Schrödinger in 1926 to have equal explanatory validity. Their formal structures were identical (as was proved in 1930 by Dirac). But Dirac himself argues that the conceptual pictures provided by these different systems are so orthogonal that one of them *must* be preferable to the other. The understanding provided by one is quite different than that provided by the other despite their formal equivalence. Successful formal derivation of phenomena is thus quite independent of explanatory adequacy (or conceptual understanding).

Generative syntax and generative semantics may be formally equivalent, but they differ greatly in explanatory adequacy. If the defenders of the EST have no arguments for it other than the "notational variant" claim, they have no arguments for it at all.

THE NATURE AND REPRESENTATION OF KNOWLEDGE AND MEANING

The strong claim of the constructive cognitive theorist, exemplified by the BMF articles, is that there is no meaning or knowledge in language *per se.* Stated another way, the claim is that language does not *carry* meaning in sentences, but rather *triggers* or releases meaning (i.e., occasions understanding) that is already in the head. Unless a hearer can generate a context which renders a sentence interpretable, the sentence has no meaning at all. To put it another way, the "dictionary" of lexical items that the linguist habitually uses as a *deus ex machina* to supplement his account of the sentence, like actual dictionaries, has no meaning in it at all. If one does not know "how words mean" in human conceptualization, then one cannot use a real dictionary: There are no meanings in dictionaries, only alternative verbalizations. Dictionaries embody paraphrase relationships, but meaning, which is what makes paraphrase a matter of paraphrastics, is already in the head that uses a dictionary. To state it in yet a fourth way, all sentences, regardless of whether the linguist marks them as such, are *inherently* ambiguous. The problem of ambiguity, though, is actually that of comprehension or understanding. Until the hearer assimilates a sentence to his conceptual framework, it has no determinate meaning at all, and is "ambiguous" in the sense of "uncomprehended."

No matter how it is formulated, this is a striking claim, the full import of which is liable to remain obscure for some time. A number of us, though, have come to believe it, and the problem is now to follow where it leads. In a sense, the future of constructive theory lies in its promise of being able to pursue this insight to a coherent picture of the nature of human knowledge and its acquisition. Pursuit of this path will simultaneously lift cognitive psychology out of the domination of linguistics and shove us out into the dark on our own. No longer may we borrow clear-cut "normal science" experiments from the latest linguistics journal and consider the role of psycholinguistics to be that of construct validation of the psychological reality of linguistic constructs.

Being too close to the BMF position I can't be a very effective critic. Instead I shall merely point out that, as should be obvious, we must now reevaluate and reinterpret a sizable number of terms that psychologists have often felt that they understood well enough. Once we though we understood what learning is all about. Then Chomsky forced us to acknowledge that our knowledge is vastly greater than our learning history can allow. The 2500-year currency of associationism as the "mechanism" of learning has come to an end with the theoretical bankruptcy of the concept. We know vastly more than we have learned, and what we learn is not associations. But what do we learn? BMF point to highly abstract relations, rules of inference, in short toward the successor concepts of Henry Head's "schemata." But what are the schemata, or the categories, of human understanding? Do we know anything that Kant didn't know in 1781? I think it fairly clear that the answer is "No," that in many ways we have learned nothing that Plato didn't know (Weimer, 1973). Memory is equally an enigma. Once we thought it was the storage of specific traces. Then we gave up traces; now storage is but an inappropriate metaphor. The BMF position points toward memory as assimilation: the assimilation of new "information" (but hardly "bits") to, or the restructuring of, abstract schematic networks. In this conception there is no storage of any "thing" at all: only the utilization of information. The problem of understanding, and the focus on context providing the cue to abstract invariants, lead inexorably to another answerless question: What is meaning, and how does language manage to trigger it? We have had these and countless other questions for over two millennia now. But we have never had any answers. The promise of the BMF approach is that it may lead to some.

Let me leave the constructive cognitive approach with two observations. The first is merely informational, and is only slightly overstated. Almost everything that Ross said in his discussion of linguistics *that was interesting* either ignored or was orthogonal to his deep structures. Conversely, everything that BMF have done in the laboratory demonstrating the constructive nature of comprehension and the reconstructive nature of memory has been independent of specific linguistic proposals. That ought to tell us something. The second concerns a question I would like to see answered. Not long ago McCawley (1970) wrote an article entitled "Where Do Noun Phrases Come From?" But no linguist has yet tackled a more difficult question: Where do verb phrases come from? I suspect that no non-question-begging answer to this question will ever be forthcoming from linguistics—that it transcends the bounds of the domain, no matter which theoretical position is endorsed. To answer where verb phrases come from will require a completed theory of pragmatics—whence will derive the theory of actions that seems to be the domain in which verbs reside. And that domain ought to be the province of cognitive psychology.

THE PROBLEM OF PERCEPTION AND THE RECONCILIATION OF GIBSON-IAN AND STRUCTURAL REALISM

On first reading, J. J. Gibson's approach to perception, direct or unmediated (as opposed to naive) realism, seems incompatible with a constructive approach to cognitive psychology. Gibson's message has been and remains that the information (in a highly abstract psychological sense of the term not to be confused with information theory) necessary to account for our perception of the external world can be found in the properties of the stimulus array itself. When this is combined with the doctrine of evolution, the program of ecological optics results. And since ecological optics is in constant conflict with traditional or image optics, it is often assumed that Gibsonian realism is incompatible with the constructive nature of the higher mental processes such as language and thought.

Such an interpretation is, I fear, completely at odds with both Gibson and constructive theory. There is no inconsistency in simultaneously asserting that all the higher mental processes are constructive in nature *and* that Gibson's is the only sane approach to perception. The resolution of the *prima facie* conflict comes in specifying the input to the CNS and the nature of its construction granted that specification of the input. Once we remind ourselves of the nature of human knowledge and our present state of scientific knowledge of the nonmental realm, it becomes clear why all perceptionn *must* be constructive in nature, despite its unmediated or direct nature (assuming Gibson is correct, at least in essentials).

Somewhat paradoxically, it is physical science, not psychology, which guarantees that all experience is a construction. Structural realism, as a thesis concerning the nature of scientific knowledge, tells us that the only properties of the nonmental realm of which we have any knowledge whatsoever are purely structural. When we see something that appears to be a perceptible object, all the qualities which we know by acquaintance are in us as percipient beings rather than in the object. Suppose a neurophysiologist performs an operation exposing the brain of a patient. What the neurophysiologist *sees*, i.e., the event he experiences, is an event in his own brain which has only an indirect causal relationship with the physical brain of the patient. Everything that he sees in seeing the other man's brain is actually wholly within his own brain. Physics does not disclose a knowledge of qualitative properties such as those that occur in "seeing": The only properties of the nonmental realm with which science deals are second-order or structural properties. The way the nonmental realm of "external" objects affects us is by causal chains of purely structural properties. The entire realm of human phenomenal experience is thus wholly within our own nervous systems, and our perceptual "knowledge" is inevitably constructed, no matter what modality is involved. Bertrand Russell put the point well:

> Suppose, for example, that I see a chair, or rather that there is an occurrence which would ordinarily be so described . . . .Common sense supposes that the chair which I perceive would still be there if I did not perceive it, for example, if I shut my eyes. Physics and physiology between them assure me that what is there independently of my seeing is something very unlike a visual experience, namely a mad dance of billions of electrons undergoing billions of quantum transitions. My relation to this object is indirect, and is known only by inference: it is not something that I directly experience whenever there is that occurrence which I call "seeing a chair." In fact the whole of what occurs when I have the experience which I call "seeing a chair" is to be counted as belonging to my mental world. If there is a chair which is outside my mental world, as I firmly believe, this is something which is not a direct object of experience. but is arrived at by a process of inference. This conclusion has odd consequences. We must distinguish between the physical world of physics, and the physical world of our everyday experience. The physical world of physics, supposing physics to be correct, exists independently of my mental life. From a metaphysical point of view, it is solid and self-subsistent, always assuming that there is such a world. Per contra, the physical world of my everyday experience is a part of my mental life [Russell, 1951, pp. 151-52].

"Unconstructed experience" is thus an impossibility in the sense analogous to that of "square circle."

It should thus be clear that Gibson's approach to perception is compatible with structural realism, and indeed virtually required by it. What structural realism says is simultaneously that human experience is a construction within the CNS and that human knowledge is of the structural properties of the nonmental realm. If there is to be such a thing as human perception at all, there must be causal chains linking the nonmental world to the CNS which models it. Gibsonian perceptual theory asserts that the information specified by those causal chains originating in external or nonmental phenomena is sufficient to produce in our CNS the perceptions which we do in fact have. All perception is a construction in the CNS, but it is a construction resulting from input that only Gibson and his students have specified intelligently. The information upon which human perception is based is specified in the stimulus array. Despite the fact that all experience is a construction, the highly abstract, ecologically significant information that we perceive is perceived directly —without the mediation of symbolic or constructive activity such as images. Structural realism makes the first claim, Gibsonian direct realism, the second.

Whoever thinks that Gibsonian perceptual psychology is incorrect should then try to account for the facts of perception on the basis of *image optics.* The "refutation" of direct realism in philosophy is entirely based upon the acceptance of image optics. That this is so is clear when one examines the "argument from illusion" as a refutation of naive representational realism. The argument from illusion claims that perception often does not represent what we have come to know *by other means* to be "really" there, and that *therefore* we should conclude that perception is a construction. But if image optics is abandoned, the force of the antecedent is entirely relocated. As Shaw, Mace, and Turvey have repeatedly pointed out, the information from which perception arises is actually present in the stimulus array, and the perceptual system is processing information directly as it always does. Thus these theorists correctly point out that the mere existence of illusion does not argue against Gibsonian realism, but in making this point they ignore the constructive nature of experience. Halwes and BMF, on the other hand, point out that perception (*all* perception) must equally be constructive (because we do not perceive what physical science tells us is the actual flora and fauna of the nonmental world), and in their haste to make this point have lost sight of the compatibility of the constructive thesis with Gibson's claim. Yet both groups have provided devastating arguments against "image" conceptions of higher mental processing, and the unanimity with which the image approach has been rejected is of far more importance than the mistaken opposition between Gibsonian and structural realism.

THE PROBLEM OF TACIT KNOWLEDGE: WILL YOUR REAL HEAD PLEASE STAND UP AND TELL US ABOUT MEANING

Moving from Mace's and Turvey's chapters through to the presentations of BMF and Halwes, the central concern of this volume comes more and more clearly to the fore: The major part of human knowledge is tacit. The problem is that we are not yet sure what is meant by saying that knowledge is largely tacit, and thus we have no theoretical framework adequate to explicate it. We can start with Polanyi's

(1958, 1966) dictum that tacit knowledge is that of which we are almost always unaware and can *never* explicitly formalize. But neither Polanyi nor anyone else has a theory of what tacit knowledge is, and I doubt that we would recognize one if we somehow fell upon it. (It wouldn't help to know it tacitly!) Without realizing it, cognitive psychology has "gone fishing" and hooked something that it cannot discern, that shows no signs of coming to gaff. Indeed, we are definitely on the line, but who is going to land whom is very much in doubt.

Tacit knowledge and the problem of meaning. We began discussing tacit knowledge in terms of perception. With regard to perceiving, tacit knowledge is the problem of thing-kind identification, of the identification of a particular X as an instance of *class* X. We can recognize an infinitude of instances of (say) faces, *as* faces, yet no one can say what is involved in such recognition. How does the mind work that it can perceive an infinitude of particulars as exemplifications of a generic concept? No one has the faintest idea. We do, I think, know certain aspects of what is involved: The mind must be operating with a set of abstract conceptual categories, and its rules of determination must assimilate particulars to these deep structural categories. The mind can never know particulars *as such* (see Hayek, 1952). Thus we "know" that the mind is primarily aware of abstract classifications (concepts) and only derivatively aware of particulars (Weimer, 1973). The Turvey and Fertig study is a case in point: Somehow we know that certain words are polarized in one direction and that others are in a different category, and yet consciously we could guess for a thousand years and never characterize either category. One's head knows the difference in categories, but *which* head? In other cases, for example triangularity, we can explicitly characterize the concept that we know (in terms of abstract rules from geometry), but we still know nothing about how triangles are perceived as such.

But tacit knowledge is not limited to perception. As both Polanyi's writing and the papers in this volume point out, it is characteristic of all conception. The problem of concept formation is an instance of it, as is our knowledge of language (Chomsky probably made his most valuable contribution to psychology by emphasizing that we know more of our language than we have learned or can tell). Comprehension or understanding simply focuses upon another aspect of the same problem. And so on throughout the entire psychological domain.

Indeed, I would like to argue that the entire problem of tacit knowledge is nothing more, nothing less, than the problem of meaning. In this sense, there is only one problem that has ever existed in psychology, and everything the field has investigated is merely a manifestation of that problem, a different aspect of the same elephant, an elephant that we have grasped at since the dawn of reflective thought without ever reaching at all.

This problem has many names. In the language of behaviorism, it is a matter of stimulus generalization or of stimulus equivalence. In the terminology of Gestalt psychology, it is the problem of contact between perceptual process and memory trace: the so-called "Hoffding step." Among philosophers, the question is usually formulated in terms of "universals" and of "abstraction from particulars." For Bruner and his associates, it is the problem of categorization. In computer technology, it is called "character recognition" when only letters and numbers are to be identified, or more generally "pattern recognition" [Neisser, 1967, p. 47].

The problem "When are stimuli equivalent?" *is* the problem of stimulus rocognition, which *is* the problem of concept formation, *ad infinitum,* all of which together constitute the problems of meaning. Stimuli are equivalent, in the final analysis, only because they mean the same thing. No matter where one goes in psychology there comes a point at which one runs straight into an insurmountable wall that is, conceptually speaking, infinitely high and wide. All we can do is look up and see that written on that wall are all the problems of the manifestations of meaning.

The behavioral or response output side of psychology is equally beset by this same problem. Take human skills: Every skilled behavior in which we engage has a characteristic signature, a style that exhibits how we behave, and every behavior is an instance, or an expression, of our categorization and construction of meaningful patterns. Skill is the competence to exhibit patterned configurations of movements that are meaningful. Everything we do, every action we perform, is a syntactically structured sequence of "movements" that are intelligible only as expressions of meaning. The problem of serial order in behavior, as Lashley (1951) pointed out, is simultaneously beyond the bounds of associationistic chaining models and intrinsically a problem of meaning.

Motor theories of the mind and the representation of information. There is at least one way to look at the mind which could provide a conceptualization of tacit knowledge and therefore of meaning. Traditional conceptions regard mind as intrinsically *sensory* and passive in nature, with a few "motor areas" that take their orders from the predominant sensory mechanism. Such a conception is tailor-made to be incapable of accounting for any of the problems of tacit knowledge, because all it attributes to mind is the linkage of stimuli to responses (or other stimuli), according to the undefined mechanism of associationism. But if mind is conceived of as a motor, actively generating not only its response outputs but also its sensory "input" through the restructuring of its own activity, the problems of pattern recognition, creativity in behavior, etc., need not be insurmountable. Such a conception explicates all higher mental processes as skills of the CNS. If the higher mental processes are seen as (motoric) skills, then the problem of meaning becomes that of the representation of information within the CNS. The motor theory of perception, when correctly formulated, states that information is represented in terms of the central neural motor command system of the modality involved (the Halwes and Wire outline shows how this relates to speech perception).

A motor theory of mind may seem to be a very strange way of construing human knowledge and understanding. There is no space to explicate the theory here, but it is appropriate to point out several things. First, a potential misconception: The motor theory is not the muscle theory of John B. Watson (or even the more nearly tenable ideomotor theory of William James). Second, it is not all that unfamiliar. For example, a direct fallout of the motor theory of the mind's operation is the motor theory of knowledge, which holds that we "know" the world and its objects in terms of our actions upon it rather than by the relations among objects *per se*. The only relations among objects that one can know are those that result from the way in which one's mind is structured. This last point has been emphasized by Kant, Cassirer, Hayek, and a host of "active" epistemologists, as well as Russell's structural realism. The motor theory of knowledge is amply represented in the work of Piaget. Another example is the motor theory of memory. The constructive theory of BMF and Halwes as well as Gibsonian theory present a motor theory of the representation of information. Since it is obvious that constructive theory entails a motor theory of memory, Gibson's agreement on this point should be considered. As Shaw and McIntyre point out, Gibson has no conception of storage. Instead, he talks of the modulation of information (as does Pribram, 1971, with holographic conceptions of memory). But the very idea that there is no storage, only modulation, *is* the motor theory! Gibson and the constructivists have a pseudo-disagreement over the role of construction, but this feud is only intelligible if the general motor theory of mind is presupposed.

Granting, however, that a conception of the mind as a motor or a generator provides a framework for understanding the higher mental processes, it certainly does not tell us what meaning is, only (at best) how it is instantiated. The concept of meaning is an undefined primitive in every conception of psychology that has ever been put forth. The explication of what meaning is, rather than the modes of its instantiation, transcends the bounds of psychology, philosophy, linguistics, or any other discipline yet known. It may be that it transcends the bounds of human comprehension entirely. If that is so, then psychology must be construed as explicating the manifestations of meaning rather than characterizing meaning intrinsically. In either case it is clearly the most difficult task science has ever undertaken.

NEW WINE AND OLD BOTTLES: SHAW, SYMMETRY THEORY, AND THE SHAPE OF THINGS TO COME

Psychologists often have a hard time understanding Robert Shaw. What he talks about is somehow related to traditional psychology, but it is so different that it seems impossible to relate the two. Shaw's thinking represents a novel approach to cognitive psychology, and it is often necessary to go back to the "experimental epistemology" of Warren S. McCulloch, the pioneering work on automata theory and the problems of complexity done by John von Neumann, and the philosophy of perception of Bertrand Russell to understand the origin of Shaw's perspective on cognitive problems. I cannot say whether it results from continued exposure to his views, or from my reaching many similar conclusions from a different perspective, but I find that more and more of what he has been saying makes very good sense, and that it has striking implications for how cognitive psychology ought to proceed. Of the many tantalizing remarks he has made in the pages above, four points seem particularly worthy of attention in their implications for the future.

The quest for a representation of mind in the natural order. Ever since John B. Watson made up his windpipe that he didn't have a mind, the "world knot" (as

Schopenhauer called the mind-body complex) has had rough sledding in psychology. The field has gone to extreme lengths to commit the operationalist's fallacy of confusing the evidence (behavior) with that which it evidences (a behaver), and to deny that there is anything at all evidenced. When the behaviorist has looked in the mirror, *he,* like Count Dracula, has not been there. My point is not just that you have to be "bats" to be a behaviorist, but that behaviorism has neglected "you" entirely. And a psychology which neglects the self as a subject of conceptual activity is so severely limited that it is no psychology at all.

As Feigl (1967) has noted, there are at least three major clusters of problems in the mind-body complex, and this volume has touched on them all. The first problem is posed by *sentience:* The mere existence of phenomenal experience, of "raw feels," as Tolman felicitously called them, cannot be reconciled with any materialistic conception of the universe. My being a sentient organism is inexplicable in physicalistic terms, and it leads to perception as a psychological problem as opposed to a physical problem. The second problem is *sapience:* The mere existence of knowledge and meaning in the world is likewise totally inexplicable in terms of physical theory. To put it paradoxically, to the question "Where is meaning in the physical universe?" the answer is simultaneously "Everywhere" and "Nowhere." Asking a simple question like "How do physical objects (such as spoken sentences) *mean?*" leads one instantly and inevitably into the mind-body problem. Sapience and sentience have returned to psychology in the last twenty years, and their presence no longer raises eyebrows. But the third aspect of the mind-body complex, *selfhood,* has yet to be acknowledged. Selfhood is a problem because persons are singular logical subjects of conceptual activity in a physical universe which is pluralistic and has only objects, but no subjects. Shaw's concern with the algorist is likely to raise eyebrows because it is a concern with selfhood, with the subject of psychological activity, rather than with an object of such activity.

The majority of psychologists would rather not acknowledge the self. Neisser (1967, for example, runs straight into the problem in the last chapter of *Cognitive Psychology,* and contents himself with a verbal sedative, saying that he has a "programulus" rather than the more traditional homunculus in the head. But it doesn't matter what we call it: What matters is that there must be a self, or an algoristic basis, in psychology. Shaw has had the courage to point out that *we* are not in current psychology at all, and has told us where to look to begin to find a scientific image of ourselves.

Control systems and modeling the mind. Traditional psychology modeled mind in terms of a linear or "chaining" control system. The concept of associationism as the mechanism of mind has just come to the end of its 2500-year currency, and many psychologists have come to accept the arguments in favor of hierarchical control systems. The evidence in favor of such systems came primarily from Chomsky's work on language, Lenneberg's (1967) documentation of the physiological bases of language and speech perception, analyses of skilled movement such as Bernstein's (1967), and the systems approach to biology (Weiss, 1971). Thus it was easy for cognitive psychologists to embrace hierarchical control systems as the "natural" (indeed the only) alternative to linear systems.

But now Shaw is telling us that when we look at the wholistic aspects of organismic integration, hierarchies aren't powerful enough to account for what we see. He proposes that we are *coalitions* rather than just hierarchies, and that such concepts as the epigenetic development of the organism and the integration of the various mental processes cannot be understood except in coalitional terms.

If this is so, then within two decades of our lives as psychologists we will have been forced to make an enormous leap, from simpleminded and intuitively obvious models of mind to models of an abstractness and complexity unparalleled in the history of human thought. How many will be able to make the transition? What will the psychology of the future look like? What are the prospects for understanding extremely complex phenomena? Will it even be possible for *human* beings to do psychology? The prospects are not very good, if we assume that psychology is to be as it is traditionally conceived of. I suggest reading Shaw (1971) and Hayek (1952, 1967) to see what can and cannot be expected in attempting to model complex phenomena such as the human mind.

Semantic and cognitive bases for logic. For centuries logic has been revered for the certainty of its inference and the elegance of its formalism. But where is logic in scientific practice? The answer is that traditional deductive logic is nowhere in actual research and discovery, and that if it applies at all, it does so only after the fact, in the writing up of a finished research report. Many philosophers have known this, and some, such as C. S. Peirce (1966) and N. R. Hanson (1958), have attempted to analyze the quasi-logical aspects of scientific discovery. But virtually no one has questioned the non-*modal* interpretation of logic, or suggested that the logic of science might be in a different mood than the traditional logic of implication. Yet, as Shaw points out, the Stoics knew that all logic is modal logic, and they analyzed a modal form that seems to fit the context in which scientific theory construction is carried out. By *interpreting* logic in the context of discovery rather than the context of justification (to use Reichenbach's famous distinction), Shaw has pointed to the direction that work in the foundations of logic must take. Logic can only be understood in its modal force, as an instrument within the pragmatic and semantic context of human affairs. When the contexts in which logic can be used are explored, it will become clear that logic, generically speaking, is much broader than traditional implication, and that there is indeed a logic of scientific postulation and inference. Shaw's contention, however, will never get a hearing among philosophers unless it can be divorced from the taint of "psychologism." Whether this can be done or not remains to be seen.

The context of constraint—the role of invariance principles in natural philosophy. Despite the fact that cognitive psychology may be extremely difficult, there is a ray of hope in Shaw's message. Some aspects of the direction of future research can be ascertained by rational reflection. If we are wise we will learn to explore and take advantage of what Shaw calls the context of constraint.

As Shaw and McIntyre have argued, there is a strong co-implication relationship among the concepts discussed by cognitive psychologists. What we know (or think we know) about (to use their terminology) the algorithmic basis constrains what we will postulate to be the algoristic basis, and vice versa. What we know about physics, for instance, imposes constraints upon models or instantiations of the algorist. Higher-order principles that one has found to apply to one domain or theory will have recognizable counterparts in another domain. But even within one given domain we can often see the shape of things to come by paying attention to symmetries and asymmetries, as the example of Mendeleev and the construction of the periodic table illustrates.

Such examples illustrate the nature and role of invariance principles in scientific inquiry. Invariance means constancy of formal properties with respect to transformations of the entity involved. Discussions of invariance require specification of the entity (or class of entities) involved and the permissible transformations which retain the invariance. Invariance principles function in science as higher-order integrative concepts that exhibit the communality of otherwise disparate domains. By knowing the form an invariance takes with regard to one domain we can make a prediction regarding the form an invariance relationship will take in another domain.

As science has progressed from the study of simple, easily isolated phenomena to that of complex organized systems, the very nature and scope of its theoretical apparatus have changed. In place of the mechanistic, deterministic, billiard-ball causal framework of Newtonian science we now see scientific understanding as a search for patterns of structural interrelations among phenomena. Mechanism left the scientific world-perspective nearly two hundred years ago, and determinism and causality have been abandoned or completely redefined after the advent of quantum mechanics. Science is in the business of discovering ordered structure in dynamic systems, and attempts to exhibit the invariant properties of such complex systems. Natural science has become a search for invariants.

But psychology has not kept pace with these changes in the natural and biological sciences. Indeed, when Kurt Lewin (1935) suggested that it abandon an Aristotelian framework in favor of a Galilean one (so that it would then be only three centuries behind the times instead of twenty-three), the dominant response was to suggest that since Aristotle had been the "father" of psychology his framework was good enough for "scientific" psychology today. The few theorists who noted that out-of-date conceptions could not account for even the simplest psychological phenomena were reviled as "vitalists" and "metaphysicians." Even within the psycholinguistic and and cognitive avant-garde today there is an almost unquestioning reliance upon a conception of science that has been out of date since before the turn of the century.

Shaw would like us to pay attention to the *form,* if not the content, of theory in the advanced sciences, and take advantage of the context of constraint imposed by symmetry theoretic considerations. This is not a new request; indeed, Cassirer (1944) told us that perception would be best understood in terms of group theory. If anything, Shaw's work is an actualization of the promise that Cassirer held forth over thirty years ago. Since Cassirer's message was so clear, and the logic of his argument so compelling, I can only ask why so few have followed his advice. The only reasonable answer I can find is Kuhn's account of methodology (specifically with regard to the factors affecting resistance to "paradigm shifts"), but that is a topic for another place.

PROBLEMS AND PROMISES OF A UNIFIED PSYCHOLOGY

Terry Halwes's chapter raises issues that will receive increasingly more attention in the future. Having touched upon the reconciliation of Gibsonian and structural realism above, I want to comment upon three related points that stem from the second part of his chapter. These points center on the unification of theoretical, academic psychology and practical, "philosophy of life"-oriented esoteric approaches.

Psychology as a pure and applied discipline. Psychology has been a self-proclaimed "science" now for one hundred years. That is a long time to live in the ivory tower of academia. Occasionally some brave souls have dared to ask whether psychology as a "science" has any function other than to keep a certain class of misfits off the streets of the real world. The usual response has been a chorus of howls that "pure research" does not have to be justified by contemporary relevance. While that is always true, it is hardly an adequate reply for the psychological sciences, which ought to be able to do something about the human condition, if anything can. That "ought," as should be clear, is the normative one of ethical responsibility.

But what have we learned in the last century that is practically relevant? Every day our "civilized" society takes another giant step toward its own destruction, by driving itself just a little more neurotic-going-on-psychotic. Has a century of academic psychology taught us how to cope with ourselves, let alone the rest of the world? That the answer is "No" is not surprising. What is surprising, and frightening, is that we don't seem to care. Indeed, when someone reminds us that the oriental "ways of life," which are really nothing but common sense, are more competent to deal with the psychological problems of daily life than we are, we become indignant. Because the mystics and yogis and Zen masters of the ages have not had PhD's from a "top twenty" university we have concluded that they must be charlatans.

Thus it is not surprising that many are pained by Halwes's essay, for here is someone with academic credentials who is a traitor to the ivory tower, who suggests that the message of the Eastern way of life must be incorporated into academic practice and ivory tower tradition. We had better get applied cognitive psychology off the ground, and its lessons incorporated into theoretical psychology. Halwes argues persuasively that the incorporation can easily be effected in the constructive approach to cognitive theory, and the ease of transition between the two parts of his chapter are evidence in favor of his message. With that message I am in complete agreement, and would urge that theoretical psychology look to the applied problems of everyday life as a test of "transfer of training." If the theoretical ideas don't pass this test, a failure of theory is indicated.

But there is one outright error and one constant danger in the new "mysticism." The error can be eliminated—and when it is, considerable clarification results—but the danger is always there. Let us consider them in turn.

The role of experience in epistemology. The error is the assumption that there is an epistemic dichotomy between discursive thought and experience (or intuition). The claim is made that *knowledge* transcends the bounds of scientific inquiry, and that true insight can be obtained by (the mystical) experience. This reasoning obscures even those works that consciously seek to reconcile Eastern insight and Western science. For example, Ornstein (1972) writes that "science as a mode of knowing involves a limitation on inquiry [p. 6]." Speaking of a contrast between independent investigators who worked exclusively during the day or night, he says: "If those who work at night look up and see the faint starlight in the sky, and concentrate on the movements of the stars, they may produce documents which predict the positions of the stars at any given time, *but these writings will be totally incomprehensible to someone who experiences only daylight* [Ornstein, 1972, p. 11, emphasis added]." These comments seek to establish an epistemic dichotomy between discursive scientific knowledge and the experience of the individual, and to place experience at the foundation of knowledge.

Now phenomenology of knowledge is one thing, but phenomenalism as an epistemology is another. A good phenomenology is indispensable to psychology, and I would recommend Ernst Cassirer's *The Phenomenology of Knowledge* (1957) as the finest cognitive psychology yet written. But phenomenalism has numerous defects and just isn't adequate as an epistemology. Bertrand Russell toyed with the position early in his career and made a distinction that, when correctly interpreted, annihilates phenomenalism. That distinction is between *knowledge by description* and *knowledge by acquaintance.* We are acquainted with phenomenal experience: the sights, sounds, smells, tastes, and touches of our sensory systems, our feelings and emotions, etc. We know these things personally, experientially; we are literally acquainted with them. But this is not the sort of knowledge that science discloses. Scientific knowledge is knowledge by description, of the structural characteristics of the nonmental realm. Scientific knowledge of the nonmental realm is *never* of the intrinsic or first-order properties of objects: We don't *experience* the objects that science discloses, and yet we *know* them as well as, if not better than, we know our own "raw feels." Knowledge, the discursive, propositional sort disclosed by both science and common sense, is not based or founded on experience, even though it ultimately refers back to the experiences of an observer. Scientific knowledge literally is the structures embodied in our heads that model the structural properties of the nonmental realm, as Hanson (1970) so beautifully shows.

Now if all the mystic were saying is that knowledge by description is not knowledge by acquaintance, his claim would be but a tautology, coupled perhaps to a lament. But apparently he wants to claim more: that experience (of the appropriate sort) can deliver knowledge of reality that is incomprehensible to science. Now this claim is simply nonsense. Knowledge by description can "capture" or, better *represent* anything we can know. If the mystic *knows* anything, it can be formulated, propositionally, in terms of knowledge by description. If the "ineffable" experience is truly that, it is not a knowledge *claim* (it is nothing more, nor less, than an experience). We may not have had the mystic's experience, to be sure, but we can know it if he can describe it. If he can't describe it, he can't know it descriptively either; he can just endure it.

Indeed, if what we know is examined, it becomes obvious that science can comprehend an infinitude of things that experience can never address. The mystic has things backward: Knowledge by description is vastly more powerful than knowledge by acquaintance, and there are many things we can know that we cannot experience. We can understand, for instance, what it would be like to see ultraviolet radiation, but we can never experience it. Or better, what experience underlies our understanding of the mathematics is indefensible: The daytime people can perfectly well understand propositions about unexperienced stars, just as you and I can understand that within the Einsteinian theoretical framework light is the limiting velocity in the universe, despite our inability ever to experience that proposition as such.

There are definitely limits to both understanding and experiencing. But they are not what the epigones of the new experientialism have assumed. The limits on understanding are imposed by the inevitability that at least part of our knowledge is tacit at any given time. But that does not mean that there are things which are not in principle knowable by discursive reasoning. Hayek is light-years ahead of most of us in exploring these issues, and I beg all to study these remarks carefully:

> It is important not to confuse the contention that any such system (the mind) must always act on some rules which it cannot communicate with the contention that there are particular rules which no such system could ever state. All the former contention means is that there will always be some rules governing a mind which that mind in its then prevailing state cannot communicate, and that, if it ever were to acquire the capacity of communicating these rules, this would presuppose that it had acquired further higher rules which make the communication of the former possible but which themselves will still be incommunicable.
>
> To those familiar with the celebrated theorem due to Kurt Gödel it will probably be obvious that these conclusions are closely related to those Gödel has shown to prevail in formalized arithmetical systems. It would thus appear that Gödel's theorem is but a special case of a more general principle applying to all conscious and particularly all rational processes, namely the principle that among their determinants there must always be some rules which cannot be stated or even be conscious. At least all we can talk about and probably all we can consciously think about presupposes the existence of a framework which determines meaning, i.e., a system of rules which operate us but which we can neither state nor form an image of and which we can merely evoke in others insofar as they already possess them [Hayek, 1967, p. 62].

On the end of enlightenment: A word of warning. There is a constant danger in the contemplative tradition that seeks nirvana or enlightenment. Enlightenment, like any other human achievement, must be used by its attainer. Used in one way, it can be of enormous benefit to mankind; used another way, it becomes a short cut to oblivion. The contrast is between inner- and outer-directedness, and between use for mankind and use for one person. Consider these points in reverse order.

Philosophy, and knowledge, make extraordinary demands upon us. One of them is that we be both unselfish and unstinting in our efforts. Plato, as we know, employed the allegory of the prisoners in the cave to convey the human epistemological condition (this is the historical source of Turvey's "prison" story). But, and this is far less well known, he was quick to admonish that those who managed to climb out of the cave, after they had ceased to be blinded by the sunlight and attained knowledge, had a duty to return to the cave to aid their fellow man. So long as the new proponents of the Eastern ways of enlightenment keep this message in mind, and having attained it come back to help the rest of us, I am all for it. But enlightenment for its own sake I cannot condone. Those who climb up the mountain must be prepared to climb back down.

The other point is closely related. It is a matter of who is in control of my life: I, or what I take to be my unconscious (or my intuition, or whatever I call that other little man inside). There is little room in either science or society for those who do not attempt to control their own lives, and who use "unconscious messages" as a rationalization (in the Freudian sense) for not working. If we get to the point where we have lost control, and some intellectually externalized source is telling us what to do, then therapy is more in order than congratulations. Self-discipline and self-mastery are integral parts of the oriental message, and anyone who seeks enlightenment must realize this.

Speaking of therapy, let me close this discussion of Halwes's message with a quotation from an early psychotherapist (and point out the commonality of his message with Spencer Brown's). This is from a selection on recommendations to physicians on how to practice therapy:

> The technique, however, is a very simple one. It disclaims the use of any special aids, even of notetaking, as we shall see, and simply consists in making no effort to concentrate the attention on anything in particular, and in maintaining in regard to all that one hears the same measure of calm, quiet attentiveness—or "evenly hovering attention," as I once before described it. In this way a strain which could not be kept up for several hours daily and a danger inseparable from deliberate attentiveness are avoided. For as soon as attention is deliberately concentrated in a certain degree, one begins to select from the material before one; one point will be fixed in the mind with particular clearness and some other consequently disregarded, and in this selection one's expectations or one's inclinations will be followed. This is just what must not be done, however; if one's expectations are followed in this selection there is the danger of never finding anything but what is already known, and if one follows one's inclinations anything which is to be perceived will most certainly be falsified. It must not be forgotten that the meaning of the things one hears is, at all events for the most part, only recognizable later on [Freud, 1959, p. 324].

How many would have guessed that Freud himself was the author?

COGNITIVE PSYCHOLOGY AND BRAIN SCIENCE

The neurosciences seem quite remote from typical cognitive investigations But this separation is detrimental to both fields. The cognitive psychologist must realize that all higher mental processes, the richness of phenomenal experience, indeed everything we can know and do, results from the CNS's ability to structure and restructure its own activity. All cognitive activity has its basis in neurophysiological functioning. Thus developments in the neurosciences' conception of how the brain and nervous system(s) function are indispensible to cognitive psychology. In perhaps the most obvious case, if psychologists had paid attention to the known complexity and organization of nervous functioning, the inadequate conceptions of reflexology and the "switchboard nervous system" that behaviorists accepted *as scientific fact* would not have hindered progress. The point remains: No cognitive psychology can be accepted as adequate which is at variance with known neurophysiological functioning.

But as Anderson's chapter argues, the relationship between the two fields need not be one way. As his example of the conflict of atomistic and wholistic approaches to perception from the neurophysiological point of view illustrates, developments in psychology and epistemology can constrain not only theorizing but interpretation of research in neurophysiology. Just as neurophysiology constrains cognitive psychology, the complexity and organization of cognitive data requires a conceptualization of neural organization of at least equal complexity and organization. Anderson's chapter shows the effects of that dialectical interplay upon our emerging conceptions of pattern perception and its problems. Hopefully both fields will profit by studying it.

MILLER AND THE MATTER OF METAPHORS AND MISTAKES

Although it was not prepared for this conference, George Miller's attitude of stopping to take stock of psycholinguistics, asking "Where do we go from here?" fits our framework so well that we are happy to be able to include his chapter. Miller's career has been exemplary, but in one respect, it gives some cause for alarm. Although he has been an outstanding pioneer, a number of the trails that Miller has blazed have gotten lost in the wilderness. He has been perceptive enough to note that our field has gone off in the wrong direction, and has then proposed a new direction that was not necessarily an improvement. Without meaning to belittle an outstanding psychologist, I think the most important thing we have learned from George Miller has been that he was wrong on some important issues. We have learned, after exploring certain approaches that he pioneered, that despite their high face validity, they have been dead ends.

Another walk down Primrose Lane? Consider some examples, which are as instructive as they are painful. At the end of the 1940's mathematical psychology was born, primarily a result of the labor of Egon Brunswik and W. K. Estes. While Brunswik concentrated on perception and Estes on learning theory, Miller attempted to tackle *Language and Communication* (1951). But what mathematics was available to psychology at that time? Simple Markov models and the much in vogue information theoretic approach of Shannon and Weaver (1948). For the better part of the fifties Miller led us down a primrose lane by the simple expedient of (*a*) having the most sophisticated psychological treatment of language, and (*b*) touting information theory as the way to go. The field ran around with that shiny new tool, looking for that aspect of language to which it would provide the key. Markov models of the mind had high face validity, added an aura of pseudo-mathematical sophistication, but delayed progress in psycholinguistics by masking the complexity of the phenomena involved.

Toward the end of the decade Miller had realized from Chomsky the futility of his earlier approach, and he attempted to redress the situation in *Plans and the Structure of Behavior* (1960) and the *Math Handbook* chapters (Chomsky & Miller, 1963; Miller & Chomsky, 1963). It was from this framework that the first transformational psycholinguistic research program grew, stemming from what is now known as the "derivational theory of complexity" (DTC). The DTC had very high face validity as a starting point for serious psycholinguistic research, but by 1966 Fodor and Garrett could write the obituary notice for the entire program. With hindsight, Miller's DTC made two very questionable assumptions: (*a*) that the relationship between competence and performance was simple and (*b*) that latency was a reliable window to the mind. At the time, each was obvious and uncontroversial; now they are instantly suspect. Nevertheless, psycholinguistic research prior to 1965 is of little systematic import to the field today.

Miller's chapter is, again, seemingly obvious and intuitively reasonable. Since it suggests yet another new direction, I hope you will see why I am perplexed. On the one hand we need another primrose lane like more holes in our heads, and on the other it is reasonable, and perhaps it is the way to go. Since he led the way down blind alleys as a defender of both the association and the communication metaphors, what is one to think of the newly proffered computation metaphor? Perhaps a comparison of Miller's metaphor with the one implicit in the BMF chapters will indicate at least my personal malaise. These latter authors (including Brewer) make comprehension their guiding metaphor rather than computation. Their key to cognition is the effort after meaning (to use Bartlett's, 1932, phrase), the attempt to construct a context that renders an input (in any mode) intelligible and meaningful, which, in short, renders incoming information *comprehensible.* To my mind the problem for Miller's approach is that the higher mental processes comprehend as well as compute. No doubt all devices that process information do in fact compute, and no doubt there are significant generalizations valid for any such processing device. But all any computer can do is calculate (or compute); it cannot comprehend. Try, for example, to handle the Brewer-BMF data with procedural semantics: The "click of comprehension" will be absent from the program and output of a computing device that attempts to model such human performance.

But regardless of which metaphor will be of most utility to the field, it is far more important to notice that we have several competing alternatives available. By exploring these alternatives we ought to learn new, theoretically motivated facts about cognitive phenomena that would not have been available in a monotheoretical framework. Thus, regardless of whether history shows Miller's approach right or wrong, he is to be applauded for providing a serious hypothesis for our consideration. It is better for our field that he make a bold conjecture which is soon overthrown than make none at all.

The importance of being wrong. It is important to note that being wrong in science is not an indication of failure. Naive methodologies have identified the two in the past, but recent explorations of the nature of science (e.g. Kuhn, 1970; Lakatos, 1970) have made it clear that proposing and articulating a false hypothesis is not "unscientific." Since all serious hypotheses in science are refuted by contrary evidence, often available when they were originally proposed, Miller cannot be faulted for having endorsed conjectures that were late abandoned. The task of science has never been to pick the one true hypothesis while discarding the false ones; rather it is more a matter of picking the least black lie from alternatives all of which are known to be falsified in advance. One should not be discouraged for making mistakes in science, but one should be encouraged for detecting them: That, in a nutshell, is Popper's methodology of *Conjectures and Refutations* (1963), and it appears to be very good methodology for a field in flux and transition (such as psycholinguistics and cognitive psychology). In this regard, much (if not all) progress in science is a matter of detecting mistakes—we learn which ways not to go. We have learned much from Miller in this regard, and although we should be as wary of his conjectures as anyone else's, we should not fault him for advancing them. But we should definitely worry about the criteria employed to assess the warrant of scientific conjectures, for this is the psychologist's problem as much as the philosopher's (see Weimer, in press a).

THERE ARE CONSPIRACIES AND THEN THERE ARE CONSPIRACIES

Life is full of conspiracies, and there were two significant ones in the conference that produced this volume. One was intentional, a part of our planning; the other unintentional, a fault of the intractability of the principal phenomenon discussed. The two are revealing: one, of where we have come from; the other, of where we must go.

In planning the conference, Palermo and I stacked the deck in favor of new theoretical approaches to the problems of cognitive psychology. We wanted to accomplish a number of tasks. Perhaps foremost in our minds was the desire to show that the "new" cognitive psychology could stand on its own theoretical and empirical feet. We also wanted to indicate that cognitive psychology need not be limited to the traditional computer modeling, visual search, short-term memory, and other paradigms, or to the mini-theorizing that has characterized it in the past. There are broad-based theoretical perspectives in the preceding pages far more powerful than the mini-models of, say, short-term memory, and they generate experiments that are simultaneously more interesting and more revealing of the nature of mental functioning. There is more to cognitive psychology than studies of imagery, associative clustering, or the latest multistage memory-store model, and we wanted to provide a forum in which part of that "something more" could be aired. A glance at the references in the chapters above is informative in this regard. One does not often encounter citations of such writers as Gibson, Russell, Hayek, Cassirer, and von Neumann in the hard-core cognitive literature. I think this is a disadvantage to the field, because these theorists have far more to say to psychology than most of the traditional sources. That is a very strong statement, and I hope it provokes some readers to go see what these thinkers have to say, and judge for themselves where the field ought to go.

The other conspiracy involves the complexity and pervasiveness of the problem of tacit knowledge. Once one abandons simpleminded perspectives such as behaviorism or information theory, it becomes obvious that the human higher mental processes are among the most complex and intractable problems known to man. Even the simplest behaviors are the result of enormously complex and abstract causal processes that result, in the last analysis, from the central nervous system's ability to structure and restructure its own activity. Having stated the problem, however, we find ourselves with very little else to say. The enormity of our ignorance conspires against us all. Perhaps the most important thing we can learn from this volume is how little we really know about the mind and its place in nature. Perhaps a future volume will be able to present a more sophisticated and complete view of our ignorance.

REFERENCES

Agassi, J. Sensationalism. *Mind,* 1966, N. S. Vol. 75, 1-24.

Bartlett, F. C. *Remembering.* Cambridge: Cambridge University Press, 1932.

Bernstein, N. *The Co-ordination and regulation of movements.* Oxford: Pergamon Press, 1967.

Cassirer, E. The concept of group and the theory of perception. *Philosophy and Phenomenological Research,* 1944, 5, 1-35.

Cassirer, E. The philosophy of symbolic forms. Vol. 3, *The phenomenology of knowledge.* New Haven: Yale University Press, 1957.

Chomsky, N. *Aspects of the theory of syntax.* Cambridge: MIT Press, 1965.

Chomsky, N. *Language and mind.* New York: Harcourt, Brance, 1968.

Chomsky, N. Deep structure, surface structure, and semantic interpretation. In D. D. Steinberg & L. A. Jakobovits (Eds.), *Semantics: An interdisciplinary reader.* Cambridge: Cambridge University Press, 1971.

Chomsky, N., & Miller, G. A. Introduction to the formal analysis of natural languages. In R. D. Luce, E. R. Bush, & E. Galanter (Eds.), *Handbook of mathematical psychology.* Vol. 2. New York: Wiley, 1963.

Dollard, J., & Miller, N. E. *Personality and psychotherapy.* New York: McGraw-Hill, 1950.

Faile, F. Correspondence of behavior planning segments, conceptual chunks and phonological phrases in spontaneous speech. Unpublished doctoral dissertation, Pennsylvania State University, 1972.

Feigl, H. *The mental and the physical: The essay and a postscript.* Minneapolis: University of Minnesota Press, 1967.

Feyerabend, P. Problems of microphysics. In R. G. Colodny (Ed.), *Frontiers of Science and philosophy.* Pittsburgh: University of Pittsburgh Press, 1962.

Feyerabend, P. Problems of empiricism. In R. G. Colodny (Ed.), *Beyond the edge of certainty.* Englewood Cliffs, N.J.: Prentice-Hall, 1965.

Fodor, J. A., & Garrett, M. Some reflections on competence and performance. In J. Lyons & R. J. Wales (Eds.), *Psycholinguistics papers.* Edinburgh: Edinburgh University Press, 1966.

Freud, S. *Collected papers.* New York: Basic Books, 1959.

Hanson, N. R. *Patterns of Discovery.* Cambridge: Cambridge University Press, 1958.

Hanson, N. R. A picture theory of theory meaning. In R. G. Colodny (Ed.), *The nature and function of scientific theories.* Pittsburgh: University of Pittsburgh Press, 1970.

Hayek, F. *The sensory order.* Chicago: University of Chicago Press, 1952.

Hayek, F. *Studies in philosophy, politics and economics.* New York: Simon & Schuster, 1967.

Hull, C. L. *Principles of behavior.* New York: Appleton-Century, 1943.

Körner, S. *Experience and theory.* New York: Humanities Press, 1966.

Kuhn, T. S. *The structure of scientific revolutions.* (2nd ed.) Chicago: University of Chicago Press, 1970.

Lakatos, I. Falsification and the methodology of scientific research programmes. In I. Lakatos & A. Musgrave (Eds.), *Criticism and the growth of knowledge.* Cambridge: Cambridge University Press, 1970.

Lakatos, I. History of science and its rational reconstructions, In R. Buck & R. S. Cohen (Eds.), *Boston studies in the philosophy of science.* Vol. 8. New York: Humanities Press, 1972.

Lashley, K. S. The problem of serial order in behavior. In L. A. Jeffress (Ed.), *Cerebral mechanisms in behavior.* New York: Wiley, 1951.

Lenneberg, E. *Biological foundations of language.* New York: Wiley, 1967.

Lewin, K. The conflict between Aristotelian and Galilean modes of thought in contemporary psychology. *Journal of General Psychology,* 1935, 5, 141-147.

McCawley, J. Where do noun phrases come from? In R. Jacobs & P. S. Rosenbaum (Eds.), *Readings in English transformational grammar.* Waltham, Mass.: Ginn, 1970.

Miller, G. A. *Language and communication.* New York: McGraw-Hill, 1951.

Miller, G. A., & Chomsky, N. Finitary models of language users. In R. D. Luce, E. R. Bush, & E. Galanter (Eds.), *Handbook of mathematical psychology.* Vol 2. New York: Wiley, 1963.

Miller, G. A., Galanter, E., & Pribram, K. H. *Plans and the structure of behavior.* New York: Holt, Rinehart & Winston 1960.

Neisser, U. *Cognitive psychology.* New York: Appleton-Century-Crofts, 1967.

Osgood, C. E. On understanding and creating sentences. *American Psychologist,* 1963, 18, 735-751.

Osgood, C. E. Toward a wedding of insufficiencies. In T. R. Dixon & D. L. Horton (Eds.), *Verbal behavior and general behavior theory.* Englewood Cliffs, N. J.: Prentice-Hall, 1968.

Ornstein, R. E. *The psychology of consciousness.* San Francisco: Freeman, 1972.

Peirce, C. S. *Collected papers.* Cambridge: Harvard University Press, 1966.

Polanyi, M. *Personal knowledge.* New York: Harper & Row, 1958.

Polanyi, M. *The tacit dimension.* Garden City, N. Y.: Doubleday, 1966.

Popper, K. R. *The logic of scientific discovery.* New York: Harper & Row, 1959.

Popper, K. R. *Conjectures and refutations.* New York: Harper & Row, 1963.

Pribram, K. H. *Languages of the brain.* Englewood Cliffs, N. J.: Prentice-Hall, 1971.

Ross, J. R. Constraints on variables in syntax. Unpublished doctoral dissertation, Massachusetts Institute of Technology, 1967.

Russell, B. *Portraits from memory.* New York: Simon & Schuster, 1951.

Shaw, R. Cognition, simulation and the problem of complexity. *Journal of Structural Learning.* 1971, 2, 31-44.

Weimer, W. B. The syntax of action: Prolegomena to the transformational analysis of behavior. Unpublished doctoral dissertation, University of Minnesota, 1969.

Weimer, W. B. Psycholinguistics and Plato's paradoxes of the *Meno. American Psychologist,* 1973, 28, 15-33.

Weimer, W. B. The psychology of inference and expectation. In G. Maxwell & R. M. Anderson (Eds.), *Minnesota studies in the philosophy of science.* Vol. 6, Minneapolis: University of Minnesota Press, in press. (a)

Weimer, W. B. *Structural analysis and the future of psychology,* Englewood Cliffs, N. J.: Prentice-Hall, in press. (b)

Weiss, P. A. The basic concept of hierarchy systems. In P. A. Weiss (Ed.), *Hierarchically organized systems in theory and practice.* New York: Hafner, 1971.

AUTHOR INDEX

Numbers in italics refer to the pages on which the complete references are listed.